Handbook of
Educational Data Mining

Chapman & Hall/CRC
Data Mining and Knowledge Discovery Series

SERIES EDITOR
Vipin Kumar
University of Minnesota
Department of Computer Science and Engineering
Minneapolis, Minnesota, U.S.A

AIMS AND SCOPE

This series aims to capture new developments and applications in data mining and knowledge discovery, while summarizing the computational tools and techniques useful in data analysis. This series encourages the integration of mathematical, statistical, and computational methods and techniques through the publication of a broad range of textbooks, reference works, and handbooks. The inclusion of concrete examples and applications is highly encouraged. The scope of the series includes, but is not limited to, titles in the areas of data mining and knowledge discovery methods and applications, modeling, algorithms, theory and foundations, data and knowledge visualization, data mining systems and tools, and privacy and security issues.

PUBLISHED TITLES

UNDERSTANDING COMPLEX DATASETS:
DATA MINING WITH MATRIX DECOMPOSITIONS
David Skillicorn

COMPUTATIONAL METHODS OF FEATURE
SELECTION
Huan Liu and Hiroshi Motoda

CONSTRAINED CLUSTERING: ADVANCES IN
ALGORITHMS, THEORY, AND APPLICATIONS
Sugato Basu, Ian Davidson, and Kiri L. Wagstaff

KNOWLEDGE DISCOVERY FOR
COUNTERTERRORISM AND LAW ENFORCEMENT
David Skillicorn

MULTIMEDIA DATA MINING: A SYSTEMATIC
INTRODUCTION TO CONCEPTS AND THEORY
Zhongfei Zhang and Ruofei Zhang

NEXT GENERATION OF DATA MINING
Hillol Kargupta, Jiawei Han, Philip S. Yu,
Rajeev Motwani, and Vipin Kumar

DATA MINING FOR DESIGN AND MARKETING
Yukio Ohsawa and Katsutoshi Yada

THE TOP TEN ALGORITHMS IN DATA MINING
Xindong Wu and Vipin Kumar

GEOGRAPHIC DATA MINING AND
KNOWLEDGE DISCOVERY, SECOND EDITION
Harvey J. Miller and Jiawei Han

TEXT MINING: CLASSIFICATION, CLUSTERING,
AND APPLICATIONS
Ashok N. Srivastava and Mehran Sahami

BIOLOGICAL DATA MINING
Jake Y. Chen and Stefano Lonardi

INFORMATION DISCOVERY ON ELECTRONIC
HEALTH RECORDS
Vagelis Hristidis

TEMPORAL DATA MINING
Theophano Mitsa

RELATIONAL DATA CLUSTERING: MODELS,
ALGORITHMS, AND APPLICATIONS
Bo Long, Zhongfei Zhang, and Philip S. Yu

KNOWLEDGE DISCOVERY FROM DATA STREAMS
João Gama

STATISTICAL DATA MINING USING SAS
APPLICATIONS, SECOND EDITION
George Fernandez

INTRODUCTION TO PRIVACY-PRESERVING DATA
PUBLISHING: CONCEPTS AND TECHNIQUES
Benjamin C. M. Fung, Ke Wang, Ada Wai-Chee Fu,
and Philip S. Yu

HANDBOOK OF EDUCATIONAL DATA MINING
Cristóbal Romero, Sebastian Ventura,
Mykola Pechenizkiy, and Ryan S.J.d. Baker

Chapman & Hall/CRC
Data Mining and Knowledge Discovery Series

Handbook of Educational Data Mining

Edited by
Cristóbal Romero, Sebastian Ventura,
Mykola Pechenizkiy, and Ryan S.J.d. Baker

CRC Press
Taylor & Francis Group
Boca Raton   London   New York

CRC Press is an imprint of the
Taylor & Francis Group, an **informa** business

A CHAPMAN & HALL BOOK

CRC Press
Taylor & Francis Group
6000 Broken Sound Parkway NW, Suite 300
Boca Raton, FL 33487-2742

© 2011 by Taylor and Francis Group, LLC
CRC Press is an imprint of Taylor & Francis Group, an Informa business

No claim to original U.S. Government works

Printed in the United States of America on acid-free paper
10 9 8 7 6 5 4 3 2 1

International Standard Book Number: 978-1-4398-0457-5 (Hardback)

Visit the Taylor & Francis Web site at
http://www.taylorandfrancis.com

and the CRC Press Web site at
http://www.crcpress.com

To my wife, Ana, and my son, Cristóbal

Cristóbal Romero

To my wife, Inma, and my daughter, Marta

Sebastián Ventura

To my wife, Ekaterina, and my daughter, Aleksandra

Mykola Pechenizkiy

To my wife, Adriana, and my daughter, Maria

Ryan S. J. d. Baker

Contents

Part II Case Studies

Preface

The Purpose of This Book

The goal of this book is to provide an overview of the current state of knowledge of educational data mining (EDM). The primary goal of EDM is to use large-scale educational data sets to better understand learning and to provide information about the learning process. Although researchers have been studying human learning for over a century, what is different about EDM is that it makes use not of experimental subjects learning a contrived task for 20 minutes in a lab setting; rather, it typically uses data from students learning school subjects, often over the course of an entire school year. For example, it is possible to observe students learning a skill over an eight-month interval and make discoveries about what types of activities result in better long-term learning, to learn about the impact of what time students start their homework has on classroom performance, or to understand how the length of time students spend reading feedback on their work impacts the quality of their later efforts.

In order to conduct EDM, researchers use a variety of sources of data such as intelligent computer tutors, classic computer-based educational systems, online class discussion forums, electronic teacher gradebooks, school-level data on student enrollment, and standardized tests. Many of these sources have existed for decades or, in the case of standardized testing, about 2000 years. What has recently changed is the rapid improvement in storage and communication provided by computers, which greatly simplifies the task of collecting and collating large data sets. This explosion of data has revolutionized the way we study the learning process.

In many ways, this change parallels that of bioinformatics 20 years earlier: an explosion of available data revolutionized how much research in biology was conducted. However, the larger number of data was only part of the story. It was also necessary to discover, adapt, or invent computational techniques for analyzing and understanding this new, vast quantity of data. Bioinformatics did this by applying computer science techniques such as data mining and pattern recognition to the data, and the result has revolutionized research in biology. Similarly, EDM has the necessary sources of data. More and more schools are using educational software that is capable of recording for later analysis every action by the student and the computer. Within the United States, an emphasis on educational accountability and high stakes standardized tests has resulted in large electronic databases of student performance. In addition to these data, we need the appropriate computational and statistical frameworks and techniques to make sense of the data, as well as researchers to ask the right questions of the data.

No one discipline has the necessary expertise to conduct EDM research. Thus, the community, as can be seen by the chapter authors of this book, is composed of people from multiple disciplines. Computer science provides expertise in working with large quantities of data, both in terms of machine learning and data-mining techniques that scale gracefully to data sets with millions of records, as well as address real-world concerns such as "scrubbing" data to ensure systematic errors in the source data do not lead to erroneous results. Statisticians and psychometricians provide expertise in understanding how to properly analyze complex study designs, and properly adjust for the fact that most educational data are not from a classic randomized controlled study. These two communities are strong in statistical and computational techniques, but techniques and data are not sufficient to advance a scientific domain; researchers with basic understanding of the teaching and learning process are also required. Thus, education researchers and psychologists are key participants in the EDM community.

Main Avenues of Research in Educational Data Mining

There are three major avenues of research in EDM. They nicely align with the classic who–what–where–when interrogatives.

The first avenue is work on developing computational tools and techniques, determining which ones are best suited to working with large educational data sets, and finding best practices for evaluation metrics and model fitting. Examples of such efforts include experimenting with different visualization techniques for how to look at and make sense of the data. Since educational data sets are often longitudinal, encompassing months and sometimes years, and rich interactions with the student can occur during that time, some means of making sense of the data is needed. Another common approach in EDM is using variants of learning curves to track changes in student knowledge. Learning curves are some of the oldest techniques in cognitive psychology, so EDM efforts focus on examining more flexible functional forms, and discovering what other factors, such as student engagement with the learning process, are important to include. One difficulty with complex modeling in EDM is there is often no way of determining the best parameters for a particular model. Well-known techniques such as hill climbing can become trapped in local maxima. Thus, empirical work about which model-fitting techniques perform well for EDM tasks is necessary.

This work on extending and better understanding our computational toolkit is a necessary foundation to EDM. Work in this area focuses on how we can extract information from data. At present, although a majority of EDM research is in this avenue, the other two are not less important—just less explored.

The second avenue is determining what questions we should ask the data. There are several obvious candidates: Does the class understand the material well enough to go on? Do any students require remedial instruction? Which students are likely to need academic counseling to complete school successfully? These are questions that have been asked and answered by teachers for millennia. EDM certainly enables us to be data driven and to answer such questions more accurately; however, EDM's potential is much greater. The enormous data and computational resources are a tremendous opportunity, and one of the hardest tasks is capitalizing on it: what are new and interesting questions we can answer by using EDM? For example, in educational settings there are many advantages of group projects. Drawbacks are that it can be hard to attribute credit and, perhaps more importantly, to determine which groups are having difficulties—perhaps even before the group itself realizes. A tool that is able to analyze student conversations and activity, and automatically highlight potential problems for the instructor would be powerful, and has no good analog in the days before computers and records of past student collaborations were easily available. Looking into the future, it would be useful if we could determine if a particular student would be better served by having a different classroom teacher, not because one teacher is overall a better choice, but because for this type of student the teacher is a better choice. The first example is at the edge of what EDM is capable; the second is, for now, beyond our capabilities.

This job of expanding our horizons and determining what are new, exciting questions to ask the data is necessary for EDM to grow.

The third avenue of EDM is finding who are educational stakeholders that could benefit from the richer reporting made possible with EDM. Obvious interested parties are students and teachers. However, what about the students' parents? Would it make sense for them to receive reports? Aside from report cards and parent–teacher conferences, there is little communication to parents about their child's performance. Most parents are too busy for a detailed report of their child's school day, but what about some distilled information? A system that informed parents if their child did not complete the homework that was due that day could be beneficial. Similarly, if a student's performance noticeably declines, such a change would be detectable using EDM and the parents could be informed. Other stakeholders include school principals, who could be informed of teachers who were struggling relative to peers, and areas in which the school was performing poorly. Finally, there are the students themselves. Although students currently receive an array of grades on homework, quizzes, and exams, they receive much less larger-grain information, such as using the student's past performance to suggest which classes to take, or that the student's homework scores are lower than expected based on exam performance. Note that such features also change the context of educational data from something that is used in the classroom, to something that is potentially used in a completely different place.

Research in this area focuses on expanding the list of stakeholders for whom we can provide information, and where this information is received. Although there is much potential work in this area that is not technically demanding, notifying parents of missed homework assignments is simple enough, such work has to integrate with a school's IT infrastructure, and changes the ground rules. Previously, teachers and students controlled information flow to parents; now parents are getting information directly. Overcoming such issues is challenging. Therefore, this area has seen some attention, but is relatively unexplored by EDM researchers.

The field of EDM has grown substantially in the past five years, with the first workshop referred to as "Educational data mining" occurring in 2005. Since then, it has held its third international conference in 2010, had one book published, has its own online journal, and is now having this book published. This growth is exciting for multiple reasons. First, education is a fundamentally important topic, rivaled only by medicine and health, which cuts across countries and cultures. Being able to better answer age-old questions in education, as well as finding ways to answer questions that have not yet been asked, is an activity that will have a broad impact on humanity. Second, doing effective educational research is no longer about having a large team of graduate assistants to score and code data, and sufficient offices with filing cabinets to store the results. There are public repositories of educational data sets for others to try their hand at EDM, and anyone with a computer and Internet connection can join the community. Thus, a much larger and broader population can participate in helping improve the state of education.

This book is a good first step for anyone wishing to join the EDM community, or for active researchers wishing to keep abreast of the field. The chapters are written by key EDM researchers, and cover many of the field's essential topics. Thus, the reader gets a broad treatment of the field by those on the front lines.

MATLAB® is a registered trademark of The MathWorks, Inc. For product information, please contact:

The MathWorks, Inc.
3 Apple Hill Drive
Natick, MA 01760-2098 USA
Tel: 508 647 7000
Fax: 508-647-7001
E-mail: info@mathworks.com
Web: www.mathworks.com

Joseph E. Beck
Worcester Polytechnic Institute, Massachusetts

Editors

Dr. Cristóbal Romero is an associate professor in the Department of Computer Science at the University of Córdoba, Spain. His research interests include applying artificial intelligence and data-mining techniques in education and e-learning systems. He received his PhD in computer science from the University of Granada, Spain, in 2003. The title of his PhD thesis was "Applying data mining techniques for improving adaptive hypermedia web-based courses." He has published several papers about educational data mining in international journals and conferences, and has served as a reviewer for journals and as a program committee (PC) member for conferences. He is a member of the International Working Group on Educational Data Mining and an organizer or PC member of conferences and workshops about EDM. He was conference chair (with Sebastián Ventura) of the Second International Conference on Educational Data Mining (EDM'09).

Dr. Sebastián Ventura is an associate professor in the Department of Computer Science at the University of Córdoba, Spain. He received his PhD in sciences from the University of Córdoba in 2003. His research interests include machine learning, data mining, and their applications, and, recently, in the application of KDD techniques in e-learning. He has published several papers about educational data mining (EDM) in international journals and conferences. He has served as a reviewer for several journals such as *User Modelling and User Adapted Interaction*, *Information Sciences*, and *Soft Computing*. He has also served as a PC member in several research EDM forums, including as conference chair (with Cristóbal Romero) of the Second International Conference on Educational Data Mining (EDM'09).

Dr. Mykola Pechenizkiy is an assistant professor in the Department of Computer Science, Eindhoven University of Technology, the Netherlands. He received his PhD in computer science and information systems from the University of Jyväskylä, Finland, in 2005. His research interests include knowledge discovery, data mining, and machine learning, and their applications. One of the particular areas of focus is on applying machine learning for modeling, changing user interests and characteristics in adaptive hypermedia applications including, but not limited to, e-learning and e-health. He has published several papers in these areas, and has been involved in the organization of conferences, workshops, and special tracks.

 **Dr. Ryan S. J. d. Baker** is an assistant professor of psychology and the learning sciences in the Department of Social Science and Policy Studies at Worcester Polytechnic Institute, Massachusetts, with a collaborative appointment in computer science. He graduated from Carnegie Mellon University, Pittsburgh, Pennsylvania, in 2005, with a PhD in human–computer interaction. He was a program chair (with Joseph Beck) of the First International Conference on Educational Data Mining, and is an associate editor of the *Journal of Educational Data Mining* and a founder of the International Working Group on Educational Data Mining. His research is at the intersection of educational data mining, machine learning, human–computer interaction, and educational psychology, and he has received five best paper awards or nominations in these areas. He is the former technical director of the Pittsburgh Science of Learning DataShop, the world's largest public repository for data on the interaction between students and educational software.

Contributors

Wil van der Aalst
Department of Mathematics and
    Computer Science
Eindhoven University of Technology
Eindhoven, the Netherlands

Analía Amandi
ISISTAN Research Institute
Universidad Nacional del Centro de la
    Provincia de Buenos Aires
Tandil, Argentina

Saleema Amershi
Department of Computer Science and
    Engineering
University of Washington
Seattle, Washington

Brigham S. Anderson
School of Computer Science
Carnegie Mellon University
Pittsburgh, Pennsylvania

Cláudia Antunes
Department of Computer Science and
    Engineering
Instituto Superior Técnico
Lisbon, Portugal

Ivon Arroyo
Department of Computer Science
University of Massachusetts Amherst
Amherst, Massachusetts

Ryan S. J. d. Baker
Department of Social Science and Policy
    Studies
Worcester Polytechnic Institute
Worcester, Massachusetts

Tiffany Barnes
Department of Computer Science
University of North Carolina at
    Charlotte
Charlotte, North Carolina

Joseph E. Beck
Computer Science Department
Worcester Polytechnic Institute
Worcester, Massachusetts

and

Machine Learning Department
Carnegie Mellon University
Pittsburgh, Pennsylvania

Javier Bravo
Escuela Politécnica Superior
Universidad Autónoma de Madrid
Madrid, Spain

Winslow Burleson
Department of Computer Science and
    Engineering
Arizona State University
Tempe, Arizona

Toon Calders
Department of Mathematics and
    Computer Science
Eindhoven University of Technology
Eindhoven, the Netherlands

Cristina Carmona
Departamento de Lenguajes y Ciencias de
    la Computación
Universidad de Málaga
Málaga, Spain

Gladys Castillo
Department of Mathematics
Centre for Research on Optimization and
    Control
University of Aveiro
Aveiro, Portugal

Carlos de Castro
Department of Computer Science and
    Numerical Analysis
University of Cordoba
Cordoba, Spain

Félix Castro
Departament de Llenguatges i Sistemes
    Informàtics
Universitat Politècnica de Catalunya
Barcelona, Spain

and

Centro de Investigación en Tecnologías de
    Información y Sistemas
Universidad Autónoma del Estado de
    Hidalgo
Hidalgo, Mexico

Mihaela Cocea
London Knowledge Lab
The University of London
London, United Kingdom

and

School of Computing
National College of Ireland
Dublin, Ireland

Cristina Conati
Department of Computer Science
University of British Columbia
Vancouver, British Columbia, Canada

David G. Cooper
Department of Computer Science
University of Massachusetts Amherst
Amherst, Massachusetts

Marvin Croy
Department of Philosophy
University of North Carolina at Charlotte
Charlotte, North Carolina

Andrew Cuneo
Robotics Institute
Carnegie Mellon University
Pittsburgh, Pennsylvania

Kyle Cunningham
Human–Computer Interaction Institute
Carnegie Mellon University
Pittsburgh, Pennsylvania

Sidney D'Mello
Institute for Intelligent Systems
The University of Memphis
Memphis, Tennessee

Philippe Fournier-Viger
Department of Computer Science
University of Quebec in Montreal
Montreal, Quebec, Canada

Enrique García
Department of Computer Science and
    Numerical Analysis
University of Cordoba
Cordoba, Spain

Daniela Godoy
ISISTAN Research Institute
Universidad Nacional del Centro de la
    Provincia de Buenos Aires
Tandil, Argentina

Evandro Gouvea
European Media Laboratory GmbH
Heidelberg, Germany

and

Robotics Institute
Carnegie Mellon University
Pittsburgh, Pennsylvania

Art Graesser
Institute for Intelligent Systems
The University of Memphis
Memphis, Tennessee

Wilhelmiina Hämäläinen
Department of Computer Science
University of Helsinki
Helsinki, Finland

Cristina L. Heffernan
Department of Computer Science
Worcester Polytechnic Institute
Worcester, Massachusetts

Neil T. Heffernan
Department of Computer Science
Worcester Polytechnic Institute
Worcester, Massachusetts

Cecily Heiner
Language Technologies Institute
Carnegie Mellon University
Pittsburgh, Pennsylvania

and

Computer Science Department
University of Utah
Salt Lake City, Utah

Arnon Hershkovitz
Knowledge Technology Lab
School of Education
Tel Aviv University
Tel Aviv, Israel

Earl Hunt
Department of Psychology
University of Washington
Seattle, Washington

Octavio Juarez
Robotics Institute
Carnegie Mellon University
Pittsburgh, Pennsylvania

Brian W. Junker
Department of Statistics
Carnegie Mellon University
Pittsburgh, Pennsylvania

Judy Kay
School of Information Technologies
University of Sydney
Sydney, New South Wales, Australia

Jihie Kim
Information Sciences Institute
University of Southern California
Marina del Rey, California

Kenneth R. Koedinger
Human–Computer Interaction Institute
Carnegie Mellon University
Pittsburgh, Pennsylvania

Irena Koprinska
School of Information Technologies
University of Sydney
Sydney, New South Wales, Australia

Brett Leber
Human–Computer Interaction Institute
Carnegie Mellon University
Pittsburgh, Pennsylvania

Tara M. Madhyastha
Department of Psychology
University of Washington
Seattle, Washington

David Masip
Department of Computer Science,
    Multimedia and Telecommunications
Universitat Oberta de Catalunya
Barcelona, Spain

Manolis Mavrikis
London Knowledge Lab
The University of London
London, United Kingdom

Riccardo Mazza
Faculty of Communication Sciences
University of Lugano
Lugano, Switzerland

and

Department of Innovative Technologies
University of Applied Sciences of Southern
    Switzerland
Manno, Switzerland

Gordon G. McCalla
Department of Computer Science
University of Saskatchewan
Saskatoon, Saskatchewan, Canada

Victor H. Menendez
Facultad de Matemáticas
Universidad Autónoma de Yucatán
Merida, Mexico

Agathe Merceron
Media and Computer Science Department
Beuth University of Applied Sciences
Berlin, Germany

Eva Millán
Departamento de Lenguajes y Ciencias de
 la Computación
Universidad de Málaga
Malaga, Spain

Julià Minguillón
Department of Computer Science,
 Multimedia and Telecommunications
Universitat Oberta de Catalunya
Barcelona, Spain

Enric Mor
Department of Computer Science,
 Multimedia and Telecommunications
Universitat Oberta de Catalunya
Barcelona, Spain

Jack Mostow
Robotics Institute
Carnegie Mellon University
Pittsburgh, Pennsylvania

Rafi Nachmias
Knowledge Technology Lab
School of Education
Tel Aviv University
Tel Aviv, Israel

Àngela Nebot
Departament de Llenguatges i Sistemes
 Informàtics
Universitat Politècnica de Catalunya
Barcelona, Spain

John C. Nesbit
Faculty of Education
Simon Fraser University
Burnaby, British Columbia, Canada

Engelbert Mephu Nguifo
Department of Computer Sciences
Université Blaise-Pascal Clermont 2
Clermont-Ferrand, France

Roger Nkambou
Department of Computer Science
University of Quebec in Montreal
Montreal, Quebec, Canada

Alvaro Ortigosa
Escuela Politécnica Superior
Universidad Autónoma de Madrid
Madrid, Spain

Zachary A. Pardos
Department of Computer Science
Worcester Polytechnic Institute
Worcester, Massachusetts

Mykola Pechenizkiy
Department of Mathematics and
 Computer Science
Eindhoven University of Technology
Eindhoven, the Netherlands

Kaska Porayska-Pomsta
London Knowledge Lab
The University of London
London, United Kingdom

Manuel E. Prieto
Escuela Superior de Informática
Universidad de Castilla-La Mancha
Ciudad Real, Spain

Sujith Ravi
Information Sciences Institute
University of Southern California
Marina del Rey, California

Cristóbal Romero
Department of Computer Science and
    Numerical Analysis
University of Cordoba
Cordoba, Spain

Richard Scheines
Department of Philosophy
Carnegie Mellon University
Pittsburgh, Pennsylvania

Erin Shaw
Information Sciences Institute
University of Southern California
Marina del Rey, California

Judy Sheard
Faculty of Information Technology
Monash University
Melbourne, Victoria, Australia

Benjamin Shih
Machine Learning Department
Carnegie Mellon University
Pittsburgh, Pennsylvania

Alida Skogsholm
Human–Computer Interaction Institute
Carnegie Mellon University
Pittsburgh, Pennsylvania

John Stamper
Human–Computer Interaction Institute
Carnegie Mellon University
Pittsburgh, Pennsylvania

Tiffany Y. Tang
Department of Computer Science
Konkuk University
Chungju-si, South Korea

Nikola Trčka
Department of Mathematics and
    Computer Science
Eindhoven University of Technology
Eindhoven, the Netherlands

Alfredo Vellido
Departament de Llenguatges i Sistemes
    Informàtics
Universitat Politècnica de Catalunya
Barcelona, Spain

Sebastián Ventura
Department of Computer Science and
    Numerical Analysis
University of Cordoba
Cordoba, Spain

César Vialardi
Facultad de Ingeniería de Sistemas
Universidad de Lima
Lima, Peru

Mikko Vinni
School of Computing
University of Eastern Finland
Joensuu, Finland

Stephan Weibelzahl
School of Computing
National College of Ireland
Dublin, Ireland

Philip H. Winne
Faculty of Education
Simon Fraser University
Burnaby, British Columbia, Canada

Beverly P. Woolf
Department of Computer Science
University of Massachusetts Amherst
Amherst, Massachusetts

Yabo Xu
School of Computing Science
Simon Fraser University
Burnaby, British Columbia, Canada

Kalina Yacef
School of Information Technologies
University of Sydney
Sydney, New South Wales, Australia

Amelia Zafra
Department of Computer Science and
    Numerical Analysis
University of Cordoba
Cordoba, Spain

Alfredo Zapata
Facultad de Educación
Universidad Autónoma de Yucatán
Merida, Mexico

Mingming Zhou
Faculty of Education
Simon Fraser University
Burnaby, British Columbia, Canada

1

Introduction

Cristóbal Romero, Sebastián Ventura, Mykola Pechenizkiy, and Ryan S. J. d. Baker

CONTENTS

1.1 Background

In the last years, researchers from a variety of disciplines (including computer science, statistics, data mining, and education) have begun to investigate how data mining can improve education and facilitate education research. Educational data mining (EDM) is increasingly recognized as an emerging discipline [10]. EDM focuses on the development of methods for exploring the unique types of data that come from an educational context. These data come from several sources, including data from traditional face-to-face classroom environments, educational software, online courseware, and summative/high-stakes tests. These sources increasingly provide vast amounts of data, which can be analyzed to easily address questions that were not previously feasible, involving differences between student populations, or involving uncommon student behaviors. EDM is contributing to education and education research in a multitude of ways, as can be seen from the diversity of educational problems considered in the following chapters of this volume. EDM's contributions have influenced thinking on pedagogy and learning, and have promoted the improvement of educational software, improving software's capacity to individualize students' learning experiences. As EDM matures as a research area, it has produced a conference series (The International Conference on Educational Data Mining—as of 2010, in its third iteration), a journal (the *Journal of Educational Data Mining*), and a number of highly cited papers (see [2] for a review of some of the most highly cited EDM papers).

These contributions in education build off of data mining's past impacts in other domains such as commerce and biology [11]. In some ways, the advent of EDM can be considered as education "catching up" to other areas, where improving methods for exploiting data have promoted transformative impacts in practice [4,7,12]. Although the discovery methods used across domains are similar (e.g. [3]), there are some important differences between them. For instance, in comparing the use of data mining within e-commerce and EDM, there are the following differences:

- *Domain.* The goal of data mining in e-commerce is to influence clients in purchasing while the educational systems purpose is to guide students in learning [10].
- *Data.* In e-commerce, typically data used is limited to web server access logs, whereas in EDM there is much more information available about the student [9], allowing for richer user (student) modeling. This data come possibly from different sources, including field observations, motivational questionnaires, measurements collected from controlled experiments, and so on. Depending on the type of the educational environment (traditional classroom education, computer-based or web-based education) and an information system that supports it (a learning management, an intelligent tutoring or adaptive hypermedia system) also different kinds of data is being collected including but not limited to student profiles, (inter)activity data, interaction (with the system, with educators and with peers), rich information about learning objects and tasks, and so on. Gathering and integrating this data together, performing its exploratory analysis, visualization, and preparation for mining are nontrivial tasks on their own.
- *Objective.* The objective of data mining in e-commerce is increasing profit. Profit is a tangible goal that can be measured in terms of amounts of money, and which leads to clear secondary measures such as the number of customers and customer loyalty. As the objective of data mining in education is largely to improve learning [10], measurements are more difficult to obtain, and must be estimated through proxies such as improved performance.
- *Techniques.* The majority of traditional data mining techniques including but not limited to classification, clustering, and association analysis techniques have been already applied successfully in the educational domain. And the most popular approaches are covered by the introductory chapters of the book. Nevertheless, educational systems have special characteristics that require a different treatment of the mining problem. Data hierarchy and nonindependence becomes particularly important to account for, as individual students contribute large amounts of data while progressing through a learning trajectory, and those students are impacted by fellow classmates and teacher and school-level effects. As a consequence, some specific data mining techniques are needed to address learning [8] and other data about learners. Some traditional techniques can be adapted, some cannot. This trend has led to psychometric methods designed to address these issues of hierarchy and nonindependence being integrated into EDM, as can be seen in several chapters in this volume. However, EDM is still an emerging research area, and we can foresee that its further development will result in a better understanding of challenges peculiar to this field and will help researchers involved in EDM to see what techniques can be adopted and what new tailored techniques have to be developed.

The application of data mining techniques to educational systems in order to improve learning can be viewed as a formative evaluation technique. Formative evaluation [1] is the evaluation of an educational program while it is still in development, and with the purpose of continually improving the program. Examining how students use the system is one way to evaluate instructional design in a formative manner and may help educational designers to improve the instructional materials [5]. Data mining techniques can be used to gather information that can be used to assist educational designers to establish a

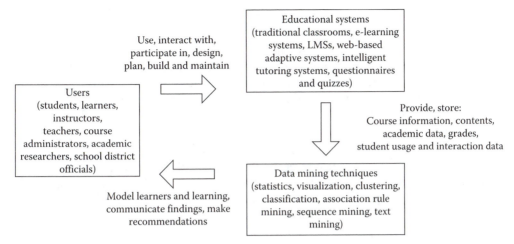

FIGURE 1.1
Applying data mining to the design of educational systems.

pedagogical basis for decisions when designing or modifying an environment's pedagogical approach.

The application of data mining to the design of educational systems is an iterative cycle of hypothesis formation, testing, and refinement (see Figure 1.1).

Mined knowledge should enter the design loop towards guiding, facilitating, and enhancing learning as a whole. In this process, the goal is not just to turn data into knowledge, but also to filter mined knowledge for decision making.

As we can see in Figure 1.1, educators and educational designers (whether in school districts, curriculum companies, or universities) design, plan, build, and maintain educational systems. Students use those educational systems to learn. Building off of the available information about courses, students, usage, and interaction, data mining techniques can be applied in order to discover useful knowledge that helps to improve educational designs. The discovered knowledge can be used not only by educational designers and teachers, but also by end users—students. Hence, the application of data mining in educational systems can be oriented to supporting the specific needs of each of these categories of stakeholders.

1.2 Educational Applications

In the last several years, EDM has been applied to address a wide number of goals. In this book we can distinguish between the following general applications or tasks:

- *Communicating to stakeholders.* The objective is to help to course administrators and educators in analyzing students' activities and usage information in courses. The most frequently used techniques for this type of goal are exploratory data analysis through statistical analysis and visualizations or reports, and process mining.

Chapters 2 through 4, 9, 12, 22, 24, and 28 discuss methods and case studies for this category of application.

- *Maintaining and improving courses.* The objective is to help to course administrators and educators in determining how to improve courses (contents, activities, links, etc.), using information (in particular) about student usage and learning. The most frequently used techniques for this type of goal are association, clustering, and classification. Chapters 7, 17, 26, and 34 discuss methods and case studies for this category of application.

- *Generating recommendation.* The objective is to recommend to students which content (or tasks or links) is most appropriate for them at the current time. The most frequently used techniques for this type of goal are association, sequencing, classification, and clustering. Chapters 6, 8, 12, 18, 19, and 32 discuss methods and case studies for this category of application.

- *Predicting student grades and learning outcomes.* The objective is to predict a student's final grades or other types of learning outcomes (such as retention in a degree program or future ability to learn), based on data from course activities. The most frequently used techniques for this type of goal are classification, clustering, and association. Chapters 5 and 13 discuss methods and case studies for this category of application.

- *Student modeling.* User modeling in the educational domain has a number of applications, including for example the detection (often in real time) of student states and characteristics such as satisfaction, motivation, learning progress, or certain types of problems that negatively impact their learning outcomes (making too many errors, misusing or underusing help, gaming the system, inefficiently exploring learning resources, etc.), affect, learning styles, and preferences. The common objective here is to create a student model from usage information. The frequently used techniques for this type of goal are not only clustering, classification, and association analysis, but also statistical analyses, Bayes networks (including Bayesian Knowledge-Tracing), psychometric models, and reinforcement learning. Chapters 6, 12, 14 through 16, 20, 21, 23, 25, 27, 31, 33, and 35 discuss methods and case studies for this category of application.

- *Domain structure analysis.* The objective is to determine domain structure, using the ability to predict student performance as a measure of the quality of a domain structure model. Performance on tests or within a learning environment is utilized for this goal. The most frequently used techniques for this type of goal are association rules, clustering methods, and space-searching algorithms. Chapters 10, 11, 29, and 30 discuss methods and case studies for this category of application.

1.3 Objectives, Content, and How to Read This Book

Our objective, in compiling this book, is to provide as complete as possible a picture of the current state of the art in the application of data mining techniques in education. Recent developments in technology enhanced learning have resulted in a widespread use of e-learning environments and educational software, within many regular university courses and primary and secondary schools. For instance, 6% of U.S. high schools now use Cognitive Tutor software for mathematics learning (cf. [6]). As these environments become more widespread, ever-larger collections of data have been obtained by educational data repositories. A case study on one of the largest of these repositories is given in the chapter on the PSLC DataShop by Koedinger and colleagues.

This expansion of data has led to increasing interest among education researchers in a variety of disciplines, and among practitioners and educational administrators, in tools and techniques for analysis of the accumulated data to improve understanding of learners and learning process, to drive the development of more effective educational software and better educational decision-making. This interest has become a driving force for EDM. We believe that this book can support researchers and practitioners in integrating EDM into their research and practice, and bringing the educational and data mining communities together, so that education experts understand what types of questions EDM can address, and data miners understand what types of questions are of importance to educational design and educational decision-making.

This volume, the *Handbook of Educational Data Mining*, consists of two parts. In the first part, we offer nine surveys and tutorials about the principal data mining techniques that have been applied in education. In the second part, we give a set of 25 case studies, offering readers a rich overview of the problems that EDM has produced leverage for.

The book is structured so that it can be read in its entirety, first introducing concepts and methods, and then showing their applications. However, readers can also focus on areas of specific interest, as have been outlined in the categorization of the educational applications. We welcome readers to the field of EDM and hope that it is of value to their research or practical goals. If you enjoy this book, we hope that you will join us at a future iteration of the Educational Data Mining conference; see www.educationaldatamining.org for the latest information, and to subscribe to our community mailing list, edm-announce.

References

1. Arruabarrena, R., Pérez, T. A., López-Cuadrado, J., and Vadillo, J. G. J. (2002). On evaluating adaptive systems for education. In *International Conference on Adaptive Hypermedia and Adaptive Web-Based Systems*, Málaga, Spain, pp. 363–367.
2. Baker, R.S.J.d. and Yacef, K. (2009). The state of educational data mining in 2009: A review and future visions. *Journal of Educational Data Mining*, 1(1), 3–17.
3. Hanna, M. (2004). Data mining in the e-learning domain. *Computers and Education Journal*, 42(3), 267–287.
4. Hirschman, L., Park, J.C., Tsujii, J., Wong, W., and Wu, C.H. (2002). Accomplishments and challenges in literature data mining for biology. *Bioinformatics*, 18(12), 1553–1561.
5. Ingram, A. (1999). Using web server logs in evaluating instructional web sites. *Journal of Educational Technology Systems*, 28(2), 137–157.
6. Koedinger, K. and Corbett, A. (2006). Cognitive tutors: Technology bringing learning science to the classroom. In K. Sawyer (Ed.), *The Cambridge Handbook of the Learning Sciences*. Cambridge, U.K.: Cambridge University Press, pp. 61–78.
7. Lewis, M. (2004). *Moneyball: The Art of Winning an Unfair Game*. New York: Norton.
8. Li, J. and Zaïane, O. (2004). Combining usage, content, and structure data to improve web site recommendation. In *International Conference on Ecommerce and Web Technologies*, Zaragoza, Spain, pp. 305–315.

9. Pahl, C. and Donnellan, C. (2003). Data mining technology for the evaluation of web-based teaching and learning systems. In *Proceedings of the Congress e-Learning*, Montreal, Canada.
10. Romero, C. and Ventura, S. (2007). Educational data mining: A survey from 1995 to 2005. *Expert Systems with Applications*, 33(1), 135–146.
11. Srivastava, J., Cooley, R., Deshpande, M., and Tan, P. (2000). Web usage mining: Discovery and applications of usage patterns from web data. *SIGKDD Explorations*, 1(2), 12–23.
12. Shaw, M.J., Subramanian, C., Tan, G.W., and Welge, M.E. (2001). Knowledge management and data management for marketing. *Decision Support Systems*, 31(1), 127–137.

Part I

Basic Techniques, Surveys and Tutorials

2

Visualization in Educational Environments

Riccardo Mazza

CONTENTS

2.1 Introduction

This chapter presents an introduction to information visualization, a new discipline with origins in the late 1980s that is part of the field of human–computer interaction. We will illustrate the purposes of this discipline, its basic concepts, and some design principles that can be applied to graphically render students' data from educational systems. The chapter starts with a description of information visualization followed by a discussion on some design principles, which are defined by outstanding scholars in the field. Finally, some systems in which visualizations have been used in learning environments to represent user models, discussions, and tracking data are described.

2.2 What Is Information Visualization?

Visualization, which may be defined as "the display of data with the aim of maximizing comprehension rather than photographic realism*", has greatly increased over the last years thanks to the availability of more and more powerful computers at low cost. The discipline of information visualization (IV) [2,16] originated in the late 1980s for the purpose of exploring the use of computers to generate interactive, visual representation to explain and understand specific features of data. The basic principle of IV is to present data in a visual form and use human perceptual abilities for their interpretation.

As in many other fields, several people have tried to give a rigorous, scientific definition of the discipline of IV. The definition that received most consensus from the community of the researchers seems to be the one given by Card et al. in their famous collection of papers on IV: *the readings* [2]. According to them, IV is "the use of computer-supported, interactive, visual representations of abstract data to amplify cognition." By this definition, four terms are the key to understand this domain: visual representation, interaction, abstract data, and cognitive amplification. We will try to analyze each of them to clearly describe the field and their applications.

2.2.1 Visual Representations

There are many situations in the real world where we try to understand some phenomena, data, and events using graphics. Some aspects, such as when people need to find a route in a city, the stock market trends over a certain period, and the weather forecast, may be understood better using graphics rather than text. Graphical representation of data, compared to the textual or tabular ones (in case of numbers), takes advantage of the human visual perception. Perception is very powerful as it conveys large amount of information to our mind, and allowing us to recognize essential features and to make important inferences. This is possible thanks to the fact that there is a series of identification and recognition operations that our brain performs in an "automatic" way without the need to focus our attention or even be conscious of them. Perceptual tasks that can be performed in a very short time lapse (typically between 200 and 250 ms or less) are called pre-attentive, since they occur without the intervention of consciousness [20].

According to Ware [20], the graphical proprieties that are pre-attentively processed can be grouped into four basic categories: color, form, movement, and spatial position. Managing properly the elements that are "pre-attentively" processed can make a difference in a user interface and is fundamental for the generation of good user interfaces and graphics.

Let us try to explain these concepts with a practical example.

In Figure 2.1 are represented a list of numbers together with bars whose length is proportional to the number on the left. Suppose we have to find the maximum and the minimum between the numbers. If we don't have the bars on the right, we need to read and understand each value, and take into account the maximum and the minimum value we read until we reach

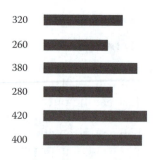

| 320 |
| 260 |
| 380 |
| 280 |
| 420 |
| 400 |

FIGURE 2.1
Comparing perception of lines with numbers.

---

* *A Dictionary of Computing*. Oxford University Press, 1996. *Oxford Reference Online*. Oxford University Press.

the end. This can be defined as a scrutiny task, because it is a conscious operation that involves memory, semantics, and symbolism.

Let us try to do the same operation, this time using the bars on the left. The length of the bars lets us to identify almost immediately the longest and the shortest thanks to the pre-attentive property of length, the length of the bars allows us to almost immediately identify the longest and the shortest.

Graphical representations are often associated with the term "visualization" (or "visualisation" in the British version of the term). It has been noted by Spence [16] that there is a diversity of uses of the term "visualization." For instance, in a dictionary the following definitions can be found:

> Visualize: form a mental image of...*
> Visualization: The display of data with the aim of maximizing comprehension rather than photographic realism.†
> Visualization: the act or process of interpreting in visual terms or of putting into visible form‡

These definitions reveal that visualization is an activity in which humans are engaged, as an internal construct of the mind [16,20]. It is something that cannot be printed on a paper or displayed on a computer screen. With these considerations, we can summarize that visualization is a cognitive activity, facilitated by graphical external representations from which people construct internal mental representation of the world [16,20].

Computers may facilitate the visualization process with some visualization tools. This is especially true in recent years with the availability of powerful computers at low cost. However, the above definition is independent from computers: although computers can facilitate visualization, it still remains an activity that happens in the mind.

2.2.2 Interaction

Recently there has been great progress in high-performance, affordable computer graphics. The common personal computer has reached a graphic power that just 10 years ago was possible only with very expensive graphic workstations specifically built for the graphic process. At the same time, there has been a rapid expansion in information that people have to process for their daily activities. This need led scientists to explore new ways to represent huge amounts of data with computers, taking advantage of the possibility of users interacting with the algorithms that create the graphical representation. Interactivity derives from the people's ability to also identify interesting facts when the visual display changes and allows them to manipulate the visualization or the underlying data to explore such changes.

2.2.3 Abstract Data

IV definitions introduce the term "abstract data," for which some clarification is needed. The data itself can have a wide variety of forms, but we can distinguish between data that have a physical correspondence and is closely related to mathematical structures and models (e.g., the airflow around the wing of an airplane, or the density of the ozone layer surrounding

---

* *The Concise Oxford Dictionary.* Ed. Judy Pearsall. Oxford University Press, 2001. *Oxford Reference Online.* Oxford University Press.
† *A Dictionary of Computing.* Oxford University Press, 1996. *Oxford Reference Online.* Oxford University Press.
‡ *Merriam-Webster Online Dictionary.* http://www.webster.com

earth), and data that is more abstract in nature (e.g., the stock market fluctuations). The former is known as scientific visualization, and the latter as IV [4,16,19].

Scientific visualization was developed in response to the needs of scientists and engineers to view experimental or phenomenal data in graphical formats (an example is given in Figure 2.2), while IV is dealing with unstructured data sets as a distinct flavor [4]. In Table 2.1 is reported a table with some examples of abstract data and physical data.

However, we ought to say that this distinction is not strict, and sometimes abstract and physical data are combined in a single representation. For instance, the results from the last Swiss federal referendum on changing the Swiss law on asylum can be considered a sort of abstract data if the goal of the graphical representation is to highlight the preference (yes or no) with respect to the social status, age, sex, etc. of the voter. But if we want to highlight the percentage that the referendum got in each town, a mapping with the geographical location might be helpful to see how the linguistic regions, cantons, and the proximity with the border influenced the choice of the electorate (see Figure 2.3).

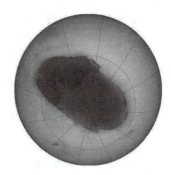

FIGURE 2.2
Example of scientific visualization: The ozone hole the South Pole on September 22, 2004. (Image from the NASA Goddard Space Center archives and reproduced with permission.)

2.2.4 Cognitive Amplification

Graphics aid thinking and reasoning in several ways. For example, let us take a multiplication (a typical mental activity), e.g., 27×42 in our head, without having a pencil and paper. This calculation made with our mind will take usually at least five times longer than when using a pencil and paper [2]. The difficulty in doing this operation in the mind is holding the partial results of the multiplication in the memory until they can be used:

$$
\begin{array}{rrrl}
 & 2 & 7 & \times \\
\hline
 & 4 & 2 & \\
\hline
 & 5 & 4 & \\
1 & 0 & 8 & - \\
\hline
1 & 1 & 3 & 4 \\
\hline
\end{array}
$$

This example shows how visual and manipulative use of the external representations and processing amplifies cognitive performance. Graphics use the visual representations that help to amplify cognition. They convey information to our minds that allows us to search

TABLE 2.1

Some Examples of Abstract Data and Physical Data

Abstract Data	Physical Data
Names	Data gathered from instruments
Grades	Simulations of wind flow
News or stories	Geographical locations
Jobs	Molecular structure

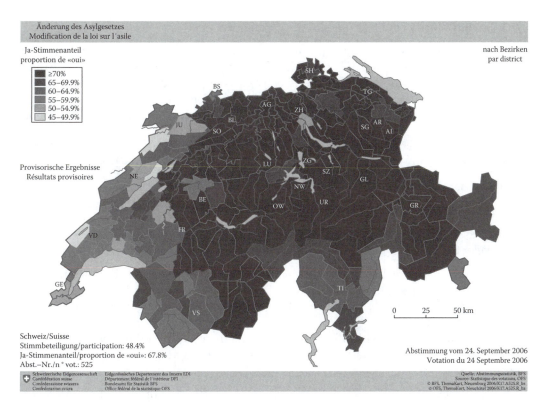

FIGURE 2.3

Graphical representation of results of federal referendum in Switzerland on September 24, 2006. (Image from the Swiss Federal Statistical Office, http://www.bfs.admin.ch. © Bundesamt für Statistik, ThemaKart 2009, reproduced with permission.)

for patterns, recognize relationship between data, and perform some inferences more easily. Card et al. [2] propose six major ways in which visualizations can amplify cognition by

1. Increasing the memory and processing resources available to users
2. Reducing the search for information
3. Using visual representations to enhance the detection of patterns
4. Enabling perceptual inference operations
5. Using perceptual mechanisms for monitoring
6. Encoding information in a manipulable medium

2.3 Design Principles

The basic principle of IV is to present data in form of graphical representations and use human perceptual abilities for their interpretation. "A picture is worth a thousand words" is a well-known old adage that everybody knows. But why (and in which situations) graphical representations are effective?

2.3.1 Spatial Clarity

Graphical representations may facilitate the way we present and understand large complex datasets. As Larkin and Simon [7] argued in their seminal paper "Why a diagram is (sometimes) worth ten thousand words," the effectiveness of graphical representations is due to their spatial clarity. Well-constructed graphical representations of data allow people to quickly to gain insights that might lead to significant discoveries as a result of spatial clarity.

Larkin and Simon compared the computational efficiency of diagrams and sentences in solving physics problems, and concluded that diagrams helped in three basic ways:

Locality is enabled by grouping together information that is used together. This avoids large amounts of search and allows different information closely located to be processed simultaneously. For example, Figure 2.4 represents the map of the Madrid metro transport system. In this map the locality principle is applied by placing metro lines and zones in the same map. The traveler can find in the same place information about lines, connections, and stations.

Minimizing labeling is enabled by using location to group information about a single element, avoiding the need to match symbolic labels and leading to reducing the working memory load. For example, the Madrid transport map (Figure 2.4) uses visual entities such as lines depicted with different colors to denote different metro lines. Connections are clearly indicated by a white circle that connects the corresponding lines. There is no need to use textual representations because the connections are explicitly represented in the graphics.

Perceptual enhancement is enabled by supporting a large number of perceptual inferences that are easy for humans to perform. For example, in Figure 2.4, a traveler who has to travel from *Nuevos Ministerios* to *Opera* can see that there are different combination of lines and connection that he can take, and probably can decide which is the fastest way to reach the destination.

2.3.2 Graphical Excellence

Sometimes graphical representations of data have been used to distort the underlying data. Tufte [18] and Bertin [1] list a number of examples of graphics that distort the underlying data or communicate incorrect ideas. Tufte indicates some principles that should be followed to build effective well-designed graphics. In particular, a graphical display should [18]

- Show the data.
- Induce the viewer to think about the substance, not the methodology.
- Avoid distorting what the data says.
- Present many data in a small space.
- Give different perspectives on the data—from a broad overview to a fine structure.
- Serve a reasonably clear purpose: description, exploration, tabulation, or decoration.
- Be closely integrated with the statistical and verbal descriptions of the data set.
- Encourage inferential processes, such as comparing different pieces of data.
- Give different perspectives on the data—from a broad overview to a fine structure.

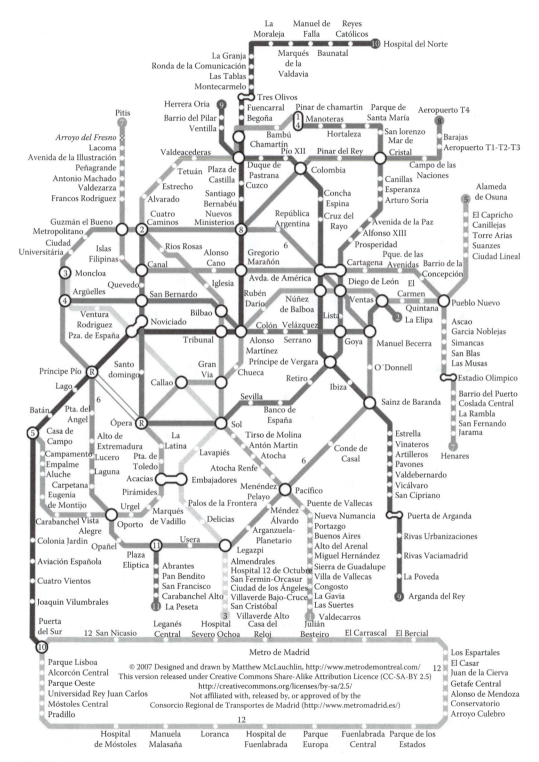

FIGURE 2.4
Map of the Madrid metro system. (Images licensed under Creative Commons Share-Alike.)

Following these principles is the key to build what Tufte calls the graphical excellence, and it consists in "giving the viewer the greatest number of ideas in the shortest time with the least ink in the smallest space" [18].

A key question in IV is how we convert abstract data into a graphical representation, preserving the underlying meaning and, at the same time, providing new insight. There is no "magic formula" that helps the researchers to build systematically a graphical representation starting from a raw set of data. It depends on the nature of the data, the type of information to be represented and its use, but more consistently, it depends on the creativity of the designer of the graphical representation. Some interesting ideas, even if innovative, have often failed in practice.

Graphics facilitate IV, but a number of issues must be considered [16,18]:

1. Data is nearly always multidimensional, while graphics represented on a computer screen or on a paper are presented in a 2D surface.

2. Sometimes we need to represent a huge dataset, while the number of data viewable on a computer screen or on a paper is limited.

3. Data may vary during the time, while graphics are static.

4. Humans have remarkable abilities to select, manipulate, and rearrange data, so the graphical representations should provide users with these features.

2.4 Visualizations in Educational Software

In this section we will explore some graphical representations that have been adopted in educational contexts. We will concentrate our analysis in software applications that aims to provide learning to students and gives the instructors some feedback on actions and improvements undertaken by students with the subject. We will consider three types of applications: visualization of user models, visualization of online communications, and visualization of students' tracking data.

2.4.1 Visualizations of User Models

A user model is a representation of a set of beliefs about the user, particularly their knowledge in various areas, and their goals and preferences. Student models are a key component of intelligent educational systems used to represent the student's understanding of material taught. Methods for user modeling are often exploited in educational systems. These models are enabling the increasing personalization of software, particularly on the Internet, where the user model is the set of information and beliefs that is used to personalize the Web site [19].

2.4.1.1 UM/QV

QV [6] is an overview interface for UM [5], a toolkit for cooperative user modeling. A model is structured as a hierarchy of elements of the domain. QV uses a hierarchical representation of concepts to present the user model. For instance, Figure 2.5 gives a graphical representation of a model showing concepts of the SAM text editor. It gives a quick overview whether the user appears to know each element of the domain. QV exploits different types

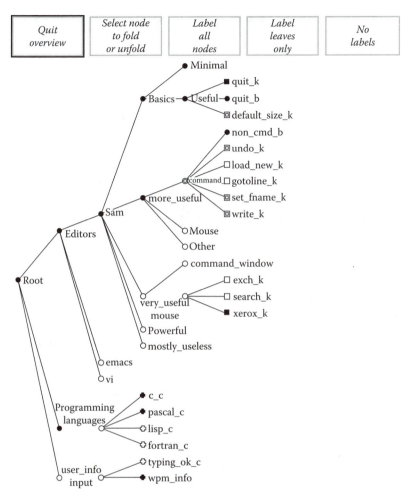

FIGURE 2.5
The QV tool showing a user model. (Image courtesy of Judy Kay.)

of geometric forms and color to represent known/unknown concepts. A square indicates a knowledge component, diamond a belief, a circle indicates a nonleaf node, and crosses indicate other component types. The filling of the shape is used to indicate the component value. For instance, in the example, the white squares show that the user knows that element, while the dark squares indicate lack of knowledge. Nested shapes, such as `default _ size _ k` or `undo _ k`, indicate that the system has not been able to determine whether the user knows it or not (e.g., if there is inconsistency in the information about the user). The view of the graph is manipulable, in particular, clicking on a nonleaf node causes the subtree to be displayed, useful in case of models having a large number of components to be displayed.

2.4.1.2 ViSMod

ViSMod [22] is an interactive visualization tool for the representation of Bayesian learner models. In ViSMod, learners and instructors can inspect the learner model using a graphical representation of the Bayesian network. ViSMod uses concept maps to render a

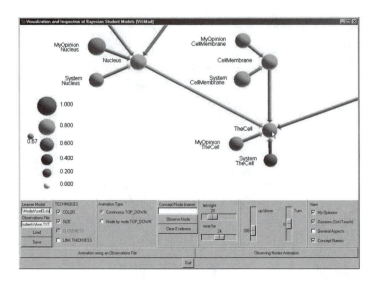

FIGURE 2.6
A screenshot of ViSMod showing a fragment of a Bayesian student model in the area of biology cell. (Image courtesy of Diego Zapata-Rivera.)

Bayesian student model and various visualization techniques such as color, size proximity link thickness, and animation to represent concepts such as marginal probability, changes in probability, probability propagation, and cause–effect relationships (Figure 2.6). One interesting aspect of this model is that the overall belief of a student knowing a particular concept is captured taking into account the students' opinion, the instructors' opinion, and the influence of social aspects of learning on each concept. By using VisMod, it is possible to inspect complex networks by focusing on a particular segment (e.g., zooming or scrolling) and using animations to represent how probability propagation occurs in a simple network in which several causes affect a single node.

2.4.1.3 E-KERMIT

KERMIT (Knowledge-based Entity Relationship Modelling Intelligent Tutor) [17] is a knowledge-based intelligent tutoring system aimed at teaching conceptual database design for university level students. KERMIT teaches the basic entity-relationship (ER) database modeling by presenting to the student the requirements for a database, and the student has to design an ER diagram for it. E-KERMIT is an extension of KERMIT developed by Hartley and Mitrovic [3] with an open student model. In E-KERMIT the student may examine with a dedicated interface the global view of the student model (see Figure 2.7). The course domain is divided in categories, representing the processes and concepts in ER modeling. In the representation of the open student model concepts of the domain are mapped with histograms. The histogram shows how much of the concrete part of the domain the student knows correctly (in black) or incorrectly (in gray) and the percentage of covered on the concepts of the category. For instance, the example shows that the student covered 32% of the concepts of the category Type, and has scored 23% out of a possible 32% on this category. This means that the student's performance on category type so far is 77% (23/320 × 100).

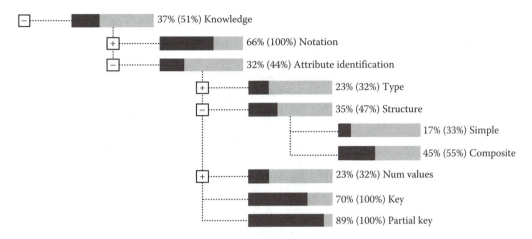

FIGURE 2.7
The main view of a student's progress in E-KERMIT. Progress bars indicate how much the student comprehends each category of the domain. (Image reproduced with permission of Tanja Mitrovic.)

2.4.2 Visualizations of Online Communications

One important aspect that should be considered in distance education is the social one. There are various types of interactions that may occur in distance learning, such as interactions between individual students and interactions between students and the instructors. In the Internet, the main tools that engage students and instructors in communicative activities are discussion forums, e-mail, and chat. Some works attempted to visualize the communications exchanged in educational settings to discover patterns, roles, and engagement of students in social activities.

2.4.2.1 Simuligne

Simuligne [12] is a research project that uses social network analysis [14] to monitor group communications in distance learning in order to help instructors detect collaboration problems or slowdown of group interactions. Social network analysis is a research field that "characterize the group's structure and, in particular, the influence of each of the members on that group, reasoning on the relationship that can be observed in that group" (Reffay and Chanier [12], p. 343). It provides both a graphical and a mathematical analysis of interactions between individuals. The graphical version can be represented with a network, where the nodes in the network are the individuals and groups while the links show relationships or flows between the nodes. The social network analysis can help to determine the prominence of a student respect to others, and other social network researcher measures, such as the cohesion factor between students. The cohesion is a statistical measure that represents how much the individuals socialize in a group that shares goals and values. Reffay and Chanier applied this theory to a list of e-mails exchanged in a class of distance learners. Figure 2.8 illustrates the graphical representation of the e-mail graph for each learning group. We can see for instance that there is no communication with Gl2 and Gl3, or the central role of the tutor in the discussions (node Gt).

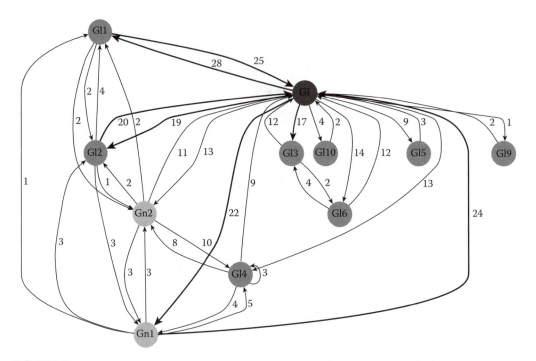

FIGURE 2.8
The communication graph of the e-mail exchanged within groups in Simuligne. (Image courtesy of Christophe Reffay.)

2.4.2.2 PeopleGarden

PeopleGarden [21] uses a flower and garden metaphor to visualize participations on a message board. The message board is visualized as a garden full of flowers. Each flower represents one individual. The height of flower denotes amount of time a user has been at the board and its petals his postings. Initial postings are shown in red, replies in blue. An example is represented in Figure 2.9. The figure can help the instructor of a course to quickly grasp the underlying situation, such as a single dominant member in discussion on the left or a group with many members at different level of participation on the right.

2.4.3 Visualizations of Student-Tracking Data

Many software environments have been produced in the latest years to facilitate the adoption of distance learning through the Web. Thanks to the diffusion and the popularity of the Web, many software environments take advantage of the client–server communication on the Internet to support distance learning. Environments called course management systems (CMSs) have been developed for this purpose. Using CMSs, instructors can distribute information to students, produce content material, prepare assignments and tests, engage in discussions, and manage distance classes.

One of the most common problems with CMSs is the difficulty for the instructor to verify what students are doing: are the students attending the course, reading materials, and performing exercises? CMSs accumulate tracking data in form of large log in a distance course, and it can be used to monitor the students' activities. This data is accessible

FIGURE 2.9
The PeopleGarden visual representations of participation on a message board. (Image by Rebecca Xiong and Judith Donath, © 1999 MIT media lab.)

to the instructor of the course, but it is commonly presented in the format of a textual log file, which is inappropriate for the instructor's needs [8]. To this end, since the log data is collected in a format that is suitable to be analyzed with IV techniques and tools, a number of approaches have been proposed to graphically represent the tracking data generated by a CMS.

Recently, a number of researches that exploits graphical representations to analyze the student tracking have been proposed. ViSION [15] is a tool that was implemented to display student interactions with a courseware website designed to assist students with their group project work. CourseVis [10] is another application that exploits graphical representations to analyze the student tracking data. CourseVis is a visual student tracking tool that transforms tracking data from a CMS into graphical representations that can be explored and manipulated by course instructors to examine social, cognitive, and behavioral aspects of distance students. CourseVis was started from a systematic investigation aimed to find out what information about distance students the instructors need when they run courses with a CMS, as well as to identify possible ways to help instructors acquire this information. This investigation was conducted with a survey, and the results were used to draw the requirements and to inform the design of the graphical representations. One of the (several) graphical representations produced by CourseVis is reported in Figure 2.10.

This comprehensive image represents in a single view the behaviors of a specific student in an online course. It takes advantage of single-axis composition method (multiple variables share an axis and are aligned using that axis) for presenting large number of variables in a 2D metric space. With a common x-axis mapping the dates of the course, a number of variables are represented. The information represented here are namely the student's access to the content pages (ordered by topics of the course), the global access to the course (content pages, quiz, discussion, etc.), a progress with the schedule of the course, messages (posted, read, follow-ups), and the submission of quizzes and assignments. For a detailed description of CourseVis, see Mazza and Dimitrova [10].

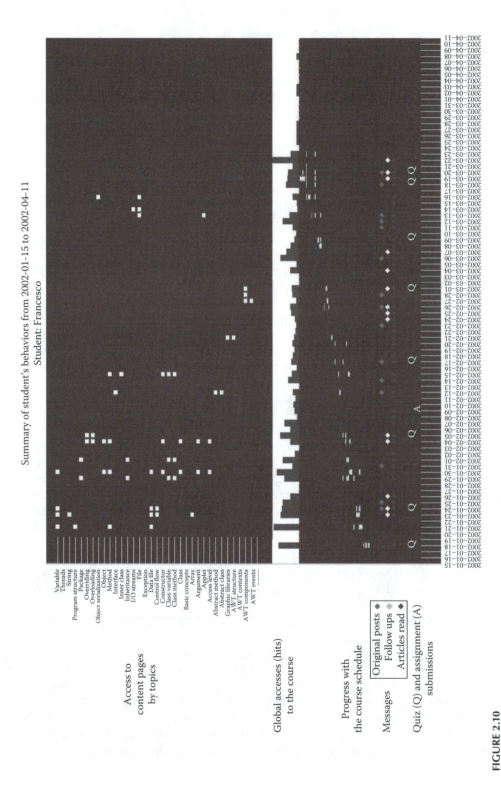

FIGURE 2.10
Graphical representation of student's behaviors in CourseVis. (Image from Mazza, R. and Dimitrova, V., Generation of graphical representations of student tracking data in course management systems, in *Proceedings of the 9th International Conference on Information Visualisation*, London, U.K., July 6–8, 2005. © 2005 IEEE.)

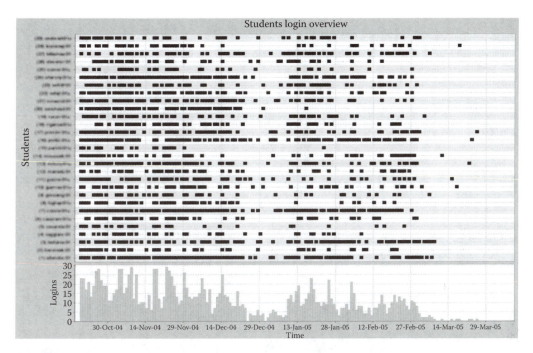

FIGURE 2.11

A graph reporting an overview of students' accesses to resources of the course in GISMO.

The produced visualizations were evaluated with an empirical study [8], which has shown that graphical representations produced with it can help instructors to identify individuals who need particular attention, discover patterns and trends in accesses and discussions, and reflect on their teaching practice. However, it revealed some limitations, such as the adoption of 3D graphics in one of the graphical representations (which was considered too problematic for the typical users of the systems), and the lack of full integration with the CMS.

For these reasons, the ideas behind CourseVis were applied in a plug-in for the CMS open source Moodle called GISMO [11]. GISMO is developed as a plug-in module fully integrated with the CMS and is available for download at http://gismo.sourceforge.net.

Figure 2.11 shows the students' accesses to the course. It reports a graph of the accesses to the course. A simple matrix formed by students' names (on *Y*-axis) and dates of the course (on *X*-axis) is used to represent the course accesses. Each blue square represents at least one access to the course made by the student on the selected date. The histogram at the bottom shows the global number of hits to the course made by all students on each date. The instructor has an overview of the global student access to the course with a clear identification of patterns and trends.

Figure 2.12 reports an overview of students' accesses to resources of the course, student names on the *Y*-axis and resource names on the *X*-axis. A mark is depicted if the student accessed this resource, and the color of the mark ranges from light color to dark color, according to the number of times he/she accessed this resource. With this picture, the instructor has an overview of the student accesses to the pages course with a clear identification of most (and last) accessed resources.

GISMO is described in detail in Mazza and Milani [9] and Mazza and Botturi [11].

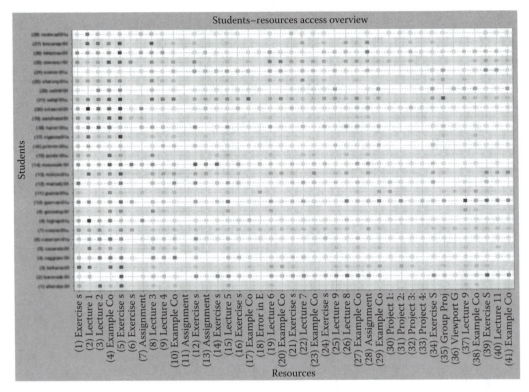

FIGURE 2.12
A graph reporting an overview of students' accesses to resources of the course.

2.5 Conclusions

Online educational systems collect a vast amount of information that is valuable for analyzing students' behavior. However, due to the vast amount of data these systems generate, it is very difficult to manage manually [13]. In the last few years, researchers have begun to investigate various methods to extract valuable information from this huge amount of data that might be helpful to instructors to manage their courses. Data mining and IV could be two approaches that might help to uncover new, interesting, and useful knowledge based on students' usage data [13].

In this chapter, we presented some ideas and principles of using IV techniques to graphically render students' data collect by web-based educational systems. Thanks to our visual perceptual abilities, we have seen how graphical representations may be very useful to quickly discover patterns, regularities, and trends on data and provide a useful overview of the whole dataset. We described some systems where visualizations have been used in learning environments to represent user models, discussions, and tracking data.

It is recognized that data mining algorithms alone are not enough, as well as it is recognized that it is infeasible to consider graphics displays alone an effective solution to the analysis of complex and large data sets. The two approaches data mining and IV could be combined together in order to build something that is greater than the sum of the parts. Future research has to consider these two approaches and merge toward a unified research stream.

References

1. Bertin, J. (1981). *Graphics and Graphic Information Processing*. Walter de Gruyter, Berlin, Germany.
2. Card K. S., Mackinlay J. D., and Shneiderman B. (1999). *Readings in Information Visualization, Using Vision to Think*. Morgan Kaufmann, San Francisco, CA.
3. Hartley, D. and Mitrovic, A. (2002). Supporting learning by opening the student model. In *Intelligent Tutoring Systems, Proceedings of the 6th International Conference, ITS 2002*, Biarritz, France and San Sebastian, Spain, June 2–7, 2002, volume 2363 of *Lecture Notes in Computer Science*, pp. 453–462. Springer, Berlin, Germany.
4. Hermann, I., Melancon, G., and Marshall, M. S. (2000). Graph visualisation and navigation in information visualisation. *IEEE Transaction on Visualization and Computer Graphics*, 1(6):24–43. http://www.cwi.nl/InfoVisu/Survey/StarGraphVisuInInfoVis.html
5. Kay, J. (1995). The um toolkit for cooperative user modelling. *User Modeling and User Adapted Interaction*, 4:149–196.
6. Kay, J. (1999). A scrutable user modelling shell for user-adapted interaction. PhD thesis, Basser Department of Computer Science, University of Sydney, Sydney, Australia.
7. Larkin, J. H. and Simon, H. A. (1987). Why a diagram is (sometimes) worth ten thousand words. In Glasgow, J., Narayahan, H., and Chandrasekaram, B., editors, *Diagrammatic Reasoning—Cognitive and Computational Perspectives*, pp. 69–109. Cambridge, MA: AAAI Press/The MIT Press. 1995. Reprinted from *Cognitive Science*, 11:65–100, 1987.
8. Mazza, R. (2004). Using information visualization to facilitate instructors in web-based distance learning. PhD thesis dissertation, Faculty of Communication Sciences, University of Lugano, Lugano, Switzerland.
9. Mazza, R. and Milani, C. (2005). Exploring usage analysis in learning systems: Gaining insights from visualisations. In *Workshop on Usage Analysis in Learning Systems. 12th International Conference on Artificial Intelligence in Education (AIED 2005)*, pp. 65–72. Amsterdam, the Netherlands, July 18, 2005.
10. Mazza, R. and Dimitrova, V. (2007). CourseVis: A graphical student monitoring tool for facilitating instructors in web-based distance courses. *International Journal in Human-Computer Studies (IJHCS)*, 65(2):125–139. Elsevier Ltd.
11. Mazza, R. and Botturi, L. (2007). Monitoring an online course with the GISMO tool: A case study. *Journal of Interactive Learning Research*, 18(2):251–265. Chesapeake, VA: AACE.
12. Reffay, C. and Chanier, T. (2003) How social network analysis can help to measure cohesion in collaborative distance learning?. *Proceeding of the Computer Supported Collaborative Learning Conference (CSCL'03)*, p. 343–352. Kluwer Academic Publishers, Bergen, Norway.
13. Romero, C. et al. (2008). Data mining in course management systems: Moodle case study and tutorial. *Computers & Education*, 51(1):368–384.
14. Scott, J. (1991). *Social Network Analysis. A Handbook*. SAGE Publication, London, U.K.
15. Sheard, J., Albrecht, D., and Butbul, E. (2005) ViSION: Visualizing student interactions online. In *The Eleventh Australasian World Wide Web Conference (AusWeb05)*. Queensland, Australia, July 2–6, 2005.
16. Spence R. (2001). *Information Visualisation*. Addison-Wesley, Harlow, U.K., 2001.
17. Suraweera, P. and Mitrovic, A. (2002). Kermit: A constraint-based tutor for database modeling. In *ITS 2002, Proceedings of 6th International Conference*, volume 2363 of *Lecture Notes in Computer Science*, pp. 377–387. Springer-Verlag, Berlin, Germany.
18. Tufte, E. R. (1983). *The Visual Display of Quantitative Information*. Graphics Press, Cheshire, CT.

19. Uther, J. (2001). On the visualisation of large user models in web based systems. PhD thesis, School of Information Technologies, University of Sydney, Sydney, Australia.

20. Ware, C. (1999). *Information Visualization. Perception for Design. Morgan Kaufmann Series in Interactive Technologies*. Morgan Kaufmann, San Francisco, CA.

21. Xiong, R. and Donath, J. (1999). Peoplegarden: Creating data portraits for users. In *Proceedings of the 12th Annual ACM Symposium on User Interface Software and Technology*. November 7–10, 1999, Asheville, NC.

22. Zapata-Rivera, J. D. and Greer, J. E. (2001). Externalising learner modelling representations. In *Workshop on External Representations in AIED: Multiple Forms and Multiple Roles*, pp. 71–76. Held with the *AI-ED 2001—10th International Conference on Artificial Intelligence in Education*, San Antonio, TX, May 19–23, 2001.

23. Mazza, R. and Dimitrova, V. (2005). Generation of graphical representations of student tracking data in course management systems. In *Proceedings of the 9th International Conference on Information Visualisation*, London, U.K., July 6–8, 2005.

3

Basics of Statistical Analysis of Interactions Data from Web-Based Learning Environments

Judy Sheard

CONTENTS

3.1 Introduction

With the enormous growth in the use of Web-based learning environments, there is a need for feedback and evaluation methods that are suitable for these environments. Traditional methods used to monitor and assess learning behavior are not necessarily effective or appropriate for an electronic learning environment. However, Web technologies have enabled a new way of collecting data about learning behavior. The automatic capture and recording of information about student interactions using computer software processes provides a rich source of data. In the 1980s, Zuboff [1], a social scientist, proposed that computer-generated interactions could be used to provide information about online learning processes. Zuboff recognized that as well as *automating* tasks, computers also generate information about the processing of those tasks. She termed this process *informating* and predicted that the capacity for a machine to "informate" about its actions would ultimately reconfigure the nature of work. Early research studies of computer interactions captured keystroke type data, which provided information about general technology usage. The focus of studies of computer interactions has now shifted from considering the technology in isolation to understanding the user in relationship to the technology.

Data of student interactions with a Web-based learning environment may be stored on a Web server log as part of normal server activity or may be captured by software processes. A common technique used is *instrumentation* in which additional code is added to webpage scripts to capture details of interactions [2]. The continuous collection of interactions data enables longitudinal views of learning behavior rather than just snapshots or summaries, which are provided by other data collection techniques. Another advantage of capturing interactions data is that it records what students have *actually* done rather than relying on their recollections or perceptions, thus eliminating problems of selective recall or inaccurate estimation [3,4]. Collecting data on log files is also an efficient technique for gathering data in the learning situation. This technique is transparent to the student and does not affect the learning process [5]. Log file data collection and recording fits the paradigm of naturalistic observation and enquiry [6]. However, monitoring use of a learning environment via log files raises the issue of privacy, particularly in cases where the students can be identified.

The main limitations with collecting data of student interactions lie in the management and interpretation of the data. Recording the online interactions of a group of students over the term of their course generates a huge volume of data. Although this data contains records of students' learning behavior, deducing information beyond what they have done, when it was done and how long it took, is difficult. Combining the interactions data with other data such as learning outcomes can help provide a fuller picture [7,8].

These issues have provided impetus for the development of methods to manage and interpret student interactions data. These methods have drawn mainly from the data mining domain. The application of data mining techniques to Web log file data has led to the development of a field called Web usage mining, which is the study of user behavior when navigating on the Web. Mobasher [9] states that the "goal of Web usage mining is to capture and model the behavioral patterns and profiles of users interacting with a Web site" (p. 3). In some respects, Web usage mining is the process of reconciling the Web site developer's view of how the Web site should be used with the way it is actually used [10]. Web usage mining typically involves preprocessing, exploration, and analysis phases. The data can be collected from Web log files, user profiles, and any other data from user interactions [11]. This typically forms a large and complex data set.

Web usage mining is often an inductive process, tending by nature to be open-ended and exploratory. Techniques such as clustering, classification, association and sequential pattern mining, text mining, and outlier detection are used to discover patterns in the data, moving from specific observations to broader generalizations and theories. However, Web usage mining may also be deductive in nature using statistical analysis to describe data and test inferences, thus working from the general to the specific [12]. In this chapter, we will focus on the use of statistical techniques and explain how these can be applied to analysis of logged interactions data.

There are many tools available to assist with usage analysis of Web log files. For example, AccessWatch, Analogue, Getstats, Gwstat, and Webstat [12,13]. Some have been designed for use on educational data, for example the Synergo and CoiAT tools [14]. In this chapter, we will explain techniques that can be applied in a standard statistical software package, for example, R, SAS or SPSS.

The chapter is organized as follows. Firstly, a review of other studies which have conducted statistical analysis of Web log file data is presented. This is followed by a description of Web log files, data that can be recorded on these files, and data abstractions that can be defined. Next an explanation of the different processes necessary to prepare Web log file data for analysis is provided. The final section gives an overview of descriptive and inferential statistical techniques, which can be applied to the analysis of data collected from a Web-based learning environment.

3.2 Studies of Statistical Analysis of Web Log Files

Many studies have conducted statistical analysis of data of student interactions with Web-based learning materials to give information about Web site usage and student learning behavior. A basic type of analysis uses simple measures of frequency of access to a Web site and individual pages. An example is a study by Nachmias and Segev [3] in which interactions with 117 courseware Web sites were analyzed. A number of studies have extended this analysis to consider the times of access, showing patterns of student behavior over time periods. For example, studies by Cockburn and McKenzie [15], Hwang and Li [16], and Nilikant and Mitovic [17].

A number of studies have calculated the duration of access to Web sites or resources to give a different picture of student use of learning resources. Studies by Gao and Lehman [18] and Monk [19] analyzed log file data to measure the total time students spent accessing learning material. A study by Grob et al. [20] analyzed trends in frequency and duration of access to an e-learning resource over a period of nearly 3 years. A study by Claypool et al. [21] found that the total time spent on a webpage reliably indicates a user's interest in the page content.

Analysis of Web log file data can incorporate data from other sources to provide a richer picture of student behavior. For example, Hwang and Li [16] combined analysis of log file data of students in an introductory computing course with information about homework tasks to gain an understanding of the study habits of students over the course of a semester. Monk [19] combined data on access to online course materials with user profiles to determine any differences in access based on age, course of study, or institution. A study by Peled and Rashty [8] found differences in the type of resources accessed based on gender. The males used interactive resources significantly more than the females, whereas females used passive resources more than males. Another study by Comunale et al. [22] found that females perceived that the courseware Web site contributed more to their learning.

An important aspect of an investigation of student usage of a courseware Web site is determining how the usage relates to task completion or learning outcomes. The study by Comunale et al. [22] found evidence to suggest that higher course grades are related to more frequent Web site use. Other examples of studies of the relationship between Web site usage and learning are by Feng et al. [23], Gao and Lehman [18], and Zhu et al. [24].

3.3 Web Log Files

A Web log file provides a continuous transcript of data on Web site usage. Each record on the log file contains specific data about a single user interaction with a Web site. An interaction here is defined as a selection of a Web site URL. An important consideration in analysis of Web log files is that the information gained will depend on the data that is contained in the log files. The data recorded are dependent on the mechanism used for collection and may be tailored by the educator. Web log files may be classified according to whether they are generated on a Web server or a client computer.

The most commonly reported log file analyses use data collected on the Web server as part of normal server activity. Web server log files hold data of interactions captured at the webpage level. A webpage is a collection of information consisting of one or more Web resources intended to be rendered simultaneously. However, Web server logs typically do not contain any data from client side user interfaces, such as Java applets and page element interactions [8,15]. Furthermore, caching by the Web browser or a proxy server may mean that a page request results in retrieval of the page from the local or proxy server cache. In either case, the request will not be recorded on the server log file.

A less common form of Web log files are those generated by the client computer using techniques such as instrumentation of webpages. Collecting data on the client side offers advantages over server side collection as it enables a greater range of data to be collected. Using client-side logging, data can be collected at a page element level. Client side logging can overcome the problem of caching, allowing all page requests to be recorded, and enable identification of *sessions* (sequences of contiguous page accesses that comprise a user visit). Furthermore, users can be identified, making possible the integration of demographic data and enabling a richer analysis of the data. However, client side logging requires installation of special software or a modified browser on the user's computer [15]. The study by Peled and Rashty [8] is an example of client-side logging.

3.3.1 Log File Data

Web log files will typically contain, at least, the following data:

- *Interaction identification.* A unique identifier for an interaction. Each interaction is recorded as a single record on the log file.
- *Page URL.* This identifies the page on the Web site that was accessed by the interaction. The page identification indicates the area of the Web site that the user is

working in and may be used to determine the type of action that the user had performed.

- *Interaction time.* This specifies the date and time of the interaction. This information may be used to calculate the time lapses between different interactions.

Client side logging makes possible the recording of additional data, enabling more sophisticated and detailed analysis of Web site usage and user behavior. The data recorded will depend on the application being monitored and the process used to record the data. The following data are useful to record:

- *Session identification.* This identifies the user session in which the interaction occurred. Identification of a session allows the interactions to be associated with a single session and a user who may or may not be identified.
- *User identification.* This identifies the user who initiated the interaction. Identification of users allows comparisons to be made between users based on available demographic information.

Other data may be recorded that provide additional information about the interaction or the user. These may be obtained from other sources and will be specific to each application.

3.3.2 Log File Data Abstractions

In an analysis of log file data, it is useful to take different views or abstractions of the data to enable more meaningful analysis. Abstractions are, in effect, groupings of records on the log file that are related in some way. The following abstractions are useful to consider:

1. *Page view*—The lowest and most common level of data abstraction. A page view is equivalent to a single interaction stored on the log file and results from a single user request. This is suitable for fine-grained analysis of Web site usage.
2. *Session*—A sequence of interactions representing a user visit to the Web site. This can be seen as a temporal abstraction of the log file data and is suitable for a coarse-grained analysis of Web site usage. Note that this definition of a session is similar to the definition of a server session in the Web Characterization Terminology & Definitions Sheet [25].
3. *Task*—A sequence of contiguous page accesses to one resource on a Web site within a user session. A resource is a page or group of linked pages that is identified logically as a function or facility within the Web site domain. This is more specific than the general definition of resource as specified in the Web Characterization Terminology & Definitions Sheet, which defines a resource as: "anything that has identity" [25]. This abstraction can be seen as a resource abstraction.
4. *Activity*—A sequence of semantically meaningful page accesses that relate to a particular activity or task that the user performs. This is, in effect, an abstraction of a discrete behavioral activity of the user.

Mobasher [9] describes three levels of abstraction that are typically used for analysis of log file data: page view, session, and transaction. The page view and session abstractions described above are the same as those defined by Mobasher [9] and are explicitly defined in the Web domain. The activity abstraction relates to the transaction abstraction described by Mobasher.

3.4 Preprocessing Log Data

Web log files are typically not in a form that can be directly analyzed using statistical or data mining techniques. An important task before analysis involves preparation of a suitable data set from the huge volume of data that is collected. The preprocessing of Web log file data generally involves a multistage and largely contextualized process. Data preparation may involve cleaning, transformation of data into a form suitable for specific analysis, identification of sessions and users, and integration of data from other sources. It may also involve identification of meaningful abstractions of the data. This section presents an overview of these processes.

3.4.1 Data Cleaning

Cleaning of Web log files involves tasks to ensure that the data is relevant and accurate, and meaningful analysis can be performed. The data preparation must exclude unnecessary data without impoverishing the data or introducing bias. This process may involve removing irrelevant records, replacing missing records, and eliminating outlying data. The following provides a brief description of each of these tasks:

3.4.1.1 Removal of Irrelevant Data

A request for a webpage may cause several entries to be recorded on the log file. For example, the loading of a single page may involve downloading separate files containing content, graphics, and frames. Including all such entries in an analysis will result in overcounting of page visits giving an inaccurate picture of user accesses. To avoid this, all data captured from file downloads other than the main page file must be removed from the data set prior to analysis [26–28].

3.4.1.2 Determining Missing Entries

The use of local and proxy server caches can distort the view of Web site usage, in particular, user navigation paths. Cooley et al. [10] suggest a method of path completion, which uses the Web site topology to fill in missing page references. This technique is based on the assumption that users rarely request a page refresh or type in a URL to access a webpage.

3.4.1.3 Removal of Outliers

Outliers may be defined as "values which seem either too large or too small as compared to the rest of the observations" [29]. Outliers may be phenomena of interest in a data set; however, they may be caused by errors such as errors in measurement. In the latter case the presence of these outliers could distort the analysis and they need to be eliminated from the dataset. Making the distinction between the outliers that should be accepted and those that should be rejected is not always easy. This requires knowledge of the domain in which the data was collected and depends on the aims of the analysis [30].

In the context of log file data, it may be important to identify and exclude outliers from analysis. For example, log files may contain long periods between successive interactions within sequences of user interactions. This typically occurs because the user pauses from their work for some reason. The inclusion of sequences containing long pauses can give misleading results when calculating time spent at a Web site and it is important to filter out these sequences before analysis. Claypool et al. [21] used a time limit between successive interactions of approximately 20 min to filter out sessions with these pauses, arguing that after this time it was likely that a user had stopped reading the page. Sheard [2] used a limit of 10 min based on an empirical study of access times. As another example of outliers, log files may contain sessions with unusually long streams of interactions. Giudici [31] filtered out the 99th percentile of the distributions of both sequence length and session times based on results of an exploratory study.

3.4.2 Data Transformation

Individual data variables may need to be transformed or new data variables derived to enable meaningful analysis of Web log file data. This may involve, for example, mapping data to numeric values to enable comparisons. The data transformations made will depend on the aims of the analysis and will be specific to each application.

Two processes that may be conducted as part of data transformation is data discretization and feature selection. Data discretization is the process of splitting continuous data into discrete values [32]. These may be categorical values to aid comprehensibility or may be ordinal values which maintain the order of the original values. Related to this is feature selection, which is the process of choosing data variables to be used in analysis and eliminating irrelevant or redundant variables from a data set [33].

3.4.3 Session Identification

In analysis of Web log file data, it is often important to distinguish between user sessions. Sessions may be identified by an identity that is allocated by the server or through the user logging into a session. However, if the server does not allocate a session identity or there is no user login mechanism, then a timeout may be used to determine the session boundaries. Using this mechanism, it is assumed that a new session has started if the time between two webpage requests for the same user exceeds a certain limit. Catledge and Pitkow [34] used empirical data to define a timeout period of 25.5 min to determine session boundaries. This was calculated by taking 1.5 standard deviations from the mean time between user interface requests. A typical timeout period used is 30 min [26,35]. However, Joshi et al. [27] used 45 min and Chan [36] used 15 min for session boundaries in their studies. These widely different values appear to have been chosen arbitrarily.

3.4.4 User Identification

Identification of the user is necessary for the inclusion of demographic data in analysis of Web log file data. A user may be identified through a login mechanism, task submission system, or by use of a cookie. A cookie is a piece of software placed on a client computer by the Web server, allowing the Web server to keep a record of the user and user actions at the Web site [37]. If these facilities are not available then the machine IP address is sometimes used. However, this is problematic for several reasons. A user may access a Web site from different computers, or several users may access a Web site from the one computer [28]. The use of proxy servers causes problems with user identification as all requests have the same identifier even when they originate from different users. At best, an IP address will provide a rough way to distinguish between users but not to identify them. Cooley et al. [10] suggest several heuristics which can be used to help distinguish between users within sequences of interactions. These include looking for a change in browser or operating system software or looking for impossible navigation steps.

3.4.5 Data Integration

Data from Web log files may be integrated with other data to enable more extensive and/or meaningful analysis. In an educational context, additional data could provide information about the students, such as age, gender, Web experience, course performance, and learning style, or could provide information about the Web site, such as webpage type and size [9].

3.5 Statistical Analysis of Log File Data

The previous section described the type of data that can be stored on Web log files and some of the different abstractions that can be taken from this data. Log data typically forms a large data set and to derive meaning from this data requires quantitative analysis. In this section, we will give an overview of statistical techniques that may be used in the analysis of log file data. This is only a brief introduction to this topic. More details of these techniques may be found in books that cover quantitative methods, for example, Burns [38] and Wiersma [39] or introductory books on statistics, for example, Kranzler et al. [40]. Details of how to apply the statistical tests in SPSS may be found in Brace et al. [41] and Coakes et al. [42].

Interactions data collected from an educational Web site can be analyzed in many different ways to provide information about Web site usage, resource usage, learning behavior, and task performance, for individuals or groups of students. The analysis conducted will be determined by the objectives of the study and will be constrained by the data collected and the levels of abstraction defined. Analysis of Web log file data will use different measures for interactions and abstractions of these interactions. A measure in this context is a one-dimensional variable that is computed from the log file records [43]. Each interaction recorded on a log file will typically identify at least the page that the user has visited and the time this occurred. The interactions can be readily analyzed to provide counts and frequencies of interactions. Abstractions of interactions defined as tasks, sessions, or activities can be analyzed to provide counts, frequency, and durations of these abstractions. These measures can be further analyzed to determine patterns and trends over time. If the users can be identified then comparisons of behavior between users or groups of users can be made.

A range of statistical techniques can be used to analyze log file data. Broadly these may be grouped into descriptive statistics, which are used to describe the data, and inferential statistics, which are used to analyze the data in order to draw inferences.

The first consideration in data analysis is determining the measurement scale of the data variable that you wish to analyze. There are four levels as follows:

- *Nominal* (or categorical)—measures without order. Data variables may be classified or grouped. For example, course of study, gender, page URL.
- *Ordinal*—measures with order. Values of the data variables may be ordered or ranked, but equal intervals between measurement scores on the scale are not established. For example, exam grade.
- *Interval*—measures with order and with equal intervals on a scale. For example, test score, time.
- *Ratio*—measures with order, with equal intervals on a scale, and a true zero point. For example, age, session duration.

These levels form a hierarchy of increasing information held in variables at each level of measurement. For each level there are different descriptive and statistical techniques that can be applied to the data.

We will now give an overview of the different statistical techniques that can be used on data from Web log files. All the tests presented for interval scale data will also apply to ratio scale data, therefore the discussion will only mention interval scale and the application to ratio scale data will be implied.

3.5.1 Descriptive Statistics

Descriptive statistics are used to describe sets of quantitative data. These provide, in effect, summaries of the data to allow interpretation and comparison. Data can be summarized to give numeric values, which can be presented in tabular or graphical form. For example, a simple summary of log file data could be a count of interactions or an average length of time between interactions.

Descriptive statistics often involve descriptions of distributions of data and relationships between distributions of variables. In analysis of log file data, a distribution is typically the set of values of one variable from the log file. The particular way the distribution is described will depend on the scale of measurement of the variable.

3.5.1.1 Describing Distributions

There are three main ways distributions of ordinal and interval data can be described. Firstly, the measure of central tendency (where it is located on the scale of measurement), secondly, the dispersion (the degree of spread), and thirdly the shape. For distributions of nominal data, only the measure of central tendency is applicable. Measures may be used to describe each of these characteristics of a distribution and often these may be shown graphically.

3.5.1.1.1 Measure of Central Tendency

The measure of central tendency gives an average of the values of the distribution. The most commonly used measures of central tendency are the mean, median, and mode.

- *Mean*—The arithmetic mean is determined by the sum of the values in the distribution divided by the number of values. The mean is used for interval scale data. However, if the distribution is asymmetrical or has outlying points, the mean may not give a good measure of the average of the values. In this case, the median should be used as the measure of central tendency. An example of log file data distributions that are often asymmetrical are frequencies of Web site access times [44].

- *Median*—The point on the scale below which half of the values lie. This is used for ordinal data and for interval data which has an *asymmetrical* distribution or the distribution contains *outlying* points.
- *Mode*—The value with the most frequent occurrence. This is typically used for nominal data.

3.5.1.1.2 Dispersion

The measure of dispersion indicates the degree of spread of the distribution. This is only used for ordinal and interval scale data. There are several measures which may be used:

- *Range*: The difference between the maximum and minimum values on the scale of measurement. This gives a measure of the spread of values but no indication of how they are distributed.
- *Interquartile range*: The data values are divided into four equal sections and the interquartile range is the range of the middle half of the data set. This is a useful measure if the data set contains outlying values.
- *Variance*: The average of the squared deviations from the mean of the distribution, where the deviation is the difference between the mean of the distribution and a value in the distribution. This is used for interval scale data.
- *Standard deviation*: The positive square root of the variance. This is used for interval scale data.

3.5.1.1.3 Shape

The shape of the distribution is important for determining the type of analysis that can be performed on the data. An important shape for interval scale data is the normal distribution or "bell curve." Normal distributions are special distributions with certain characteristics, which are required for tests on interval scale variables. Other relevant descriptions of the shape of a distribution are as follows:

- *Skewness*—extent to which the distribution is asymmetrical
- *Kurtosis*—extent to which the distribution is flat or peaked
- *Modality*—number of peaks in the distribution

3.5.1.2 Relationships between Variables

In analysis of data we are often interested in the relationship between variables. For example, "Is an increase in number of interactions with study material associated with an increase in exam performance?" The degree of relationship is called a correlation and is measured by a correlation coefficient r. Correlation coefficients can take values from +1.0 to −1.0. The absolute value indicates the strength of the relationship and the sign indicates whether it is a positive or negative relationship. Zero indicates no linear relationship.

The proportion of variance of one variable that is predictable from the other variable is called the coefficient of determination and is calculated as the square of the correlation coefficient (r^2). The coefficient of determination gives a measure of the strength of association between two variables and can take a value from 0 to 1. For example, we will consider the relationship between exam performance and use of study material. If r equals 0.75, then r^2 equals 0.57, which means that 57% of the total variation in exam performance can be explained by the linear relationship between exam performance and interactions with the study material.

3.5.1.3 Graphical Descriptions of Data

One of the most common graphical forms used to describe a distribution is the bar graph or histogram. On a bar graph, the vertical axis represents the frequency of values and the horizontal axis has a point for each value (see an example in [45]). For interval data, which can usually take many values, the data can be summarized further with each point on the horizontal axis representing a range of values (see examples in [3,17]). There are a number of other types of graphs suitable for displaying distributions. For example, a stem and leaf plot. A useful graph to show the variability of a distribution is a box plot (see example in [21]). Relationships between distributions can be shown using a scatterplot, which is a two-dimensional graph showing the values of one variable plotted against the values of the other variable (see examples in [17,23]).

3.5.2 Inferential Statistics

Inferential statistics are used to make inferences from the data, commonly through hypothesis testing. The role of hypothesis testing is to determine whether the result obtained from analysis occurred by chance. The null hypothesis, which is the hypothesis of no difference or no relationship, is tested through these statistical tests. A level of significance is used to establish whether the null hypothesis should be accepted or not. The level of significance is the point which determines whether the observed difference or relationship is too large to be attributed to chance. There are many inferential statistical tests, which can be grouped into two broad categories:

- *Parametric analyses*: Used for data on the interval scale which meet specific assumptions.
- *Nonparametric analyses*: Typically used for nominal or ordinal scale variables.

In analysis of log file data, we are often interested in testing for differences between variables, for example, "Is the there any difference in the number of accesses to learning resources between the male and female students?" We may also be interested in relationships between variables. We will now give an overview of analysis for testing for differences and testing for relationships.

3.5.2.1 Testing for Differences between Distributions Using Parametric Tests

In testing for differences between two or more distributions on the interval scale, we are testing for a difference between the means of these distributions. This is a simplification of what is actually happening and for more explanation, see Burns [38], Wiersma [39], and Kranzler et al. [40]. There are different tests that may be used depending on the number of distributions we are testing, the number of variables we are testing, and whether these are related. An example of related variables are pre- and posttest scores for a group of students. See Table 3.1 for a summary of the most common parametric tests used to test for differences between distributions.

TABLE 3.1

Parametric Tests for Difference

Statistical Test	Hypothesis Tested	Example
t-Test (independent-samples)	There is no difference between the mean values of two distributions.	There is no difference in the access times for course materials between the on-campus and distance education students.
t-Test (paired-samples)	There is no difference between the means of two distributions of related variables. The paired samples may be formed when one group of students has been tested twice or when students are paired on similar characteristics.	There is no difference in the mid semester and final exam results for a class of students.
ANOVA (one-way)	There is no difference between the mean values of two or more distributions. Only one factor (independent variable) is tested.	There is no difference in mean weekly online access times between students across five degree programs.
ANOVA (two-way)	There is no difference between the means values of two or more distributions. In this case, two factors (A and B) are included in the analysis. The possible null hypotheses are: 1. There is no difference in the means of factor A. 2. There is no difference in means of factor B. 3. There is no interaction between factors A and B.	1. There is no difference in mean weekly online access times between students across five degree programs. 2. There is no difference in mean weekly online access times between male and female students in these degree programs. 3. The weekly access times of male and female students are not influenced by program of study.

The data and distributions we are testing should meet the following assumptions:

- Data values are independent. This does not apply to paired-samples *t*-tests.
- Data values are selected from a normally distributed population. A normal distribution will have one peak and low absolute values for skewness and kurtosis. A test that may be used to test for normality is the Shapiro–Wilk test [41,42].
- Homogeneity of variance: The variance across two or more distributions is equal. This may be tested Levene's test [41,42]. See Feng and Heffernan [46] for examples of parametric tests.

3.5.2.2 Testing for Differences between Distributions Using Nonparametric Tests

Nonparametric tests are used for nominal and ordinal scale data. They are also used for interval scale data, which does not meet the assumptions necessary for parametric tests. See Table 3.2 for a summary of the most common nonparametric tests.

In testing for differences between two or more distributions on the ordinal (or interval) scales we are testing for a difference between the medians of these distributions. Once again, this is a simplification of what is actually happening and for more explanation, see Burns [38], Wiersma [39], and Kranzler et al. [40]. There are different tests that may be used depending on the number of distributions we are testing and whether they are related. See Claypool et al. for examples of nonparametric tests [21].

TABLE 3.2

Nonparametric Tests for Difference

Statistical Test	Hypothesis Tested
χ^2 test for independence	Two variables are independent.
Mann–Whitney U	There is no difference between two distributions. Mann–Whitney U is the nonparametric equivalent of the independent samples t-test.
Wilcoxon matched-pairs signed rank test	There is no difference between two distributions of related samples. This is the nonparametric equivalent of the paired-samples t-test.
Kruskal–Wallis	There is no difference between the values from three or more distributions. This is the nonparametric equivalent of the one-way ANOVA.

TABLE 3.3

Correlation Tests

Level of Measurement	Correlation Coefficient
Both distributions on the interval scale	Pearson product-moment
Both distributions on the ordinal scale	Spearman rank order
Both distributions on the nominal scale	Contingency coefficient

In testing for differences in distributions of nominal variables, we are testing that the relative proportions of values of one variable are independent from the relative proportions of values of another variable. For example, "Are the proportions of accesses to each resource the same for each day of the week?"

3.5.2.3 Testing for Relationships

Correlation was previously presented as a descriptive statistic. However, correlations can also be conducted in the context of inferential statistics. There are different correlation tests, depending on the measurement scale of the data used. If there is a difference in the level of measurement, then the test appropriate for the lower measure should be used. For example, if one variable is measured on the interval scale and the other on the ordinal scale then a Spearman Rank order correlation should be used. See Table 3.3 for a summary of the most common tests.

3.6 Conclusions

This chapter has outlined common techniques for descriptive and inferential statistical analysis, which may be applied to log file data. Also explained are processes necessary for preparing the log file data for analysis using standard statistical software. Statistical analysis of log file data of student interactions can be used to provide information about Web site usage, resource usage, learning behavior, and task performance.

References

1. Zuboff, S., *In the Age of the Smart Machine: The Future of Work and Power*. Basic Books, New York, 1984, 468 pp.
2. Sheard, J., *An Investigation of Student Behaviour in Web-Based Learning Environments, in Faculty of Information Technology*. PhD thesis, Monash University, Melbourne, Australia, 2006.
3. Nachmias, R. and Segev, L., Students' use of content in Web-supported academic courses. *The Internet and Higher Education* 6: 145–157, 2003.
4. Yi, M.Y. and Hwang, Y., Predicting the use of Web-based information systems: Efficacy, enjoyment, learning goal orientation, and the technology acceptance model. *International Journal of Human-Computer Studies* 59: 431–449, 2003.
5. Federico, P.-A., Hypermedia environments and adaptive instruction. *Computers in Human Behavior* 15(6): 653–692, 1999.
6. Sarantakos, S., *Social Research*, 2nd edn. MacMillan Publishers Australia Pty Ltd., Melbourne, Australia, 1998.
7. Ingram, A.L., Using Web server logs in evaluating instructional Web sites. *Journal of Educational Technology Systems* 28(2): 137–157, 1999–2000.
8. Peled, A. and Rashty, D., Logging for success: Advancing the use of WWW logs to improve computer mediated distance learning. *Journal of Educational Computing Research* 21(4): 413–431, 1999.
9. Mobasher, B., *Web Usage Mining and Personalization, in Practical Handbook of Internet Computing*, M.P. Singh, Editor. CRC Press, Boca Raton, FL, 2004, pp. 1–35.
10. Cooley, R., Mobasher, B., and Srivastava, J. Web mining: Information and pattern discovery on the World Wide Web. In *Proceedings of 9th IEEE International Conference Tools and Artificial Intelligence (ICTAI'97)*, Newport Beach, CA, November 1997, pp. 558–567.
11. Kosala, R. and Blockeel, H., Web mining research: A survey. *ACM SIGKDD Explorations* 2(1): 1–15, 2000.
12. Romero, C. and Ventura, S., Educational data mining: A survey from 1995 to 2005. *Expert Systems with Applications* 33: 135–146, 2007.
13. Zaïane, O.R., Xin, M., and Han, J., Discovering Web access patterns and trends by applying OLAP and data mining technology on web logs. In *Proceedings of Advances in Digital Libraries*, Santa Barbara, CA, April 1998, pp. 19–29.
14. Avouris, N., Komis, V., Fiotakis, G., Margaritis, M., and Voyiatzaki, E., Logging of fingertip actions is not enough for analysis of learning activities. In *Proceedings of 12th International Conference on Artificial Intelligence in Education*, Amsterdam, the Netherlands, July 2005, pp. 1–8.
15. Cockburn, A. and McKenzie, B., What do Web users do? An empirical analysis of Web use. *International Journal of Human-Computer Studies* 54(6): 903–922, 2001.
16. Hwang, W.-Y. and Li, C.-C., What the user log shows based on learning time distribution. *Journal of Computer Assisted Learning* 18: 232–236, 2002.
17. Nilakant, K. and Mitovic, A., Application of data mining in constraint-based intelligent tutoring systems. In *Proceedings of Artificial Intelligence in Education*. Amsterdam, the Netherlands, July 2005, pp. 896–898.
18. Gao, T. and Lehman, J.D., The effects of different levels of interaction on the achievement and motivational perceptions of college students in a Web-based learning environment. *Journal of Interactive Learning Research* 14(4): 367–386, 2003.
19. Monk, D., Using data mining for e-learning decision making. *Electronic Journal of e-Learning* 3(1): 41–45, 2005.
20. Grob, H.L., Bensberg, F., and Kaderali, F., Controlling open source intermediaries—A Web log mining approach. In *Proceedings of International Conference on Information Technology Interfaces*, Zagreb, Croatia, 2004, pp. 233–242.

21. Claypool, M., Brown, D., Le, P., and Waseda, M., Inferring user interest. *IEEE Internet Computing* **5**(6): 32–39, 2001.
22. Comunale, C.L., Sexton, T.R., and Voss, D.J.P., The effectiveness of course Web sites in higher education: An exploratory study. *Journal of Educational Technology Systems* **30**(2): 171–190, 2001–2002.
23. Feng, M., Heffernan, N., and Koedinger, K., Looking for sources of error in predicting student's knowledge. In *Proceedings of AAAI Workshop on Educational Data Mining*, Menlo Park, CA, 2005, pp. 1–8.
24. Zhu, J.J.H., Stokes, M., and Lu, A.X.Y., The use and effects of Web-based instruction: Evidence from a single-source study. *Journal of Interactive Learning Research* **11**(2): 197–218, 2000.
25. W3C. *Web Characterization Terminology & Definitions Sheet.* 1999 [cited December 29, 2009]. Available from: http://www.w3.org/1999/05/WCA-terms/
26. Cooley, R., Mobasher, B., and Srivastava, J., Data preparation for mining World Wide Web browsing patterns. *Knowledge and Information Systems* **1**(1): 1–27, 1999.
27. Joshi, K.P., Joshi, A., Yesha, Y., and Krishnapuram, R., Warehousing and mining Web logs. In *Proceedings of ACM CIKM'99 2nd Workshop on Web Information and Data Management (WIDM'99) Conference*, Kansas City, MO, 1999, pp. 63–68.
28. Srivastava, J., Cooley, R., Deshpande, M., and Tan, P.-N., Web usage mining: Discovery and applications of usage patterns from Web data. *SIGKDD Explorations* **1**(2): 12–23, 2000.
29. Gumbel, E.J., Discussion on "Rejection of Outliers" by Anscombe, F.J. *Technometrics* **2**: 165–166, 1960.
30. Redpath, R. and Sheard, J., Domain knowledge to support understanding and treatment of outliers. In *Proceedings of International Conference on Information and Automation (ICIA 2005)*, Colombo, Sri Lanka, 2005, pp. 398–403.
31. Giudici, P., *Applied Data Mining: Statistical Methods for Business and Industry.* John Wiley & Sons Inc., West Sussex, U.K., 2003.
32. Ribeiro, M.X., Traina, A.J.M., and Caetano Traina, J., A new algorithm for data discretization and feature selection. In *Proceedings of the 2008 ACM Symposium on Applied Computing.* ACM, Fortaleza, Brazil, 2008.
33. Piramuthu, S., Evaluating feature selection methods for learning in data mining applications. *European Journal of Operational Research* **156**: 483–494, 2004.
34. Catledge, L.D. and Pitkow, J.E., Characterizing browsing strategies in the World-Wide Web. *Computer Networks and ISDN Systems* **27**(6): 1065–1073, 1995.
35. Cohen, L.B., A two-tiered model for analyzing library website usage statistics, Part 1: Web server logs. *Portal: Libraries and the Academy* **3**(2): 315–326, 2003.
36. Chan, P.K. Constructing Web user profiles: A non-invasive learning approach to building Web user profiles. In *Proceedings of Workshop on Web Usage Analysis and User Profiling (WEBKDD'99)*, San Diego, CA, 1999, pp. 39–55.
37. Eirinaki, M. and Vazirgiannis, M., Web mining for Web personalization. *ACM Transactions on Internet Technology* **3**(1): 1–27, 2003.
38. Burns, R., *Introduction to Research Methods.* 4th edn. Sage Publications Ltd., London, U.K., 2000.
39. Wiersma, W., *Research Methods in Education: An Introduction*, 6th ed. Allyn & Bacon, Boston, MA, 1995, 480 pp.
40. Kranzler, J.H., Moursund, J., and Kranzler, J., *Statistics for the Terrified*, 4th ed. Pearson Prentice Hall, Upper Saddle River, NJ, 2007, 224 pp.
41. Brace, N., Kemp, R., and Snelgar, R., *SPSS for Psychologists.* 3rd ed. Palgrave McMillan, Hampshire, U.K., 2006.
42. Coakes, S.J., Steed, L., and Ong, C., *SPSS version 16.0 for Windows: Analysis without Anguish.* John Wiley & Sons, Milton, Australia, 2009.
43. Berendt, B. and Brenstein, E., Visualizing individual differences in Web navigation: STRATDYN, a tool for analysing navigation patterns. *Behavior Research Methods, Instruments & Computers* **33**(2): 243–257, 2001.

44. Sheard, J., Ceddia, J., Hurst, J., and Tuovinen, J., Determining Website usage time from interactions: Data preparation and analysis. *Journal of Educational Technology Systems* **32**(1): 101–121, 2003.
45. Romero, C., Ventura, S., and Garcia, E., Data mining in course management systems: Moodle case study and tutorial. *Science Direct* **51**(1): 368–384, 2008.
46. Feng, M. and Heffernan, N., Informing teachers live about student learning: Reporting in the Assistment system. *Technology, Instruction, Cognition and Learning* **3**: 1–8, 2005.

4

A Data Repository for the EDM Community: The PSLC DataShop

Kenneth R. Koedinger, Ryan S. J. d. Baker, Kyle Cunningham,
Alida Skogsholm, Brett Leber, and John Stamper

CONTENTS

4.1 Introduction

In recent years, educational data mining has emerged as a burgeoning new area for scientific investigation. One reason for the emerging excitement about educational data mining (EDM) is the increasing availability of fine-grained, extensive, and longitudinal data on student learning. These data come from many sources, including standardized tests combined with student demographic data (for instance, www.icpsr.umich.edu/IAED), and videos of classroom interactions [22]. Extensive new data sources have been transformational in science [5] and business (being a major part of the success of key businesses such as Google, FedEx, and Wal-Mart).

In this chapter, we present an open data repository of learning data—the Pittsburgh Science of Learning Center DataShop (http://pslcdatashop.org)—which we have designed to have characteristics that make it particularly useful for EDM. We discuss the ways in which members of the EDM community are currently utilizing this resource, and how DataShop's tools support both exploratory data analysis and EDM.

At present, DataShop specializes in data on the interaction between students and educational software, including data from online courses, intelligent tutoring systems, virtual labs, online assessment systems, collaborative learning environments, and simulations. Historically, educational data of this nature have been stored in a wide variety of formats, including streamed log files directly from web-based or non-web-based educational software, summary log files (sometimes including outputs from student models), and researcher-specific database formats (both flat and relational). Moving toward a common set of standards for sharing data, student models, and the results of EDM analyses—key goals of the DataShop project—will facilitate more efficient, extensive storage and use of such data, and more effective collaboration within the community.

DataShop contains data with three attributes that make it particularly useful for EDM analyses. First, *the data is fine-grained*, at the grain size of semantically meaningful "transactions" between the student and the software, including both the student's action, and the software's response. Second, *the data is longitudinal*, involving student behavior and learning, in many cases, over the span of an entire semester or year of study. Third, *the data is extensive*, involving millions of transactions for some of the educational software packages for which DataShop has data. These three characteristics have made the PSLC DataShop useful to many educational data miners, both involved with the PSLC and external to it. We have the ambition of becoming the key venue for sharing educational interaction data and collaborating on its progressive analysis to support scientific discovery in education.

4.2 The Pittsburgh Science of Learning Center DataShop

DataShop is a data repository and web application for learning science researchers and EDM researchers. It provides secure data storage as well as an array of analysis and visualization tools available through a web-based interface. Data is collected from the PSLC's six ongoing courses: algebra (intelligent tutors and collaborative learning), chemistry (virtual labs, online course interactions, and intelligent tutors), Chinese (online course interactions and optimized drill), English (intelligent tutors and optimized drill), geometry (intelligent tutors), and physics (intelligent tutors and collaborative learning). There are also sources external to the PSLC that regularly contribute data to DataShop, such as middle school math data from the ASSISTments project (http://www.assistment.org) [18] and college online course data (e.g., in statistics) from the Open Learning Initiative (http://cmu.edu/oli). Many other studies and researchers also use DataShop to analyze their data.

DataShop can store a wide variety of types of data associated with a computerized course or study. This includes student–software interaction data (which is capable of being analyzed through the analysis and visualization tools) as well as any related publications, files, presentations, or electronic artifacts a researcher would like to store. In many cases, pre- and posttests, questionnaire responses, system screen shots, and demographic data are associated with student interaction data. Mappings between problem steps and knowledge components (either skills or concepts) can be created by researchers and statistically compared to one another.

Courses and studies are represented as datasets, which are organized by project, when relevant. For example, one dataset that has been used in several EDM analyses [cf. 6,7,9,10,23,24] is the "Algebra 1 2005–2006" dataset, which is grouped with similar datasets under the "Algebra Course" project.

The amount of data in DataShop is constantly growing. As of June 2009, DataShop offers 164 datasets under 50 projects. Across datasets, there are 25 million software–student transactions, representing over 111,000 student hours.

Researchers have utilized DataShop to explore learning issues in a variety of educational domains. These include, but are not limited to, collaborative problem solving in algebra [30], self-explanation in physics [20], the effectiveness of worked examples and polite language in a stoichiometry tutor [25], and the optimization of knowledge component learning in Chinese [27].

4.3 Logging and Storage Methods

Software–student interaction data is typically parsed from messages logged by educational software—such as the intelligent tutor shown in Figure 4.1—into the DataShop XML format. While the student learns from the software, the student's actions and the tutor's responses are stored in a log database or file, which is imported into DataShop for storage and analysis.

The DataShop logging format differs from many other educational data formatting standards in that it attempts to capture student–computer interaction history at a fine-grained level, while also providing data on the interactions' context. The format does not attempt to describe, a priori, learning resources and how they are transferred [cf. 1,16], or test content [cf. 31]. In this way, the format is essentially descriptive, not prescriptive. The DataShop logging model is represented by the following constructs [cf. 30]:

- *Context message*: The student, problem, and session with the tutor
- *Tool message*: Represents an action in the tool performed by a student or tutor
- *Tutor message*: Represents a tutor's response to a student action

Below we see example context, tool, and tutor messages in the DataShop XML format:

```
<context_message context_message_id="C2badca9c5c:-7fe5" name=
"START_PROBLEM">
  <dataset> <name>Geometry Hampton 2005-2006</name>
    <level type="Lesson"> <name>PACT-AREA</name>
      <level type="Section"> <name>PACT-AREA-6</name>
        <problem> <name>MAKING-CANS</name> </problem>
      </level>
    </level>
  </dataset>
</context_message>
<tool_message context_message_id="C2badca9c5c:-7fe5">
    <semantic_event transaction_id="T2a9c5c:-7fe7" name="ATTEMPT" />
    <event_descriptor>
      <selection>(POG-AREA QUESTION2)</selection>
      <action>INPUT-CELL-VALUE</action>
      <input>200.96</input>
    </event_descriptor>
  </tool_message>
<tutor_message context_message_id="C2badca9c5c:-7fe5">
    <semantic_event transaction_id="T2a9c5c:-7fe7" name="RESULT" />
    <event_descriptor> … [as above] … </event_descriptor>
    <action_evaluation>CORRECT</action_evaluation>
  </tutor_message>
```

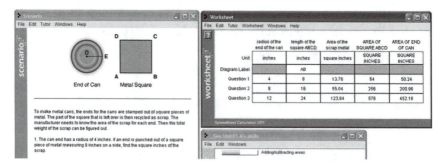

FIGURE 4.1
A problem from Carnegie Learning's Cognitive Tutor Geometry (2005 version).

In this example, the student attempted problem "MAKING-CANS" in the "PACT-AREA" lesson of the geometry tutor (shown in Figure 4.1). Looking at the tool and tutor message pair, we see the student correctly entered "200.96" as the answer. Tool and tutor messages are paired with each other (by the context message), allowing DataShop to interpret the student action and the tutor's response in conjunction. These pairs are then stored as a single *tutor transaction* in the database. Table 4.1 illustrates how actions from the MAKING-CANS example are interpreted and stored as tutor transactions.

A tutor transaction stores details such as the student identifier, session, time, problem name, problem step (or subgoal) identifier, attempt number, transaction type (e.g., attempt or hint request), student input, tutor response, hint number (if this transaction was a hint request) conditions assigned to the problem step, as well as the knowledge components (skills or concepts) relevant to the transaction. DataShop can also store "untutored" student actions, which include a student clicking "play" on an audio or video segment, navigating through pages of online course content, or taking an action in an untutored virtual lab like pouring the contents of one virtual beaker into another. These actions are logged as unpaired tool messages (i.e., there is no corresponding tutor message) and are stored in the repository as well.

Multiple tool and tutor messages are typically logged for a single problem-solving activity. Problem-solving activity is broken down into "steps" that represent completion of possible subgoals or pieces of a problem solution. Students often make multiple attempts at a step or get instructional help on a step, and each of these attempts or help requests are stored as a separate tutor transaction in the database. In the "MAKING-CANS" example, we see the student attempted the "(SCRAP-METAL-AREA Q1)" step three times (transaction numbers 2, 3, and 6 in Table 4.1). We can ascertain from the transactions that the student was unsuccessful in her first two attempts, providing an answer of "32" and "4," both labeled as incorrect by the tutor. On the third attempt, the student successfully completed the problem step, providing an input of "13.76" (as can be seen in Figure 4.1).

To allow for fast and easy analysis of data and distillation into visualizations (discussed later in this chapter), tutor transactions are aggregated into a student-step rollup table. This "denormalized" table aggregates the data into a record of each step (of each problem) executed by each student. This table is used by many of the DataShop tools, such as the Performance Profiler and Learning Curve. An example of how the "MAKING-CANS" tutor transactions are aggregated by student-step is depicted in Table 4.2.

One other key type of information stored in DataShop is information on the "knowledge components" involved in steps. Each step in a problem requires the student to know something—a relevant concept or skill—to perform the step correctly. This small unit of

TABLE 4.1

A Simplified Tutor Transaction Excerpt from the "Making-Cans" Example

#	Student	Problem	Step	Attempt #	Student Input	Evaluation	Knowledge Component
1	S01	MAKING-CANS	(SQUARE-BASE Q1)	1	8	CORRECT	Enter-Given
2	S01	MAKING-CANS	(SCRAP-METAL-AREA Q1)	1	32	INCORRECT	
3	S01	MAKING-CANS	(SCRAP-METAL-AREA Q1)	2	4	INCORRECT	
4	S01	MAKING-CANS	(SQUARE-AREA Q1)	1	64	CORRECT	Square-Area
5	S01	MAKING-CANS	(POG-AREA Q1)	1	50.24	CORRECT	Circle-Area
6	S01	MAKING-CANS	(SCRAP-METAL-AREA Q1)	3	13.76	CORRECT	Compose-Areas
7	S01	MAKING-CANS	(POG-RADIUS Q2)	1	8	CORRECT	Enter-Given
8	S01	MAKING-CANS	(SQUARE-BASE Q2)	1	16	CORRECT	Enter-Given
9	S01	MAKING-CANS	(SQUARE-AREA 02)	1	256	CORRECT	Square-Area
10	S01	MAKING-CANS	(POG-AREA Q2)	1	200.96	CORRECT	Circle-Area
11	S01	MAKING-CANS	(SCRAP-METAL-AREA Q2)	1	55.04	CORRECT	Compose-Areas
12	S01	MAKING-CANS	(POG-RADIUS Q3)	1	12	CORRECT	Enter-Given
13	S01	MAKING-CANS	(SQUARE-BASE Q3)	1	24	CORRECT	Enter-Given
14	S01	MAKING-CANS	(SQUARE-AREA Q3)	1	576	CORRECT	Square-Area
15	S01	MAKING-CANS	(POG-AREA Q3)	1	452.16	CORRECT	Circle-Area
16	S01	MAKING-CANS	(SCRAP-METAL-AREA Q3)	1	123.84	CORRECT	Compose-Areas
17	S01	MAKING-CANS	DONE	1	DONE	CORRECT	Determine-Done

TABLE 4.2

Data from the "Making-Cans" Example, Aggregated by Student-Step

#	Student	Problem	Step	Opportunity Count	Total Incorrects	Total Hints	Assistance Score	Error Rate	Knowledge Component
1	S01	WATERING_VEGGIES	(WATERED-AREA Q1)	1	0	0	0	0	Circle-Area
2	S01	WATERING_VEGGIES	(TOTAL-GARDEN Q1)	1	2	1	3	1	Rectangle-Area
3	S01	WATERING_VEGGIES	(UNWATERED-AREA Q1)	1	0	0	0	0	Compose-Areas
4	S01	WATERING_VEGGIES	DONE	1	0	0	0	0	Determine-Done
5	S01	MAKING-CANS	(POG-RADIUS Q1)	1	0	0	0	0	Enter-Given
6	S01	MAKING-CANS	(SQUARE-BASE Q1)	1	0	0	0	0	Enter-Given
7	S01	MAKING-CANS	(SQUARE-AREA Q1)	1	0	0	0	0	Square-Area
8	S01	MAKING-CANS	(POG-AREA Q1)	2	0	0	0	0	Circle-Area
9	S01	MAKING-CANS	(SCRAP-METAL-AREA Q1)	2	2	0	2	1	Compose-Areas
10	S01	MAKING-CANS	(POG-RADIUS Q2)	2	0	0	0	0	Enter-Given
11	S01	MAKING-CANS	(SQUARE-BASE Q2)	2	0	0	0	0	Enter-Given
12	S01	MAKING-CANS	(SQUARE-AREA Q2)	2	0	0	0	0	Square-Area
13	S01	MAKING-CANS	(POG-AREA Q2)	3	0	0	0	0	Circle-Area
14	S01	MAKING-CANS	(SCRAP-METAL-AREA Q2)	3	0	0	0	0	Compose-Areas
15	S01	MAKING-CANS	(POG-RADIUS Q3)	3	0	0	0	0	Enter-Given
16	S01	MAKING-CANS	(SQUARE-BASE Q3)	3	0	0	0	0	Enter-Given
17	S01	MAKING-CANS	(SQUARE-AREA Q3)	3	0	0	0	0	Square-Area
18	S01	MAKING-CANS	(POG-AREA Q3)	4	0	0	0	0	Circle-Area
19	S01	MAKING-CANS	(SCRAP-METAL-AREA Q3)	4	0	0	0	0	Compose-Areas
20	S01	MAKING-CANS	DONE	2	0	0	0	0	Determine-Done

knowledge is termed a "knowledge component" (see http://www.learnlab.org/research/ wiki for more detail on this construct). In the "MAKING-CANS" example, we see the knowledge component "Compose-Areas" assigned to the correct transaction (row 6 of Table 4.1) for the "(SCRAP-METAL-AREA Q1)" step. A knowledge component codes for a general student capability to accomplish steps in tasks. Knowledge component modeling, the process of assigning knowledge components to steps, bolsters the usefulness of intelligent tutor data, increasing the feasibility of assessing a student's knowledge relevant to a given step [cf. 7,8]. A step can have zero, one, or multiple knowledge components associated with it.

To document this required concept or skill, a tutor author can label steps with the hypothesized knowledge component(s) required for correct completion of the step, and this encoding can be imported into DataShop along with the data. Alternatively, researchers can develop their own knowledge component to step mappings, either through knowledge engineering, exploratory data analysis (using DataShop's Performance Profiler—more on this later), or EDM [cf. 14], and import these mappings into DataShop through the web application. DataShop provides researchers with an assessment of the goodness of each model (e.g., the Bayesian Information Criterion [cf. 29]), which can be used to determine which model best represents the data. Some datasets now have as many as 10 different knowledge component models associated with them by researchers at multiple universities (for instance, the "Geometry Area (1996–1997)" dataset).

4.4 Importing and Exporting Learning Data

Data may be imported into the DataShop repository through XML or a tab-delimited text file format. Logging to DataShop XML provides the richest and most complete data. If logging via XML, educational software can send messages directly to the DataShop logging server in real time. This approach is used by example-tracing tutors built in the Cognitive Tutor Authoring Tools (CTAT) framework (ctat.pact.cs.cmu.edu) [cf. 3]. Logs are automatically processed on a nightly basis, making them available for analysis or export through the web application. Alternatively, a computer tutor can write XML to files on the local hard disk (for example, if a tutor is running off-line) and then send the data to the logging server at a later time. Data in a preexisting log format can also be converted to DataShop XML and then imported into the repository. This procedure has worked well for data collected by several types of educational software including Andes (www.andes.pitt.edu) [19], mathematics Cognitive Tutors (carnegielearning.com) [4], REAP (reap.cs.cmu.edu) [13], optimized vocabulary practice [27], and ASSISTments (assistments.org) [18]. The tab-delimited format of a transaction table can alternatively be used to import from a preexisting source.

DataShop offers various data export options through the web application, each delivered in a tab-delimited text file. These include transaction and student-step level exports (as illustrated in Tables 4.1 and 4.2), and a student-problem aggregate export.

4.5 Analysis and Visualization Tools

The DataShop web application provides several tools to assist with analyzing and visualizing repository data. These tools can be used in conjunction to jump-start data analysis: A researcher can determine if students are learning by viewing learning curves, then drill down on individual problems, knowledge components, and students to analyze performance in greater detail.

The following DataShop tools are available for exploratory data analysis:

- *Dataset info*: Provides dataset metrics, contextual information, demographics, high-level descriptive information (number of students, transactions, knowledge components, etc.), as well as papers, files, a problem summary table, and the ability to export and import knowledge component models.

- *Error report*: Presents each student's first attempt at a problem or knowledge component, including if he or she was correct, the number of students or observations, and the details of the student's answer.

- *Performance profiler*: Multipurpose tool that visualizes student performance at various grain sizes (problem, step, curriculum level, knowledge component, and student) and offers a choice of measures of performance (error rate, assistance score, average number of incorrect actions, average number of hints, and residual error rate). There is support for selecting subsets of interest ("samples") among the problems or knowledge components in a curriculum. Figure 4.2 shows student performance (proportion of correct answers, errors, and hint requests) on a subset of the problems in Cognitive Tutor Algebra; the *y*-axis ("Problem") represents individual problems, and the proportion of each performance category is shown along the *x*-axis.

- *Learning curve*: Visualizes student learning changes over time. The tool can visualize the change over time in error rate, assistance score, correct step time, and

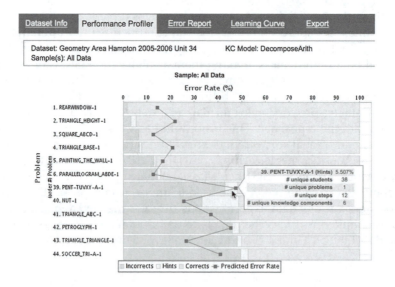

FIGURE 4.2

Performance Profiler tool showing the average error rate, which is the incorrect entries (left side of bar) plus hints (middle of bar) on students' first attempt at each step across a selection of problems from a Geometry Area dataset. Using controls not pictured, the user has selected to view the six problems with the lowest error rate and the six with the highest error rate. The blue points are predictions based a particular knowledge component model and the statistical model behind the LFA [14] algorithm.

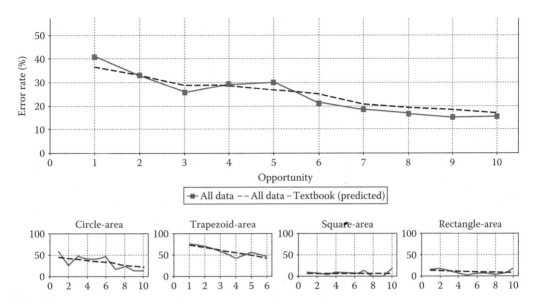

FIGURE 4.3
Error rate learning curve with predicted values from a Geometry Area dataset. The solid curve represents the actual values, each point is an average across all students and knowledge components for the given opportunity. The dashed curve represents the predicted curve values, based on the LFA model [14], a variant of Item Response Theory.

other metrics as well. The Learning Factors Analysis (LFA) model [14] can provide predicted values for error rate learning curves. Figure 4.3 depicts error rate learning curves generated by DataShop. In this graph, "error rate," or the percentage of students that asked for a hint or made an incorrect attempt on their first attempt on steps associated with a specific knowledge component, is shown on the y-axis. The x-axis ("Opportunity") indicates the nth time (e.g., 4 is the 4th time) a student has (according to the current model) had an opportunity to use a knowledge component to solve a step in a problem. Each unique step in a problem is distinct from other problem-solving steps, even if they involve the same knowledge component(s).

4.6　Uses of the PSLC DataShop

As indicated above, many recent analyses of data from DataShop have been performed in a variety of domains. A number of other studies have used, tested, or extended the analysis techniques employed in DataShop including investigations in reading [21], physics [26], and geometry [28]. Often analyses have been targeted at finding ways to improve student learning. In some cases, the work has been taken full circle such that an analysis led to an instructional redesign that was demonstrated to improve student learning beyond that realized by the original instruction. We provide a couple of examples.

Cen, Junker, and Koedinger performed a learning curve analysis using the LFA algorithm based on data from the area unit of the Geometry Cognitive Tutor [15]. They noticed that while students were required to over-practice some easy target knowledge components or skills (see square-area in Figure 4.3), they under-practiced some harder skills (see trapezoid-area in Figure 4.3). Based on observation and further analysis, they created a new version of the geometry tutor by resetting parameters that determine how often skills are practiced. They ran a classroom experiment where students in a course were pre- and posttested and randomly assigned to use either the previous or the new tutor version. Students using the new version took 20% less time to finish the same curriculum units (because over-practice was eliminated) and learned just as much as measured by normal, transfer, and long-term retention tests.

A second demonstration of a data mining project that "closed the loop" is a work by Baker et al. [8] who had done formal observations of student behavior in computer labs while working through lessons of a middle school math Cognitive Tutor. Among a number of categories of disengaged behavior, he found that "gaming the system" had the largest correlation with poor learning outcomes. Gaming refers to student behavior that appears to avoid thinking and learning through systematic guessing or fast and repeated requests for increasing help. Baker used machine learning techniques to build a "detector" capable of processing student log information, in real time, to determine when students were gaming. The detector became the basis for an intervention system, a "meta tutor," designed to discourage gaming and engage students in supplementary instruction on topics they had gamed. A controlled experiment demonstrated student-learning benefits associated with this adaptive selection of supplementary instruction for students observed to be gaming. Since then, the gaming detector has been used within analyses of why students game [11], and precisely how gaming leads to poorer learning.

Broadly, the data available in DataShop is driving the development of more precise computational models of human cognition, motivation, and learning. In particular, an ongoing area of research using DataShop data is the empirical evaluation and improvement of knowledge representations [cf. 12,17,32]. As noted in a major national report, "psychometric validation of [online] assessments is needed so they can be compared with conventional assessments, and complement and ultimately supplant them" [2].

4.7 Data Annotation: A Key Upcoming Feature

Over the next year, one of our key development goals is to make it possible for researchers to easily upload the results of data mining and computational modeling projects to the datasets where those analyses took place, annotating transactions, problem steps, and students with reference to any cognitive, meta-cognitive, or motivational constructs that can be expressed at these grain sizes. Functionality will be added to enable researchers to connect to DataShop either programmatically (via a web service) or by uploading annotations within the web application (as is currently possible for knowledge component models). We believe that adding this capacity to DataShop will increase its utility, as today's analyses often build on yesterday's analyses. For instance, models of gaming the system and off-task behavior have relied upon estimates of the probability that the student knew the relevant knowledge components at the time of the behavior. It will also allow for a larger number of competitive analyses [cf. 6], where multiple modeling methods are applied to the same dataset and evaluated for comparative goodness of fit.

4.8 Conclusions

We have described PSLC's DataShop, an open repository and web-based tool suite for storing and analyzing click-stream data, fine-grained longitudinal data generated by online courses, assessments, intelligent tutoring systems, virtual labs, simulations, and other forms of educational technology. In contrast to other types of educational data such as video and school-level data, data in DataShop include a rich set of semantic codes that facilitate automated analysis and meaningful interpretation.

The PSLC DataShop uniform data format is an initial attempt to develop a common standard that we hope will be useful to the field if not as is, then in driving better or more useful common standards. In addition to being a source for learning data, it is also a place where researchers can deposit data and then get help from other researchers who can perform secondary analysis on this data.

DataShop allows free access to a wide variety of datasets and analysis tools. These tools help researchers visualize student performance, difficulties, and learning over time. Such analyses can lead to demonstrably better instructional designs. The data can also drive improved models of student cognition, affect, and learning that can be used to improve online assessment and online learning. We take as a premise that the human brain constructs knowledge based on a variety of input sources (e.g., verbal, visual, and physical) and in a fashion and at a grain size that may or may not conform to the structure as conceived by an instructor or domain expert. The question of how the latent nature and content of human knowledge representation can be discovered from data is a deep and important scientific question, like for instance, the nature of the human genome. To answer this question requires a vast collection of relevant data, associated analysis methods, and new theory.

Acknowledgment

The research for this chapter was supported by the National Science Foundation award number SBE-0354420 for the Pittsburgh Science of Learning Center.

References

1. Advanced Distributed Learning. 2003. *SCORM Overview*. Unpublished white paper. Alexandria, VA: Advanced Distributed Learning.
2. Ainsworth, S., Honey, M., Johnson, W.L., Koedinger, K.R., Muramatsu, B., Pea, R., Recker, M., and Weimar, S. 2005. *Cyberinfrastructure for Education and Learning for the Future (CELF): A Vision and Research Agenda*. Washington, DC: Computing Research Association.
3. Aleven, V., McLaren, B., Sewall, J., and Koedinger, K. 2006. The Cognitive Tutor Authoring Tools (CTAT): Preliminary evaluation of efficiency gains. In: *Proceedings of the Eighth International Conference on Intelligent Tutoring Systems*, Jhongli, Taiwan, pp. 61–70.
4. Anderson, J.R., Corbett, A.T., Koedinger, K.R., and Pelletier, R. 1995. Cognitive tutors: Lessons learned. *The Journal of the Learning Sciences* 4 (2): 167–207.

5. Atkins, D.E. (ed.). 2003. *Revolutionizing Science and Engineering through Cyberinfrastructure: Report on the National Science Foundation Blue-Ribbon Advisory Panel on Cyberinfrastructure*. Arlington, VA: National Science Foundation. http://www.cise.nsf.gov/sci/reports/atkins.pdf

6. Baker, R.S.J.d., Corbett, A.T., and Aleven, V. 2008. Improving contextual models of guessing and slipping with a truncated training set. In: *Proceedings of the First International Conference on Educational Data Mining*, Montreal, Canada, pp. 67–76.

7. Baker, R.S.J.d., Corbett, A.T., and Aleven, V. 2008. More accurate student modeling through contextual estimation of slip and guess probabilities in Bayesian knowledge tracing. In: *Proceedings of the Ninth International Conference on Intelligent Tutoring Systems*, Montreal, Canada, pp.406–415.

8. Baker, R., Corbett, A., Koedinger, K.R., Evenson, S., Roll, I., Wagner, A., Naim, M., Raspat, J., Baker, D., and Beck, J. 2006. Adapting to when students game an intelligent tutoring system. In M. Ikeda, K. D. Ashley, and T.-W. Chan (Eds.), *Proceedings of the Eighth International Conference on Intelligent Tutoring Systems*, Jhongli, Taiwan, pp. 392–401.

9. Baker, R.S.J.d. and de Carvalho, A.M.J.A. 2008. Labeling student behavior faster and more precisely with text replays. In: *Proceedings of the First International Conference on Educational Data Mining*, Montreal, Canada, pp. 38–47.

10. Baker, R.S.J.d., de Carvalho, A.M.J.A., Raspat, J., Aleven, V., Corbett, A.T., and Koedinger, K.R. 2009. Educational Software Features that Encourage and Discourage "Gaming the System". In: *Proceedings of the 14th International Conference on Artificial Intelligence in Education*, Brighton, U.K., pp. 475–482.

11. Baker, R., Walonoski, J., Heffernan, N., Roll, I., Corbett, A., and Koedinger, K. 2008. Why students engage in "Gaming the System" behavior in interactive learning environments. *Journal of Interactive Learning Research* 19 (2): 185–224.

12. Barnes, T., Bitzer, D., and Vouk, M. 2005. Experimental analysis of the q-matrix method in knowledge discovery. In: *Proceedings of the 15th International Symposium on Methodologies for Intelligent Systems*, May 25–28, 2005, Saratoga Springs, NY.

13. Brown, J., Frishkoff, G., and Eskenazi, M. 2005. Automatic question generation for vocabulary assessment. In: *Proceedings of the Annual Human Language Technology Meeting*, Vancouver, Canada, 249–254.

14. Cen, H., Koedinger, K., and Junker, B. 2006. Learning Factors Analysis—A general method for cognitive model evaluation and improvement. *Proceedings of the Eighth International Conference on Intelligent Tutoring Systems*, Jhongli, Taiwan.

15. Cen, H., Koedinger, K., and Junker, B. 2007. Is over practice necessary?—Improving learning efficiency with the cognitive tutor through educational data mining. In R. Luckin and K. Koedinger (eds.), *Proceedings of the 13th International Conference on Artificial Intelligence in Education*, Los Angeles, CA, pp. 511–518.

16. Duval, E. and Hodgins, W. 2003. A LOM research agenda. In: *Proceedings of the WWW2003— Twelfth International World Wide Web Conference*, 20–24 May 2003, Budapest, Hungary.

17. Falmagne, J.-C., Koppen, M., Villano, M., and Doignon, J.-P. 1990. Introduction to knowledge spaces: How to build, test, and search them. *Psychological Review* 97: 201–224.

18. Feng, M. and Heffernan, N.T. 2007. Towards live informing and automatic analyzing of student learning: Reporting in ASSISTment system. *Journal of Interactive Learning Research* 18 (2): 207–230.

19. Gertner, A.S. and VanLehn, K. 2000. Andes: A coached problem-solving environment for physics. In: *Proceedings of the Fifth International Conference on Intelligent Tutoring Systems*, Montreal, Canada, pp.133–142.

20. Hausmann, R. and VanLehn, K. 2007. Self-explaining in the classroom: Learning curve evidence. In McNamara and Trafton (eds.), *Proceedings of the 29th Annual Cognitive Science Society*, Nashville, TN, pp. 1067–1072.

21. Leszczenski, J. M. and Beck J. E. 2007. What's in a word? Extending learning factors analysis to model reading transfer. In: *Proceedings of the Educational Data Mining Workshop at the 14th International Conference on Artificial Intelligence in Education*, Los Angeles, CA, pp. 31–39.

22. MacWhinney, B., Bird, S., Cieri, C., and Martell, C. 2004. TalkBank: Building an open unified multimodal database of communicative interaction. *Proceedings of the Fourth International Conference on Language Resources and Evaluation*, Lisbon, Portugal.

23. Matsuda, N., Cohen, W., Sewall, J., Lacerda, G., and Koedinger, K. R. 2007. Evaluating a simulated student using real students data for training and testing. In: C. Conati, K. McCoy, and G. Paliouras (eds.), *Proceedings of the 11th International Conference on User Modeling, UM2007*, Corfu, Greece, pp. 107–116.

24. Matsuda, N., Cohen, W., Sewall, J., Lacerda, G., and Koedinger, K. R. 2007. Predicting students' performance with SimStudent: Learning cognitive skills from observation. In: R. Lukin, K.R. Koedinger, and J. Greer (eds.), *Proceedings of the 13th International Conference on Artificial Intelligence in Education*, Los Angeles, CA, pp. 467–476.

25. McLaren, B. M., Lim, S., Yaron, D., and Koedinger, K. R. 2007. Can a polite intelligent tutoring system lead to improved learning outside of the lab? In R. Luckin and K.R. Koedinger (eds.), *Proceedings of the 13th International Conference on Artificial Intelligence in Education*, Los Angeles, CA, pp. 433–440.

26. Nwaigwe, A., Koedinger, K.R., VanLehn, K., Hausmann, R., and Weinstein, A. 2007. Exploring alternative methods for error attribution in learning curves analyses in intelligent tutoring systems. In R. Luckin and K.R. Koedinger (eds.), *Proceedings of the 13th International Conference on Artificial Intelligence in Education*, Los Angeles, CA, pp. 246–253.

27. Pavlik Jr. P. I., Presson, N., and Koedinger, K. R. 2007. Optimizing knowledge component learning using a dynamic structural model of practice. In R. Lewis and T. Polk (eds.), *Proceedings of the Eighth International Conference of Cognitive Modeling*, Ann Arbor, MI.

28. Rafferty, A. N. and Yudelson, M. 2007. Applying learning factors analysis to build stereotypic student models. In: *Proceedings of the 13th International Conference on Artificial Intelligence in Education*, Los Angeles, CA.

29. Raftery, A. 1995. Bayesian model selection in social science research. *Sociological Methodology* 28: 111–163.

30. Ritter, S. and Koedinger, K. R. 1998. An architecture for plug-in tutor agents. *Journal of Artificial Intelligence in Education* 7 (3–4): 315–347.

31. Smythe, C. and Roberts, P. 2000. An overview of the IMS question & test interoperability specification. In: *Proceedings of the Conference on Computer Aided Assessment (CAA'2000)*, Leicestershire, U.K.

32. Tatsuoka, K. 1983. Rule space: An approach for dealing with misconceptions based on item response theory. *Journal of Educational Measurement* 20 (4): 345–354.

5

Classifiers for Educational Data Mining

Wilhelmiina Hämäläinen and Mikko Vinni

CONTENTS

5.1 Introduction

The idea of classification is to place an object into one class or category, based on its other characteristics. In education, teachers and instructors are always classifying their students on their knowledge, motivation, and behavior. Assessing exam answers is also a classification task, where a mark is determined according to certain evaluation criteria.

Automatic classification is an inevitable part of intelligent tutoring systems and adaptive learning environments. Before the system can select any adaptation action such as selecting tasks, learning material, or advice, it should first classify the learner's current situation. For this purpose, we need a *classifier*—a model that predicts the class value from other *explanatory* attributes. For example, one can derive the student's motivation level from his or her actions within the tutoring system or predict the students who are likely to fail or drop out from their task scores. Such predictions are equally useful in traditional teaching, but computerized learning systems often serve larger classes and collect more data for deriving classifiers.

Classifiers can be designed manually, based on experts' knowledge, but nowadays it is more common to *learn* them from real data. The basic idea is the following: First, we have to choose the classification method, like decision trees, Bayesian networks, or neural networks. Second, we need a sample of data, where all class values are known. The data is divided into two parts, a *training set* and a *test set*. The training set is given to a learning algorithm, which derives a classifier. Then the classifier is tested with the test set, where all class values are hidden. If the classifier classifies most cases in the test set correctly, we can assume that it will also work accurately on future data. On the other hand, if the classifier makes too many errors (misclassifications) in the test data, we can assume that it was a wrong model. A better model can be searched after modifying the data, changing the settings of the learning algorithm, or by using another classification method.

Typically the learning task—like any data mining task—is an iterative process, where one has to try different data manipulations, classification approaches, and algorithm settings before a good classifier is found. However, there exists a vast amount of both practical and theoretical knowledge that can guide the search process. In this chapter, we try to summarize and apply this knowledge on the educational context and give good recipes for ways to succeed in classification.

The rest of the chapter is organized as follows: In Section 5.2, we survey the previous research where classifiers for educational purposes have been learned from data. In Section 5.3, we recall the main principles affecting the model accuracy and give several guidelines for accurate classification. In Section 5.4, we introduce the main approaches for classification and analyze their suitability to the educational domain. The final conclusions are drawn in Section 5.5.

5.2 Background

We begin with a literature survey on how data-driven classification has been applied in the educational context. We consider four types of classification problems that have often occurred in the previous research. For each group of experiments, we describe the classification problems solved, type and size of data, main classification methods, and achieved accuracy (expected proportion of correct classifications in the future data).

5.2.1 Predicting Academic Success

The first group consists of experiments where the task was to classify the student's academic success at the university level. The objectives were to predict dropouts in the beginning of studies [8,19,43], graduation in time [2,19], general performance [36], or need for remedial classes [32].

The data sets were relatively large (500–20,000 rows, in average 7,200 rows), because they were collected from the entire university or several universities, possibly during several years. The number of available attributes was also large (40–375), and only the most important were used. In addition to demographic data and course scores, the data often contained questionnaire data on students' perceptions, experiences, and financial situation.

All experiments compared several classification methods. Decision trees were the most common, but also Bayesian networks and neural networks were popular. The achieved accuracy was in average 79%, which is a good result for such difficult and important tasks. In the largest data sets (>15,000 rows), 93%–94% accuracy was achieved.

5.2.2 Predicting the Course Outcomes

The second group consists of experiments where the task was to classify the student's success in one course. The objectives were to predict passing/failing a course [4,14,15,49], dropouts [28], or the student's score [33,35,41]. In most cases, the course was implemented as a distance learning course, where failure and dropout are especially serious problems.

The data sets were relatively small (50–350 rows, in average 200), because they were restricted by the number of students who take the same course. Usually the data consisted of just one class of students, but if the course had remained unchanged, it was possible to pool data from several classes.

The main attributes concerned were not only exercise tasks and the student's activity in the course, but also demographic and questionnaire data were used. The original number of attributes could be large (>50), but was reduced to 3–10 before any model was learned.

A large variety of classification methods were tried and compared in these experiments. The most common methods were decision trees, Bayesian networks, neural networks, *K*-nearest neighbor classifiers, and regression-based methods. The average accuracy was only 72%, but in the best cases nearly 90%. The most important factors affecting the classification accuracy were the number of class values used (best for the binary case) and at how early a stage the predictions were done (best at the end of the course, when all attributes are available).

5.2.3 Succeeding in the Next Task

In the third group of experiments the task was to predict the student's success in the next task, given his or her answers to previous tasks. This is an important problem especially in computerized adaptive testing, where the idea is to select the next question according to the student's current knowledge level. In [9,26,46], just the correctness of the student's answer was predicted, while [31] predicted the student's score in the next task.

The data sets were relatively small (40–360 rows, in average 130). The data consisted of students' answers in the previous tasks (measured skill and achieved score) and possibly other attributes concerning the student's activities within the learning system.

All experiments used probabilistic classification methods (Bayesian networks or Hidden Markov models). The accuracy was reported only in the last three experiments and varied between 73% and 90%.

5.2.4 Metacognitive Skills, Habits, and Motivation

The fourth group covers experiments, where the task was to classify metacognitive skills and other factors which affect learning. The objectives were to predict the student's motivation or engagement level [5,6], cognitive style [29], expertise in using the learning system [7], "gaming" the system [1], or recommended intervention strategy [22].

Real log data was used in the first five experiments. The size of data varied (30–950 rows, in average 160), because some experiments pooled all data on one student's actions, while others could use even short sequences of sessions. The attributes concerned navigation habits, time spent in different activities, number of pages read, number of times a task was tried, etc. Only a small number of attributes (4–7) was used to learn models.

In [22], a large set of artificial data was simulated. Four attributes were used to describe the student's metacognitive skills (self-efficacy, goal orientation, locus of control, perceived task difficulty). The idea was that later these attributes could be derived from log data.

The most common classification methods were decision trees, Bayesian networks, K-nearest neighbor classifiers, and regression-based techniques. Classification accuracy was reported only in four experiments and varied between 88% and 98%. One explanation for the high accuracy is that the class values were often decided by experts using some rules and the same attributes as the classifier used.

5.2.5 Summary

These 24 reviewed experiments give a good overview of the typical educational data and the most popular classification methods used.

In most cases the class attribute concerned a student, and there was just one row of data per student. In the university level studies, the size of the data was still large, but in the course level studies, the data sets were small (50–350 rows). Larger data sets were available for tasks, where each sequence of log data was classified separately.

Typically, the original data contained both categorical and numeric attributes. Often, the data was discretized before modeling, but sometimes both numeric and categorical versions of the data were modeled and compared. Purely numeric data occurred when all attributes were task scores or statistics on log data (frequencies of actions, time spent in actions). However, the task scores had often just a few values, and the data was discrete. This is an important feature, because different classification methods suit for discrete and continuous data.

The most common classification methods were decisions trees (16 experiments), Bayesian networks (13), neural networks (6), K-nearest neighbor classifiers (6), support vector machines (SVMs) (3), and different kinds of regression-based techniques (10).

5.3 Main Principles

In this section, we discuss the general principles that affect the selection of classification method and achieved classification accuracy. The main concerns are whether to choose a discriminative or probabilistic classifier, how to estimate the real accuracy, the tradeoff between overfitting and underfitting, and the impact of data preprocessing.

5.3.1 Discriminative or Probabilistic Classifier?

The basic form of classifiers is called *discriminative*, because they determine just one class value for each row of data. If M is a classifier (model), $C = \{c_1, \ldots, c_l\}$ the set of class values, and t a row of data, then the predicted class is $M(t) = c_i$ for just one i.

An alternative is a *probabilistic* classifier, which defines the probability of classes for all classified rows. Now $M(t) = [P(C = c_1|t), ..., P(C = c_i|t)]$, where $P(C = c_i|t)$ is the probability that t belongs to class c_i.

Probabilistic classification contains more information, which can be useful in some applications. One example is the task where one should predict the student's performance in a course, before the course has finished. The data often contains many inconsistent rows, where all other attribute values are the same, but the class values are different. Therefore, the class values cannot be determined accurately, and it is more informative for the course instructors to know how likely the student will pass the course. It can also be pedagogically wiser to tell the student that she or he has 48% probability to pass the course than to inform that she or he is going to fail.

Another example occurs in intelligent tutoring systems (or computerized adaptive testing) where one should select the most suitable action (next task) based on the learner's current situation. Now each row of data t describes the learner profile. For each situation (class c_i) there can be several recommendable actions b_j with probabilities $P(B = b_j|C = c_i)$, which tell how useful action b_j is in class c_i. Now we can easily calculate the total probability $P(B = b_j|t)$ that action b_j is useful, given learner profile t.

5.3.2 Classification Accuracy

The classification accuracy in set r is measured by *classification rate*, which defines the proportion of correctly classified rows in set r. If the predicted class by classifier M for row t is $M(t)$ and the actual class is $C(t)$, then the accuracy is

$$cr = \frac{\text{\# rows in } r \text{ where } M(t) = C(t)}{\text{\# rows in } r}$$

where # rows is an abbreviation for the number of rows.

The *classification error* in set r is simply the proportion of misclassified rows in r: $err = 1 - cr$.

If the class value is binary (e.g., the student passes or fails the course), the rates have special names:

	Predicted Class c_1	Predicted Class c_2
True class c_1	True positive rate $\dfrac{\text{\# rows where } M(t) = c_1 = C(t)}{\text{\# rows where } M(t) = c_1}$	False negative rate $\dfrac{\text{\# rows where } M(t) = c_2 \neq C(t) = c_1}{\text{\# rows where } M(t) = c_2}$
True class c_2	False positive rate $\dfrac{\text{\# rows where } M(t) = c_1 \neq C(t) = c_2}{\text{\# rows where } M(t) = c_1}$	True negative rate $\dfrac{\text{\# rows where } M(t) = c_2 = C(t)}{\text{\# rows where } M(t) = c_2}$

If the accuracy in one class is more critical (e.g., all possible failures or dropouts should be identified), we can often bias the model to minimize false positive (false negative) rate in the cost of large false negative (positive) rate (see e.g., [47, Chapter 5.7]).

When r is the training set, the error is called the *training error*. If r has the same distribution as the whole population (e.g., all future students in a similar course), the training error gives a good estimate for the *generalization error* also. Unfortunately, this is seldom the case in the educational domain. The training sets are so small that they cannot capture the real distribution and the resulting classifier is seriously biased. Therefore, we should somehow estimate the generalization error on unseen data.

A common solution is to reserve a part of the data as a test set. However, if the data set is already small, it is not advisable to reduce the training set any more. In this case, *m-fold cross-validation* is a better solution. The idea is that we partition the original data set of size n to m disjoint subsets of size n/m. Then we reserve one subset for validation and learn the model with other $m - 1$ subsets. The procedure is repeated m times with different validation sets and finally we calculate the mean of classification errors. An extreme case is *leave-one-out* cross-validation, where just one row is saved for validation and the model is learned from the remaining $n - 1$ rows.

5.3.3 Overfitting

Overfitting is an important problem related to accuracy. Overfitting means that the model has fitted to the training data too much so that it expresses even the rarest special cases and errors in data. The resulting model is so specialized that it cannot generalize to future data. For example, a data set that was collected for predicting the student's success in a programming course contained one female student, who had good IT skills and self-efficacy, and knew the idea of programming beforehand, but still dropped out the course. Still, we could not assume that all future students with the same characteristics would drop out. (In fact, all the other female students with good self-efficacy passed the course.)

Overfitting happens when the model is too complex relative to the data size. The reason is that complex models have higher *representative power*, and they can represent all data peculiarities, including errors. On the other hand, simple models have lower representative power but they generalize well to future data. If the model is too simple, it cannot catch any essential patterns in the data, but *underfits*. It means that the model approximates poorly the true model or there does not exist a true model.

Figure 5.1 demonstrates the effects of overfitting and underrating when the model complexity increases. In this example, we used the previously mentioned data set from a programming course. The attributes were added to the model in the order of their importance (measured by Information Gain) and a decision tree was learned with *ID3* algorithm [39]. The simplest model used just one attribute (exercises points in applets), while the last model used 23 attributes. In the simplest models both the training and testing errors were large, because there were not enough attributes to discriminate the classes, and the models underfitted. On the other hand, the most complex models achieved a small training error, because they could fit the training data well. In the same time, the testing error increased, because the models had overfitted.

In the educational domain, overfitting is a critical problem, because there are many attributes available to construct a complex model, but only a little data to learn it accurately. As a rule of thumb it is often suggested (e.g., [12,24]) that we should have at least 5–10 rows of data per model parameter. The simpler the model is, fewer the parameters needed. For example, if we have k binary-valued attributes, a naive Bayes classifier contains $O(k)$ parameters, while a general Bayesian classifier has in the worst case $O(2^k)$ parameters. In the first case, it is enough that $n > 5k$ $(10k)$, while in the latter case, we need at least $n > 5 \cdot 2^k$ $(10 \cdot 2^k)$ rows of data. If the attributes are not binary-valued, more data is needed.

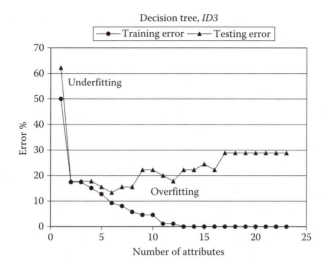

FIGURE 5.1
Effects of underfitting and overfitting. The training error decreases but testing error increases with the number of attributes.

In practice, there are two things we can do: (1) use simple classification methods requiring fewer model parameters, and (2) reduce the number of attributes and their domains by feature selection and feature extraction.

5.3.4 Linear and Nonlinear Class Boundaries

The main aspect of representative power is the form of class boundaries that can be represented. Linear classifiers can separate two classes only, if they are *linearly separable*, that is, there exists a hyperplane (in two-dimensional case, just a straight line) that separates the data points in both classes. Otherwise, the classes are *linearly inseparable* (Figure 5.2). It is still possible that only few data points are in the wrong side of the hyperplane, and thus the error in assuming a linear boundary is small. Depending on the degree of error, a linear classifier can still be preferable, because the resulting model is simpler and thus

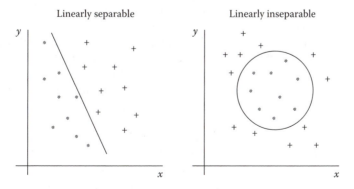

FIGURE 5.2
Linearly separable and inseparable class boundaries.

less sensitive to overfitting. However, some classes can be separated only by a nonlinear boundary and a nonlinear classifier is needed.

5.3.5 Data Preprocessing

Before the modeling paradigm can be selected, we should know what kind of data is available. Typically, educational data is discrete-valued, either numeric or categorical. The numeric values such as exercise points are either integers or represented with a low precision (e.g., half or one-fourth points). Log-based data can contain also continuous values such as time spent on a task or average reading speed.

Real data is often incomplete in several ways. It can contain missing or erroneous attribute values. Erroneous values are generally called *noise*, but in some contexts noise means only measurement errors. Educational data is usually quite clean (free of noise), because it is either collected automatically (log data) or checked carefully (student's scores). Missing values occur more frequently, especially when we combine data from different sources. For example, questionnaire data on students' attitudes and habits could be combined with their performance data, but it is possible that some students have skipped the whole questionnaire or answered only some questions.

Outliers refer to data points that deviate significantly from the majority so that they do not fit the same model as others. Outliers can be due to noise, but in educational data they are often true observations. There are always exceptional students, who succeed with little effort or fail against all expectations.

The goal of data preprocessing is to improve the quality of data and produce good attributes for classification. The main tasks are *data cleaning, feature extraction*, and *feature selection*. In data cleaning, one should fill in the missing values and try to identify and correct errors. In feature extraction, new attributes are produced by transforming and combining the original ones. In feature selection, an optimal set of attributes is selected.

The most commonly used feature extraction technique in educational classification is discretization. In discretization, the range of numeric values is divided into intervals, which will be used as new attribute values. In the extreme case, all attributes can be binarized. For example, the exercise points can be divided into two categories, low (0) and high (1). Even if some information is lost, the resulting model can produce a more accurate classification. The reason is that small variation in exercise points or exact point values are not important, but the general tendency is; that is, if the student has done a little or a lot of them. Generally, discretization smooths out the effect of noise and enables simpler models, which are less prone to overfitting.

Feature selection can be done by analyzing the dependencies between the class attribute and explanatory attributes (e.g., correlation analysis, information gain, or association rules). Another approach is to use a learning algorithm and select the most important attributes in the resulting classifier. For example, one can first learn a decision tree and then use its attributes for a *K*-nearest neighbor classifier [47].

Some techniques perform feature extraction and feature selection simultaneously. For example, in *principal component analysis (PCA)* [25] and *independent component analysis (ICA)* [27] new attributes are produced as linear combinations of the original ones. Simultaneously, they suggest which of the new attributes describe the data best.

The dilemma is that the goodness of feature extraction and selection cannot be evaluated before the classifier is learned and tested. If the number of attributes is large, all possibilities cannot be tested. That is why all feature extraction and selection methods are more or less heuristic. Overviews of feature extraction and selection techniques can be found in [16, Chapter 3] and [47, Chapters 7.1 through 7.3].

5.4 Classification Approaches

In the following, we will briefly introduce the main approaches for classification: decision trees, Bayesian classifiers, neural networks, nearest neighbor classifiers, SVMs, and linear regression. The approaches are compared for their suitability to classify typical educational data.

5.4.1 Decision Trees

Decision trees (see e.g., [47, Chapter 6.1]) are maybe the best-known classification paradigm. A decision tree represents a set of classification rules in a tree form. Each root-leaf path corresponds to a rule of form $T_{i_1} \wedge \ldots \wedge T_{i_l} \rightarrow (C = c)$, where c is the class value in the leaf and each T_{i_1} is a Boolean-valued test on attribute A_{i_j}.

The earliest decision trees were constructed by human experts, but nowadays they are usually learned from data. The best known algorithms are *ID3* [39] and *C4.5* [40]. The basic idea in all learning algorithms is to partition the attribute space until some termination criterion is reached in each leaf. Usually, the criterion is that all points in the leaf belong to one class. However, if the data contains inconsistencies, this is not possible. As a solution, the most common class among the data points in the leaf is selected. An alternative is to report the class probabilities according to relative frequencies in the node.

Decision trees have many advantages: they are simple and easy to understand, they can handle mixed variables (i.e., both numeric and categorical variables), they can classify new examples quickly, and they are flexible. Enlargements of decision trees can easily handle small noise and missing attribute values. Decision trees have high representative power, because they can approximate nonlinear class boundaries, even if the boundaries are everywhere piecewise parallel to attribute axes. However, it should be remembered that the resulting model can be seriously overfitted, especially if we have a small training set.

The main restriction of decision trees is the assumption that all data points in the domain can be classified deterministically into exactly one class. As a result, all inconsistencies are interpreted as errors, and decision trees are not suitable for intrinsically nondeterministic domains. One such example is course performance data, where a significant proportion of rows can be inconsistent. Class probabilities have sometimes been suggested as a solution, but the resulting system is very unstable, because each leaf node has its own probability distribution [17, p. 346]. Thus, even a minor change in one of the input variables can change the probabilities totally, when the data point is assigned to another leaf node.

Another problem is that decision trees are very sensitive to overfitting, especially in small data sets. In educational applications, the future data seldom follows the same distribution as the training set and we would need more robust models. For example, [10] recommend the use of naive Bayes instead of decision trees for small data sets, even if the attributes were not independent, as naive Bayes assumes.

Often overfitting can be avoided if we learn a collection of decision trees and average their predictions. This approach is generally called *model averaging* or *ensemble learning* (see e.g., [44]). In ensemble learning, we can combine several models with different structures, and even from different modeling paradigms. In practice, these methods can remarkably improve classification accuracy.

Finally, we recall that learning a globally optimal decision tree is a nondeterministic polynomial time (*NP*)-complete problem [23]. That is why all the common decision tree algorithms employ some heuristics and can produce suboptimal results.

5.4.2 Bayesian Classifiers

In *Bayesian networks* (see e.g., [38]), statistical dependencies are represented visually as a graph structure. The idea is that we take into account all information about conditional independencies and represent a minimal dependency-structure of attributes. Each vertex in the graph corresponds to an attribute, and the incoming edges define the set of attributes on which it depends. The strength of dependencies is defined by conditional probabilities. For example, if A_1 depends on attributes A_2 and A_3, the model has to define conditional probabilities $P(A_1|A_2, A_3)$ for all value combinations of A_1, A_2, and A_3.

When the Bayesian network is used for classification, we should first learn the dependency structure between explanatory attributes A_1, ..., A_k and the class attribute C. In the educational technology, it has been quite common to define an ad hoc graph structure by experts. However, there is a high risk that the resulting network imposes irrelevant dependencies while skipping actually-strong dependencies.

When the structure has been selected, the parameters are learned from the data. The parameters define the class-conditional distributions $P(t|C=c)$ for all possible data points $t \in S$ and all class values c. When a new data point is classified, it is enough to calculate class probabilities $P(C=c|t)$ by the Bayes rule:

$$P(C = c|t) = \frac{P(C = c)P(t|C = c)}{P(t)}$$

In practice, the problem is the large number of probabilities we have to estimate. For example, if all attributes A_1, ..., A_k have v different values and all A_i's are mutually dependent, we have to define $O(v^k)$ probabilities. This means that we also need a large training set to estimate the required joint probability accurately.

Another problem that decreases the classification accuracy of Bayesian networks is the use of *Minimum Description Length* (*MDL*) score function for model selection [13]. *MDL* measures the error in the model over all variables, but it does not necessarily minimize the error in the class variable. This problem occurs especially when the model contains several attributes and the accuracy of estimates $P(A_1, ..., A_k)$ begins to dominate the score.

The *naive Bayes model* solves both problems. The model complexity is restricted by a strong independence assumption: we assume that all attributes A_1, ..., A_k are conditionally independent, given the class attribute C, that is, $P(A_1,...,A_k|C) = \prod_{i=1}^{k} P(A_i|C)$. This *naive Bayes assumption* can be represented as a two-layer Bayesian network (Figure 5.3), with the class variable C as the root node and all the other variables as leaf nodes. Now we have to estimate only $O(kv)$ probabilities per class. The use of *MDL* score function in the model selection is also avoided, because the model structure is fixed, once we have decided the explanatory variables A_i.

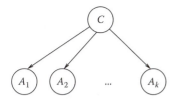

FIGURE 5.3
A naive Bayes model with class attribute C and explanatory-attributes $A_1,...,A_k$.

In practice, the naive Bayes assumption holds very seldom, but still the naive Bayes classifiers have achieved good results. In fact, [10] have shown that naive Bayes assumption is only a sufficient but not a necessary condition for the optimality of the naive Bayes classifier. In addition, if we are only interested in the ranked order of the classes, it does not matter if the estimated probabilities are biased.

As a consequence of naive Bayes assumption, the representative power of the naive Bayes model is lower than that of decision trees. If the model uses categorical data, it can recognize linear class boundaries. However, in some special cases the class boundaries can be more complex, and the exact representative power of the naive Bayes classifier with categorical data is not known [30]. When numeric data is used, more complex (nonlinear) boundaries can be represented.

Otherwise, the naive Bayes model has many advantages: it is very simple, efficient, robust to noise, and easy to interpret. It is especially suitable for small data sets, because it combines small complexity with a flexible probabilistic model. The basic model suits only for discrete data and the numeric data should be discretized. Alternatively, we can learn a continuous model by estimating densities instead of distributions. However, continuous Bayesian networks assume some general form of distribution, typically the normal distribution, which is often unrealistic. Usually, discretization is a better solution, because it also simplifies the model and the resulting classifier is more robust to overfitting.

5.4.3 Neural Networks

Artificial neural networks (see e.g., [11]) are very popular in pattern recognition, and justly so. According to a classical phrase (J. Denker, quoted in [42, p. 585]), they are "the second best way of doing just about anything." Still, they can be problematic when applied to educational technology, unless you have a lot of numeric data and know exactly how to train the model.

Feed-forward neural networks (*FFNNs*) are the most widely used type of neural networks. The *FFNN* architecture consists of layers of nodes: one for input nodes, one for output nodes, and at least one layer of *hidden nodes*. On each hidden layer the nodes are connected to the previous and next layer nodes and the edges are associated with individual weights. The most general model contains just one hidden layer. This is usually sufficient, because in principle *any function can be represented by a three-layer network*, given sufficiently many hidden nodes [18]. This implies that we can also represent any kind of (nonlinear) class boundaries. However, in practice, learning a highly nonlinear network is very difficult or even impossible. For linearly separable classes it is sufficient to use a *perceptron*, an *FFNN* with no hidden layers.

The learning algorithm is an essential part of the neural network model. Even if neural networks can represent any kind of classifiers, we are seldom able to learn the optimal model. The learning is computationally difficult and the results depend on several open parameters such as the number of hidden layers, number of hidden nodes on each layer, initial weights, and the termination criterion. Especially the selection of the architecture (network topology) and the termination criterion are critical, because neural networks are very sensitive to overfitting. Unfortunately, there are no foolproof instructions and the parameters have to be defined by trial and error. However, there are some general rules of thumb, which restrict the number of trials needed. For example, [11, p. 317] suggest to use a three-layer network as a default and add layers only for serious reasons. For stopping criterion (deciding when the model is ready), a popular strategy is to use a separate test set [34, p. 111].

FFNNs have several attractive features. They can easily learn nonlinear boundaries and in principle represent any kind of classifiers. If the original variables are not discriminatory, *FFNN* transforms them implicitly. In addition, *FFNNs* are robust to noise and can be updated with new data.

The main disadvantage is that *FFNNs* need a lot of data—much more than typical educational data sets contain. They are very sensitive to overfitting and the problem is even more critical with small training sets. The data should be numeric and categorical data must be somehow quantized before it can be used. However, this increases the model complexity and the results are sensitive to the quantization method used.

The neural network model is a black box and it is difficult for people to understand the explanations for the outcomes. In addition, neural networks are unstable and achieve good results only in good hands [12]. Finally, we recall that finding an optimal *FFNN* is an *NP*-complete problem [3] and the learning algorithm can get stuck at a local optimum. Still, the training can be time consuming, especially if we want to circumvent overfitting.

5.4.4 *K*-Nearest Neighbor Classifiers

K-nearest neighbor classifiers (see e.g., [17, pp. 347–352]) represent a totally different approach to classification. They do not build any explicit global model, but approximate it only locally and implicitly. The main idea is to classify a new object by examining the class values of the K most similar data points. The selected class can be either the most common class among the neighbors or a class distribution in the neighborhood.

The only learning task in *K*-nearest neighbor classifiers is to select two important parameters: the number of neighbors K and distance metric d.

An appropriate K value can be selected by trying different values and validating the results in a separate test set. When data sets are small, a good strategy is to use leave-one-out cross-validation. If K is fixed, then the size of the neighborhood varies. In sparse areas, the nearest neighbors are more remote than in dense areas. However, defining different K's for different areas is even more difficult. If K is very small, then the neighborhood is also small and the classification is based on just a few data points. As a result the classifier is unstable, because these few neighbors can vary a lot. On the other hand, if K is very large, then the most likely class in the neighborhood can deviate much from the real class. For small dimensional data sets, suitable K is usually between 5 and 10. One solution is to weigh the neighbors by their distances. In this case, the neighborhood can cover all data points so far and all neighborhoods are equally large. The only disadvantage is that the computation becomes slower.

Defining the distance metric d is another more critical problem. Usually, the metrics take into account all attributes, even if some attributes were irrelevant. Now it is possible that the most similar neighbors become remote and the "wrong neighbors" corrupt the classification. The problem becomes more serious when more attributes are used and the attribute space is sparse. When all points are far, it is hard to recognize real neighbors from other points and the predictions become inaccurate. As a solution, it has been suggested (e.g., [20]) to give relevance weights for attributes, but the relevant attributes can also vary from class to class. In practice, appropriate feature selection can produce better results.

The nearest neighborhood classifiers have several advantages: there are only two parameters to learn (or select), the classification accuracy can be very good in some problems, and the classification is quite robust to noise and missing values. Especially weighted distance smooths the noise in attribute values and missing values can be simply skipped. Nearest neighbor classifiers have very high representative power, because they can work with any kind of class boundaries, given sufficient data.

The main disadvantage is the difficulty to select distance function *d*. Educational data often consists of both numeric and categorical data, and numeric attributes can be in different scales. It means that we not only need a weighted distance function, but also a large data set to learn the weights accurately. Irrelevant attributes are also common in some educational data sets (e.g., questionnaire data) and they should be removed first.

The lack of an explicit model can be either an advantage or a disadvantage. If the model is very complex, it is often easier to approximate it only locally. In addition, there is no need to update the classifier when new data is added. However, this kind of "lazy methods" are slower in classification than model-based approaches. If the data set is large, we need some index to find the nearest neighbors efficiently. It is also noteworthy that an explicit model is useful for human evaluators and designers of the system.

5.4.5 Support Vector Machines

SVMs [45] are an ideal method when the class boundaries are nonlinear but here is too little data to learn complex nonlinear models. The underlying idea is that when the data is mapped to a higher dimension, the classes become linearly separable. In practice, the mapping is done only implicitly, using kernel functions.

SVMs concentrate on only the class boundaries; points that are any way easily classified are skipped. The goal is to find the "thickest hyperplane" (with the largest margin), which separates the classes. Often, better results are achieved with "soft" margins, which allow some misclassified data points. When the optimal margin is determined, it is enough to save the *support vectors,* that is, data points that define the class boundaries.

The main advantage of *SVMs* is that they always find the global optimum, because there are no local optima in maximizing the margin. Another benefit is that the accuracy does not depend on the dimensionality of data and the system is very robust to overfitting. This is an important advantage when the class boundary is nonlinear. Most other classification paradigms produce too complex models for nonlinear boundaries.

However, *SVMs* have the same restriction as neural networks: the data should be continuous numerical (or quantized), the model is not easily interpreted, and selecting the appropriate parameters (especially the kernel function) can be difficult. Outliers can cause problems, because they are used to define the class borders. Usually, the problem is avoided by soft margins.

5.4.6 Linear Regression

Linear regression is actually not a classification method, but it works well, when all attributes are numeric. For example, passing a course depends on the student's points, and the points can be predicted by linear regression.

In linear regression, it is assumed that the target attribute (e.g., total points) is a linear function of other, mutually independent attributes. However, the model is very flexible and can work well, even if the actual dependency is only approximately linear or the other attributes are weakly correlated (e.g., [48]). The reason is that linear regression produces very simple models, which are not as risky for overfitting as more complex models.

However, the data should not contain large gaps (empty areas) and the number of outliers should be small [21, p. 162].

5.4.7 Comparison

Selecting the most appropriate classification method for the given task is a difficult problem and no general answer can be given. In Table 5.1, we have evaluated the main classification methods according to eight general criteria, which are often relevant when educational data is classified.

The first criterion concerns the *form of class boundaries*. Decision trees, general Bayesian networks, *FFNNs*, nearest neighbor classifiers, and *SVMs* can represent highly nonlinear boundaries. Naive Bayes model using nominal data can represent only a subset of linear boundaries, but with numeric data it can represent quite complex nonlinear boundaries. Linear regression is restricted to only linear boundaries, but it tolerates small deviations from the linearity. It should be noticed that strong representative power is not desirable if we have only little data and a simpler, linear model would suffice. The reason is that complex, nonlinear models are also more sensitive to overfitting.

The second criterion, *accuracy on small data sets*, is crucial for the educational domain. An accurate classifier cannot be learned if there is insufficient data. The sufficient amount of data depends on the model complexity. In practice, we should favor simple models, such as naive Bayes classifiers or linear regression. Support vector machines can produce extremely good results if the model parameters are correctly selected. On the other hand, decision trees, *FFNNs*, and nearest neighbor classifiers require much larger data sets to work accurately. The accuracy of general Bayesian classifiers depends on the complexity of the structure used.

The third criterion concerns whether the method can handle *incomplete data*, that is, noise (errors), outliers (which can be due to noise), and missing values. Educational data is usually clean, but outliers and missing values occur frequently. Naive and general Bayesian

TABLE 5.1

Comparison of Different Classification Paradigms

	DT	NB	GB	FFNN	K-nn	SVM	LR
Nonlinear boundaries	+	(+)	+	+	+	+	−
Accuracy on small data sets	−	+	+/−	−	−	+	+
Works with incomplete data	−	+	+	+	+	−	−
Supports mixed variables	+	+	+	−	+	−	−
Natural interpretation	+	+	+	−	(+)	−	+
Efficient reasoning	+	+	+	+	−	+	+
Efficient learning	+/−	+	−	−	+/−	+	+
Efficient updating	−	+	+	+	+	−	+

Sign + means that the method supports the property, − that it does not. The abbreviations are *DT*, decision tree; *NB*, naive Bayes classifier; *GB*, general Bayesian classifier; *FFNN*, feed-forward neural network; *K-nn*, *K*-nearest neighbor classifier; *SVM*, support vector machine; *LR*, linear regression.

classifiers, *FFNNs*, and nearest neighbor models are especially robust to noise in the data. Bayesian classifiers, nearest neighbor models, and some enlargements of decision trees can also handle missing values quite well. However, decision trees are generally very sensitive to small changes such as noise in the data. Linear regression cannot handle missing attribute values at all and serious outliers can corrupt the whole model. *SVMs* are also sensitive to outliers.

The fourth criterion tells whether the method *supports mixed variables*, that is, both numeric and categorical. All methods can handle numeric attributes, but categorical attributes are problematic for *FFNNs*, linear regression, and *SVMs*.

Natural interpretation is also an important criterion, since all educational models should be transparent to the learner (e.g., [37]). All the other paradigms except neural networks and *SVMs* offer more or less understandable models. Especially decision trees and Bayesian networks have a comprehensive visual representation.

The last criteria concern the *computational efficiency* of classification, learning, and updating the model. The most important is efficient classification, because the system should adapt to the learner's current situation immediately. For example, if the system offers individual exercises for learners, it should detect when easier or more challenging tasks are desired. Nearest neighbor classifier is the only one that lacks this property. The efficiency of learning is not so critical, because it is not done in real time. In some methods, the models can be efficiently updated, given new data. This is an attractive feature because often we can collect new data when the model is already in use.

5.5 Conclusions

Classification has many applications in both traditional education and modern educational technology. The best results are achieved when classifiers can be learned from real data, but in educational domain the data sets are often too small for accurate learning.

In this chapter, we have discussed the main principles that affect classification accuracy. The most important concern is to select a sufficiently powerful model, which catches the dependencies between the class attribute and other attributes, but which is sufficiently simple to avoid overfitting. Both data preprocessing and the selected classification method affect this goal. To help the reader, we have analyzed the suitability of different classification methods for typical educational data and problems.

References

1. R.S. Baker, A.T. Corbett, and K.R. Koedinger. Detecting student misuse of intelligent tutoring systems. In *Proceedings of the 7th International Conference on Intelligent Tutoring Systems (ITS'04)*, pp. 531–540. Springer Verlag, Berlin, Germany, 2004.
2. K. Barker, T. Trafalis, and T.R. Rhoads. Learning from student data. In *Proceedings of the 2004 IEEE Systems and Information Engineering Design Symposium*, pp. 79–86. University of Virginia, Charlottesville, VA, 2004.
3. A. Blum and R.L. Rivest. Training 3-node neural network is NP-complete. In *Proceedings of the 1988 Workshop on Computational Learning Theory (COLT)*, pp. 9–18. MIT, Cambridge, MA, 1988.

4. V.P. Bresfelean, M. Bresfelean, N. Ghisoiu, and C.-A. Comes. Determining students' academic failure profile founded on data mining methods. In *Proceedings of the 30th International Conference on Information Technology Interfaces (ITI 2008)*, pp. 317–322. Dubrovnik, Croatia, 2008.

5. M. Cocea and S. Weibelzahl. Can log files analysis estimate learners' level of motivation? In *Proceedings of Lernen–Wissensentdeckung–Adaptivität (LWA2006)*, pp. 32–35, Hildesheim, Germany, 2006.

6. M. Cocea and S. Weibelzahl. Cross-system validation of engagement prediction from log files. In *Creating New Learning Experiences on a Global Scale, Proceedings of the 2nd European Conference on Technology Enhanced Learning (EC-TEL2007)*, volume 4753, *Lecture Notes in Computer Science*, pp. 14–25. Springer, Heidelberg, Germany, 2007.

7. M. Damez, T.H. Dang, C. Marsala, and B. Bouchon-Meunier. Fuzzy decision tree for user modeling from human-computer interactions. In *Proceedings of the 5th International Conference on Human System Learning (ICHSL'05)*, pp. 287–302. Marrakech, Maroc, 2005.

8. G. Dekker, M. Pechenizkiy, and J. Vleeshouwers. Predicting students drop out: A case study. In *Educational Data Mining 2009: Proceedings of the 2nd International Conference on Educational Data Mining (EDM'09)*, pp. 41–50. Cordoba, Spain, July 1–3, 2009.

9. M.C. Desmarais and X. Pu. A Bayesian student model without hidden nodes and its comparison with item response theory. *International Journal of Artificial Intelligence in Education*, 15:291–323, 2005.

10. P. Domingos and M. Pazzani. On the optimality of the simple Bayesian classifier under zero-one loss. *Machine Learning*, 29:103–130, 1997.

11. R.O. Duda, P.E. Hart, and D.G. Stork. *Pattern Classification*, 2nd ed. Wiley-Interscience Publication, New York, 2000.

12. R. Duin. Learned from neural networks. In *Proceedings of the 6th Annual Conference of the Advanced School for Computing and Imaging (ASCI-2000)*, pp. 9–13. Advanced School for Computing and Imaging (ASCI), Delft, the Netherlands, 2000.

13. N. Friedman, D. Geiger, and M. Goldszmidt. Bayesian network classifiers. *Machine Learning*, 29(2–3):131–163, 1997.

14. W. Hämäläinen, T.H. Laine, and E. Sutinen. Data mining in personalizing distance education courses. In C. Romero and S. Ventura, editors, *Data Mining in e-Learning*, pp. 157–171. WitPress, Southampton, U.K., 2006.

15. W. Hämäläinen and M. Vinni. Comparison of machine learning methods for intelligent tutoring systems. In *Proceedings of the 8th International Conference on Intelligent Tutoring Systems*, volume 4053, *Lecture Notes in Computer Science*, pp. 525–534. Springer-Verlag, Berlin, Germany, 2006.

16. J. Han and M. Kamber. *Data Mining: Concepts and Techniques*, 2nd edn. Morgan Kaufmann, San Francisco, CA, 2006.

17. D. Hand, H. Mannila, and P. Smyth. *Principles of Data Mining*. MIT Press, Cambridge, MA, 2002.

18. R. Hecht-Nielsen. Theory of the backpropagation neural network. In *Proceedings of the International Joint Conference on Neural Networks (IJCNN)*, volume 1, pp. 593–605. IEEE, Washington, DC, 1989.

19. S. Herzog. Estimating student retention and degree-completion time: Decision trees and neural networks vis-a-vis regression. *New Directions for Institutional Research*, 131:17–33, 2006.

20. A. Hinneburg, C.C. Aggarwal, and D.A. Kleim. What is the nearest neighbor in high dimensional spaces? In *Proceedings of 26th International Conference on Very Large Data Bases (VLDB 2000)*, pp. 506–515. Morgan Kaufmann, Cairo, Egypt, September 10–14, 2000.

21. P.J. Huber. *Robust Statistics*. Wiley Series in Probability and Mathematical Statistics. John Wiley & Sons, New York, 1981.

22. T. Hurley and S. Weibelzahl. Eliciting adaptation knowledge from online tutors to increase motivation. In *Proceedings of 11th International Conference on User Modeling (UM2007)*, volume 4511, *Lecture Notes in Artificial Intelligence*, pp. 370–374. Springer Verlag, Berlin, Germany, 2007.

23. L. Hyafil and R.L. Rivest. Constructing optimal binary decision trees is NP-complete. *Information Processing Letters*, 5(1):15–17, 1976.

24. A.K. Jain, P.W. Duin, and J. Mao. Statistical pattern recognition: A review. *IEEE Transactions on Pattern Analysis and Machine Intelligence*, 22(1):4–37, 2000.

25. I.T. Jolliffe. *Principal Component Analysis*. Springer-Verlag, New York, 1986.

26. A. Jonsson, J. Johns, H. Mehranian, I. Arroyo, B. Woolf, A.G. Barto, D. Fisher, and S. Mahadevan. Evaluating the feasibility of learning student models from data. In *Papers from the 2005 AAAI Workshop on Educational Data Mining*, pp. 1–6. AAAI Press, Menlo Park, CA, 2005.

27. C. Jutten and J. Herault. An adaptive algorithm based on neuromimetic architecture. *Signal Processing*, 24:1–10, 1991.

28. S.B. Kotsiantis, C.J. Pierrakeas, and P.E. Pintelas. Preventing student dropout in distance learning using machine learning techniques. In *Proceedings of 7th International Conference on Knowledge-Based Intelligent Information and Engineering Systems (KES-2003)*, volume 2774, *Lecture Notes in Computer Science*, pp. 267–274. Springer-Verlag, Heidelberg, Germany, 2003.

29. M.-G. Lee. Profiling students' adaption styles in web-based learning. *Computers & Education*, 36:121–132, 2001.

30. C.X. Ling and H. Zhang. The representational power of discrete Bayesian networks. *The Journal of Machine Learning Research*, 3:709–721, 2003.

31. C.-C. Liu. Knowledge discovery from web portfolios: Tools for learning performance assessment. PhD thesis, Department of Computer Science Information Engineering Yuan Ze University, Taiwan, 2000.

32. Y. Ma, B. Liu, C.K. Wong, P.S. Yu, and S.M. Lee. Targeting the right students using data mining. In *Proceedings of the Sixth ACM SIGKDD International Conference on Knowledge Discovery and Data Mining (KDD'00)*, pp. 457–464. ACM Press, New York, 2000.

33. B. Minaei-Bidgoli, D.A. Kashy, G. Kortemeyer, and W. Punch. Predicting student performance: An application of data mining methods with an educational web-based system. In *Proceedings of 33rd Frontiers in Education Conference*, pp. T2A-13–T2A-18. Westminster, CO, November 5–8, 2003.

34. T.M. Mitchell. *Machine Learning*. McGraw-Hill Companies, New York, 1997.

35. M. Mühlenbrock. Automatic action analysis in an interactive learning environment. In *Proceedings of the Workshop on Usage Analysis in Learning Systems at AIED-2005*, pp. 73–80. Amsterdam, the Netherlands, 2005.

36. N. Thai Nghe, P. Janecek, and P. Haddawy. A comparative analysis of techniques for predicting academic performance. In *Proceedings of the 37th Conference on ASEE/IEEE Frontiers in Education*, pp. T2G-7–T2G-12. Milwaukee, WI, October 10–13, 2007.

37. T. O'Shea, R. Bornat, B. Boulay, and M. Eisenstad. Tools for creating intelligent computer tutors. In *Proceedings of the International NATO Symposium on Artificial and Human Intelligence*, pp. 181–199. Elsevier North-Holland, Inc., New York, 1984.

38. J. Pearl. *Probabilistic Reasoning in Intelligent Systems: Networks of Plausible Inference*. Morgan Kaufman Publishers, San Mateo, CA, 1988.

39. J.R. Quinlan. Induction of decision trees. *Machine Learning*, 1(1):81–106, 1986.

40. J.R. Quinlan. *C4.5: Programs for Machine Learning*. Morgan Kaufmann, San Mateo, CA, 1993.

41. C. Romero, S. Ventura, P.G. Espejo, and C. Hervas. Data mining algorithms to classify students. In *Educational Data Mining 2008: Proceedings of the 1st International Conference on Educational Data Mining*, pp. 8–17. Montreal, Canada, June 20–21, 2008.

42. S.J. Russell and P. Norvig. *Artificial Intelligence: A Modern Approach*, 2nd edn. Prentice Hall, Englewood Cliffs, NJ, 2002.

43. J.F. Superby, J.-P. Vandamme, and N. Meskens. Determination of factors influencing the achievement of the first-year university students using data mining methods. In *Proceedings of the Workshop on Educational Data Mining at ITS'06*, pp. 37–44. Jhongali, Taiwan, 2006.

44. G. Valentini and F. Masulli. *Ensembles of Learning Machines*, volume 2486, *Lecture Notes in Computer Science*, pp. 3–22. Springer-Verlag, Berlin, Germany, 2002. Invited Review.

45. V.N. Vapnik. *Statistical Learning Theory*. John Wiley & Sons, New York, 1998.

46. J. Vomlel. Bayesian networks in educational testing. *International Journal of Uncertainty, Fuzziness and Knowledge Based Systems*, (Supplementary Issue 1):83–100, 2004.

47. I.H. Witten and E. Frank. *Data Mining: Practical Machine Learning Tools and Techniques*, 2nd ed. Morgan Kaufmann, San Francisco, CA, 2005.
48. Xycoon. Linear regression techniques. Chapter II. In *Statistics – Econometrics – Forecasting (Online Econometrics Textbook)*, Office for Research Development and Education, 2000–2006. Available on http://www.xycoon.com/. Retrieved on January 1, 2006.
49. W. Zang and F. Lin. Investigation of web-based teaching and learning by-boosting algorithms. In *Proceedings of IEEE International Conference on Information Technology: Research and Education (ITRE 2003)*, pp. 445–449. Malaga, Spain, August 11–13, 2003.

6

Clustering Educational Data

Alfredo Vellido, Félix Castro, and Àngela Nebot

CONTENTS

6.1 Introduction

The Internet and the advance of telecommunication technologies allow us to share and manipulate information in nearly real time. This reality is determining the next generation of distance education tools. Distance education arose from traditional education in order to cover the necessities of remote students and/or help the teaching–learning process, reinforcing or replacing traditional education. The Internet takes this process of delocalization of the educative experience to a new realm, where the lack of face-to-face interaction is, at least partially, replaced by an increased level of technology-mediated interaction. Furthermore, telecommunications allow this interaction to take forms that were not available to traditional presential and distance learning teachers and learners.

Most e-learning processes generate vast amounts of data that could well be used to better understand the learners and their needs, as well as to improve e-learning systems. Data mining was conceived to tackle this type of problem. As a field of research, it is almost contemporary to e-learning, and somehow vaguely defined. Not because of its complexity, but because it places its roots in the ever-shifting world of business studies. In its most formal definition, it can be understood not just as a collection of data analysis methods, but as a data analysis process that encompasses anything from data understanding, preprocessing, and modeling to process evaluation and implementation [1]. It is nevertheless usual to pay preferential attention to the data mining methods themselves. These commonly bridge the fields of traditional statistics, pattern recognition, and machine learning to provide analytical solutions to problems in areas as diverse as biomedicine, engineering, and business, to name just a few. An aspect that perhaps makes data mining unique is that it pays special attention to the compatibility of the data modeling techniques with new information technologies (IT) and database development and operation, often focusing on large, heterogeneous, and complex databases. e-Learning databases often fit this description.

Therefore, data mining can be used to extract knowledge from e-learning systems through the analysis of the information available in the form of data generated by their users. In this case, the main objective becomes finding the patterns of teachers' and students' system usage and, perhaps most importantly, discovering the students' learning behavior patterns. For a detailed insight into data mining applied to e-learning systems, the reader is referred to [2].

e-Learning has become a social process connecting students to communities of devices, people, and situations, so that they can construct relevant and meaningful learning experiences that they co-author themselves. Collaborative learning is one of the components of pervasive learning, the others being autonomy, location, and relationship. There are a variety of approaches in education that involve joint intellectual effort by students of similar performance. Groups of students work together to understand concepts, share ideas, and ultimately succeed as a whole. Students of similar performance can be identified and grouped by the assessment of their abilities.

The process of grouping students is, therefore, one of relevance for data mining. This naturally refers to an area of data analysis, namely data clustering, which is aimed at discovering the natural grouping structure of data. This chapter is devoted to this area of data mining and its corresponding analytical methods, which hold the promise of providing useful knowledge to the community of e-learning practitioners. Clustering and visualization methods can enhance the e-learning experience, due to the capacity of the former to group similar actors based on their similarities, and the ability of the latter to describe and explore these groups intuitively.

The remaining of the chapter is organized as follows: In Section 6.2, we provide a brief account of the clustering problem and some of the most popular clustering techniques. Section 6.3 provides a broad review of clustering in e-learning. Finally, Section 6.4 wraps up the chapter by drawing some general conclusions.

6.2 The Clustering Problem in Data Mining

Grouping and labeling aspects of reality seem to be two of the most standard occupations of the human brain and, therefore, of natural learning. When dividing the existing reality into different categories, we are seamlessly performing grouping and classification tasks that can be improved over time through learning. Clustering is specifically characterized by the fact that class labeling information is not considered in the process of group definition.

From a data mining point of view, grouping processes concern the theory of multivariate data clustering. It is well beyond the aim of this chapter to provide a detailed account of the manifold branches of clustering research and the broad palette offered by the state-of-the-art techniques in this area. Suffice at this point to provide a general overview of this field.

In an extremely simplified way, the problem of data clustering may be defined as that of assigning each of N data items to one of K possible clusters. Mind you, this definition falls short in the case of some fuzzy or probabilistic clustering methods in which, instead of *hard* assignments, the result is a measure or a probability of cluster membership. This assignment must be the result of applying similarity measures such as, in the most standard case, an Euclidean distance between points. We cannot ignore that, often, similarity is a tricky concept in clustering, given that, beyond data density, often we must also consider cluster shape and size.

In terms of processes, we could broadly separate *hierarchical* and *partitional* methods. Hierarchical clustering assumes that cluster structure appears at different, usually nested structural levels. Partitional clustering considers a single common level for all clusters and it can therefore be considered as a special case of hierarchical clustering. Among partitional methods, k-means is perhaps the most popular one [3]. Plenty of extensions of this method have been developed over the last decades, including fuzzy versions that avoid hard cluster assignments, such as Fuzzy c-means [4] or even adaptations to hierarchical processing such as Bisecting k-means [5].

Another way of discriminating between different clustering techniques is according to the objective function they usually aim to optimize. Also, and this may perhaps be a neater criterion, clustering methods can be either stochastic in nature (probabilistic techniques) or heuristic (mostly algorithmic). The former resort to the definition of probability density distributions and, among their advantages, most of their adaptive parameters can be estimated in an automated and principled manner. Mixture models are a basic example of these [6] and they often entail Bayesian methods, e.g., [7]. Heuristic methods are plentiful, very different in terms of origin (theoretically and application-wise) and, therefore, far too varied for a basic review such as this. One of the most successful ones [8] is Kohonen's self-organizing map (SOM [9]), in its many forms. The roots of this model are in the field of neuroscience, but it has become extremely successful as a tool for simultaneous data clustering and visualization. A probabilistic alternative to SOM, namely generative topographic mapping (GTM [10]) was defined to preserve SOM's functionality while avoiding many of its limitations.

The evaluation of clustering processes is not straightforward. In classification or prediction, evaluation is usually performed on the basis of the available class label information in test sets. This is not the case in clustering. The validity of a clustering solution often depends on the expert domain point of view. Quantifying this can be difficult, since the interpretation of how interesting a clustering is, will inevitably be an application-dependent matter and therefore subjective to some degree.

However, there are many issues that are relevant for the choice of clustering technique. One of them is data heterogeneity. Different data require different methods and, often, data come in different modalities simultaneously. Some examples include the analysis of data streams [11], and rank data [12]. Data sample size is also important, as not all methods are suited to deal with large data collections (see, for instance, [13]). The methods capable of handling very large data sets can be grouped in different categories, according to [14] efficient nearest-neighbor (NN) search, data summarization, distributed computing, incremental clustering, and sampling-based methods. Sometimes, we have to analyze structured data, for which there are semantic relationships within each object that must be considered, or data for which graphs are a natural representation. Graphical clustering methods can be of use in these cases [15,16].

Next, we single out some popular clustering techniques and describe them in further detail. They are k-means, fuzzy c-means (FCM), SOM, and GTM. They represent rather different methodological approaches to the common target problem of multivariate data grouping.

6.2.1 *k*-Means Clustering

k-Means is one of the best-known and widely used clustering algorithms. Notwithstanding the fact that it was proposed over 50 years ago and that literally hundreds of clustering algorithms have been defined since, *k*-means remains popular. Some of the main characteristics behind its reputation are the ease of implementation, its simplicity, efficiency, and empirical success.

As all partitional clustering algorithms, *k*-means aims to divide a data set $D = \{x_1, x_2, ..., x_n\}$ into K disjoint clusters, $C = \{C_1, C_2, ..., C_K\}$, where each data case, x_i, is assigned to a unique cluster C_k. The algorithm attempts to find a user-specified number of clusters, K, which are represented by their centroids. *k*-Means iteratively moves cluster centers of a pattern or observation neighborhood until convergence of the position of the centers is achieved, which should aim to minimize the squared error over all K clusters. As a starting point, the algorithm chooses the means of the clusters identified by group-average clustering. Its operation is illustrated in Figure 6.1, which shows how, starting from three centroids, the final clusters are found in three iteration steps.

k-Means can be summarized as follows:

1. *Chose random K* points as cluster centers.
2. Assign all observations to their closest cluster center according to a similarity measure.
3. Recompute new cluster centers.
4. Repeat steps 2 and 3 until the cluster membership becomes stable.

Similarity is a fundamental topic in the definition of a cluster; a measure of the similarity between two observations from the same feature space is essential to most clustering

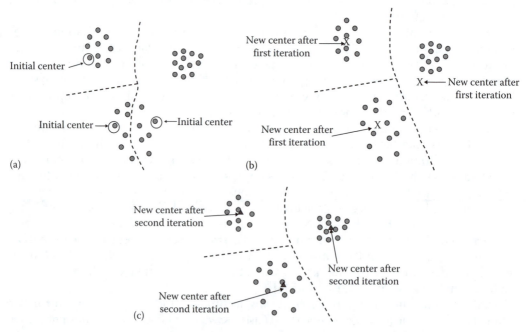

FIGURE 6.1
k-Means results to find three clusters in a simple data set.

procedures. The most popular metric in clustering analysis is the Euclidean distance. It works well when a data set has intuitive compact and/or isolated clusters. *k*-Means typically resorts to the Euclidean metric for computing the distance between points and cluster centers. Therefore, *k*-means tends to find hyperspherical or ball-shaped clusters in data. Alternatively, *k*-means with the Mahalanobis distance metric has been used to detect hyperellipsoidal clusters [17].

As was stated above, the basic *k*-means requires as initial parameter the number of clusters, i.e., the *K* value; this is a critical decision, due to the fact that different initializations can lead to different clustering solutions, as the algorithm has no guarantee of converging to a global minimum. The final clustering solution is, therefore, rather sensitive to the initialization of the cluster centers.

To deal with the original *k*-means drawbacks, many variants or extensions have been developed. Some of these extensions deal with both the selection of a good initial partition and allowing splitting and merging clusters, all of them with the ultimate goal to find global minimum value. Two well-known variants of *k*-means are ISODATA [18] and FORGY [19]. In *k*-means, each data point is assigned to a single cluster (hard assignment). Fuzzy *c*-means, proposed by Dunn [4], is an extension of *k*-means where each data point can be a member of multiple clusters with a membership value (soft assignment). Data reduction by replacing group examples with their centroids before clustering them was used to speed up *k*-means and fuzzy *c*-means in [20]. Other variants produce a hierarchical clustering by applying the algorithm with $K=2$ to the overall data set and then repeating the procedure recursively within each cluster [21].

6.2.2 Fuzzy c-Means Clustering

Traditional partitional clustering approaches generate partitions; in a partition, each data sample belongs to one and only one cluster. Therefore, the clusters in a hard-clustering approach are disjoint. Fuzzy clustering extends this notion to associate each pattern with every cluster using a membership function. The output of such algorithms is a clustering, but not a partition. FCM is a fuzzy clustering method that allows one observation or data sample to belong to two or more clusters with a membership degree to each one. FCM is a fuzzification version of the *k*-means algorithm.

In fuzzy clustering, each cluster corresponds to a fuzzy set of the entire data sample. Figure 6.2 illustrates this idea. The rectangles include two hard clusters in the data set: $H_1 = \{1, 2, 3, 4, 5\}$ and $H_2 = \{6, 7, 8, 9\}$. A fuzzy clustering algorithm, for instance FCM, could produce two fuzzy clusters: F_1 and F_2 represented by ellipses. Each data sample will have a membership value between 0 and 1 for each fuzzy cluster. Larger membership values indicate higher confidence in the assignment of the observation to the cluster.

In FCM, the points on the edge of a cluster may be in the cluster to a lesser degree than points in the center of cluster. For each data point *x*, there is a coefficient indicating the degree of being in the *k*th cluster $u_k(x)$. Often, the sum of those coefficients for any given *x* should be 1, such is expressed in (6.1):

$$\forall x \left(\sum_{k=1}^{Num\ clusters} u_k(x) = 1 \right) \tag{6.1}$$

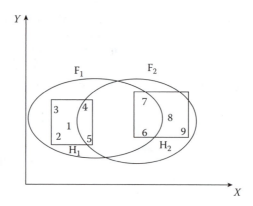

FIGURE 6.2
Fuzzy and hard clusters representation.

With FCM, the centroid of a cluster is the mean of all points, weighted by their degree of belonging to the cluster, as shown in (6.2):

$$\text{center}_k = \frac{\sum_x u_k(x)^m x}{\sum_x u_k(x)^m} \qquad (6.2)$$

The degree of belonging is related to the inverse of the distance to the cluster center, as it is presented in (6.3):

$$u_k(x) = \frac{1}{d(\text{center}_k, x)} \qquad (6.3)$$

The coefficients are normalized and fuzzified with a real parameter $m > 1$ so that their sum is 1:

$$u_k(x) = \frac{1}{\sum_j \left(d(\text{center}_k, x) / d(\text{center}_j, x) \right)^{2/(m-1)}} \qquad (6.4)$$

When m is close to 1, then cluster center closest to a given data point receives much more weight than the rest, and the algorithm becomes similar to k-means.

The FCM algorithm could be summarized in the following steps [22]:

1. Select an initial fuzzy partition of the N objects into K clusters by selecting the $N \times K$ membership matrix U. An element u_{ij} of this matrix represents the grade of membership of object x_i in cluster C_j. Where u_{ij} have values between 0 and 1.
2. Reassign data samples to clusters to reduce a criterion function value and recompute U. To perform this, using U, find the value of a fuzzy criterion function, e.g., a weighted squared error criterion function, associated with the corresponding partition. One possible fuzzy criterion function is show in (6.5).

$$E^2(x,U) = \sum_{i=1}^{N}\sum_{k=1}^{N} u_{ij}\|x_i - c_k\|^2 \tag{6.5}$$

where $center_k$ is the kth fuzzy cluster center.
3. Repeat step 2 until entries in U have a stable value.

FCM can still converge to local minima of the squared error criterion. The design of membership functions is the most important problem in fuzzy clustering; different choices include those based on similarity decomposition and centroids of clusters [22].

6.2.3 Kohonen Self-Organizing Maps

The SOM [9] is a successful artificial neural network model that has been used in a wide variety of applications, mostly for engineering problems but also for multivariate data analysis. SOM is an unsupervised learning model that projects p-dimensional input data points into a q-dimensional (usually $q=1$ or 2) discrete map in a topologically ordered fashion. Each lattice cell is represented by a neuron that has a p-dimensional weight vector associated. Every input pattern is compared to the weight vector of each neuron and the closest neuron (according to a similarity measure) is declared the winner. The activation of the winning neuron is spread (according to a function; usually a Gaussian centered in the winning neuron) to neurons in its immediate neighborhood and their weight vectors are adjusted to be more similar to the input patterns. Initially, the size of the neighborhood is large but, over the iterations, the neighborhood size is gradually reduced [23]. Figure 6.3 illustrates the architecture of a basic SOM model.

SOM represents data structures in a different manner to, e.g., multidimensional scaling, a more traditional multivariate data analysis methodology. The SOM algorithm concentrates on preserving the neighborhood relations in the data instead of trying to preserve the distances between the data items. In other words, in SOM, the mapping is topology-preserving in the sense that neighboring neurons respond to similar input patterns.

There are two basic versions of the SOM algorithm: online and batch. The batch version is often used when all the data are available at once. In the online algorithm, the data samples are presented in order until convergence is reached. The k-means algorithm could be seen as a specific instance of SOM in which the assignment of a data point to a given

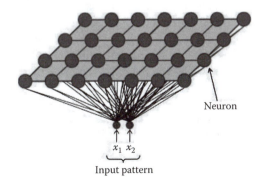

FIGURE 6.3
Simple SOM model.

cluster is based on a delta function, i.e., *on a winner-takes-all* in which only the winning neuron is updated to become closer to the observed data point in each iteration.

6.2.4 Generative Topographic Mapping

The GTM [10] was originally formulated both as a probabilistic clustering model alternative to the heuristic SOM [9] and as a constrained mixture of Gaussian distributions. It is precisely these constraints that create a projective manifold for cluster visualization, overcoming a limitation of generic finite mixture models. The GTM can also be seen as a nonlinear latent variable model that defines a mapping from a low-dimensional latent space onto the multivariate data space. The mapping is carried out by a set of basis functions generating a density distribution. The functional form of this mapping for each variable *d* can be expressed as

$$y_d(\mathbf{u},\mathbf{W}) = \sum_m^M \phi_m(\mathbf{u}) w_{md}, \tag{6.6}$$

where
- Φ are basis functions $\Phi(\mathbf{u}) = (\phi_1(\mathbf{u}), \ldots, \phi_M(\mathbf{u}))$ that introduce the nonlinearity in the mapping
- $\mathbf{W}$ is the matrix of adaptive weights w_{md} that defines the mapping
- $\mathbf{u}$ is a point in latent space

In order to provide an alternative to the visualization space defined by the characteristic SOM lattice, the latent space of the GTM is discretized as a regular grid of K latent points $\mathbf{u}_k$. The mixture density for a data point $\mathbf{x}$, given Gaussian basis functions, can be written as

$$p(\mathbf{x}|\mathbf{W},\beta) = \frac{1}{K} \sum_{k=1}^K \left(\frac{\beta}{2\pi}\right)^{D/2} \exp\left\{-\frac{\beta}{2}\|y_k - x\|^2\right\} \tag{6.7}$$

where the D elements of $\mathbf{y}$ are given by (6.6). This density allows for the definition of a model likelihood, and the well-known Expectation-Maximization (EM [24]) algorithm can be used to obtain the maximum likelihood estimates of the adaptive parameters ($\mathbf{W}$ and β) of the model. See [10] for details on these calculations.

Model interpretation usually requires a drastic reduction in the dimensionality of the data. Latent variable models can provide such interpretation through visualization, as they describe the data in intrinsically low-dimensional latent spaces. Each of the latent points $\mathbf{u}_k$ in the latent visualization space is mapped, following (6.6), as $\mathbf{y}_k = \Phi(\mathbf{u}_k)\mathbf{W}$. The $\mathbf{y}_k$ points are usually known as reference vectors or prototypes. Each of the reference vector elements corresponds to one of the input variables, and their values over the latent visualization space can be color-coded to produce reference maps that provide information on the behavior of each variable and its influence on the clustering results. Each of the latent space points can be considered by itself as a cluster representative.

The probability theory foundations of GTM allow the definition of principle alternatives for the automatic detection of outliers [25] and for unsupervised feature relevance determination and feature selection [26].

6.3 Clustering in e-Learning

Unlike in classification problems, in data grouping or cluster analysis we are not interested in modeling a relation between a set of multivariate data items and a certain set of outcomes for each of them. Instead, we usually aim to discover and model the groups in which the data items are often clustered, according to some similarity measure. Data clustering is usually dealt with unsupervised learning techniques (i.e., class label information is usually unavailable) and it is a problem that becomes more challenging (or even intractable) as the input space dimensionality increases and, as a result, data become more sparsely represented. This situation is far from uncommon in e-learning systems.

From a fairly detailed literature review, we can generalize that most studies dealing with clustering problems in the e-learning context fall into three main categories: (1) works devoted to group e-learning material based on their similarities; (2) works that attempt to group students according to their navigational and/or learning behavior; and (3) works that propose clustering analysis as part of an e-learning strategy but do not present any practical application results.

6.3.1 Cluster Analysis of e-Learning Material

In this subsection, we analyze, in certain detail, the current state of research in clustering techniques as applied to the analysis of e-learning material. This analysis has the ultimate goal of improving the use of these materials and, beyond that, the discovery of similarities between topics and the creation of new links between them. Table 6.1 summarizes some of the reviewed research.

Some researchers [27–29] have proposed the use of clustering techniques to group similar course materials: An ontology-based tool, within a Web Semantics framework, was implemented in [29] with the goal of helping e-learning users to find and organize distributed courseware resources. An element of this tool was the implementation of the bisection *k*-means algorithm, used for the grouping of similar learning materials. Kohonen's well-known SOM algorithm was used in [27] to devise an intelligent searching tool to cluster similar learning material into classes, based on its semantic similarities. Clustering was proposed in [28] to group similar learning documents based on their topics and similarities. A Document Index Graph (DIG) for document representation was introduced, and some classical clustering algorithms (hierarchical agglomerative clustering, single-pass clustering and *k*-NN) were implemented.

In [30], a network-based testing and diagnostic system was implemented. It entails a multiple-criteria test-sheet-generating problem and a dynamic programming approach to generate test sheets. The proposed approach employs fuzzy logic theory to determine the difficulty levels of test items according to the learning status and personal features of each student, and then applies an advanced artificial neural network model: fuzzy adaptive resonance theory (Fuzzy ART) [31] to cluster the test items into groups, as well as dynamic programming [32] for test sheet construction.

Kim et al. [33], in order to group students into levels and identify the knowledge that each group needs to learn, redefined the Distribution Sensitive Clustering (DISC) [34] algorithm for clustering numerical values by minimizing the relaxation error. The applied algorithm starts from one cluster consisting of all the values of an attribute, and then finds "cuts" to recursively partition the cluster.

TABLE 6.1

Research in Clustering Analysis of e-Learning Material

References	Clustering Method	e-Learning Objective
[20]	Bisection k-means	To find and organize distributed courseware resources.
[18]	SOM	To cluster similar learning material into classes, based on semantic similarities.
[19]	Hierarchical agglomerative clustering, single-pass clustering and k-NN	To group similar learning documents based on their topics and similarities. A DIG for document representation is introduced.
[21]	Fuzzy ART	To generate test sheets. Fuzzy logic theory is used to determine the difficulty levels of test items, and fuzzy ART to cluster the test items into groups. Dynamic programming is used for the test sheet construction.
[24]	Conceptual clustering algorithm (DISC)	Reorganization of learning content by means of a computerized adaptive test. The concept of knowledge unit extracted from each course topic is introduced.
[26]	SOM	The clustering of the course materials using a measure of the similarity between the terms they contain.
[27]	FCM	The organization of online learning material.
[28,29]	Agglomerative, Direct k-way, repeated bisection and graph partitional from the clustering CLUTO package	To cluster e-learning documents into meaningful groups to find out more refined subconcepts. This information is used for improving the content search in e-learning platforms.
[30]	Hierarchical agglomerative clustering	To construct an e-learning FAQ concept hierarchy. Rough set theory is used to classify users' queries.
[31]	Web text clustering based on maximal frequent itemsets	To group e-learning documents based on their frequent word similarities.

In [35], a scheme and an integrated architecture for information representation in e-learning applications were presented. In order to describe knowledge about the course-related topics, the authors propose three levels: content, symbolic, and conceptual. To bridge the content and the symbolic levels, the topics are represented by a concept map, implemented as a SOM model. The goal here is clustering the course materials using a measure of the similarity between the terms they contain. In the proposed approach, the concept space is built over the SOM map exploiting the property that semantically related concepts are close to each other; therefore, the SOM contains the basic elements of the course.

In [36], a framework for the organization of online learning material is presented. Mendes and colleagues propose the FCM clustering algorithm to discover knowledge and the topic map standard to represent it.

The authors in [37,38] put forward an approach for personalized search in e-learning platforms. The proposal includes semantic web technologies to represent the e-learning content and the students' profiles using an ontology from navigation logs that record which lectures have been accessed. Based on these activities, three entropy-based clustering techniques are applied to group the documents in order to discover more refined semantic subconcepts.

An approach to define an e-learning frequently asked questions (FAQ) retrieval system is proposed in [39]. Here, a hierarchical agglomerative clustering method is applied to construct a FAQ concept hierarchy; and rough set theory is used to classify users' queries. In [40], a web text clustering method based on maximal frequent itemsets is introduced in order to provide a personalized e-learning experience.

In order to improve the content and organization of the resources of virtual courses, clustering methods concerned with the evaluation of learning materials, such as those presented here, could be used to the advantage of all those involved in the learning process. It is our opinion that, beyond the application of clustering techniques, a sensible improvement in the development of course material evaluation processes may come from the exploration of groups according to their web usage patterns. Subsequently, association rules, for instance, could be applied to explore the relationships between the usability of the course materials and the students' learning performance, on the basis of the information gathered from the interaction between the user and the learning environment.

Moreover, if we can perform students' evaluation from their system usability behavior, this outcome could also indirectly be used to improve the course resources. For instance, if the students' evaluation was unsatisfactory, it could hint to the fact that the course resources and learning materials are inadequate and therefore should be changed and/or improved based on the successful students' navigational paths.

6.3.2 Clustering of Students according to Their e-Learning Behavior

The studies reviewed in Section 6.3.1 could be considered as a form of text- or keywords-driven information retrieving. In these approaches, students' learning behavior and dynamics are usually not considered, despite the fact that they are key factors to improve the teaching–learning process. In this subsection, we review research work dealing with the grouping of students based on their learning behavior. Table 6.2 summarizes some of this research.

The results obtained from this clustering process could be used by teachers to provide specialized advice to students belonging to each cluster. Moreover, clustering and visualization methods can enhance the e-learning experience, due to the capacity of the former to group similar actors based on their similarities and the ability of the latter to describe and explore these groups intuitively. The simplifying assumption that students belonging to homogeneous groups or clusters that would share web usage behavior, makes personalization strategies more scalable. Furthermore, tools to group students based on their navigational and/or learning behavior may be an effective and efficient way to promote greater academic accomplishment.

In [41,42], an in-depth study describing the usability of artificial neural networks and, more specifically, of Kohonen's SOM [9] for the evaluation of students in a tutorial supervisor (TS) system, as well as the ability of a fuzzy TS to adapt question difficulty in the evaluation process, was carried out. An investigation on how data mining techniques could be successfully incorporated into e-learning environments, and how this could improve the learning processes was presented in [43,44]. Here, data clustering is suggested as a means to promote group-based collaborative learning and to provide incremental student diagnosis. SOM is also the clustering technique of choice in [45], as part of an e-learning recommendation system called SOM/DM. Once groups of related interests are established, an association rule mining approach, based on the a priori algorithm, is used to find out the rules describing each cluster and perform the recommendation process.

The different variants of the GTM model were used in [46–48] for the clustering and visualization of multivariate data concerning the behavior of the students of a virtual course. In these experiments, the t-GTM [25] model was used for simultaneous student's data clustering, visualization, outlier detection, and feature relative relevance determination of the variables involved in a real virtual course. The goal of the experiments was twofold: On the one hand, the authors wanted to perform an identification and characterization

TABLE 6.2

Research in Clustering Analysis to Group e-Learning Students

References	Clustering Method	e-Learning Objective
[32,33]	SOM	Students' evaluation in a tutorial supervisor system.
[34]	Weighted Euclidian distance-based clustering	To group students according to the purpose of the recommendation in collaborative environments.
[35]	Weighted Euclidian distance-based clustering	To promote group-based collaborative learning and to provide incremental student diagnosis.
[36]	SOM	To group students based on their background. After that, association rule mining (a priori) is performed to provide course recommendations.
[37–39]	GTM, t-GTM, and FRD-GTM	The clustering and visualization of multivariate data concerning the behavior of the students of a virtual course, including atypical learning behavior analysis and feature relevance ranking.
[40]	EM	To group students into clusters according to their browsing behaviors.
[41]	EM	To discover user behavior patterns in collaborative activities.
[42]	FCM	To group students based on student' characteristics. Although the proposed tool is able to work with n-dimensional spaces, at the moment of publication, it is able to use a maximum of three attributes.
[43]	FCM	To group students based on their personality and learning strategy.
[44]	Fuzzy set clustering	To group similar students into homogeneous classes and to provide personalized learning to students.
[45]	Matrix-based clustering method	To group students based on personal attributes.
[46]	Hierarchical Euclidean distance-based clustering	To group students' levels in ICT based on the answers provided from e-questionnaires.
[47]	Weighted Euclidian distance-based clustering	To provide students' grouping according to their navigational behavior. In this study, the authors generated and used simulated navigational data.
[48]	k-Means	To cluster students based on the performance similarities.
[49]	k-Means	To improve webpage access prediction performance. Association rule mining and Markov models.
[50]	Two-phase hierarchical clustering	To group students based on their learning styles and usability preferences.
[51]	Naïve Bayes	To form e-learning interactive students' groups.

of atypical (outlier) students. On the other hand, they were interested in estimating the relative relevance of the available data features [46]. The results showed that useful knowledge can be extracted from the t-GTM combination of outlier detection, feature relevance determination, and data clustering and visualization [48]. This knowledge could be fed back into the e-learning system in order to provide students with personalized guidance, tailored to their inhomogeneous needs and requirements.

In [49], user actions associated to students' web usage were gathered and preprocessed as part of a data mining process. The EM algorithm was then used to group the users into clusters according to their behaviors. These results could be used by teachers to provide specialized advice to students belonging to each cluster. The EM algorithm was also the method of choice in [50], where clustering was used to discover user behavior patterns in collaborative activities in e-learning applications.

Christodoulopoulos and Papanikolaou [51] designed a web-based group formation tool that uses low-complexity algorithms for students' groupings. To make each student fit in different groups, FCM was applied. This clustering information is also provided to teachers for them to switch students between groups. Teachers can select the grouping method (manually or automatically) and then define the number of groups to be created. FCM is again used in [52] to cluster the students based on both, their personality and learning strategy. A deeper analysis based on frequent patterns is introduced to confirm the result of the proposed clustering method. Fuzzy models are also considered in [53], where an e-learning system based on a fuzzy set clustering algorithm to group similar students into homogeneous classes and to provide personalized learning to students was presented.

An approach that performs an improvement of the Matrix-based Clustering Method was outlined in [54]. This introduces the concept of "agglomerate strength" for further cluster cohesion measurement. The authors propose a learner mode that includes five factors: personality, motivation, style, concept, and strategy.

In [55], a hierarchical Euclidean distance-based clustering algorithm able to tackle a large number of features (a common characteristic of web-based education systems) was introduced. The authors propose a novel method for gathering and estimating the information and communications technologies (ICT) level of students in all fields of education through a web-based interface, which takes into account personalized and profile-based schemes. Clustering is applied to group students on the basis of the answers provided in e-questionnaires. A weighted Euclidian distance clustering algorithm is also used by Tang and Chan [56], who describe a student grouping technique based on students' navigational behaviors. In the proposed approach, the authors generated simulated navigational student data and used the clustering algorithm to discover students' groups according to their abilities.

In [57], an intelligent e-learning system that groups students of similar performance was presented. It is based on six-dimensional items (prerequisite knowledge, memory capacity, marks secured in the previous exams, interestedness, read amount, and reading speed) representing the performance of a student. *k*-Means clustering is applied to group of people with similar learning performance profiles. This algorithm is also used in [58], for an approach that includes clustering, association rules, and a Markov model to achieve better webpage access prediction performance. The obtained clusters help to improve the Markov model prediction accuracy.

In [59], a set of students were clustered according to their learning styles and usability preferences in an e-learning system. The proposed approach applies two versions of a two-phase hierarchical clustering algorithm. In [60], a student's grouping approach based on naïve Bayesian methods was presented. According to the authors, it should help virtual teachers to form highly interactive students' groups. Four different attributes of high-interaction and high-satisfaction groups are identified: learning periods (favorite periods chosen to interact with the educational system), region, age, and value types (related to a value-scale of concepts).

One of the most difficult and time-consuming activities for teachers in distance education courses is the evaluation process, due to the fact that, in this type of course, the review process is better accomplished through collaborative resources such as e-mail, discussion forums, chats, etc. As a result, this evaluation usually has to be carried out according to a large number of parameters, whose influence in the final mark is not always well defined and/or understood. Therefore, it would be helpful to discover features that are highly relevant for the evaluation of groups (clusters) of students. In this way, it would be possible for teachers to provide feedback to students, on their learning activity, online and in real time, in a more effective way than if we tried to do it individually. This option, using clustering methods, could reduce teachers' workload.

6.3.3 Clustering Analysis as a Tool to Improve e-Learning Environments

Several researchers have suggested that group interaction is a vital element in team success. However, courses often suffer from a lack group coherency and identity that impacts information exchange and knowledge sharing, especially in a problem-solving scenario. Instructors of online courses usually find that their class size is larger than that of traditional classes and that students rarely interact effectively. The formation of groups with high interaction levels becomes difficult for most students because of the limitations of social intercommunication on the Internet.

Some authors have proposed the application of clustering analysis techniques for the improvement of e-learning environments [61,62]. Fu and Foghlu [61] integrate the techniques of subspace clustering and conceptual clustering to define an algorithm, called conceptual subspace clustering (CSC), which extracts conceptual clusters in dense subspaces and describes clusters through overlapping concepts. CSC selects subspaces based on data density and exploits hierarchical overlapping clusters that can be described by concepts. A framework for representing assessment results and usage patterns by a hierarchy of flow graphs was introduced in [62]. It can be used as a decision algorithm for evaluating relationships between usage patterns and the performance of students. In their work, these authors propose the use of web usage mining techniques, specifically flow graphs, to identify student groups, based on their usage sequences. However, no proper educational experiments are shown.

Myszkowski et al. [63] directly propose the use of data mining techniques to make learning more effective. For instance, as an automatic intrusion detection tool, the clustering of user action–time sequences is proposed to discover patterns of standard and nonstandard (considered here as potential malicious) behavior.

From the virtual teacher standpoint, valuable information could be gathered from the e-mail or discussion forum resources in e-learning courses. However, there is still a lack of automated tools with this purpose, probably due to the difficulty of analyzing the learning behavior from the aforementioned sources. Such tools would entail the use of Text Mining (or Web Mining) techniques. Natural Language Processing (NLP) methods would be of potential interest to tackle this problem in e-learning, due their ability to automatically extract useful information that would be difficult, or almost impossible to obtain, through other techniques. Unfortunately, NLP techniques have not been applied extensively in e-learning. Some exceptions can be found in [27,28], where NLP and clustering models were proposed for grouping similar learning materials based on their topics and semantic similarities.

6.4 Conclusions

The pervasiveness of the Internet has enabled online distance education to become far more mainstream than it used to be, and that has happened in a surprisingly short time. e-Learning course offerings are now plentiful, and many new e-learning platforms and systems have been developed and implemented with varying degrees of success. These systems generate an exponentially increasing amount of data, and much of this information has the potential to become new and usable knowledge to improve all instances of e-learning. Data mining clustering processes should enable the extraction of this knowledge and facilitate its use.

It is still early days for the integration of data mining in e-learning systems and not many real and fully operative implementations are available. Nevertheless, a good deal of academic research in this area has been published over the last few years. Much of it concerns the design and application of clustering methods. In this chapter, we have reviewed, in some detail, recent research on clustering as applied to e-learning, dealing with problems of students' learning assessment, learning materials and course evaluation, and course adaptation based on students' learning behavior. It has been argued that the use of clustering strategies should ease the reutilization of the knowledge generated by data mining processes, as well as reduce the costs of educative personalization processes.

Acknowledgment

Félix Castro is a research fellow within the PROMEP program of the Mexican Secretary of Public Education.

References

1. Chapman, P., Clinton, J., Kerber, R., Khabaza, T., Reinartz, T., Shearer, C., and Wirth, R., CRIPS-DM 1.0 step by step data mining guide. *CRISP-DM Consortium*, August 2000.
2. Castro, F., Vellido, A., Nebot, A., and Mugica, F., Applying data mining techniques to e-learning problems, in *Evolution of Teaching and Learning Paradigms in Intelligent Environment*, Studies in Computational Intelligence (SCI), Vol. 62, Jain, L.C., Tedman, R.A. and Tedman, D.K. (Eds.), pp. 183–221, 2007.
3. MacQueen, J., Some methods for classification and analysis of multivariate observations, in *Fifth Berkeley Symposium on Mathematics, Statistics and Probability*, University of California Press, Berkeley, CA, pp. 281–297, 1967.
4. Dunn, J.C., A fuzzy relative of the ISODATA process and its use in detecting compact well-separated clusters. *J. Cybern.* 3, 32–57, 1973.
5. Pelleg, D. and Moore, A., Accelerating exact k-means algorithms with geometric reasoning, in *The Fifth International Conference on Knowledge Discovery in Databases*, AAAI Press, Menlo Park, CA, pp. 277–281, 1999.
6. McLachlan, G.J. and Basford, K.E., *Mixture Models: Inference and Applications to Clustering*. Marcel Dekker, New York, 1988.
7. Blei, D.M., Ng, A.Y., and Jordan, M.I., Latent dirichlet allocation. *J. Mach. Learn. Res.* 3, 993–1022, 2003.
8. Oja, M., Kaski, S., and Kohonen, T., Bibliography of self-organizing map (SOM). *Neural Comput. Surveys* 3, 1–156, 2002.
9. Kohonen, T., *Self-Organizing Maps*, 3rd edn., Springer-Verlag, Berlin, Germany, 2001.
10. Bishop, C.M., Svensén, M., and Williams, C.K.I., GTM: The generative topographic mapping. *Neural Comput.* 10(1), 215–234, 1998.
11. Hore, P., Hall, L.O., and Goldgof, D.B., A scalable framework for cluster ensembles. *Pattern Recogn.* 42(5), 676–688, 2009.

12. Busse, L.M., Orbanz, P., and Buhmann, J.M., Cluster analysis of heterogeneous rank data, in *Proceedings of the 24th International Conference on Machine Learning (ICML)*, ACM, New York, pp. 113–120, 2007.
13. Andrews, N.O. and Fox, E.A., Recent developments in document clustering. Technical Report, TR-07-35. Department of Computer Science, Virginia Tech, Blacksburg, VA, 2007.
14. Jain, A.K., Data clustering: 50 years beyond K-means. *Pattern Recogn. Lett.* 31(8), 651–666, 2010.
15. Tsuda, K. and Kudo, T., Clustering graphs by weighted substructure mining, in *Proceedings of the 23rd International Conference on Machine Learning (ICML)*, ACM, New York, pp. 953–960, 2006.
16. Backstrom, L., Huttenlocher, D., Kleinberg, J., and Lan, X., Group formation in large social networks: Membership, growth, and evolution, in *Proceedings of the 12th International Conference on Knowledge Discovery and Data Mining*, Philadelphia, PA, 2006.
17. Mao, J. and Jain, A.K., A self-organizing network for hyperellipsoidal clustering (HEC), *IEEE Trans. Neural Netw.* 7, 16–29, 1996.
18. Ball, G. and Hall, D., ISODATA, a novel method of data analysis and pattern classification. Technical report NTIS AD 699616. Stanford Research Institute, Stanford, CA, 1965.
19. Forgy, E.W., Cluster analysis of multivariate data: Efficiency vs. interpretability of classifications. *Biometrics* 21, 768–769, 1965.
20. Eschrich, S., Ke, J., Hall, L.O., and Goldgof, D.B., Fast accurate fuzzy clustering through data reduction. *IEEE Trans. Fuzzy Syst.* 11(2), 262–270, 2003.
21. Witten, I.H. and Eibe, F., *Data Mining: Practical Machine Learning Tools and Techniques*, 2nd ed. Morgan Kaufman-Elsevier, San Francisco, CA, 2005.
22. Jain, A.K., Murty, M.N., and Flynn, P.J., Data clustering: A review. *ACM Comput. Serv.* 31(3), 264–323, 1999.
23. Mitra, S. and Acharya, T., *Data Mining: Multimedia, Soft Computing, and Bioinformatics*. John Wiley & Sons, Hoboken, NJ, 2003.
24. Dempster, A.P., Laird, M.N., and Rubin, D.B., Maximum likelihood from incomplete data via the EM algorithm. *J. R. Stat. Soc.* 39(1), 1–38, 1977.
25. Vellido, A., Missing data imputation through gtm as a mixture of t-distributions. *Neural Netw.* 19(10), 1624–1635, 2006.
26. Vellido, A., Assessment of an unsupervised feature selection method for generative topographic mapping, in *The 16th International Conference on Artificial Neural Networks (ICANN'2006)*, Athens, Greece, LNCS (4132) Springer-Verlag, Berlin, Germany, pp. 361–370, 2006.
27. Drigas, A. and Vrettaros, J., An intelligent tool for building e-learning contend-material using natural language in digital libraries. *WSEAS Trans. Inf. Sci. Appl.* 5(1), 1197–1205, 2004.
28. Hammouda, K. and Kamel, M., Data mining in e-learning, in *e-Learning Networked Environments and Architectures: A Knowledge Processing Perspective*, Pierre, S. (Ed.). Springer-Verlag, Berlin, Germany, 2005.
29. Tane, J., Schmitz, C., and Stumme, G., Semantic resource management for the web: An e-learning application, in *The Proceedings 13th World Wide Web Conference, WWW2004*, Fieldman, S., Uretsky, M. (Eds.). ACM Press, New York, pp. 1–10, 2004.
30. Hwang, G.J., A test-sheet-generating algorithm for multiple assessment requirements. *IEEE Trans. Educ.* 46(3), 329–337, 2003.
31. Carpenter, G., Grossberg, S., and Rosen, D.B., Fuzzy ART: Fast stable learning and categorization of analog patterns by an adaptive resonance system. *Neural Netw.* 4, 759–771, 1991.
32. Dreyfus, S.E. and Law, A.M., *The Art and Theory of Dynamic Programming*, Academic Press, New York, 1977.
33. Kim, J., Chern, G., Feng, D., Shaw, E., and Hovy, E., Mining and assessing discussions on the web through speech act analysis, in *The AAAI Workshop on Web Content Mining with Human Language Technology*, Athens, GA, pp. 1–8, 2006.
34. Chu, W.W. and Chiang, K., Abstraction of high level concepts from numerical values in databases, in *The AAAI Workshop on Knowledge Discovery in Databases*, Seattle, WA, July 1994.

35. Pirrone, R., Cossentino, M., Pilato, G., and Rizzo, R., Concept maps and course ontology: A multi-level approach to e-learning, in *The II AI*IA Workshop on Artificial Intelligence and E-learning*, Pisa, Italy, September 23–26, 2003.

36. Mendes, M.E.S., Martinez, E., and Sacks, L., Knowledge-based content navigation in e-learning applications, in *The London Communication Symposium*, London, U.K., September 9–10, 2002.

37. Zhuhadar, L. and Nasraoui, O., Personalized cluster-based semantically enriched web search for e-learning, in *The ONISW'08*, Napa Valley, CA, ACM, New York, pp. 105–111, 2008.

38. Zhuhadar, L. and Nasraoui, O., Semantic information retrieval for personalized e-learning, in *The 20th IEEE International Conference on Tools with Artificial Intelligence*, IEEE Computer Society, Dayton, OH, pp. 364–368, November 3–5, 2008.

39. Chiu, D.Y., Pan, Y.C., and Chang, W.C., Using rough set theory to construct e-learning FAQ retrieval infrastructure, in *The First IEEE International Conference on Ubi-Media Computing*, Lanzhou, China, pp. 547–552, July 15–16, 2008.

40. Su, Z., Song, W., Lin, M., and Li, J., Web text clustering for personalized e-learning based on maximal frequent itemsets, in *The International Conference on Computer Science and Software Engineering*, IEEE Computer Science, Hubei, China, pp. 452–455, December 12–14, 2008.

41. Mullier, D., A tutorial supervisor for automatic assessment in educational systems. *Int. J. e-Learn.* 2(1), 37–49, 2003.

42. Mullier, D., Moore, D., and Hobbs, D., A neural-network system for automatically assessing students, in *World Conference on Educational Multimedia, Hypermedia and Telecommunications*, Kommers, P. and Richards, G. (Eds.), AACE, Chesapeake, VA, pp. 1366–1371, 2001.

43. Tang, T.Y. and McCalla, G., Smart recommendation for an evolving e-learning system: Architecture and experiment. *Int. J. e-Learn.* 4(1), 105–129, 2005.

44. McCalla, G., The ecological approach to the design of e-learning environments: Purpose-based capture and use of information about learners. *J. Int. Media Educ.*, Special Issue on the Educational Semantic Web, 2004.

45. Tai, D.W.S., Wu, H.J., and Li, P.H., A hybrid system: Neural network with data mining in an e-learning environment, in *KES'2007/WIRN'2007*, Part II, B. Apolloni et al. (Eds.), LNAI 4693, Springer-Verlag, Berlin, Germany, pp. 42–49, 2007.

46. Castro, F., Vellido, A., Nebot, A., and Minguillón, J., Finding relevant features to characterize student behavior on an e-learning system, in *The International Conference on Frontiers in Education: Computer Science and Computer Engineering (FECS'05)*, Hamid, R.A. (Ed.), Las Vegas, NV, pp. 210–216, 2005.

47. Castro, F., Vellido, A., Nebot, A., and Minguillón, J., Detecting atypical student behaviour on an e-learning system, in *VI Congreso Nacional de Informática Educativa, Simposio Nacional de Tecnologías de la Información y las Comunicaciones en la Educación (SINTICE'2005)*, Granada, Spain, pp. 153–160, 2005.

48. Vellido, A., Castro, F., Nebot, A., and Mugica, F., Characterization of atypical virtual campus usage behavior through robust generative relevance analysis, in *The 5th IASTED International Conference on Web-Based Education (WBE'2006)*, Puerto Vallarta, Mexico, pp. 183–188, 2006.

49. Teng, C., Lin, C., Cheng, S., and Heh, J., Analyzing user behavior distribution on e-learning platform with techniques of clustering, in *Society for Information Technology and Teacher Education International Conference*, Atlanta, GA, pp. 3052–3058, 2004.

50. Talavera, L. and Gaudioso, E., Mining student data to characterize similar behavior groups in unstructured collaboration spaces, in *Workshop in Artificial Intelligence in Computer Supported Collaborative Learning*, in conjunction with *16th European Conference on Artificial Intelligence (ECAI'2003)*, Valencia, Spain, pp. 17–22, 2004.

51. Christodoulopoulos, C.E. and Papanikolaou, K.A., A group formation tool in a e-learning context, in *The 19th IEEE International Conference on Tools with Artificial Intelligence*, IEEE Computer Society, Patras, Greece, pp. 117–123, October 29–31, 2007.

52. Tian, F., Wang, S., Zheng, C., and Zheng, Q., Research on e-learner personality grouping based on fuzzy clustering analysis, in *The 12th International Conference on Computer Supported Cooperative Work in Design (CSCWD'2008)*, Xi'an, China, pp. 1035–1040, April 16–18, 2008.

53. Lu, F., Li, X., Liu, Q., Yang, Z., Tan, G., and He, T., Research on personalized e-learning system using fuzzy set based clustering algorithm, in *ICCS'2007*, Y. Shi et al. (Eds.), Part III, LNCS (4489), Springer-Verlag, Berlin, Germany, pp. 587–590, 2007.

54. Zhang, K., Cui, L., Wang, H., and Sui, Q., An improvement of matrix-based clustering method for grouping learners in e-learning, in *The 11th International Conference on Computer Supported Cooperative Work in Design (CSCWD'2007)*, Melbourne, Australia, pp. 1010–1015, April 26–28, 2007.

55. Mylonas, P., Tzouveli, P., and Kollias, S., Intelligent content adaptation in the framework of an integrated e-learning system, in *The International Workshop in Combining Intelligent and Adaptive Hypermedia Methods/Techniques in Web Based Education Systems (CIAH'2005)*, Salzburg, Austria, pp. 59–66, September 6–9, 2005.

56. Tang, T.Y. and Chan, K.C., Feature construction for student group forming based on their browsing behaviors in an e-learning system, in *PRICAI'2002*, Ishizuka, M. and Sattar, A. (Eds.), LNAI (2417), Springer-Verlag, Berlin, Germany, pp. 512–521, 2002.

57. Manikandan, C., Sundaram, M.A.S., and Mahesh, B.M., Collaborative e-learning for remote education-an approach for realizing pervasive learning environments, in *2nd International Conference on Information and Automation (ICIA'2006)*, Colombo, Srilanka, pp. 274–278, December 14–17, 2006.

58. Khalil, F., Li, J., and Wang, H., Integrating recommendation models for improved web page prediction accuracy, in *The 31st Australasian Computer Science Conference (ACSC'2008)*, *Conference in Research and Practice in Information Technology (CRPIT'2008)*, Vol. 74, Wollongong, Australia, pp. 91–100, 2008.

59. Zakrzewska, D., Using clustering techniques for students' grouping in intelligent e-learning systems, in *USAB 2008*, Holzinger, A. (Ed.), LNCS (5298), Springer-Verlag, Berlin, Germany, pp. 403–410, 2008.

60. Yang, Q., Zheng, S., Huang, J., and Li, J., A design to promote group learning in e-learning by naive Bayesian, *Comput. Intel. Des.* 2, 379–382, 2008.

61. Fu, H., and Foghlu, M.O., A conceptual subspace clustering algorithm in e-learning, in *The 10th International Conference on Advances in Communication Technology (ICACT'2008)*, IEEE Conference Proceeding, Phoenix Park, Republic of Korea, pp. 1983–1988, 2008.

62. Chan, C., A Framework for assessing usage of web-based e-learning systems, in *The Second International Conference on Innovative Computing, Information and Control (ICICIC'2007)*, Kumamoto, Japan, pp. 147–150, September 5–7, 2007.

63. Myszkowski, P.B., Kwaśnicka, H., and Markowska, U.K., Data mining techniques in e-learning CelGrid system, in *The 7th Computer Information Systems and Industrial Management Applications*, IEEE Computer Science, Ostrava, the Czech Republic, pp. 315–319, June 26–28, 2008.

7

Association Rule Mining in Learning Management Systems

Enrique García, Cristóbal Romero, Sebastián Ventura,
Carlos de Castro, and Toon Calders

CONTENTS

7.1 Introduction

Learning management systems (LMSs) can offer a great variety of channels and workspaces to facilitate information sharing and communication among participants in a course. They let educators distribute information to students, produce content material, prepare assignments and tests, engage in discussions, manage distance classes, and enable collaborative learning with forums, chats, file storage areas, news services, etc. Some examples of commercial systems are Blackboard [1], WebCT [2], and Top-Class [3], while some examples of free systems are Moodle [4], Ilias [5], and Claroline [6]. One of the most commonly used is Moodle (modular object–oriented developmental learning environment), a free learning management system enabling the creation of powerful, flexible, and engaging online courses and experiences [42].

These e-learning systems accumulate a vast amount of information that is very valuable for analyzing students' behavior and could create a gold mine of educational data [7]. They can record any student activities involved, such as reading, writing, taking tests, performing various tasks, and even communicating with peers. They normally also provide a database that stores all the system's information: personal information about the users (profile), and academic results and users' interaction data. However, due to the vast quantities of data these systems can generate daily, it is very difficult to manage data analysis manually.

Instructors and course authors demand tools to assist them in this task, preferably on a continual basis. Although some platforms offer some reporting tools, it becomes hard for a tutor to extract useful information when there are a great number of students [8]. The current LMSs do not provide specific tools allowing educators to thoroughly track and assess all learners' activities while evaluating the structure and contents of the course and its effectiveness for the learning process [9]. A very promising area for attaining this objective is the use of data mining. Data mining or knowledge discovery in databases (KDD) is the automatic extraction of implicit and interesting patterns from large data collections. Next to statistics and data visualization, there are many data mining techniques for analyzing the data. Some of the most useful data mining tasks and methods are clustering, classification, and association rule mining. These methods uncover new, interesting, and useful knowledge based on users' usage data. In the last few years, researchers have begun to apply data mining methods to help instructors and administrators to improve e-learning systems [10].

Association rule mining has been applied to e-learning systems traditionally for association analysis (finding correlations between items in a dataset), including, e.g., the following tasks: building recommender agents for online learning activities or shortcuts [11], automatically guiding the learner's activities and intelligently generating and recommending learning materials [12], identifying attributes characterizing patterns of performance disparity between various groups of students [13], discovering interesting relationships from a student's usage information in order to provide feedback to the course author [14], finding out the relationships between each pattern of a learner's behavior [15], finding student mistakes often occurring together [16], guiding the search for the best fitting transfer model of student learning [17], optimizing the content of an e-learning portal by determining the content of most interest to the user [18], extracting useful patterns to help educators and web masters evaluating and interpreting online course activities [11], and personalizing e-learning based on aggregate usage profiles and a domain ontology [19].

Association rules mining is one of the most well studied data mining tasks. It discovers relationships among attributes in databases, producing if-then statements concerning attribute-values [20]. Association rule mining has been applied to web-based education systems from two points of view: (1) help professors to obtain detailed feedback of the e-learning process: e.g., finding out how the students learn on the web, to evaluate the students based on their navigation patterns, to classify the students into groups, and to restructure the contents of the Web site to personalize the courses; and (2) help students in their interaction with the e-learning system: e.g., adaptation of the course according to the apprentice's progress, e.g., by recommending to them personalized learning paths based on the previous experiences by other similar students.

This paper is organized in the following way: First, we describe the background of association rule mining in general and more specifically its application to e-learning. Then, we describe the main drawbacks and some possible solutions for applying association rule algorithms in LMSs. Next, we show a practical tutorial of using an association rule mining algorithm over data generated from a Moodle system. Finally, the conclusions and further research are outlined.

7.2 Background

IF–THEN rules are one of the most popular ways of knowledge representation, due to their simplicity and comprehensibility [21]. There are different types of rules according to the

TABLE 7.1

IF-THEN Rule Format

<rule>	::=	IF <antecedent> THEN <consequent>
<antecedent>	::=	<condition> +
<consequent>	::=	<condition> +
<condition>	::=	<attribute> <operator> <value>
<attribute>	::=	Each one of the possible attributes set
<value>	::=	Each one of the possible values of the attributes set
<operator>	::=	= | > | < | ≥ | ≤ | ≠

data mining technique used, for example: classification, association, sequential pattern analysis, prediction, causality induction, optimization, etc. In the area of KDD, the most studied ones are association rules, classifiers, and predictors. An example of a generic rule format IF-THEN in Extend Backus Naur Form (EBNF) notation is shown in Table 7.1.

Before beginning the study in depth of the main association rule mining algorithms, we first formally define what an association rule is [22].

Let $I = \{i_1, i_2, \ldots, i_m\}$ be a set of literals, called items. Let D be a set of transactions, where each transaction T is a set of items such that $T \subseteq I$. Each transaction is associated with a unique identifier, called its *TID*. We say that a transaction T *contains* X, a set of some items in I, if $X \subseteq I$. An association rule is an implication of the form $X \Rightarrow Y$, where $X \subset I$, $Y \subset I$, and $X \cap Y = \emptyset$. The rule $X \Rightarrow Y$ holds in the transaction set D with confidence c if $c\%$ of transactions in D that contain X also contain Y. The rule $X \Rightarrow Y$ has support s in the transaction set D if $s\%$ of transactions in D contain $X \cup Y$. An example association rule is: "IF diapers in a transaction, THEN beer is in the transaction as well in 30% of the cases. Diapers and beer are bought together in 11% of the rows in the database." In this example, support and confidence of the rule are

$$s = P(X \cup Y) = 11\%$$

$$c = P\left(\frac{Y}{X}\right) = \frac{P(X \cup Y)}{P(X)} = \frac{s(X \cup Y)}{s(X)} = 30\%$$

Given a set of transactions D, and user-specified thresholds minimum support (called *minsup*) and minimum confidence (called *minconf*), the problem of mining association rules is to generate all association rules that have support and confidence greater than *minsup* and *minconf*, respectively. Our discussion is neutral with respect to the representation of D. For example, D could be a data file, a relational table, or the result of a relational expression.

The previous problem is solved by the Apriori algorithm [20] that is the first and simplest association rule mining algorithm. For an overview of different association rule mining algorithms and implementations, see the frequent itemset mining implementations (FIMI) repository (http://fimi.cs.helsinki.fi/). Figure 7.1 shows the Apriori algorithm. The first pass of the algorithm simply counts item occurrences to determine the frequent itemsets of size (cardinality) 1. A frequent itemset of size k is in literature also called a *large k-itemset*. All subsequent passes consist of two phases. First, the large itemsets L_k found in the (k)th

C_k: Candidate itemsets of size k;
L_k: Frequent itemsets of size k
L_1 = {frequent items};
for ($k = 1$; L_k != $\varnothing$; k++) **do begin**
    C_{k+1} = {candidates generated from L_k};
    for each transaction t in the database **do**
        increment the count of all candidates in C_{k+1}
        that are *contained* in t;
    L_{k+1} = {candidates in C_{k+1} with *minsup*}
end
return $\cup_k L_k$;

FIGURE 7.1
Pseudo-code of Apriori algorithm.

Let us consider a set L_3 = {*abc, abd, acd, ace, bcd*}
The join step:
  - C_{k+1} is generated by joining L_k with itself
Self-joining: L_3*L_3 (Items must be in lexicographic order.)
  - *abcd* from *abc* and *abd*
  - *acde* from *acd* and *ace*
The prune step:
  - Any k-itemset that is not frequent cannot be a subset of a frequent
  ($k + 1$)-itemset
  - Pruning C_4: *acde* is removed because *ade* is not in L_3
The final candidate set: C_4={*abcd*}

FIGURE 7.2
Apriori candidate generation.

pass are used to generate the candidate itemsets C_{k+1} as it is shown in Figure 7.2. Next, the database is scanned and the support of candidates in C_{k+1} is counted.

There are a lot of different association rule algorithms. A comparative study between the main algorithms that are currently used to discover association rules can be found in [23]: Apriori [22], FP-Growth [24], MagnumOpus [25], and Closet [26]. Most of these algorithms require the user to set two thresholds, the minimal support and the minimal confidence, and find all the rules that exceed the thresholds specified by the user. Therefore, the user must possess a certain amount of expertise in order to find the right settings for support and confidence to obtain the best rules.

7.3 Drawbacks of Applying Association Rule in e-Learning

In the association rule mining area, most of the research efforts went in the first place to improving the algorithmic performance [27], and in the second place into reducing the output set by allowing the possibility to express constraints on the desired results. Over the past decade, a variety of algorithms that address these issues through the refinement of search strategies, pruning techniques, and data structures have been developed. While most algorithms focus on the explicit discovery of all rules that satisfy minimal support and confidence constraints for a given dataset, increasing consideration is being given to specialized algorithms that attempt to improve processing time or facilitate user interpretation by reducing the result set size and by incorporating domain knowledge [28].

Most of the current data mining tools are too complex for educators to use, and their features go well beyond the scope of what an educator might require. As a result, the course administrator is more likely to apply data mining techniques in order to produce reports for instructors who then use these reports to make decisions about how to improve the student's learning and the online courses. Nowadays, normally, data mining tools are designed more for power and flexibility than for simplicity. There are also other specific problems related to the application of association rule mining to e-learning data.

Next, we are going to describe some of the main drawbacks of association rule algorithms in e-learning.

7.3.1 Finding the Appropriate Parameter Settings of the Mining Algorithm

Association rule mining algorithms need to be configured before they are executed. So, the user has to give appropriate values for the parameters in advance (often leading to too many or too few rules) in order to obtain a good number of rules. Most of these algorithms require the user to set two thresholds, the minimal support and the minimal confidence, and then find all the rules that exceed the thresholds specified by the user. Therefore, the user must possess a certain amount of expertise in order to find the right settings for support and confidence to obtain the best rules.

One possible solution to this problem can be to use a parameter-free algorithm. For example, the Weka [29] package implements an Apriori-type algorithm that solves this problem partially. This algorithm reduces iteratively the minimum support, by a factor delta support (Δs) introduced by the user, until a minimum support is reached or a required number of rules has been generated.

Another improved version of the Apriori algorithm is the Predictive Apriori algorithm [30], which automatically resolves the problem of balance between these two parameters, maximizing the probability of making an accurate prediction for the dataset. In order to achieve this, a parameter called the exact expected predictive accuracy is defined and calculated using the Bayesian method, which provides information about the accuracy of the rule found.

In [31], experimental tests were performed on a Moodle course by comparing the two previous algorithms. The final results demonstrated better performance for Predictive Apriori than the Apriori-type algorithm using the Δs factor.

7.3.2 Discovering Too Many Rules

Educational datasets are normally very small if we compare them with databases used in other data mining fields—typical sizes are the size of one class, which is often only 50–100 exemplars. In very few cases, we get data from 200 to 300 students. Therefore, the application of traditional association algorithms will be simple and efficient. However, association rule mining algorithms normally discover a huge quantity of rules and do not guarantee that all the rules found are relevant.

Event though support and confidence already allow for pruning many associations, often it is desirable to apply other constraints as well; for example, on the attributes that must or cannot be present in the antecedent or consequent of the discovered rules.

Another solution is to evaluate and post-prune the obtained rules in order to find the most interesting rules for a specific problem. Traditionally, the use of objective interestingness measures has been suggested [32], such as support and confidence, mentioned previously, as well as purely statistical measures such as the chi-square statistic and the correlation coefficient in order to measure the dependency inference between data variables. Subjective measures are becoming increasingly important [33], in other words measures that are based on subjective factors controlled by the user.

Most of the subjective approaches involve user participation in order to express, in accordance with his or her previous knowledge, which rules are of interest. Some suggested subjective measures [34] are: unexpectedness (rules are interesting if they are unknown to the user or contradict the user's knowledge) and actionability (rules are interesting if users can do something with them to their advantage).

Liu et al. [34] proposed an interestingness analysis system (IAS) that compares rules discovered with the user's knowledge about the area of interest. Let U be the set of a user's specification representing his or her knowledge space, and A be the set of discovered association rules, this algorithm implements a pruning technique for removing redundant or insignificant rules by ranking and classifying them into four categories: conforming rules, unexpected consequent rules, unexpected condition rules, and both-side unexpected rules. The degrees of membership into each of these four categories are used for ranking the rules. Using their own specification language, they indicate their knowledge about the matter in question, through relationships among the fields or items in the database.

Finally, another approximation is that we can see the knowledge database as a rule repository on the basis of which subjective analysis of the rules discovered can be performed [35]. Before running the association rule mining algorithm, the teacher could download the relevant knowledge database, in accordance with his or her profile. The personalization of the rules returned is based on filtering parameters, associated with the type of the course to be analyzed, such as the area of knowledge, the level of education, the difficulty of the course, etc. The rules repository is created on the server in a collaborative way where the experts can vote for each rule in the repository, based on the educational considerations and their experience gained in other similar e-learning courses.

7.3.3 Discovery of Poorly Understandable Rules

A factor that is of major importance in determining the quality of the extracted rules is their comprehensibility. Although the main motivation for rule extraction is to obtain a comprehensible description of the underlying model's hypothesis, this aspect of rule quality is often overlooked due to the subjective nature of comprehensibility, which cannot be measured independently of the person using the system [36]. Prior experience and domain knowledge of this person play an important role in assessing the comprehensibility. This contrasts with accuracy that can be considered as a property of the rules and which can be evaluated independently of the users.

There are some traditional techniques that have been used in order to improve the comprehensibility of discovered rules, such as constraining the number of items in the antecedent or consequent of the rule, or performing a discretization of numerical values. Discretization [37] divides the numerical data into categorical classes that are easier to understand for the instructor (categorical values are more user-friendly for the instructor than precise magnitudes and ranges).

Another way to improve the comprehensibility of the rules is to incorporate domain knowledge and semantics, and to use a common and well-known vocabulary for the teacher. In the context of web-based educational systems, we can identify some common attributes to a variety of e-learning systems such as LMS and adaptive hypermedia courses, such as visited, time, score, difficulty level, knowledge level, attempts, number of messages, etc. In this context, the use of standard metadata for e-learning [38] allows the creation and maintenance of a common knowledge base with a common vocabulary susceptible to sharing among different communities of instructors or creators of e-learning courses.

The Sharable Content Object Reference Model (SCORM) [39] standard describes a content aggregation model and a tracking model for reusable learning objects to support adaptive instruction based on the learner's objectives, preferences, performance, and other factors like instructional techniques. One of the most important features of SCORM is that it allows the instructional content designer to specify sequencing rules and navigation behavior while maintaining the possibility of reusing learning resources within multiple and different aggregation contexts. While SCORM provides a framework for the representation and processing of the metadata, it falls short in including the needed support for more specific pedagogical tracking such as the use of collaborative resources. We thus argue that the use of a more specific pedagogical ontology provides a higher level of decision support analysis and mining, based in qualitative issues like the collaborative degree of activities.

Lastly, we consider very important to mention another aspect that can facilitate the comprehensibility of discovered rules, the visualization. The goal of visualization is to help analysts in inspecting the data after applying the mining task [40] by means of some visual representation to the corpus of rules extracted. A range of visual representations is used, such as tables, two-dimensional matrices, graphs, bar charts, grids, mosaic plots, parallel coordinates, etc. Association rule mining can be integrated with visualization techniques [41] in order to allow users to drive the association rule finding process, giving them control and visual cues to ease understanding of both the process and its results. However, the visualization methods are still difficult to understand for a non-expert in data mining, such as a teacher. Therefore, we consider that this question needs to be addressed in the near future, and the challenge will be to apply these techniques in a more intuitive way, identifying within these data structures the rules that are relevant and meaningful in the context of the e-learning analysis, and representing them in a simple way such as icons, colors, etc., using interactive bidimensional and three-dimensional representations.

7.3.4 Statistical Significance of Discovered Rules

One aspect that is often overlooked when applying data mining techniques on small datasets is that of *overfitting*. When there is only limited data available, and the hypothesis space (i.e., the total number of possible rules) is huge, it is inevitable in a statistical sense to get false discoveries because every rule has a small chance of being true in the given data, and the number of rules is huge. The smaller the dataset, the larger the danger for these so-called type-I errors: false rules that accidentally hold in the small dataset. To address this problem, it is more than advisable to restrict the hypothesis space by inserting as much as possible background knowledge; i.e.: restricting the body and heads of the rules as much as possible, and maybe, in the worst case, even removing numerous attributes from the dataset. When evaluating the outcome of an association rule mining operation, one also has to take very well into account that without further controlled experiments the found associations are, at least, open to debate.

7.4 An Introduction to Association Rule Mining with Weka in a Moodle LMS

We are going to use Weka over Moodle data in order to show a practical example of applying association rule mining in an educational environment.

Moodle [42] is a well-known, freeware learning management system and an open-source software package designed using sound pedagogical principles, to help educators create effective online learning communities. Moodle has a flexible array of module activities and resources to create five kinds of static course material (a text page, a web page, a link to anything on the Web, a view into one of the course's directories, and a label that displays any text or image), six types of interactive course material (assignments, choice, journal, lesson, quiz, and survey), and five kinds of activities where students interact with each other (chat, forum, glossary, wiki, and workshop).

On the other hand, Weka [29] is an open-source software platform that provides a collection of machine learning and data mining algorithms for data pre-processing, classification, regression, clustering, association rules, and visualization.

The process of applying association rule mining over the Moodle data consists of the same four steps as the general data mining process (see Figure 7.3):

- **Collect data**. The LMS system is used by students, and the usage and interaction information is stored in the database. We are going to use the students' usage data of the Moodle system.

- **Preprocess the data**. The data are cleaned and transformed into a mineable format. In order to preprocess the Moodle data, we used the MySQL System Tray Monitor and Administrator tools [43] and the Open DB Preprocess task in the Weka Explorer [29].

- **Apply association rule mining**. The data mining algorithms are applied to discover and summarize knowledge of interest to the teacher.

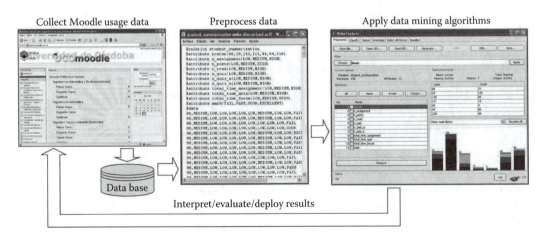

FIGURE 7.3
Mining Moodle data.

- **Interpret, evaluate, and deploy the results**. The obtained results or model are interpreted and used by the teacher for further actions. The teacher can use the discovered information for making decision about the students and the Moodle activities of the course in order to improve the students' learning.

Our objective is to use the students' usage data of the Moodle system. Moodle has a lot of detailed information about content, users, usage, etc. that is stored in a relational database. The data is stored in a single database: MySQL and PostgreSQL are best supported, but it can also be used with Oracle, Access, and Interbase, any database supporting Open DataBase Connectivity (ODBC) connections and others. We have used MySQL because it is the world's most popular open source database. Moodle has more than 150 tables, some of the most important are *mdl_log, mdl_assignement, mdl_chat, mdl_forum, mdl_message*, and *mdl_quiz*.

Data preprocessing allows for transforming the original data into a suitable shape to be used by a particular data mining algorithm or framework. So, before applying a data mining algorithm, a number of general data preprocessing tasks have to be addressed (data cleaning, user identification, session identification, path completion, transaction identification, data transformation and enrichment, data integration, and data reduction). Data preprocessing of LMS-generated data has some specific issues:

- Moodle and most of the LMSs use user authentication (password protection) in which logs have entries identified by users since the users have to log-in, and sessions are already identified since users may also have to log-out. So, we can remove the typical user and session identification tasks of preprocessing data of web-based systems.
- Moodle and most of the LMSs record the students' usage information not only in log files but also directly in relational databases. The tracking module can store user interactions at a higher level than simple page access. Databases are more powerful, flexible and less bug-prone that typical log text files for data gathering and integration.

Therefore, the data gathered by an LMS may require less cleaning and preprocessing than data collected in other systems based on log files. In our case, we are going to do the following preprocessing tasks:

- *Selecting data*. The first task is to choose in what specific Moodle courses we are interested to use for mining.
- *Creating summary tables*. Starting from the selected course, we create summarization tables that aggregate the information at the required level (e.g., student). Student and interaction data are spread over several tables. We have created a new summary table that integrates the most important information for our objective. This table has a summary, by row, about all the activities done by each student in the course and the final obtained mark by the student in the same course. In order to create this table, it is necessary to do several queries to the database in order to obtain the information of the desired students (userid value from mdl_user_students table) and courses (id value of the mdl_course table). Table 7.2 shows the main attributes used to create summarization tables.

TABLE 7.2

Attributes Used for Each Student

Name	Description
course	Identification number of the course
n_assigment	Number of realized assignments
n_quiz	Number of realized quizzes
n_quiz_a	Number of passed quizzes
n_quiz_s	Number of failed quizzes
n_messages	Number of send messages to the chat
n_messages_ap	Number of send messages to the teacher
n_posts	Number of send messages to the forum
n_read	Number or read messages of the forum
total_time_assignment	Total time used in assignment
total_time_quiz	Total time used in quiz
total_time_forum	Total time used in forum
mark	Final mark the student obtained in the course

- *Discretizing data.* Next, we perform a discretization of numerical values in order to increase the interpretation and comprehensibility. Discretization divides the data in categorical classes that are easier to understand for the teacher (categorical values are more familiar to the teacher than precise magnitudes and ranges). In our experiments, we discretized all the numerical values of the summarization table (except for course identification value). There are several unsupervised global methods [37] for transforming continuous attributes into discrete attributes, such as the equal-width method, equal-frequency method, or the manual method (in which you have to specify the cut-off points). In this case, we have used the manual method for the mark attribute and the equal-width method for the other attributes. The labels that we have used in the mark attribute are FAIL, PASS, GOOD, and EXCELLENT, and in all the other attributes: LOW, MEDIUM, and HIGH.

- *Transforming the data.* Finally, we transform the data to the required format used by the data mining algorithm or framework in order to be mineable. In this case, we have exported the summary table to a text file with ARFF (Attribute-Relation File Format) format used by Weka. An ARFF file is an ASCII text file that describes a list of instances sharing a set of attributes [44].

Once the data is prepared, we can apply the association rule mining algorithm. In order to do so, it is necessary (1) to choose the specific association rule mining algorithm; (2) to configure the parameters of the algorithm; (3) to identify which table will be used for the mining; (4) and to specify some other restrictions, such as the maximum number of items and what specific attributes can be present in the antecedent or consequent of the discovered rules.

In this case, we have used the Apriori algorithm [20] for finding association rules over the discretized summarization table of the course 110 (Projects), executing this algorithm with a minimum support of 0.3 and a minimum confidence of 0.9 as parameters.

Projects is a 3° course subjects of computer science studies oriented to design, develop, document, and maintain a full computer science project. Students have to use Moodle

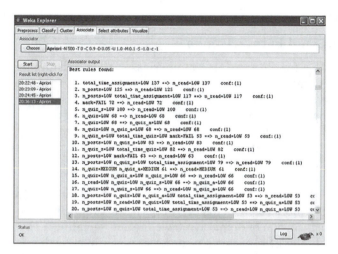

FIGURE 7.4
Results of Apriori algorithm.

to read/download documents/notes, do activities, do quizzes, and send/read message to forums in order to complement traditional (face-to-face) classrooms. The instructor can use all the collected data by Moodle for doing data mining; in our case, association rule mining. Association rules can discover, for example, interesting relationships between the Moodle usage and the student's final marks. It can show what type of students actions predict good final marks (if activities done then marks good) or bad final marks (if not message send/read to forum then marks bad) and can be used to detect on-time student with problem in order to help them and motivate them.

Finally, we do a data post-processing step in which the obtained results and models are interpreted, evaluated, and used by the teacher for further actions. The teacher can use the discovered information for making decisions about the students and the LMS activities of the course in order to improve the students' learning. Next, we are going to explain the meaning of some obtained rules. Figure 7.4 shows how a huge number of association rules can be discovered. There are also a lot of uninteresting rules, like a great number of redundant rules (rules with a generalization of relationships of several rules, like rule 3 with rules 1 and 2, and rule 6 with rule 7 and 8). There are some similar rules (rules with the same element in antecedent and consequent but interchanged, such as rules 15, 16, and 17, and rules 18, 19, and 20). And there are some random relationships (rules with random relations between variables, such as rules 1 and 5). But there are also rules that show relevant information for educational purposes, like those that show expected or conforming relationships (if a student does not send messages, it is logical that he or she does not read them either, such as rule 2, and, similarly, rules 10, 11, and 13). There are also rules that show unexpected relationships (such as rules 4, 12, 14, and 9), which can be very useful for the instructor in decision making about the activities and detecting students with learning problems, like rules 4, 12, and 9 that show that if the number of messages read and messages sent in the forum is very low, and the total time and number of passed quizzes are very low, then the final mark obtained is a failing grade. Starting from this information, the instructor can pay more attention to these students because they are prone to failure. As a result, the instructor can motivate them, in time, to pass the course.

7.5 Conclusions and Future Trends

It is still the early days for the total integration of association rule mining in e-learning systems, and not many real and fully operative implementations are available. Nevertheless, a good deal of academic research in this area has been published over the last few years. In this paper, we have outlined some of the main drawbacks of the application of association rule mining to data generated by learning management systems. We have proposed some possible solutions for each problem. Furthermore, we have given general outlines and explained how to carry out a particular KDD process for association rule mining in an LMS system.

We believe that some future research lines will focus on developing an association rule mining tool that can more easily be used by educators; proposing new specific measures of interest with the inclusion of domain knowledge and semantic information; integrating the mining tool into the LMS systems in order to give direct feedback; developing iterative and interactive or guided mining to help educators to apply KDD processes, or even developing an automatic mining system that can perform the mining automatically in an unattended way, such that the teacher only has to use the proposed recommendations in order to improve the students' learning.

Acknowledgments

The authors gratefully acknowledge the financial support provided by the Spanish Department of Research under TIN2008-06681-C06-03 and P08-TIC-3720 Projects.

References

1. BlackBoard, available at http://www.blackboard.com/ (accessed March 16), 2009.
2. WebCT, available at http://www.webct.com/ (accessed March 16), 2009.
3. TopClass, available at http://www.topclass.nl/ (accessed March 16), 2009.
4. Moodle, available at http://moodle.org/ (accessed March 16), 2009.
5. Ilias, available at http://www.ilias.de/ (accessed March 16), 2009.
6. Claroline, available at http://www.claroline.net/ (accessed March 16), 2009.
7. Mostow, J. and Beck, J., Some useful tactics to modify, map and mine data from intelligent tutors. *Natural Language Engineering* 12(2), 195–208, 2006.
8. Dringus, L. and Ellis, T., Using data mining as a strategy for assessing asynchronous discussion forums. *Computer & Education Journal* 45, 141–160, 2005.
9. Zorrilla, M.E., Menasalvas, E., Marin, D., Mora, E., and Segovia, J., Web usage mining project for improving web-based learning sites. In *Web Mining Workshop*, Cataluña, Spain, 2005, pp. 1–22.
10. Romero, C. and Ventura, S., *Data Mining in E-Learning*, Wit Press, Southampton, U.K., 2006.
11. Zaïane, O., Building a recommender agent for e-learning systems. In *Proceedings of the International Conference in Education (ICCE)*, Auckland, Nueva Zelanda, IEEE Press, New York, 2002, pp. 55–59.

12. Lu, J., Personalized e-learning material recommender system. In *International Conference on Information Technology for Application*, Harbin, China, 2004, pp. 374–379.

13. Minaei-Bidgoli, B., Tan, P., and Punch, W., Mining interesting contrast rules for a web-based educational system. In *International Conference on Machine Learning Applications*, Louisville, KY, December 16–18, 2004.

14. Romero, C., Ventura, S., and De Bra, P., Knowledge discovery with genetic programming for providing feedback to courseware author. *User Modeling and User-Adapted Interaction: The Journal of Personalization Research* 14(5), 425–464, 2004.

15. Yu, P., Own, C., and Lin, L., On learning behavior analysis of web based interactive environment. In *Proceedings of the ICCEE*, Oslo, Norway, August 6–10, 2001.

16. Merceron, A. and Yacef, K., Mining student data captured from a web-based tutoring tool: Initial exploration and results. *Journal of Interactive Learning Research* 15(4), 319–346, 2004.

17. Freyberger, J., Heffernan, N., and Ruiz, C., Using association rules to guide a search for best fitting transfer models of student learning. In *Workshop on Analyzing Student-Tutor Interactions Logs to Improve Educational Outcomes at ITS Conference*, Maceio, Brazil, August 30, 2004.

18. Ramli, A.A., Web usage mining using Apriori algorithm: UUM learning care portal case. *International Conference on Knowledge Management*, Malaysia, 2005, pp. 1–19.

19. Markellou, P., Mousourouli, I., Spiros, S., and Tsakalidis, A., Using semantic web mining technologies for personalized e-learning experiences. In *The 4th IASTED Conference on Web-Based Education, WBE-2005*, Grindelwald, Switzerland, February 21–23, 2005.

20. Agrawal, R., Imielinski, T., and Swami, A.N., Mining association rules between sets of items in large databases. In *Proceedings of SIGMOD*, Washington, DC, 1993, pp. 207–216.

21. Klosgen, W. and Zytkow, J., *Handbook of Data Mining and Knowledge Discovery*, Oxford University Press, New York, 2002.

22. Agrawal, R. and Srikant, R., Fast algorithms for mining association rules. In *Proceedings of the Conference on Very Large Data Bases*, Santiago, Chile, September 12–15, 1994.

23. Zheng, Z., Kohavi, R., and Mason, L., Real world performance of association rule algorithms. In *Proceedings of the 7th ACM SIGKDD International Conference on Knowledge Discovery & Data Mining*, San Francisco, CA, ACM, New York, 2001, pp. 401–406.

24. Han, J., Pei, J., and Yin, Y., Mining frequent patterns without candidate generation. In *Proceedings of the ACM-SIGMOD International Conference on Management of Data (SIGMOD'99)*, Philadelphia, PA, June, 1999, pp. 359–370.

25. Webb, G.I., OPUS: An efficient admissible algorithm for unordered search. *Journal of Artificial Intelligence Research*, 3, 431–465, 1995.

26. Pei, J., Han, J., and Mao, R. CLOSET: An efficient algorithm for mining frequent closed itemsets. In *Proceedings of ACM_SIGMOD International DMKD'00*, Dallas, TX, 2000.

27. Ceglar, A. and Roddick, J.F., Association mining. *ACM Computing Surveys*, 38(2), 1–42, 2006.

28. Calders, T. and Goethals, B., Non-derivable itemset mining. *Data Mining and Knowledge Discovery* 14, 171–206, 2007.

29. Weka, available at http://www.cs.waikato.ac.nz/ml/weka/ (accessed March 16), 2009.

30. Scheffer, T., Finding association rules that trade support optimally against confidence. *Lecture Notes in Computer Science* 2168, 424–435, 2001.

31. García, E., Romero, C., Ventura, S., and De Castro, C., Using rules discovery for the continuous improvement of e-learning courses. In *Proceedings of the 7th International Conference on Intelligent Data Engineering and Automated Learning-IDEAL 2006*, LNCS 4224, Burgos, Spain, September 20–23, 2006, Springer-Verlag, Berlin, Germany, pp. 887–895.

32. Tan, P. and Kumar, V., *Interesting Measures for Association Patterns: A Perspectiva*, Technical Report TR00-036. Department of Computer Science, University of Minnesota, Minneapolis, MN, 2000.

33. Silberschatz, A. and Tuzhilin, A., What makes patterns interesting in Knowledge discovery systems. *IEEE Transactions on Knowledge and Data Engineering* 8(6), 970–974, 1996.

34. Liu, B., Wynne, H., Shu, C., and Yiming, M., Analyzing the subjective interestingness of association rules. *IEEE Intelligent Systems and their Applications* 15(5), 47–55, 2000.

35. García, E., Romero, C., Ventura, S., and De Castro, C., An architecture for making recommendations to courseware authors through association rule mining and collaborative filtering. *UMUAI: User Modelling and User Adapted Interaction* 19(99), 100–132, 2009.

36. Huysmans, J., Baesens, B., and Vanthienen, J., Using Rule Extraction to Improve the Comprehensibility of Predictive Models. http://ssrn.com/abstract=961358 (accessed January 20, 2008), 2006.

37. Dougherty, J., Kohavi, M., and Sahami, M., Supervised and unsupervised discretization of continuous features. *International Conference on Machine Learning*, Tahoe City, CA, 1995, pp. 194–202.

38. Brase, J. and Nejdl, W., Ontologies and metadata for e-learning. In *Handbook on Ontologies*, Springer Verlag, Berlin, Germany, 2003, pp. 579–598.

39. SCORM, *Advanced Distributed Learning. Shareable Content Object Reference Model: The SCORM Overview*, ADL Co-Laboratory, Alexandria, VA, available at http://www.adlnet.org (accessed March 16, 2009), 2005.

40. De Oliveira, M.C.F. and Levkowitz, H., From visual data exploration to visual data mining: A survey. *IEEE Transactions on Visualization and Computer Graphics* 9(3), 378–394, 2003.

41. Yamamoto, C.H. and De Oliveira, M.C.F., Visualization to assist users in association rule mining tasks. PhD dissertation, Arizona State Mathematics and Computer Sciences Institute, Sao Paulo University, Sao Paulo, Brazil. http://www.sbbd-sbes2005.ufu.br/arquivos/11866.pdf (accessed March 16, 2009), 2004.

42. Rice, W.H., Moodle e-learning course development. In *A Complete Guide to Successful Learning Using Moodle*, Packt Publishing, Birmingham, U.K./Mumbai, India, 2006.

43. Ullman, L., *Guía de aprendizaje MySQL*, Pearson Prentice Hall, Madrid, Spain, 2003.

44. Witten, I.H. and Frank, E., *Data Mining: Practical Machine Learning Tools and Techniques*, Morgan Kaufman, San Francisco, CA, 2005.

8

Sequential Pattern Analysis of Learning Logs: Methodology and Applications

Mingming Zhou, Yabo Xu, John C. Nesbit, and Philip H. Winne

CONTENTS

8.1 Introduction

Sequential pattern mining is an important challenge in the field of knowledge discovery and data mining. It is a process of discovering and displaying previously unknown interrelationships, clusters, and data patterns with the goal of supporting improved decision-making [1]. The mined knowledge can be used in a wide range of practical applications, such as analyzing DNA sequences [2,3], stock price fluctuations [4], telecommunication network intrusion detection [5], web usage patterns [6], customers' transaction history [7], and software structure evaluation [8].

The concept of sequential pattern analysis was first introduced by Agrawal and Srikant [9], based on their study of customer purchase sequences. Briefly, given a set of sequences, the problem is to discover subsequences that are frequent, in the sense that the occurrence of such subsequences among data sequences exceeds a user-specified minimum *support*. The support of a sequential pattern is the percentage of sequences that contain the pattern [10]. In their classic example of book purchase records, a sequential pattern could be manifested by customers who bought Asimov's novels *Foundation*, *Foundation and Empire*, and *Second Foundation* in that order. Customers who bought other books in between these three transactions are still counted as manifesting the sequential pattern. As well, a set of items can be an element of a sequential pattern, for example, *Foundation* and *Ringworld*, followed by *Foundation and Empire* and *Ringworld Engineers*, followed by *Second Foundation*. Note that all the items in an element of a sequential pattern must be present in a single transaction to support the pattern.

TABLE 8.1

A Sequence Database

Sequence_id	Sequence
s1	A, C, D, F, B, C, D
s2	A, D, E, B, A, D
s3	C, D, C, B, C, D
s4	A, C, D, B, B, D

In sequential data mining, a *sequence* is an ordering of events, and each event in this ordered list is called an *item*. A sequence, α, is a subsequence of another sequence, β, if α can be formed from β by leaving out some events without disturbing the relative positions of the remaining events. For example, if $\alpha = <$ C, E, G, E $>$ and $\beta = <$ A, C, B, D, E, G, C, E, D, B, G $>$, α is a subsequence of β. We may also say β contains α if α is a subsequence of β. Given a set of sequences S, the support of a sequence α in S is the number of sequences containing α, denoted as support(α). Given a percentage *min_sup* as the minimum support threshold, a sequence α is a *sequential pattern* observed in S if support(α) $\geq$ *min_sup*$^*|S|$, where $|S|$ is the total number of sequences in S. That is, for sequence α to be classified as a pattern, it must occur in at least *min_sup* percentage of sequences in S.

Imagine the sequence database to be S given in Table 8.1 and *min_sup* = 3. The items in the database are {A, B, C, D, E, F}. Sequence s1 has seven items, and contributes one to the support of subsequences <A, C> and <A, D, B, D>. Since all sequences s1, s3, s4 contain subsequence s = <A, D, B, D>, s is a sequential pattern of length 4. <A, C> is not a pattern as it is supported only by two sequences s1 and s4.

The main approaches to sequential pattern mining are a priori based [10] and pattern-growth based [11,12]. Among a priori based algorithms, *AprioriAll* requires the use of all frequent subsequences of the previous pass to create new candidate sequences in each pass, and only those candidates with maximum support are kept. In *AprioriSome*, only subsequences of certain lengths are counted in the forward phase, while the subsequences for the skipped lengths are counted in the backward phase. All subsequences that are contained in other large subsequences are removed in advance. In contrast, *DynamicSome* only counts subsequences of certain lengths in the forward phase. All multiples of a *step* value are then counted. In the following steps of the algorithm, sequences are generated by joining sequences of the lower length steps [9]. As an extension, generalized sequential pattern (GSP) considers time constraints to specify minimum and maximum time periods between elements in the pattern and introduce item taxonomies and thus the possibility to mine generalized patterns that include items from different levels of a taxonomy [10,13]. The pattern-growth method is represented by *PrefixSpan* (prefix projected sequential pattern mining) [12]. It reduces the candidate subsequence generation efforts by exploring a prefix projection and thus also reduces the database sizes for future scans. The advantages of *PrefixSpan* are that it does not create (and test) any candidate sequence that does not occur in a projected database, but only "grows longer sequential patterns from the shorter frequent ones" [12] (p. 221) and that the projected databases get smaller with each step, thus leading to more efficient processing.

8.2 Sequential Pattern Analysis in Education

8.2.1 Background

Initial attempts to determine learning behavior and motivation took the form of learners' responses to survey items, probes in an interview, or content revealed in think aloud protocols. Problems intrinsically arise in interpreting and generalizing such data, because the content of thoughts that learners report in self-report protocols on learning behavior only describes what they *perceive* about themselves in the context of *remembered* task conditions. Yet, memory is subject to loss (forgetting), distortion (biased sampling of memories), and reconstruction, which undermines the accuracy and reliability of responses. For these reasons, direct evidence of learning strategies and motivations has been difficult to collect and study with traditional methods.

In recent years, there has been increasing interest in the use of data mining to investigate scientific questions in educational settings, fostering a new and growing research community for educational data mining [14]. With the emergence of computer-based learning environments, traces of learners' activities and behavior that are automatically generated by computer systems allow researchers to make this latent knowledge explicit. The unobtrusiveness of this method enables researchers to track learning events in a nonlinear environment without disrupting the learner's thinking or navigation through content. More importantly, data obtained in real time allow "virtual" re-creation of learners' actions, which support grounded interpretations about how learners construct knowledge, and track their actual choices as well as methods they use to express agency through self-regulated learning within a particular context.

The extraction of sequential patterns in e-learning contributes to educational research in various ways. It helps to evaluate learner's activities and accordingly to adapt and customize resource delivery [15], to be compared with expected behavioral patterns and theoretically appropriate learning paths [16], to indicate how to best organize educational interfaces and be able to make suggestions to learners who share similar characteristics [17], to generate personalized activities to different groups of learners [18], to identify interaction sequences indicative of problems and patterns that are markers of success [19], to recommend to a student the most appropriate links or web pages within an adaptive web-based course to visit next [20], to improve e-learning systems [21], and to identify predictors of success by analyzing transfer student records [22]. All these applications suggest that educational data mining has the potential to extend a much wider tool set to the analysis of important questions in education.

8.2.2 Tracing the Contextualized Learning Process

Many types of educational software are capable of writing event records to log files as learners interact with the software's features and information conveyed by the software, such as web pages shown in a browser. Well-designed methods for capturing data to log files can potentially generate data that is very valuable to researchers investigating how learners access and manipulate information. One example of such software is nStudy [23], a web application for researching self-regulated learning in solo and collaborative settings (see Figure 8.1). In nStudy, as learners study, they operate on multimedia documents using tools to create information objects and link those information objects into structured units. nStudy's tools include those used for making notes based on a choice of schemas (e.g., question and answer, summary, etc.), tagging selected content to classify its properties (e.g., important, review this, do not understand, etc.), hyperlinks that expose new information according to the content developer's model of the domain, constructing new terms in a glossary, drawing and manipulating concept maps to assemble information within and across information objects (e.g., selections in a text; among notes, terms, etc.), a powerful multifaceted search tool, and a chatting tool, to name a few. In short, students have access to a wide variety of cognitive tools

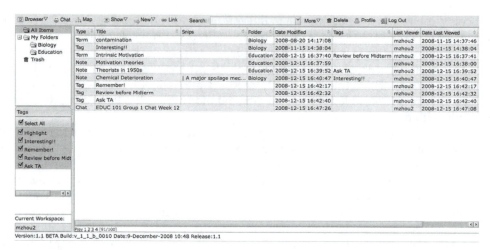

FIGURE 8.1
A screenshot of nStudy user interface.

that afford multiple and varied options for exercising and expressing agency as they construct knowledge.

As students select and use tools in nStudy, the system collects data on the fly about their choices and constructions. Data are logged at the level of a software event and written to an XML file time-stamped to the millisecond. The XML file is a transcript containing the events that trace students' interaction with information—the way it was operated on by using nStudy's tools and the time when that event occurred (see Figure 8.2). These events represent small-grained traces such as moving from one web page to another, clicking a button, opening a new window, or tagging a selected text.

As a learner uses each tool, nStudy records in detail all the events involved that make up a composite studying action. For instance, when the student adds a label to information selected in a sentence from the web page, nStudy logs information about which sentence is being annotated, which tag is applied, the time when the tag is applied, and how long it takes to complete the action. The whole series of actions logged during the student's studying session can be examined to make inferences about the students' interactive goals, strategies, and beliefs. These records support grounded interpretations about how a learner constructs knowledge. Trace data reflect what learners do in ways that reveal more accurately, although not perfectly, whether, when, and how learners access prior knowledge to process new information. With sufficient samples of trace data, it may be possible to identify standards learners use to make these decisions [24].

Given the complexity of learning logs captured in multimedia learning environments and the intricacy of the cognitive processes that take place during information processing, there are several challenges to be met when applying sequential pattern analysis to learning logs. The first challenge for any software is that given its broad functionality (such as nStudy), the events recorded in the log file are unlikely to correspond exactly to the learning tactics being examined by the researcher. If every mouse-click and keystroke is recorded as a log event, each tactic is likely to generate multiple log events. The simple tactic of labeling a text segment as "critical" might generate at least a text selection event followed by a menu selection event, when the learner selects "critical" from a menu. It is even possible that the sequence of log events generated by a tactic is interrupted by events a researcher deems extraneous, such as repetitive attempts to select a piece of text due to unskilled mouse

```
- <lg: ViewEvent container= "Browser Window z_ci_2:nStudy Browser[User Homepage]: Mechanisms for Food
  Preservation"
  timeStamp="2008-12-15T13:18:11.733-08:00">
    <lg:ButtonAction/>
    <lg:componentId ID="ID: BrowserWindow.ToolBar.FastMarkButton.NotePopupMenu.MenuItem —
      Description: Menu item"/>
  </lg:View Event>
- <lg:View Event container="Browser Window z_ci_2:nStudy Browser[User Homepage]: Mechanisms for Food
  Preservation"
  timeStamp="2008-12-15T13:18:13.327-08:00">
    <lg:Window Action action="FocusLost"/>
    <lg:componentId ID="ID: BrowserWindow — Description: browser window"/>
  </lg:View Event>
- <lg:ModelEvent action="created" target="link" timeStamp="2008-12-15T13:18:13.770-08:00" user="mzhou2">
  - <lg:targetObject>
    - <lg:link>
      - <lg:end0>
        <lg:url>/mzhou2/section3.htm</lg:url>
      - <lg:xpath>
        xpointer(string-range(/html[1]/body[1]/div[1]/p[3]/span[1], " ", 2, 7))
        </lg:xpath>
        <lg:snip>he need</lg:snip>
      </lg:end0>
      - <lg:end1>
        - <lg:mo>
          <nt:Note author="mzhou2" dateCreated="2008-12-15T13:18:13.643-08:00"
            dateModified="2008-12-15T13:18:13.646-08:00"
          templateRef="fdgdfghh"/>
        </lg:mo>
        <lg:moID>10918</lg:moID>
      </lg:end1>
    </lg:link>
  </lg:targetObject>
</lg:ModelEvent>
- <lg:ModelEvent action="created" target="link" timeStamp="2008-12-15T13:18:16.875-08:00" user="mzhou2">
  - <lg:targetObject>
    - <lg:link>
      - <lg:end0>
        <lg:url>/mzhou2/section3.htm</lg:url>
      - <lg:xpath>
        xpointer(string-range(/html[1]/body[1]/div[1]/p[3], " ", 279, 7))
```

FIGURE 8.2
A screenshot of nStudy logs.

control. Hence, it is necessary to identify the train of log events corresponding to a tactic and match that train to a stream of logged events infiltrated with noise. The challenge is to model the sequence at a coarser level—to generate a sequence of higher-level actions from the raw event logs—such that each action corresponds to a tactic deployed by a learner.

Second, existing sequential pattern mining algorithms, if applied directly in our scenario, may generate excessive instances of irrelevant patterns that add to the difficulties of producing a meaningful pattern analysis. This relates to a third and greater challenge, namely, that learning strategies used by students are in general unknown a priori, and, unlike the sequence of events corresponding to a tactic, are difficult to predict. Given a large sample of learning logs, it is common for sequential mining to return thousands of patterns, only a portion of which are educationally meaningful. The challenge is to use the action stream produced by the previous step in the analysis to detect patterns of actions corresponding to learning strategies. This is made more difficult by nonstrategic or extraneous actions that act as noise in the action stream. Thus, it is necessary for educational researchers to either inject their domain knowledge during the sequential mining phase or apply the domain knowledge post hoc to effectively filter out relevant patterns that address their research questions. Further, we must find the patterns (strategies) that are repeated with relatively high frequency across a set of log files that might correspond to, say, the learning sessions generated by all students enrolled in the same course.

Learning logs like those generated as students study using nStudy offer a wealth of data about how students process information during learning. Each learning log can be viewed as a sequence of students' self-directed interactions, called *events*, with their learning environment. Sequential pattern analysis can be used to identify frequently occurring sequences of events. In the following sections, we propose a complete methodology to address these challenges in sequential pattern analysis of learning logs, including a flexible schema for modeling learning sequences at different levels. We introduce two effective mechanisms for injecting research contexts and domain knowledge into the pattern discovery process, and a constraint-based pattern filtering process using nStudy log files generated by university students as examples to identify their studying patterns.

8.3 Learning Log Analysis Using Data Mining Approach

Educational researchers have explored several techniques for analyzing log files of trace data [25,26], especially in investigations of self-regulated learning [27–29]. In this chapter, we extend these approaches to describe a method for identifying and characterizing sequential patterns of studying activities.

Sequential pattern analysis of learning logs is a three-step process consisting of three consecutive steps, namely, preprocessing, pattern discovery, and pattern analysis–evaluation, with the high-level flow shown in Figure 8.3:

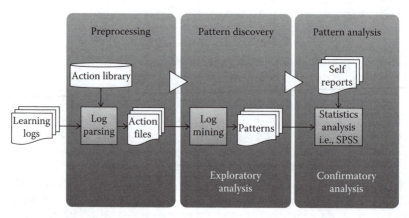

FIGURE 8.3
Flow of sequential pattern analysis on learning logs.

1. **Preprocessing**. In this step, the raw learning logs are taken as the input, consisting of a complex series of low-level events spaced along a time dimension. They are modeled at the behavioral unit or grain size that the educational researcher wishes to study. This is done by a log parsing mechanism, which matches events in a learning log to canonical action patterns predefined by the researcher in the *action library* and generates a sequence of temporally ordered learner actions.

2. **Pattern Discovery**. These sequences are then fed into our sequential mining algorithm to discover patterns across the learning logs.

3. **Pattern Analysis–Evaluation**. With the abundant sequential pattern generated in the previous step, educational researchers identify interesting patterns in this step, test research hypotheses, and perform conventional confirmatory data analysis (compared to the exploratory data analysis in step 2) with the help of other statistic tools such as SPSS.

8.3.1 Preprocessing: From Events to Learning Actions

The raw learning logs collected by the computer system (e.g., nStudy) may be excessively detailed. To analyze these logs at the behavioral unit or grain size that education researchers wish to study, we need to reformat the raw learning logs by systematically aggregating them. An *action library* is created for this purpose by defining sets of sequential event traces (see Figure 8.4). For example, consider creating a critique note containing several fields in nStudy. As a learner uses this tool, the system traces the following events: which content was selected and linked to the note, when the selection was made, how the learner directed nStudy to open a note window (e.g., a choice from the menu bar or a selection from a contextual pop-up menu), which type of note the learner chose among the options available ("critique note," in this example), which fields of the note the learner filled in, what information was entered in each field, what other online sources the learner consulted during the completion of this note, and when the learner closed the note window. Together, these events constitute the action of making a critique note. By specifying all the events for each action as pre-validated sequences in the action library, the raw log files can be translated into a format that consists solely of actions, has all irrelevant and misleading events eliminated, and is suitable for input to sequential mining algorithms.

Educational data mining methods often differ from methods from the broader data mining literature, as they explicitly exploit the multiple levels of meaningful hierarchy in educational data [30]. The issue of granularity arises not because of the operational definitions of the examined constructs but because researchers intend to model how an individual learns [31]. An important feature of the action library is the flexible control of grain size, which is the level of detail at which researchers decide a priori to address research questions in learning science. In the action library, researchers can aggregate finer-grained learning events into bigger chunks. They can also divide coarser-grained events into smaller units to increase granularity. We believe this flexibility for exploring grain size is critical to new investigations of learning in multimedia environments.

As the action library defines the syntax of actions on which researchers wish to focus, the log parsing process translates low-level events to higher-level actions. This process is similar to that performed by a computer language compiler. A common approach adopted in language compilation is the bottom-up parsing strategy, also known as shift-reduce parsing. It attempts to identify the most fundamental units first, and then infer higher-order structures from lower ones. However, noise and extraneous events in logs of natural

```
– <lv:Actions>
  – <lv:Action name="View_Term">
    <lv:Description> View a glossary term in the glossary view. </lv:Description>
    – <lv:Parameters>
    <lv:Parameter name="Template" srcEvent="0" path="ListViewSelection/targetObject/Name:name"
      display="True"/>
    </lv:Parameters>
    – <lv:Events>
      <lv:ViewEvent target="MainWindow.GlossaryView.GlossaryList" action="ListViewSelection"/>
      <lv:ViewEvent target="MainWindow.GlossaryView.DetailPanel.Template Combo"
        action="ListViewSelection"/>
      <lv:ViewEvent target="MainWindow.GlossaryView.DetailPanel.Template Combo"
        action="ListViewSelection"/>
      <lv:ViewEvent target="MainWindow.GlossaryView.DetailPanel" action="DataPanelModelChange"/>
    </lv:Events>
  </lv:Action>
  – <lv:Action name="Update_Term">
    – <lv:Description>
      In the glossary view, select a glossary from the list and update.
    </lv:Description>
    – <lv:Parameters>
      <lv:Parameter name="Template" srcEvent="0" path="DataFieldSelectionAction/targetObject/Name:name"
        display="True"/>
    </lv:Parameters>
    – <lv:Events>
      <lv:ViewEvent target="MainWindow.GlossaryView.DetailPanel" action="DataFieldSelectionAction"/>
      <lv:ModelEvent target="term" action="updated"/>
    </lv:Events>
  </lv:Action>
```

FIGURE 8.4
A snapshot of the action library.

data would normally halt the shift-reduce parsing process, because traditional compilers terminate with failure as soon as an error is detected in the input. To avoid this problem, we incorporate the following mechanisms into our adapted shift-reduce parser to make it robust enough to continue parsing in the presence of noise:

1. **Halt after m consecutive unmatched logs**. If unmatched logs occur consecutively more than m times, parsing will stop and the current sequences in the stack are taken as a broken action.

2. **Backtrack and rematch**. One way to deal with the broken action is to backtrack to the first unmatched log, skip the current log to be matched, and continue the matching. Whether the broken action will be output depends on the portion of the valid sequences that are matched. Then the parsing will restart on the first unmatched sequence.

The output of this parsing analysis is a time-sequenced list of actions that represents the students' studying (see Figure 8.5). These action sequences then serve as input in the next *pattern discovery* stage.

8.3.2 Pattern Discovery

In the pattern discovery stage, a researcher applies sequential pattern mining algorithms to the sequences of parsed actions from the preprocessing step. The objective is to discover

Action List	Parse Result	Statistics	Patterns

Action Name	Template	Start Time	Duration(sec)
Browser	./html/07chapter_b.html	2007.10.22*T*10.31.27.405	0.00
Browser	./html/07chapter_b.html	2007.10.22*T*10.31.30.790	0.00
View_Term	Allan Paivio	2007.10.22*T*10.31.51.089	0.00
Make_Term	Glossary Term_3	2007.10.22*T*10.31.51.109	2.38
Browser	./html/01chapter.html	2007.10.22*T*10.31.56.497	0.00
Browser	./html/01chapter.html	2007.10.22*T*10.31.56.497	0.00
Update_Term	Long-term working memory	2007.10.22*T*10.26.06.113	0.00
Update_Term	Glossary Term_3	2007.10.22*T*10.32.03.186	3.34
Update_Term	Glossary Term_3	2007.10.22*T*10.32.03.166	19.06
View_Term	Cognitive Theory of Multimedi...	2007.10.22*T*10.32.22.254	0.02
View_Term	Cognitive Theory of Multimedi...	2007.10.22*T*10.32.22.284	0.01
Update_Term	Cognitive Theory of Multimedi...	2007.10.22*T*10.32.22.324	6.39
Update_Term	Cognitive Theory of Multimedi...	2007.10.22*T*10.32.28.743	4.55
Browser	./html/07chapter_b.html	2007.10.22*T*10.34.48.484	0.00
Update_Term	Cognitive Theory of Multimedi...	2007.10.22*T*10.32.33.320	0.00
Browser	./html/07chapter_b.html	2007.10.22*T*10.35.38.626	0.00
Browser	./html/07chapter_b.html	2007.10.22*T*10.35.39.437	0.00
Browser	./html/07chapter_b.html	2007.10.22*T*10.35.42.001	0.00
Browser	./html/07chapter_b.html	2007.10.22*T*10.36.06.697	0.00
Browser	./html/07chapter_b.html	2007.10.22*T*10.36.20.917	0.00
Browser	./html/07chapter_b.html	2007.10.22*T*10.36.21.878	0.00
Browser	./html/07chapter_b.html	2007.10.22*T*10.36.23.561	0.00
Make_Term	Glossary Term_4	2007.10.22*T*10.37.05.521	1.37
View_Term	Explicit Memory	2007.10.22*T*10.37.24.589	0.01
Update_Term	Explicit Memory	2007.10.22*T*10.37.24.609	9.87
Make_Term	Glossary Term_5	2007.10.22*T*10.38.04.746	1.33
Update_Term	Implicit memory	2007.10.22*T*10.38.17.314	3.03
Update_Term	Implicit memory	2007.10.22*T*10.38.20.369	30.05

FIGURE 8.5
A screenshot of the parsing output—action list.

meaningful and relevant patterns. "Meaningful" patterns are those that are interpretable in a particular research context. However, only some of the meaningful patterns found are likely to be relevant to the research questions pursued by the researcher. In the field of data mining, sequential pattern mining has long been identified as an important topic, with a focus on developing efficient and scalable sequential pattern mining algorithms. These algorithms, if applied directly in our scenario, are insufficient, not because of their algorithm inefficiency, but due to their inability to introduce research contexts and domain knowledge into the pattern discovery process. We propose two effective mechanisms to address this problem.

Incorporate research context into sequence modeling. Sequence modeling can be applied in various ways that depend on how the log data are aggregated. For example, all sessions (log files) from each student in a group could be combined to create a single sequence for that group, so that the data mining algorithm will find sequential patterns that are common in that group's studying activities. Alternatively, the separate sessions (log files) from a single student could be mined to find sequential patterns that are common to that student. In short, there are various ways to model input sequences according to researchers' needs, and the semantics of sequential patterns is determined by the way input sequences are modeled. The following are the common ways of modeling sequences under different research contexts:

1. **Student-based sequence modeling**. All actions from a single student are taken as a sequence of temporarily ordered actions. The discovered sequential patterns across a group of students indicate common learning behaviors within this group.
2. **Session-based sequence modeling**. Given that a student engages in different sessions, actions from one single session are treated as a sequence. Corresponding sequential patterns across sessions identify the typical learning behavior of this student. Alternatively, combined with student-based sequence modeling, session-based modeling allows us to find common learning behaviors within a particular session for a group of students.

3. **Object-based sequence modeling**. The action sequences produced from the parsing process preserve the links between actions and objects. For instance, a "make a note" action would be distinguished from a "make a glossary" action by the object type on which an action is performed, that is, note versus glossary. With such information, we can construct a sequence of actions performed on a particular type of object. If we constrain input sequences by the object type, for example, note, glossary term, concept map, or even a segment of text, the sequential patterns offer information at a micro level. In particular, research questions could be answered such as whether students review previous notes before making new notes, or how frequently students revise a glossary after the glossary is first constructed.

Enforce educational domain knowledge as constraints. In a sense, all patterns are interesting and meaningful as they reflect students' real learning processes. However, not every pattern makes a significant contribution to educational research in understanding how individuals learn, given current development of educational theories. Constraints are thus often used in sequential pattern mining to limit the search space to those patterns with which researchers are likely to produce thought-provoking findings [32]. Two types of constraints are particularly relevant in educational contexts:

1. **Position constraint**. This type of constraint emphasizes the importance of *where* and *when* the patterns are detected. Specifically, our framework allows researchers to specify any part of the input sequence (in the unit of location or time) they want to include or exclude in the pattern discovery process, so that patterns observed at a certain position can be extracted. For instance, a researcher interested in the strategy students adopt in the revision phase of essay writing could locate patterns among sequences within the last 15 min in a session, by imposing time constraints. Or, a researcher curious about whether students make more notes about the most difficult passage during reading could constrain the input sequences to notes linked to the specified paragraph.

2. **Distance constraint**. This type of constraint specifies a distance relationship between the actions within a pattern. For example, a researcher who wants to find out the immediate antecedent or subsequent action in a learning behavior pattern could request each single action occurring in the pattern to be within a certain distance from the target/central action. This information will better inform researchers of students' learning style and estimate the predictive power of an action of the target action. For example, the further away an action is from the target, the less chance this action would occur before or after the target action occurs.

Formulating these constraints effectively requires the support of domain knowledge to determine the type of constraint to be applied and, more importantly, to set the constraint in a way that is suited to the research problem. Deft use of constraints can remove "non-meaningful" patterns and enable researchers to customize and refine their strategy of analyzing log data.

8.3.3 Pattern Analysis: From Exploratory to Confirmatory Approach

The process of analyzing learning strategies has two phases analogous to the exploratory and confirmatory phases in factor analysis. In the exploratory phase, the problem is to use one data set to discover action patterns that correspond to strategies. Sequential pattern mining discovers patterns that may or may not be useful to the researcher. As we observed in our previous studies [32–35], the patterns generated from mining algorithms usually number in the hundreds, or even more. We note the following observations when massive arrays of patterns are generated:

1. A significant portion of patterns detected offers little insight into students' strategic intent. For example, it is very usual for students to scroll up and down to browse the content when reading a web page. Yet the pattern consisting of a series of "browse" actions does not, by itself, convey useful information.

2. Researchers could display interest beyond the discovered patterns. A sequential pattern captures only the sequential property of a group of students. A sequential pattern captures only sequences. Findings about sequences could be combined with other variables, such as individual characteristics of students, to discover more about their learning processes. Sometimes, additional analyses can improve the interpretation of a pattern. For example, by profiling overconfident and underconfident learners in terms of their sequential learning patterns, additional contrasts can be framed about the learning styles of these two different groups.

To respond the first issue, we add an ad hoc query language that allows separating irrelevant or nonmeaningful patterns or identifying specific patterns based on theoretical assumptions. In the top bar of the parser output, researchers can specify the minimum frequency, minimum length of a pattern, and/or particular actions contained in a pattern. For example, in Figure 8.6, when the minimum frequency is set to be 22, 21211 patterns were filtered out. If we take the length of pattern into account, the 9th and 23rd will be of most interest to a researcher. The 9th pattern depicts a process of "browsing the content → creating a glossary term → updating that term → continue browsing the content", whereas the 23rd pattern describes "browsing the content → creating a glossary term → continue

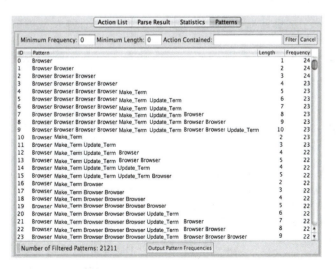

FIGURE 8.6
A screenshot of the sequential pattern output.

Pattern / Sequence	Make_Term-> Browser-> Update_Term	Make_Term-> Browser-> Update_Term ->Browser	Browser-> Make_Term-> Browser-> Update_Term	Make_Term-> Browser-> Make_Term-> ->Update_Term	Make_Term-> Browser-> Browser-> Update_Term	
001	2	1	0	0	1	...
002	1	0	1	0	0	...
003	0	0	0	1	0	...
004	1	0	1	0	2	...
005	1	1	0	0	1	...
...	...	...	...	...	...	...

FIGURE 8.7
Partial sequence-pattern matrix.

browsing the content → updating that term." These patterns of sequenced actions can then be aggregated to infer higher-order structures, such as a surface learning approach versus a deep learning approach, or performance-oriented learning tactics versus mastery-oriented learning tactics. The patterns in Figure 8.6 represent a deep learning approach wherein learners create glossary terms to aid understanding and revisit them with further reading. This method allows building up even larger strategies, based on how students' behavior expresses motivation.

The second issue concerns moving from exploratory to confirmatory data analysis. In the confirmatory phase, the problem is to show that the discovered action patterns are evident in subsequent data sets. Once patterns have been identified, they can be counted and statistically analyzed like any other psychoeducational measure. As shown in Figure 8.7, the sequence-pattern matrix indicates the occurrence of each pattern in each sequence. In this phase, the software searches for the patterns in the current or subsequent data sets and counts the frequency of the patterns for each learner (or other unit of observation). The data from this phase can be exported to statistical software for further analysis. Our next step is to implement intuitive graphic charts and tables for pattern visualization that promote better understanding of pattern-based results.

8.4 Educational Implications

Green [36] criticized methodologies used in studying learning: "What is required is a more sophisticated approach to conceptual analysis in general. Phenomena such as learning, memory, reasoning, perception, and emotion can be neither adequately defined in terms of, nor reduced to, a small set of measurement operations" (p. 315). Recent advances in technology have broadened opportunities for measuring processes involved in learning. Although we are just beginning to understand how students go about learning over the course of studying sessions, sufficient attention has not been paid to strengths and weaknesses of different types of data and means for analyzing them. Self-report is essential because these are the data learners have "in mind" when they engage in self-regulated learning. However, to provide a fuller account of how learning processes entwine and vary over the course of learning, we need to augment those self-report methods for gathering data with techniques that are sensitive to dynamic manifestations of psychological engagement over the course of engaging complex learning activities.

Many researchers adopt qualitative methods to analyze log data [37,38], whereas others generate frequency counts of actions that learners perform [28,39,40]. However, these approaches to analysis fail to capture either patterns of an individual's study tactics or navigation in hypermedia environments [41]. Tracing methodology takes promising steps toward this goal of capturing the elements of such dynamic learning processes and advancing educational research. Because it has the potential to capture the dynamics of the learning process, log analysis addresses concerns that have been expressed about gathering point samples using concurrent think-aloud protocols, free descriptions, or self-report questionnaires [24,42]. Further, the application of data mining algorithms multiplies the power to interpret these process data and broadens views about learning and other processes that relate to learning. Thus, analyzing traces in log files and identifying patterns of activities they contain help researchers to elaborate descriptions of learning processes by generating a more accurate picture of what is "going on" during learning and offer educational researchers insights into students' learning strategies and motivation, and how their strategies and motivation change within a session or across sessions.

8.5 Conclusions and Future Research Directions

We have explained how learning event logs can be used to collect detailed and potentially critical data about what students do as they interact with learning materials. We also have shown how sequential data mining algorithms enable educational researchers to obtain accurate and meaningful information about how individuals learn. The application of data mining in education has requirements not present in other domains, mainly the need to take into account pedagogical aspects of the learner and the system [14], as well as individual characteristics of learners, such as motivation, cognition, and so forth. An obvious next step in developing this methodology involves mapping a variety of learning-relevant factors (e.g., motivation) onto patterns of actions over the course of learning. If a correspondence emerges between motivation patterns and patterns of actions, then predictions may be made about motivation based on actions collected on the fly. This brings theorizing closer to the phenomena at hand. Due to inevitable conceptual ambiguities in some motivational constructs (such as goals), the mapping between motivation patterns and patterns of actions should have an empirical as well as a rational or logical basis. We believe this new kind of "thick description" can provide multiple levels of integrated information about learners' attitudes, beliefs, and interactions with the content. Future work should continue to collect data to validate this methodology.

Acknowledgments

Support for this research was provided by grants to Philip H. Winne from the Social Sciences and Humanities Research Council of Canada (410-2002-1787 and 512-2003-1012), the Canada Research Chair Program, and Simon Fraser University.

References

1. Benoit, G. Data mining. *Annu. Rev. Infor. Sci. Tech.* 36: 265–310, 2002.
2. Wang, K., Y. Xu, and J. X. Yu. Scalable sequential pattern mining for biological sequences. In *Proceedings of the Conference on Information Knowledge Management*, ed. D. A. Evans, L. Gravano, O. Herzog, C. Zhai, and M. Ronthaler, pp. 178–187. New York: Assoc. Comput. Machinery, 2004.
3. Zaki, M. Mining data in bioinformatics. In *Handbook of Data Mining*, ed. N. Ye, pp. 573–596. Mahwah, NJ: Lawrence Earlbaum Associates, 2003.
4. Zhao, Q. and S. S. Bhowmick. Sequential pattern mining: A survey. Technical Report, CAIS, Nanyang Technological University, Singapore, No. 2003118, 2003.
5. Hu, Y. and B. Panda. A data mining approach for database intrusion detection. In *Proceedings of the 19th ACM Symposium on Applied Computing*, Nicosia, Cyprus, pp. 711–716, 2004.
6. Pei, J., J. Han, B. Mortazavi-Asl, and H. Zhu. Mining access patterns efficiently from web logs. *Lect. Notes. Compt. Sci.* 1805: 396–407, 2000.
7. Tsantis, L. and J. Castellani. Enhancing learning environments through solution-based knowledge discovery tools: Forecasting for self-perpetuating systemic reform. *J. Special. Educ. Tech.* 16: 39–52, 2001.
8. Sartipi, K. and H. Safyallah. Application of execution pattern mining and concept lattice analysis on software structure evaluation. In *Proc. of the International Conference on Software Engineering and Knowledge Engineering*, ed. K. Zhang, G. Spanoudakis, and G. Visaggio, pp. 302–308. Skokie: KSI press, 2006.
9. Agrawal, R. and R. Srikant. Mining sequential patterns. In *Proceedings of 11th International Conference on Data Engineering*, ed. P. S. Yu and A. S. P. Chen, pp. 3–14. Washington: IEEE Comput. Soc. Press, 1995.
10. Srikant R. and R. Agrawal. Mining sequential patterns: Generalizations and performance improvements. In *Proceedings of the 5th International Conference on Extending Database Technology (EDBT'96)*, Avignon, France, pp. 3–17, 1996.
11. Han, J., J. Pei, and Y. Yin. Mining frequent patterns without candidate generation. In *Proceedings of the 2000 ACM-SIGMOD International Conference on Management of Data (SIGMOD'00)*, Dallas, TX, pp. 1–12, 2000.
12. Pei, J., J. Han, B. Mortazavi-Asl, H. Pinto, Q. Chen, U. Dayal, and M.-C. Hsu. PrefixSpan: Mining sequential patterns efficiently by prefix-projected pattern growth. In *Proceedings of the 2001 International Conference on Data Engineering (ICDE'01)*, Heidelberg, Germany, pp. 215–224, 2001.
13. Pei, J., J. Han, B. Mortazavi-Asl, and H. Zhu. Mining access patterns efficiently from web logs. In *Proc Pacific-Asia Conf on Knowledge Discovery and Data Mining*, ed. T. Terano, H. Liu, and A. L. P. Chen, pp. 396–407. London, U.K.: Springer-Verlag, 2000.
14. Romero, C. and S. Ventura. Educational data mining: A survey from 1995 to 2005. *Expert Syst. Appl.* 33: 135–146, 2007.
15. Zaïane, O. and J. Luo. Web usage mining for a better web-based learning environment. In *Proceedings of Conference on Advanced Technology for Education*, Banff, Alberta, pp. 60–64, 2001.
16. Pahl, C. and C. Donnellan. Data mining technology for the evaluation of web-based teaching and learning systems. In *Proceedings of Congress E-learning*, Montreal, Canada, pp. 1–7, 2003.
17. Ha, S., S. Bae, and S. Park. Web mining for distance education. In *IEEE International Conference on Management of Innovation and Technology*, Singapore, pp. 715–719, 2000.
18. Wang, W., J. Weng, J. Su, and S. Tseng. Learning portfolio analysis and mining in SCORM compliant environment. In *ASEE/IEEE Frontiers in Education Conference*, Savannah, Georgia, pp. 17–24, 2004.
19. Kay, J., N. Maisonneuve, K. Yacef, and O. R. Zaiane. Mining patterns of events in students' teamwork data. In *Proceedings of Educational Data Mining Workshop*, Taiwan, pp. 1–8, 2006.
20. Romero, C., S. Ventura, A. Zafra, and P. de Bra. Applying web usage mining for personalizing hyperlinks in web-based adaptive educational systems. *Comput. Educ.* 53: 828–840, 2009.

21. Romero, C. and S. Ventura. *Data Mining in E-learning*. Wit Press, Southampton, U.K., 2006.
22. Luan, J. Data mining and its applications in higher education. *New Directions Institut. Res.*, 113: 17–36, 2002.
23. Winne, P. H. and A. F. Hadwin. *nStudy: A Web Application for Researching and Promoting Self-Regulated Learning* (version 1.01) [computer program]. Simon Fraser University, Burnaby, Canada, 2009.
24. Winne, P. H. How software technologies can improve research on learning and bolster school reform. *Educ. Psychol.* 41: 5–17, 2006.
25. Nesbit, J. C. and A. F. Hadwin. Methodological issues in educational psychology. In *Handbook of Educational Psychology*, ed, P. A. Alexander and P. H. Winne, pp. 825–847. Mahwah, NJ: Erlbaum, 2006.
26. Hadwin, A. F., P. H. Winne, and J. C. Nesbit. Annual review: Roles for software technologies in advancing research and theory in educational psychology. *Br. J. Educ. Psychol.* 75: 1–24, 2005.
27. Hadwin, A. F., J. C. Nesbit, J. Code, D. Jamieson-Noel, and P. H. Winne. Examining trace data to explore self-regulated learning. *Metacogn. Learn.* 2: 107–124, 2007.
28. Nesbit, J. C., P. H. Winne, D. Jamieson-Noel et al. Using cognitive tools in gStudy to investigate how study activities covary with achievement goals. *J. Educ. Comput. Res.* 35: 339–358, 2007.
29. Winne, P. H., L. Gupta, and J. C. Nesbit. Exploring individual differences in studying strategies using graph theoretic statistics. *Alberta. J. Educ. Res.* 40: 177–193, 1994.
30. Baker, R. S. J. d. Data mining for education. In *International Encyclopedia of Education* (3rd edition), ed. B. McGaw, P. Peterson, and E. Baker. Oxford, U.K.: Elsevier, in press.
31. Winne, P. H. Meeting challenges to researching learning from instruction by increasing the complexity of research. In *Handling Complexity in Learning Environments: Research and Theory*, ed. J. Elen and R. E. Clark, pp. 221–236. Amsterdam, the Netharlands: Pergamon, 2006.
32. Pei, J., J. Han, and W. Wang. Constraint-based sequential pattern mining: The pattern-growth methods. *J. Intell. Info. Syst.* 28: 133–160, 2007.
33. Nesbit, J. C., Y. Xu, P. H. Winne, and M. Zhou. Sequential pattern analysis software for educational event data. *Paper Presented at 6th International Conference on Methods and Techniques in Behavioral Research*, Maastricht, the Netherlands, 2008.
34. Zhou, M. and P. H. Winne. Differences in achievement goal-setting among high-achievers and low-achievers. *Paper Presented at the American Educational Research Association* 2008 Annual Meeting, New York, 2008.
35. Zhou, M. and P. H. Winne. Tracing motivation in multimedia learning contexts. *Poster Presented at 6th International Conference on Methods and Techniques in Behavioral Research*, Maastricht, the Netherlands, 2008.
36. Green, C. D. Of immortal mythological beasts: Operationism in psychology. *Theor. Psychol.* 2: 291–320, 1992.
37. MacGregor, S. K. Hypermedia navigation profiles: Cognitive characteristics and information processing strategies. *J. Educ. Comput. Res.* 20: 189–206, 1999.
38. Schroeder, E. E. and B. L. Grabowski. Patterns of exploration and learning with hypermedia. *J. Educ. Comput. Res.* 13: 313–335, 1995.
39. Lawless, K. A. and J. M. Kulikowich. Understanding hypertext navigation through cluster analysis. *J. Educ. Comput. Res.* 14: 385–399, 1996.
40. Barab, S. A., M. F. Bowdish, M. Young, and S. V. Owen. Understanding kiosk navigation: Using log files to capture hypermedia searches. *Instr. Sci.* 24: 377–395, 1996.
41. Barab, S. A., B. R. Fajen, J. M. Kulikowich, and M. Young. Assessing hypermedia navigation through pathfinder: Prospects and limitations. *J. Educ. Comput. Res.* 15: 185–205, 1996.
42. Winne, P. H., D. L. Jamieson-Noel, and K. Muis. Methodological issues and advances in researching tactics, strategies, and self-regulated learning. In *Advances in Motivation and Achievement: New Directions in Measures and Methods*, ed. P. R. Pintrich and M. L. Maehr, pp. 121–155. Greenwich, CT: JAI, 2002.

9

Process Mining from Educational Data

Nikola Trčka, Mykola Pechenizkiy, and Wil van der Aalst

CONTENTS

9.1 Introduction

In modern education, various information systems are used to support educational processes. In the majority of cases, these systems have logging capabilities to audit and monitor the processes they support. At the level of a university, administrative information systems collect information about students, their enrollment in particular programs and courses, and performance like examination grades. In addition, the information about the lectures, instructors, study programs, courses, and prerequisites are typically available as well. These data can be analyzed from various levels and perspectives, showing different aspects of organization, and giving us more insight into the overall educational system. From the level of an individual course, we can consider participation in lectures, accomplishing assignments, and enrolling in midterm and final exams. However, with the development and increasing popularity of blended learning and e-learning, information systems enable us to capture activities also at different levels of granularity. Besides more traditional tasks like overall student performance or dropout prediction [1], it becomes possible to track how different learning resources (videolectures, handouts, wikis, hypermedia, quizzes) are used [2], how students progress with (software) project assignments (svn commits) [3], and self-assessment test and questionnaires [4].

More recently, traditional data-mining techniques have been extensively applied to find interesting patterns, build descriptive and predictive models from large volumes of data accumulated through the use of different information systems [5,6]. The results of data

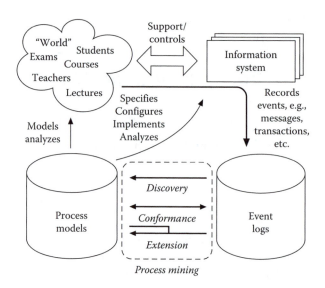

FIGURE 9.1
Process mining concepts.

mining can be used for getting a better understanding of the underlying educational processes, for generating recommendations and advices to students, for improving resource management, etc. However, most of the traditional data-mining techniques do not focus on the process as a whole. They do not aim at discovering or analyzing the complete educational process, and it is, e.g., not clear how, given a study curriculum, we could check automatically whether the students always follow it. It is also not possible to have a clear visual representation of the whole process. To allow for these types of analysis (in which the process plays the central role), a new line of data-mining research, called *process mining*, has been invented [9].

Process mining has emerged from the business community. It focuses on the development of a set of intelligent tools and techniques aimed at extracting process-related knowledge from event logs* recorded by an information system. The complete overview of process mining is illustrated in Figure 9.1. The three major types of process mining applications are

1. *Conformance checking:* reflecting on the observed reality, i.e., checking whether the modeled behavior matches the observed behavior.
2. *Process model discovery:* constructing complete and compact process models able to reproduce the observed behavior.
3. *Process model extension:* projection of information extracted from the logs onto the model, to make the tacit knowledge explicit and facilitate better understanding of the process model.

Process mining is supported by the powerful open-source framework ProM [7]. This framework includes a vast number of different techniques for process discovery, conformance

---

* Typical examples of event logs may include resource usage and activity logs in an e-learning environment, an intelligent tutoring system, or an educational adaptive hypermedia system.

analysis and model extension, as well as many other tools like convertors, visualizers, etc. The tool allowed for a wide use of process mining in industry.

In this chapter, we exemplify the applicability of process mining, and the ProM framework in particular, for educational data-mining context. We discuss some of their potential for extracting knowledge from a particular type of an educational information system, considering an (oversimplified) educational processes reflecting students behavior only in terms of their *examination traces*. We focus on process model conformance and process model discovery, and do not consider model extensions.

The structure of the chapter is as follows. In the next section, we explain process mining in more detail and we present the ProM framework. Then, we discuss how we applied some process mining techniques on our educational data set, establishing some useful results. Finally, the last section is for discussions.

9.2 Process Mining and ProM Framework

As explained in the introduction, process mining consists of three subfields: conformance checking, model discovery, and model extension. We only use the first two and we now explain them in more detail.

Conformance analysis: While process mining can be used to discover a process model from a given event log, explicit process specifications describing how a process should (or is expected to) be executed are often available. Together with the data recorded in the log, this situation raises the interesting question "Do the specification and the log *conform* to each other?" As a result, analyzing the gap between the modeled and the real world helps both to detect violations (i.e., the real world does not "behave properly") and to check whether the existing specification is not outdated [8].

Process model discovery: Conformance analysis is useful only if we have a model of the supposed process. In many cases, however, the starting point is not a model but the observed reality recorded in an event log. There exist several algorithms that use this log as input and automatically construct a depiction of an organization's current business processes. This process representation typically comes in the form of a (formal) mathematical model supporting concurrency, sequential, and alternative behavior (like, e.g., the model of Petri nets) [9].

ProM framework: ProM is an extensible framework that supports a wide variety of process mining techniques in the form of plug-ins. It consolidates the state of the art of process mining. The framework is platform independent, open source, and can be downloaded and used free of charge. We would also like to draw your attention to the availability of online help, demos, and tutorials that thoroughly describe how the ProM plug-ins can be used.

Figure 9.2 gives an overview of the framework indicating the relations between different plug-ins.

ProM logs must be in the MXML format (to be exemplified in the following section) and can be loaded (and filtered if necessary) through the use of *log filter.*

The *mining* plug-ins are the core functionality of the framework. They implement process discovery algorithms that construct process models from an event log.

These algorithms can mine several process perspectives, such as control-flow or data perspective. The *export* plug-ins implement some form of "save as" functionality for objects, while the *import* plug-ins implement the "open" functionality for exported objects. The *conversion* plug-ins implement conversion algorithms between different data/model

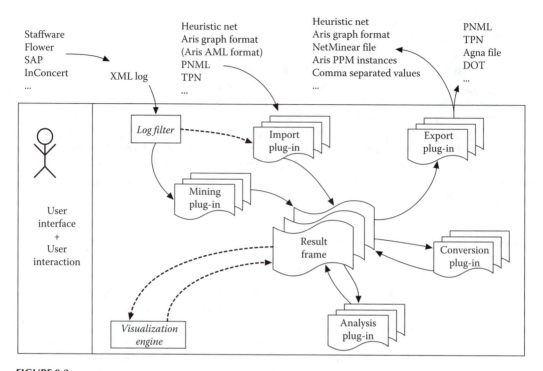

FIGURE 9.2
ProM framework. (From van Dongen, B.F. et al., The ProM framework: A new era in process mining tool support, in *Proceedings of the ICATPN 2005*, Ciardo, G. and Darondeau, P. (eds.), LNCS 3536, Springer, Heidelberg, Germany, pp. 444–454, 2005. With permission.)

formats, for example, from EPCs to Petri nets. The *analysis* plug-ins include various analysis methods, checking both qualitative and quantitative properties of models, logs, or combined. Conformance checkers, e.g., are implemented as analysis plug-ins requiring both a model and a log. In addition to this, ProM has a visualization engine to display logs and different types of (discovered) process models, and comes with ProMimport, a separate tool that converts database data to ProM-recognizable MXML format.

Figure 9.3 shows the snapshot of ProM 5.0 screen with a few plug-ins running.

It is not reasonable to give a complete overview of all of ProM plug-ins here (there are around 250 of them at this moment). We, therefore, just mention those that we think are the most relevant plug-ins in the context of educational data mining. These include (1) plug-ins for importing the data from a database to MXML file (ProM import); (2) plug-ins for log inspection and filtering; (3) conformance analysis plug-ins, in particular those that compare Petri nets with logs, and those based on linear temporal logic (LTL) model checking; (4) process model discovery with Heuristic and Fuzzy Miner [10]; and (5) Dot Chart visualization [11]. How we applied these plug-ins on our educational data set is the subject of the next section.

9.3 Process Mining Educational Data Set

In this section, we show how a real-world educational data set can be imported into ProM, and how some useful results can be obtained from this set using the standard process

FIGURE 9.3
ProM screenshot with some plug-ins executing.

mining techniques. We first describe some of the important data preparation steps, and then we consider examples of visual data exploration, conformance checking, and process discovery.

9.3.1 Data Preparation

The data being collected by our educational information system is stored in a relational database and contains different information starting from preuniversity education (high school grades, name of the school), demographics data, performance throughout the different study phases, etc. We show here the way how it can be transformed into the MXML format by using the ProM Import plug-in [12]. We use for our study only the data about the examination results, i.e., a selection of *course id*, *timestamp*, and *grade* triplets for selected students. However, the data preparation procedure is generic with respect to ProM requirement.

Four tables (see Figure 9.4) having a similar structure as that of fields in the MXML format have to be created. These are the (1) *Process_Instances* table, which needs to be filled with the identifier of a certain process instance (*PI-ID* is primary key) and, if available, its accompanying description; (2) *Data_Attributes_Process_Instances* table, which needs to be filled with additional information about each process instance, i.e., with the so-called data attributes (*PI-ID* is needed to identify to which process instance each data attribute belongs, i.e., *PI-ID* is a foreign key; *name* represents the name of the data attribute and the *value* represents the value of the data attribute); (3) *Audit_Trail_Entries* table, which needs to

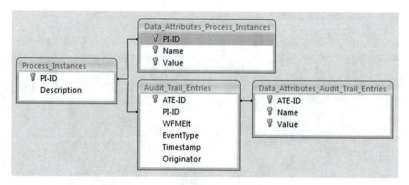

FIGURE 9.4
Database schema for preparing data to be converted to MXML format.

be filled with data about tasks that have been performed during the execution of a process instance (*WFMElt* contains the name of the task, *EventType* the task event type, *Timestamp* the time in which the task changed its state, and *Originator* the person or system that caused the change in the task state, and *ATE-ID* the primary key); and (4) *Data_Attributes_ Audit_Trail_Entries* table, which needs to be filled with additional information about each audit trail entry (if such information exists).

Note that it is not required that systems log all of this information; e.g., some systems do not record transactional information, related data, or timestamps. In the MXML format, only the *ProcessInstance* (i.e., case) field and the *WorkflowModelElement* (i.e., activity) field are obligatory; all other fields (data, timestamps, resources, etc.) are optional.

Having all the data filled into these tables, ProM import automatically transforms the database to an MXML file.*

In our case, *PI-ID* corresponds to a student, *WFMElt* to a course identified for which an examination took place at time recorded in *Timestamp*. Additionally, we can preserve information about the grades, intermediate and final graduation, and semester identifies.

Figure 9.5 illustrates a log example composed of process instances (i.e., students in our case) with corresponding audit trail entries or events (i.e., examinations in our case) with various attributes (grade for the exam, attempt, etc.).

9.3.2 Visual Mining with Dotted Chart Analysis

After building the log file and importing it into ProM, we can start our analysis. It is always advisable to start with visual techniques to get some insight over the complete set of data. We, therefore, choose to represent the log as a dotted chart first.

The dotted chart is a chart similar to a Gantt chart. It shows the spread of events over time by plotting a dot for each event in the log. The chart has three (orthogonal) dimensions: one showing the time of the event, and the other two showing (possibly different) components (such as *instance ID*, *originator*, or *task ID*) of the event. Time is measured along the horizontal axis. The first considered component is shown along the vertical axis, in boxes. The second component of the event is given by the color of the dot.

---

* We omit here many details of data cleaning and data selection steps, which are common for a data mining process.

```
<?xml version="1.0" encoding="UTF-8" ?>
<WorkflowLog xmlns:xsi= http://www.w3.org/2001/XMLSchema-instance…/>
<Process id="GLOBAL" description="This log is converted from the tables
'Process _ Instances and Audit _ Trail _ Entries and
Data _ Attributes _ Process _ Instances and
Data _ Attributes _ Audit _ Trail _ Entries' at the database '
jdbc:odbc:edm13012009' ">
<ProcessInstance id="1663">
<AuditTrailEntry>
<Data>
  <Attribute name="rounded _ result">9</Attribute>
  <Attribute name="trimester _ id">1996-1</Attribute>
  </Data>
  <WorkflowModelElement>2M104</WorkflowModelElement>
  <EventType unknowntype="J">unknown</EventType>
  <Timestamp>1996-10-07T00:00:00.000+02:00</Timestamp>
  <Originator>9</Originator>
  </AuditTrailEntry>
  <AuditTrailEntry>
<Data>
<Attribute name="rounded _ result">8</Attribute>
  <Attribute name="trimester _ id">1996-1</Attribute>
  </Data>
  <WorkflowModelElement>5A015</WorkflowModelElement>
  <EventType unknowntype="J">unknown</EventType>
  <Timestamp>1996-10-08T00:00:00.000+02:00</Timestamp>
  <Originator>8</Originator>
  </AuditTrailEntry>
<AuditTrailEntry>
<Data>
  <Attribute name="rounded _ result">7</Attribute>
  <Attribute name="trimester _ id">1996-1</Attribute>
  </Data>
  <WorkflowModelElement>2Y345</WorkflowModelElement>
  <EventType unknowntype="J">unknown</EventType>
  <Timestamp>1996-10-11T00:00:00.000+02:00</Timestamp>
  <Originator>7</Originator>
  </AuditTrailEntry>
<AuditTrailEntry>
```

FIGURE 9.5
Fragment of the MXML log containing data about students' examinations.

The dotted chart analysis plug-in of ProM is fully configurable (see Figures 9.6 and 9.7). It is always possible to choose which components are considered, enabling us to quickly focus on a particular aspect of the event log. Multiple time options are offered to determine the position of the event in the horizontal time dimension. For example, time can be set to be actual (the time when the event actually happened is used to position the corresponding dot), or relative (the first event of an instance is time-stamped to zero). Sorting of the vertical axes can be done in multiple ways, e.g., based on instance durations or the number of events. Dot coloring is flexible.

The dotted chart analysis can show some interesting patterns present in the event log. For example, if the instance is used as the first component type, the spread of events within each instance can be identified. The users can easily identify which instance takes longer, which instances have many events, etc. We now show how this type of analysis is useful for our data set.

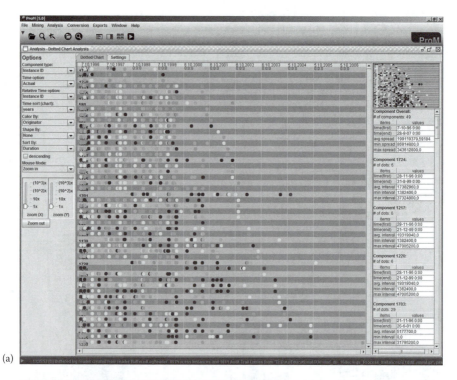

(a)

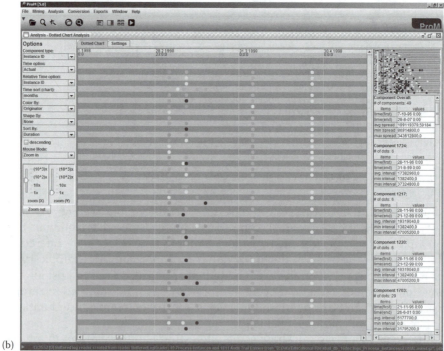

(b)

FIGURE 9.6

DCA of students (who started in the same year) performance; instances (one per student) are sorted by duration (of their studies): (a) all the data and (b) the zoomed region.

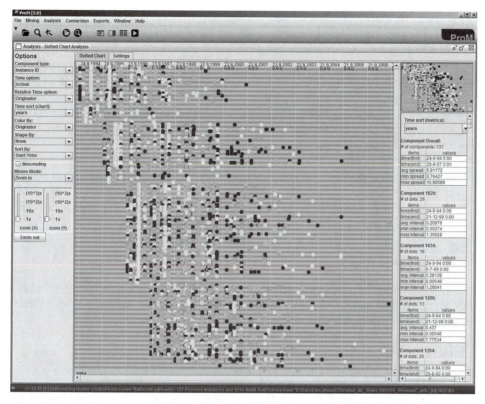

FIGURE 9.7
DCA of four different "generations" of students started at different years.

Recall that in our case, the events in the log represent exams, different log instances correspond to different students, tasks are course names, and originators correspond to the obtained grades.

Figure 9.6 illustrated the output of the dot chart analysis of the subset of students who started their studies in the same year. All the instances (one per student) are sorted by the duration of studies.

A point in black color denotes the situation when a student receives a grade for the particular examination that is not enough to pass the course. The white color denotes grades that are close to borderline but good enough to pass, and the grey color denotes really good grades. We can clearly see from Figure 9.6a that the students who studied longer had (on average) lower grades.

The zoomed region (Figure 9.6b) allows us to see vertical black and white "lines" indicating that some exams were correspondingly hard or easy, and what is important to note, not much discriminating.

Figure 9.7 shows four consequent generations of students. From this figure we are, e.g., able to compare the number of students started in each year, or to find which generation had more good or bad grades in certain study phases.

9.3.3 Conformance Analysis

As we have seen, the dotted chart analysis can provide us with many useful insights on the student data set. However, it cannot (directly) show us which paths the students typically take, what are the choices they make, nor whether the order of exams always agreed with the prerequisites specified in the curriculum. For this, we need some more advanced techniques.

The purpose of conformance analysis is to find out whether the information in the log is as specified by the process model, a set of constraints in the study curricular in our case. As we discussed in the introduction, this analysis may be used to detect deviations, to locate and explain these deviations, and to measure the severity of these deviations. ProM supports various types of conformance analysis; for this chapter, we use the *Conformance Checker* and *LTL Checker* plug-ins.

Conformance checker requires, in addition to an event log, some a priori model. This model may be handcrafted or obtained through process discovery. Whatever its source, ProM provides various ways of checking whether reality (information in the log) conforms to such a model. On the other side, the LTL Checker does not compare a model with the log, but a set of requirements described by the (linear) temporal logic LTL.

9.3.3.1 Conformance Checking

The conformance checker supports analysis of the model fitness, precision (or behavioral appropriateness), and structure (or structural appropriateness) via log replay, state space analysis, and structural analysis.

Generally, the evaluation of conformance can take place in different, orthogonal dimensions. First of all, the behavior allowed by the process model can be assessed. It may be both "too much" and "too little" compared to the behavior recorded in the event log. Second, we can evaluate the structure of the process model.

Fitness analysis is concerned with the investigation whether a process model is able to reproduce all execution sequences that are in the log, or, viewed from the other angle, whether the log traces comply with the description in the model, i.e., the fitness is 100% if every trace in the log "fits" the model description. So, fitness analysis aims at the detection of mismatches between the process specification and the execution of particular process instances.

There are two perspectives of the fitness analysis results: *model* perspective (Figure 9.9) and *log* perspective (Figure 9.10).

From a model perspective, the degree of fitness relates the amount of missing and consumed tokens, and the amount of remaining and produced tokens. So, if the log can be replayed correctly, i.e., there were tokens neither missing nor remaining, fitness is equal to 1. In the worst case, every produced and consumed token is remaining or missing, the fitness is equal to 0.

There are a number of options, which can be used to enhance the visualization of the process model. So the visualization of token counters indicating the missing and remaining tokens during log replay for each place, *failed tasks* (the transitions that were not enabled during log replay and therefore could not be successfully executed) and *remaining tasks* (the transitions that remained enabled after log replay, which indicates non-proper completion of the specified process, and hints that this task should have been executed), *path coverage* and *passed edges* allows seeing popular roots and localizing those parts in the model where the mismatch took place (if any).

From a log perspective, the degree of fitness is estimated as the fraction of successfully executed process instances named *successful execution* and the fraction of properly completed process instances named *proper completion* in each case (taking the number of occurrences per trace into account). The *failed log events* option allows highlighting events that could not be replayed correctly and corresponds to the failed tasks in the model view.

Precision analysis deals with the detection of "extra behavior," discovering for example alternative branches that were never used when executing the process. The precision is 100% if the model "precisely" allows for the behavior observed in the log.

The *simple behavioral appropriateness*, which is based on the mean number of enabled transitions during log replay (the greater the value the less behavior is allowed by the process model and the more precisely the behavior observed in the log is captured), and *the advanced behavioral appropriateness*, which is based on the detection of model flexibility (that is, alternative or parallel behavior) that was not used during real executions observed in the log, are used to measure the degree of precision (or behavioral appropriateness).

Furthermore, there are a number of options, which can be used to enhance the visualization of the process model; by the indication of *always/never precedes* and *always/never follows* options, we can highlight corresponding activities.

Besides fitness and precision, the *structural properties* of the model and its semantics can be analyzed. In a process model, structure is the syntactic means by which behavior (i.e., the semantics) can be specified, using the vocabulary of the modeling language (for example, routing nodes such as AND or exclusive OR). However, often there are several syntactic ways to express the same behavior, and there may be representations easier or harder to understand. Clearly, this evaluation dimension highly depends on the process modeling formalism and is difficult to assess in an objective way.

We now show how conformance checking can be used to check whether the students follow the study curriculum. The idea is to construct a Petri net model of (a small part of) the curriculum, and then fit it into the plug-in to look for discrepancies.

A study curriculum typically describes different possibilities students have and contains different types of constrains that students are expected to obey. The most popular constraints perhaps are the course prerequisites, i.e., we may want to prohibit a student to take a more advanced course before an introductory course is passed. Figure 9.8 shows a very small part of the study curriculum in the form of the Petri net (drawn also with the ProM plug-in), representing a constraint that each student has to take at least two courses from 2Y420, 2F725, and 2IH20. In general, any *m-out-of-n* items constraint can be expressed with a similar approach.

Figure 9.9 gives the output of the conformance checking (the Model view) of the corresponding Petri nets from Figure 9.8. We can see from the figure the places in the model where problems occurred during the log replay and many interesting characteristics, including path coverage, passed edges, failed and remaining tasks, and token counters. In

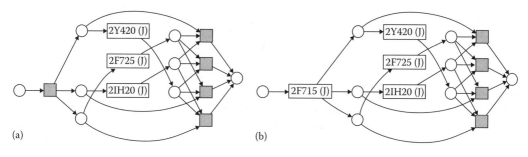

FIGURE 9.8
Petri nets representing a small part of the study curricular: (a) *2 out of 3* constraint and (b) *2 out of 3* constraint with prerequisite constraint.

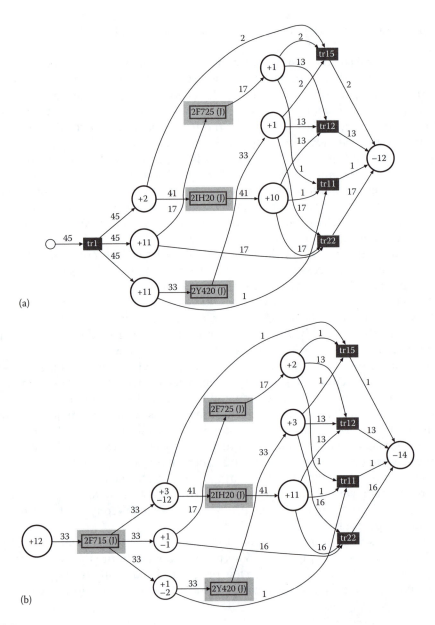

FIGURE 9.9
Conformance analysis of the Petri nets from Figure 9.8—model view: (a) *2 out of 3* constraint and (b) *2 out of 3* constraint with the prerequisite.

Figure 9.9b, we see that the prerequisite constraint that 2F715 should be taken (and passed) before *2 out of 3* choice is to be made was violated quite often. The course 2IH20 was passed in 12 cases (2F725 once and 2Y420 twice) before the prerequisite 2F715. Figure 9.9a on the other hand indicates that there are no problems in the log (the *2 out of 3* constraint was always satisfied).

Figure 9.10b shows the log view of the result where, for the case with the prerequisite constrains, we can see some log replay problems (marked here as dark rectangles) occurred

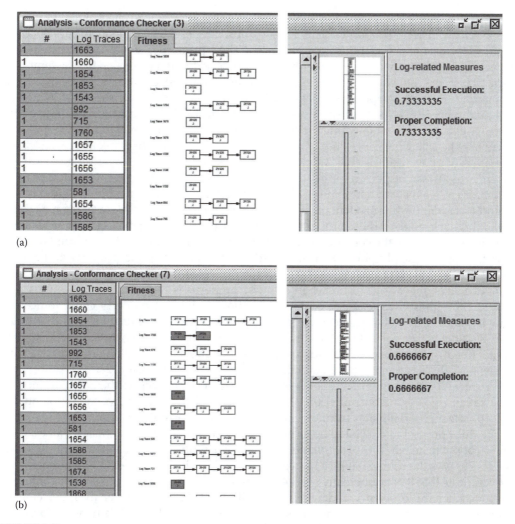

FIGURE 9.10
Conformance analysis of the Petri nets from Figure 9.8—log view: (a) two courses out of three constraint and (b) two courses out of three constraint with prerequisite constraint.

in the log (instances 2, 6, 8, and 12). Figure 9.10a shows no "dark" tasks as the log complies with the first model.

9.3.3.2 LTL Analysis

As already explained, to check whether the order of exams (the observed reality) had always complied with the curriculum (the assumed behavior), we can apply the conformance. However, the actual model of the curriculum rarely exists, and so a different compliance check is needed. Moreover, we sometimes want to answer very complicated questions about our data set that, in general, would be hard to fit into any of the existing forms of conformance checking. In these situations, the LTL Checker plug-in of ProM can be used.

The LTL Checker plug-in is a log-analysis plug-in that allows us to check whether the log satisfies a given set of properties. This plug-in, thus, does not need a model to run, but only requires the user to define the desired properties. These properties, which in our case should reflect the requirements of the curriculum, are described in (an extension of) the temporal logic LTL. In the context of a generic log, this powerful and very expressive logic can specify things like "if task A happens, then task B will happen within 5 time units," "Task A always eventually performs," or "Person A never performs task B." As we now show, using this logic we can also verify many interesting properties of our educational data set.

We use the LTL Checker to check (1) if there are any students that took more than three exams on one day; (2) if the rule "Logic 1 must be passed before the exam for Logic 2 can be taken" was always respected (prerequisite check); (3) if there is a course A that is a prerequisite for course B such that many students have got a low grade in A but a high grade in B; and (4) to identify the students that have passed some course twice, second time with a lower/higher grade. All these properties can be easily coded using the LTL language of the plug-in; an excerpt of the code file is given in Figure 9.11. This file can be imported into the user interface of the plug-in, which shows a description of a selected property and allows the user to add the input parameters (in our case, the courses).

Figure 9.12a shows the result when the first property is checked. As it is impossible to take more than three exams per day, a violation of the first property could indicate a flaw in the way the data has been entered into the database. The result shows that there are 38 students (i.e., correct case instances) that satisfy this property, and 11 students that do not (incorrect case instances). We can select each student now, and find the day when he or she took these exams; one such situation is highlighted in Figure 9.12a.

Figure 9.12b shows that all students but one have been respecting the curriculum, and have taken, e.g., Logic 2 only after they have passed Logic 1. Note that we could potentially incorporate all prerequisites from the curriculum in this formula.

The third property is meant to be used to check whether some prerequisites make sense, and to possibly help in future adaptations of the curriculum. The case when many students are able to pass the course B with a high grade, even though they almost failed the course A, may indicate that B does not really need A as a prerequisite. Of course, if B is just a continuation of A, then this problem could indicate a significant difference between the requirements for these courses. In either case, normalization issues may need to be taken into account.

The fourth property simply checks whether someone was trying to pass an exam that he or she has passed already. Finally, the last property can be used to advise students to either try or not try with another exam if they are not satisfied with their current grade (or in a different setting to see whether many student are willing to improve their grade).

Note that the LTL Checker plug-in can also be used to filter out some unwanted instances (i.e., the students) from the log. We have indeed used this feature for the dotted chart analysis, where we selected the "good" students as log instances that do not satisfy the LTL formula.

9.3.3.3 Process Discovery with Fuzzy Miner

The techniques of conformance checking are very useful if we want to check whether some property holds of the log. The techniques of process discovery aim at extracting the complete model (a Petri net, e.g.), thus capturing all relevant properties. For our educational data set, these techniques can be used to extract the actual (i.e., the followed) curriculum.

ProM offers several plug-ins that can be used for process discovery from an event log. These plug-ins have been designed to mine different aspect of the log, and to use different

```
formula exists_ student_ taking_ more_ than_ three_ exams_ per_ day():=
{<h2>Is there a student taking more than three exams per day?</h2>}
            exists[d: day |
                <> ( (d == day /\ _ O ( (d == day /\ _ O (d == day) ) ) ) )];
formula course_ c1_ always_ before_ c2(c1: course, c2:course):=
{<h2>Prerequisite check: Is the course c1 always taken before the course c2?</h2>}
      (<> (course == c2)
       ->
       ! ( (course != c1 _ U course == c2) )
      );
formula prerequisite_ with_ low_ grade_ but_ course_ with_ high_ grade(c1:course,
c2:course):=
{<h2>Can a low grade for a prerequisite follow a high grade for the course?</h2>}
      (course_ c1_ always_ before_ c2(c1,c2)
       /\
       <> ( ( (c1 == course /\ grade <= 60)
           /\
           <> ( (c2 == course /\ grade >= 80) )
           )
         )
      );
formula exams_ passed_ twice():=
{<h2>Can an exam be passed twice?</h2>}
    exists[c: course | <> ( ( (c == course /\ grade >= 60)
                          /\ _ O (<> ( (c == course) ) ) ) )];
formula exams_ passed_ twice_ second_ grade_ higher():=
{<h2>Exams that are passed twice and the second time the grade was higher?</h2>}
    exists[c: course | ( (<> ( ( (c == course /\ grade == 60)
                        /\ _ O (<> ( (c == course /\ grade > 60) ) ) ) )
              \/
               <> ( ( (c == course /\ grade == 70)
                  /\ _ O (<> ( (c == course /\ grade > 70) ) ) ) ) )
           \/
            (<> ( ( (c == course /\ grade == 80)
               /\ _ O (<> ( (c == course /\ grade > 80) ) ) ) )
           \/
            <> ( ( (c == course /\ grade == 90)
               /\ _ O (<> ( (c == course /\ grade > 90) ) ) ) ) ) )];
```

FIGURE 9.11
Conformance analysis of constraints expressed with LTL.

algorithms to achieve so. As our log is expected to be highly unstructured, and to contain a lot of rare and uninteresting behavior, we decided to demonstrate the use of the Fuzzy Miner plug-in. This, fully parameterizable, plug-in has capabilities to abstract from, or to aggregate, less significant behavior, focusing only on the important parts. In this way, we are able to avoid the unreadable, "spaghetti-like," process models that would result from using some other (standard) discovery plug-ins. Of course, if the visual representation of the process is not an ultimate goal (if the model is, e.g., not to be read by humans), other plug-ins would apply here as well.

Mining with Fuzzy Miner is an interactive and explorative process, where the user configures the parameters until the desired level of abstraction is reached. There are several metrics that can be taken into account for mining, like frequency, routing, distance, or data, each with a desired strength.

The graph notation used is fairly straightforward. Square nodes represent event classes, with their significance (maximal value is 1.0) provided below the event class name. Less

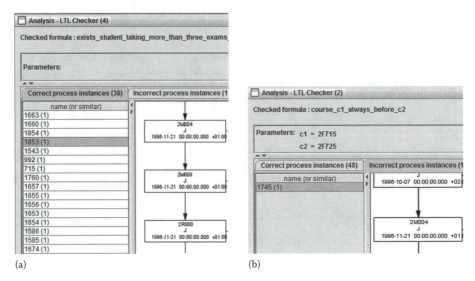

FIGURE 9.12
Output of the LTL checker: (a) not more than three exams per day and (b) a course prerequisite check.

significant and lowly correlated behavior is discarded from the process model, i.e., nodes and arcs that fall into this category are removed from the graph. Coherent groups of less significant but highly correlated behavior are represented in aggregated form as clusters. Cluster nodes are represented as octagons, displaying the mean significance of the clustered elements and their amount. The internal components of clusters and their structure can be explored by clicking on the corresponding cluster nodes. Links, or arcs, drawn between nodes are decorated with the significance and correlation represented by each relation. Additionally, arcs are colored in a gray shade; the lower the significance of the relation the lighter the gray.

We used Fuzzy Miner in a very modest way and included only the metric related to the total frequency of a task, i.e., in our case to the "popularity" of a course. Figure 9.13 shows two discovered models of the curriculum with different threshold values that determine the level of abstraction (by grouping together the courses that were infrequently taken and thus focusing only on the important parts).

The semantics of Fuzzy Miner models is similar to the semantics of Petri nets. So, the models from Figure 9.13 allow us to see all the paths the students took and the choices they made (with corresponding frequencies).

One nice feature of the Fuzzy Miner plug-in is its ability to show the animation of instances (a snapshot is given in the right upper part of Figure 9.3) flowing through the process model (either student by student or all at once). The domain experts say that this is one of the best ways to illustrate the most common paths.

9.4 Discussion and Further Work

Different institutions involved in traditional education or e-learning (or both) started to collect more and more data about various aspects of educational processes. Data-mining techniques have been successfully applied to different types of educational data and have

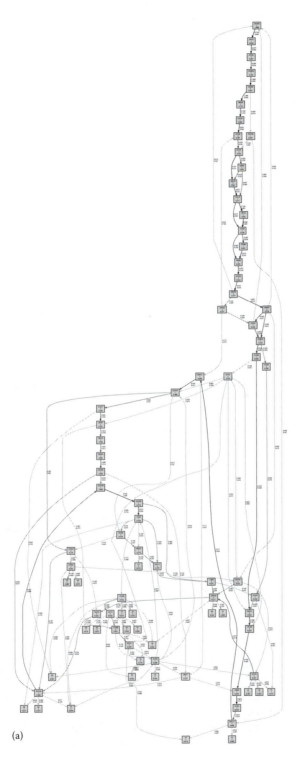

(a)

FIGURE 9.13
The outputs of the Fuzzy Miner plug-in with two different levels of abstraction.

(*continued*)

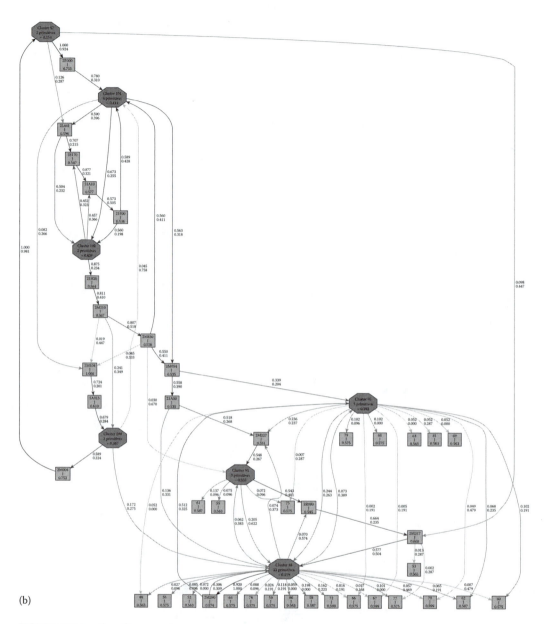

(b)

FIGURE 9.13 (continued)

helped to address many issues with use of traditional classification, clustering, and association analysis techniques.

Process perspective in educational domains has also drawn attention of several researchers; however, most of the traditional intelligent data analysis approaches discussed so far in the context of educational data mining rarely focus on a process as a whole.

In this chapter, we presented a comprehensive introduction into process mining framework and ProM tool and we discussed some of its potential for extracting knowledge from a particular type of the educational information system. We considered only a simplified educational processes reflecting students behavior in terms of their examination traces consisting of a sequence of course, grade, and timestamp triplets for each student. However, we hope that a reader can see how the same technique can be applied to many other types of datasets including learning resources usage logs, various interaction logs (e.g., with an intelligent tutoring system), etc. For example, in [4] we illustrated some of the potential of process mining techniques applied to online assessment data, where students in one of the tests were able to receive tailored immediate elaborative feedback after answering each of the questions in the test one by one in a strict order, and in the other test to receive no feedback but to answer question in a flexible order.

ProM 5.0 provides a plugable environment for process mining, offering a wide variety of plug-ins for process discovery, conformance checking, model extension, and model transformation. Our further work includes the development of EDM-tailored ProM plug-ins, which, from the one hand, would help to bring process mining tools closer to the domain experts (i.e., educational specialists and researchers who not necessarily have all the technical background), helping them analyze educational processes in a principled way based on formal modeling, and from the other hand would allow to better address some of the EDM-specific challenges related to data preprocessing, namely, dealing with duplicate events, "synonyms," parallelism, pseudo-dependencies, relatively large diversity, and small sample. One particular focus is on integrating domain knowledge into process mining. Some preliminary work in this direction can be found in [13], where we introduced a new domain-driven framework for educational process mining, which assumes that a set of *pattern templates* can be predefined to focus the mining in a desired way and make it more effective and efficient.

Acknowledgments

This work is supported by NWO. We would like to thank STU for providing the data, and the many people involved in the development of ProM.

References

1. Dekker, G., Pechenizkiy M., and Vleeshouwers, J., Predicting students drop out: A case study, in *Proceedings of the 2nd International Conference on Educational Data Mining* (EDM'09), Cordoba, Spain, pp. 41–50, July 1–3, 2009.
2. Zafra, A. and Ventura, S., Predicting student grades in learning management systems with multiple instance genetic programming, in *Proceedings of the 2nd International Conference on Educational Data Mining* (EDM'09), Cordoba, Spain, pp. 309–318, July 1–3, 2009.
3. Perera, D., Kay, J., Koprinska, I., Yacef, K., and Zaïane, O.R., Clustering and sequential pattern mining of online collaborative learning data. *IEEE Trans. Knowl. Data Eng.* 21(6), 759–772, 2009.
4. Pechenizkiy, M., Trcka, N., Vasilyeva, E., van der Aalst, W., and De Bra, P., Process mining the student assessment data, in *Proceedings of the 2nd International Conference on Educational Data Mining* (EDM'09), Cordoba, Spain, pp. 279–288, July 1–3, 2009.
5. Romero, C., Ventura, S., and García, E., Data mining in course management systems: MOODLE case study and tutorial. *Comput. Educ.* 51, 368–384, 2008.
6. Romero, C. and S. Ventura, S., Educational data mining: A survey from 1995 to 2005. *Expert Syst. Appl.* 33(1), 135–146, 2007.

7. van Dongen, B.F., de Medeiros, A.K.A., Verbeek, H.M.W., Weijters, A.J.M.M., and van der Aalst, W.M.P., The ProM framework: A new era in process mining tool support, in *Proceedings of the ICATPN 2005*, Ciardo, G., Darondeau, P., Eds., LNCS 3536, Springer, Heidelberg, Germany, 2005, pp. 444–454.
8. Rozinat, A. and van der Aalst, W.M.P., Conformance checking of processes based on monitoring real behavior. *Inform. Syst.* 33(1), 64–95, 2008.
9. van der Aalst, W.M.P., Weijters, A.J.M.M., and Maruster, L., Workflow mining: Discovering process models from event logs. *IEEE Trans. Knowl. Data Eng.* 16(9), 1128–1142, 2004.
10. Günther, C.W. and van der Aalst, W.M.P., Fuzzy mining: Adaptive process simplification based on multi-perspective metrics, in *Proceedings of the International Conference on Business Process Management (BPM 2007)*, Alonso, G., Dadam, P., and Rosemann, M., Eds., LNCS 4714, Springer-Verlag, Berlin, Germany, 2007, pp. 328–343.
11. Song, M. and van der Aalst, W.M.P., Supporting process mining by showing events at a glance, in *Proceedings of the 7th Annual Workshop on Information Technologies and Systems (WITS'07)*, Chari, K. and Kumar, A., Eds., Montreal, Canada, 2007, pp. 139–145.
12. Günther, C.W. and van der Aalst, W.M.P., A generic import framework for process event logs, in *Proceedings of the Business Process Management Workshop*, 2006, pp. 81–92 (see also http://promimport.sourceforge.net/).
13. Trcka, N. and Pechenizkiy, M., From local patterns to global models: Towards domain driven educational process mining, in *Proceedings of the 9th International Conference on Intelligent Systems Design and Applications (ISDA'09)*, Pisa, Italy, IEEE CS Press, November 30–December 2, 2009.

10

Modeling Hierarchy and Dependence among Task Responses in Educational Data Mining

Brian W. Junker

CONTENTS

10.1 Introduction

Modern educational systems, especially those mediated by human–computer interaction systems such as web-based courses, learning content management systems, and adaptive and intelligent educational systems, make large data streams available by recording student actions at microgenetic [25, p. 100] timescales* for days, weeks, and months at a time. Educational data mining (EDM) [31] aims to exploit these data streams to provide feedback and guidance to students and teachers and to provide data for educational researchers to better understand the nature of teaching and learning.

Most empirical problems in EDM can be decomposed into three types: making inferences about the characteristics of tasks (e.g., does the task measure what we want? does it do so well or poorly? for which students? etc.); making inferences about the characteristics of students (e.g., what skills, proficiencies, or other knowledge components (KCs) do they possess? does an intervention improve performance?); and making predictions about students' performance on future tasks (e.g., which students will perform well in a downstream assessment?). Unfortunately, progress on any of these inferential problems is hampered by two sources of statistical dependence. First, different student actions may not provide independent pieces of information about that individual student. For example, if the student

---

* That is, recording students' actions at high frequency as they are learning rather than taking a single cross-sectional measurement or infrequent longitudinal measurements.

correctly calculates the area from the lengths of the two sides of the rectangle, we may get little additional independent information from another multiplication task. Second, there may be dependence among multiple responses (from the same or different students), due to common cognitive, social, or institutional contexts. The two kinds of dependence may be combined hierarchically in building models for educational data, and each kind of dependence should be accounted for in making any kind of inferences in EDM.

In this chapter, I illustrate the consequences of failing to account for these sources of dependence in making inferences about task and student characteristics, using examples from the literature. In Section 10.2.1, I have expressed the cost in terms of the number of additional tasks that students would need to perform, in order to achieve the precision promised by an excessively simple model. In Section 10.3.1, I have highlighted a substantial classification bias that arises from the use of a model that ignores hierarchy. In Section 10.3.2, I consider an example in which ignoring dependence produces a false statistical significance for the effect of an intervention. I am not aware of correspondingly careful studies of predictive inference using under-specified models. In situations in which the predictive criterion is itself less complex (e.g., [3] and [18]), simpler models that ignore dependence and hierarchy can be quite successful. When models in EDM are expected to predict fine-grained outcomes, or make precise and accurate predictions over a range of outcomes, I expect that accounting for dependence and hierarchy will be as important for prediction as it already is for other EDM inferential tasks.

10.2 Dependence between Task Responses

10.2.1 Conditional Independence and Marginal Dependence

Figure 10.1 provides three questions or tasks that may be encountered in one section of the Assistment online tutoring system [39]. It is easy to infer that this section of the tutor has something to do with elementary probability calculations. However, no one question in the figure is dispositive about the student's knowledge of (or progress in learning) elementary probability.

Moreover, whatever our beliefs going in about how hard or easy these questions are, if we know how a student does on one of these three problems, we would revise our prediction of how the student would do on the others. For example, we may feel that a student

---

1. *Of the 640 students in a school, 428 were born in Massachusetts. If a newspaper reporter interviews one student at random, which is the best estimate of the probability that the student was born in Massachusetts?*
2. *A bag contains three red, two green, and four blue balls. John is going to draw out a ball without looking in the bag. What is the probability that he will draw either a green or a blue ball?*
3. *A bag contains three blue, four red, and two white marbles. Karin is going to draw out a marble without looking in the bag. What is the probability that she will not draw a red marble?*

FIGURE 10.1

Three questions encountered in the Assistments online tutoring system. (From Worcester Polytechnic Institute, *Assistment: Assisting Students with their Assessments*, 2009. Retrieved January 2009 from http://www.assistment.org/. With permission.)

who correctly answers question #2 in Figure 10.1 is much more likely to get question #3 correct, and somewhat more likely to get question #1 correct. This is an example of *non-independence* between student responses. It is not certain, however, that the student will get either problem #3 or problem #1 correct; the dependence between responses is clearly probabilistic, not deterministic.

Let y_{ij} denote the scored response or performance of the ith student ($i=1,\ldots, N$) to the jth question or task ($j=1,\ldots, J$). Because the outcome y_{ij} is probabilistic, we specify a stochastic model for it,

$$P\left[y_{ij}=y\right]=f\left(y|\theta_i,\beta_j,\psi\right), \tag{10.1}$$

where

    y is a possible score or coding of the student response
    θ_i is a parameter (or parameters) related to the student
    β_j is a parameter (or parameters) related to the task
    ψ is whatever parameters remain (here and throughout, we use ψ to represent incidental
        parameters in any part of the model)

Any of these parameters may be continuous or discrete, unidimensional or multidimensional, or missing.

If $y_{ij} \in \{0, 1\}$, then $f(y|\theta_i, \beta_j, \psi)$ has the general form

$$f\left(y|\theta_i,\beta_j,\psi\right)=g\left(\theta_i,\beta_j,\psi\right)^y\left[1-g\left(\theta_i,\beta_j,\psi\right)\right]^{(1-y)},$$

where $g(\theta_i, \beta_j, \psi)=f(1|\theta_i, \beta_j, \psi)$. Examples of models of this type include

- *Item response models* (IRMs) [35], also called item response theory (IRT) models, typically take $g(\theta_i,\beta_j,\psi)$ to be a logistic or other sigmoidal function, such as

$$g\left(\theta_i,\beta_j,\psi\right)=\frac{\exp\left[a_j\left(\theta_i-b_j\right)\right]}{1+\exp\left[a_j\left(\theta_i-b_j\right)\right]}, \tag{10.2}$$

where

    θ_i is a continuous index of student i's general facility in the task domain (perhaps interpretable as a crude measure of the aggregation of skills or other knowledge components needed to succeed in that domain)
    $\beta_j=(a_j, b_j)$ characterizes the task (a_j is related to the power of the task response to classify high/low facility students; and b_j is a measure of task difficulty—it indicates the value of θ for which a student has a 50% chance of succeeding on the task)

When θ_i has only one component, the model is called a unidimensional IRM; otherwise it is a multidimensional IRM. Examples of applications of IRMs to online tutoring data include Ayers and Junker [3] and Feng et al. [11]. Chang and Ying [8] consider the use of IRMs to select "the next task" in a computerized adaptive test (CAT).

- *Latent class models* (LCMs) [14], also known as latent class analysis (LCA) models, take θ_i as a discrete "class membership" variable, $\theta_i \in \{1, ..., C\}$, and take $\beta_j = (b_{j1}, ..., b_{jC})$ to be the success probabilities in each class, so that

$$g\left(\theta_i, \beta_j, \psi\right) = b_{j\theta_i}. \tag{10.3}$$

  That is to say, if student i is in class $c(\theta_i = c)$, then $P[y_{ij} = 1] = b_{jc}$. LCMs have been used extensively for decades; Langeheine and Rost [19] and Rost and Langeheine [30] provide recent reviews, and van der Maas and Straatemeier [36] give an example of using LCMs to detect different cognitive strategies (see also [25, Chapter 4]).

- *Cognitive diagnosis models* (CDMs) [7] posit a set of latent, discrete skills, or more generally KCs, that underlie task performance. A typical model is the reparameterized unified model (RUM) [7, pp. 1010ff.], in which

$$g\left(\theta_i, \beta_j, \psi\right) = \pi_j \prod_{k=1}^{k} r_{jk}^{(1-\theta_{ik})q_{jk}}, \tag{10.4}$$

  where
  $\theta_i \in \{0, 1\}^K$ is a vector of K binary indicators of presence/absence of each KC
  $\beta_j = (\pi_j, r_{j1}, ..., r_{jK})$ contains the probability π_j of success if all KCs are present and the discounts r_{jk} associated with absence of each KC
  $\psi = Q = [q_{jk}]$ is an incidence matrix indicating connections between KCs and this y_{ij} [4,34]

It is easy to see that this model is also an LCM with $C = 2^K$ latent classes and constraints on the b_{jc}'s determined by the right-hand side of (10.3) [20].

Other extensions and elaborations of these may be found in [33]. For example, models for discrete multi-valued $y_{ij} \in \{1,..., R\}$ [41, pp. 115ff.], continuous y_{ij} [40], and other forms of y_{ij} are also in use.

The generative model for J tasks is usually obtained by multiplying the per-task models together,

$$P\left(y_{i1},..., y_{ij} | \theta_i, \beta, \psi\right) = \prod_{j=1}^{J} f\left(y_{ij} | \theta_i, \beta_j, \psi\right), \tag{10.5}$$

where $\beta = (\beta_1,..., \beta_J)$. In probabilistic language, we say the responses are conditionally independent given the parameters θ, β, and ψ. Figure 10.2 shows the typical structure of (10.5) for a unidimensional IRM; and Figure 10.3 shows a possible structure for a CDM.* Especially in the latter case, it is clear that these models can be thought of as layers in a Bayes net with observable (y_{ij}) and hidden (θ_i) nodes and links between them characterized by β and ψ. A formal approach linking Bayes net modeling to educational assessment, and leading to many interesting elaborations of these models, is provided by Mislevy et al. [23].

---

* Following the usual semantics for graphical models, if deleting a subset S of nodes in the graph produces disconnected subgraphs, then the subgraphs are conditionally independent given S [10].

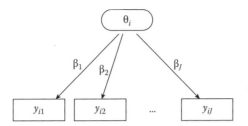

FIGURE 10.2
Typical conditional independence structure for a single latent variable θ_i and multiple task responses y_{ij} (e.g., unidimensional item response model). β_j's control model for the edges of the graph, as in (10.1). Directed edges point to variables that are conditionally independent, given the variables from which the edges emanate.

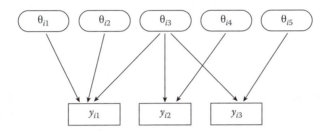

FIGURE 10.3
Typical conditional independence structure for multiple discrete latent KCs $\theta_{i1}, \ldots, \theta_{iK}$ ($K = 5$ in this example) and multiple task responses y_{ij}. β_j's (not shown, to reduce clutter) control model for the edges of the graph, as in (10.1).

Given their differing roles, it is convenient, and important practically, to distinguish inferential tasks involving β and ϕ, which relate to the structure of the model, from inferential tasks involving θ_i, which relate to the cognitive status of a student, as defined by that model. Methodology for estimating β and ϕ is wide and deep, ranging from direct maximum likelihood, E–M, and variational methods, to moment-based clustering, simulation, and Monte Carlo methods. While it is beyond the scope of this chapter to review these methods (useful general reviews and tutorials are provided by Andrieu et al. [2], Minka [21,22], and Murphy [24]), two remarks are worth making. First, it is still challenging to determine entirely empirically what the dependence structure of multivariate response data is. Moreover, there is a data/model complexity tradeoff: if there is too little data, it is difficult to (dis)confirm simpler models that ignore some dependencies, and it may not generalize well to larger data sets; on the other hand, if there is too much data, conventional estimation algorithms may become intractable. (Weaver [38] considers this problem for ACT-R models, which underlie many online tutoring systems, for example.) Second, however, it is often possible to anticipate and build the right kind of dependence structure a priori into the model, which facilitates estimation of β and ϕ and leads to better inferences about θ. Indeed, inference on θ with the wrong dependence structure, or assuming independence when it is not true, can lead to unrealistic conclusions about the precision and accuracy of θ estimates.

To see the kinds of structures that are fruitful to build into the models, consider the ideal setting in which β and ψ may be taken to be known, from good training data or reliable expert opinion; however, θ_i is not known and is the object of inference. Usually, it is possible to specify a prior distribution for θ_i, for example, indicating the relative likelihood of various values of θ, the distribution of θ in a student population of interest, etc. In that case, the generative model for the two-stage "experiment" of randomly sampling a student and observing that student's task response is

$$P_{\beta,\psi}\left(y_{i1},\ldots,y_{iJ}\right)=\int P\left(y_{i1},\ldots,y_{iJ}\mid\theta_i,\beta,\psi\right)p\left(\theta_i\right)d\theta_i, \qquad (10.6)$$

where $P(y_{i1},\ldots,y_{iJ}\mid\theta_i,\beta,\psi)$ is as in (10.5). If θ_i is discrete instead of continuous, the integral here should be replaced with a sum.

The dependence between task responses suggested in Figure 10.1 now becomes clear, using components from (10.6). For example,

$$P_{\beta,\psi}\left(y_{i1}\mid y_{i2}\right)=\frac{P_{\beta,\psi}\left(y_{i1}\mid y_{i2}\right)}{P_{\beta,\psi}\left(y_{i2}\right)}=\frac{\int P\left(y_{i1},y_{i2}\mid\theta_i,\beta,\psi\right)p\left(\theta_i\right)d\theta_i}{\int P\left(y_{i2}\mid\theta_i,\beta,\psi\right)p\left(\theta_i\right)d\theta_i}, \qquad (10.7)$$

and in most cases this will depend on the value of y_{i2}. Whenever, as would usually be the case, $P[y_{ij}=1]$ is a nondecreasing function of θ_i, there can be a very strong positive dependence between the y_{ij}'s for each i, as shown by Holland and Rosenbaum [15].

The dependence here is a mathematical consequence of not "clamping" θ_i to a fixed value. If we assume θ_i is fixed, then we would use components from (10.5) instead of (10.6) in (10.7), and we would find that $P_{\beta,\psi}(y_{i1}\mid y_{i2})=P_{\beta,\psi}(y_{i1})$, i.e., the responses are independent when θ_i is fixed (and β and ψ are known). This is the psychometric principle of *local independence*.

If we wish to make inferences about θ_i, for fixed and known β and ψ, we have a choice between working with (10.5) or (10.6). Generally speaking, if $y_{i1},\ldots,y_{iJ}$ are positively correlated as in (10.6), they will not provide J independent pieces of information, and inferences about θ_i will be less certain—higher standard errors of estimation—than if the y_{ij} are independent as in (10.5). On the other hand, the prior distribution $p(\theta_i)$ in (10.6) can incorporate additional information about the student and drive standard errors of estimation down again. The decision about whether to use (10.5) or (10.6) may depend to some extent on the tradeoff between the effects of dependence and prior information on inferences about θ_i.

10.2.2 Nuisance Dependence

Extra dependence between scored task responses may arise because of commonalities in the tasks or task scoring that are not captured by the latent quantity θ of interest. For example:

- If tasks can be grouped by context (e.g., reading comprehension questions related to the same reading passage) or other features into $c=1,\ldots,C$ groups or "testlets" of J_c tasks each, the model (10.5) no longer holds exactly, and instead a model of the form

$$P\left(y_{i1},\ldots,y_{iJ}\mid\theta_i,\beta,\psi\right)=\prod_{c=1}^{C}\int\prod_{jc=1}^{J_c}f\left(y_{ijc}\mid\theta_i,\gamma_{i(c)},\beta_j,\psi\right)p\left(\gamma_{i(c)}\right)d\gamma_{i(c)} \qquad (10.8)$$

may hold, in which $\gamma_{i(c)}$ is an additional latent variable interpretable as individual facility unique to each context c. Averaging over the new latent variables $\gamma_{i(c)}$ induces additional dependence in the data, increasing standard errors of estimation for θ_i. Wang et al. [37] explore this model and its consequences for inference.

Wang et al. [37, Figure 1] illustrate the effect of ignoring context effects in a computer skills assessment in which students perform approximately 10 tasks in each of four situations. Ignoring this grouping of tasks in the model understates the standard errors for estimating students' computer proficiencies by a factor of about 1.4 for typical students. The number of tasks performed by students would need to roughly double, to obtain estimates with standard errors this small, using a model that correctly accounts for the context effects.

- If students' task performances are rated by multiple raters of varying quality (e.g., human raters), then a variable similar to γ_{ic} in (10.8) can be incorporated to model individual differences in severity and internal consistency of multiple raters. As before, the additional dependence due to averaging over $\gamma_{i(j)}$ increases standard errors of estimation for θ_i. Patz et al. [26] develop this approach in detail and compare it to models that ignore this extra dependence.

  Patz et al. [26, Table 3] show, in a simulated example, that 95% intervals fail to cover four out of five true task "difficulty" parameters (β_j's) when dependence due to rater variability is ignored in the model—indicating severe estimation bias—whereas a model that accounts for this dependence covers all of the β_j's with mostly narrower intervals.* In the same example [26, Table 4], they show that 95% intervals for estimating θ_i's are, on average, about half as wide in the model that ignores the dependence structure,[†] as in the model that accounts for it—indicating unrealistic optimism in the simpler model about how precisely θ_i's have been estimated. In order to obtain intervals this narrow in the model that correctly accounts for the dependence, we would need roughly three times as many task responses from each student.

- If multiple tasks are generated from the same task model (sometimes referred to as "clones" or "morphs" or "item families"; e.g., questions #2 and #3 in Figure 10.1), then they may share dependence similar to that of (10.8), but expressed through latent variables $\gamma_{j(c)}$ for the common part of β_j for tasks from the same item model c. Johnson and Sinharay [16] explore this model in detail. In empirical examples (Figures 10.3 and 10.4), they find that ignoring this source of dependence produces biased and less certain estimates of task parameters (β_j's) analogous to those in Patz et al. [26], but has a negligible effect on inferences for θ_i's.

In each situation, some aspect of the way the tasks are generated or scored produces extra dependence that increases our uncertainty (standard error) in making inferences about θ_i. Whether the increase is enough to worry about depends on preliminary analysis in each possible context. Johnson et al. [17] provide a useful review of this class of models.

---

* The narrower intervals arise from "borrowing" or "pooling" information across multiple ratings of the same task, in the dependence model, for estimating that task's difficulty.

† The intervals are narrower because the simpler model treats each task rating as an independent piece of information; whereas different ratings of the same task do not contribute independent information about students' cognitive status.

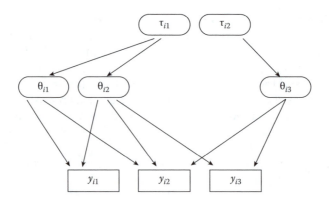

FIGURE 10.4
Hierarchical elaboration of the model in Figure 10.3. Here τ_{i1} and τ_{i2} are higher-order latent variables that model dependence between groups of KC variables θ_{iK}, and again y_{ij} are task responses.

10.2.3 Aggregation Dependence

The dependence illustrated in (10.7) is not only due to Bayesian modeling assumptions. As illustrated by Darroch et al. [9, equation (7)], the same type of dependence among response variables occurs whenever many students are aggregated together into a single data set. Even if (10.5) is the correct model for each individual, the corresponding model for a sample of N such individuals would be of the form

$$\frac{1}{N}\sum_{i=1}^{N}\prod_{j=1}^{J}f\left(y_{ij}\,|\,\theta_i,\beta_j,\psi\right), \qquad (10.9)$$

which exhibits the same sort of nonindependence among response variables as (10.6) (since, in essence, it replaces integration against the density $p(\theta_i)$ with summation against the uniform weights $1/N$).

This dependence due to aggregation is critical to many data-driven approaches to inferring latent structure. Desmarais' POKS algorithm, for example as described in [6], finds "surmise" or prerequisite relationships among tasks by testing for aggregation dependence, which can be traced to latent structure if desired. Pavlik et al. [27] apply a similar procedure to improve the KC model of an existing tutor.

10.3 Hierarchy

While statistical dependence between task responses may be due to a common source of uncertainty, as in (10.6), or to a common source of variation that we do not try to condition on in the model, as in (10.8) or (10.9), tasks may also become dependent because of a hierarchical relationship between them, or between the KCs that underlie performance on them. I now turn to these sources of dependence.

10.3.1 Hierarchy of Knowledge Structure

When multiple KCs are present, as in Figure 10.3, a natural assumption in the absence of additional information is that the KCs themselves occur independently of one another. However, in many situations, we may be willing to assume more.

If there is a strong empirical or substantive theory about which KCs tend to be learned together, a long-standing approach to encoding this is to use a Bayes net with at least two layers of discrete hidden nodes; this is a hierarchical version of the model in Figure 10.3. In such models, the KCs themselves are dependent, because of the common between-persons variation at higher levels of the Bayes net. Schematically, the model will be of the form of Figure 10.4, where the directed edges again lead to variables that are conditionally independent, given the variables they lead from. Pearl [28] did much to formalize this approach; Almond et al. [1] recently reviewed the use of hierarchical Bayes net modeling in educational assessments generally.

Even when there is not much theory about which KCs go together, there may still be positive dependence among the KCs. A simpler modeling structure may be appropriate then, for example, a model of the form of Figure 10.4 with only one continuous τ_i connected to all the KC variables θ_{ik}. This might arise, for example, if KC's are generally learned in the same order by most students as a curriculum progresses from skills that are easier to master to those that are more difficult. Variations of this model, which can also be viewed as stacking Figure 10.2 on top of Figure 10.3, have been explored by de la Torre and Douglas [5].

In an application of the DINA model to fraction subtraction data, they show [5, Tables 9 and 10] that ignoring this dependence between KCs has relatively little impact on estimates of slip and guess parameters in the DINA model, but tends to vastly overstate the proportion of students who know each of the eight skills involved; classification agreement between the two models ranges from $\kappa = 0.00$ to $\kappa = 0.59$ (with all but one κ below 0.33), so the models are also not classifying the same students as knowing each skill. A comparison of models using the BIC criterion provides quite strong evidence in favor of the dependent-skills model for this data.

I am not aware of any detailed studies comparing precision and accuracy of inferences about KCs when more complex hierarchical structures such as those in Figure 10.3 are ignored. The evidence from simpler cases such as [5] suggests, however, that such dependence is very likely to be present and the effects of ignoring it clearly need to be understood for CDMs and related models.

10.3.2 Hierarchy of Institutional/Social Structure

Many studies of interventions in education occur in an institutional context. Multiple students are grouped within classes, multiple classes taught by teachers, teachers exist within buildings, buildings within districts, etc. These social and institutional groupings are well known to lead to additional dependence between observations. Just as with the dependence between task responses reviewed above, social and institutional dependence tends to increase uncertainty in inference: for example, differences in outcomes between a treatment group and a control group must be larger to be reliably detected.

These hierarchical models also go by other names: multilevel models, mixed-effects models, and variance components models. Formally, they are closely related to the models for between-task dependence described in Section 10.2: all are instances of Bayes net models, suitably generalized to allow for a variety of distributions of the random variables at the nodes of the network. However, differing data collection methodologies and differing computational details mean that the models are not usually treated in the same literatures. One exception is the text by Gelman and Hill [13], which is nearly unique in suggesting models that include both hierarchical structure for social/institutional dependence as well as some structures for between-task dependence. Singer and Willet [32] provide another excellent resource, especially for using hierarchical models to study change over time.

Feng et al. [11] apply multilevel models to choose among KC sets of varying granularity for online tutoring data that include a time component. In their model, individual differences in the learning curve are modeled as in (10.6), creating between-task dependence. The model could easily be expanded to incorporate dependence due to clustering of students within different classrooms, schools, etc.

Fox [12] illustrates the use of models that incorporate both between-task dependence as well as dependence due to clustering of students within schools in three educational studies: a comparison of mathematics task performance among students in Dutch schools that do or do not participate in an exit exam program; an examination of the effect of an adaptive teaching technique on fourth grade mathematics achievement; and an exploration of differences within and between schools in the West Bank, in seventh grade mathematics achievement.

Correctly accounting for dependence in such studies will lead to some increased effect sizes and greater statistical significance and some lower effect sizes and lesser statistical significance, even in the same study. For example, Fox [12, Table 5] compares a model that fully accounts for both the hierarchical structure of the data and the dependence between tasks within student, with a model that ignores this dependence by working with total scores instead of task scores. (Both models account for dependence due to hierarchical nesting of students within schools due to institutional structure; ignoring this would produce many falsely significant comparisons.) The model that fully accounts for dependence has moderately high standard errors for most parameters, and in some cases produces offsetting increases in the parameter estimates themselves. A baseline aptitude measure is found to have a small but significant effect on student achievement in the simpler model, whereas in the model that accounts for between-task dependence, it has a larger, still significant effect. On the other hand, the adaptive instruction intervention was found to have a positive, significant effect in the simpler model; however, it was marginally lower and not significant (due to a greater standard error estimate) in the dependence-aware model. Thus, accounting for dependence is not always a "win" and not always a "loss" for detecting effects. It will, however, produce more defensible and more generalizable inferences.

10.4 Conclusions

In this chapter, I have reviewed two commonly-seen dependence phenomena for task response data in EDM: between-task dependence due to common underlying structure (skills, knowledge components) or common contexts (common topic or task model, common scoring procedure), and between-student dependence due to common social or institutional settings. The statistical models used to account for these sources of dependence are mathematically similar, though often treated in different parts of the literature.

The models I have considered are static in nature. In many EDM settings, dynamic models that account for change over time, such as latent Markov learning models, are also appropriate. Although a review of learning models is beyond the scope of this chapter, Rijmen et al. [29] (and the references therein) provide recent, interesting examples of formally combining response models with latent learning models, and adapting modern computational methods for complete inferences that appropriately account for sources of dependence.

Dependence between tasks in aggregated student response data can be exploited to learn about the latent structure underlying the responses (how many skills or knowledge components, how are they related to particular tasks, etc.). However, when the latent structure is taken as known and the goal is to make inferences about individual students' proficiencies, or about differences between different groups of students (say, a treatment and a control group), the effect of dependence between tasks or between students is usually to increase uncertainty (standard errors of estimation). Analyses that do not account for this dependence tend to produce answers that are too optimistic about what can be detected; and that in any event are more difficult to defend and less likely to generalize.

Acknowledgments

Parts of this work were supported by the U.S. Department of Education Grants #R305K030140 and #R305B04063, and by the National Science Foundation Award #DMS-0240019.

References

1. Almond, R.G., DiBello, L.V., Mouder, B., and Zapata-Rivera, J.-D. (2007). Modeling diagnostic assessments with Bayesian networks. *Journal of Educational Measurement*, 44, 341–359.
2. Andrieu, C., de Freitas, N., Doucet, A., and Jordan, M.I. (2003). An introduction to MCMC for machine learning. *Machine Learning*, 50, 5–43. Retrieved June 2008 from http://www.springer-link.com/content/100309/
3. Ayers, E. and Junker, B.W. (2008). IRT modeling of tutor performance to predict end-of-year exam scores. *Educational and Psychological Measurement*, 68, 972–987.
4. Barnes, T. (2005). Q-matrix method: Mining student response data for knowledge. In: *Proceedings of the AAAI-05 Workshop on Educational Data Mining*, Pittsburgh, PA (AAAI Technical Report #WS-05-02).
5. de la Torre, J. and Douglas, J.A. (2004). Higher-order latent trait models for cognitive diagnosis. *Psychometrika*, 69, 333–353.
6. Desmarais M.C. and Pu, X. (2005). A Bayesian inference adaptive testing framework and its comparison with item response theory. *International Journal of Artificial Intelligence in Education*, 15, 291–323.
7. DiBello, L.V., Roussos, L.A., and Stout, W.F. (2007). Review of cognitively diagnostic assessment and a summary of psychometric models. In: Rao, C.R. and Sinharay, S. (eds.), *Handbook of Statistics*, Vol. 26 (Psychometrics). New York: Elsevier, Chapter 31, pp. 979–1030.
8. Chang, H.-H. and Ying, Z. (2009). Nonlinear sequential designs for logistic item response theory models with applications to computerized adaptive tests. *Annals of Statistics*, 37, 1466–1488.
9. Darroch, J.N., Fienberg, S.E., Glonek, G.F.V., and Junker, B.W. (1993). A three-sample multiple recapture approach to census population estimation with heterogeneous catchability. *Journal of the American Statistical Association*, 88, 1137–1148.

10. Edwards, D. (2000). *Introduction to Graphical Modeling*, 2nd edn. New York: Springer.
11. Feng, M., Heffernan, N.T., Mani, M., and Heffernan, C. (2006). Using mixed-effects modeling to compare different grain-sized skill models. In: Beck, J., Aimeur, E., and Barnes, T. (eds.), *Educational Data Mining: Papers from the AAAI Workshop*. Menlo Park, CA: AAAI Press, pp. 57–66. Technical Report WS-06-05. ISBN 978-1-57735-287-7. Preprint obtained from http://www.assistment.org
12. Fox, J.-P. (2004). Applications of multilevel IRT modeling. *School Effectiveness and School Improvement*, 15, 261–280. Preprint obtained from http://users.edte.utwente.nl/fox/
13. Gelman, A. and Hill, J. (2007). *Data Analysis Using Regression and Multilevel/Hierarchical Models*. New York: Cambridge University Press.
14. Hagenaars, J. and McCutcheon, A.L. (eds.) (2002). *Applied Latent Class Analysis*. New York: Cambridge University Press.
15. Holland, P.W. and Rosenbaum, P.R. (1986). Conditional association and unidimensionality in monotone latent variable models. *Annals of Statistics*, 14, 1523–1543.
16. Johnson, M.S. and Sinharay, S. (2005). Calibration of polytomous item families using Bayesian hierarchical modeling. *Applied Psychological Measurement*, 29, 369–400.
17. Johnson, M.S., Sinharay, S., and Bradlow, E.T. (2007). Hierarchical item response models. In: Rao, C.R. and Sinharay, S. (eds.), *Handbook of Statistics*, Vol. 26 (Psychometrics). New York: Elsevier, Chapter 17, pp. 587–606.
18. Junker, B.W. (2007). Using on-line tutoring records to predict end-of-year exam scores: Experience with the ASSISTments project and MCAS 8th grade mathematics. In Lissitz, R.W. (ed.), *Assessing and Modeling Cognitive Development in School: Intellectual Growth and Standard Settings*. Maple Grove, MN: JAM Press.
19. Langeheine, R. and Rost, J. (eds.) (1988). *Latent Trait and Latent Class Models*. New York/London: Plenum Press.
20. Maris, E. (1999). Estimating multiple classification latent class models. *Psychometrika*, 64, 187–212.
21. Minka, T. (2009). *Tutorials on Bayesian Inference*. Retrieved July 2009 from http://www.research.microsoft.com/~minka/papers/
22. Minka, T. (2009). Automating variational inference for statistics and data mining. In: *Invited Presentation, 74th Annual Meeting of the Psychometric Society*. Cambridge, England, July 2009. Abstract retrieved September 2009 from http://www.thepsychometricscentre.com/
23. Mislevy, R.J., Steinberg, L.S., and Almond, R.G. (2003). On the structure of educational assessment. *Measurement: Interdisciplinary Research and Perspective*, 1, 3–62.
24. Murphy, K.P. (2001). The Bayes net toolbox for MATLAB. In Wegman, E.J., Braverman, A., Goodman, A., and Smyth, P. (eds.), *Computing Science and Statistics 33: Proceedings of the 33rd Symposium on the Interface*, Costa Mesa, CA, June 13–16, 2001, pp. 331–350. Retrieved September 2009 from http://www.galaxy.gmu.edu/interface/I01/master.pdf
25. National Research Council (2001). *Knowing What Students Know: The Science and Design of Educational Assessment*. Washington, DC: National Academy Press.
26. Patz, R.J., Junker, B.W., Johnson, M.S., and Mariano, L.T. (2002). The hierarchical rater model for rated test items and its application to large-scale educational assessment data. *Journal of Educational and Behavioral Statistics*, 27, 341–384.
27. Pavlik, P., Cen, H., Wu, L., and Koedinger, L. (2008). Using item-type performance covariance to improve the skill model of an existing tutor. In: Baker, R.S.J.D., Barnes, T., and Beck, J.E. (eds.), *Educational Data Mining 2008: First International Conference on Educational Data Mining, Proceedings*, Montreal, Canada, June 20–21, 2008, pp. 77–86.
28. Pearl, J. (1988). *Probabilistic Reasoning in Intelligent Systems: Networks of Plausible Inference*. San Mateo, CA: Morgan Kaufman Publishers.
29. Rijmen, F., Vansteelandt, K., and Paul De Boeck, P. (2008). Latent class models for diary method data: Parameter estimation by local computations. *Psychometrika*, 73, 167–182.
30. Rost, J. and Langeheine, R. (eds.) (1997). *Applications of Latent Trait and Latent Class Models in the Social Sciences*. New York: Waxmann.

31. Romero, C. and Ventura, S. (2007). Educational data mining: A survey from 1995 to 2005. *Expert Systems with Applications*, 33, 135–146.
32. Singer, J.D. and Willett, J.B. (2003). *Applied Longitudinal Data Analysis: Modeling Change and Occurrence*. New York: Oxford University Press.
33. Rao, C.R. and Sinharay, S. (eds.) (2002). *Handbook of Statistics*, Vol. 26 (Psychometrics). New York: Elsevier.
34. Tatsuoka, K.K. (1990). Toward an integration of item response theory and cognitive error diagnosis. In: Frederiksen, N., Glaser, R., Lesgold, A., and Shafto, M.G. (eds.), *Diagnostic Monitoring of Skill and Knowledge Acquisition*. Hillsdale, NJ: Erlbaum, pp. 453–488.
35. van der Linden, W.J. and Hambleton, R.K. (eds.) (1997). *Handbook of Modern Item Response Theory*. New York: Springer.
36. van der Maas, H.L.J. and Straatemeier, M. (2008). How to detect cognitive strategies: Commentary on 'Differentiation and integration: Guiding principles for analyzing cognitive change'. *Developmental Science*, 11, 449–453.
37. Wang, X., Bradlow, E.T., and Wainer, H. (2002). A general Bayesian model for testlets: Theory and applications. *Applied Psychological Measurement*, 26, 109–128.
38. Weaver, R. (2008). Parameters, predictions, and evidence in computational modeling: A statistical view informed by ACT-R. *Cognitive Science*, 32, 1349–1375.
39. Worcester Polytechnic Institute. (2009). *Assistment: Assisting Students with their Assessments*. Retrieved January 2009 from http://www.assistment.org/
40. Yanai, H. and Ichikawa, M. (2007). Factor analysis. In: Rao, C.R. and Sinharay, S. (eds.), *Handbook of Statistics*, Vol. 26 (Psychometrics). New York: Elsevier, Chapter 9, pp. 257–296.
41. Yen, W.M. and Fitzpatrick, A.R. (2006). Item response theory. In: Brennan, R.L. (ed.), *Educational Measurement*, 4th edn. Westport, CT: American Council on Education & Praeger Publishers, Chapter 4, pp. 111–154.

Part II

Case Studies

11

Novel Derivation and Application of Skill Matrices: The q-Matrix Method

Tiffany Barnes

CONTENTS

11.1 Introduction

For a tutor or computer-aided instructional tool, a skill matrix represents the relationship between tutor problems and the underlying skills students need to solve those problems. Skill matrices are used in knowledge assessment to help determine probabilities that skills are learned and to select problems in mastery learning environments. Typically, skill matrices are determined by subject experts, who create a list of target skills to be taught and associate each problem with its related skills in the skill matrix. Experts can disagree widely about the skills needed to solve certain problems, and using two very different skill matrices in the same tutor could result in very different knowledge assessments and student learning experiences. We argue that skill matrices can be empirically derived from student data in ways that best predict student knowledge states and problem-solving success, while still assuming that students may have made slips or guesses while working on problems.

In this chapter, we describe the q-matrix method, an educational data-mining technique to extract skill matrices from student problem-solving data and use these derived skill matrices, or q-matrices, in novel ways to automatically assess, understand, and correct student knowledge. Through exploiting the underlying assumption that students usually "have a skill or not," the q-matrix method effectively groups students according to similar performance on tutor problems and presents a concise and human-understandable summary of these groups in matrix form. Using this data-derived skill matrix, new students can be automatically classified into one of the derived groups, which is associated with a skill profile, and this profile can be used with the skill matrix to automatically determine which problems a student should work to increase his or her skill levels. This technique can be used in a mastery learning environment to iteratively choose problems until a student has attained the threshold mastery level on every skill.

We present a suite of case studies comparing the q-matrix method to other automated and expert methods for clustering students and evaluating the q-matrix method for directing student studies. The chapter concludes with a discussion of the ways the q-matrix method can be used to augment existing computer-aided instructional tools with adaptive feedback and individualized instruction.

11.2 Relation to Prior Work

Through adaptation to individual students, intelligent tutoring systems (ITSs) can have significant effects on learning, but there are several challenges and trade-offs in their development, notably the considerable time they take to construct [14]. A number of approaches have been taken to automate the creation of ITSs. Some systems seek to augment computer-aided instruction (CAI) tools with adaptive capabilities. REDEEM, one of the first authoring tools, was built to reduce the time needed to create an ITS by allowing teachers to add their own teaching strategies to existing computer-based training systems in a variety of domains [1]. ASSERT uses a machine learning technique called theory refinement to automatically revise a knowledge base that correctly defines a domain to be consistent with examples of students work in that domain. The ASSERT model allows for automatic generation of feedback that indicates how student answers differ from the correct domain knowledge. The q-matrix does not have a full domain model, but rather models patterns in student answers [2]. The ADVISOR tutor applies machine learning to student data to model the probability that a student will answer a problem correctly and how long this response will take. Teachers can set pedagogical goals to balance learning and time, and ADVISOR will learn help strategies from student data to support teacher-set goals. Students using the REDEEM, ASSERT, and ADVISOR systems perform better than those without adapted feedback. Similar to these systems, the q-matrix method is used to model student responses and provide feedback [9]. The Cognitive Tutor Authoring Tool (CTAT) provides an interface for building a problem-solving environment and constructs example-based rules from teacher-solved problems [13].

Although these approaches automate portions of ITS creation, many of them still rely upon expert-derived skill matrices that represent relationships between skills and problems. For the ASSISTment system, an expert rates each problem according to the hierarchical levels of skills needed to solve it and the resulting skill matrices are used along with tutor data to predict student performance on standardized middle school math tests [12,15]. With the q-matrix method, we derive skill matrices from data to automated knowledge assessment and evaluate learning tools.

The q-matrix method is a natural extension of the rule space model. The rule space model plots the results of predicted "good" and "bad" rule applications in problem solving on a

TABLE 11.1

Example q-Matrix

	$q1$	$q2$	$q3$	$q4$	$q5$	$q6$	$q7$
con1	1	0	0	0	0	1	1
con2	1	1	0	1	0	0	1
con3	1	1	1	0	0	0	0

graph and compares these points with student work [10,17]. This plotting allows for direct comparison of hypothesized rules and actual errors, without having to catalog every possible mistake. For example, for the sum $-1 + -7$, a mistaken rule to add absolute values yields an answer of 8 and the correct rule gives -8. Each such answer can be compared to student results, and the rule with the closest predicted answer is assumed to correspond to the one the student is using.

This idea of determining a student's knowledge state from question responses inspired the creation of a q-matrix, a binary matrix showing the relationship between test items and latent attributes, or concepts. Students were assigned knowledge states based on their test answers and the manually constructed q-matrix. Since this method was used primarily for diagnosis on tests, no learning was assumed to occur between problems.

A q-matrix is a matrix that represents relationships between a set of observed variables (e.g., questions) and latent variables that relate these observations. We call these latent variables "concepts." A q-matrix, also known as a skill matrix or "attribute-by item incidence matrix," contains a one if a question is related to the concept, and a zero if not. An example q-matrix is given in Table 11.1. In this q-matrix, the observed variables are seven questions $q1-q7$, and the concepts are $c1-c3$. For simplicity, this example is given with binary values.

Brewer extended q-matrix values to range from zero to one, representing the probability that a student will answer a question incorrectly if he or she does not understand the concept [11]. For a given q-matrix Q, the value of $Q(Con,Ques)$ represents the conditional probability that a student will miss the question $Ques$ given that they do not understand concept Con. In Table 11.1, this means that question $q1$ will not be answered correctly unless a student understands all three concepts $c1-c3$. Question $q2$ will not be answered correctly unless a student understands concepts $c2$ and $c3$, even if the student does not understand concept $c1$. In contrast, question $q5$ can be answered correctly without understanding any of the concepts $c1-c3$. This indicates that prerequisite knowledge not represented in the q-matrix affects the answer to $q5$. In a more general setting, q-matrix "concepts" can be thought of similarly to the components extracted in principal components analysis, since they represent abstract data vectors that can be used to understand a larger set. These concepts can also be used to describe different clusters of observed data.

Birenbaum et al.'s rule space research showed that it is possible to automate the diagnosis of student knowledge states, based solely on student item-response patterns and the relationship between questions and their concepts [10,17]. Though promising, the rule space method is time consuming and topic-specific, and requires expert analysis of questions. The rule space method provides no way to show that the relationships derived by experts are those used by students, or that different experts will create the same rules.

To better understand what q-matrix might explain student behavior, Brewer created a method to extract a q-matrix from student data and found that the method could be used to recover knowledge states of simulated students [11]. Sellers designed the binary relations tutorial (BRT) and conducted an experiment to determine if the q-matrices extracted from student responses corresponded well with expert-created q-matrices for each of the three sections of the BRT [16]. With a small sample of 17 students, she found that Sections 1 and 2 corresponded well with expert analysis but that Section 3 did not [16]. Barnes and Bitzer applied the method to larger groups of students [6] and found the method comparable to standard knowledge discovery techniques for grouping student data [4,7]. In particular, the q-matrix method outperformed factor analysis in modeling student data and resulted in much more understandable concepts (when compared to factors), but had higher error than k-means cluster analysis on the data. However, to use cluster analysis for automated remediation, experts would have to analyze the clusters to determine what misconceptions each cluster represented, and then determine what material to present to students in the cluster. With the q-matrix method, each cluster directly corresponds to its own representative answer and concept state that can be used for remediation, as described below.

Barnes later applied the q-matrix method in a novel way to understand strategies for solving propositional proofs [3]. Barnes et al. also compared the method to facets for giving teachers feedback on student misconceptions [8]. In this chapter, we detail the q-matrix method and its use in a computer-aided instructional tutorial [5].

11.3 Method

11.3.1 q-Matrix Algorithm

The q-matrix algorithm is a simple hill-climbing algorithm that creates a matrix representing relationships between concepts and questions directly from student response data [11]. The algorithm varies c, the number of concepts, and the values in the q-matrix, minimizing the total error for all students for a given set of n questions. To avoid local minima, each search is seeded with different random q-matrices and the best search result is kept.

In the q-matrix algorithm, we first set c, the number of concepts, to one, and then generate a random q-matrix of concepts versus questions, with values ranging from zero to one. We then calculate the concept states, which are binary strings representing the presence (1) or absence (0) of each concept. For each concept state, we calculate a corresponding predicted answer or ideal response vector (*IDR*). We compare each student response to each *IDR* and assign the response to the closest *IDR* and parent concept state, with an "error" being the distance from the response to the *IDR*. The total q-matrix error is the sum of these errors associated with assigning students to concept states, over all students.

We then perform hill-climbing by adding or subtracting a small fixed delta to a single q-matrix value, and recomputing its error. If the overall q-matrix error is improved, the change is saved. This process is repeated for all the values in the q-matrix several times until the error in the q-matrix is not changing significantly. After a q-matrix is computed in this fashion, the algorithm is run again with a new random initial q-matrix several times, and the q-matrix with minimum error is saved, to avoid local minima. The final result is not guaranteed to be the absolute minimum, but provides an acceptable q-matrix for c, the current given number of concepts.

To determine the best number of concepts to use in the q-matrix, this algorithm is repeated for increasing values of c, until a stopping criterion is met. There are two stopping criteria to consider: either stopping when the q-matrix error falls below a pre-set threshold, such as that of less than 1 per student as used here, or by looking for a decrease in the marginal reduction of error by adding more concepts. In all cases, the number of concepts should be as small as possible to avoid over-fitting to particular student responses, since

TABLE 11.2

q-Matrix Method Pseudo-Code for Fixed *NumCon*

Set *MinError* = *LargeNumber*;
For *Starts* = 1 to *NumStarts*
    Randomly initialize *Q[NumCon][NumQues]*;
    Set $Q^* = Q$; Set *CurrError* = *Error(Q)*;
    For *Iter* = 1 to *NumIter*;
        For *c* = 1 to *NumCon*
            For *q* = 1 to *NumQues*
                $Q^*[c][q] = Q[c][q] + Delta$;
                If *(Error(Q*) < CurrError)*
                    Do
                        Set $Q = Q^*$; Set *CurrError* = *Error(Q*)*;
                        $Q^*[c][q] = Q[c][q] + Delta$;
                    While *(Error(Q*) < CurrError)*;
                Else
                    $Q^*[c][q] = Q[c][q] - Delta$;
                    While *(Error(Q*) < CurrError)*
                        Set $Q = Q^*$; Set *CurrError* = *Error(Q*)*;
                        $Q^*[c][q] = Q[c][q] - Delta$;
    If *(CurrError < MinError)*
        Set *BestQ* = *Q*; Set *MinError* = *CurrError*;

we do not assume that student responses are free from guesses and slips. Pseudocode for the hill-climbing algorithm is given in Table 11.2 for a set number of concepts, *NumCon*, until we meet the pre-set stopping criterion.

The parameter *NumStarts* allows enough random starts to avoid local minima. In the interior loop, single values in the q-matrix are optimized (by *Delta* at a time) while the rest of the q-matrix is held constant. Therefore, several (*NumIter*) passes through the entire q-matrix are made. In these experiments, *NumStarts* was 50, *Delta* was 0.1, and *NumIter* was 5.

11.3.2 Computing q-Matrix Error

Once a q-matrix is constructed, we can use it to group student responses into clusters by concept states. Each cluster is represented by its *IDR*, the response a student in the given cluster would give assuming no slips or guesses. We determine this *IDR* using the q-matrix with the cluster's concept state, a vector of bits where the kth bit is 1 if concept *k* is understood, and 0 otherwise. For each question *q* in the q-matrix, we examine the concepts needed to answer that question. If the concept state contains all those needed for *q*, we set bit *q* in the *IDR* to 1, and otherwise to 0. There are 2^c concept states for a q-matrix with *c* concepts.

When the q-matrix contains only binary values (not probabilities between 0 and 1), this can be calculated for a concept state *s* and the q-matrix *Q* by composing $\neg s$ with *Q*:

$$IDR = \neg((\neg s)Q)$$

For example, given concept state *s* = 0110 and the q-matrix *Q* given in Table 11.1, $\neg s = 1001$, $(\neg s)Q = 101001$. Therefore, *IDR* = 010110. $(\neg s)Q$ can be viewed as a vector of all the questions that require concepts that are unknown for a student in concept state *s*. Thus, the *IDR* for *s* is exactly the remaining questions, since none of them require concepts that are unknown for a student in concept state *s*.

When the *q*-matrix consists of continuous probabilities, for a given question *q*, for each unknown concept *c*, we compute the conditional probability that the student will miss question *q* given that concept *c* is unknown by $1 - Q(c, q)$, where $Q(c, q)$ is the *q*-matrix value for concept *c* and question *q*. Then, since we assume concept–question relationships to be independent, the probability that question *q* will be missed is the product of $1 - Q(c, q)$ over all unknown concepts *c*. The final prediction that *q* will be answered correctly is 1 minus this product. Mathematically, given a *q*-matrix *Q* with *NumCon* concepts, and a concept state *S*, where *S(c)* denotes whether concept *c* is understood, we calculate the ideal response (*IDR*) for each question *q*:

$$IDR(q) = \prod_{c=1}^{NumCon} \begin{Bmatrix} 1 & S(c) = 1 \\ 1 - Q(c,q) & S(c) = 0 \end{Bmatrix} \tag{11.1}$$

An *IDR* can be constructed then by using these probabilities as predicted answers (which will always be incorrect since we assume no partial credit is given), or they can be rounded to 1 or 0 according to a threshold. In our work, we use the probabilities as predictions, since we wish to accumulate a more accurate reflection of our prediction error for each *q*-matrix.

Table 11.3 lists the *IDR*s for all the possible concept states for the *q*-matrix given in Table 11.1. The all-zero concept state 000 describes the "default" knowledge not accounted for in the model, while the all-one concept state 111 describes full understanding of all concepts. Concept state 011's *IDR* corresponds to a binary OR of the *IDR*s for concept states 001 and 010, plus the addition of a 1 for *q2*, which requires both concepts *c2* and *c3* for a correct outcome.

To evaluate the fit of a given *q*-matrix to a data set, we compute its concept states and *IDR*s as in Table 11.3 and determine each data point's nearest neighbor from the set of *IDR*s. The response is then assigned to the corresponding concept state, with an associated error, which is the L_1 distance between the *IDR* and the response. In other words, the distance *d(r,IDR)* between response vector *RESP* and its *IDR*, where *k* ranges over all questions, is

$$d(RESP, IDR) = \sum_{k} |RESP(k) - IDR(k)| \tag{11.2}$$

For example, for a response vector 0111110 and the *q*-matrix given in Table 11.1, the nearest *IDR* would be 0111100 in concept state 011, and the error associated with this assignment is 1, since there is only one difference between the response and its nearest *IDR*. The total error for a *q*-matrix on a given data set is the sum of the errors over all data points.

TABLE 11.3

Ideal Response Vectors for Each Concept State

Concept State	IDR	Concept State	IDR
000	0000100	100	0000110
001	0010100	101	0010110
010	0001100	110	0001111
011	0111100	111	1111111

11.3.3 Hypotheses and Experiment

To demonstrate the application and analysis of the q-matrix method, we present an experiment using the BRT with over 100 students in a discrete mathematics course at North Carolina State University in Fall 2002. The tutorial was required for credit in the class, but credit was awarded simply for attempting all questions and completing a survey, which asked students whether they felt the tutorial "knew" which questions they least understood. Our hypotheses were: (1) expert and extracted q-matrices will differ, but extracted q-matrices will be useful in interpreting student data, and (2) the q-matrix method can be effective in guiding student remediation (at least as effective as a student directing his own learning).

The BRT consists of three sections, with five parts in Section 1 and eight parts in each of Sections 2 and 3. In each part, instructional text and examples are given, and the students practice sample questions with feedback three or more times. A sample question in section BRT-3 would give students a set and a matrix representing a relation and ask the student if the relation has a given property (e.g., transitive). The questions are procedurally generated to allow for a different question each time. At the end of each section, a quiz with one question per part is given, where responses are marked as correct or incorrect, but other feedback is not given. Students were randomly assigned to guided or self-guided groups. In the guided group, the section quiz responses were used with the q-matrix to compute which part was most likely to be where students had misconceptions, and the BRT returned the student to that part for a review and more practice. In the self-guided group, students were asked to choose which question on the quiz they least understood, but were not redirected to review any particular items. All students were then allowed to review any topics they wished.

In the BRT, we used the q-matrices derived in a pilot experiment [16] to choose remediation material for review after each section quiz. We used the new student responses from this experiment to compute a new set of q-matrices. In the next section, we compare these q-matrices to expert q-matrices to check our hypothesis that student concepts do not always correspond to expert analysis. We also discuss how extracted q-matrices can be used to understand student behavior. To better understand the effects of automated remediation using q-matrices, we compare the choices of self-guided students to those the BRT would make. We also discuss student survey results.

11.4 Comparing Expert and Extracted q-Matrices

In this section, we compare the matrices extracted from our Fall 2002 data set with those from the pilot and those created by experts. Three experts independently created section q-matrices, and then collaborated to agree upon a final expert q-matrix for each section.

11.4.1 Binary Relations Tutorial, Section 1 (BRT-1)

The first section, BRT-1, covers Cartesian products, relations, and composition of relations. Table 11.4 lists the expert BRT-1 q-matrix. In both the pilot and our current experiment, the q-matrix method extracted only the "composites" concept listed in row 3. This tells us that most students answered the first four questions correctly, but many missed question $q1.5$. This corresponds with the expert analysis of this tutorial, and the lack of variation among student responses explains how no other concepts could be extracted.

TABLE 11.4

BRT-1 Expert and Extracted q-Matrices

	$q1.1$ Cart. Prod.	$q1.2$ Cart. Prod.	$q1.3$ Relations	$q1.4$ Matrix Rep. of Relations	$q1.5$ Composites
Cartesian products	1	1	1	1	1
Relations	0	0	1	1	1
Composites, only concept extracted	0	0	0	0	1

11.4.2 Binary Relations Tutorial, Section 2 (BRT-2)

For the second section, BRT-2, we extracted q-matrices with 2, 3, and 4 concepts, as shown in Table 11.5. The expert and pilot q-matrices corresponded in all but one value. For instructors, the "multiple properties" concept indicated the application of more than one definition. However, the pilot q-matrix reflects that students find applying the definition of $q2.6$, transitive, more complex. The experts agreed that the extracted pilot q-matrix was appropriate.

The 4-concept q-matrix in Table 11.5 meets the "less than one error per student" criterion, but is quite different from both the expert and pilot q-matrices. The 4-concept q-matrix separates out three concepts relating to only one question each. These three questions were the biggest separators among students, since 74 out of 142 students missed only one question. Out of the remaining students, 39 missed only two questions. This skew toward missing only one question caused the q-matrix analysis to work harder to separate these large groups of students, demonstrating the method's sensitivity to characteristics of the data set and questions.

Although each run of the q-matrix algorithm starts with random values, it is often the case that q-matrices with increasing numbers of concepts have similar or even identical concepts. For example, the 4-concept q-matrix uses concepts 1 and 2 from the 2-concept q-matrix and concept 5 from the 3-concept q-matrix. This repetition in concept usage reflects the ability of the method to find reproducible concepts that explain student behavior.

Although experts created a concept that seemingly represented definition complexity (e.g., having to check more than one property), there are properties whose definitions are complex to understand and check. Each of the extracted q-matrices show asymmetric and transitive grouped together, suggesting that student miss these questions at the same time. This could be because they are at similar levels of complexity or difficulty. However, questions that "separate" groups of students, which may be of a similar difficulty level, can often be separated into their own concepts, as seen with concepts 2, 5, and 6. Therefore, context experts should always check conclusions drawn from extracted q-matrices with their own experience. Here, the properties in order of difficulty are poset ($q2.8$), equivalence relation ($q2.7$), transitive ($q2.6$), asymmetric ($q2.5$), antisymmetric ($q2.4$), and irreflexive ($q2.3$). Questions $q2.1$ and $q2.2$ are the easiest; this is reflected in the q-matrices since they require no "concepts" to solve them. This means that most students got these questions correct.

11.4.3 Binary Relations Tutorial, Section 3 (BRT-3)

The 3-concept, 7-question expert-generated q-matrix for BRT-3 is shown in Table 11.6. The "Hasse diagrams" concept contained all questions. The second concept grouped questions

TABLE 11.5

BRT-2 Expert, Pilot, and Extracted *q*-Matrices

Concept	q2.1 Reflexive	q2.2 Symmetric	q2.3 Irreflexive	q2.4 Antisymmetric	q2.5 Asymmetric	q2.6 Transitive	q2.7 Equiv. Rel.	q2.8 Posets
Expert and pilot q-matrices								
Special properties of relations	1	1	1	1	1	1	1	1
Multiple properties	0	0	0	0	1	exp 0/pilot 1	1	1
2-Concept q-matrix, 1.27 errors/student								
1: Irr-Asym-Trans	0	0	1	0	1	1	0	0
2: Poset	0	0	0	0	0	0	0	1
3-Concept q-matrix, 1.11 errors/student								
3: Poset-Asym-Trans	0	0	0	0	1	1	0	1
4: Irr-Equiv. Rel.-Trans	0	0	1	0	0	1	1	0
5: Antisymmetric	0	0	0	1	0	0	0	0
4-Concept q-matrix, 0.74 errors/student								
1: Irr-Asym-Trans	0	0	1	0	1	1	0	0
2: Poset	0	0	0	0	0	0	0	1
5: Antisymmetric	0	0	0	1	0	0	0	0
6: Equiv. Rel.	0	0	0	0	0	0	1	0

TABLE 11.6

BRT-3 Extracted q-Matrix, 4 Concepts, Err/Stud: 0.72

Concept #: Description	q3.1 Hasse Diagrams	q3.2 Maximal Elements	q3.3 Minimal Elements	q3.4 Upper Bounds	q3.5 Lower Bounds	q3.6 Least Upper Bounds	q3.7 Greatest Lower Bounds
BRT-3 Expert q-matrix							
1: Hasse diagrams	1	1	1	1	1	1	1
2: Groups of elements	0	1	1	1	1	0	0
3: Max and min	0	0	0	0	0	1	1
BRT-3 Four-concept extracted q-matrix, 0.72 errors/student							
1: Hasse diagrams	1	0	0	0	0	0	0
2: Maximal, upper, lub	0	1	0	1	0	1	0
3: Upper bounds, lub, glb	0	0	0	1	0	1	1
4: Lower bounds	0	0	0	0	1	0	0

that examined subsets of partially ordered sets for upper and lower bounds. The third concept grouped together questions that combined the ideas of maximal and minimal elements with upper and lower bounds.

Of the 194 students who completed the BRT-3 quiz, only 78 had distinct response vectors. The extracted 4-concept q-matrix is given in Table 11.6. When we compare the extracted and expert q-matrices, we find that concept 3 is similar in both of these—in both, $q3.6$ and $q3.7$ are related, but in the extracted q-matrix, these are also related to $q3.4$. Question $q3.3$ relates to no concepts, implying that most students got this (easy) question correct. Questions $q3.4$ and $q3.6$ are related to 2 concepts each, implying that they are more difficult (since questions that require more concepts are less likely to be correct). Concepts 1 and 4 both relate to one question each, suggesting that no other questions were missed when a student missed one of these.

Using the q-matrix method, we would be very unlikely to extract the "Hasse diagrams" concept from this tutorial, since every concept state where this concept was unknown would have an *IDR* of all zeroes. However, the all-zero concept state would also have an all-zero *IDR* if every question relates to at least one concept, and given equal-error choices, we preferentially assign students to the all-zero state to simplify the model created.

11.4.4 How Many Concepts and How Much Data?

Although we have presented two criteria for selecting the number of concepts, the final number should be based on a few considerations, including: (1) the amount of data available, (2) somewhat even distribution of student responses among concept states, (3) a small number of concepts relative to the number of questions, and (4) the accuracy of matching responses to concept states. Several of these criteria can be examined based on the number of concept states. There are 2^c concept states for any q-matrix with c concepts. If we divide the number of unique responses by the number of states, we get the average number of responses per state. Assuming at least one response per concept state gives a maximum number of concepts as the logarithm, base 2, of the number of response vectors in the data. Therefore, if you have 10 responses, there should be no more than 4 concepts.

We should also consider the number of questions in limiting the number of concepts. The most fitted (and likely over-fitted) model would assign one concept to each question, so there should be no more concepts than there are questions. Based on a preference for a more concise concept matrix, we use the rule of thumb that the number of concepts should be proportional to the logarithm, base 2, of the number of questions. We can understand differences in the IDR and a student response in terms of guess and slip rates, where a guess is when the IDR predicts an incorrect answer but the student guesses the correct one, and a slip is when we predict a correct answer but observe an incorrect one. To simplify our discussion, let's assume the two rates are equal and are about 20%. Therefore, the error associated with assigning any given response to a concept state has an expected rate of 20% of answers being different than those in the *IDR*. If the number of questions is 5, then the error rate would be 1 per student. With 10 questions, the error rate would be 2 per student. If we expect high guess and slip rates, we would choose fewer concepts to encompass more general groups of students. However, if we intend to tailor responses more individually and expect low guess and slip rates, we would choose the larger number of concepts.

Several characteristics are assumed about data sets when using the *q*-matrix method. First, the data set should be representative of a class of students, with many levels of ability and stages of learning present. Second, it is assumed that learning is not occurring between questions. Third, concepts are assumed to be conjunctive, in other words, that all skills needed for a problem must be present for the student to solve it. Fourth, it is assumed that the questions in the quiz or test are good questions that test concepts of interest, and that widely divergent material is not included on the same test (though analysis of the extracted *q*-matrix can help identify cases where this is not true). In simulations where the method was used to simulate student data sets with varied sizes, guess, and slip rates, as few as 25 unique responses were needed to recover the original *q*-matrix [11]. However, as we have shown here in BRT-3, a pairing of complex material with little or no repetition of the concepts being tested means that more data is needed to make an accurate or low-error *q*-matrix.

11.4.5 Summary of Expert-Extracted Comparison

Because of the differences in novice and expert models of a domain, we would not expect expert *q*-matrices to correspond particularly well with those extracted from student data. Where these models agree, it is on the questions that are the most difficult or complex, since difficulty is a large factor in determining the variance among a diverse population of students. To better model how questions relate to concepts for a particular knowledge level, *q*-matrices could be extracted for a sub-population of students at a certain knowledge level.

Questions where expert and extracted *q*-matrices disagree the most are areas that should be further considered: Do the extracted *q*-matrices make sense? If not, is there some underlying structure to the questions that can explain similar student behavior, such as using examples from an unrelated domain that some students know but others do not? Or, do the related problems have special cases in them, such as the case of 0 in multiplication problems? If so, instructors should consider adding questions to better diagnose student knowledge.

11.5 Evaluating Remediation

To give a baseline indication of the acceptability of automatic redirection, a minimum standard of "do no harm" was measured. To do this, we compared student choices of topics for further study with those we would have chosen automatically using the concept with the lowest probability of being understood. All of these selected q-matrix review choices were reviewed by instructors and were deemed appropriate. Some students were randomly assigned to a self-guided option, where they select the question they least understood upon completion of each section of the binary relations tutorial. Most of these students chose a question related to concept the q-matrix predicted least likely to be understood. In BRT-1, only 7% of self-guided students chose to review a different question than selected by the q-matrix. Since our BRT-1 q-matrix was a one-concept q-matrix relating only to question 5, the most difficult on the quiz, this is not a surprising result. In BRT-2, 30% of self-guided students chose a different question to review than the q-matrix would have. This means that 70% of the time the q-matrix method predicted the same concept to review as students did. In BRT-3, however, 43% of students chose differently than our automated choice. This result is not discouraging, though, since on a more complex topic such as this one, students may need to review more than one concept. Further experiments are needed to measure the effects of automatic remediation on student knowledge.

In the survey, students were asked to agree or disagree with the statement, "I felt like the program knew which concepts I did not understand and directed me back to lessons on concepts I understood the least." Forty-six percent of respondents agreed that the BRT seemed to know what they did not understand and directed them to study the concepts they least understood, while only 13% of students disagreed.

Six percent felt that the best aspect of the tutorial was its ability to take students back to review material they did not understand. Some pointed out that it would be more useful to review these sections a different way, or that they wanted to review more than just one topic after taking a section test. Future work will address these concerns and take into account more sophisticated pedagogical strategies for selecting topics for review.

11.6 Conclusions

This research represents an initial study of the effectiveness of data-derived q-matrices in understanding and directing student learning. The method can be used with small data sets of as few as 25 student responses to make usable q-matrices, though those derived will work best with groups of students with similar performance and ability levels. Using larger data sets with varied student profiles will make the derived q-matrices more general but less tailored to a particular semester or instructor.

The questions used to collect the data are important; we assume that they are appropriate, related, and written to test student knowledge of a domain. The q-matrix method can highlight the need to adjust questions to make the test more balanced in terms of measuring proficiency in several skills. Examining derived q-matrices can also help instructional designers identify places where student behavior shows that there may be unintended relationships among questions.

As we predicted, expert and extracted q-matrices did not often coincide. However, we were able to use extracted q-matrices to understand patterns of student responses, such as frequently correct or incorrect questions, and could compare the extracted concepts with our understanding of the domain to determine whether the observed patterns made sense. We also compared the questions that self-guided students chose to review with the questions that we would have chosen for them based on our estimates of concept understanding. We found that the q-matrix method often chose the same questions for review as the self-guided students chose for themselves. Based on survey results, a majority of students felt as if the tutorial adapted to their individual knowledge.

Future work will address several important questions about the q-matrix method. Although the method has been validated using simulated students, a comparison of q-matrix results on varying class sizes would yield a measure of the robustness of the method. We also plan to compare error for expert models in explaining student performance with q-matrix models. It would also be interesting to use the q-matrix method to compare skill matrices derived for the same class taught by different professors.

References

1. Ainsworth, S.E., Major, N., Grimshaw, S.K., Hayes, M., Underwood, J.D., Williams, B., and Wood, D.J. 2003. REDEEM: Simple intelligent tutoring systems from usable tools, in T. Murray, S. Blessing, and S.E. Ainsworth (eds), *Advanced Tools for Advanced Technology Learning Environments*, pp. 205–232. Amsterdam, the Netherlands: Kluwer Academic Publishers.
2. Baffes, P. and Mooney, R.J. 1996. A novel application of theory refinement to student modeling, in *Proceedings of the 13th National Conference on Artificial Intelligence*, Portland, OR, pp. 403–408.
3. Barnes, T. 2006. Evaluation of the q-matrix method in understanding student logic proofs, in *Proceedings of the 19th International Conference of the Florida Artificial Intelligence Research Society (FLAIRS 2006)*, Melbourne Beach, FL, May 11–13, 2006.
4. Barnes, T. 2005. Experimental analysis of the q-matrix method in automated knowledge assessment, in *Proceedings IASTED International Conference on Computers and Advanced Technology in Education (CATE 2005)*, Oranjestad, Aruba, August 29–31, 2005.
5. Barnes, T. 2005. The q-matrix method: Mining student response data for knowledge, in *Proceedings of the AAAI-2005 Workshop on Educational Data Mining*, Pittsburgh, PA, July 9–13, 2005.
6. Barnes, T. and Bitzer, D. 2002. Fault tolerant teaching and automated knowledge assessment, in *Proceedings of the ACM Southeast Conference*, Raleigh, NC, April, 2002.
7. Barnes, T., Bitzer, D., and Vouk, M. 2005. Experimental analysis of the q-matrix method in knowledge discovery, in *Proceedings of the International Symposium of Methodologies for Intelligent Systems*, Saratoga Springs, NY.
8. Barnes, T., Stamper, J., and Madhyastha, T. 2006. Comparative analysis of concept derivation using the q-matrix method and facets, in *Proceedings of the AAAI 21st National Conference on Artificial Intelligence Educational Data Mining Workshop*, Boston, MA, July 17, 2006.
9. Beck, J., Woolf, B.P., and Beal, C.R. 2000. ADVISOR: A machine learning architecture for intelligent tutor construction, in *7th National Conference on Artificial Intelligence*, pp. 552–557. Saint Paul, MN: AAAI Press/The MIT Press.
10. Birenbaum, M., Kelly, A., and Tatsuoka, K. 1993. Diagnosing knowledge states in algebra using the rule-space model. *Journal for Research in Mathematics Education*, 24(5): 442–459.
11. Brewer, P. 1996. Methods for concept mapping in computer based education. Computer Science Masters thesis, North Carolina State University, Raleigh, NC.

12. Feng, M., Beck, J., Heffernan, N., and Koedinger, K. 2008. Can an intelligent tutoring system predict math proficiency as well as a standardized test? in *Proceedings of the 1st International Conference on Educational Data Mining*, Montreal, Canada, June 20–21, 2008, p. 107–116.

13. Koedinger, K.R., Aleven, V., Heffernan., T., McLaren, B., and Hockenberry, M. 2004. Opening the door to non-programmers: Authoring intelligent tutor behavior by demonstration, in *Proceedings of the 7th International Conference on Intelligent Tutoring Systems*, Alagoas, Brazil, pp. 162–173.

14. Murray, T. 1999. Authoring intelligent tutoring systems: An analysis of the state of the art. *International Journal of Artificial Intelligence in Education*, 10: 98–129.

15. Razzaq, L., Heffernan, N., Feng, M., and Pardos, Z. 2007. Developing fine-grained transfer models in the ASSISTment system. *Journal of Technology, Instruction, Cognition, and Learning*, 5(3): 289–304.

16. Sellers, J. 1998. An empirical evaluation of a fault-tolerant approach to computer-assisted teaching of binary relations. Masters thesis, North Carolina State University, Raleigh, NC.

17. Tatsuoka, K. 1983. Rule space: An approach for dealing with misconceptions based on item response theory. *Journal of Educational Measurement*, 20(4): 345–354.

12

Educational Data Mining to Support Group Work in Software Development Projects

Judy Kay, Irena Koprinska, and Kalina Yacef

CONTENTS

12.1 Introduction

Educational data mining is the process of converting data from educational systems to useful information to inform pedagogical design decisions and answer educational questions. With the increasing use of technology in education, there is a large amount of content and electronic traces generated by student interaction with computer learning environments such as collaborative learning systems, project management systems, intelligent teaching systems, simulators, and educational game environments. The challenge is how to effectively mine these large amounts of data, find meaningful patterns, and present them to teachers and students in a useful form.

In this chapter, we focus on supporting the teaching and learning of group work skills. Group work is central in many aspects of life. It is especially important in the workplace where most often the combined efforts of a group of people are required to complete a complex task in a given time. The context of our study is a senior software development project, where students work in groups to develop a software solution for a real industry client over a semester. Students use a state-of-the art online group collaboration environment with tools such as a wiki for sharing web pages, ticketing coordination and planning tool, and software repository with version control. Our goal was threefold:

1. To provide a high-level overview of the activity of each group member. The teachers can use this overview at the weekly meetings to provide a starting point for review of the group's recent progress and also to help identify potential problems early enough for remedial actions to be effective. Individual students can also use the overview for self-monitoring to check if they are contributing effectively and if they are fulfilling their allocated roles, e.g., leader, tracker, software developer.

2. To identify patterns of activities associated with strong and weak groups. Using historic data from previous courses, patterns characterizing the behavior of strong and weak groups can be identified at various levels (e.g., individual students or groups) and in different forms (e.g., as a sequence of temporal events or a summary of characteristics, ignoring the time aspect). The teacher monitoring the current group can recognize such patterns and provide timely feedback during the semester, e.g., identify ineffective patterns and work with the group to rectify them; identify positive patterns and reinforce them. These patterns can also improve the teaching of group skills by providing concrete examples illustrating key principles such as effective leadership and monitoring activity.

3. To improve our understanding of how the strong groups make use of the online collaboration tool. This can be used by teachers in future courses to customize the online environment and assessment, in order to improve student learning.

To achieve these goals, we applied three approaches: (1) mirroring visualizations to summarize the huge amounts of longitudinal data and give students and teachers a bird's-eye view of the activity of the group; (2) sequential pattern mining to identify interactions between team members and action sequences, characterizing strong and weak groups; and (3) clustering of the students and groups according to their activity to find nontemporal patterns characterizing student and group behavior.

The next section describes the theoretical underpinning of our work and the related work. Then, we present the context of our study and the data used. The following sections explain the application of the three data mining techniques, highlight the important findings, and discuss how the results can be used to improve group work skills.

12.2 Theoretical Underpinning and Related Work

Our approach was driven by two forms of theoretical underpinning. The first one is the Big Five theory of group work [1]. It states five key factors for success of group work: *leadership, mutual performance monitoring, backup behavior, adaptability,* and *team orientation*. Backup behavior involves reallocating work between members as their different loads and progress become recognized. Adaptability is a broader form of changing plans as new information about group and external issues are identified. Team orientation covers aspects such as commitment to the group. The Big Five theory also identifies three supporting mechanisms: *shared mental models* (e.g., shared understanding of how the group should operate); *mutual trust, closed loop communication* (e.g., a person posting a message on any media receives feedback about it and confirms this). This theory provides a language with which to discuss group work and also guides our data mining.

The second theoretical underpinning is based on Extreme Programming [2], a successful software development methodology. Some of its key principles are: constant communication within the group and with customers, simple clean design, pair programming, testing the software from day one, delivering the code to customers as early as possible, and implementing changes as suggested. These principles helped us to identify the features of activity that should be extracted, used in the analysis, and presented in the visualizations.

Some researchers have investigated the use of data mining to analyze collaborative interactions. Talavera and Gaudioso [3] applied clustering to student interaction data to build profiles of student behaviors in a course teaching the use of Internet. Data was collected from forums, email, and chat. The goal was to support evaluation of collaborative activities and, although only preliminary results were presented, their work confirmed the potential of data mining to extract useful patterns and get insight into collaboration profiles. In [4] a method based on clustering and statistical indicators was proposed. The aim was to infer information about the collaboration process in an online collaborative learning environment. Prata et al. [5] have developed a machine-learned model, which automatically detects students' speech acts in a collaborative learning environment, and found a positive correlation between speech acts denoting interpersonal conflict and learning gains. Soller [6] analyzed knowledge sharing conversations using Hidden Markov models and multidimensional scaling. However, her approach required group members to use a special interface using sentence starters. The DEGREE system [7] allows students to submit text proposals, coedit, and refine them, until agreement is reached. However, it also requires a special interface and user classified utterances and is also limited to a single collaboration medium. By contrast, we wanted to ensure that the learners used collections of conventional collaboration tools in an authentic manner, as they are intended to be used to support group work; we did not want to add interface restrictions or additional activities for learners as a support for the data mining. These goals ensure the potential generality of the tools we want to create. It also means that we can explore the use of a range of collaboration tools, not just a single medium, such as chat.

Mirroring visualizations to support group collaboration have been used previously [8,9]. In [10], the goal is to improve participation rate by creating an adaptive rewards system using mirrored group and individual models. However, it significantly differs from our goal of supporting small groups for which learning group work skills is one of the learning objectives and the group work is the key focus. In our previous work, we found that mirroring of simple overall information about a group is valuable [11]. The work on social translucence [12,13] has also shown the value of mirroring in helping group members to realize how their attitude affect the group and to alter their behavior.

12.3 Data

The context of this study is a senior level capstone software development project course, which runs over a semester. There were 43 students, working in 7 groups of 5–7. The task was to develop a software solution for a client. The topics varied from creating a computer-based driving ability test to developing an object tracking system for an art installation.

The groups were required to use Trac [14], an open-source, web-based, project management system for professional software development. It consists of three parts, tightly integrated through hyperlinks:

- A group wiki supporting communication and documentation. It allows the group members to add, remove, or edit shared web pages, linked from the main group page.
- A ticket system supporting task management. A ticket is created for each task that the team has to do and is assigned to a person for completion. The team can also add comments on it, reassign it to somebody else or close it.
- Subversion (SVN) is for source code management. It provides a repository for the software created by the group and manages the changes. It allows recovery of older versions of the software and a view of the history of how the files and directories were changed.

The Trac usage data contained roughly 15,000 events and its size was 1.6 MB in mySQL format. We also had the progressive and final student marks, which take into account both the quality of the product and the group management process followed. Based on them, the groups were ranked and named accordingly—Group 1 is the best group and Group 7 is the weakest.

12.4 Data Mining Approaches and Results

12.4.1 Mirroring Visualizations

One of the important challenges facing teachers and students in the context of group work is to see the big picture—whether group members are all contributing effectively and fulfilling their allocated roles. During a semester long project, using a system such as Trac, the groups generate a large amount of electronic traces. These data contain rich and valuable information that can help in determining group progress and in identifying problems early enough to intervene effectively. However, the raw data cannot be used directly by teachers and students due to its large quantities and overwhelming amount of details.

To address this problem, we designed a high-level visual summary (*mirror*) of the activities of each group member over time. Our goal was to extract an overview of the huge amount of group activity data and present it in a form that is a useful starting point for exploring if the group is working effectively. For example, at the weekly meetings with the groups, the teachers can point to the summary and ask students to explain how it relates to the work done.

Given the multifaceted nature of group interactions, especially in our context where students work for months on complex projects, we needed to decide what data to mine to provide the information needed for our goals of facilitating group operation, identifying potential group problems early, and presenting an effective starting point for review of the group's recent progress. The five key factors for success from the analysis of group work and the key elements of group management from Extreme Programming pointed to the key elements that teachers and students should be able to learn from the mirror visualizations.

We concluded that we should (1) summarize each student's activity (daily and cumulatively) on each of the media (wiki, task planning tickets, and version control actions in the software repository) and (2) summarize the flow of interaction between the team members. We expected that some group members would have different patterns of activity from others, e.g., the group leaders should have appeared more active on planning tasks, reflected in creation of tickets; the absence of this pattern would suggest that the leaders are not doing their job. We also expected that better groups would show a higher interactivity than the weaker ones.

We designed a set of visualizations to meet these goals. We describe two of them. Figure 12.1 shows our main visualization, the Wattle Tree (named after an Australian native plant with fluffy golden-yellow round flowers). Each person in the team appears as a "tree" that climbs up the page over time. The tree starts when the user first does an action on any of the three media considered. The vertical axis shows the date and the day number. Wiki-related activity is represented by yellow "flowers," circles on the left of the trees. SVN-related activity is similarly represented, as orange flowers on the right of the trees. The size of the flower indicates the size of the contribution. Ticket actions are represented by leaves—the green lines: a dark green leaf on the left indicates a ticket was open by the user and a light green leaf on the right indicates the user closed a ticket. The length of the left leaf is proportional to the time it remained opened. Those still open are shown at a standard, maximal size (e.g., the ones around day 41 in Figure 12.1).

As already discussed, a good team leader will typically take the responsibility for opening most of the tickets. We see that the leftmost person in Figure 12.1 has opened many tickets while the closing of tickets is more evenly distributed across the team. Although these visualizations are intended to be meaningful for the team, rather than the outsider viewing them, there are some features we can identify in Figure 12.1. The two students at the left appear to have been the most active in management aspects at the wiki and tickets: knowledge of the group bears this out. The fourth student from the left is particularly active on SVN corresponding to a larger role in the technical development. The fifth student from the left has a hiatus from about Day 27, corresponding to too little activity. This group had times when several members were ill or had other difficulties and they could see the effect of these problems in the Wattle diagram. The team member with responsibility for tracking progress could use the Wattle tree to get an overview of activity at a glance. This serves as a starting point for delving into the details, as needed, by checking individual tickets, wiki pages and SVN documents and their histories.

Wattle trees do not contain information on who issued tickets to whom, and who contributes to a wiki page. In order to visualize these activities, we use what we call an interaction network, inspired by the graphical notations used in Social Network Analysis [15], and showing relationships and flows between entities. An example for one group is shown in Figure 12.2. The nodes represent team members and the lines between them indicate interaction between the team members, as they modify the same wiki page, SVN file or ticket. The width of the edge is proportional to the number of interactions between them.

These interaction graphs can be used for reflective group activities in class. They may indicate different patterns and require deep knowledge for interpretation. For example, a tick line may correspond to a group member writing poor code with the others having to fix it or a group member who does not trust the others and frequently edits their code.

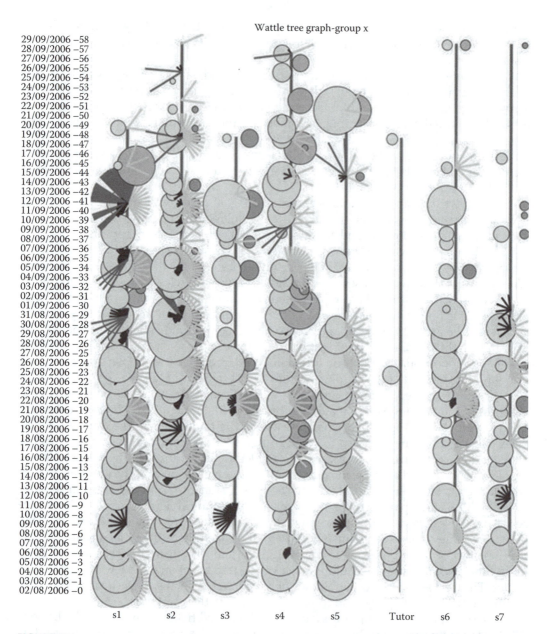

FIGURE 12.1
Wattle diagram.

The Wattle tree and interaction networks were available during the semester and were used in the weekly meetings between student groups and teachers. Individual students found that they could see what they and the other students in the group have been doing and whether they have been performing at appropriate levels. Teachers found that they could identify group problems very early and help address them.

The visualization tools that we developed were also used successfully in the context of postgraduate courses in educational technology, where groups worked collaboratively to write essays. Thus, they have a broader value.

Future work will include making the Wattle trees and interaction networks more interactive. We have recently developed an interactive visualization, called Narcissus [16]. It supports views at three levels: group, project, and ticket, and the user can also click on the components and see the supporting evidence.

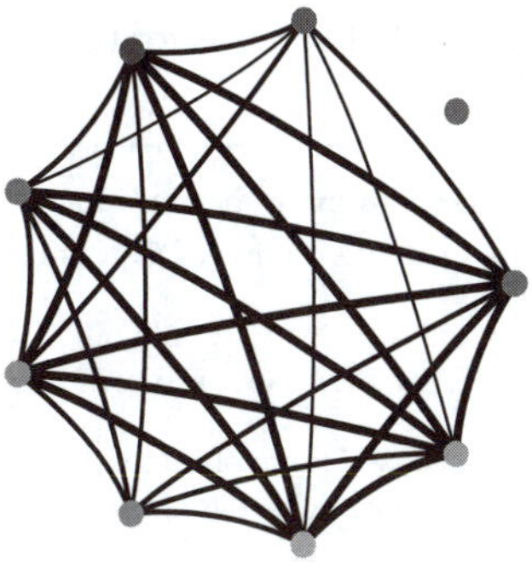

Interaction graph-medium wiki

FIGURE 12.2
Interaction network.

12.4.2 Sequential Pattern Mining

The temporal order of events is an important aspect of group work. We investigated if there are recurrent sequences of events distinguishing the stronger from the weaker groups. For instance, we expected to see the following pattern in the strong groups: the leader amends a wiki page, creates tickets, allocates them to group members who accept the ticket, act on it (activity on the wiki and/or the SVN), then comment on the ticket, and close it. To find such temporal patterns we used sequential pattern mining [17]. A sequence is defined as an ordered set of elements (events). Given a sequence dataset and a threshold s (called support), it finds all sequences that occur at least s times in the dataset. Sequential pattern mining has been previously used in e-learning although for different goals than ours: to support personalized course delivery based on the learner characteristics [18] and to recommend sequences of resources for users to view in order to learn about a given topic [19].

We used the Generalized Sequential Pattern (GSP) Mining algorithm [17], which is a multiple-pass, candidate generation-and-test approach, based on the so called apriori property. We have slightly modified the standard GSP, as described in [20], to better suit our context.

Before the sequential pattern mining can be performed, the data need to be suitably preprocessed. This involved three critical steps summarized below (for more details see [20]):

1. Abstraction of the raw data into a list of events for each group (a unique, chronological sequence of events). The resulting sequence for each group consisted of 1416–3395 events.

2. Splitting these long sequences into a dataset of several meaningful sequences. We formed three types of sequences: (1) for the same resource (e.g., the same wiki page or ticket); (2) for a group session (a session is formed by cutting the group event sequence where gaps of minimum length of time occurred); and (3) for the same task (a task is defined by a ticket and comprising all events linked from and to that ticket).

3. Encoding the events suitably to facilitate data mining. We developed and used several alphabets to describe our events in a way that could compress our data meaningfully and we ran the GSP algorithm using all these alphabets.

Table 12.1 summarizes some of the distinctive patterns we found for the strong and weak groups and their explanation.

After the extraction of these patterns, the teachers examined in detail the actions on Trac and confirmed the meaningfulness of the results. The results can be used in future teaching to provide concrete examples of patterns associated with good and poor practice, e.g., to illustrate general principles such as effective leadership and monitoring in terms

TABLE 12.1

Sequential Patterns for Best and Weak Groups

Patterns	Explanation
Patterns found in best groups	
Frequent alternation of SVN and wiki events	Documentation in wiki about SVN commits to group repository
Frequent alteration of SVN and ticket events	Tickets being updated following SVM commits
Tickets used more often than wiki, and many consecutive ticket events	Higher and better use of the ticketing system; tickets are more task-oriented than wiki and ticketing system is better indicator of the work actually done
Many consecutive SVN events	Work more often committed to group repository
Many SVN events on the same files	Regular commits to the repository (software development done)
High ticketing activity for Leaders—tickets created by Leader, accepted by another member, Leaders commenting on tickets and following up assigned work.	Effective leadership
Patterns found in weak groups	
Frequent alternation of wiki and ticket events and lack of sequences containing SVN events	The wiki and tickets were not used to support software development
Lack of SVN events	Less actual work done
Wiki used more often than tickets	Wikis are less focused and task-oriented than tickets
Leaders involved in too much technical work. Tickets created by Leader, followed by ticketing events by other members (e.g., open, edit, close), before completing work.	Less effective leadership.
Tracker rather than Leader creating and editing many tickets	Tracker performing leadership duties

of wikis, tickets, and SVN activity. The patterns can also be extracted and presented to students during the semester as formative feedback to help rectify poor group operation and encourage effective practices.

12.4.3 Clustering

We applied clustering to find patters characterizing the student behavior at two levels: groups of students and individual students. Clustering is an unsupervised method for finding groups of similar objects using multiple data attributes. We used the classical *k*-means clustering algorithm as it is simple, effective, and relatively efficient [21].

12.4.3.1 Clustering Groups

Two key issues critically affect the performance of clustering algorithms: attribute selection and number of clusters. We experimented with various sets of attributes [20] and found a set of 11 attributes based on all media (wiki, ticket, and SVN) to be the most informative. These attributes were derived from the number of events per ticket, number of

TABLE 12.2

Clustering Groups of Students

| Cluster | Distinguishing Characteristics | | |
	Tickets	Wiki	SVN
1: Group 1	Very frequent activity	High edits per wiki page	Very frequent activity
	High events per ticket	High wiki page usage span	
	High % of ticket update and ticket accepting events		
2: Groups 5 and 7	Moderately frequent activity	High edits per wiki page	Moderately frequent activity
	Low number of events per ticket and low % of ticket update events	Low number of lines added/ deleted per wiki edit	
3: Groups 2, 3, 4, and 6	Infrequent activity	Moderate number of lines added/deleted per wiki edit	Infrequent activity
	Moderate number of events per ticket and moderate % of ticket update events		

days ticketing occurred, number of events per wiki page, wiki page usage span, number of lines edited/deleted per wiki edit, number of days SVN activity occurred, and others.

The number of clusters was set to 3, based on our knowledge about the groups, e.g., their progressive and final marks, which reflected the quality of the processes followed and the quality of the final product. The resulting clusters for *k*-means and their distinguishing characteristics are shown in Table 12.2. It should be noted that we also experimented with hierarchical clustering and EM for *k* = 3 and obtained the same clusters.

The first cluster contains only Group 1 (the top group) and is characterized with active use of the three media and high number of active events such as ticket acceptance and update, wiki page edits, and SVN activities. The second cluster contains Groups 5 and 7 and it is characterized with moderately frequent use of tickets and SVN and low number of active events. Although there were many edits of wiki pages as in cluster 1, they involved small modifications (lines added/deleted). The third cluster contains the remaining groups and is characterized by overall low ticketing and SVN activity. While low ticketing activity is typically associated with weaker groups, Group 2, the second best group, also showed this characteristic as it was reluctant to use the ticketing system.

These results were useful for the teachers. For example, the teachers had some sense that Group 1 was well managed but this cluster analysis pointed to some interesting behaviors distinguishing this group that we did not noticed before. For example, we found that the group made extensive use of the wiki on each ticket for communication about the task associated with it, which is a novel and effective way to use TRAC. This new understanding was used in subsequent teaching and was evaluated by the teachers as helpful.

12.4.3.2 Clustering Students

To gain insight into the group composition, we also conducted clustering of the individual students. We selected 14 attributes, similar to the attributes used in the clustering of the groups but characterizing individual not group activity; for more details see [20]. Table 12.3 shows the clusters obtained with *k*-means for *k* = 4 (set empirically), together

TABLE 12.3

Clustering Individual Students

Cluster Label	Cluster Size	Distinguishing Characteristics		
		Tickets	**Wiki**	**SVN**
Managers	8 students	High ticketing activity Involved in many tickets	High wiki activity	Moderate SVN activity
Trac-Oriented Developers	9 students	Moderately high ticketing activity Ticketing occurring on many different days	Moderate wiki activity	Very high SVN activity
Loafers	11 students	Low ticketing activity	Low wiki activity	Low SVN activity
Others	15 students	Moderately low ticketing activity	Moderately low wiki activity Many wiki events on days which wiki events occurred	Many SVN events on days which SVN events occurred

with their characteristics. Based on our interpretation of the cluster characteristics, a cluster label was assigned ("Managers," "Trac-oriented developers," "Loafers," and "Others"). We then looked at the group composition, taking into account the labels assigned to each student; see Table 12.4. The stars (*) show where the group's designated manager (leader) was placed by the clustering. This role was allocated to one person after the initial start-up period. For example, Group 7 consisted of 7 students; 1 of them was clustered as "Manager," 0 as "Trac-oriented developer," 2 as "Loafers" and 4 as "Others"; the designated manager was clustered as "Manager."

Some new interesting differences between the groups emerged. Groups 2 and 3 (placed in the same cluster, see Table 12.2) differ by Group 3's lack of a manager and Group 2's lack of Trac-oriented developers. The first finding was consistent with our knowledge of the leadership problems this group encountered, with the original manager leaving the course and another student taking over. The second finding was validated in a group interview, where the main developers expressed a reluctance to use Trac. Group 5 is also

TABLE 12.4

Group Composition

	Managers	Trac-Oriented Developers	Loafers	Others
Group 1	*1	3	1	1
Group 2	*1	0	1	3
Group 3	0	1	2	*3
Group 4	*1	3	2	0
Group 5	3	*1	0	3
Group 6	*1	1	3	1
Group 7	*1	0	2	4

distinctive in its excess of managers, which was further complicated by their designated manager being placed in the "Trac-oriented developers" cluster. It appears that this weak leadership resulted in others reacting to fill the manager's role, with their technical work subsequently being compromised, which is a pattern to be aware of in future groups.

To verify if these patterns were evident earlier, we ran the clustering using the data only from the first seven weeks. We found that some of these key results had already emerged. For example, the Group 5 leader was already showing the developer's behaviors. Had the teachers been aware of this, they may have been able to help this group deal with this problem early enough to have made a difference. The presence of three loafers was also apparent in Group 6. The early data also showed leadership's behaviors by all other leaders at that stage. These results have great value not only for the teachers but also for the individuals to understand their behavior and change it, if needed.

In conclusion, we found clustering to be useful, revealing interesting patterns characterizing the behavior of the groups and individual students. Strong groups are characterized by effective group leadership and frequent use of the three media, with high number of active events. Some important results are evident in early data, in time for timely problem identification and intervention.

12.4.4 Limitations

The data have several limitations that affected the results.

First, the Trac data do not capture all group communication. In addition to Trac, students collaborated and communicated via other media to which we do not have access, such as face-to-face meetings twice a week, instant messaging, telephone conversations, SMS, and others. An addition of a chat tool to Trac can capture some of this communication and also increase the use of Trac.

Second, the data mining results revealed insufficient use of Trac by some of the groups (e.g., Group 2) and subsequent interviews revealed that they were reluctant to use Trac as they felt it was cumbersome and preferred to communicate by other means.

Third, there were not enough instances for the cluster analysis, especially for the clustering of groups. Although our data contained more than 15,000 events, there were only for 7 groups and 43 students to cluster. Nevertheless, we think that clustering by using the collected data and selected attributes allowed for uncovering useful patterns, characterizing the work of stronger and weaker students as already discussed. The follow-up interviews were very helpful for interpreting and validating the patterns.

12.5 Conclusions

This chapter describes our work on mining of student group interaction data. Our goal was to improve teaching and learning of group work skills in the context of a capstone software development project course. Students used Trac, a state-of-the art collaborative platform for software development, which includes wiki for shared web pages, ticket task management system, and software repository system. We applied three data mining approaches: mirroring visualization, sequential pattern mining, and clustering. We found that they enabled us to achieve the goals of early identification of problems in groups, improving monitoring and self-monitoring of student progress throughout the semester, and helping students to learn to work effectively in groups.

More specifically, mirroring visualizations such as Wattle trees and interaction networks helped us to understand how well individual members are contributing to the group and how well this visualization can be used for reflective activities in class. The clustering and sequential mining results revealed interesting patterns distinguishing between the strong and weak groups, and we also found that some of them can be mined from early data, in time to rectify problems. The next step will be to automate the discovery of patterns during the semester, match them with the patterns we validated, and present regular formative feedback to students, including useful links and remedial exercises. Future work will also include systematic evaluation of the impact of the results on student learning in future cohorts.

Our work also highlighted some of the challenges in analyzing and visualizing educational data. Educational data is temporal, noisy, and lacking enough data for some tasks. For example, one of the groups was reluctant to use the ticket system, which resulted in non-representative ticket data; there were not enough samples for the clustering of the groups (i.e., many events but a small number of students and groups). Good understanding of the educational domain and data and using suitable preprocessing for data abstraction, representation, and feature selection are critical for the success.

Our approach and results may be valuable not only for software development projects using online collaboration systems similar to Trac, but also to the much broader area of Computer Supported Collaborative Learning, where teachers need to address many of the same concerns that were drivers for this work, e.g., to identify groups that are functioning poorly, whether individuals are not contributing or are doing so in ways that do not match their assigned group role and responsibilities.

References

1. Salas, E., D.E. Sims, and C.S. Burke, Is there a "Big Five" in teamwork? *Small Group Research* **36**: 555–599, 2005.
2. XP—Extreme Programming. [cited 2009]; Available from: www.extremeprogramming.org
3. Talavera, L. and E. Gaudioso, Mining student data to characterize similar behavior groups in unstructured collaboration spaces, in *Proceedings of European Conference on Artificial Intelligence*, Valencia, Spain, 2004, pp. 17–23.
4. Anaya, A.R. and J.G. Boticario, A data mining approach to reveal representative collaboration indicators in open collaboration frameworks, in *Proceedings of Educational Data Mining Conference*, Cordoba, Spain, 2009, pp. 210–219.
5. Prata, D.N., R.S.d. Baker, E.d.B. Costa, C.P. Rose, Y. Cui, and A.M.J.B.d. Carvalho, Detecting and understanding the impact of cognitive and interpersonal conflict in computer supported collaborative environments, in *Proceedings of 2nd International Conference on Educational Data Mining*, T. Barnes, M. Desmarais, C. Romero, and S. Ventura, Editors, Cordoba, Spain, 2009, pp. 131–140.
6. Soller, A., Computational modeling and analysis of knowledge sharing in collaborative distance learning. *User Modeling and User-Adapted Interaction* **14**(4): 351–381, 2004.
7. Barros, B. and M.F. Verdejo, Analysing student interaction processes in order to improve collaboration. The DEGREE approach. *International Journal of Artificial Intelligence in Education* **11**: 221–241, 2000.
8. Jermann, P., A. Soller, and M. Muehlenbrock, From mirroring to guiding: A review of state of the art technology for supporting collaborative learning, in *Proceedings of 1st European Conference on Computer-Supported Collaborative Learning*, Maastricht, the Netherlands, 2001, pp. 324–331.

9. Bratisis, T., A. Dimitracopoulou, A. Martinez-Mones, J.A. Marcos-Garcia, and Y. Dimitriadis, Supporting members of a learning community using interaction analysis tools: The example of the Kaleidoscope NoE scientific network, in *Proceedings of International Conference on Advanced Technologies (IICALT)*, Santander, Spain, 2008, pp. 809–813.

10. Cheng, R. and J. Vassileva, Design and evaluation of an adaptive incentive mechanism for sustained educational online communities. *User Modeling and User-Adapted Interaction* **16**(3): 321–348, 2006.

11. Kay, J., P. Reimann, and K. Yacef. Mirroring of group activity to support learning as participation, in *International Conference on Artificial Intelligence in Education (AIED'07)*, IOS Press, Los Angeles, CA, 2007.

12. Erickson, T., C. Halverson, W.A. Kellogg, M. Laff, and T. Wolf, Social translucence: Designing social infrastructures that make collective activity visible. *Communications of the ACM* **45**(4): 40–44, 2002.

13. Erickson, T. and W.A. Kellogg, Social translucence: An approach to designing systems that mesh with social processes. *ACM Transactions on Computer-Human Interaction* **7**(1): 59–83, 2000.

14. TRAC. 2007 [cited December 2009]; Available from: http://trac.edgewall.org/

15. Scott, J., *Social Network Analysis: A Handbook*. Sage, London, U.K., 1991.

16. Upton, K. and J. Kay, Narcissus: Interactive activity mirror for small groups, in *Proceedings of International Conference on User Modelling, Adaptation and Personalisation*, Trento, Italy, June 22–26, 2009, pp. 54–65.

17. Srikant, R. and R. Agrawal, Mining sequential patterns: Generalizations and performance improvements, in *Proceedings of 5th International Conference on Extending Database Technology (EDBT)*, Avignon, France, March 25–29, 1996.

18. Wang, W., J.-F. Weng, J.-M. Su, and S.-S. Tseng, Learning portfolio analysis and mining in SCORM complaint environment, in *Proceedings of 34th ASEE/IEEE Frontiers in Education Conference*, IEEE, Savannah, GA, October 20–23, 2004.

19. Cummins, D., K. Yacef, and I. Koprinska, A sequence based recommender system for learning resources. *Australian Journal of Intelligent Information Processing Systems* **9**(2): 49–56, 2006.

20. Perera, D., J. Kay, I. Koprinska, K. Yacef, and O. Zaiane, Clustering and sequential pattern mining of online collaborative learning data. *IEEE Transactions on Knowledge and Data Engineering* **21**(6): 759–772, 2009.

21. Tan, P.-N., M. Steinback, and V. Kumar, *Introduction to Data Mining*. Pearson Addison Wesley, Boston, MA, 2006.

13

Multi-Instance Learning versus Single-Instance Learning for Predicting the Student's Performance

Amelia Zafra, Cristóbal Romero, and Sebastián Ventura

CONTENTS

13.1 Introduction

Advances in technology and the impact of the Internet in the last few years have both affected all aspects of our lives. In particular, the implications in educational circles are of an incalculable magnitude, making the relationship between technology and education more and more obvious and necessary. In this respect, it is important to mention the appearance of the virtual learning environment (VLE) or e-learning platforms [1]. These systems can potentially eliminate barriers and provide flexibility, constantly updated material, student memory retention, individualized learning, and feedback superior to the traditional classroom [2]. The design and implementation of e-learning platforms have grown exponentially in the last few years becoming an essential accessory to support both face-to-face classrooms and distance learning. The use of these applications accumulates a great amount of information, because they can record all the information about students' actions and interactions in log files and data sets.

Ever since this problem was identified, there has been a growing interest in analyzing this valuable information to detect possible errors, shortcomings, and improvements in student performance, and discover how the student's motivation affects the way he or she interacts with the software. Promoted by this appreciable interest, a considerable number of automatic tools that make possible to work with vast quantities of data have appeared. Fausett and Elwasif [3] predicted students' grades (classified into five classes: A, B, C, D, and E or F from test scores using neural networks); Martínez [4] predicted student academic success (classes that are successful or not) using discriminant function analysis; Minaei-Bidgoli and Punch [5] classified students by using genetic algorithms to predict their final grade; Superby et al. [6] predicted a student's academic success (classified into low, medium, and high risk classes) using different data mining methods; Kotsiantis and Pintelas [7] predicted a student's marks (pass and fail classes) using regression techniques in Hellenic Open University data; and Delgado et al. [8] used neural network models from Moodle logs. Further information can be found in a very complete survey developed by Romero and Ventura [9]; it provides a good review of the main works (from 1995 to 2005) using data mining techniques grouped by task in e-learning environments.

The main property that all studies share about solving this problem to date is to use a traditional learning perspective with a single-instance representation. However, the essential particularity when facing this problem is that the information is incomplete because each course has different types and numbers of activities, and each student carries out the number of activities considered most interesting, dedicating more or less time to resolve them. Multi-instance learning (MIL) allows a more appropriate representation of this information by storing the general information of each pattern by means of bag attributes and specific information about the student's work of each pattern by means of a variable number of instances. This paper presents both traditional supervised learning representation and the first proposal to work in a MIL scenario. Algorithms of the most representative paradigms in both traditional supervised learning and MIL are compared. Experimental results show how MIL is more effective in obtaining more accurate models as well as a more optimized representation.

The chapter is organized as follows. Section 13.2 introduces MIL and its main definitions and techniques. Section 13.3 presents the problem of classifying students' performance from single-instance and multi-instance perspectives. Section 13.4 reports experimental results for all the algorithms tested and compares them. Finally, Section 13.5 summarizes the main contributions of this paper and raises some future research directions.

13.2 Multi-Instance Learning

This section gives a definition and notation of MIL and reviews the most important developments in MIL in recent years.

13.2.1 Definition and Notation of Multi-Instance Learning

MIL was introduced by Dieterich et al. [10] and is designed to solve the same problems as single-instance learning: learning a concept that correctly classifies training data and generalizes about unseen data. Although the actual learning process is quite similar, the two approaches differ in the available labels from which they learn. In a traditional supervised learning setting, an object m_i is represented by a feature vector v_i, which is associated with a label $f(m_i)$. However, in the multi-instance setting, each object m_i may have V_i various instances denoted $m_{i,1}, m_{i,2}, \ldots, m_{i,vi}$. Each of these variants will be represented by a (usually) distinct feature vector $V(m_{i,j})$. A complete training example is therefore written as $(V(m_{i,1}), V(m_{i,2}), \ldots, V(m_{i,vi}), f(m_i))$.

The goal of learning is to find a good approximation of function $f(m_i)$, $f'(m_i)$, analyzing a set of training examples and labeled by $f(m_i)$. To obtain this function, Dietterich defines an hypothesis that assumes that if the result observed is *positive*, then at least one of the variant instances must have produced that positive result. Furthermore, if the result observed is *negative*, then none of the variant instances could have produced a positive result. This can be modeled by introducing a second function $g(V(m_{i,j}))$ that takes a single variant instance and produces a result. The externally observed result, $f(m_i)$, can then be defined as follows:

$$f(m_i) = \begin{cases} 1, & \text{if exists} \quad g(V(m_{i,j})) \\ 0, & \text{otherwise} \end{cases}$$

In the early years of research on MIL, all multi-instance classification works were based on this assumption, which is known as the standard multi-instance or Dietterich hypothesis. More recently, generalized MIL models have been formalized [11,12] where a bag is qualified to be positive if instances in the bag satisfy some sophisticated constraints other than simply having at least one positive instance.

13.2.2 Literature Review of Multi-Instance Learning

During the last decade, this recent learning framework has found an interested audience in the machine learning community, and numerous works are drawing widespread attention because of the numerous real-world applications that have found in MIL a natural way of being represented. Among these tasks are text categorization [13], content-based image retrieval [14,15], drug activity prediction [16,17], image annotation [18], web index page recommendation [19], stock selection [16], landmark matching [20], and computer security [21].

In order to solve these problems, an extensive number of methods have been proposed in the literature. If we go through them, we can find specifically developed algorithms for solving MIL problems, such as APR algorithms [10], the first proposal in MIL; Diverse density (DD) [16], one of the most popular algorithms in this learning; and some variants, such as EM-DD [17], which combine DD with expectation maximization (EM) and a more recent proposal by Pao et al. [14]. On the other hand, there are contributions that adapt popular machine learning paradigms to the MIL context, such as multi-instance lazy learning algorithms, which extend k nearest-neighbor algorithms (kNN) [22]; multi-instance tree learners, which adapt classic methods, ID3-MI [23] and C4.5 [21]; multi-instance rule inducers, which adapt the RIPPER algorithm [23]; multi-instance neural networks, which extend standard neural networks [24,25]; multi-instance kernel methods, which adapt classic support vector machines (SMO) [13,18]; and multi-instance ensembles, which show the use of ensembles in this learning [26,27]. Finally, we can find a multi-instance evolutionary algorithm that adapts grammar-guided genetic programming to this scenario [19,28].

13.3 Problem of Predicting Students' Results Based on Their Virtual Learning Platform Performance

Predicting the performance of students based on their work on the virtual learning platform is an issue under much research. This problem allows interesting relationships to be obtained that can suggest activities and resources to students and educators that favor and improve both learning and the effective learning process. Thus, it can be determined if all the additional material provided to the students (web-based homework) helps them to delve into the concepts and subjects developed in the classroom or if some activities are more worthwhile for improving the final results.

The problem could be formulated in the following way. A student could do different activities in a course to enable him or her to acquire and strengthen the concepts acquired in class. Later, at the end of the course, students face a final exam. A student with a mark over a fixed threshold passes a module, while a student with a mark lower than that threshold fails that lesson or module. With this premise, the problem consists of predicting if the student will pass or fail the module considering the number, time, and type of activities the student has undertaken during the course.

In continuation, the information available is set out in detail and both traditional supervised learning and MIL will be described.

13.3.1 Components of the Moodle Virtual Learning Platform

There is an enormous variety of e-learning platforms and most of them have common features and services. Nowadays, one of the most commonly used is Moodle (modular object-oriented developmental learning environment), a free learning management system enabling the creation of powerful, flexible, and engaging online courses and experiences [29].

The Moodle system stores a great deal of detailed information about course content, users, and usage in a relational database. This study is based on the information stored about three activities: quizzes, assignments, and forums. The quizzes are a useful tool for students to test their level of knowledge and review each of the subjects studied. They are a great tool for giving students rapid feedback on their performance and for gauging their comprehension of materials. In our study, both passed and failed quizzes are taken into consideration. Assignments are a tool for collecting student work. The assignment module gives an easy way to allow students to upload digital content for grading. They can be asked to submit essays, spreadsheets, presentations, web pages, photographs, or small audio or video clips. Research indicates that online assignment submission increases student motivation and performance. Finally, forums are a powerful communication tool within a Moodle course. They allow educators and students to communicate with each other at any time, from anywhere with an Internet connection. Students do not have to be logged on at the same time to communicate with the teacher or their classmates. Thus, students can take their time composing replies, which can lead to more thoughtful discussions. A lot of research indicates that more students are willing to participate in an asynchronous forum than are willing to speak up in class. Forums create many opportunities to replicate the conversations you have in class, to formulate project discussions between groups of students, or to bring the best ideas and questions from the forum into your classroom. There are lots of strategies and studies for the effective use of this tool.

TABLE 13.1

Information Summary Considered in Our Study

	Attributes	
Activity	Name	Description
Assignment	*numberAssignment*	Number of practices/tasks done by the user in the course
	timeAssignment	Total time in seconds that the user has been in the assignment section
Forum	*numberPosts*	Number of messages sent by the user forum
	numberRead	Number of messages read by the user forum
	timeForum	Total time in seconds that the user has been in the forum section
Quiz	*numberQuiz*	Number of quizzes seen by the user
	numberQuiz_a	Number of quizzes passed by the user
	numberQuiz_s	Number of quizzes failed by the user
	timeQuiz	Total time in seconds that the user has been in the quiz section

A summary of the information considered for each activity in our study is shown in Table 13.1.

13.3.2 Representation of Information for Working with Machine Learning Algorithms

Two representations of the problem are developed, contemplating the information in Table 13.1. One of them is a classical representation to solve the problem with traditional supervised learning algorithms. This representation considers a student by pattern/instance; the information in each instance represents all activities that the student might carry out. In this problem, each student could execute a different number of activities: a hardworking student may do all the activities available and, on the other hand, there can be students who have not done any activity. Moreover, there are some courses with only a few activities along with others with an enormous variety and number of activities. With this representation, in spite of the different information on each student and course, all instances share the same information. This means that most examples have empty attribute values either because the student did not do any activity of a certain type or because that course did not have any available activity of that type. The main problem is that the information is not displayed according to the characteristic of the problem; therefore, the representation does not fit the information available in each example.

This problem could be viewed as a multi-instance problem where each pattern is composed of a student registered in each course. In this case, each student is regarded as a bag that represents the work carried out. Each bag is composed of one or several instances. Each instance represents the different types of work that the student has done. Therefore, each pattern/bag will have activities of different types as instances done by the student. This representation fits the problem perfectly because general student and course information is stored as bag attributes, and variable information is stored as instance attributes. A summary of the attributes (features) that belong to the bag and the information that corresponds to the instances are presented in Figure 13.1. Each instance is divided into three attributes: the type of activity, the number of exercises in that activity, and the time devoted to completing that activity. Eight activity types are considered (therefore, a pattern will have a maximum number of eight instances). They are as follows: *ASSIGNMENT_S*, number of assignments that the student has submitted; *ASSIGNMENT*, referring to the number of times the student has visited the activity without finally submitting any file;

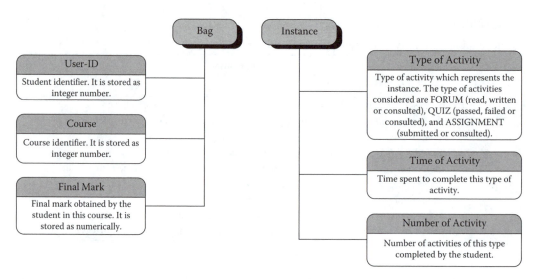

FIGURE 13.1
Information about bags and information about instances.

QUIZ_P, number of quizzes passed by the student; *QUIZ_F*, number of quizzes failed by the student; *QUIZ*, referring to the times the student has visited a survey without actually answering it; *FORUM_POST*, number of messages that the student has submitted; *FORUM_READ*, number of messages that the student has read; and *FORUM*, referring to the times the student has seen different forums without entering them. In addition, the bag contains three attributes: student identification, course identification, and the final mark obtained by the student in that course.

This information could be represented in a natural way from the MIL perspective. It is a flexible representation where new activities can be added without affecting the patterns that do not consider this new type of activity. The information about the types of activities carried out is stored as instances, and the number of instances per student is variable. Thus, activities that are not very common in the courses could be studied without increasing the general information about each pattern.

Figure 13.2 shows available information about two students. Figure 13.2a shows the information according to traditional supervised learning; each student is a pattern that contains all the information considered, even though this student may not have actually done any type of activity. Figure 13.2b and c shows the information according to MIL representation. Figure 13.2b shows a user who has carried out only one, and we can see the information that belongs to the bag or the instance in each case. Figure 13.2c shows a user that has carried out all the activities along with his or her information with respect to the bag and instances.

13.4 Experimentation and Results

Two types of experiments are carried out. The first experiment compares algorithms using a single-instance representation, while the second one evaluates multi-instance proposals

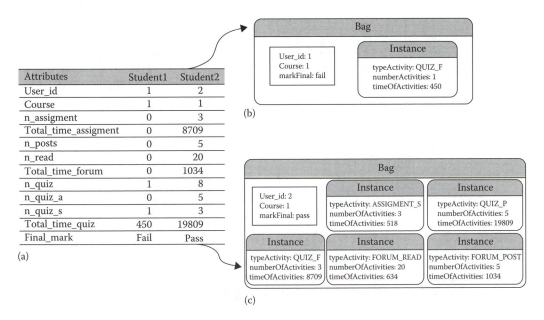

(a)

Attributes	Student1	Student2
User_id	1	2
Course	1	1
n_assigment	0	3
Total_time_assigment	0	8709
n_posts	0	5
n_read	0	20
Total_time_forum	0	1034
n_quiz	1	8
n_quiz_a	0	5
n_quiz_s	1	3
Total_time_quiz	450	19809
Final_mark	Fail	Pass

(b)

(c)

FIGURE 13.2

Information about two students (a) Available information for student 1 and student 2 to traditional supervised learning. (b) Information about bag and instances for student 1 to MIL. (c) Information about bag and instances for student 2 to MIL.

for solving this problem. Finally, single-instance and multi-instance proposals are compared. All experiments are carried out using 10-fold stratified cross validation, [30] and the average values of accuracy, sensitivity, and specificity are reported below. These measurements are widely used in classification and evaluate different parts of a classifier; therefore, an acceptable classifier must obtain an appropriate value in each one of them. *Accuracy* is the proportion of cases correctly identified, *sensitivity* is the proportion of cases correctly identified as meeting a certain condition, and *specificity* is the proportion correctly identified as not meeting a certain condition.

In this section, first the problem domain is described briefly and then the results are shown and discussed.

13.4.1 Problem Domain Used in Experimentation

This study uses the students' usage data from the VLE at the Cordoba University. Currently, the Cordoba University Moodle system has about 580 courses with over 19,000 students taking different courses offered by this university. From among all the courses available, a selection is made of those offering at least two types of activities considered and with different number of activities and resources. Thus, this study has used the information generated by Moodle for 7 courses with 419 students. The final marks obtained by students in these courses are also available. The details about the seven e-learning courses, the number of students enrolled in each course, and the number of assignments, forums, and quizzes are given in Table 13.2. For the purpose of our study, the collection of data was carried out during an academic year from September to June, just before the final examinations. All information about each student for both representations is exported to a text file using Weka ARFF format [31].

TABLE 13.2

General Information about the Courses

Course Identifier	Number of Students	Number of Assignments	Number of Forums	Number of Quizzes
ICT-29	118	11	2	0
ICT-46	9	0	3	6
ICT-88	72	12	2	0
ICT-94	66	2	3	31
ICT-110	62	7	9	12
ICT-111	13	19	4	0
ICT-218	79	4	5	30

13.4.2 Comparison with Supervised Learning Algorithms

This study has considered different and representative paradigms used in traditional supervised learning. The following methods have shown good results in other applications. *Methods based on trees*: RandomTree [31], DecisionStump [31], RandomForest [32], C4.5 (*J48*) [33], and grafted C4.5 (*J48graft*) [34]; *Methods based on rules*: NNge [35], Ridor [36], ZeroR [31], and OneR [37]; *Methods based on SMO* [38]; *Methods based on Naive Bayes*: NaiveBayesSimple [39], NaiveBayes [40], NaiveBayesMultinomial [41], and NaiveBayesUpdatebale [40]; and *Methods based on neural network*: RBFNetwork [31]. More information can be consulted on the WEKA workbench [31] where they were designed. To compare the different proposals, we consider three very common measurements used in classification: accuracy, sensitivity, and specificity [42]. Accuracy measures the proportion of correct predictions to the total number of cases evaluated, sensitivity measures the proportion of cases correctly identified as meeting a certain condition, and specificity is the proportion of cases correctly identified as not meeting a certain condition.

In Table 13.3 are reported the average results for the considered measurements of all algorithms employed in this study. In traditional supervised learning, an SMO algorithm obtains the best accuracy with a percentage of 69.76%. In general, sensitivity values are better optimized at the expense of a decrease in specific values. This demonstrates that the models do not correctly classify negative examples because they identify students as passing the course when they actually finally fail it. This case is especially difficult to classify because there are hard-working students that do not manage to finally pass the course. Different paradigms used in experimentations produce similar results; all paradigms considered contain some algorithms with results similar to the best proposal. The results of accuracy of each algorithm are shown in Figure 13.3. In this figure, the algorithms are sorted according to their values with respect to accuracy. We can compare the different proposals and find the best and the worst proposal; moreover, the differences between the different algorithms also are appreciated.

13.4.3 Comparison with Multi-Instance Learning

In the case of MIL representation, the most relevant proposals presented to date are considered to solve this problem. The different paradigms compared included *Methods based on Diverse Density*: MIDD[16], MIEMDD[17], and MDD[31]; *Methods based on Logistic Regression*: MILR[43]; *Methods based on SMO*: MISMO uses the SMO algorithm [38] for SVM learning in conjunction with an MI kernel [44]; *Distance-based*

TABLE 13.3

Results for Supervised Learning Algorithms

	Algorithms	Accuracy	Sensitivity	Specificity
Trees	DecisionStump	0.6690	0.8889	0.3651
	RandomForest	0.6667	0.7573	0.5426
	RandomTree	0.6476	0.6996	0.5755
	J48 graft	0.6881	0.7950	0.5408
	J48	0.6857	0.7950	0.5345
Rules	NNge	0.6952	0.7329	0.6434
	Ridor	0.6810	0.8648	0.4310
	OneR	0.6476	0.7665	0.4835
	ZeroR	0.5810	1.0000	0.0000
Naive Bayes	NaiveBayes	0.6857	0.8232	0.4944
	NaiveBayesMultinomial	0.6929	0.7662	0.5918
	NaiveBayesSimple	0.6810	0.8232	0.4832
	NaiveBayesUpdateable	0.6857	0.8232	0.4944
Others	RBFNetwork	0.6929	0.8227	0.5114
	SMO	0.6976	0.8842	0.4374

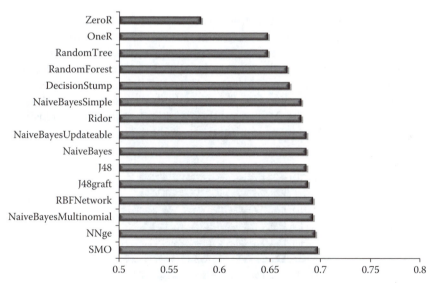

FIGURE 13.3
Accuracy obtained by single-instance algorithms.

Approaches: CitationKNN [22] and MIOptimalBall [45]; *Methods based on Supervised Learning Algorithms*: MIWrapper [46] using different learners, such as Bagging, PART, SMO, AdaBoost, and NaiveBayes; MISimple [31] using PART and AdaBoost as learners; and MIBoost [26]. More information could be consulted at the WEKA workbench [31] where these techniques are designed. The average results of accuracy, sensitivity, and specificity are reported in Table 13.4.

As in single-instance learning, better sensitivity values are obtained at the expense of specificity. In fact, these measurements have a trade-off that would be interesting to

TABLE 13.4

Results for Multi-Instance Learning Algorithms

	Algorithm	Accuracy	Sensitivity	Specificity
Methods based on supervised learning (Simple)	PART	0.7357	0.8387	0.5920
	AdaBoostM1&PART	0.7262	0.8187	0.5992
Methods based on supervised learning (Wrapper)	Bagging&PART	0.7167	0.7733	0.6361
	AdaBoostM1&PART	0.7071	0.7735	0.6136
	PART	0.7024	0.7857	0.5842
	SMO	0.6810	0.8644	0.4270
	NaiveBayes	0.6786	0.8515	0.4371
Methods based on distance	MIOptimalBall	0.7071	0.7218	0.6877
	CitationKNN	0.7000	0.7977	0.5631
Methods based on trees	DecisionStump	0.6762	0.7820	0.5277
	RepTree	0.6595	0.7127	0.5866
Logistic regression	MILR	0.6952	0.8183	0.5218
Methods based on diverse density	MIDD	0.6976	0.8552	0.4783
	MIEMDD	0.6762	0.8549	0.4250
	MDD	0.6571	0.7864	0.4757

optimize by using multi-objective strategies. With respect to the different paradigms used, the methods based on rules (PART) or a combination of this method with other proposals obtain the best results for this learning. The results of accuracy obtained by each algorithm are shown in Figure 13.4. In this figure, the algorithms are sorted according to their values with respect to accuracy measurement. Thus, the differences between algorithms are easier to understand, and we can check that methods based on systems based on rules as PART achieve the best results. Moreover, these methods add comprehensibility to the problem generating rules that a user can interpret easily.

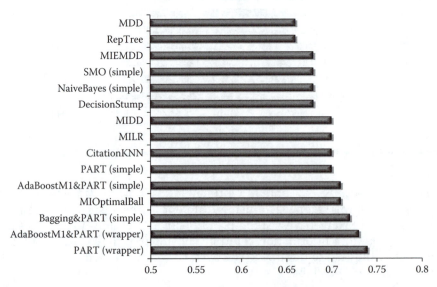

FIGURE 13.4

Accuracy obtained by multi-instance algorithms.

It can be seen that some of the paradigms used in single-instance and multi-instance representation are similar in both proposals. However, these methods are not comparable directly because they are not exactly the same implementations. Therefore, it is necessary to evaluate the results obtained by each representation considering the different algorithms evaluated to draw a final conclusion (in Section 13.4.4 we perform the comparison). At first sight, it is interesting to see in the graphics showed that generally the algorithms with multi-instance representation yield higher values of accuracy.

13.4.4 Comparison between Single- and Multi-Instance Learning

In this section, a statistical study is carried out with the purpose of demonstrating if the representation with multiple instances is more appropriate than single-instance representations to solve the problem of predicting the students' performance according their work in a virtual learning platform. Both representations have considered 15 of the most representative algorithms of various paradigms developed to date, which include systems based on tree, on decision tree, logistic regression, neural network, SMO, and others. Their results about accuracy, sensitivity, and specificity values have been shown in the previous sections. The idea is to check if there are significant differences between the accuracy values obtained by the different algorithms using the MIL representation and the traditional supervised learning representation with single instance.

The Wilcoxon rank sum test is used to look for differences between the accuracy values obtained by both representations. This test is a nonparametric recommended in the study performed by Demsar [47] that allows us to address the question of whether there are significant differences between the accuracy values obtained by the algorithms using both representations. To do this, the null hypothesis of this test assures that there are not significant differences between the accuracy values of each representation, and the alternative hypothesis assures that if there are.

This test evaluates the differences of performance between the two representations evaluating the obtained results by the algorithms with each representation. Table 13.5 shows the mean ranks and the sum of ranks for each representation. The scores are ranked from lowest to highest. Therefore, we can see that algorithms using single-instance representation get a lower mean rank than algorithms using multi-instance representation. Therefore, this information can be used to ascertain a priori that multi-instance representation has a greater number of algorithms that obtains a higher accuracy value.

Table 13.6 provides the actual test statistical Wilcoxon procedure and the corresponding z-score. Moreover, we show the significant value of the test that gives the two-tailed probability to determine if we accept or reject the null hypothesis. According to this value, the results are highly significant (p-value < 0.05). Therefore, with a 95% level of confidence we reject the null hypothesis and we can determine that there are significant differences between the results obtained by both representations. Consequently, the multi-instance representation has significantly higher accuracy values than the single-instance

TABLE 13.5

Sum of Ranks and Mean Rank of the Two Representations

	Mean Rank	Sum of Ranks
Multi-instance representation	18.67	280
Single-instance representation	12.33	185

TABLE 13.6

Wilcoxon Rank–Sum Test Results

	Wilcoxon W	Z-Score	Asymp Sig (2-Tailed) (*p*-Value)
Accuracy for both representations	185	−1.973	0.048

representation. This conclusion is reached by noting that for multi-instance representation scores, the mean rank is higher in the algorithms using multi-instance representation (with a value of 18.67) than in single-instance representation (with a value of 12.33).

13.5 Conclusions and Future Work

This chapter describes a first proposal using a MIL representation for the problem of predicting a student's performance based on his or her work in VLE. To check effectiveness, both traditional supervised learning and MIL representations are described. The most representative paradigms considering 15 different algorithms of each learning are applied to solve this problem, and the results are compared. A statistical study comparing the two representations shows that the results of algorithms using multi-instance representation obtain higher accuracy values and the differences are significant. These results confirm that MIL representation is a more appropriate representation that is able to represent available information in a well-suited approach and improve the results of the algorithms remarkably.

References

1. Nagi, K. and Suesawaluk, P. Research analysis of Moodle reports to gauge the level of interactivity in eLearning courses at Assumption University, Thailand. In *ICCN'08: Proceedings of the 18th International Conference on Computer and Communication Engineering*, Kuala Lumpur, Malaysia, 2008.
2. Chou, S. and Liu, S. Learning effectiveness in Web-based technology-mediated virtual learning environment. In *HICSS'05: Proceedings of the 38th Hawaii International Conference on System Sciences*, Washington, DC, January 3–6, 2005.
3. Fausett, L. and Elwasif, W. Predicting performance from test scores using backpropagation and counterpropagation. In *WCCI'94: IEEE World Congress on Computational Intelligence*, Orlando, FL, 1994, pp. 3398–3402.
4. Martínez, D. Predicting student outcomes using discriminant function analysis. In *Annual Meeting of the Research and Planning Group*, San Francisco, CA, 2001, pp. 163–173.
5. Minaei-Bidgoli, B. and Punch, W. Using genetic algorithms for data mining optimization in an educational Web-based system. *Genetic and Evolutionary Computation*, 2, 2252–2263, 2003.
6. Superby, J.F., Vandamme, J.P., and Meskens, N. Determination of factors influencing the achievement of the first-year university students using data mining methods. In *EDM'06: Workshop on Educational Data Mining*, Hong Kong, China, 2006, pp. 37–44.
7. Kotsiantis, S.B. and Pintelas, P.E. Predicting students marks in Hellenic Open University. In *ICALT'05: The 5th International Conference on Advanced Learning Technologies*, Kaohsiung, Taiwan, July 5–8, 2005, pp. 664–668.

8. Delgado, M., Gibaja, E., Pegalajar, M.C., and Pérez, O. Predicting students' marks from Moodle Logs using neural network models. In *Current Developments in Technology-Assisted Education*, FORMATEX, Badajoz, Spain, 2006, pp. 586–590.

9. Romero, C. and Ventura, S. Educational data mining: A survey from 1995 to 2005. *Expert Systems with Applications*, 33(1), 135–146, 2007.

10. Dietterich, T.G., Lathrop, R.H., and Lozano-Perez, T. Solving the multiple instance problem with axis-parallel rectangles. *Artificial Intelligence*, 89(1–2), 31–71, 1997.

11. Weidmann, N., Frank, E., and Pfahringer, B. A two-level learning method for generalized multi-instance problems. In *ECML'03: Proceedings of the 14th European Conference on Machine Learning*, Cavtat-Dubrovnik, Croatia, 2003, pp. 468–479.

12. Scott, S., Zhang, J., and Brown, J. On generalized multiple-instance learning. *International Journal of Computational Intelligence and Applications*, 5, 21–35, 2005.

13. Andrews, S., Tsochantaridis, I., and Hofmann, T. Support vector machines for multiple-instance learning. In *NIPS'02: Proceedings of Neural Information Processing System*, Vancouver, Canada, 2000, pp. 561–568.

14. Pao, H.T., Chuang, S.C., Xu, Y.Y., and Fu, H. An EM based multiple instance learning method for image classification. *Expert Systems with Applications*, 35(3), 1468–1472, 2008.

15. Chen, Y. and Wang, J.Z. Image categorization by learning and reasoning with regions. *Journal of Machine Learning Research*, 5, 913–939, 2004.

16. Maron, O. and Lozano-Pérez, T. A framework for multiple-instance learning. In *NIPS'97: Proceedings of Neural Information Processing System 10*, Denver, CO, 1997, pp. 570–576.

17. Zhang, Q. and Goldman, S. EM-DD: An improved multiple-instance learning technique. In *NIPS'01: Proceedings of Neural Information Processing System 14*, Vancouver, Canada, 2001, pp. 1073–1080.

18. Han, Q.Y. Incorporating multiple SVMs for automatic image annotation. *Pattern Recognition*, 40(2), 728–741, 2007.

19. Zafra, A., Ventura, S., Romero, C., and Herrera-Viedma, E. Multi-instance genetic programming for web index recommendation. *Expert System with Applications*, 36, 11470–11479, 2009.

20. Goldman, S.A. and Scott, S.D. Multiple-instance learning of real valued geometric patterns. *Annals of Mathematics and Artificial Intelligence*, 39, 259–290, 2001.

21. Ruffo, G. Learning single and multiple instance decision tree for computer security applications. PhD dissertation, Department of Computer Science, University of Turin, Torino, Italy, 2000.

22. Wang, J. and Zucker, J.-D. Solving the multiple-instance problem: A lazy learning approach. In *ICML'00: Proceedings of the 17th International Conference on Machine Learning*, Stanford, CA, 2000, pp. 1119–1126.

23. Chevaleyre, Y.-Z. and Zucker, J.-D. Solving multiple-instance and multiple-part learning problems with decision trees and decision rules. Application to the mutagenesis problem. In *AI'01: Proceedings of the 14th of the Canadian Society for Computational Studies of Intelligence, LNCS 2056*, Ottawa, Canada 2001, pp. 204–214.

24. Ramon, J. and De Raedt, L. Multi-instance neural networks. In *ICML'00: A Workshop on Attribute-Value and Relational Learning at the 17th Conference on Machine Learning*, San Francisco, CA, 2000.

25. Chai, Y.M. and Yang, Z.-W. A multi-instance learning algorithm based on normalized radial basis function network. In *ISSN'07: Proceedings of the 4th International Symposium on Neural Networks. LNCS 4491*, Nanjing, China, 2007, pp. 1162–1172.

26. Xu, X. and Frank, E. Logistic regression and boosting for labelled bags of instances. In *PAKDD'04: Proceedings of the 8th Conference of Pacific-Asia. LNCS 3056*, Sydney, Australia, 2004, pp. 272–281.

27. Zhou, Z.-H. and Zhang, M.-L. Solving multi-instance problems with classifier ensemble based on constructive clustering. *Knowledge and Information Systems*, 11(2), 155–170, 2007.

28. Zafra, A. and Ventura, S. Multi-objective genetic programming for multiple instance learning. In *EMCL'07: Proceedings of the 18th European Conference on Machine Learning, LNAI 4701*, Warsaw, Poland, 2007, pp. 790–797.

29. Rice, W.H. *Moodle e-Learning Course Development. A Complete Guide to Successful Learning Using Moodle.* Pack Publishing, Birmingham, U.K., 2006.
30. Wiens, T.S., Dale, B.C., Boyce, M.S., and Kershaw, P.G. Three way k-fold cross-validation of resource selection functions. *Ecological Modelling*, 3–4, 244–255, 2007.
31. Witten, I.H. and Frank, E. *Data Mining: Practical Machine Learning Tools and Techniques*, 2nd edn. Morgan Kaufmann, San Francisco, CA, 2005.
32. Breiman, L. Random forests. *Machine Learning*, 45(1), 5–32, 2001.
33. Quinlan, R. *C4.5: Programs for Machine Learning*. Morgan Kaufmann Publishers, San Mateo, CA, 1993.
34. Webb, G. Decision tree grafting from the all-tests-but-one partition. In *IJCAI'99: Proceedings of the 16th International Joint Conference on Artificial Intelligence*, San Francisco, CA, 1999, pp. 702–707.
35. Martin, B. Instance-based learning: Nearest neighbor with generalization. PhD thesis, Department of Computer Science. University of Waikato, Hamilton, New Zealand, 1995.
36. Gaines, B.R. and Compton, P. Induction of ripple-down rules applied to modeling large databases. *Journal of Intelligence Information System*, 5(3), 211–228, 1995.
37. Holte, R.C. Very simple classification rules perform well on most commonly used datasets. *Machine Learning*, 11, 63–91, 1993.
38. Keerthi, S.S., Shevade, S.K., Bhattacharyya, C., and Murthy, K.R.K. Improvements to Platt's SMO algorithm for SVM classifier design. *Neural Computation*, 13(3), 637–649, 2001.
39. Duda, R. and Hart, P. *Pattern Classification and Scene Analysis*. Wiley, New York, 1973.
40. George, H.J. and Langley, P. Estimating continuous distributions in Bayesian classifiers. In *UAI'95: Proceedings of the 11th Conference on Uncertainty in Artificial Intelligence*, San Mateo, CA, 1995, pp. 338–345.
41. McCallum, A. and Nigam, K. A comparison of event models for naive Bayes text classification. In *AAAI'98: Workshop on Learning for Text Categorization*, Orlando, FL, 1998, pp. 41–48.
42. Tan, K.C., Tay, A., Lee, T., and Heng, C.M., Mining multiple comprehensible classification rules using genetic programming. In *CEC'02: Proceedings of the 2002 Congress on Evolutionary Computation*, Honolulu, HI, 2002, Vol. 2, pp. 1302–1307.
43. Xu, X. Statistical learning in multiple instance problems. PhD thesis, Department of Computer Science, University of Waikato, Hamilton, New Zealand, 2003.
44. Gärtner, T., Flach, P.A., Kowalczyk, A., and Smola, A.J. Multi-instance kernels. In *ICML'02: Proceedings of the 19th International Conference on Machine Learning*, Morgan Kaufmann, Sydney, Australia, 2002, pp. 179–186.
45. Auer, P. and Ortner, R. A boosting approach to multiple instance learning. In *ECML'04: Proceedings of the 5th European Conference on Machine Learning. Lecture Notes in Computer Science*, Pisa, Italy, 2004, Vol. 3201, pp. 63–74.
46. Frank, E. and Xu, X. Applying propositional learning algorithms to multi-instance data, Technical report, Department of Computer Science, University of Waikato, 2003.
47. Demsar, J. Statistical comparisons of classifiers over multiple data sets. *Journal of Machine Learning Research*, 17, 1–30, 2006.

14

A Response-Time Model for Bottom-Out Hints as Worked Examples

Benjamin Shih, Kenneth R. Koedinger, and Richard Scheines

CONTENTS

14.1 Introduction

Students sometimes use an educational system's help in unexpected ways. For example, they may bypass abstract hints in search of a concrete example. This behavior has traditionally been labeled as gaming or help abuse. In this chapter, we propose that some examples of this behavior are not abusive and that bottom-out hints can serve as worked examples. To demonstrate this, we create a model for distinguishing good bottom-out hint use from bad bottom-out hint use by analyzing logged response times. This model not only predicts learning, but captures behaviors related to self-explanation.

There is a large body of research on measuring students' affective and metacognitive states. The goals of this research range from adapting instruction to individual needs to designing interventions that change affective states. One technique is to build classification models for affective states using tutor interaction data, often with student response times as an independent variable [3,5,6,13]. Several lines of research using this approach have targeted tutor help abuse as a behavior negatively correlated with learning [3,13], but these classification rules for help abuse can be quite broad and thus proscribe behaviors that may actually benefit learning. For example, students that drill down to the most detailed hint may not be gaming the system, but instead searching for a worked example. The goal of this chapter is to show that a simple response-time-based indicator can discern some good bottom-out hint behaviors. We also provide a case study on the construction of models for unobserved states or traits.

An indicator for good bottom-out hint behaviors would be useful in several ways. It could indicate general traits, such as good metacognitive self-regulation, or it might serve as a proxy for students' affective states. In general, even an indicator that does not directly guide educational interventions could still be useful as a component in existing models, possibly replacing or augmenting present estimates of self-explanation and reasoning. For example, Mavrikis proposed a model that included a reflection-on-hints feature derived from the total time spent after hints [10]. The indicator proposed here could offer an improved estimate of that reflection time, and thus improve the entire model. However, the indicator might be most useful for improving the design of computer-based educational scaffolding. There is significant evidence to suggest that optimal learning comes from a mix of worked examples and scaffolded problems [11,12]. A response-time indicator for self-explanation behavior could help determine the conditions under which worked examples or scaffolded problems are more effective.

In this chapter, we discuss the existing research, focused on the discrepancy between existing tutor models and results from the worked example and self-explanation literature. We then describe our data with an emphasis on the timing information available in the log files. Next, we focus on a simple student model that leads to an equally simple indicator for good bottom-out hint behaviors. We show that the indicator has a high correlation with learning gain in the aforementioned data, and that the original study's experimental condition provides strong evidence that the indicator captures some form of reasoning or self-explanation behavior.

14.2 Background

Usually, a response-time is defined as the time required for a subject to respond to a stimulus. For educational systems, this is often calculated at the transaction level. How long does it take a student to perform a task, such as request help or enter an answer? The limitations of log data mean that many details are obscure, such as the student's thought process or the presence of distractions. The student's actions may have been triggered by an event outside the systems' purview or the student may be engaging in other off-task behavior. While a limitation, it is exactly this off-task aspect of response times that makes them so valuable for estimating students' affective states [6].

There is a large body of prior work on response-time-based models for affective and metacognitive states. For example, Beck modeled student disengagement using a response-time-based model [6]. His work is particularly relevant because, like this study, he used a combination of model building and elimination of irrelevant examples to construct his detector. There are also a number of help-seeking models that utilize response times in their design to better detect gaming behavior, particularly behaviors that involve drilling through scaffolding or repeated guessing [3,13]. Still, we know of no examples of models that can detect help abuse aimed at soliciting a worked example. To the contrary, one rule shared by many models is that bypassing the traditional scaffold structure to retrieve the bottom-out hint, which is often the final answer, is considered an undesirable behavior [3].

In the literature on worked examples, particularly, for self-explanation, help abuse is not always bad for learning. If a student truly needs a worked example, drilling down through the help system may be the easiest available means of getting one. There is a significant body of research on worked examples to suggest that this is true [11]. There have also been attempts to apply worked examples to computerized educational systems [4,9]. For this chapter, however, the focus is restricted to considering worked examples as improving learning through self-explanation. In the original self-explanation studies, students were given worked examples and then asked to explain the examples to themselves [7]. Later interventions resulted in improved pre-post gain [8], but extending the direct self-explanation intervention to computerized educational systems has been less successful [9]. Using self-explanation interventions in other situations, such as with students explaining their own work, has found some success in computerized systems [2]. One study by Schworm and Renkl found that students did learn from worked examples, but only if they were prompted to self-explain; so long as students were prompted for self-explanations, there was a learning effect regardless of the type of worked example presented [12]. This result is particularly important because of its 2×2 design, which found that explicit instruction could reduce self-explanation and, thus, be detrimental to learning. This suggests that neither self-explanation of worked examples nor explicit instruction within scaffolded problems is necessarily an optimal strategy. Thus, the mechanism relating self-explanation behavior to learning in computer tutors is complex, but clearly vital to the successful integration of worked examples into computerized educational systems.

14.3 Data

Our data consists of logs of student interactions with the Geometry Cognitive Tutor [1]. In the tutor, students are presented with a geometry problem displayed above several empty text fields. A step in the problem requires filling in a text field. The fields are arranged systematically on each problem page and might, for example, ask for the values of angles in a polygon or for the intermediate values required to calculate the circumference of a circle. In the tutor, a transaction is defined as interacting with the glossary, requesting a hint, entering an answer, or pressing "done." The done transaction is only required to start a new problem, not to start a new step.

The data itself comes from Aleven and Koedinger [1]. They studied the addition of required explanation steps to the Geometry Cognitive Tutor. In the experimental condition, after entering a correct answer, students were asked to justify their answer by citing a theorem. This could be done either by searching the glossary or by directly inputting the theorem into a text field. The tutor labeled the theorem as correct if it was a perfect, letter-by-letter match for the tutor's stored answer. This type of reasoning or justification transaction is the study's version of self-explanation (albeit with feedback). In their study, Aleven and Koedinger found that students in the experimental condition "learned with greater understanding compared to students who did not explain steps" [1].

The hints are arranged in levels, with each later level providing a more specific suggestion about how to proceed on that step. While the early hint levels can be quite abstract, the bottom-out hint does everything short of entering the answer. The only required work to finish a step after receiving a bottom-out hint is to input the answer itself into the text field. This type of transaction is the study's version of a simple worked example.

There were 39 students in the study that had both pretest and posttest scores. They were split into 20 and 19 between the two conditions. All times were measured in hundredth's of a second. The other details of the data are introduced in the discussion of results, Section 4.5.

14.4 Model

The core assumption underlying this work is that bottom-out hints can serve as worked examples. In our data, a bottom-out hint is defined to be the last hint available for a given step. The number of hints available differs from step to step, but the frequency of bottom-out hint requests suggests that students were comfortable drilling down to the last hint.

Assuming that bottom-out hints sometimes serve as worked examples, there are a couple of ways to detect desirable bottom-out hint behaviors. The first method is to detect when a student's goal is to retrieve a worked example. This method is sensitive to properly modeling student intentions. The second method, which is the focus of this work, is to detect when a student is *learning* from a bottom-out hint, regardless of their intent in retrieving the hint. This assumes that learning derives from the act of self-explanation or through a similar mechanism, and can occur even if the student purposefully gamed the system to retrieve the bottom-out hint. We estimate the amount of learning by using the time spent thinking about a hint. This makes the approach dependent only on student's time spent and independent of a student's intention.

To detect learning from bottom-out hints, our model requires estimates of the time students spend thinking about hints. Call the hint time $HINT_t$, where $HINT_t$ is the time spent thinking about a hint requested on transaction t. Estimating $HINT_t$ is nontrivial. Students may spend some of their time engaged in activities unobserved in the log, like chatting with a neighbor. However, even assuming no external activities or any off-task behavior whatsoever, $HINT_t$ is still not directly observable in the data.

To illustrate this, consider the following model for student cognition. On an answer transaction, the student first thinks about an answer, then enters an answer, and then reflects on their solution. Call this model TER for think–enter–reflect. An illustration of how the TER model would underlie observed data is shown in Figure 14.1. The reflection time for the second transaction is part of the logged time for the third transaction. Under the TER model, the reflection time for one transaction is indistinguishable from the thinking and entry times associated with the next transaction. Nevertheless, we need an estimate for the think and reflect times to approximate student learning from bottom-out hints.

The full problem, including external factors, is illustrated in Table 14.1. It shows a series of actual student transactions on a pair of problem steps along with hypothetical, unobserved student cognition. Entries in italics are observed in the log, while those in normal face are unobserved, and ellipses represent data not relevant to the example. The time the student spends thinking and reflecting on the bottom-out hint is about 6s, but the available *observed* durations are 0.347, 15.152, and 4.944s. In a case like this, the log data's observed response times include a mixture of think and reflect times across multiple steps. Unfortunately, while the reflection time is important for properly estimating $HINT_t$, it is

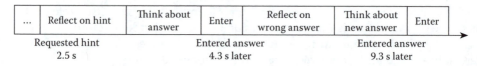

FIGURE 14.1
TER model.

TABLE 14.1

Hypothetical Student Transactions (*Observed Data*, Unobserved Data)

Step	Transaction	Observed *T*	Cognition	Hypothetical *T*
Step 1	*Request hint*	0.347	...	...
			Thinking about hint	3
			Looking at clock	2
			Thinking about date	9
Step 1	*Enter answer*	15.152	Typing answer	1.152
			Thinking about last step	2
			Thinking about next step	1
Step 2	*Enter answer*	4.944	Typing answer	1.944

categorized improperly. The reflection time for transaction *t* is actually part of the logged time for transaction $(t+1)$, that is, after receiving a hint, thinking about the hint, and entering the answer, the tutor records a time stamp, but the student may continue thinking about the hint as long as they wish. Teasing apart these transaction times requires some creative rearranging of terms. Rather than estimating $HINT_t$ directly, we will estimate a number of other values and calculate $HINT_t$ accordingly.

The first part of our model separates out two types of bottom-out hint cognition: think and reflect. Thinking is defined as all hint cognition before entering the answer; reflecting is all hint cognition after entering the answer. Let think time be denoted by K_t and reflect time be denoted by R_t. We define $HINT_t = K_t + R_t$.

The task reduces to estimating K_t and R_t. As shown earlier, this can be difficult for an arbitrary transaction. However, the task is easier if we restrict our focus to bottom-out hints. Let the time to enter an answer be denoted by E_t. Table 14.2 provides an example of how bottom-out hints differ from other transactions: the absence of a reflect time, R_{t-1}, in the bottom-out case. Except for the time spent on answer entry and the time spent off-task, the time between receiving a hint and entering the answer is K_t. This is because, after receiving a bottom-out hint, a student does not need to engage in reflection about the step before, eliminating the confound R_{t-1}. A similar, but slightly more complicated result applies to R_t. For now, assume the off-task time is zero—it will be properly addressed later. Let the total time for a transaction be T_t. Then the equation for $HINT_t$ becomes

TABLE 14.2

TER Model with Estimators

Transaction	Cognition	Notation
Hint	...	
	Think about step	K_t
	Off-task	E_t
Enter answer	Enter answer	
	Reflect on previous step	R_t
	Think about new step	K_{t+1}
	Off-task	E_{t+1}
Enter answer	Enter answer	

$$HINT_t = K_t + R_t$$
$$= (T_t - E_t) + R_t$$
$$= (T_t - E_t) + (T_{t+1} - (K_{t+1} + E_{t+1}))$$

where T_t and T_{t+1} are the observed times in the log data. The first term consists of replacing K_t with measured and unmeasured times from before the answer is submitted (row 2 of Table 14.2). The second term consists of times from after the answer is submitted (row 3 of Table 14.2). We have reduced the problem to something tractable. Now, if we have an estimate for E_t, we can estimate K_t. Similarly, if we have an estimate for K_{t+1} and E_{t+1}, we can estimate R_t.

Constructing reliable estimates for the above values is impossible on a per transaction basis. However, if we aggregate across all transactions performed by a given student, then the estimators become feasible. There are two important points regarding the estimators we will use. First, response times, because of their open-ended nature, are extremely prone to outliers. For example, the longest recorded transaction is over 25 min in length. Thus, we require our estimators to be robust. Second, some students have relatively few (≈10) bottom-out hint transactions that will fit our eventual criteria, so our estimators must converge quickly.

Now we require new notations. We use the s subscript, where s represents a student. We also use the $\hat{E}_s$ notation for estimators and the $m(E_t)$ notation for medians. You can think of the median of E_t, $m(E_t)$, as approximating the mean, but always use the median because of outliers. $\hat{E}_s$, the per student estimator, will represent some measure of the usual E_t for a student s. Also, let A be the set of all transactions and A_s be the set of all transactions for a given student. We will further subdivide these sets into correct answers transactions immediately following a bottom-out hint and transactions following those transactions. These two types of transactions are generalizations of the last two transactions shown in Table 14.2. Let A_s^1 be the set of all correct answer transactions by a student s where the transaction immediately follows a bottom-out hint. These are transactions corresponding to row 2 of Table 14.2. Similarly, let A_s^2 be the set of all transactions that follow a transaction $t \in A_s^1$. These are transactions corresponding to row 3 of Table 14.2. Essentially, a bottom-out hint transaction is followed by a transaction of type A_s^1, which is in turn followed by a transaction of type A_s^2. For convenience, we will let $T_s^1 = m(T_t), t \in A_s^1$ be the median time for transactions of the first type and $T_s^2 = m(T_t), t \in A_s^2$ be the median time for transactions of the second type. This gives an equation for our estimator:

$$HI\hat{N}T_S = (T_s^1 - E_s) + (T_s^2 - (K_s^2 + E_s))$$

where $K_s^2 = m(K_t), t \in A_s^2$ is the thinking time during transaction $t \in A_s^2$.

Consider $\hat{E}_s$, the median time for student s to enter an answer. Most answers are short and require very little time to type. If we assume that the variance is small, then $\hat{E}_s \approx \min (E_t), t \in A_s$, that is, because the variance is small, E_t can be treated as a constant. We use the minimum rather than a more common measure, like the mean, because we cannot directly observe E_t and must avoid outliers. If $K_t \approx 0$, then the total time spent on a post-hint transaction is approximately E_t, as shown in Table 14.2. Thus, the minimum time student s spends on any answer step is a good approximation of E_s. In practice, the observed $\hat{E}_s$ is about 1 s. Using $\hat{E}_s$, we can now estimate K_t for $t \in A_s^1$.

To isolate the reflection time, R_s, we need an approximation for K_s^2, the thinking time for transactions $t \in A_s^2$. Unfortunately, K_s^2 is difficult to estimate. Instead, we will estimate a value related to K_s^2. The key observation is that if a student has already thought through an answer on their own, without using any system help, they presumably engage in very little reflection after they enter their solution. Mathematically, let N_s be the set of transactions for a student s where they do not use a bottom-out hint. For cases $t \in N_s$, we can assume that $R_t \approx 0$, that is, that students do not reflect. We can now use the following estimator to isolate R_s:

$$R_s = T_s^2 - \left(K_s^2 + E_s\right)$$
$$= m\left(T_t^2\right) - \left(K_s^2 + E_s\right)$$
$$\approx m\left(T_t^2\right) - m\left(T_t^N\right)$$

where the substitution from the first to the second line derives from the assumption $R_t \approx 0$, $t \in N_s$. This is the last estimator we require: we can estimate R_s using the median time on the first transaction of a step where the prior step was completed without worked examples, that is, where $t \in N_s$. This approach avoids directly estimating K_s^2, and estimates the sum $\left(K_s^2 + E_s\right)$ instead.

There is still the problem of off-task time. We have so far assumed that the off-task time is approximately zero. We will continue to hold this assumption. While students engage in long periods of off-task behavior, we assume that for most transactions, students are on-task. This implies that transactions with off-task behaviors are rare, albeit potentially of long duration. Since we use medians, we eliminate these outliers from consideration entirely, and thus continue to assume that on any given transaction, off-task time is close to zero.

A subtle point is that the model will not fit well for end-of-problem transactions. At the end of a problem there is a "done" step, where the student has to decide to hit "done." The model no longer accurately represents the student's cognitive process as it does not include the "done" decision. These transactions could be valuable to an extended version of the model, but for this study, all end-of-problem transactions are simply dropped.

14.5 Results

We first demonstrate the model for students in the control condition. These students were not required to perform any formal reasoning steps. The goal is to predict the adjusted pretest to posttest gain, which is the max of (post-pre)/(1 − pre) and (post-pre)/(pre). We will not use Z-scores because the pretest suffered from a floor effect; so the pretest scores are very non-normal (Shapiro–Wilks: $p < 0.005$). Two students were removed from the population for having fewer than five bottom-out hint requests, bringing the population down to 18. The results are shown in Table 14.3.

TABLE 14.3

Indicator Correlations in the Control Condition

	Pre	Post	Adjusted Gain
K_s	−0.11	0.37*	0.34*
R_s	0.29	0.42**	0.36*
$HINT_s$	0.04	0.53**	0.48**

*$p<0.10$, **$p<0.05$.

The first result of interest is that none of the indicators have statistically significant correlations with the pretest. This suggests that they measure some state or trait of the students that is not well captured by the pretest. The second result is that all three indicators correlate strongly with both the posttest and learning gain. Notably, $HINT_s$, our main indicator, has a correlation of about 0.5 with both the posttest and the learning gain. To the extent that $HINT_s$ does distinguish between "good" and "bad" bottom-out hint behaviors, this correlation suggests that the two types of behaviors are useful classifications.

It is possible that these indicators might only be achieving correlations comparable to time-on-task or average transaction time. As Table 14.4 shows, this is clearly not the case. All three hint time indicators outperform the traditional time-on-task measures, with the minimum correlation in Table 14.3 equal to 0.34.

Nevertheless, these results still do not clarify whether the indicator $HINT_s$ is actually measuring what it purports to measure: self-explanation on worked examples. To explore this question, we use the experimental condition. In the experimental condition, students were asked to justify their solutions by providing the mathematical theorem associated with their answer. This changes the basic pattern of transactions from HINT-GUESS-GUESS to HINT-GUESS-JUSTIFY-GUESS. We can now directly measure R_s using the time spent on the new JUSTIFY step, since, in the experimental condition, the new justify step requires a reasoning process. R_s is now the median time students spend on a correct justification step after a bottom-out hint, subtracting the minimum time they ever spend on correct justifications. We use the minimum for reasons analogous to those of $\hat{E}_s$. In this condition, there were sufficient observations for all 19 students. The resulting correlations are shown in Table 14.5.

There is almost no correlation between our indicators and the pretest score, again showing that our indicators are detecting phenomena not effectively measured by the pretest. The correlations with the posttest and learning gain are also high for both R_s and $HINT_s$. While R_s by itself has a statistically significant correlation at $p < 0.10$, K_s and R_s combined demonstrate a statistically significant correlation at $p < 0.05$. This suggests that while some students think about a bottom-out hint before entering the answer and some students think about the hint after entering the answer, all students, regardless of style, benefit from the time spent thinking about bottom-out hints when such hints are requested. The corollary is that some bottom-out hints are beneficial to learning.

TABLE 14.4

Time-on-Task Correlations in the Control Condition

	Pre	Post	Adjusted Gain
Time-on-task	−0.31	−0.10	0.23
Average transaction time	−0.03	0.27	0.20

TABLE 14.5

Correlations in the Experimental
Condition

	Pre	Post	Adjusted Gain
K_s	−0.02	0.23	0.25
R_s	0.02	0.31*	0.35*
$HINT_s$	0.00	0.38*	0.41**

*$p < 0.10$, **$p < 0.05$.

TABLE 14.6

Changes in Behavior in the Experimental Condition

	Mean	Var	Pre	Post	Adjusted Gain
$\Delta HINT_s$	0.56	5.06	0.41*	0.47**	0.38*

*$p < 0.10$, **$p < 0.05$.

So far, we have shown that the indicator $HINT_s$ is robust enough to show strong correlations with learning gain despite being measured in two different ways across two separate conditions. The first set of results demonstrated that $HINT_s$ can be measured without any direct observation of reasoning steps. The second set of results showed that direct observation of $HINT_s$ was similarly effective. Our data, however, allows us access to two other interesting questions. First, does prompting students to explain their reasoning change their bottom-out hint behavior? Second, do changes in this behavior correlate with learning gain?

To answer both questions, we look at the indicators trained on only the first 20% of each student's transactions. For this, we use only the experimental condition, since, when 80% of the data is removed, the control condition has very few remaining students with very few observations. Even in the experimental condition, only 15 students have more than five bottom-out hint requests in the reduced data set. The results are shown in Table 14.6, with $\Delta HINT_s$ representing the difference between $HINT_s$ trained on the first 20% of the data and $HINT_s$ trained on the full data.

To answer the first question, the change in $HINT_s$ due to the Aleven and Koedinger intervention is not statistically different from zero. Their intervention, requiring ungraded self-explanations, does not appear to encourage longer response times in the presence of bottom-out hints, so this mechanism does not explain their experimental results [1]. However, some students do change behavior. As seen in Table 14.6, students who increased their $HINT_s$ time had higher learning gains.

14.6 Conclusions and Future Work

In this chapter, we presented evidence that some bottom-out hint use can be beneficial for learning. The correlations between our indicators and pre–post learning gain represent one form of evidence; the correlations between changes in our indicators and pre-post learning gain represent another. Both sets of results show that thinking about bottom-out hints predicts learning. However, extending our results to practical use requires additional work.

Our indicators provide estimates for student thinking about bottom-out hints. However, these estimates are aggregated across transactions, providing a student-level indicator. The indicator could already be used for categorizing students and potentially offering them individualized help; it could also be an informative component within a higher-granularity model. However, at present, the indicator does not provide the level of granularity required to choose specific moments for tutor intervention. To achieve that level of granularity, a better distributional understanding of student response times would be helpful, as would an indicator capable of distinguishing between students seeking worked examples versus engaging in gaming. Exploring how the distribution of response times differs between high-learning bottom-out hint students and low-learning bottom-out hint students would help solve both problems.

This issue aside, our indicators for student self-explanation time have proven remarkably effective. They not only predict learning gain, they do so better than traditional time-on-task measures, they are uncorrelated with pretest scores, and changes in our indicators over time also predict learning gain. The indicators achieve these goals without inherent assumptions about domain or system design, facilitating adaptation to other educational systems in other domains. However, the actual results presented are derived from only one well-defined domain and one heavily scaffolded tutoring system. While easily adapted to other domains and systems, the indicators may or may not be accurate outside of geometry or in other types of tutoring systems.

The inclusion of two conditions, one without justification steps and one with justification steps, allowed us to show that the indicators do measure phenomena related to reasoning or self-explanation. We estimated the indicators for the two conditions in different ways; yet, both times, the results were significant. This provides a substantial degree of validity. However, one direction for future work is to show that the indicators correlate with other measures of self-explanation or worked example cognition. One useful study would be to compare these indicators with human estimates of student self-explanation.

References

1. Aleven, V. and Koedinger, K. R. An effective meta-cognitive strategy: Learning by doing and explaining with a computer-based cognitive tutor. *Cognitive Science*, 26(2), 2002, 147–179.
2. Aleven, V., Koedinger, K. R., and Cross, K. Tutoring answer explanation fosters learning with understanding. In: *Proceedings of the Ninth International Conference on Artificial Intelligence in Education*, LeMans, France, 1999.
3. Aleven, V., McLaren, B. M., Roll, I., and Koedinger, K. R. Toward tutoring help seeking—Applying cognitive modeling to meta-cognitive skills. In: *Proceedings of the Seventh Conference on Intelligent Tutoring Systems*, Alagoas, Brazil, 2004, pp. 227–239.
4. Atkinson, R. K., Renkl, A., and Merrill, M. M. Transitioning from studying examples to solving problems: Effects of self-explanation prompts and fading worked-out steps. *Journal of Educational Psychology*, 95(4), 2003, 774–783.
5. Baker, R. S., Corbett, A. T., and Koedinger, K. R. Detecting student misuse of intelligent tutoring systems. *Proceedings of the Seventh International Conference on Intelligent Tutoring Systems*, Alagoas, Brazil, 2004, pp. 531–540.

6. Beck, J. Engagement tracing: Using response times to model student disengagement. *Proceedings of the 12th International Conference on Artificial Intelligence in Education*, Amsterdam, the Netherlands, 2005, pp. 88–95.

7. Chi, M. T. H., Bassok, M., Lewis, M., Reimann, P., and Glaser, R. Self-explanations: How students study and use examples in learning to solve problems. *Cognitive Science*, 13, 1989, 145–182.

8. Chi, M. T. H., deLeeuw, N., Chiu, M. H., and LaVancher, C. Eliciting self-explanations improves understanding. *Cognitive Science*, 18, 1994, 439–477.

9. Conati, C. and VanLehn, K. Teaching meta-cognitive skills: Implementation and evaluation of a tutoring system to guide self-explanation while learning from examples. In: *Proceedings of the Ninth International Conference on Artificial Intelligence in Education*, LeMans, France, 1999, pp. 297–304.

10. Mavrikis, M. Data-driven modelling of students' interactions in an ILE. In: *Proceedings of the First International Conference on Educational Data Mining*, Montreal, Canada, 2008, pp. 87–96.

11. Paas, F. G. W. C. and VanMeerienboer, J. J. G. Variability of worked examples and transfer of geometrical problem-solving skills: A cognitive-load approach. *Journal of Educational Psychology*, 86(1), 1994, 122–133.

12. Schworm, S. and Renkl, A. Learning by solved example problems: Instructional explanations reduce self-explanation activity. In: *Proceedings of the 24th Annual Conference of the Cognitive Science Society*, Fairfax, VA, 2002, pp. 816–821.

13. Walonoski, J. A. and Heffernan, N. T. Detection and analysis of off-task gaming behavior in intelligent tutoring systems. In: *Proceedings of the Eighth International Conference on Intelligent Tutoring Systems*, Jhongli, Taiwan, 2006, pp. 722–724.

15

Automatic Recognition of Learner Types in Exploratory Learning Environments

Saleema Amershi and Cristina Conati

CONTENTS

15.1 Introduction

Exploratory learning environments (ELEs) provide facilities for student-led exploration of a target domain with the premise that active discovery of knowledge promotes deeper understandings than more controlled instruction [32]. Through the use of graphs and animations, algorithm visualization (AV) systems aim to better demonstrate algorithm dynamics than traditionally static media, and there has been interest in using them within ELEs to promote interactive learning of algorithms [15,34]. Despite theories and intuitions behind AVs and ELEs, reports on their pedagogical effectiveness have been mixed [8,34]. Research has suggested that pedagogical effectiveness is influenced by distinguishing student characteristics such as metacognitive abilities [8] and learning styles [15,34]. For example, some students often find such unstructured environments difficult to navigate effectively and so they may not learn well with them [20]. Such findings highlight the need for ELEs in general, and specifically for ELEs that use interactive AVs, to provide adaptive support for students with diverse abilities or learning styles. This is a challenging goal because of the difficulty in observing distinct student behaviors in such highly unstructured environments. The few efforts that have been made toward this goal mostly rely on hand-constructing detailed student models that can monitor student behaviors, assess individual needs, and inform adaptive help facilities [8,31]. This is a complex and time-consuming task that typically requires the collaborative efforts of domain, application, and model experts.

The authors in [10] explored an approach based on supervised machine learning, where domain experts manually labeled interaction episodes based on whether or not students reflected on the outcome of their exploratory actions. The resulting dataset was then used to train a classifier for student reflection behavior that was integrated with a previously developed knowledge-based model of student exploratory behavior. While the addition of the classifier significantly improved model accuracy, this approach suffers from the same drawbacks of knowledge-based approaches described earlier. It is time consuming and error prone, because humans have to supply the labels for the dataset, and it needs a priori definitions of relevant behaviors when there is limited knowledge of what these behaviors may be.

In this chapter, we explore an alternative approach that addresses the above limitations by relying on data mining to automatically identify common interaction behaviors, and then using these behaviors to train a user model. The key distinction between our modeling approach and knowledge-based or supervised approaches with hand-labeled data is that human intervention is delayed until after a data mining algorithm has automatically identified behavioral patterns. This means, instead of having to observe individual student behaviors in search of meaningful patterns to model or to input to a supervised classifier, the developer is automatically presented with a picture of common behavioral patterns that can then be analyzed in terms of learning effects. Expert effort is potentially reduced further by using supervised learning to build the user model from the identified patterns. While these models are generally not as fine-grained as those generated by more laborious approaches based on experts' knowledge or labeled data, they may still provide enough information to inform soft forms of adaptivity in-line with the unstructured nature of the interaction with ELEs.

In recent years, there has been a growing interest in exploring the usage of data mining for educational technologies, or *educational data mining* (EDM). Much of the work on EDM to date has focused on traditional intelligent tutoring systems (ITSs) that support structured problem solving [5,33,39] or drill-and-practice activities (e.g., [6]) where students receive feedback and hints based on the correctness of their answers. In contrast, our work aims to model students as they interact with environments that support learning via exploratory activities, like interactive simulations, where there is no clear notion of correct or incorrect behavior.

In this chapter, we present the results of applying this approach to an ELE called the AIspace Constraint Satisfaction Problem (CSP) Applet [1]. We show that by applying unsupervised clustering to log data, we identify interaction patterns that are meaningful to discriminate different types of learners and that would be hard to detect based on intuition or a basic correlation analysis. We also show preliminary results on using the identified learner groups for online classification of new users. Our long-term goal is automatic interface adaptations to encourage effective behaviors and prevent detrimental ones.

This chapter is organized as follows. Section 15.2 reports on related work. Section 15.3 describes the CSP Applet. Section 15.4 describes the application of unsupervised learning for off-line identification of meaningful clusters of users. Section 15.5 illustrates how the clusters identified in the off-line phase are used directly in a classifier student model. And finally, in Section 15.6, we conclude with a summary and a discussion of future research directions.

15.2 Related Work

Much of the research on data-based approaches to student modeling has employed supervised machine-learning techniques that require labeled example data for training the model. If the activities to be modeled allow for a clear definition of correctness of students' behaviors, and the target learning environments can judge for correctness, the labeled training data can be derived directly from the system by recoding student interactions along with the relevant system's feedback. This is the approach adopted in, for instance, the AnimalWatch (an ITS for teaching arithmetic [7]), the Reading Tutor [6], and the CAPIT system for teaching punctuation and capitalization rules [22]. The work closest to ours in this pool is that of [14] those who also use a data-based approach to automatically learn a user model for the AIspace CSP Applet. Their goal, however, was to predict future user actions, and so they were not concerned with if and how these actions related to learning. Their approach relies on training a stochastic state space user model on sequences of interface actions, and therefore can be considered a supervised approach with system-provided labels, where the labels are future user interface actions.

When output labels are not readily available from the system, supervised data-based approaches require that data labels be provided by hand. An example is provided by research on detecting specific types of behaviors known as "gaming the system" during interaction with learning environments. In this research, the gaming observations correspond to labels of the input data (logged interface events, such as user actions and latency between actions). The labeled data is then used to train a regression model that can predict instances of gaming [5,6,18,30,37]. It should be noted that in this line of research, it was possible to predefine which behaviors were instances of gaming the system, because the target systems supported a structured, well-studied, problem-solving or drill-and-practice type of pedagogical interaction.

Unsupervised machine-learning techniques sidestep the problem of obtaining labeled data altogether. These methods have been applied quite extensively in user modeling for noneducational applications (see, for instance, [23]). While the application of these techniques for student modeling is not as widespread, there are already several attempts in this direction. The author in [39] proposes an approach to recommend web pages to users of e-learning environments based on association rules between user actions and web pages learned from Weblogs. The approach has yet to be put into practice. Similar to what we do, both [36] and [25] use clustering on interface action frequencies to detect meaningful behavioral patterns in an environment for collaborative learning. In [28], the authors use unsupervised clustering on action frequencies to identify groups of students with common learning and affective behaviors while using a tutoring system for algebra, providing initial evidence that it may be possible to detect states such as flow and engaged work from basic action frequency information. Our work differs from these research efforts because we use higher-dimensional data including action latency and measures of variance, as well as because we take the data mining process one step further to automatically build a user model that can be used to provide automatic, online adaptive support.

One common application of EDM relates to discover useful patterns by clustering student test scores or students' solutions labeled based on their correctness [4,16,27]. The Multistrategy Error Detection and Discovery (MEDD) system [33] goes a step forward and uses unsupervised clustering to build a library of Prolog programming errors that can then be used to direct system interventions. Suarez and Sison [35] have successfully transferred this approach to create bug libraries and detect programming errors in Java. Our approach to user modeling differs from these in that we are modeling student interaction behaviors in unstructured environments with no clear definition of correct behavior instead of static student solutions and errors.

15.3 The AIspace CSP Applet Learning Environment

The CSP Applet is part of AIspace, a collection of interactive tools that use AV to help students explore the dynamics of common artificial intelligence (AI) algorithms (including algorithms for search, machine learning, and reasoning under uncertainty) [1]. A CSP consists of a set of variables, variable domains, and a set of constraints on legal variable–value assignments. The goal is to find an assignment of values to variables that satisfies all constraints. A CSP can be naturally represented as a graph where nodes are the variables of interest and constraints are defined by arcs between the corresponding nodes.

The CSP Applet demonstrates the Arc Consistency 3 (AC-3) algorithm for solving CSPs on graphs [26]. AC-3 defines an arc as consistent if it represents a satisfied constraint. The algorithm iteratively makes individual arcs consistent by removing variable domain values inconsistent with corresponding constraints. The process continues until all arcs have been considered and the network is consistent. If there are variables left with more than one domain value, a procedure called *Domain Splitting* can be applied to any of these variables to split the CSP into disjoint cases, so that AC-3 can recursively solve each resulting case.

Figure 15.1 [3] shows a sample CSP as it is graphically represented in the CSP Applet. Initially, all the arcs in the network are colored blue, indicating that they need to be tested for consistency. As the AC-3 algorithm runs, state changes in the graph are represented via the use of color and highlighting. The CSP Applet provides several mechanisms for the interactive execution of the AC-3 algorithm, accessible through the button toolbar shown at the top of Figure 15.1, or through a direct manipulation of graph elements. Note that the Applet also provides functionalities for creating CSP networks, but, in this research, we

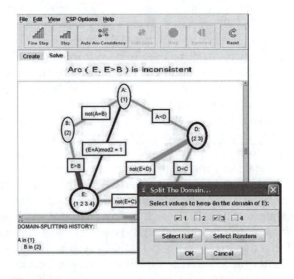

FIGURE 15.1
AIspace CSP Applet interface. (From Amershi, S. and Conati, C., *J. Educ. Data Mining*, 1, 1, 2009. With permission.)

limit our analysis to only those relevant to solving a predefined CSP. Here, we provide a brief description of these functionalities necessary to understand the results of applying our user modeling framework to this environment.

- *Fine Step.* Allows the student to manually advance through the AC-3 algorithm at a fine scale. *Fine Step* cycles through three stages, triggered by consecutive clicks of the *Fine Step* button. First, the CSP Applet selects one of the existing blue (untested) arcs and highlights it. Second, the arc is tested for consistency. If the arc is consistent, its color will change to green and the *Fine Step* cycle terminates. Otherwise, its color changes to red and a third *Fine Step* is needed. In this final stage, the CSP Applet removes the inconsistency by reducing the domain of one of the variables involved in the constraint, and turns the arc green. Because other arcs connected to the reduced variable may have become inconsistent as a result of this step, they must be retested and thus are turned back to blue. The effect of each *Fine Step* is reinforced explicitly in text through a panel above the graph (see message above the CSP in Figure 15.1).
- *Step.* Executes the AC-3 algorithm in coarser detail. One *Step* performs all three stages of *Fine Step* at once, on a blue arc chosen by the algorithm.
- *Direct Arc Click.* Allows the student to choose which arc to *Step* on by clicking directly on it.
- *Domain Split.* Allows a student to divide the network into smaller subproblems by splitting a variable's domain. This is done by clicking directly on a node in the network, and then selecting values to keep in the dialog box that appears (see dialog box at the lower-right corner of the CSP Applet in Figure 15.1). The choice of variables to split on and values to keep affect the algorithm's efficiency in finding a solution.
- *Backtrack.* Recovers the alternate subproblem set aside by *Domain Splitting*, allowing for a recursive application of AC-3.
- *Auto Arc Consistency (Auto AC).* Automatically *Fine Steps* through the CSP network, at a user-specified speed, until it is consistent.
- *Auto Solve.* Iterates between *Fine Stepping* to reach graph consistency and automatically *Domain Splitting* until a solution is found.
- *Stop.* Lets the student stop execution of *Auto AC* or *Auto Solve* at any time.
- *Reset.* Restores the CSP to its initial state so that the student can reexamine the initial problem and restart the algorithm.

The data we use for the research described in this chapter was obtained from a previous user study investigating user attitudes for the CSP Applet [1]. In Section 15.4, we describe how we use logged data from this study to identify different groups of learners via unsupervised clustering.

15.4 Off-Line Clustering

Our proposed student modeling approach divides the modeling process into two major phases: off-line identification of clusters of students in unlabeled data, representing distinct interaction behaviors, and online classification of new students based on these clusters. In this section, we focus on the off-line phase. This phase starts with the collection and preprocessing of raw, unlabeled data from student interaction with the target environment. The result of preprocessing is a set of feature vectors representing individual students in terms of their interaction behavior. These vectors are then used as input to a clustering algorithm that groups them according to their similarity. The resulting groups, or "clusters," represent students who interact similarly with the environment. These clusters are then analyzed by the model developer in order to determine whether and how they represent interaction behaviors that are effective or ineffective for learning.

In Sections 15.4.1 through 15.4.3, we detail the various steps involved in the off-line phase in the context of student interaction with the CSP Applet.

15.4.1 Data Collection and Preprocessing

As mentioned in Section 15.3, the data we use for this research was obtained from a previous experiment investigating the effects of studying sample problems with the CSP Applet [1]. A total of 24 undergraduate computer science and engineering students participated in the user study, which typified a scenario where a student learns about a set of target concepts from text-based materials, studies relevant sample problems, and finally is tested on the target concepts. First, students had one hour to read a textbook chapter on CSP problems [26]. Next, they took a 20 min pretest on the material. After the pretest, students studied sample problems using the CSP Applet, and finally they were given a posttest almost identical to the pretest except for a few different domain values or arcs. For the current experiment, we used both the time-stamped logged data of user interactions with the CSP Applet, as well as results from the pre- and posttests. From the logged data, we obtained 1931 user actions over 205.3 min. It should be noted that we had disabled the *Step* and *Auto Solve* mechanisms for the user study, because we had seen students misusing them during pilot studies. Thus, the actions included in the log files were limited to *Fine Step, Direct Arc Click, Auto AC, Stop, Reset, Domain Split,* and *Backtrack.* While it would have been useful to see if our modeling approach could capture the misuse of *Step* and *Auto Solve,* remarkably it was still able to identify several other behaviors potentially detrimental for learning (as we discuss below). The fact that our approach discovered suboptimal learning behaviors that we could not catch by observing the interactions, highlights how difficult it can be to recognize distinct learning behaviors in this type of environment.

Clustering operates on data points in a feature space, where features can be any measurable property of the data [17]. Therefore, in order to find clusters of students who interact with the CSP Applet in similar ways, each student must be represented by a multidimensional data point or "feature vector." The second step in the off-line phase is to generate these feature vectors by computing low-level features from the data collected. From the logged user study data, we computed 24 feature vectors corresponding to the 24 study participants. The feature vectors had 21 dimensions, resulting from deriving three features for each of the actions described in Section 15.3: (1) action frequency, (2) the average latency after the action, and (3) the standard deviation of the latency after the action. The latency dimensions are intended to measure if and how a student is reflecting on action results. Specifically, the second dimension is an indicator of student reflection, and the third dimension is an indicator of reflection selectiveness, since varied latency may indicate planned rather than impulsive or inattentive behavior (e.g., consistently rushing through actions versus selectively attending to the results of actions).

15.4.2 Unsupervised Clustering

After forming the feature vector representation of the data, the next step in the off-line phase is to perform clustering on the feature vectors to discover patterns in the students' interaction behaviors. Clustering works by grouping feature vectors by their similarity; here, we define similarity to be the Euclidean distance between feature vectors in the normalized feature space. While there exist numerous clustering algorithms (see [17] for a survey), we chose the popular partition-based *k*-means [11] clustering algorithm as a proof of concept for this step.

K-means converges to different local optima depending on the selection of the initial cluster centroids, and so, in this research, we execute 20 trials (with randomly selected initial cluster centroids) and use the highest-quality clusters as the final cluster set. We measure the quality based on Fisher's criterion [13] in a discriminant analysis, which reflects the ratio of between-cluster/within-cluster scatter, that is, high-quality clusters are defined as having maximum between-cluster variance and minimum within-cluster variance. We applied *k*-means clustering to the study data with *k* set to 2, 3, and 4 because we only expected to find a few distinct clusters with our small sample size. The clusters found by *k* set to 4 were the same as those with *k* set to 3 with the exception of one data point forming a singleton cluster. This essentially corresponds to an outlier in the data, and so, in Section 15.4.3 on cluster analysis, we report only the results for *k* set to 2 and *k* set to 3.

15.4.3 Cluster Analysis

In this phase, clusters are first analyzed to determine which ones represent students showing effective versus ineffective interaction behaviors. In this research, we use learning gains from application use (e.g., improvements from pre- to posttests) to determine which clusters of students were successful learners and which were not. It should be noted, however, that the approach may still be used if learning gains are unknown, but, in this case, the intuition or expert evaluation is required to analyze and label the clusters in terms of learning outcomes.

The second step in cluster analysis is to explicitly characterize the interaction behaviors in the different clusters by evaluating cluster similarities and dissimilarities along each of the feature dimensions. While this step is not strictly necessary for online user recognition based on supervised classification, it is useful to help educators and developers gain insights into the different learning behaviors and devise appropriate adaptive interventions targeting them. In this research, we use formal statistical tests to compare clusters in terms of learning and feature similarity. For measuring statistical significance, we use Welch's t-test for unequal sample variances when comparing two clusters, and a one-way analysis of variances (ANOVAs) with Tukey HSD adjustments (p_{HSD}) for post hoc pair-wise comparison [12] to compare multiple clusters. To compute the effect size (a measure of the practical significance of a difference), we use Cohen's *d* [9] for two clusters (where $d > .8$ is considered a large effect, and *d* between .5 and .8 is a medium effect). For multiple clusters, we use partial eta-squared (partial η^2 [9], where partial $\eta^2 > .14$ is considered a large effect, and a value between .06 and .14 is a medium effect).

15.4.3.1 Cluster Analysis for the CSP Applet (k = 2)

When we compared average learning gains between the clusters found by *k*-means with *k* set to 2 (*k*-2 clusters from now on), we found that one cluster (4 students) had (statistically and practically) significantly ($p < .05$ and $d > .8$, respectively) higher learning gains (7 points) than the other cluster (20 students, 3.08 points gain). Hereafter, we will refer to these clusters as 'HL' (high learning) cluster, and 'LL' (low learning) cluster respectively.

In order to characterize the HL and LL clusters in terms of distinguishing student interaction behaviors, we did a pair-wise analysis of the differences between the clusters along each of the 21 dimensions. Table 15.1 summarizes the results of this analysis, where the features reported are those for which we found statistically or practically significant differences. Here, we interpret the differences along these individual feature dimensions, or discuss combinations of dimensions that yielded sensible results. The results on the use of the *Fine Step* feature are quite intuitive. From Table 15.1, we can see that the LL students used this feature significantly more frequently than the HL students. In addition, both the latency averages and standard deviations after a *Fine Step* were significantly shorter for the LL students, indicating that they *Fine Stepped* frequently and consistently too quickly. These results plausibly indicate that LL students may be using this feature mechanically, without pausing long enough to consider the effects of each *Fine Step*, a behavior that may contribute to the LL gains achieved by these students.

The HL students used the *Auto AC* feature more frequently than the LL students, although the difference is not statistically significant. In isolation, this result appears unintuitive considering that simply watching the AC-3 algorithm in execution is an inactive form of learner engagement [24]. However, in combination with the significantly higher frequency of *Stopping* (see "*Stop* frequency" in Table 15.1), this behavior suggests that the HL students could be using these features to forward through the AC-3 algorithm in larger steps to analyze it at a coarser scale, rather than just passively watching the algorithm progress.

The HL students also paused longer and more selectively after *Resetting* than the LL students (see "*Reset* latency average" and "*Reset* latency SD" entries in Table 15.1). With the hindsight that these students were successful learners, we can interpret this behavior as an indication that they were reflecting on each problem more than the LL students. However, without the prescience of learning outcomes, it is likely that an application expert or educator observing the students would overlook this less obvious behavior.

There was also a significant difference in the frequency of *Domain Splitting* between the HL and LL clusters of students, with the LL cluster frequency being higher (see "*Domain Split* frequency" in Table 15.1). As it is, it is hard to find an intuitive explanation for this result in terms of learning. However, the analysis of the clusters found with $k=3$ in Section 15.4.3.2 shows finer distinctions along this dimension, as well as along the latency

TABLE 15.1

Pair-Wise Feature Comparisons between HL and LL Clusters for $k=2$

Feature Description	HL Average	LL Average	p	Cohen's d
Fine Step frequency	.025	.118	**6e-4***	**1.34***
Fine Step latency average	10.2	3.08	**.013***	**1.90***
Fine Step latency SD	12.2	4.06	**.005***	**2.04***
Stop frequency	.003	7e-4	.058	**.935***
Stop latency SD	1.06	0	.051	**1.16***
Reset latency average	46.6	11.4	.086	**.866***
Reset latency SD	24.4	9.56	**.003***	**1.51***
Domain Split frequency	.003	.009	**.012***	.783

Source: Amershi, S. and Conati, C., *J. Educ. Data Mining*, 1, 1, 2009. With permission.
* Significant at $p < .05$ or $d > .8$ (values in bold).

dimensions after a *Domain Split* action. These latter findings are more revealing, indicating that there are likely more than two learning patterns.

15.4.3.2 Cluster Analysis for the CSP Applet (k = 3)

As for the *k*-2 clusters, we found significant differences in learning outcomes with the clusters found with *k* set to 3 (*k*-3 clusters from now on). One of these clusters coincides with the HL cluster found with *k* = 2. A post hoc pair-wise analysis showed that students in this cluster have significantly higher learning gains ($p_{HSD} < .05$ and $d > .8$) than students in the other two clusters. We found no significant learning difference between the two LL clusters, which we will label as LL1 (8 students, 2.94 points gain) and LL2 (12 students, 3.17 points gain).

Table 15.2 summarizes the three-way comparisons amongst the three clusters along each of the 21 dimensions. Table 15.3 summarizes the post hoc pair-wise comparisons between the clusters (i.e., HL compared to LL1, HL compared to LL2, and LL1 compared to LL2) along each of the dimensions. Both tables include only those features that yield significant differences.

As before, here we discuss the results in Tables 15.2 and 15.3 for an individual dimension or combinations of dimensions, in order to characterize the interaction behaviors of students in each cluster. We found distinguishing *Fine Step* behaviors between the HL students and students in both LL clusters, similar to what we had found for the *k*-2 clusters. First, there was a nonsignificant trend of both the LL1 and LL2 students having a higher frequency of *Fine Stepping* than the HL students. Both the average and the standard deviation of the latency after a *Fine Step* were significantly higher for the HL students than for both the LL1 and LL2 students, suggesting that LL students consistently pause less than HL students after a *Fine Step*, and that this reduced attention may have negatively affected their learning.

The patterns of usage for the *Auto AC, Stop,* and *Reset* functionalities were also similar to those we found with the *k*-2 clusters, that is, the HL students used the *Auto AC* feature more frequently than students in both LL clusters (the difference is statistically significant

TABLE 15.2

Three-Way Comparisons between HL, LL1, and LL2 Clusters

Feature Description	HL Average	LL1 Average	LL2 Average	F	p	Partial η^2
Fine Step frequency	.025	.111	.122	1.98	.162	.159*
Fine Step latency average	10.2	3.07	3.08	20.4	1e-5*	.660*
Fine Step latency SD	12.2	4.82	3.55	12.1	3e-4*	.536*
Auto AC frequency	.007	.003	.004	2.66	.093	.202*
Stop frequency	.003	3e-4	9e-4	3.00	.071	.222*
Stop latency SD	1.06	0	0	15.8	6e-4*	.600*
Reset latency average	46.6	18.7	6.52	6.94	.005*	.398*
Reset latency SD	24.4	14.2	6.43	5.09	.016*	.327*
Domain Split frequency	.003	.018	.003	12.0	3e-4*	.532*
Domain Split latency average	6.75	8.68	1.89	12.0	3e-4*	.533*
Domain Split latency SD	1.37	6.66	.622	27.7	1e-6*	.725*
Backtrack latency average	1.75	8.90	.202	3.21	.061	.234*
Backtrack latency SD	0	7.96	.138	2.92	.076	.218*

Source: Amershi, S. and Conati, C., *J. Educ. Data Mining*, 1, 1, 2009. With permission.

* Significant at $p < .05$ or *partial* $\eta^2 > .14$ (values in bold).

TABLE 15.3

Post Hoc Pair-Wise Comparisons between HL, LL1, and LL2 Clusters

Feature Description	HL versus LL1		HL versus LL2		LL1 versus LL2	
	p_{HSD}	d	p_{HSD}	d	p_{HSD}	d
Fine Step frequency	.142	**1.10***	.078	**1.48***	.691	.106
Fine Step latency average	**1e-5***	**1.98***	**1e-5***	**1.85***	.818	.007
Fine Step latency SD	**.001***	**1.68***	**1e-4***	**2.33***	.395	.356
Auto AC frequency	**.046***	.745	.076	.666	.595	.228
Stop frequency	**.031***	**1.21***	.081	.783	.449	.296
Stop latency average	.552	**.966***	.692	.169	.287	.387
Stop latency SD	**5e-5***	**1.16***	**3e-5***	**1.16***	.823	0
Reset latency average	**.031***	.673	**.002***	**1.01***	.194	.867
Reset latency SD	.136	**1.08***	**.007***	**1.84***	.125	.601
Domain Split frequency	**.003***	**1.91***	.820	.011	**2e-4***	**1.69***
Domain Split latency average	.350	.483	**.019***	**1.24***	**1e-4***	**1.79***
Domain Split latency SD	**1e-4***	**2.83***	.488	.527	**0***	**2.73***
Backtrack latency average	.167	.745	.667	.648	**.028***	**.934***
Backtrack latency SD	.118	**.867***	.811	.556	**.042***	**.851***

Source: Amershi, S. and Conati, C., *J. Educ. Data Mining*, 1, 1, 2009. With permission.
* Significant at $p_{HSD} < .05$ or $d > .8$ (values in bold).

between the HL and LL1 clusters), suggesting that the HL students were using these features to selectively forward through the AC-3 algorithm to learn. The HL students also paused longer and more selectively after *Resetting* than both the LL1 and LL2 students, suggesting that the HL students may be reflecting more on each problem.

The k-3 clustering also reveals several additional patterns, not only between the HL and LL clusters, but also between the two LL clusters, indicating that $k = 3$ was better at discriminating relevant student behaviors. For example, the k-2 clusters showed that the LL students used the *Domain Split* feature more frequently than the HL students; however, the k-3 clustering reveals a more complex pattern. This pattern is summarized by the following combination of findings:

- LL1 students used the *Domain Split* feature significantly more than the HL students.
- HL and LL2 students used the *Domain Split* feature comparably frequently.
- HL and LL1 students had similar pausing averages after a domain split, and paused significantly longer than the LL2 students.
- LL1 students paused significantly more selectively (had a higher standard deviation for pause latency) than both HL and LL2 students.
- LL1 had longer pauses after *Backtracking* than both HL and LL2 clusters.

Effective *Domain Splitting* is intended to require thought about efficiency in solving a CSP given different possible splits, and so the HL students' longer pauses may have contributed to their better learning as compared to LL2 students. However, it is interesting that the LL1 students paused for just as long after *Domain Splitting* as the HL students, and more selectively than both the HL and LL2 students, yet still had LL gains. The fact that the LL1 cluster is also characterized by longer pauses after *Backtracking* may indicate that long pauses for LL1 students indicated confusion about these Applet features or the concepts of *Domain Splitting* and backtracking, rather than effective reflection. This is indeed a complex behavior that may have been difficult to identify through mere observation.

15.5 Online Recognition

The second phase of our modeling approach uses the clusters identified in the off-line phase to train a supervised classifier user model for online classification of new users into successful/unsuccessful learner groups. As a proof of concept for this phase, we devised an online k-means classifier that incrementally updates the classification of a new student into one of the clusters from the off-line phase, as the student interacts with the target ELE. As an action occurs, the feature vector representing the student's behavior thus far is updated to reflect the new observation, that is, all feature dimensions related to the current action (e.g., action frequency and the various latency dimensions) are recomputed to take into account the current action. After updating the feature vector, the student is (re)classified by simply recalculating the distances between the updated vector and each cluster's centroid, and then assigning the feature vector to the cluster with the nearest centroid. We built and evaluated both a two- and three-class k-means classifier corresponding to the two-cluster and three-cluster setup described in Section 5.4.3.

To evaluate the models, we performed a 24-fold leave-one-out cross validation (LOOCV), as follows. In each fold, we removed one student's data from the set of N available feature vectors, and used k-means to re-cluster the reduced feature vector set. Next, the removed student's data (the test data) was fed into a classifier user model trained on the reduced set, and online predictions were made for the incoming actions as described above. Model accuracy is evaluated by checking after every action whether the current student is correctly classified into the cluster to which he/she was assigned in the off-line phase. Aggregate model accuracy is reported as the percentage of students correctly classified as a function of the number of actions seen by the classifier.

It should be noted, however, that by using the LOOCV strategy, we run the risk of altering the original clusters detected in the off-line phase (*off-line clusters* from now on) by using the entire feature vector set. Therefore, we should not expect to achieve 100% accuracy even after seeing all the actions, because the user models are classifying incoming test data given the clusters found by LOOCV using the reduced set of feature vectors. In supervised machine learning, this issue is known as *hypothesis stability* [19]. In [21], the authors extend this notion to the unsupervised setting by defining a stability cost (SC), or expected empirical risk, which essentially quantifies the inconsistency between the original clusters and those produced by LOOCV. Perfect stability (SC = 0) occurs when the off-line clusters are unchanged by LOOCV. Conversely, maximum instability (SC = 1) occurs when none of the original data labels (as defined by the original off-line clusters) are maintained by LOOCV. In other words, a low SC helps to ensure that the off-line clusters are relatively resistant to distortions caused by the removal of one feature vector. We compute the SC prior to assessing predictive accuracy to ensure that the models are essentially predicting what we would like them to predict, that is, the membership of the removed student's behavioral patterns in one of the off-line clusters.

15.5.1 Model Evaluation ($k = 2$)

The estimated SC of using the LOOCV strategy to evaluate the classifier user model trained with the k-2 clusters (two-class k-means classifier from now on) is .05 (averaging over the 24-folds). As discussed earlier, this is considered a very low cost, indicating that our k-2 clusters are relatively stable during the LOOCV evaluation. Therefore, a classification by the two-class k-means classifier means that a new student's learning behaviors are similar to those of either the HL or LL clusters identified in the off-line phase.

Figure 15.2 shows the average accuracy of the two-class k-means classifier in predicting the correct classifications of each of our 24 students (using the LOOCV strategy) as they interact with the CSP Applet.

The percentage of correct classifications is shown as a function of the percentage of student actions the model has seen (solid line labeled "Overall" in the figure's legend). The figure also shows the model's performance in classifying HL students into the HL cluster (dashed line) and LL students into the LL cluster (dotted line). For comparison purposes, the figure also shows the performance of a baseline model using a most-likely class classification method where new student actions are always classified into the most-likely, or largest, class, that is, the LL cluster in our case (20 students). This is shown in Figure 15.2 by the dashed line straight across at the 83.3% (20 out of 24) classification accuracy level. The trends in Figure 15.2 show that the overall accuracy of this classifier improves as more evidence is accumulated, converging to 87.5% after seeing all of the student's actions. Initially, the classifier performs slightly worse than the baseline model, but then it starts outperforming the baseline model after seeing about 30% of the student's actions. The accuracy of the classifier model in recognizing LL students remains relatively consistent over time, converging to approximately 90%. In contrast, the accuracy of the model in recognizing HL students begins very low, reaches a relatively acceptable performance after seeing approximately 40% of the student's actions, and eventually converges to approximately 75% after seeing all of the student's actions. It should be noted that the baseline approach would consistently misclassify HL students, and thus interfere with the unconstrained nature of ELE interaction for these students. While the performance of the classifier in detecting

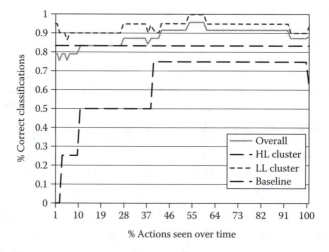

FIGURE 15.2
Performance of CSP Applet user models ($k=2$) over time. (From Amershi, S. and Conati, C., *J. Educ. Data Mining*, 1, 1, 2009. With permission.)

HL students is better than the baseline, it may still cause a system based on this model to interfere with an HL student's natural learning behavior, thus hindering student control, one of the key aspects of ELEs. The imbalance between accuracy in classifying LL and HL students is likely due to the distribution of the sample data [38] as the HL cluster has fewer data points than the LL cluster (4 compared to 20). This is a common phenomenon observed in classifier learning. Collecting more training data to correct for this imbalance, even if the cluster sizes are representative of the natural population distributions, may help to increase the classifier user model's accuracy on HL students [38].

15.5.2 Model Evaluation for the CSP Applet ($k = 3$)

The SC for using the LOOCV strategy to evaluate the three-class classifier user model is estimated at .09. The SC for this classifier is still low, although slightly higher than for the two-class classifier. This likely reflects the fact that the k-3 clusters are smaller than the k-2 clusters and, thus, less stable (i.e., removing a data point is more likely to produce different clusterings during LOOCV).

Figure 15.3 shows the overall prediction accuracy as a function of the number of observed student actions for this classifier user model (solid line). For comparison purposes, the figure also shows the performance of a most-likely class baseline user model (dashed line), which always classifies student actions into the largest class (LL2, with 12 students). Again, the classifier's accuracy improves with more observations, starting off at about 50% accuracy, but then reaching approximately 83.3% after seeing all of the actions. After seeing approximately 30% of the student actions, the classifier user model outperforms the baseline model, which has a consistent, 50% (12 out of 24) accuracy rate.

Figure 15.4 shows the prediction accuracy trends for the individual clusters. For the HL cluster, the classification accuracy (dashed line) again begins very low, but reaches 75% after seeing about 40% of the actions, and then eventually reaches 100% after seeing all of

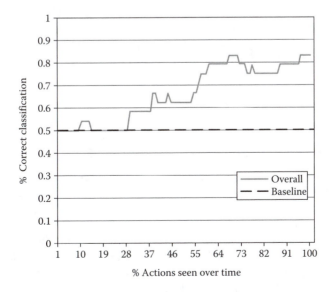

FIGURE 15.3
Performance of CSP Applet user models ($k = 3$) over time. (From Amershi, S. and Conati, C., *J. Educ. Data Mining*, 1, 1, 2009. With permission.)

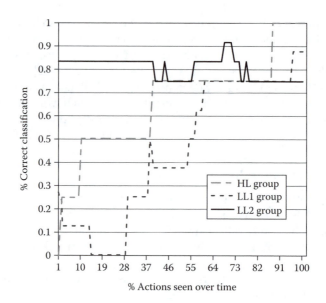

FIGURE 15.4
Performance of CSP Applet user models ($k=3$) over time for individual clusters. (From Amershi, S. and Conati, C., *J. Educ. Data Mining*, 1, 1, 2009. With permission.)

the actions. The accuracy of the model at classifying LL1 students (dotted line) also begins low, but then reaches approximately 75% after seeing about 60% of the actions, and converges to approximately 85%. The accuracy for the LL2 students (solid line) remains relatively consistent as actions are observed, eventually reaching approximately 75%. As with the increase in the SC, the lower accuracy, sensitivity, and specificity of this classifier user model is likely an artifact of the fewer data points within each cluster. Further supporting this hypothesis is the fact that the LL2 cluster, which had 12 members, had the highest classification accuracy (80.3% averaged over time), whereas the HL and LL1 clusters, which had only four and eight members, respectively, had visibly lower classification accuracies (66.3% and 44.9% averaged over time, respectively). Therefore, more training data should be collected and used, particularly as the number of clusters increases, when applying our user modeling framework.

15.6 Conclusions and Future Work

In this chapter, we have presented a data-based user model that uses both unsupervised and supervised machine learning to discover and capture effective or ineffective student behaviors while interacting with an ELE. Building models for these educational systems is especially challenging because of both the unconstrained nature of the interaction with ELE and the lack of a clear definition of correctness for student behaviors that makes it hard to foresee how the many possible user behaviors may relate to learning. The few existing approaches to this problem have been very knowledge intensive, relying on a time-consuming, detailed analysis of the target system; instructional domain; and learning processes. Since these approaches are so domain/application specific, they are difficult to generalize to other domains and applications.

We applied our approach to build the user model for the CSP Applet, an exploratory environment that uses interactive visualizations to help students understand an algorithm for constraint satisfaction. We presented results showing that, despite limitations due to the availability of data, our approach is capable of detecting meaningful clusters of student behaviors, and can achieve reasonable accuracy for the online categorization of new students in terms of the effectiveness of their learning behaviors.

The next steps of this research include testing our proposed approach with larger datasets, and experimenting with other clustering algorithms, in particular, a probabilistic variant of *k*-means called expectation maximization (EM) [11].

We will then investigate how to use the results of the online student modeling phase to provide adaptive support during interaction with AIspace. We are planning to experiment with a multilayered interface design [29], where each layer's mechanisms and help resources are tailored to facilitate learning for a given learner group identified by clustering. Then, based on a new learner's classification, the environment could select the most appropriate interface layer for that learner. For instance, the AIspace CSP Applet may select a layer with *Fine Step* disabled or with a subsequent delay to encourage careful thought for those students classified as ineffective learners by the two-class classifier user model described in Section 15.5.1. Similarly, for the three-class case, the CSP Applet could disable or introduce a delay after *Fine Step* for students classified into either of the ineffective learner groups. Additionally, in this case, the CSP Applet could also include a delay after *Domain Splitting* for students classified into the LL2 (low learning 2) group, as these students were consistently hasty in using this feature (see Section 15.4.2.3). The other ineffective learner group, LL1 (low learning 1), discovered by our framework in this experiment was characterized by lengthy pauses after *Domain Splitting* as well as *Backtracking*, indicating confusion about these CSP Applet mechanisms or concepts (see Section 15.4.2.2). Therefore, general tips about *Domain Splitting* and *Backtracking* could be made more prominent for these particular students for clarification purposes.

Finally, we want to test the generality of our approach by applying it to other learning environments. We have already obtained positive results similar to those described in the paper with an ELE for mathematical functions [2]. We now want to experiment with applying the approach to educational computer games, educational environments in which the exploratory component is integrated into gamelike activities.

References

1. Amershi, S., Carenini, C., Conati, C., Mackworth, A., and Poole, D. 2008. Pedagogy and usability in interactive visualizations—Designing and evaluating CIspace. *Interacting with Computers— The Interdisciplinary Journal of Human-Computer Interaction* 20 (1), 64–96.
2. Amershi, S. and Conati, C. 2007. Unsupervised and supervised machine learning in user modeling for intelligent learning environments. *Proceedings of Intelligent User Interfaces*, Honolulu, HI, pp. 72–81.
3. Amershi, S. and Conati, C. 2009. Combining unsupervised and supervised machine learning to build user models for exploratory learning environments. *The Journal of Educational Data Mining*, 1, 1.
4. Ayers, E., Nugent, R., and Dean, N. 2008. Skill set profile clustering based on weighted student responses. *Proceedings of the 1st International Conference on Educational Data Mining*, Montreal, Quebec, Canada, pp. 210–217.

5. Baker, R. S. J. D., Corbett, A. T., Roll, I., and Koedinger, K. R. 2008. Developing a generalizable detector of when students game the system. *User Modeling and User-Adapted Interaction* 18 (3), 287–314.
6. Beck, J. 2005. Engagement tracing: Using response times to model student disengagement. *Proceedings of the International Conference on Artificial Intelligence in Education*, Amsterdam, the Netherlands.
7. Beck, J. and Woolf, B. P. 2000. High-level student modeling with machine learning. *Proceedings of Intelligent Tutoring Systems*, Montreal, Quebec, Canada.
8. Bunt, A. and Conati, C. 2003. Probabilistic student modeling to improve exploratory behavior. *UMUAI* 13 (3), 269–309.
9. Cohen, J. 1988. *Statistical Power Analysis for the Behavioral Sciences*, 2nd edn. Hillsdale, NJ: Lawrence Erlbaum Associates.
10. Conati, C. and Merten, C. 2007. Eye-tracking for user modeling in exploratory learning environments: An empirical evaluation. *Knowledge Based Systems* 20(6), 557–574.
11. Duda, R. O., Hart, P. E., and Stork, D. G. 2001. *Pattern Classification*, 2nd edn. New York: Wiley-Interscience.
12. Faraway, J. J. 2002. *Practical Regression and ANOVA Using R*. http://www.maths.bath.ac.uk/~jjf23/book/pra.pdf
13. Fisher, R. A. 1936. The use of multiple measurements in taxonomic problems. *Annals of Eugenics* 7 (2), 179–188.
14. Gorniak, P. J. and Poole, D. 2000. Building a stochastic dynamic model of application use. *Proceedings of UAI*, San Francisco, CA.
15. Hundhausen, C. D., Douglas, S. A., and Stasko, J. T. 2002. A meta-study of algorithm visualization effectiveness. *Visual Languages and Computing* 13 (3), 259–290.
16. Hunt, E. and Madhyastha, T. 2005. Data mining patterns of thought. *Proceedings of the AAAI Workshop on Educational Data Mining*, Pittsburgh, PA.
17. Jain, A. K., Murty, M. N., and Flynn, P. J. 1999. Data clustering: A review. *ACM Computing Surveys* 31 (3), 264–323.
18. Johns, J. and Woolf, B. 2006. A dynamic mixture model to detect student motivation and proficiency. *Proceedings of the 21st National Conference on Artificial Intelligence*, Boston, MA, pp. 163–168.
19. Kearns, M. and Ron, D. 1997. Algorithmic stability and sanity-check bounds for leave-one-out cross-validation. *Proceedings of Computational Learning Theory*, Nashville, TN.
20. Kirschner, P., Sweller, J., and Clark, R. 2006. Why minimal guidance during instruction does not work: An analysis of the failure of constructivist, discovery, problem-based, experimental and inquiry-based teaching. *Educational Psychologist* 41 (2), 75–86.
21. Lange, T., Braun, M. L., Roth, V., and Buhmann, J. M. 2003. Stability-based model selection. *Proceedings of NIPS*, Vancouver, Whistler, Canada.
22. Mayo, M. and Mitrovic, A. 2001. Optimising ITS behavior with Bayesian networks and decision theory. *Artificial Intelligence in Education* 12, 124–153.
23. Mobasher, B. and Tuzhilin A. 2009. Special issue on data mining for personalization, *Journal of User Modeling and User-Adapted Interaction*, 19 (1–2).
24. Naps, T. L., Rodger, S., Velzquez-Iturbide, J., Rößling, G., Almstrum, V., Dann, W. et al. 2003. Exploring the role of visualization and engagement in computer science education. *ACM SIGCSE Bulletin* 35 (2), 131–152.
25. Perera, D., Kay, J., Yacef, K., Koprinska, I., and Zaiane, O. 2009. Clustering and sequential pattern mining of online collaborative learning data. *Proceedings of the IEEE Transactions on Knowledge and Data Engineering*, 21(6), 759–772.
26. Poole, D., Mackworth, A., and Goebel, R. 1998. *Computational Intelligence: A Logical Approach*. New York: Oxford University Press.
27. Romero, C., Ventura, S., Espejo, P. G., and Hervas, C. 2008. Data mining algorithms to classify students. *Proceedings of Educational Data Mining*, Montreal, Quebec, Canada, pp. 8–17.

28. Rodrigo, M. M. T., Anglo, E. A., Sugay, J. O., and Baker, R. S. J. D. 2008. Use of unsupervised clustering to characterize learner behaviors and affective states while using an intelligent tutoring system. *Proceedings of International Conference on Computers in Education*, Taipei, Taiwan.

29. Schneiderman, B. 2003. Promoting universal usability with multi-layer interface design. *Proceedings of the ACM Conference on Universal Usability*, Vancouver, British Columbia, Canada.

30. Shih, B., Koedinger, K., and Scheines, R. 2008. A response time model for bottom-out hints as worked examples. *Proceedings of the 2nd International Conference on Educational Data Mining*, Montreal, Quebec, Canada.

31. Shute, V. 1994. Discovery learning environments: Appropriate for all? *Proceedings of the American Educational Research Association*, New Orleans, LA.

32. Shute, V. and Glaser, V. 1990. A large-scale evaluation of an intelligent discovery world. *Interactive Learning Environments* 1, 51–76.

33. Sison, R., Numao, M., and Shimura, M. 2000. Multistrategy discovery and detection of novice programmer errors. *Machine Learning* 38, 157–180.

34. Stern, L., Markham, S., and Hanewald, R. 2005. You can lead a horse to water: How students really use pedagogical software. *Proceedings of the ACM SIGCSE Conference on Innovation and Technology in Computer Science Education*, St-Louis, MO.

35. Suarez, M. and Sison, R. 2008. Automatic construction of a bug library for object oriented novice java programming errors. *Proceedings of Intelligent Tutoring Systems*, Montreal, Quebec, Canada.

36. Talavera, L. and Gaudioso, E. 2004. Mining student data to characterize similar behavior groups in unstructured collaboration spaces. *Proceedings of the European Conference on AI Workshop on AI in CSCL*, Valencia, Spain.

37. Walonoski, J. A. and Heffernan, N. T. 2006. Detection and analysis of off-task gaming behavior in intelligent tutoring systems. *Proceedings of the 8th International Conference on Intelligent Tutoring Systems*, Jhongli, Taiwan.

38. Weiss, G. M. and Provost, F. 2001. The effect of class distribution on classifier learning: An empirical study. (Technical No. ML-TR-44). Rutgers University, New Brunswick, NJ.

39. Zaiane, O. 2002. Building a recommender agent for e-learning systems. *Proceedings of the International Conference on Computers in Education*, Auckland, New Zealand.

16

Modeling Affect by Mining Students' Interactions within Learning Environments

Manolis Mavrikis, Sidney D'Mello, Kaska Porayska-Pomsta, Mihaela Cocea, and Art Graesser

CONTENTS

16.1 Introduction

In the past decade, research on affect-sensitive learning environments has emerged as an important area in artificial intelligence in education (AIEd) and intelligent tutoring systems (ITS) [1–6]. These systems aspire to enhance the effectiveness of computer-mediated tutorial interactions by dynamically adapting to individual learners' affective and cognitive states [7] thereby emulating accomplished human tutors [7,8]. Such dynamic adaptation requires the implementation of an *affective loop* [9], consisting of (1) detection of the learner's affective states, (2) selection of systems actions that are sensitive to a learner's affective and cognitive states, and sometimes (3) synthesis of emotional expressions by animated pedagogical agents that simulate human tutors or peer learning companions [9,10].

The design of affect-sensitive learning environments is grounded in research that states that the complex interplay between affect and cognition during learning activities is of crucial importance to facilitating learning of complex topics, particularly at deeper levels of comprehension [11–17]. Within this research, one particular area of interest is concerned with the ways in which human tutors detect and respond to learners' affective states: robust detection of learners' affect is critical to enabling the development of affect-sensitive ITSs. In this chapter, we will examine the state-of-the art methods by which such detection can be facilitated. In particular, we examine the issues that arise from the use of supervised machine-learning techniques as a method for inferring learners' affective states based on features extracted from students' naturalistic interactions with computerized learning environments. Our focus is on general methodological questions related to educational data mining (EDM) with an emphasis on data collection protocols and machine-learning techniques for modeling learners' affective states. We present two case studies that demonstrate how particular EDM techniques are used to detect learners' affective states based on parameters that are collected during learners' interactions with different learning environments. We conclude with a critical analysis of the specific research outcomes afforded by the methods and techniques employed in the case studies that we present.

16.2 Background

There is an increasing body of research that is concerned with identifying the affective states that accompany learning and devising ways to automatically detect them during real interactions within different educational systems [18–24].

Different approaches to detecting affect focus on monitoring facial expressions, acoustic–prosodic features of speech, gross body language, and physiological measures such as skin conductivity or heart-rate monitoring. For extensive reviews, the reader is referred to [25–31]. Another approach involves an analysis of a combination of lexical and discourse features with acoustic–prosodic and lexical features obtained through a learner's interaction with spoken dialogue systems. A number of research groups have reported that appending an acoustic–prosodic and lexical feature vector with dialogue features results in a 1%–4% improvement in classification accuracy [32–34]. While these approaches have been shown to be relatively successful in detecting affective states of the learners, some tend to be quite expensive and some of them can be intrusive and may interfere with the learning process.

An interesting alternative to physiological and bodily measures for affect detection is to focus on learners' actions that are observable in the heat of the moment, i.e., at the time at which they are produced by the learner in the specific learning environment [6]. One obvious advantage of referring to these actions is that the technology required is less expensive and less intrusive than physiological sensors. Furthermore, by recording learner's actions as they occur, it is possible to avoid imposing additional constraints on the learner (i.e., no cameras, gloves, head gear, etc.), thereby also reducing the risk of interference with the actual learning process, and it somewhat alleviates the concern that learners might disguise the expression of certain negative emotions.

In this chapter, we present two case studies that differ from the previous research in that we focus on interaction logs as this primarily means to infer learner affect. The first study considers a broad set of features, including lexical, semantic, and contextual cues, as the basis for detecting learners' affective states. The second case study employs an approach that relies only on student actions on the interactive feature of the environment such as hint or information buttons to infer learner affect.

Section 16.3 discusses general methodological considerations behind these two approaches before presenting the two case studies in more detail.

16.3 Methodological Considerations

One of the most important considerations when attempting to detect affect from interaction features is the context in which the data are collected. Ideally, a study through which such data is collected would achieve high ecological validity, i.e., it should approximate the situation under which the results are expected to generalize [35]. It is also desirable that studies of learners' affect would involve learners who are familiar with a specific learning environment, who can use the environment in their own time and location over an extended period of time, and who have real learning objectives in relation to the domain under investigation. While achieving ecological validity is desirable in many studies, it is essential in any investigation of human affect. Context influences affective states, hence, modeling the contextual underpinnings of learners' affective experiences is critical to obtaining valid and generalizable research results [35–38].

However, such flexibility and familiarity with both the domain and the environment is not always possible given the requirements of the data-mining techniques currently available. For example, supervised learning, the most widely used data-mining technique, requires training based on labeled instances (also referred to as *ground truth*) in order to relate affect categories to the interaction parameters and bodily and physiological channels. Collecting these affect labels requires a compromise on ecological validity. We illustrate this issue by examining the two main methods used to collect affect labels.

The first method involves concurrent reports of affective states provided either by the learners themselves (self-report) or by external observers (e.g., tutors or peer students). For example, [39] implemented an *emote-aloud* protocol that allowed for the collection of self-reports in real time while students are interacting with AutoTutor, an ITS with conversational dialogue [40]. The emote-aloud procedure is a modification of the *think-aloud* procedure [41], which involves participants talking about their cognitive states and processes while working on tasks that require deeper cognitive engagement, such as solving problems [41] or comprehending text [42]. Emoting aloud involves participants verbalizing their states on a moment-by-moment basis while interacting with a learning environment, except that the verbalizations are of affective rather than cognitive states and processes. A similar technique during a computer-mediated tutorial for recording tutors' annotations of learner's affect was employed in [6]. Online affect judgments by observers, such as observations of students in a classroom environment [43], can provide an alternative to self-reports.

The second method is to employ a retrospective affect judgment protocol as an offline measure of learners' affect [44]. Specific techniques might involve students watching replays of their interactions with a learning environment in order to report on their affective states (e.g., [45]). A more elaborate example is provided in [39], where videos of participant's face and computer screen were synchronized and displayed to the learners after the tutoring session with AutoTutor in order to enable them to make judgments on which affective states were present at various points in the session. In addition to self-reports retrospective *post-task* annotations can involve peers and/or tutors in walk-throughs on replays of learners' interactions. For example, in [46], experienced tutors were asked to annotate replays of students' interactions with a web-based interactive learning environment, while [47] used an untrained peer and two trained judges to obtain affect labels. Alternatively, it is also possible to annotate for affect appropriate log files [24].

The methods listed above have possible advantages and disadvantages. The reader is referred to [46,48], where these are discussed in detail. The rest of this chapter presents two case studies that demonstrate the use of the data-collection methodology and data-mining techniques.

16.4 Case Studies

16.4.1 Case Study 1: Detecting Affect from Dialogues with AutoTutor

16.4.1.1 Context

This case study is derived from a larger project that aspires to integrate state-of-the-art affect-sensing devices into an existing ITS called AutoTutor [40]. AutoTutor is a fully automated computer tutor that helps students learn Newtonian physics, computer literacy, and critical thinking by presenting challenging problems (or questions) that require reasoning and explanations in the answers. AutoTutor and the learner collaboratively answer these difficult questions via a mixed-initiative dialogue that is dynamically adaptive to the cognitive states of the learner.

The AutoTutor research team is currently working on a version of AutoTutor that is sensitive to the affective as well as the cognitive states of the learner [5]. The affective states being tracked are boredom, engagement/flow, confusion, frustration, and delight. These were the most prominent affective states that were observed across multiple studies with AutoTutor and other learning environments [39,49,50].

16.4.1.2 Mining Dialogue Features from AutoTutor's Log Files

The data analysis described here was conducted on a corpora obtained by conducting two studies where learners' affective states and dialogue patterns were recorded during interactions with AutoTutor. The first study [39] implemented an emote-aloud protocol with seven participants. The second ($N=28$) implemented an offline retrospective affect judgment protocol where the affect judges were the participants, an untrained peer, and two trained judges. In both studies, participants were tutored on computer literacy topics (hardware, internet, and operating systems) with AutoTutor.

Several features from AutoTutor's log files were mined in order to explore the links between the dialogue features and the affective states of the learners. These features included temporal assessments for each student–tutor turn such as the *subtopic number*, the *turn number*, and the student's *reaction time* (interval between the presentation of the question and the submission of the student's answer). The assessments of response verbosity included the *number of characters* (letters, numbers) and *speech act* (i.e., whether the student's response was a contribution toward an answer versus a frozen expression, e.g., "I don't know," "Uh huh"). The conceptual quality of the student's response was evaluated by Latent Semantic Analysis (LSA) [51]. LSA is a statistical technique that measures the conceptual similarity of two text sources. LSA-based measures included a *local good score* (the conceptual similarity between the student's current response and the particular expectation, i.e., ideal answer, being covered) and a *global good score* (the similarity of set of student responses to a problem and the set of expectations in a good answer). Additionally, changes in these measures when compared to the previous turn were also included as the *delta local good score* and the *delta global good* score. AutoTutor's major dialogue moves were ordered onto a scale of conversational *directness*, ranging from –1 to 1, in terms of the amount of information the tutor explicitly provides the student. AutoTutor's short *feedback* (negative, neutral negative, neutral, neutral positive, positive) is manifested in its verbal content, intonation, and a host of other nonverbal cues. The feedback was aligned on a 5 point scale ranging from –1 (negative) to 5 (positive feedback).

16.4.1.3 Automated Dialogue-Based Affect Classifiers

Statistical patterns between the affective states and dialogue features are extensively discussed in previous publications [39,52]. For example, boredom occurs later in the session (high subtopic number), after multiple attempts to answer the main question (high turn number), and when AutoTutor gives more direct dialogue moves (high directness). The focus of this chapter is on the accuracy by which several standard classification algorithms could individually distinguish each affective state from neutral (no affect) as well as collectively discriminate between the affective states. The classification algorithms tested were selected from a list of categories including Bayesian classifiers (naive Bayes and naive Bayes updatable), functions (logistic regression, multilayer perceptron, and support vector machines), instance-based techniques (nearest neighbor, K*, locally weighted learning), meta classification schemes (AdaBoost, Bagging predictors, additive logistic regression), trees (C4.5 decision trees, logistic model trees, REP tree), and rules (decision tables, nearest neighbor generalization, PART).

Machine-learning experiments indicated that classifiers were moderately successful in discriminating the affective states of boredom, confusion, flow, frustration, and neutral, yielding a peak accuracy of 42% with neutral (chance = 20%) and 54% without neutral (chance = 25%). Individual detections of boredom, confusion, flow, and frustration, when contrasted with neutral, had maximum accuracies of 69%, 68%, 71%, and 78%, respectively (chance = 50%). These results support the notion that dialogue features is a reasonable source for measuring the affective states that a learner is experiencing. Comparisons among the different types of classifiers indicated that functions-, meta-, and tree-based classifiers were similar quantitatively and yielded significantly higher performance than the other categories. Classification accuracy scores for the instance-based learning were significantly lower than the other five classifier categories. Bayesian classifiers outperformed rule-based classification schemes. In general AdaBoost, logistic regression, and C4.5 decision trees yielded the best performance.

16.4.2 Case Study 2: Predictive Modeling of Student-Reported Affect from Web-Based Interactions in WaLLiS

16.4.2.1 Context

This case study is derived from a research project aiming at the enhancement of an existing web-based intelligent learning environment (WaLLiS [53]) with low-cost capabilities for affect detection and affect-sensitive responses. For a brief description of WaLLiS, see also Chapter 31 of this book.

One of the aims of the research described here was to develop a methodology particularly suited for investigating affective factors under ecologically valid situations. In response to a desire to record data under the most realistic conditions, and because of the difficulty of conducting emote-aloud protocols at students' homes, retrospective walk-throughs with students and tutors were conducted. A representative sample of 18 students was obtained out of 209 students who were already familiar with WaLLiS. These students were using the system at their own time and location, while they were studying for a real course of their immediate interest. The sample was selected on the basis of disproportionate stratified random sampling [54] and included students with different mathematical abilities and awareness of their own abilities.

Similar to the previous case study, data was collected from two studies, one with students retrospectively reporting on their own affect and one with tutors watching replays of students' interactions. Only the first study collected substantial amount of data to conduct a machine-learning analysis. The second met significant difficulties, because, in the absence of other information (e.g., participants' face) tutors found it very difficult to provide judgments of students' affect. Hence, this study was only used for qualitative analysis and to validate the models derived from the machine-learning procedures as described below.

16.4.2.2 Machine Learned Models from Student–System Interactions

Similar to Case Study 1, comparisons of different machine-learning techniques were performed. The overall aim of this research was to (a) derive hypotheses for future research and (b) enable triangulation of the results with a qualitative analysis of the students' and tutors' walkthroughs. For this reason, decision trees were chosen as the classification method. This choice was motivated by the fact that decision trees are relatively inspectable and afford easy comparison and consolidation of derived models.

Separate models were derived for each affective factor rather than, as is usually the case, relying on one model that would predict all the factors. Accordingly, the machine-learning algorithm is presented with pre-processed vectors (instances) automatically constructed from the raw data by an extraction tool that matched the timestamps of contextual factors (correctness of answer, question difficulty, time spent) with the corresponding student's report. These vectors consist of the contextual factors as features and a nominal class that encodes students' reports. In the case of the affective factors, the values are binary indicating the presence of the absence of *frustration*, *boredom*, and *confusion*. For *confidence*, *interest*, and *effort*, the class takes values that depict the relative change of each factor: *decrease*, *increase* and *extreme_decrease*, *extreme_increase*.

Due to the limited size of the data, the majority of the reported affective characteristics pertain to the *confidence* and *effort* factors and therefore the machine-learning analysis exclusively focused on these two factors.

As mentioned above, there was an explicit attempt to take into account the history of students' actions. History is represented as a vector, the elements of which encode the number of times that each type of action (e.g., a hint) occurred in a time window. This window spans back to the last change of the factor under investigation or (if it has not recently changed) to the start of the relevant situation or exercise.

Space constraints prevent us from discussing all the results that constitute the rules and future hypothesis that were derived from the decision trees. These are discussed in detail in other publications [45,46]. Here, we use confidence as an example to depict the methodology and the type of results that were obtained.

In total, there were 289 reports in relation to confidence; these comprise set A. Running the algorithm on this set of data leads to biased rules since it contains only instances where changes in affective states are reported. It is important, however, to train the model with instances of the same patterns where there are no changes to the affective characteristics. Therefore, we extracted the instances (249 in total) where the same actions as these of set A occurred but were not associated with a particular report; these comprise set B. Figure 16.1

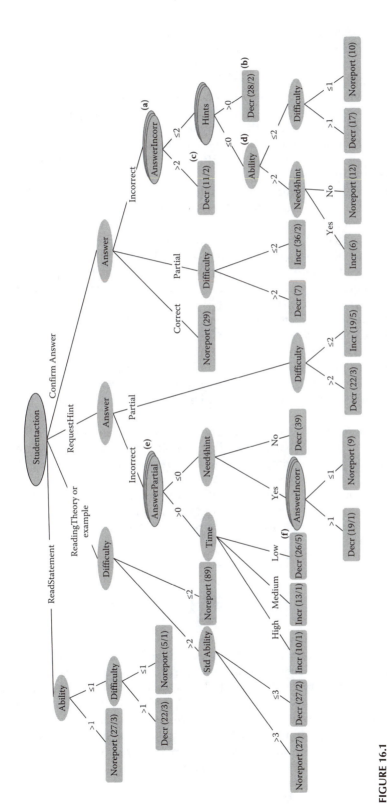

FIGURE 16.1

Graphical representation of the decision tree for confidence. Each node represents an attribute, and the labels on the edges between nodes indicate the possible values of the parent attribute. Following the path from a root to a leaf results in a rule that shows the value of the factor over the values of the attributes in the path. The numbers in brackets next to the designated class indicate the number of instances correctly classified by this rule over the misclassified ones. Nodes with layers (e.g., node a) originate from a *history* vector. For example, AnswerIncorr > 2 shows that in the relevant time window, more than two incorrect answers were provided by the student.

shows a graphic representation of the tree resulting from the merged sets of instances with attributes *action, difficulty, student ability, last answer, last feedback, time,* and the *history* vector. As an example, the rules associated with the confirm-answer action of students are described. The tree suggests that when students confirm an incorrect answer (node a) after having requested at least one hint previously, their confidence decreases (leaf b). If no hints were requested, leaf (c) suggests that if they previously had many (more than two) incorrect answers, then they report that their confidence decreases (the two misclassified instances in leaf (c) are of an extreme decrease). Otherwise, it seems that the outcome depends on students' previous knowledge, the difficulty of the question, and the necessity of the help request (node d).

The rest of the tree can be interpreted in a similar fashion. For example, the rule associated with node (e), where students are requesting hints after submitting a wrong answer shows that students' reports vary depending on whether or not their previous answer was partially correct. A closer inspection of the rule suggests that in situations where the students provided a partially correct answer, and where the system responds to such an answer with negative feedback, the students' confidence level tends to drop. This is particularly the case for students who do not spend sufficient time to read and interpret the hints provided by the system (node f).

Overall, with the addition of history in the vector, cross-validation performed in the decision tree for confidence indicated that the tree correctly classified 90.91% of the cases (Kappa = 0.87). Accuracy for effort was 89.16%, Kappa = 0.79; these can be considered as satisfactory results. Although, in this case, the addition of history did not improve the results significantly, such information can be very useful in situations like open-learner modeling where it would be important to communicate to the student the rationale behind the system's decisions.

The results demonstrate that rule induction provides a mechanism for deriving a predictive model in the form of rules that is based on students' actions with the system. Most of these rules are intuitive but defining them by hand would have required a thorough, operational understanding of the processes involved, not easily achieved by experts in the field. Although the process for collecting data was time consuming and led to small amount of unequivocal rules, the methodology and machine-learning method is generalizable to different situations resulting in at least hypotheses about rules that can guide the design of future studies.

16.5 Discussion

The case studies presented in this chapter demonstrate the benefits of using EDM techniques to monitor complex mental states in educational settings. They also identify several important challenges for the EDM field, particularly in relation to the prediction of learner affect. We highlighted different methods for collecting and annotating data of students' interaction, the importance of ecological validity, as well as the difficulty of achieving it. Several chapters in this book provide examples of the types of analysis and research that recently has become possible owing to the availability of data from systems integrated in real pedagogical situations. However, compared to other applications of EDM, affect prediction from data introduces additional challenges to the ones faced when investigating, e.g., the effects of the interaction in learning.

Although supervised learning approaches require a measure of ground truth in the phenomenon being predicted, additional challenges arise in affect measurement. We discussed the need for employing data that are representative of the behavioral evidence to which an ITS has runtime access. However, affect is a psychological construct that is notoriously difficult to measure since human judgments of affect are often vague, ill-defined, and possibly indeterminate. Self-reports, commonly used to elicit such judgments, also present a number of possible problems, such as the bias of subjectivity resulting from the fact that each affective characteristic may have a different meaning for different learners. Therefore, it is important to look at protocols that extend beyond self reports for monitoring affective states. For example, in case study 1, the video recordings of learners' facial expressions and the dialogue cues enabled the judges to make more informed ratings. Furthermore, reliable physiological sensors can also be employed. Although this may involve violating the ecological validity principle, it may be necessary for deriving models that can be introduced and evaluated subsequently in more ecologically valid situations.

Another important consideration comes from the use of qualitative methods for data collecting. These often result in limited and sparse data. Therefore, it is common to employ cross-validation to assess the quality of the predictive method. Since any evaluation influences the validity of the results, the stratified cross-validation that is typically employed in the field could benefit from being performed in a way that takes into account that we are dealing with educational data. The "off-the-shelf" methods for cross-validation could potentially introduce biases in the evaluation by including instances of the same learner in both training and testing sets. Although in some cases this is not a problem, in situations where the nature of the predicted class can be affected by latent inherent characteristics of the learner (such as affective traits or prolonged mood states), the evaluation can be biased.

Furthermore, instead of "blindly" evaluating a model's performance in relation to existing data, cost-sensitive classification [55] can provide more practical results. That is, instead of assuming equality between the costs of false positives and false negatives, it may be worth taking into account the cost of misclassifications. For example, [45] describe the use of such an approach based on rules derived from experts who evaluated the effect of false positives for a model of confidence prediction in various situations. The estimated "cost" is then employed at prediction time to inform the pedagogical decisions of the system. Having a cost function also enables the implementation of algorithms that take the cost into account during learning, thus leading to a model that is optimized with respect to the cost of the adaptive decisions taken rather than just against the data available alone.

A related question refers to the extent to which valid affect diagnosis facilitates adaptation of tutoring. Further research should investigate methodologies that incorporate several of the protocols described in this chapter simultaneously, to enable a sufficient degree of convergent validity in affect measurement [48]. To this effect, [6,46] discuss various attempts to take into account the perspective of the tutor. Similarly, [56] recruited two trained teachers to provide judgments of learners' affective states, while [52] used pedagogical experts to recommend strategies to regulate learners' affective states.

While the results of those attempts are encouraging, the development of research protocols to collect tutors' inferences is not trivial. One difficulty lies in the assumptions made about immediacy and accuracy of human reasoning [57]. To date, most efforts in the field assume that tutors respond to observable actions of the learners, thus making actions the critical features for analysis. However, as a related analysis in [6] shows, this is not always true; there are many cases where tutors accumulate evidence over a series of actions. In addition, there is sometimes anticipatory behavior that is not easily captured or directly perceivable from observable actions. Case study 2 provides a first step toward taking history of a tutorial interaction into account, but further investigation reveals that even the antecedent values of reported factors also play a role in tutors' diagnosis—even for the same sequence of events, tutors' actions (and their subsequent verbalizations and reports) are affected by values reported earlier for the same factor [46].

A possible solution that is emerging is to compare, aggregate and consolidate models developed from different sources of data (e.g., self-reports and peer or tutor reports). On the one hand, learners are a more valid source of evidence for reporting their own affective states such as their level of confidence, than the tutors. On the other hand, tutors may be better suited than the learners to judge learners' boredom or effort as well as to report on how such judgments can be used to support learning. Actor–observer biases may also play an important role in the judgments of fuzzy, vague, ill-defined constructs such as affective states. Learners might provide one set of categories by attributing their states to situational factors, while observers (peers and trained judges) might make attributions to stable dispositional factors, thereby obtaining an alternate set of categories [58].

Despite these qualifications, examples of how to derive models from different sources of data, can be found in [6], where different branches of decision trees are manually aggregated. Similar examples appear in [50]. If done using automatic methods, this approach has the potential to increase the precision of the models generated. The issue of automatically aggregating models automatically has been investigated in detail in the field of data mining [59,60]. In addition, the need to consider and merge different perspectives resembles the emerging requirements behind reconciling models in the field of ontologies e.g., [61,62]. Insights of how this could be achieved appear in [63]. A particularly relevant example is the work presented in [64], where a user's and an expert's conceptual model are compared. Developing formal ways to perform such measurements is necessary to enable the reduction of the bias introduced by researchers' intuitions.

16.6 Conclusions

As illustrated by the case studies, monitoring students' interaction parameters can provide a cost-effective, nonintrusive, efficient, and effective method to automatically detect complex phenomena such as the affective states that accompany learning. However, several methodological issues emerged and were discussed in this chapter. One important aspect to consider was the context of data collection and the inevitable interference created by affective labels collection. Another important issue that was flagged is students' familiarity with the learning environment and their goals when using it. Finally, two methods of monitoring affective states were described and employed in the case studies: (a) real-time measurements by means of emote-aloud protocols or observations and (b) retrospective affect judgment by participant and/or tutors.

Although the studies used specific systems and measured certain affective states, the methodology for data collection and machine-learning methods employed are generalizable and could serve as guidance for the design of other studies. However, several important questions still remain. There is the question of how these features can be coupled with the bodily measures such as facial features, speech contours, and body language, as well as physiological measures such as galvanic skin response, heart rate, respiration rate, etc. Detection accuracies could be increased by implementing hybrid models and consolidating their outputs. There is also the question of how computer tutors might adapt their pedagogical and motivational strategies to be responsive to assessments of learners' affective and cognitive states to heighten engagement and optimize learning gains. The accuracy as well as the type of response has to be interpreted in the context of the likely educational consequences of incorrect predictions. It is clear that although computer tutors that respond in this fashion represent a significant advance over ITSs that are mere cognitive machines; these advances await further research and technological development.

Acknowledgments

D'Mello and Graesser would like to acknowledge the National Science Foundation (REC 0106965, ITR 0325428, HCC 0834847) for funding this research. Any opinions, findings and conclusions, or recommendations expressed in this chapter are those of the authors and do not necessarily reflect the views of NSF.

References

1. Arroyo, I., Cooper, D., Burleson, W., Woolf, B., Muldner, K., and Christopherson, R., Emotion sensors go to school, in Dimitrova, V., Mizoguchi, R., du Boulay, B., and Graesser, A. (eds.), *Proceedings of the 14th International Conference on Artificial Intelligence in Education: Building Learning Systems that Care: From Knowledge Representation to Affective Modelling*, Vol. 200, Brighton, U.K., IOS Press, Amsterdam, the Netherlands, 2009, pp. 17–24.
2. Forbes-Riley, K., Rotaru, M., and Litman, D., The relative impact of student affect on performance models in a spoken dialogue tutoring system, *User Modeling and User-Adapted Interaction* 18(1), 11–43, 2008.
3. Conati, C. and Maclaren, H., Empirically building and evaluating a probabilistic model of user affect, *User Modeling and User-Adapted Interaction* 19(3), 267–303, 2009.
4. Robison, J., McQuiggan, S., and Lester, J., Evaluating the consequences of affective feedback in intelligent tutoring systems, in *International Conference on Affective Computing and Intelligent Interaction*, Amsterdam, the Netherlands, 2009, pp. 1–6.
5. D'Mello, S., Craig, S., Fike, K., Graesser, A., and Jacko, J., Responding to learners' cognitive-affective states with supportive and shakeup dialogues, *Human-Computer Interaction: Ambient, Ubiquitous and Intelligent Interaction*, Springer, Berlin/ Heidelberg, Germany, 2009, pp. 595–604.
6. Porayska-Pomsta, K., Mavrikis, M., and Pain, H., Diagnosing and acting on student affect: The tutor's perspective, *User Modeling and User-Adapted Interaction* 18(1), 125–173, 2008.
7. Lepper, M. R., Woolverton, M., Mumme, D. L., Gurtner, J., Lajoie, S. P., and Derry, S. J., Motivational techniques of expert human tutors: Lessons for the design of computer-based tutors, *Computers as Cognitive Tools*, Lawrence Erlbaum Associates, Hillsdale, NJ, 1993, pp. 75–107.
8. Goleman, D., *Emotional Intelligence: Why It Can Matter More than IQ*, Boomsbury, London, U.K., 1996.
9. Conati, C., Marsella, S., and Paiva, A., Affective interactions: The computer in the affective loop, in *Proceedings of the 10th International Conference on Intelligent User Interfaces*, ACM Press, San Diego, CA, 2005, p. 7.
10. Conati, C., Probabilistic assessment of user's emotions in educational games, *Journal of Applied Artificial Intelligence* 16(7–8), 555–575, 2002.

11. Carver, C., Negative affects deriving from the behavioral approach system, *Emotion* 4(1), 3–22, 2004.
12. Deci, E. L., Ryan, R. M., and Aronson, J., The paradox of achievement: The harder you push, the worse it gets, *Improving Academic Achievement: Impact of Psychological Factors on Education*, Academic Press, Orlando, FL, 2002, pp. 61–87.
13. Dweck, C. S. and Aronson, J., Messages that motivate: How praise molds students' beliefs, motivation, and performance (in surprising ways), in Aronson, J. (ed.), *Improving Academic Achievement: Impact of Psychological Factors on Education*, Academic Press, New York, 2002.
14. Stein, N. L., Hernandez, M. W., Trabasso, T., Lewis, M., Haviland-Jones, J. M., and Barrett, L. F., Advances in modeling emotions and thought: The importance of developmental, online, and multilevel analysis, *Handbook of Emotions*, Guilford Press, New York, 2008, pp. 574–586.
15. Keller, J. M. and Reigeluth, C. M., Motivational design of instruction, *Instructional-Design Theories and Models: An Overview of Their Current Status*, Lawrence Erlbaum Associates Hillsdale, NJ, 1983, pp. 383–434.
16. Ames, C., Classrooms: Goals, structures, and student motivation, *Journal of Educational Psychology* 84(3), 261–271, 1992.
17. Rosiek, J., Emotional scaffolding: An exploration of the teacher knowledge at the intersection of student emotion and the subject matter, *Journal of Teacher Education* 54(5), 399–412, 2003.
18. Qu, L., Wang, N., and Johnson, L., Using learner focus of attention to detect learner motivation factors, in *Proceedings of the User Modeling Conference 2005*, Edinburgh, U.K., 2005, pp. 70–73.
19. Beck, J., Engagement tracing: Using response times to model student disengagement, in *Proceedings of the 2005 conference on Artificial Intelligence in Education: Supporting Learning through Intelligent and Socially Informed Technology*, Amsterdam, the Netherlands, 2005, pp. 88–95.
20. Johns, J. and Woolf, P., A dynamic mixture model to detect student motivation and proficiency, in *AAAI*, Boston, MA, pp. 163–168, 2006.
21. de Baker, R. S. J., Corbett, A., Roll, I., and Koedinger, K., Developing a generalizable detector of when students game the system, *User Modeling and User-Adapted Interaction* 18(3), 287–314, 2008.
22. Walonoski, J. and Heffernan, N., Detection and analysis of off-task gaming behavior in intelligent tutoring systems, in *Proceedings of the 8th Conference on Intelligent Tutoring Systems*, Jhongli, Taiwan, 2006, pp. 382–391.
23. Arroyo, I. and Woolf, B., Inferring learning and attitudes with a Bayesian Network of log files data, in Looi, C. K., McCalla, G., Bredeweg, B., and Breuker, J (eds.) *Proceedings of the Artificial Intelligence in Education: Supporting Learning through Intelligent and Socially Informed Technology (AIED-2005 Conference)*, July 18–22, 2005, Amsterdam, the Netherlands, IOS Press, Amsterda, the Netherlands, 2005, pp. 33–40.
24. Cocea, M. and Weibelzahl, S., Eliciting motivation knowledge from log files towards motivation diagnosis for adaptive systems, in *Proceedings of the 11th International Conference on User Modeling 2007*, Corfu, Greece, 2007, pp. 197–206.
25. Picard, R.W. and Scheirer, J., The galvactivator: A glove that senses and communicates skin conductivity, in *Proceedings of the 9th International Conference on HCI*, New Orleans, LA, pp. 1538–1542. 2001.
26. Pantic, M. and Rothkrantz, L., Toward an affect-sensitive multimodal human-computer interaction, *Proceedings of the IEEE* 91(9), 1370–1390, 2003.
27. Zeng, Z., Pantic, M., Roisman, G., and Huang, T., A survey of affect recognition methods: Audio, visual, and spontaneous expressions, *IEEE Transactions on Pattern Analysis and Machine Intelligence* 31(1), 39–58, 2009.
28. Kapoor, A., Picard, R. W., and Ivanov, Y., Probabilistic combination of multiple modalities to detect interest, in *International Conference on Pattern Recognition*, Cambridge, U.K., 2004, pp. 969–972.
29. Messom, C. H., Sarrafzadeh, A., Johnson, M. J., and Chao, F., Affective state estimation from facial images using neural networks and fuzzy logic, in Wang, D. and Lee, N. K. (eds.), *Neural Networks Applications in Information Technology and Web Engineering*, Borneo Publications, 2005.

30. Litman, D. J., Recognizing student emotions and attitudes on the basis of utterances in spoken tutoring dialogues with both human and computer tutors, *Speech communication* 28(5), 559–590, 2006.

31. D'Mello, S., Graesser, A., and Picard, R. W., Toward an affect-sensitive AutoTutor, *Intelligent Systems, IEEE* 22(4), 53–61, 2007.

32. Ang, J., Dhillon, R., Krupski, A., Shriberg, E., and Stolcke, A., Prosody-based automatic detection of annoyance and frustration in human-computer dialog, in *Proceedings of the International Conference on Spoken Language Processing*, Vol 3, Denver, CO, 2002, pp. 2037–2039.

33. Forbes-Riley, K. and Litman, D. J., Predicting emotion in spoken dialogue from multiple knowledge sources, in *Proceedings of Human Language Technology Conference of the North American Chapter of the Association for Computational Linguistics* (HLT/NAACL), Boston, MA, 2004, pp. 201–208.

34. Liscombe, J., Riccardi, G., and Hakkani-Tür, D., Using context to improve emotion detection in spoken dialog systems, in *Ninth European Conference on Speech Communication and Technology* (EUROSPEECH'05), Lisbon, Portugal, 2005, pp. 1845–1848.

35. Barrett, F., Are emotions natural kinds?, *Perspectives on Psychological Science* 1, 28–58, 2006.

36. Aviezer, H., Ran, H., Ryan, J., Grady, C., Susskind, J. M., Anderson, A. K., and Moscovitch, M., Angry, disgusted or afraid?, *Studies on the Malleability of Facial Expression Perception* 19(7), 724–732, 2008.

37. Russell, J. A., Core affect and the psychological construction of emotion, *Psychological Review* 110(1), 145–172, 2003.

38. Stemmler, G., Heldmann, M., Pauls, C. A., and Scherer, T., Constraints for emotion specificity in fear and anger: The context counts, *Psychophysiology* 38(2), 275–291, 2001.

39. D'Mello, S. K., Craig, S. D., Sullins, C. J., and Graesser, A. C., Predicting affective states expressed through an emote-aloud procedure from AutoTutor's mixed initiative dialogue, *International Journal of Artificial Intelligence in Education* 16(1), 3–28, 2006.

40. Graesser, A. C., Chipman, P., Haynes, B. C., and Olney, A., AutoTutor: An intelligent tutoring system with mixed-initiative dialogue, *IEEE Transactions on Education* 48(4), 612–618, 2005.

41. Ericsson, K. A. and Simon, H. A., *Protocol Analysis: Verbal Reports as Data*, MIT Press, Cambridge, MA, 1993.

42. Trabasso, T. and Magliano, J. P., Conscious understanding during comprehension, *Discourse Processes* 21(3), 255–287, 1996.

43. Baker, R., Rodrigo, M., and Xolocotzin, U., The dynamics of affective transitions in simulation problem-solving environments, in Paiva, A. P. R. P. R. W. (ed.), *2nd International Conference on Affective Computing and Intelligent Interaction* 2007, Lisbon, Portugal, 666–677.

44. Conati, C., Chabbal, R., and Maclaren, H., A Study on using biometric sensors for monitoring user emotions in educational games, in *Workshop on Assessing and Adapting to User Attitudes and Affect: Why, When and How? in conjunction with User Modeling* (UM-03), Johnstown, PA, 2003.

45. Mavrikis, M., Maciocia, A., and Lee, J., Towards predictive modelling of student affect from web-based interactions, in Luckin, R., Koedinger, K., and Greer, J. (eds.), *Proceedings of the 13th International Conference on Artificial Intelligence in Education,: Building Technology Rich Learning Contexts that Work* (AIED2007), Vol. 158, Los Angeles, CA, IOS Press, Amsterdam, the Netherlands, 2007, pp. 169–176.

46. Mavrikis, M., Modelling students' behaviour and affective states in ILEs through educational data mining, PhD thesis, The University of Edinburgh, Edinburgh, U.K., 2008.

47. Dimitrova, V., Mizoguchi, R., du Boulay, B., and Graesser, A. (eds.), *Proceedings of the 14th International Conference on Artificial Intelligence in Education Building Learning Systems that Care: From Knowledge Representation to Affective Modelling* (AIED 2009), Vol. 200, July 6–10, 2009, Brighton, U.K., IOS Press, Amsterdam, the Netherlands, 2009.

48. D'Mello, S., Craig, S., and Graesser, A., Multimethod assessment of affective experience and expression during deep learning, *International Journal of Learning Technology* 4(3/4), 165–187, 2009.

49. Baker, R. S., Corbett, A. T., Koedinger, K. R., and Wagner, A. Z., Off-task behavior in the cognitive tutor classroom: When students "game the system," in *Proceedings of ACM CHI 2004: Computer-Human Interaction*, Vienna, Austria, 2004, pp. 383–390.

50. Graesser, A. C., McDaniel, B., Chipman, P., Witherspoon, A., D'Mello, S., and Gholson, B., Detection of emotions during learning with AutoTutor, in *Proceedings of the 28th Annual Conference of the Cognitive Science Society*, Mahwah, NJ, 2006, pp. 285–290.

51. Landauer, T. and Dumais, S., A Solution to plato's problem: The latent semantic analysis theory of acquisition, induction, and representation of knowledge, *Psychological Review* 104(2), 211–240, 1997.

52. D'Mello, S., Craig, S., Witherspoon, A., McDaniel, B., and Graesser, A., Automatic detection of learner's affect from conversational cues, *User Modeling and User-Adapted Interaction* 18(1–2), 45–80, 2008.

53. Mavrikis, M. and Maciocia, A., WALLIS: A Web-based ILE for science and engineering students studying mathematics, in *Workshop of Advanced Technologies for Mathematics Education in 11th International Conference on Artificial Intelligence in Education*, Sydney, Australia, 2003.

54. Lohr, S., *Sampling: Design and Analysis*, Duxbury Press, Pacific Grove, CA, 1999.

55. Witten, I. and Frank, E., *Data Mining: Practical Machine Learning Tools and Techniques*, Morgan Kaufmann, San Francisco, CA, 2005.

56. D'Mello, S., Taylor, R., Davidson, K., and Graesser, A., Self versus teacher judgments of learner emotions during a tutoring session with AutoTutor, in Woolf, B. P., Aimeur, E., Nkambou, R., and Lajoie, S. (eds.) *Proceedings of the 9th International Conference on Intelligent Tutoring Systems*, Montreal, Canada, 2008, pp. 9–18.

57. Porayska-Pomsta, K., Influence of situational context on language production: Modelling teachers' corrective responses, PhD thesis, School of Informatics, The University of Edinburgh, Edinburgh, U.K., 2003.

58. Jones, E. and Nisbett, R., *The Actor and the Observer: Divergent Perceptions of the Causes of Behavior*, General Learning Press, New York, 1971.

59. Williams, G. J., *Inducing and Combining Decision Structures for Expert Systems*, PhD thesis, The Australian National University, Canberra, Australia, 1990.

60. Vannoorenberghe, P., On aggregating belief decision trees, *Information Fusion* 5(3), 179–188, 2004.

61. Ehrig, M. and Sure, Y., Ontology mapping—An integrated approach, in *European Semantic Web Symposium (ESWS)*, Heraklion, Greece, 2004, pp. 76–91.

62. Klein, M., Combining and relating ontologies: An analysis of problems and solutions, in Perez, G., Gruninger, M., Stuckenschmidt, H., and Uschold, M. (eds.), *Workshop on Ontologies and Information Sharing (IJCAI'01)*, Seattle, WA, 2001.

63. Agarwal, P., Huang, Y., and Dimitrova, V., Formal approach to reconciliation of individual ontologies for personalisation of geospatial semantic web, in Rodriguez, M.A (ed.), *Proceedings of GeoS 2005, LNCS 3799*, Mexico, 2005, pp. 195–210.

64. Arroyo, A., Denaux, R., Dimitrova, V., and Pye, M., Interactive ontology-based user knowledge acquisition: A case study, in Sure, Y. and Dominguez, J. (eds.), *Semantic Web: Research and Applications, Proceedings of the Third European Semantic Web Conference (ESWC 2006)*, Budva, Montenegro, 2006, pp. 560–574.

17

Measuring Correlation of Strong Symmetric Association Rules in Educational Data

Agathe Merceron and Kalina Yacef

CONTENTS

17.1 Introduction

Association rules are very useful in educational data mining since they extract associations between educational items and present the results in an intuitive form to the teachers. They can be used for a range of purposes: In [1,2], they are used, combined with other methods, to personalize students' recommendation while browsing the Web. In [15], they were used to find various associations of students' behavior in the Web-based educational system LON-CAPA. The work in [4] used fuzzy rules in a personalized e-learning material recommender system to discover associations between students' requirements and learning materials. They were used in [5] to find mistakes often made together while students solve exercises in propositional logic, in order to provide proactive feedback and understand underlying learning difficulties. In [6], they were combined with genetic programming to discover relations between knowledge levels, times, and scores that help the teacher modify the course's original structure and content.

Like any other data mining technique, association rules require that one understands the data well: What is the content and the structure of the data? Does it need cleaning? Does it need transformation? Which attributes and values should be used to extract the association rules? Do the results, here the association rules, make sense or, in other words, can we rate them? Can the results be deployed to improve teaching and learning? Unlike other data mining techniques, there is mainly one algorithm to extract association rules from data (a priori, [7]). In comparison with a classification task, for example, there are many classifiers that, with the same set of data, use different algorithms and thus can give different results [3].

A pitfall in applying association rules regards the selection of "interesting" rules among all extracted rules. Let us clarify that the level of interestingness of a rule as measured by an objective measure describes how the associated items are correlated, not how useful the rule ends up being for the task. Indeed, the algorithm, depending on the thresholds given for the support and the confidence, which we will describe in the next section, can extract a large amount of rules, and the task of filtering the meaningful ones can be arduous. This is a common concern for which a range of objective measures exist, depending on the context [8,9]. However, these measures can give conflicting results about whether a rule should be retained or discarded. In such cases, how do we know which measure to follow?

We explore in this paper several objective measures in the context of our data in order to understand which are better suited for it. We extracted association rules from the data stored by the Logic-ITA, an intelligent tutoring system for formal proof in propositional logic [10]. Our aim was to find out whether some mistakes often occurred together or sequentially during practice. The results gave *strong symmetric* associations between three mistakes. *Strong* means that all associations had a strong support and a strong confidence. *Symmetric* means that $X \rightarrow Y$ and $Y \rightarrow X$ were both associations extracted. Puzzlingly, measures of interestingness such as lift, correlation, or chi-square indicated poor or no correlation. However cosine, Jaccard, and all-confidence were systematically high, implying a high correlation between the mistakes. In this chapter, we investigate why measures such as lift, correlation, and chi-square, to some extent, work poorly with our data, and we show that our data has quite a special shape. Further, chi-square on larger datasets with the same properties gives an interesting perspective on our rules. We also show that cosine, Jaccard, and all-confidence rate our rules as interesting. These latter measures, in opposition to the former measures, have the null-invariant property. This means that they are not sensitive to transactions that do not contain neither X nor Y. This fact is relevant when items are not symmetric, in the sense that the information conveyed by the presence of X is more important than the information conveyed by its absence, which is the case with the data of Logic-ITA and quite often the case with educational data in general. A preliminary version of this work has appeared in [11].

17.1.1 Association Rules Obtained with Logic-ITA

We have captured four years of data from the Logic-ITA [10], a tool to practice logic formal proofs. We have, among other analysis, extracted association rules about the mistakes made by our students in order to support our teaching. Before we describe the elements of this data, let us first present the basic concepts that we use about association rules.

17.1.1.1 Association Rules and Associated Concepts

Association rule mining comes from market basket analysis [7] and captures information such as "if customers buy beer, they also buy diapers," written as *beer → diapers*. Association rule mining finds interesting associations among large set of data items. Two measures are used to extract association rules: support and confidence. We introduce these concepts now.

Let $I = \{I_1, I_2, \ldots, I_m\}$ be a set of m items and $T = \{t_1, t_2, \ldots, t_n\}$ be a set of n transactions, with each t_i being a subset of I.

An *association rule* is a rule of the form $X \to Y$, where X and Y are disjoint subsets of I having a support and a confidence above a minimum threshold.

Support:

$$\sup(X \to Y) = \frac{|\{t_i : X, Y \in t_i\}|}{n},$$

where $|A|$ denotes the cardinality of the set A. In other words, the support of a rule $X \to Y$ is the proportion of transactions that contain both X and Y. This is also called $P(X, Y)$, the probability that a transaction contains both X and Y. Support is symmetric: $\sup(X \to Y) = \sup(Y \to X)$.

Confidence:

$$\mathrm{conf}(X \to Y) = \frac{|\{t_i : X, Y \in t_i\}|}{|\{t_i : X \in t_i\}|}.$$

In other words, the confidence of a rule $X \to Y$ is the proportion of transactions that contain both X and Y among those that contain X. An equivalent definition is

$$\mathrm{conf}(X \to Y) = \frac{P(X, Y)}{P(X)}$$

with

$$P(X) = \frac{|\{t_i : X \in t_i\}|}{n},$$

which is the probability that a transaction contains Y knowing that it already contains X. Confidence is not symmetric. Usually $\mathrm{conf}(X \to Y)$ is different from $\mathrm{conf}(Y \to X)$.

Each of the two above measures plays a role in the construction of the rules. Support makes sure that only items occurring often enough in the data will be taken into account to establish the association rules. Confidence makes sure that the occurrence of X implies in some sense the occurrence of Y.

Symmetric association rule: We call a rule $X \to Y$ a *symmetric* association rule if $\sup(X \to Y)$ is above a given minimum threshold and both $\mathrm{conf}(X \to Y)$ and $\mathrm{conf}(Y \to X)$ are above a given minimum threshold. This is the kind of association rules we obtained with the Logic-ITA.

17.1.1.2 Data from Logic-ITA

The Logic-ITA was used at Sydney University from 2001 to 2004 in a course formerly taught by the authors. Over these four years, around 860 students attended the course and used the tool, trying to construct formal proofs in propositional logic.

An exercise consists of a set of formulas (called premises) and another formula (called the conclusion). The aim is to prove that the conclusion can validly be derived from the premises. For this, the student has to construct new formulas, step by step, using logic rules and formulas previously established in the proof, until the conclusion is derived. There is no unique solution and any valid path is acceptable. Steps are checked on the fly and, if incorrect, an error message and possibly a tip are displayed. Students used the tool at their own discretion. A consequence is that there is neither a fixed number nor a fixed set of exercises done by all students.

All steps, whether correct or not, are stored for each user, and each attempted exercise as well as their error messages. A very interesting task was to analyze the mistakes made and try to detect associations within them. This is why we used association rules. We defined the set of items *I* as the set of possible mistakes or error messages and a transaction as the set of mistakes made by one student on one exercise. Therefore, we obtain as many transactions as exercises attempted with the Logic-ITA during the semester, which is about 2000. Data did not need to be cleaned but put in the proper form to extract association rules: a file containing a list of transactions, i.e., a list of mistakes per attempted exercise, was created from the database stored by Logic-ITA.

17.1.1.3 Association Rules Obtained with Logic-ITA

We used association rules to find mistakes often occurring together while solving exercises. The purpose of looking for these associations was for the teacher to ponder and, may be, to review the course material or emphasize subtleties while explaining concepts to students. Thus, it made sense to have a support that is not too low. The strongest rules for 2004 are shown in Table 17.1. "Mistake M10: *Premise set incorrect*" means that a student has not given the correct premises while applying a logic rule. "Mistake M11: *Rule can be applied, but deduction incorrect*" means that the logic rule chosen by the student can be applied but the student has entered a formula that does not match the logic rule. One type of logic rules, the deduction rules, can be applied up to two formulas previously established while other logic rules, the equivalence rules, can only be applied to one previously established formula. When a student makes a mistake regarding the number of previously established formulas, "Mistake M12: *Wrong number of line references given*" occurs.

The first association rule says that if students make mistake, *Rule can be applied, but deduction incorrect* while solving an exercise, then they also made the mistake *Wrong number of line references given* while solving the same exercise. As we can see in the small subset of three pairs of rules shown in this table, the rules are symmetric and display comparable support and confidence. Findings were quite similar across the years (2001–2004).

TABLE 17.1

Some Association Rules for Year 2004

M11 ==> M12 [sup: 77%, conf: 89%]	
M12 ==> M11 [sup: 77%, conf: 87%]	M10: Premise set incorrect
M11 ==> M10 [sup: 74%, conf: 86%]	M11: Rule can be applied, but deduction incorrect
M10 ==> M11 [sup: 78%, conf: 93%]	M12: Wrong number of line references given
M12 ==> M10 [sup: 78%, conf: 89%]	
M10 ==> M12 [sup: 74%, conf: 88%]	

17.2 Measuring Interestingness

It is a fact that association rules are not necessarily interesting and that confidence is not enough to measure how well the occurrence of X implies the occurrence of Y [8,12]. Several measures, beside confidence, have been proposed to better measure the correlation between X and Y. Here, we consider the following objective interestingness measures: lift, correlation, chi-square testing, cosine, Jaccard, and all-confidence.

17.2.1 Some Measures of Interestingness

Let us describe the measures that we explored in this chapter. Some of the measures we consider have the so-called null-invariant, or null-addition, property [8,12]. A measure has the null-invariant property if its calculation uses only the number of transactions containing X or Y, or both. A consequence is that the total number of transactions n does not impact on the result. As in the preceding section, X and Y are item sets, which means that they are disjoint subsets of I, the set of items.

- $\text{lift}(X \rightarrow Y) = \dfrac{\text{conf}(X \rightarrow Y)}{P(Y)}.$

  An equivalent definition is

$$\frac{P(X,Y)}{P(X)P(Y)}.$$

  Lift is a symmetric measure for rules of the form $X \rightarrow Y$. **A lift well above 1 indicates a strong correlation between X and Y.** A lift around 1 says that $P(X, Y) = P(X)P(Y)$. In terms of probability, this means that the occurrence of X and the occurrence of Y in the same transaction are independent events, hence X and Y are not correlated. Lift($X \rightarrow Y$) can be seen as the summary AV($X \rightarrow Y$) and AV($Y \rightarrow X$), where AV is another objective measure called Added Value [13].

- $\text{Correlation}(X \rightarrow Y) = \dfrac{P(X,Y) - P(X)P(Y)}{\sqrt{P(X)P(Y)(1 - P(X))(1 - P(Y))}}.$

  Correlation is a symmetric measure and is a straightforward application of Pearson correlation to association rules when X and Y are interpreted as vectors: $X \cup$ (respectively Y) is a vector of dimension n; coordinate i takes value 1 if transaction t_i contains X (respectively Y) and takes value 0 otherwise. A correlation around 0 indicates that X and Y are not correlated, a negative figure indicates that X and Y are negatively correlated, and **a value close to 1 that they are positively correlated**. Note that the denominator of the division is positive and smaller than 1. Thus, the absolute value $|\text{cor}(X \rightarrow Y)|$ is greater than $|P(X, Y) - P(X)P(Y)|$. In other words, if the lift is around 1, correlation can still be significantly different from 0.

- *Chi-square.* To perform the chi-square test, a table of expected frequencies is first calculated using $P(X)$ and $P(Y)$ from the contingency table. A contingency table summarizes the number of transactions that contain X and Y, X but not

Y, Y but not X, and finally that contain neither X nor Y. The expected frequency for $(X \cap Y)$ is given by the product $nP(X)P(Y)$. Performing a grand total over observed frequencies versus expected frequencies gives a number, which we denote by chi. Consider the contingency table shown in Table 17.2. The X column reads as follows: 500 transactions contain X and Y, while 50 transactions contain X but not Y. Altogether there are 550 transactions that contain X and the total number of transactions is 2000. The following column reads similarly for the transactions that do not contain X.

Here $P(X) = P(Y) = \dfrac{550}{2000}$.

Therefore the expected frequency $(X_e \cap Y_e)$ is

$$\frac{550 \times 550}{2000} = 151.25,$$

TABLE 17.2

A Contingency Table

	X	¬X	Total
Y	500	50	550
¬Y	50	1400	1450
Total	550	1450	2000

TABLE 17.3

Expected Frequencies for Table 17.2

	X_e	$¬X_e$	Total
Y_e	151.25	398.75	550
$¬Y_e$	398.75	1051.25	1450
Total	550	1450	2000

as shown in Table 17.3.

We calculate the other frequencies similarly. The grand total for chi is therefore

$$\text{Chi} = \frac{2(500 - 151.25)}{151.25} + \frac{2(50 - 398.75)}{398.75} + \frac{2(50 - 398.75)}{398.75} + \frac{2(1400 - 1051.25)}{1051.25} = 1529.87.$$

The obtained number chi is compared with a cut-off value read from a chi-square table. For the probability value of 0.05 with one degree of freedom, the cut-off value is 3.84. If chi is greater than 3.84, then X and Y are regarded as correlated with a 95% confidence level. Otherwise they are regarded as noncorrelated also with a 95% confidence level. Therefore, in our example, X and Y are highly correlated.

- $\text{Cosine}(X \rightarrow Y) = \dfrac{P(X,Y)}{\sqrt{P(X)P(Y)}}$.

An equivalent definition is

$$\text{Cosine}(X \rightarrow Y) = \frac{\left|\{t_i : X, Y \in t_i\}\right|}{\sqrt{\left|\{t_i : X \in t_i\}\right|\left|\{t_i : Y \in t_i\}\right|}}.$$

As correlation, cosine is a straightforward application of cosine in geometry to association rules when X and Y are interpreted as vectors. Cosine is a number between 0 and 1. This is due to the fact that both $P(X, Y) \le P(X)$ and $P(X, Y) \le P(Y)$. **A value close to 1 indicates a good correlation between X and Y.** In contrast to the measures considered so far, cosine has the null-invariant property.

- Jaccard $(X \rightarrow Y) = \dfrac{|X,Y|}{|X|+|Y|-|X,Y|}$,

  where

  $|X, Y|$ is the number of transactions that contain both X and Y
  $|X|$ is the number of transactions that contain X
  $|Y|$ is the number of transactions that contain Y

  Jaccard is a number between 0 and 1, which gives the proportion of transactions that contains both X and Y among the transactions that contains X or Y or both. It can be thought of as the support of (X, Y) dismissing all transactions that do not contain neither X nor Y. Like cosine, Jaccard has the null-invariant property. **A rule is rated as interesting if Jaccard is greater than 0.5.**

- All-confidence $(X \rightarrow Y) = \min\left(\dfrac{|X,Y|}{|X|}, \dfrac{|X,Y|}{|Y|}\right)$,

  where *min* denotes the minimum of the two numbers. All-confidence is a number between 0 and 1, which gives the proportion of transactions that contains both X and Y among the transactions that contains X or among the transactions that contain Y, depending on which one is smallest. Like cosine and Jaccard, all-confidence has the null-invariant property. **A rule is rated as interesting if all-confidence is greater than 0.5.**

17.2.2 How These Measures Perform on Our Datasets

Measures for interestingness as given in the previous section differ not only in their definition but also in their result. They do not rate the same sets the same way. In [8,12], the authors have done some extensive work in exploring those measures and how well they capture the dependencies between variables across various datasets. They considered 10 sets and 19 interestingness measures and, for each measure, gave a ranking for the 10 sets. Out of these 10 sets, the first 3 sets (for convenience let us call them E1, E2, and E3 as they did in their article [8]) bear much similarity with the data from the Logic-ITA because they lead to strong symmetric rules. However, there is still a substantial difference between these three sets and our sets from the Logic-ITA. In [8]'s datasets E1, E2, and E3, the values for $P(X, Y)$, $P(X)$, and $P(Y)$ are very similar, meaning that X and Y do not occur often one without the other. In contrast, in the sets from the Logic-ITA, $P(X)$ and $P(Y)$ are significantly bigger than $P(X, Y)$. As we will see, this fact has consequences on the correlation.

Since none of the datasets from [8] represented the case of our dataset, we also explored the interestingness measures under different variants of the datasets. We created various examples of contingency tables giving symmetric association rules for a minimum confidence threshold of 80% and looked at the various interestingness results that we obtained. These are shown in Table 17.4. The sets S3 and S4 are the ones that best match our data from the Logic-ITA. To complete the picture, we included symmetric rules with a relatively low support of 25%, though we are interested in strong rules with a minimum support of 60%.

Table 17.4 is to be interpreted as follows (remember that an item is, in our context, a mistake and therefore X and Y are sets of mistakes): 2000 solutions to exercises have been submitted by about 230 students. (X, Y) gives the number of solutions in which both, all mistakes from set X and all mistakes from set Y, were made, $(X, \neg Y)$ the number of

TABLE 17.4

Contingency Tables Giving Symmetric Rules with Strong Confidence

	X, Y ▤	X, ¬Y ■	¬X, Y ▧	¬X, ¬Y ☐	Pictorial Representation
S1	500	50	50	1,400	
S2	1,340	300	300	60	
S3	1,340	270	330	60	
S4	1,340	200	400	60	
S5	1,340	0	0	660	
S6	2,000	0	0	0	
S7	13,400	3,000	3,000	600	
S8	13,400	2,700	3,300	600	
S9	13,400	2,000	4,000	600	

solutions in which all mistakes from set X were made but no mistake from set Y, and so on. For the set S3, for example, 1340 solutions contain both all mistakes from set X and all mistakes from set Y, 270 contain all mistakes from set X but no mistake from Y, 330 contain all mistakes from Y but no mistakes from X, and 60 attempted solutions contain neither mistakes from X nor mistakes from Y. The last three lines, S7 to S9, are the same as S2 to S4 with a multiplying factor of 10. To help visualizing the differences of distribution between the first six datasets, we included a pictorial representation of the distributions in the last column. The last three datasets have the same distribution as S2, S3, and S4, and they are not shown again.

For each of these datasets, we calculated the various measures of interestingness we exposed earlier. Results are shown in Table 17.5. Expected frequencies are calculated assuming the independence of X and Y. Note that expected frequencies coincide with

TABLE 17.5

Measures for All Contingency Tables

	sup	conf(X→Y) conf(Y→X)	lift	Corr	Chi	cos	Jac.	All – c.
S1	0.25	0.90	**3.31**	**0.87**	1522.88	0.91	0.83	0.91
S2	0.67	0.82 0.82	1.00	−0.02	0.53	0.82	0.69	0.82
S3	0.67	0.83 0.82	1.00	−0.01	0.44	0.82	0.69	0.8
S4	0.67	0.87 0.77	1.00	0	0,00	0.82	0.69	0.77
S5	0.67	1.00 1.00	1.49	1	2000	1	1	1
S6	1.00	1.00 1.00	1.00	—	—	1	1	1
S7	0.67	0.82 0.82	1.00	−0.02	5.29	0.82	0.69	0.82
S8	0.67	0.83 0.80	1.00	−0.01	4.37	0.82	0.69	0.8
S9	0.67	0.87 0.77	1.00	0	0.01	0.82	0.69	0.77

observed frequencies for S6, so chi-square cannot be calculated. We have put in bold the results that indicate a positive dependency between X and Y. We have also highlighted the lines for S3 and S4, representing our data from the Logic-ITA and, in a lighter shade, S8 and S9, which have the same characteristics but with a multiplying factor of 10.

Our results are aligned with the ones of [8] for lift, cosine, and Jaccard: these measures confirm that the occurrence of X implies the occurrence of Y, as seen in the last three columns of Table 17.5.

However they disagree for correlation, as shown in column "Corr" of Table 17.5. Except for S1 and S5, the correlation measure indicates a poor relationship between X and Y. Note that $P(X)$ and $P(Y)$ are positive numbers smaller than 1, hence their product is smaller than $P(X)$ and $P(Y)$. If $P(X, Y)$ is significantly smaller than $P(X)$ and $P(Y)$, the difference between the product $P(X)P(Y)$ and $P(X, Y)$ is very small, and, as a result, correlation is around 0. This is exactly what happens with our data, and this fact leads to a strong difference with [8]'s E1, E2, and E3 sets, where the correlation was highly ranked: except for S1 and S5, our correlation results are around 0.

Finally, chi-square and all-confidence are not considered in [8]. It is well known that chi-square is not invariant under the row-column scaling property, as opposed to all the other measures that yield the same results as shown for S2 and S7, S3 and S8, and S4 and S9. Chi-square rates X and Y as independent for S2 and S3, but rates them as dependent in S7 and S8. As the numbers increase, the chi-square finds increasing dependency between the variables. Due to a change in the curriculum, we were not able to collect and mine association rules over more years. However, one can make the following projection: with a similar trend over a few more years, one would obtain set similar to S8 and S9. Chi-square would rate X and Y as correlated when X and Y are symmetric enough as for S3 and S8.

All-confidence always rate X and Y as correlated as cosine and Jaccard do. These three measures have the null-invariant property. These measures are particularly well-suited for nonsymmetric items, nonsymmetric in the sense that it is more important to be aware of the presence of item X than of its absence. This is actually the case of the association rules obtained with the Logic-ITA. We are looking for information concerning the occurrence of mistakes, not for their nonoccurrence. Therefore, these measures are better suited to our data than the lift, for example, and the rules should be interpreted accordingly.

17.2.3 Contrast Rules

In [15], contrast rules have been put forward to discover interesting rules that do not have necessarily a strong support. One aspect of contrast rules is to define a neighborhood to which the base rule is compared. We overtake this idea and consider the neighborhood $\{\neg X \rightarrow Y, X \rightarrow \neg Y, \neg X \rightarrow \neg Y\}$ assuming that $X \rightarrow Y$ is a symmetric rule with strong support and strong confidence. Taking the set S3, we get

$\sup(\neg X \rightarrow Y) = 0.17$	$\sup(X \rightarrow \neg Y) = 0.14$	$\sup(\neg X \rightarrow \neg Y) = 0.03$
$\mathrm{conf}(\neg X \rightarrow Y) = 0.85$	$\mathrm{conf}(X \rightarrow \neg Y) = 0.17$	$\mathrm{conf}(\neg X \rightarrow \neg Y) = 0.15$

These rules give complementary information allowing to better judge on the dependency of X and Y. They tell us that from the attempted solutions not containing mistake X, 85% of them contain mistake Y, while from the attempted solutions containing mistake X, only 17% do not contain mistake Y. Furthermore, only 3% of the attempted solutions contain neither mistake X nor mistake Y. The neighborhood $\{\neg Y \rightarrow X, \ Y \rightarrow \neg X, \ \neg Y \rightarrow \neg X\}$ behaves similarly, supporting the hypothesis that X and Y are positively correlated.

17.2.4 Pedagogical Use of the Association Rules

We have shown in earlier papers how the patterns extracted were used for improving teaching [16,17] and we recall here the main evaluation and deployment of the findings. Note that since our goal was to improve the course as much as possible, our experiment did not test the sole impact of using the association rules but the impact of all other patterns found in the data. After we first extracted association rules from 2001 and 2002 data, we used these rules to redesign the course and provide more adaptive teaching. One finding was that mistakes related to the structure of the formal proof (as opposed to, for instance, the use and applicability of a logic rule) were associated together. This led us to realize that the very concept of formal proofs was causing problems and that some concepts such as the difference between the two types of logic rules, the deduction rules and the equivalence rules, might not be clear enough. In 2003, that portion of the course was redesigned to take this problem into account and the role of each part of the proof was emphasized. After the end of the semester, mining for mistakes associations was conducted again. Surprisingly, results did not change much (a slight decrease in support and confidence levels in 2003 followed by a slight increase in 2004). However, marks in the final exam questions related to formal proofs continued increasing. We concluded that making mistakes, especially while using a training tool, is simply part of the learning process and this interpretation was supported by the fact that the number of completed exercises per student increased in 2003 and 2004.

17.3 Conclusions

In this chapter, we investigated the interestingness of the association rules found in the data from the Logic-ITA, an intelligent tutoring system for propositional logic. We used this data-mining technique to look for mistakes often made together while solving an exercise, and found strong rules associating three specific mistakes.

Taking an inquisitive look at our data, it turns out that it has quite a special shape. First, it gives strong symmetric association rules. Second, $P(X)$ and $P(Y)$, the proportion of exercises where mistake X was made and the proportion of exercises where mistake Y was made, respectively, is significantly higher than $P(X, Y)$, the proportion of exercises where both mistakes were made. A consequence is that many interestingness measures resting on probabilities or statistics such as lift, correlation, or even chi-square to a certain extent rate X and Y as noncorrelated. However cosine, Jaccard, or all-confidence, which have the null-invariant property and thus are not sensitive to transactions containing neither X nor Y, rate X and Y as positively correlated. Further, we observe that mining associations on data cumulated over several years could lead to a positive correlation with the chi-square test. Finally, contrast rules give interesting complementary information: rules not containing any mistake or making only one mistake are very weak. This is further investigated in [18]. The use of these rules to change parts of our course seemed to contribute to better learning as we have observed an increase of the marks in the final exam as well as an increase of completely finished exercises with Logic-ITA.

This really indicates that the notion of interestingness is very sensitive to the context. Since educational data often has relatively small number of instances, measures based on statistical correlation may have to be handled with care for this domain.

We come to a similar conclusion as in [19]: the interestingness of a rule should be first measured by measures with the null-invariant property such as cosine, Jacquard, or all-confidence, then with a measure from the probability field such as lift if the first ones rated the rule as uninteresting. In case of conflict between the two types of measures, the user needs to take into account the intuitive information provided by each measure and decide upon it. In particular, if knowing the presence of X is more important that knowing its absence, then it is best to follow an interestingness measure having the null-invariant property like cosine; if not, then it is better to follow an interestingness measure based on statistics like lift.

As a further thought, in an educational context, is it important to consider only objective interestingness measures to filter associations? When the rule $X \rightarrow Y$ is found, the pragmatically oriented teacher will first look at the support: in our case, it showed that over 60% of the exercises contained at least three different mistakes. This is a good reason to ponder. The analysis of whether these three mistakes are correlated with some objective measure is in fact not necessarily relevant to the remedial actions the teacher will take, and may even be better judged by the teacher. Therefore, we think that further subjective measures or criteria such as actionability should also be taken into account to filter associations.

References

1. Wang, F., On using Data Mining for browsing log analysis in learning environments. In *Data Mining in E-Learning. Series: Advances in Management Information*, C. Romero and S. Ventura, editors. WIT Press, Southampton, U.K., pp. 57–75, 2006.
2. Wang, F.-H. and H.-M. Shao, Effective personalized recommendation based on time-framed navigation clustering and association mining. *Expert Systems with Applications* **27**(3): 365–377, 2004.
3. Minaei-Bidgoli, B., D.A. Kashy, G. Kortemeyer, and W.F. Punch, Predicting student performance: an application of data mining methods with the educational web-based system LON-CAPA. In *ASEE/IEEE Frontiers in Education Conference*, IEEE, Boulder, CO, 2003.
4. Lu, J., Personalized e-learning material recommender system. In *International Conference on Information Technology for Application (ICITA'04)*, Harbin, China, pp. 374–379, 2004.
5. Merceron, A. and K. Yacef, Mining student data captured from a Web-based tutoring tool: Initial exploration and results. *Journal of Interactive Learning Research (JILR)* **15**(4): 319–346, 2004.
6. Romero, C., S. Ventura, C. de Castro, W. Hall, and M.H. Ng, Using genetic algorithms for data mining in Web-based educational hypermedia systems. In *Adaptive Systems for Web-based Education*, Malaga, Spain, May 2002.
7. Agrawal, R. and R. Srikant, Fast algorithms for mining association rules. In *VLDB*, Santiago, Chile, 1994.
8. Tan, P.N., V. Kumar, and J. Srivastava, Selecting the right interestingness measure for association patterns. In *8th ACM SIGKDD International Conference on Knowledge Discovery and Data Mining*, San Francisco, CA, pp. 67–76, 2001.

9. Brijs, T., K. Vanhoof, and G. Wets, Defining interestingness for association rules. *International Journal of Information Theories and Applications* **10**(4): 370–376, 2003.
10. Yacef, K., The Logic-ITA in the classroom: a medium scale experiment. *International Journal on Artificial Intelligence in Education* **15**: 41–60, 2005.
11. Merceron, A. and K. Yacef, Revisiting interestingness of strong symmetric association rules in educational data. In *International Workshop on Applying Data Mining in e-Learning (ADML'07)*, Crete, Greece, 2007.
12. Tan, P.N., M. Steinbach, and V. Kumar, *Introduction to Data Mining*. Pearson Education, Boston, MA, 2006.
13. Merceron, A. and K. Yacef, Interestingness measures for association rules in educational data. In *International Conference on Educational Data Mining*, R. Baker and J. Beck, editors, Montreal, Canada, pp. 57–66, 2008.
14. Tan, P.N., V. Kumar, and J. Srivastava, Selecting the right interestingness measure for association patterns. In *8th ACM SIGKDD International Conference on Knowledge Discovery and Data Mining*, San Francisco, CA, August 26–29, 2001.
15. Minaei-Bidgoli, T.B., P-N., and W.F. Punch, Mining interesting contrast rules for a Web-based educational system. In *International Conference on Machine Learning Applications (ICMLA 2004)*, Louisville, KY, December 16–18, 2004.
16. Merceron, A. and K. Yacef, A Web-based tutoring tool with mining facilities to improve learning and teaching. In *11th International Conference on Artificial Intelligence in Education*, F. Verdejo and U. Hoppe, editors, IOS Press, Sydney, Australia, pp. 201–208, 2003.
17. Merceron, A. and K. Yacef, Educational data mining: A case study. In *Artificial Intelligence in Education (AIED2005)*, C.-K. Looi, G. McCalla, B. Bredeweg, and J. Breuker, editors. IOS Press, Amsterdam, the Netherlands, pp. 467–474, 2005.
18. Merceron, A., Strong symmetric association rules and interestingness measures. In *Advances in Data Warehousing and Mining (ADWM) Book Series, Rare Association Rule Mining and Knowledge Discovery: Technologies for Infrequent and Critical Event Detection*, Y.S. Koh and N. Rountree, editors. IGI Global, Hershey, PA, 2009.
19. Han, J. and M. Kamber, *Data Mining: Concepts and Techniques*. Morgan Kaufman, San Francisco, CA, 2001.

18

Data Mining for Contextual Educational Recommendation and Evaluation Strategies

Tiffany Y. Tang and Gordon G. McCalla

CONTENTS

18.1 Introduction

When information overload intensifies, users are overwhelmed by the information pouring out from various sources, including the Internet, and are usually confused by which information should be consumed; that is, users find it difficult to pick something appropriate when the number of choices increases. Fortunately, a recommender system offers a feasible solution to this problem. For example, if a user explicitly indicates that he or she favors action movies starring *Sean Penn*, then he or she could be recommended movies like *The Interpreter*. In this case, the system is able to match user preferences to content features of the movies, which is a content-based filtering approach. In another major recommendation approach called collaborative filtering, the system constructs a group of like-minded users with whom the target user shares similar interests and makes recommendations based on an analysis of them.

For learners engaging in senior-level courses, tutors, in many cases, would like to pick some articles as supplementary reading materials for them each week. Unlike researchers "Googling" research papers matching their interests from the Internet, tutors, when making recommendations, should consider the course syllabus and their assessment of learners along many dimensions. As such, simply Googling articles from the Internet is far from enough. Suppose, a paper recommender system can carefully assess and compare both learner and candidate paper characteristics (through instructions from tutors), and make recommendations accordingly. In other words, learner models of each individual, including their learning interest, knowledge, goals, etc., will be created. Paper models will also be created based on the topic, degree of peer recommendation, etc. The recommendation is carried out by matching the learner characteristics with the paper topics to achieve appropriate pedagogical goals such as "the technical level of the paper should not impede the learner in understanding it." Therefore, the suitability of a paper for a learner is calculated in terms of the appropriateness of it to help the learner in general. This type of recommendation system is called a pedagogical paper recommender. In this chapter, we mainly discuss the potentials of data mining techniques in making personalized recommendations in the e-learning domain and highlight the importance of conducting appropriate evaluations.

The organization of this chapter is as follows. In the next section, a discussion on educational recommendation techniques is presented. Section 18.3 focuses on system design and architecture; key recommendation techniques are also presented. Section 18.4 includes the empirical studies conducted and discusses the results. Implications of our study are also pointed out. Section 18.5 concludes this chapter.

18.2 Data Mining in Educational Recommendation

Various data mining techniques have been adopted to help educators pick up tailored educational materials. In this section, we will survey two broad research efforts on making paper/article recommendations: non-multidimensional and multidimensional recommendations.

18.2.1 Non-Multidimensional Paper Recommendation

Basu et al. [1] studied paper recommendation in the context of assigning conference paper submissions to reviewing committee members. Essentially, the recommendation process is cast as extracting information about reviewers' expertise and papers' main topics, and formulating queries to obtain the recommended paper(s). Bollacker et al. [2] refine CiteSeer* through an automatic personalized paper-tracking module that retrieves each user's interests from well-maintained heterogeneous user profiles. Some commonly known text processing algorithms were adopted, such as TF-IDF, keyword matching, the use of papers' metadata, citation analysis, to track and maintain a user's notion of "relatedness" when submitting a query to search for documents. A profile of the user's behavior is then maintained while searching for papers when he or she begins to use the interface, as a cookie will be uniquely assigned to a user once he or she begins surfing through the CiteSeer user interface. Superficially, CiteSeer is similar to Google™ in its ability to find a set of papers similar to a user's query. As such, CiteSeer can be regarded as a general paper searching system, requiring a user to formulate appropriate keywords to facilitate the searching. This makes such a system, not that suitable for learners without much research experience. Woodruff et al. [3] discuss an enhanced digital book consisting of 43 articles

---

* CiteSeer is a publicly available paper searching tool, and can be accessed at: http://citeseer.ist.psu.edu/cs

with a spreading-activation-geared mechanism to make customized recommendations for readers with different types of background and knowledge. User scenarios are created indicating user goals and research experiences, based on which the system will then deliver lists of recommended articles that users should read next. Since the recommender mechanism also makes use of the citations a paper receives, the users are asked to explicitly list the papers they liked.

Two conditions essentially support the performance of the recommender. The first is that the user should be able to specify the seed paper, based on which the recommendation process will start to apply the spreading-activation mechanism. The second condition lies in the fact that the user should be well motivated and have clear goals, and be able to specify the context in which they seek recommendation (as shown in the table, the scenario is very clear and fine grained). The relaxation of either of these conditions would greatly compromise the effectiveness of the recommendations made. The paper recommender proposed in Woodruff et al. [3] is relatively inapplicable in the e-learning domain, where students are relatively novice learners, and it is not reasonable to assume that students are able to describe appropriate paper-seeking context.

McNee et al. [4] investigate the adoption of a nearest-neighbor approach, that is, collaborative filtering (CF) technique to recommend papers for researchers; although researchers do not need to explicitly specify the details of the papers they like. However, McNee et al. [4] did not address the issue of how to recommend a research paper; but how to recommend *additional references* for a *target research paper*. In the context of an e-learning system, additional readings cannot be recommended purely through an analysis of the citation matrix of a target paper. A similar study of recommending research papers by Torres et al. [5] investigates cross-culture, cross-language, and cross-research-experience research-paper recommendations. Generally, the CF adopted in the study is the citation and co-citation analysis of the active paper and its citations. And the content-based filtering (CBF) applied in the paper recommender is based on the pure textual analysis of a paper's abstract and title only. The recommendation techniques in Torres et al. [5] are quite similar to some of the authors' previous study [4] in which their core techniques fall into two categories: (1) citation and co-citation analysis; and (2) pure paper content-based approach (TF-IDF similarity measures).

Torres et al. [5] did not, however, study how users responded to the paper classes, but only demonstrated that it is important for the RS to generate high quality recommendations consistently, although not every single recommendation needs to be good. Indeed, in their post evaluations, they found out that "professionals were not as happy as students toward the recommendations." A similar study by Middleton et al. [6] also focuses on recommending on-line research papers to academic staff and students with the major aim of searching for relevant research papers and continuing to work as new papers come out. Their approach is to carry out a dynamic "match-making" between user and paper ontology. User profiles are inferred dynamically by using built-in tools tracing users' browsing behaviors through the system interface. Essentially, the recommendations are made through classical information retrieval (IR) techniques.

18.2.2 Contextual Recommendation with Multidimensional Nearest-Neighbor Approach

The majority of recommendation systems make recommendations purely based on item–item, user–user, and/or item–user correlations without considering the contextual information where the decision making happens. In other words, the RS works as a black box, only matching the interests of the target users, without probing into the details of why the users like it, or how the users will like it. For example, a user does not like animated movies, but likes to watch them during nonworking days with his or her kids. Therefore, he or she should be recommended *The Incredibles* on Saturdays and Sundays. As another example, Joe normally does not like romantic comedy movies, especially those starring *Meg Ryan*; but he will be willing and happy to watch one during holidays with his wife Sarah, who enjoys movies starring *Meg Ryan* (of any genre). Thus, on weekends, *You've Got Mail* can be recommended to Joe.

In the e-learning domain, a learner does not like software testing in general, but because he or she is taking a class on software engineering, and he or she is expecting three credits to complete the class, he or she should be recommended an article on software testing. In these cases, incorporating *contextual information* is very important and helpful in inform-ing the recommender to provide high quality recommendations to users because they vary in their decision making based on the "usage situation, the use of the good or service (for family, for gift, for self) and purchase situation" (Lilien et al. [7]). For instance, customers' *seasonal buying patterns* are classical examples of how customers change their buying hab-its based on the situation. A context-aware recommender can provide a smart shopping environment, since the recommendations are location-aware, that is, of the recommended shopping date/time, location of the stores, etc. As such, a shopper can receive personal-ized shopping recommendations in the stores of the neighborhood where he or she is. Adomavicius et al. [8] argue that dimensions of contextual information can include when, how, and with whom the users will consume the recommended items, which, therefore, directly affect users' satisfaction toward the system performance. In particular, the recom-mendation space now consists of not only item and user dimensions, but also many other contextual dimensions, such as location, time, and so on.* An example on user profile and interests could be as follows: John, age 25, enjoys watching action movies in theatres during holidays. Hence, recommendations can be of the following form: John is recommended *The Departed* during a Saturday night show at UA IFC mall. To deal with the multidimensional CF, data warehouse and OLAP application concepts drawn from database approaches are proposed [8]. Essentially, we have to transform the multidimensional CF into traditional 2D recommendations. Simply put, using our previous 3D-CF examples, we can first elimi-nate the *Time* dimension by only considering votes delivered on *weekdays* from the rating database. The resulting problem becomes the traditional 2D users vs. items CF case. In fact, from a data warehousing perspective, this approach is similar to a slicing operation on a multidimensional database. The rationale behind the *slicing* operation is straightforward: if we only want to predict whether a user will prefer to, say, watch a movie on weekdays, we should only consider the historical "weekday" ratings for this purpose.

Pazzani [10] also studied an earlier "version" of multidimensional CF through the aggre-gation of users' demographic information such as their gender, age, education, address, etc. There are a number of ways to obtain demographic data either through explicit ways such as questionnaires or implicit ways such as analyzing their behavioral data (purchas-ing data). For instance, from users' browsing behaviors, we can easily know where the users come from; hence, the recommendations become *location-aware*, which is widely used especially for recommendations to be served on mobile devices. In order to make predictions to a target user, the demographic-based CF [10] learns a relationship between each item and the type of people who tend to like it. Then, out of "that" type of people, the

---

* There are no agreed terms on what to call these additional aspects in recommender systems. Names that have been used include contextual information [8], lifestyle [9], and demographic data [10].

CF identifies the neighbors for the target user, and makes recommendations accordingly. Clearly, the difference between traditional CF and demographically based CF is the preprocessing step of *grouping* similar users.

The most recent effort in incorporating context information in making a recommendation is a study by Lekakos and Giaglis [9], in which users' *lifestyle* is considered. Lifestyle includes users' living and spending patterns, which are in turn affected by some external factors such as culture, family, etc., and internal factors such as their personality, emotions, attitudes, etc. The system will first compute the *Pearson correlation of users' lifestyles* to relate one user to another. In particular, the closeness between users is measured in terms of their lifestyle instead of ratings in traditional CF: the chance that users with the same lifestyle tend to have similar tastes will be higher. Based on it, the system will select those users who score above a certain threshold. After this filtering process, the system will make predictions on items for the target user based on ratings from neighbors. This approach is essentially similar to that in [10], which is to make use of the additional information (i.e., lifestyle, demography) to determine the closeness between users.

18.3 Contextual Paper Recommendation with Multidimensional Nearest-Neighbor Approach

Drawing upon existing research, we proposed a contextual multidimensional CF [11,12]. Figure 18.1 compares the traditional one-dimensional CF for movie recommendation and our approach.

When making a movie recommendation, the information space allows users to review both the textual comments and the numerical rating toward the movie. However, the recommendation mechanism only considers the latter in addressing users' needs. In contrast, our pedagogical paper recommender works by incorporating learners' additional impression over each paper [11,12]. That is, not only is the overall rating of the paper considered, but also ratings pertaining to the paper's *situated factors*, including its usefulness in

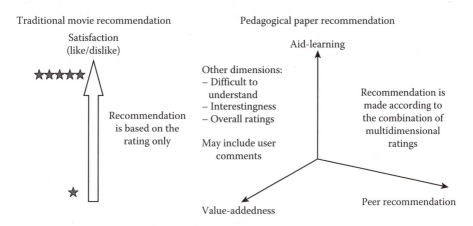

FIGURE 18.1
An illustration of users' relevance evaluation of a paper in the pedagogical paper recommender. (From Tang, T. Y., and McCalla, G. I. A multi-dimensional paper recommender, in *Proceedings of the 13th International Conference on Artificial Intelligence in Education (AIED 2007)*, Marina Del Rey, CA, 2007.)

helping learners gain new knowledge (referred to as *Value_addedness*) and strengthening their understandings of the course topics (referred to as *Aid_learning*), value in practice (referred to as *Job_relate*, as learners were all part-time degree students), and the degree of peer recommendation (referred to as *Peer_rec*), as shown in Figure 18.1.

In addition, since recommendation in a pedagogical context differs from those in other domains, we need to modify the traditional techniques according to the characteristics of the learning domain. Broadly speaking, these characteristics are due to (1) the limited number of users, (2) the large number of unrated or new items, (3) the likelihood of the learners' difficulty in understanding the items, and (4) the numerous purposes of the recommendation.

With respect to the limited number of users and the large number of unrated/new items, our recommender system has taken the cold-start problem seriously, and hence cannot rely solely on rating-based CF. For this reason, we considered content-based filtering, user-model-based CF, or other techniques that do not need many learner ratings.

In addition, we also take into consideration paper popularity in an attempt to start up the recommendation when there are not many ratings in the system. Factors that are considered in our multidimensional CF will mainly be used to correlate one user with another; that is to find the similarity between users and make recommendations accordingly. These factors include the following:

- A paper's ratings on *overall, value-addedness*, and *peer recommendations*
- Features about a learner including learner interest and background knowledge
- The average of a paper's overall ratings (paper popularity, $\tilde{r}$)

The possibility that our learners may encounter difficulty in understanding the papers has pushed us to consider their background knowledge, and hence to adopt content-based and hybrid filtering techniques that incorporate this factor.

With respect to the numerous purposes of recommendation, a tutor may aim at the learners' overall satisfaction (the highest possible overall ratings), or to stimulate learners' interest only (the highest possible interest ratings), or to help the learners to gain new information only (the highest possible value-added ratings), etc. Given the fact of numerous recommendation purposes, it is imperative and appealing to collect multidimensional ratings and to study multidimensional CF that can utilize the ratings. Table 18.1 lists out the factors considered in the multidimensional CF.

TABLE 18.1

Factors That Are Considered in Our Multidimensional CF

Dimension	Recommendation Type	Factors
3D	Collaborative filtering	Overall rating, value-addedness, peer recommendations
5D	User-model-based collaborative filtering	Overall rating, value-addedness, peer recommendations, learner interest, learner background knowledge
Popularity-incorporated 3D	Hybrid filtering	Overall rating, value-addedness, peer recommendations, paper popularity $\tilde{r}$
Popularity-incorporated 5D	Hybrid filtering	Overall rating, value-addedness, peer recommendations, learner interest, learner background knowledge, paper popularity $\tilde{r}$

As shown in Table 18.1, in multidimensional rating-based collaborative filtering, we consider ratings on overall, value_added, and peer_rec ratings, in both finding neighbors and calculating the predicted recommended papers. The weighted sum three-dimensional CF (denoted 3D-CF) Pearson correlation is

$$P_{3D}(a,b) = w_{\text{overall}} P_{\text{overall}}(a,b) + w_{\text{valueadd}} P_{\text{valueadd}}(a,b) + w_{\text{peer\_rec}} P_{\text{peer\_rec}}(a,b) \qquad (18.1)$$

where
$r_{i,k}$ is the rating by user i on co-rated item k on dimension d
P_d (a, b) is the Pearson correlation based on the rating r on dimension d

P_d (a, b) is computed with the following formula (18.2):

$$P_d(a,b) = \frac{\sum_{K}(r_{a,k} - \overline{r_a})(r_{b,k} - \overline{r_b})}{\sqrt{\sum_{K}(r_{a,k} - \overline{r_a})^2 \sum_{K}(r_{b,k} - \overline{r_b})^2}} \qquad (18.2)$$

Note that $w_{\text{overall}} + w_{\text{valueadd}} + w_{\text{peer\_rec}} = 1$, and the values are determined by the tutor manually or the system automatically. In our experiment, these weights are tuned manually following a series of trials, in which those weights reported in this chapter are representative ones. In our experiments, the number of neighbors used by this method is also set to be from 2 to 15, where they are selected according to the weighted sum Pearson correlation $P_{3D}(a, b)$ in formula (18.1). After we identify the closest neighbors for a target user a, we then calculate the *aggregate rating* of each paper to make recommendations. The selection method is by calculating the sum of weighted ratings by all closest neighbors

$$r_j^{3D} = \sum_{B} P_{3D}(a,b) r_{b,j} \qquad (18.3)$$

where
r_j^{3D} is the aggregate rating to paper j from all neighbors in set B
$P_{3D}(a, b)$ is the weighted Pearson correlation between target user a and his or her neighbor b
$r_{b,j}$ is the rating given to paper j by neighbor b

After we calculate r_j^{3D} for all papers, we can find the best paper(s) for recommendation, that is, paper(s) with the highest r_j^{3D}.

By combining Pearson correlations of 3D rating-based CF and 2D Pearson correlation between learners based on their student models, $P_{2D}(a, b)$ in a linear form, we have five-dimensional collaborative filtering method (denoted as 5D-CF). That is, we compute the aggregated Pearson correlation in this method as follows:

$$P_{5D}(a,b) = P_{3D}(a,b) + w_{2D} P_{2D\text{stdModel}}(a,b) \qquad (18.4)$$

It is clear that 5D-CF can be regarded as a user-model-based collaborative filtering method. In addition, we regard the injection of paper popularity (the average overall ratings of a

TABLE 18.2

Comparison of Our Approach with Other Multidimensional CF Approaches

	Type of Additional Information	Method of Finding Neighbors for a Target User
Adomavicius et al. (2005)	• Users' demographic data	• Users' overall rating toward each item
	• Item information	
	• Consuming information	
Pazzani (1999)	• Users' demographic data	• Learned user profile based on content information
	• Content information	• Users' overall rating toward each item
Lekakos and Giaglis (2006)	• Users' demographic data	• Learned user profile based on content information
	• Lifestyle data	• Users' overall rating toward each item
Our approach	• User models	• Learned user profile based on content information
	• Paper features	• Users' overall rating toward each item
		• The popularity of each paper

paper) as a nonpersonalized method; but under certain circumstances, it is very useful to start up the recommendation and therefore suitable for cold-start problems (see Table 18.1). That is, if the resulting estimated rating from a CF method is combined with the average rating (popularity) given by all users in a group, then we will have hybrid recommendations (denoted as Pop3D or Pop5D according to the multidimensional CF method it is attached to). Hence, recommendations from Pop3D, r_j^{Pop3D} is given by the following formula: a rating calculated from 3D-CF, that is, r_j^{3D},

$$r_j^{Pop3D} = r_j^{3D} + w_r n \tilde{r}_j \tag{18.5}$$

where

$w_{\bar{r}}$ is the weight of linear combination and is the control variable in our experiment

n is the number of neighbors in CF, that is, $n = |B|$

Our reason for combining CF with the nonpersonalized method is to remedy the low accuracy of CF, especially when the number of co-rated papers is low, that is, by considering the "authority" of a given paper according to people who have rated it: if the paper has been well received, then the "authority" level of it is high. That is, if a given paper is popular among all the users, then the target user might also be interested in it. Although this popular paper cannot be used to differentiate the different tastes of users, it is worth recommending (Table 18.2).

18.4 Empirical Studies and Results

We performed several empirical studies aimed at exploring the multidimensionality of paper recommendations. In particular, the following two aspects were investigated:

1. Exploring the characteristics of pedagogical paper recommendations. We focused on three issues: (1) Will learners be happy with papers that can expand their knowledge (i.e., teach them something new)? The ultimate goal of E-learning is fulfilling the user's knowledge needs. (2) How important is learner interest in the recommendation? For instance, how much will a learner be willing to tolerate a paper that isn't interesting? (3) Will a learner be comfortable with a highly technical paper, even if it matches the learner's interest or is required reading (for instance, a seminal paper on a topic)? In other words, we're looking for important *interactions* among the pedagogical variables that might help accurately rank a paper for a learner. To achieve this, we performed four statistical analyses to probe the interactivity among variables that we are interested in: partial correlation, structural equation modeling, principal components analysis (PCA), and partial least squares regression (PLS). As our study shows [13], user interest isn't the key factor in boosting recommendation performance. Instead, some learners accept recommendations that they don't perceive to directly match their interests.

2. Testing various recommendation techniques in a pedagogical context; that is, comparing traditional recommendation techniques with our proposed ones. A number of recommendation techniques including those presented in Table 18.1 were studied, and they have been categorized into five main types: nonpersonalized recommendation, content-based filtering, collaborative filtering, hybrid filtering, and model-based filtering. Due to space limitations, we present some key results in this section.

18.4.1 Data Collection

The study was conducted in the Hong Kong Polytechnic University. The course is a graduate foundation course in software engineering, where the author is the instructor of the course. There were altogether 48 students, and out of a pool of more than 40 papers, 23 candidate papers related to software engineering and Internet computing were selected. The length of the papers varied from 2 to 15 pages. And the features of the papers were manually added into the tables.

In order to collect learners' pedagogical features, such as eliciting the contextual information about the learners, that is, learner interest I, learning goal G, job experience E, background knowledge B, we first distribute 48 surveys to learners to fill in. And then later in making recommendations, these contextual features were incorporated. Forty-one surveys were selected, and they are used later in our experiment.

In our experiment, each student was required to read a set of two papers, that is, a recommended paper and a randomly selected one as a control treatment in our experiment for comparison. After reading these two papers, each student was required to rate the papers (see Figure 18.2). The feedback form basically collected their evaluation on a number of issues (see Q1 through Q7 in Figure 18.2). In addition, students were also given the options to write some critical comments about the papers, which could reflect their seriousness in reading the papers. Learners did not know that one of the papers was selected randomly, but they did know that the articles were personalized, and can be used for their group projects for this course. Figure 18.3 takes the screenshot of our paper recommender.

18.4.2 Evaluation Results

Aligning with our research goals, the evaluation will mostly be performed by investigating the following three pedagogical outcomes from reading, that is, *overall*, *value-addedness*, and

1. Does the paper match your interest?
   4. very much   3. relatively   2. not really   1. not at all

2. Is the paper difficult to understand?
   4. very difficult 3. difficult   2. easy   1. very easy

3. Is the paper useful to your project?
   4. very much   3. relatively   2. not really   1. not at all

4. Is the paper useful to aid your understanding of the SE concepts and techniques learned in the class?
   4. very much   3. relatively   2. not really   1. not at all

5. Would you recommend the paper to your fellow group members or other fellow classmates?
   4. absolutely   3. relatively   2. not really   1. not at all

6. Did you learn something "new" after reading this paper?
   4. absolutely   3. relatively   2. not really   1. not at all

7. What is your overall rating toward this paper?
   4. very good   3. good   2. relatively   1. bad

Please give several sentences of critical comments on the paper.

FIGURE 18.2
Paper feedback form.

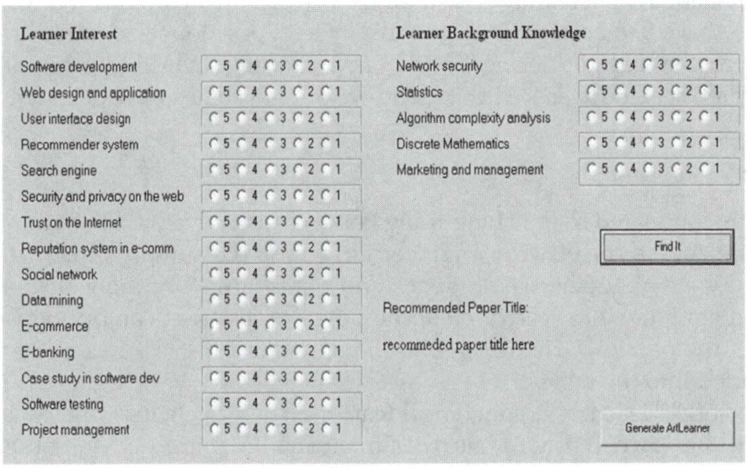

FIGURE 18.3
The paper recommender user interface.

aid_learning. We provide a general comparison of various recommendation techniques. For the sake of simplicity, we will only use average overall ratings as the metric for comparison. Some techniques involve several combinations of parameters, which have been tested in our experiments. However, we will only use some parameter settings in our analysis, those that we have remaining after discarding those with less significant results.

Table 18.3 lists the partial results of our comparison. The values higher than their corresponding best-case benchmark value are highlighted in bold. Some of them are accompanied by a *p*-value (obtained after doing a one-tail *t*-test, assuming homoscedasticity). We should be careful in comparing these results with the best-case benchmark, because the best-case benchmark assumes that all papers are completely rated, while some methods in our comparison are not. From this table, we observe that most results are worse than the best-case benchmark (second row), but all results are better than the worst-case benchmark (third row). Moreover, those that are better than the best-case benchmark are

TABLE 18.3

Average Overall Ratings Obtained from Various Recommendation Methods, Where $|K|$ Is the Number of Co-Rated Papers

Methods	Average Overall Ratings When Top-n Papers Are Recommended, $n = \{1, 3, 5\}$		
	Top 1	Top 3	Top 5
Best-case benchmark (*Popularity* only)	3.167	3.055	2.992
Worst-case benchmark (random)	2.708	2.708	2.708
3D-CF ($|K| = 2$)	2.946	2.884	2.851
3D-CF ($|K| = 4$)	3.105	2.984	2.934
3D-CF ($|K| = 8$)	**3.210** ($p = .34$)	**3.085** ($p = .31$)	**3.007** ($p = .38$)
5D-CF (($0.8_{overall}$, $0.1_{valueadd}$, 0.1_{peer_rec}), $w_{2D} = 1$, $|K| = 8$)	3.131	**3.064**	**3.011** ($p = .35$)
5D-CF (($1_{overall}$, $0_{valueadd}$, 0_{peer_rec}), $w_{2D} = 1$, $|K| = 8$)	3.146	**3.068**	**3.015** ($p = .32$)
Pop3D ($|K| = 2$)	3.160	3.047	**2.995**
Pop3D ($|K| = 4$)	3.160	**3.071** ($p = .40$)	**2.995**
Pop3D ($|K| = 8$)	3.160	**3.088** ($p = .29$)	**2.995**
Pop5D ($|K| = 2$)	3.081	3.035	2.969
Pop5D ($|K| = 4$)	3.129	**3.067**	**2.997**
Pop5D ($|K| = 8$)	3.158	**3.099** ($p = .23$)	**3.019** ($p = .29$)
Ceiling	3.560	3.347	3.248

not statistically significant (p-value ≥ 0.22), but most results better than the worst-case benchmark are significantly better (p-value < 0.05, not shown here).

For 3D-CF, when the number of co-rated papers increases, the system has done well in making recommendations, among them, the best result is when the system is making the top 1 recommendation. Compared to the performances of 3D-CF, the other three methods are less satisfactory. The reason is that when the quantity of information injected into the system increases, it might not help or even bring up noises that may reduce the effectiveness of finding close neighbors. This phenomenon might not be true in the traditional recommendation systems where a large number of data is present. In our domain, the number of papers and students are limited, therefore, injecting just-enough information into the system might generate quality recommendations. Nevertheless, we speculate that when the database increases, multidimensional filtering techniques are expected to shine.

18.4.3 Discussions

Due to the limited number of students, papers, and other learning restrictions, a tutor cannot require students to read too many papers in order to stuff the database. As such, the majority of typical recommender systems might not work well in the pedagogical domain. Through experimental studies and prototypical analysis, we draw a number of important conclusions regarding the design and evaluation of these techniques in our domain. Although our studies help peel our knowledge, more studies are needed to further our understanding of it.

For instance, we realized that one of the biggest challenges is the difficulty of testing the effectiveness or appropriateness of a recommendation method due to a low number of available ratings. Testing the method with more students, say, in two or three more semesters, may not be helpful, because the results are still not enough to draw conclusions as strong as those from other domains where the ratings can be as many as millions. We are also eager to see the collaborations from different institutions in using the system in a more distributed and larger-scale fashion (as it is very difficult to achieve it in using one class each time and in one institution). Through it, our future work includes the design of a movie lens–like benchmark database as a test-bed on which more algorithms can be tested (including ours).

Meanwhile, under those environments where a wider range of learning scenarios exist, evaluations can be performed in a more systematic way; for instance, to continuously ask students to engage in "on-line reevaluation," the reevaluation is by using a strategy similar to the all-but-one by hiding the ratings of a target user on each round through running all applicable methods on existing data (known ratings). The idea is as follows: suppose we have some ratings from the previous year's learners and we want to recommend papers to new learners. Suppose we have several applicable methods but we do not know which one is the best. This situation may arise when we have collected enough data (ratings) in the middle or near the end of the class, or when we want to use this prototype for classes other than software engineering. Then we may pick a learner from the previous year (i.e., an old learner), whose ratings are known, to test these methods. If any of the methods is superior to the rest in making recommendation, in terms of the ratings given by the old learner, then the method may also be the best for making a recommendation to the new learner.

We can also perform more task-oriented evaluations, such as evaluating the appropriateness of recommendations through a group-oriented task, where learners will be asked to design and implement an automatic tool for, say, a family calendar. In this case, learners would be required to write a research paper documenting their experiences as well as lessons learned from the task. Both the after-project questionnaire and the analysis of the report could help to evaluate the actual "uses" of the recommended papers for learning. Another task can be asking learners to conduct a research study on a topic of their choice in 3 weeks, say, the adoption of the CASE tool for software testing and present their work in front of the class. In another example, where multiple institutions are involved, we may divide students into groups from different institutions (or even different countries), and each group is then required to undertake a distributed software project, where a number of CASE tools can be used to coordinate their actions. In this case, reference articles can be supplied weekly as in our settings, though more papers can be included. Then, by the end of their project, learners will be asked to not only turn in a workable system, but also document what they have learned in a research paper.

Then, in each of these tasks, learners will be asked to evaluate the pedagogical usefulness of the recommended papers in, among others: how the papers can help their understanding of the lecture topics, how the knowledge they learned can be used to guide their joint software development effort, and how the papers can be used as "seed" ones to help them "Google" more.

We believe that the task-oriented evaluation framework is more appropriate than purely presenting the traditional metrics such as precision, recall, etc., in directly assessing user satisfaction and acceptance over the recommended items. In spite of it, we think that the factors we have considered so far (e.g., interestingness and value-addedness) represent the most typical factors that need to be taken into consideration when making recommendations in the pedagogical domain. The issues and conclusions we suggest can enlighten future studies on it, and finally further our understanding in making recommendations in this domain.

18.4.4 Implication of the Pedagogical Paper Recommender

Currently, we only investigate the recommendation of research articles. Nevertheless, we believe that the study can be extended for other educational resources, such as learning objects, chapters with different related topics in a digital book, tutorial materials, etc. In fact, almost all educational resources can be regarded as learning objects with different granularity, situated environments, and purposes. Hence, the various recommendation mechanisms can be extended to make personalized recommendations of learning objects to individual learners of different needs.

However, when considering, especially the reusability of learning objects, some other interesting yet challenging issues arise. When both the number of learners and learning objects grow, data preprocessing should be performed, for example, to pre-cluster the learners as well as the learning objects based on their corresponding models, so as to make "purposed" recommendations. While learners are represented by their pedagogical features, learning objects are annotated by multiple dimensional ratings including overall rating, degree of peer recommendation, etc. [14]. It is obvious that as more and more learners have read and rated an item, the amount of user feedback with respect to the item will accumulate. These data can be processed through an intelligent data processor for mining patterns in the cross-product of page usage and user models (see Figure 18.4),

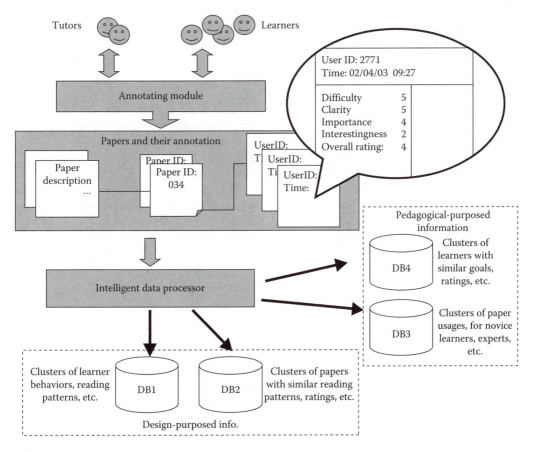

FIGURE 18.4
Paper annotations with temporal sequences of user models.

and recommendations made accordingly [15]. For instance, patterns could be found such as learning objects that are highly rated by learners with a deep understanding of some knowledge, by learners with unusual tastes, etc. The sequence of a learner's interactions with various learning objects forms a "foot print" of that learner's activity in the system [11,16].

The research-paper recommender system has been one of the core inspirations for the ecological approach, the learner centered, adaptive, reactive, and collaborative learning framework, proposed in [15]. Specifically, in the ecological approach, it is assumed that there are a large number of learning objects (research papers, web learning resources, online quiz banks, etc.) and a number of different applications that support learners including learning object recommenders (similar to the paper recommender), collaborative activities such as reading, editing, expert and expert finders, and so on. When a learner interacts with a learning object, the object is "annotated" with an instance of the learning model. After a learner has socialized with other learners, corresponding information can also be tagged. These tagged pieces of information embedded in a learner-model instance can include the following:

- Features about the learner, including cognitive, and social characteristics and most importantly their goal(s) in making the encounters.
- Learner feedback on the information content of the learning object, including its information and cognitive quality. For instance, the information quality such as the content accuracy, and up-to-dateness; the cognitive quality such as the appropriateness of the object for learners "like" him or her and the efficacy of the object with respect to their goal(s) in accessing the object, etc.

Over time, each learning object slowly accumulates learner-model instances that collectively form a record of the experiences of all sorts of learners as they have interacted with the learning object as well as their various interactions.

In sum, then, the ecological approach highlights the vision that information gradually accumulates about learning objects, the interactions, and the users. These pieces of information capture "on-the-fly" information about various activities in the system and therefore should be interpreted in the context of end use during the active learning modeling [17]. Gradually, through mechanisms like natural selection, the system will determine what information is useful and what is not, for which purpose.

18.5 Concluding Remarks

Compared to music/book/movie recommendations, paper recommendation is a relatively new, interesting, yet potentially more challenging area due to the many subtle human factors that go into making a pedagogically sound recommendation.

Finding a "good" paper is not trivial: it is not about the simple fact that the user will either accept the recommended items. Rather, it is a multiple-step process that typically entails the users navigating the paper collections, understanding the recommended items, seeing what others like/dislike, and making decisions. In addition, the prerequisite structure underlying most courses, if combined with the pedagogical paper recommendation approaches, might better help in predicting which papers would be useful and suitable to the current topic. For instance, in a syllabus, it is stated that the students have taken an introductory software engineering course and a programming language course before; in other words, the knowledge background of students is known.

It is our hope that the studies we initiated here can open up opportunities for researchers to probe into the use of automated social tools to support active learning and teaching in future networked learning environments [18], where *the flow of knowledge will be governed by the speed of human to human interaction* (p. 179) as well as human to system interaction.

References

1. Basu, C., Hirsh, H., Cohen, W., and Nevill-Manning, C. (2001). Technical paper recommendations: A study in combining multiple information sources. *Journal of Artificial Intelligence Research (JAIR)*, 1: 231–252.
2. Bollacker, K., Lawrence, S., and Giles, C. L. (1999). A system for automatic personalized tracking of scientific literature on the web. In *Proceedings of IEEE/ACM Joint Conference on Digital Libraries (ACM/IEEE JCDL'1999)*, Berkeley, CA, pp. 105–113.
3. Woodruff, A., Gossweiler, R., Pitkow, J., Chi, E., and Card, S. (2000). Enhancing a digital book with a reading recommender. In *Proceedings of ACM Conference on Human Factors in Computing Systems (ACM CHI'00)*, the Hague, the Netherlands, pp. 153–160.
4. McNee, S., Albert, I., Cosley, D., Gopalkrishnan, P., Lam, S., Rashid, A., Konstan, J. and Riedl, J. (2002). On the recommending of citations for research papers. In *Proceedings of ACM Conference on Computer Supported Collaborative Work (CSCW'02)*, New Orleans, LA, pp. 116–125.
5. Torres, R., McNee, S. M., Abel, M., Konstan, J. A., and Riedl, J. (2004). Enhancing digital libraries with TechLens. In *Proceedings of IEEE/ACM Joint Conference on Digital Libraries (ACM/IEEE JCDL'2004)*, Tuscon, AZ, pp. 228–236.
6. Middleton, S. E., Shadbolt, N. R., and De Roure, D. C. (2004). Ontological user profiling in recommender systems. *ACM Transactions on Information Systems*, 22(1): 54–88, January 2004.
7. Lilien, G. L., Kotler, P., and Moorthy, S. K. (1992). *Marketing Models*. Prentice Hall, Englewood Cliffs, NJ, pp. 22–23.
8. Adomavicius, G., Sankarayanan, R., Sen, S., and Tuzhilin, A. (2005). Incorporating contextual information in recommender systems using a multidimensional approach. *ACM Transactions on Information Systems*, 23(1): 103–145. January 2005.
9. Lekakos, G. and Giaglis, G. (2006). Improving the prediction accuracy of recommendation algorithms: Approaches anchored on human factors. *Interacting with Computers*, 18(3): 410–431, 2006.
10. Pazzani, M. (1999). A framework for collaborative, content-based, and demographic filtering. *Artificial Intelligence Review*, 13: 393–408, December 1999.
11. Tang, T. Y. and McCalla, G. I. (2007). A multidimensional paper recommender. In *Proceedings of the 13th International Conference on Artificial Intelligence in Education (AIED 2007)*, Marina Del Rey, CA.
12. Tang, T. Y. (2008). The design and study of pedagogical paper recommendation. PhD thesis. Department of Computer Science, University of Saskatchewan, May 2008.
13. Tang, T. Y. and McCalla, G. I. (2009). A multidimensional paper recommender: Experiments and evaluations. *IEEE Internet Computing*, 13(4): 34–41, IEEE Press.
14. Tang, T. Y. and McCalla, G. I. (2005). Paper annotations with learner models. In *Proceedings of the 12th International Conference on Artificial Intelligence in Education (AIED 2005)*, Amsterdam, the Netherlands, pp. 654–661.

15. McCalla, G. I. (2004). The ecological approach to the design of e-learning environments: Purpose-based capture and use of information about learners. *Journal of Interactive Media in Education (JIME)*, 7, Special issue on the educational semantic web.
16. Tang, T. Y. and McCalla, G. I. (2006). Active, context-dependent, data centered techniques for e-learning: A case study of a research paper recommender system. In C. Romero and S. Ventura (Eds.), *Data Mining in E-Learning*, WIT Press, Southampton, U.K., pp. 97–116.
17. Vassileva, J., McCalla, G. I., and Greer, J. (2003). Multi-agent multiuser modeling in I-Help. *Journal of User Modeling and User-Adapted Interaction*, 13: 179–210, Springer.
18. McCalla, G. I. (2000). The fragmentation of culture, learning, teaching and technology: Implications for the artificial intelligence in education research agenda in 2010. Special Millennium Issue on AIED in 2010, *International Journal of Artificial Intelligence in Education*, 11: 177–196.

19

Link Recommendation in E-Learning Systems Based on Content-Based Student Profiles

Daniela Godoy and Analía Amandi

CONTENTS

19.1 Introduction

E-learning systems offer students an opportunity to engage in an interactive learning process in which they can interact with each other, teachers, and the learning material. Most of these systems allow students to navigate the available material organized based on the criteria of teachers and, possibly, the student learning style and background. However, the Web is an immense source of information that can be used to enrich the learning process of students and, thus, expand the imparted knowledge and acquired skills provided by the E-learning systems. In order to exploit the information available on the Web in a fruitful way, material should be carefully selected and presented to students in the proper time not to overload them with irrelevant information.

Many approaches have emerged in the past few years taking advantage of data mining (DM) and recommendation technologies to suggest relevant material to students according to their needs, preferences, or behaviors. These techniques analyze logs of student behaviors, their individual characteristics, behavior and learning styles, and other data to discover patterns of behavior regarding content in the system that are later applied to personalize the student's interaction with the system. Learning of association rules, induction of classifiers, and data clustering have been used in several works to enhance the effectiveness in the presentation and navigation of content in E-learning systems, consequently enriching the learning experience of students.

In this chapter, we present a recommendation approach for suggesting relevant learning material to students. This approach aims at acquiring comprehensible content-based profiles capturing student interests starting from observation of their behavior in an E-learning system. These profiles are conceptual representations of the material read by the students as they take the courses offered in the system. Not only long-term interests represented in the profiles are considered to make recommendations in this approach, but also the context in which the student is acting at a certain moment. To accomplish this goal, the context of student activities is described using his or her profile, and novel information is gathered from the Web matching their active interests.

The rest of the chapter is organized as follows. Section 19.2 discusses related works on recommendation approaches used in the context of E-learning systems. Section 19.3 describes the proposed approach for recommendation and its integration with user profiling. Both the construction of content-based profiles and the detection of the active interests of a student are described in Section 19.3, which also introduces the mechanisms to generate and deliver recommendations. Section 19.4 shows the results obtained in a course. Finally, concluding remarks are stated in Section 19.5.

19.2 Related Works

Methods for building recommender systems are usually classified as content-based or collaborative filtering (CF) approaches [1]. The former is based on the intuition that users exhibit particular behaviors under given circumstances, which are likely to be repeated under similar circumstances. The latter is based on the intuition that people belonging to a certain group tend to behave alike under similar circumstances. Thus, content-based approaches recommend items similar to the ones the user liked in the past, while CF approaches recommend items liked by people with similar interests.

Content-based approaches are based in the comparison of items with user profiles containing representations of user interests, preferences, and habits. In E-learning systems, content-based recommendation aims to delivering the most appropriate content to learners according to their interests and needs. The problem of learning user profiles has been addressed using diverse techniques mostly from the DM and machine learning (ML) fields. For example, similarities and dissimilarities among user preferences and contents of the learning resources are exploited in [8] to compute automatic recommendations online to an active learner based on his or her recent navigation history.

Collaborative filtering, also known as social filtering, is one of the most successful recommendation technology and it is used in several E-commerce systems on the Web to sell a variety of items such as music, movies, and products. CF relies on users describing their interests by assigning numerical ratings to items; the assigned ratings constitute the user profile, which is compared with other profiles to locate users with similar tastes. SlopeOne CF algorithm is used in [10] to customize learning object selection from repositories, in which students specify their tastes or interests in the learning objects through explicit ratings.

Methods of recommendation based collaboration can also be divided into memory-based or model-based approaches [1]. Memory-based algorithms operate over the entire rating database to find a set of users, known as neighbors, that have a history of agreeing with the target user and make predictions based on the aggregation of the rating given by these users. Conversely, model-based algorithms learn a model for the prediction of ratings. Typically, the model building process is performed by different ML and DM algorithms such as Bayesian networks, clustering, and rule-based approaches.

In several works, clustering algorithms have been employed to group students with similar navigation behavior or learning sessions and learn group profiles characterizing each cluster properties. An example is presented in [2], in which unsupervised learning is used to automatically identify common learning behaviors and then train a classifier user model that can inform an adaptive component of an intelligent learning environment. Talavera and Gaudioso [19] present experiments using clustering techniques to automatically discover useful groups from students to obtain profiles of student behaviors.

Other examples of model-based recommendation approaches employed in E-learning systems use association rules, sequential learning, or Bayesian networks. Shen and Shen [18] organize contents into small atomic units called learning objects and use rules to guide the learning resource recommendation service based on simple sequencing specification. In [9], the extraction of sequential patterns has been used to find patterns of characteristic behaviors of students that are used for recommending relevant concepts to these students in an adaptive hypermedia educational system. The discovery of association rules in the activity logs of students has been used in an agent assisting the online learning process [23] to recommend online learning activities or shortcuts on a course Web site. In an opposite direction, mining of association rules has also been used to discover patterns of usage in courses [3]. This approach aims to help professors to improve the structure and contents of an E-learning course. Likewise, rules denoting dependence relationships among the usage data during student sessions to improve courses [15]. In [12], sequential pattern mining algorithms are applied to discover the most used path by students and recommend links to the new students as they browse the course. Hämäläinen et al. [7] construct a Bayesian network to describe the learning process of students in order to classify them according to their skills and characteristics and offer guidance according to their particularities.

Hybrid schemes combining recommendation methods belonging to different recommendation approaches are frequently used to better exploit their advantages. For example, clusters of students with similar learning characteristics are created in the research paper recommender system presented in [20] as a previous step to CF with the goal of scaling down the candidate users to those clustered together and obtained more personalized recommendation. CF is based on the ratings or feedback given by students toward the recommended papers. In [4], association rule mining is used to discover interesting information in usage data registered by students in the form of IF–THEN recommendation rules. Then, a collaborative recommender system is applied to share and score the recommendation rules obtained by teachers with similar profiles along with other experts in education. A personalized recommendation method integrating user clustering and association mining techniques is presented in [22]. This work propose a novel clustering algorithm to group users based on their historical navigation sessions partitioned according to specific time intervals. Association rules are then mined from navigation sessions of the groups to establish a recommendation model for similar students in the future. Romero et al. [16] cluster students showing common behavior and knowledge, and then try to discover sequential patterns in each cluster for generating personalized recommendation links.

19.3 Recommendation Approach

In order to recommend links relevant to the material the student is reading, the interest areas of students are described in their profiles. Thus, recommendations are made based on comparison of the active interests and the content of Web pages. Student profiles support proactive, context-aware retrieval in which relevant documents are automatically retrieved from the Web and presented to users according to their activities.

Figure 19.1 illustrates the overall recommendation scheme. In order to provide personalized assistance to students using an E-learning system, a hierarchical representation of the material read by these students is generated by observing their browsing behavior over the offered material along the courses taken. Web pages resulting from a traditional keyword-based search are filtered according to the active user goal or interests, i.e., the material a student is reading in a given context given by the current browsing session. A number of recommendations, each with a certain associated confidence, are presented to the student as result of this process. Optionally, students can provide feedback about the recommended Web pages in order to adapt their profiles accordingly.

In this work, we considered content-based profiles providing a hierarchical representation of the learning material read by the student in an E-learning system and supporting the categorization these material into semantically meaningful concepts. Ontology-based user profiling approaches [11] as well as techniques based on clustering algorithms [6] are possible approaches for obtaining such hierarchies. We also applied this approach for filtering Web pages according to content-based profiles representing general interests of Web users; for details of the clustering algorithm refer to [6].

In the following subsections we describe the approach used for recommendation of relevant material used in this work in which learning of content-based profiles is based on clustering of the documents read by students.

19.3.1 Capturing Learning Experiences

Learning material read by a student is obtained through nonintrusive observation of his or her activities in the E-learning system. In the observation process, Web pages a student

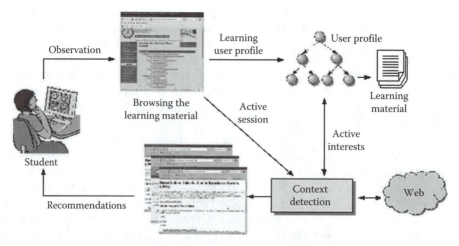

FIGURE 19.1
Overview of the recommendation approach.

read in an online Web-based course are captured and considered different learning experiences of this student. In other words, a student profile is composed of a set of learning experiences $E = \langle e_1, e_2, ..., e_l \rangle$ hierarchically organized in a set of categories. From a content analysis of these experiences comes out the knowledge to be modeled in student profiles.

Each experience encapsulates both the specific and contextual knowledge that describes a particular situation denoting a student reading of a certain piece of information. Experiences can be divided into three main parts: the description of the Web page content, the description of the associated contextual information, and the outcome of applying the experience for suggesting information. The first part enables content-based recommendation by discovering and retrieving topical related information, whereas the second and third parts allow the recommendation method to take into consideration the current student contexts and determine a level of confidence in recommendations generated using each individual experience.

The content of Web pages read by student as part of a course is represented according to the vector space model (VSM) [17]. In this model, each document is identified by a feature vector in a space in which each dimension corresponds to a distinct term associated with a numerical value or weight which indicates its importance. The resulting representation of a Web page and the corresponding learning experience is, therefore, equivalent to a t-dimensional vector:

$$e_i = \langle (t_1, w_1), ..., (t_t, w_t) \rangle$$

where w_i represents the weight of the term t_i in the page or document d_j. In a previous step, noninformative words such as prepositions, conjunctions, pronouns, and very common verbs, commonly referred to as stop-words, are removed using a standard stop-word list and a stemming algorithm is applied to the remaining words in order to reduce the morphological variants of words to their common roots [13].

Learning experiences also describe the contextual information of the situation in which the Web page was captured, including the page address, date and time it was registered, and the level of interest the user showed in the page according to some preestablished criteria.

In the description of a learning experience, the patterns of received feedback regarding suggestions given based on the knowledge provided by them are also kept track of. Basically, each experience e_i has an associated relevance rel_i, which is a function of the initial interest of the experience, the number of successful and failed recommendations made based on this experience, and the time that passes from the moment in which the experience was captured or used for the last time. Figure 19.2 shows an example of a learning experience. Then, the user profile consists of pairs $\langle e_i, rel_i \rangle$, where e_i is the user experience encoding mainly the Web page the user found interesting, and rel_i represents the evidence about the user interest in that experience, confined to the [0,1] interval, according to the collected evidence.

19.3.2 Learning Content-Based Profiles

Student profiles provide a conceptual representation of the material read by a student during the learning process carried out while attending Web-based courses. The acquisition of such profiles is based on a clustering algorithm, named WebDCC (Web document

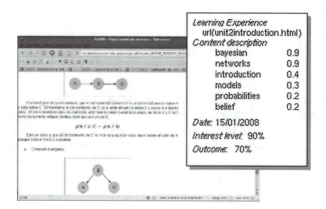

FIGURE 19.2
Example of a learning experience.

conceptual clustering) [6], with structures and procedures specifically designed for user profiling on the Web. Modeling learning material using conceptual clustering allows acquiring descriptions of the topics learned by students without their intervention through observation of student activities.

WebDCC carries out incremental, unsupervised concept learning over the collected experiences. Conceptual clustering includes not only clustering, but also characterization, i.e., the formation of intentional concept descriptions for extensionally defined clusters. It is defined as the task of, given a sequential presentation of experiences and their associated descriptions, finding clusters that group these experiences into concepts or categories, a summary description of each concept and a hierarchical organization of them [21].

The advantage of using this algorithm is twofold. Incremental learning of student profiles allows acquiring and maintaining knowledge over time as well as deal with subject areas that cannot be preestablished beforehand. Also, the result of characterization is a readable description of the learning material the student read as a means of understanding further information needs.

WebDCC algorithm takes the learning experiences captured through observation in an online fashion. Experiences are analyzed to learn a conceptual description of their content and organized within the student profiles. Identification of categories or topics in the material the student read is based on clustering of similar past experiences.

In document clustering, clusters are distinct groups of similar documents and it is generally assumed that clusters represent coherent topics. Leaves in the hierarchy correspond to clusters of experiences belonging to all ancestor concepts. This is, clusters group highly similar experiences observed by the algorithm so that a set of n_i experiences or documents belonging to a concept c_i and denoted by $E = \{e_1, e_2, \ldots, e_{ni}\}$ is organized into a collection of k clusters, $U_{ji} = \{u_{1i}, u_{2i}, \ldots, u_{ki}\}$, containing elements of E_i such that $u_{li} \cap u_{pi} = \phi$, $\forall\, l \neq p$. As relevant experiences appear, they are assigned to clusters in the student profile. Each experience can be incorporated to either some of the existent clusters or to a novel cluster depending on its similarity with the current categories represented in the profile.

Hierarchies of concepts are classification trees in which internal nodes represent concepts and leaf nodes represent clusters of experiences. The root of the hierarchy corresponds to the most general concept, which comprises all the experiences the algorithm has seen, whereas inner concepts become increasingly specific as they are placed lower in the hierarchy, covering only subsets of experiences by themselves. Finally, terminal concepts are those with no child concepts but clusters.

WebDCC generates text-like description of categories by observing the common features of Web pages in these categories and those a novel experience should have in order to belong to them. For this algorithm, concept descriptions consist in a set of terms with an associated weight indicating their importance. These descriptions facilitate both interpretation since they are easy to understand for users, and classification as standard text classification methods are applicable to either include novel experiences in the existing categories or determine the relevance of a new piece of information.

Concepts in the hierarchy, denoted by $C = \{c_1, c_2, \ldots, c_n\}$, are gradually discovered by the algorithm as new experiences become available, i.e., the student read more material in a Web-based course. In order to automatically assign experiences to concepts, the algorithm associates each of them with a description given by a set of terms, $c_i = \langle (t_1, w_1), \ldots, (t_m, w_m) \rangle$, weighted according to their importance in accurately describing the concept. Thus, WebDCC builds a hierarchical set of classifiers, each based on its own set of relevant features, as a combined result of a feature selection algorithm for deciding on the appropriate set of terms at each node in the tree and a supervised learning algorithm for constructing a classifier for such node. An instantiation of Rocchio classifier [14] in which the prototype of a category is the plain average of all training experiences is used for learning classifiers.

In user profiles, the student interest categories are extensionally defined by highly similar experiences that conform to clusters. This partition reduces the total number of experiences to a relatively small number of clusters, which are analyzed to discover topical information. The right side of Figure 19.3 shows an example of a profile for a hypothetical student who has learning experiences in three categories, corresponding to three different courses, *Logic*, *Bayesian networks*, and *Data mining*, the two last ones in a more general category of artificial intelligence (AI).

Learning experiences are integrated to the user profile by sorting it through the concept hierarchy and simultaneously updating this hierarchy. First, an experience is incorporated below the root of the existing hierarchy and then it is recursively classified in the child concepts as it descends the tree. When the experience cannot be further classified down, the algorithm considers whether to incorporate the experience into a cluster or create a new singleton cluster or category.

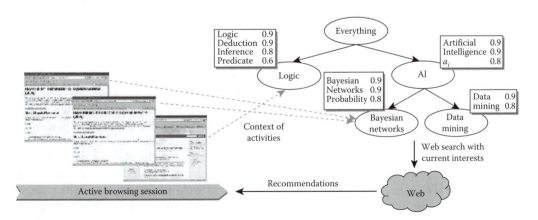

FIGURE 19.3
Context-aware recommendation.

After incorporating a new learning experience, the current hierarchy is evaluated from a structural point of view. In this evaluation, new concepts can be created or concepts can be merged, split, or promoted. Concept formation is driven by the notion of conceptual cohesiveness. Highly cohesive clusters are assumed to contain similar experiences belonging to a same category, whereas clusters exhibiting low cohesiveness are assumed to contain experiences concerning distinctive aspects of more general categories. In the last case, a concept summarizing the cluster is extracted, enabling a new partitioning of experiences and the identification of subcategories. A merge operation takes two concepts and combines them into a single one, whereas splitting takes place when a concept is no longer useful to describe experiences in a category and then it can be removed. The promotion of concepts to become siblings of their parent concepts is also taken into account in order to place concepts at the appropriate hierarchical level.

19.3.3 Detecting Active Interests

In order to generate recommendations, it is necessary first to determine which the current interests of a student are in the E-learning system, i.e., the learning material he or she is accessing. Thus, the recommendation method can take advantage of the knowledge gained from observing the student actions in conjunction with the undertaken learning process to retrieve context-relevant information from the Web.

The student browsing session in a course is composed of a set of page references. For example, the sequence of pages accessed from a log-in to a log-out in the system. Information collected from a single session is assumed to belong to a same context, providing a good foundation for inferring and applying context in recommendation. The E-learning system needs to record student actions so that the content of Web pages the student read, access time, time spent on each page, actions performed in the browser (e.g., scrolling, etc.) are available to delimit context. Each session S_j, $S_j = \{p_1, p_2, ..., p_n\}$, is considered to be a list of pages a user accessed.

To detect the topical context of a student browsing the learning material each page p_i is associated to the set of categories C_i it belongs to, defined by all of the categories c_i in the path from the root of the hierarchy to the leaf cluster in which the page p_i can be classified into. The categories a document belongs to are subsequently determined at each level going downward in the hierarchy. Namely, once having selected a category at a certain level, only its children should be considered as prospective categories at the next level.

WebDCC trains classifiers to recognize constitutive features of categories as experiences are captured and then discriminate documents belonging to these categories. For each node in the hierarchical structure, a separate classifier is induced during the learning process to distinguish documents that should be assigned to the category it represents from other documents. At each decision point in the hierarchy, a classifier is concerned with a binary classification problem where a document is either relevant or not to a given category. Figure 19.3 illustrates a set of classifiers in a hierarchical setting representing the student interests. In the figure, the top level classifier decides on the classification of documents into the root category, the second level classifiers into the Logic or AI categories, and the third level classifiers below AI into the *Bayesian networks* and *Data mining* categories. Each classifier only requires to be focused on a small number of features, which best discriminate documents belonging to the category from other documents. For example, a fairly small set of terms such as *artificial* and *intelligence* clearly determines whether a document belongs to the AI category, but these terms are unlikely to be useful for either a classifier at the same hierarchical level (e.g., *Logic*) or a classifier at the next hierarchical level (e.g., *Bayesian networks*).

Linear classifiers, which embody an explicit or declarative representation of the category based on which categorization decisions are taken, are applied in WebDCC algorithm. Learning in linear classification consists in examining the training pages (i.e., pages read by the student) a finite number of times to construct a prototype for the category, which is later compared against the pages to be classified. A prototype p_{c_i} for a category c_i consists in a vector of weighted terms, $p_{c_i} = \langle (t_1, w_1), \ldots, (t_p, w_p) \rangle$, where w_j is the weight associated to the term t_j in the category. This kind of classifiers are both efficient, since classification is linear on the number of terms, documents and categories, and easy to interpret, since it is assumed that terms with higher weights are considered better predictors for the category than those with lower weights as can be observed in the figure. WebDCC builds a hierarchical set of classifiers, each based on its own set of relevant features, as a combined result of a feature selection algorithm for deciding on the appropriate set of terms at each node in the tree and a supervised learning algorithm for constructing a classifier for such node. Rocchio classifier is used in this algorithm to train classifiers with $\beta = 1$ and $\gamma = 0$, since no negative examples are available and there is no initial query, yielding

$$p_{c_i} = \frac{1}{c_i} \sum_{d \in c_i} d$$

as a prototype for each class $c_i \in C$. Hence, each prototype p_{c_i} is the plain average of all training pages belonging to the class c_i, and the weight of each term is simply the average of its weights in positive pages of the category. To categorize a new page into a given category, its closeness to the prototype vector of the category is computed using the standard cosine similarity measure [17]. The prototype vectors of categories are attached with the classification threshold τ, which indicates the minimum similarity to the prototype of each category pages should have in order to fall into these categories. The induction of classifiers for hierarchical categories is carried out during the learning of the student profile.

19.3.4 Context-Aware Recommendation

The main goal of the recommendation approach described in this chapter is to present relevant information to students based on the knowledge of their interests. However, agents have to be also aware of the student context in order to provide learning material which is relevant at a given moment. Then, the goal is to proactively retrieve Web pages matching the active interests of students to compute a set of recommendations for the current student activity in the system. Context is described in this approach as the subset of categories in the student profile, which match the student's last visited pages. These categories represent the current interest of the student and, therefore, recommended Web pages should belong to the same categories.

Figure 19.3 illustrates the complete approach for recommendation based on the student context. The student in this example seems to be taken a course about *Bayesian networks* first and *Logic* after that, but not about *Data mining* in this particular occasion. These two concepts are detected as current interests and Web pages are searched on the Web about them. Thus, recommendations are delivered to the student as the result of the Web search carried out.

In order to capture the current user context so that recommendations can be delivered in the precise moment they are needed, a fixed-size sliding window is used over the active session. For a sliding window of size n, the active session ensures that only the last n visited pages influence recommendation. In Figure 19.3, for example, a small sliding window will allow to eliminate *Bayesian networks* as an active interest if the student continues reading some more pages about *Logic* in a course.

In contrast to student profile learning, recommendation is an online process in which the E-learning system needs to determine a set of candidate recommendations beforehand or trigger a Web search. To gather potential learning material to recommend in advance, an agent might perform a Web search to retrieve pages belonging to the concepts the student is interested in during idle computer time. For example, the system can retrieve pages from some fixed sites periodically (e.g., university Web pages) or find nearest neighbor documents by using some experiences in the profile as query (e.g., asking "more documents like this" to specialized search engines such as Google Scholar).

In order to evaluate whether a candidate Web page resulting from the Web search should be recommended to a given student, the system searches for similar learning experiences in the profile of this student assuming that the interest in a new page will resemble the interest in similar material read in the past. The existing categories in the profile bias the search toward the most relevant experiences.

The comparison between previous learning experiences and Web pages to be recommended is performed across a number of dimensions that describes them, the most important being the one that measures the similarity between the item contents, which is estimated using the cosine similarity. The n best experiences, $E = \{e_1, e_2, ..., e_k\}$, which exceed a minimum similarity threshold, are selected to determine the convenience of making a recommendation. To assess the confidence in recommending a candidate Web page r_i given the experiences in E, a weighted sum of the confidence value of each similar retrieved experience is then calculated as follows:

$$\text{conf}(r_i) = \frac{\sum_{k=1}^{n} w_k * \text{rel}_k}{\sum_{k=1}^{n} w_k}$$

where n is the number of similar experiences retrieved, rel_k is the relevance in the profile of the experience e_k and w_k is the contribution of each experience according to its similarity. This method to estimate the confidence in a recommendation is based on the well-known distance-weighted nearest neighbor algorithm.

Each experience has a weight w_k according to the inverse square of its distance from r_i. Thus, the more similar and relevant pages are the more important for assessing the confidence in a recommendation. If the confidence value of recommending r_j is greater than a certain confidence threshold, which can be customized in the E-learning system, the page is recommended.

From the moment that users provide either explicit or implicit feedback about recommendations, agents start learning from their actions. If the result of a recommendation is successful, then the system learns from the success by increasing the relevance of the corresponding experiences in the profile and, possibly, incorporating new experiences. If the result of a recommendation is a failure, the system learns from the mistake by decreasing the relevance of the experiences that has led to the unsuccessful recommendation or even removing them.

19.4 Case Study

We evaluate the link recommendation approach described in this chapter using the material of a curse designed for an education system, named SAVER* (acronym for Software de Asistencia Virtual para Educación Remota). The course is an introduction to Bayesian networks; it contains theoretical and practical material so that students can learn this topic by using the system. This course was also used for experimentation in [5].

Figure 19.4 shows a screenshot exemplifying the assistance that is provided to students during browsing. In this figure, the student is reading about reasoning under uncertainty in AI and receives recommendations about additional readings in this subject. For each suggested link, an expected level of interest is displayed, which is calculated based on the confidence of recommendation given by content similarity and the relevance of past related readings.

In order to evaluate the recommendation approach based on student profiles, we simulate a student accessing to the course material in a sequential order and the system delivering suggestions about relevant material extracted from the Web. Each time the student access a new page with content of the course, a Web search is triggered to retrieve candidate links for recommendation. For this experiment, keyword-based queries were attached to each page in the course according to their topic (extracted from the page title) so that pages matching these queries can be obtained and analyzed in a further step. It is worth noticing that these queries can be created by the content designer given its knowledge of the Web page or automatically generated according to the more frequent terms in the page. All pages gathered from the Web were compared against the user profile to determine whether it should be recommended to the student.

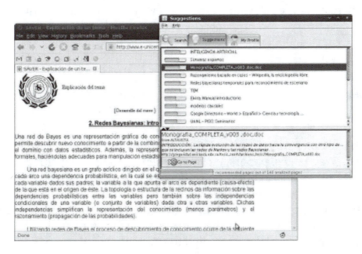

FIGURE 19.4
Screenshot showing suggestions to students.

---

* www.e-unicen.edu.ar

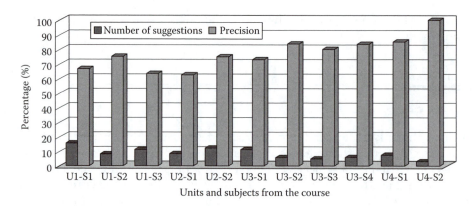

FIGURE 19.5
Experimental results in a case study.

Figure 19.5 shows the variation of precision in the generated recommendations as the student advances in the course and the profile is learned. Precision measures the proportion of relevant material recommended to the student out of the total of recommendations made. A relevance judgment was established by manually visiting each suggested Web page and assessing its importance regarding the reading material. For this experiment, we limited the number of candidate Web pages retrieved from the Web to 100, i.e., we retrieve the top 100 pages return by a search engine, and those recommendations exceeding a confidence threshold of 50% were finally suggested. Both the percentage of recommended pages as well as the precision achieved with these suggestions is depicted in the figure. Although more experimentation is needed, it is possible to observe that a small number of pages are recommended out of the top 100 Web pages (more pages can be found by extending the set of candidate pages analyzing pages placed lower in the search engine list of results), this number is even smaller for more specific subjects. However, these recommendations are made with a high level of precision. In addition, precision can be improved even more by increasing the relevance threshold, which can be manually done in the user interface.

19.5 Conclusions

In summary, this chapter presents a recommendation approach to suggest relevant learning material (e.g., Web pages, papers, etc.) to students interacting with an E-learning system. This approach is based on building content-based profiles starting from observation of student readings and behavior in the system offered courses. Whereas profiles provide a characterization of the material accessed by a student and read during the learning process, recommendations are based on the portion of such interests that are active a given moment. Thus, relevant material is presented to students according to their current context of activities given by the information they are actually reading in the system so that they can enrich their knowledge about a subject by exploiting relevant material existing on the Web and not only the one offered through the E-learning system.

References

1. G. Adomavicius and A. Tuzhilin. Toward the next generation of recommender systems: A survey of the state-of-the-art and possible extensions. *IEEE Transactions on Knowledge and Data Engineering*, 17(6):734–749, 2005.
2. S. Amershi and C. Conati. Unsupervised and supervised machine learning in user modeling for intelligent learning environments. In *Proceedings of the 2007 International Conference on Intelligent User Interfaces*. ACM Press, New York, 2007, pp. 72–81.
3. E. García, C. Romero, S. Ventura, and C. de Castro. Using rules discovery for the continuous improvement of e-learning courses. In *Intelligent Data Engineering and Automated Learning IDEAL 2006*, Volume 4224. LNCS, Burgos, Spain, 2006, pp. 887–895.
4. E. García, C. Romero, S. Ventura, and C. de Castro. An architecture for making recommendations to courseware authors using association rule mining and collaborative filtering. *User Modeling and User-Adapted Interaction*, 19(1–2):99–132, 2009.
5. P. García, S. Schiaffino, and A. Amandi. An enhanced bayesian model to detect students' learning styles in Web-based courses. *Journal of Computer Assisted Learning*, 24(4):305–315, 2008.
6. D. Godoy and A. Amandi. Modeling user interests by conceptual clustering. *Information Systems*, 31(4–5):247–265, 2006.
7. W. Hämäläinen, T. H. Laine, and E. Sutinen. Data mining in personalizing distance education courses. In *Data Mining in E-Learning*. WIT Press, Southampton, U.K., 2005, pp. 157–172.
8. M. K. Khribi, M. Jemni, and O. Nasraoui. Automatic recommendations for e-learning personalization based on web usage mining techniques and information retrieval. In *Proceedings of the 8th IEEE International Conference on Advanced Learning Technologies (ICALT'08)*. Santander, Spain, July 1–5, 2008, pp. 241–245.
9. A. Ksristofic. Recommender system for adaptive hypermedia applications. In *Proceeding of Informatics and Information Technology Student Research Conference*. Brisbane, Australia, 2005, pp. 229–234.
10. D. Lemire, H. Boley, S. Mcgrath, and M. Ball. Collaborative filtering and inference rules for context-aware learning object recommendation. *International Journal of Interactive Technology and Smart Education*, 2(3):179–188, 2005.
11. S. Middleton, N. Shadbolt, and D. Roure. Ontological user profiling in recommender systems. *ACM Transactions on Information Systems*, 22(1):54–88, 2004.
12. C. Romero Morales, A. R. Porras Pérez, S. Ventura Soto, C. Hervás Martínez, and A. Zafra Gómez. Using sequential pattern mining for links recommendation in adaptive hypermedia educational systems. In *Current Developments in Technology-Assisted Education*. Sevilla, Spain, 2006, pp. 1016–1020.
13. M. Porter. An algorithm for suffix stripping program. *Program*, 14(3):130–137, 1980.
14. J. J. Rocchio. Relevance feedback in information retrieval. In G. Salton, editor, *The SMART Retrieval System: Experiments in Automatic Document Processing*. Prentice-Hall, Englewood Cliffs, NJ, 1971, pp. 313–323.
15. C. Romero, S. Ventura, and P. De Bra. Knowledge discovery with genetic programming for providing feedback to courseware authors. *User Modeling and User-Adapted Interaction*, 14(5):425–464, 2004.
16. C. Romero, S. Ventura, J. A. Delgado, and P. De Bra. Personalized links recommendation based on data mining in adaptive educational hypermedia systems. In *Creating New Learning Experiences on a Global Scale*, volume 4753. LNCS, Crete, Greece, 2007, pp. 292–306.
17. G. Salton, A. Wong, and C. S. Yang. A vector space model for automatic indexing. *Communications of the ACM*, 18:613–620, 1975.
18. L. Shen and R. Shen. Learning content recommendation service based-on simple sequencing specification. In *Advances in Web-Based Learning ICWL 2004*, volume 3143. LNCS, Beijing, China, August, 2004, pp. 363–370.

19. L. Talavera and E. Gaudioso. Mining student data to characterize similar behavior groups in unstructured collaboration spaces. In *Workshop on AI in CSCL*. Valencia, Spain, 2004, pp. 17–23.

20. T. Tang and G. McCalla. Smart recommendation for an evolving E-learning system: Architecture and experiment. *International Journal on E-Learning*, 4(1):105–129, 2005.

21. K. Thompson and P. Langley. Concept formation in structured domains. In D. Fisher, M. Pazzani, and P. Langley, editors, *Concept Formation: Knowledge and Experience in Unsupervised Learning*. Morgan Kaufmann, San Francisco, CA, 1991, pp. 127–161.

22. F-H. Wang and H-M. Shao. Effective personalized recommendation based on time-framed navigation clustering and association mining. *Expert Systems with Applications*, 27(3):365–377, 2004.

23. O. R. Zaïane. Building a recommender agent for e-learning systems. In *Proceedings of the 7th International Conference on Computers in Education (ICCE'02)*. AACE, December 3–6, 2002, p. 55.

20

Log-Based Assessment of Motivation in Online Learning

Arnon Hershkovitz and Rafi Nachmias

CONTENTS

20.1 Introduction

It has been suggested that affective aspects play a critical role in effective learning and that they are an important factor in explaining individual differences between learners' behavior and educational outcomes [1,2]. Emotional and/or affective states (e.g., motivation, anxiety, boredom, frustration, self-efficacy, and enthusiasm) are sometimes easily noticed in the classroom (e.g., by facial expressions), but they are hard to measure and evaluate. This becomes even harder when we try to assess affective aspects of learning in Web-based or computer-based learning environments, which lack face-to-face interaction. However, the traces constituted by students' log file records offer us new possibilities to meet this challenge. This chapter presents the development of a student motivation measuring tool for Web-based or computer-based learning environments, where data is taken solely from log files. This feature of our research is part of the emerging field of educational data mining, which focuses on the use of data mining tools and techniques in order to answer education-related questions.

Being able to identify motivation, as well as other affective components of students' learning, as they are interacting with Web-based or computer-based learning environments, carries a great potential for instructors, system developers, and researchers. And above all, learners will have the benefit of better adapted education. In this chapter, we provide a review of previous research on motivation-related measuring in computer-based learning configurations and suggest a way of developing a log-based motivation measuring tool by using the *Learnogram*—a visual representation of the learning process.

20.2 Motivation Measurement in Computer-Based Learning Configurations

Affect and cognition have been shown to be related in a way that impacts the quality and the effectiveness of learning. Earlier studies laid the foundations for an understanding of the relations between certain affective states/components and aspects of learning/instructing. For example, generating motivation was suggested as an important factor for making instruction more appealing [3]; the importance of intrinsic motivation stimulation was proposed as a key factor in designing learning environments [4]; and flow, a state in which people are so involved in an activity that nothing else seems to matter, was considered an important element of understanding human–technology interaction, including students' interaction with technology [5]. Later, the relationships between emotions or affective states and learning were modeled, predicting that learning almost always occurs during an emotional episode and explaining the spiral nature of learning, as it evolves in a two-axes system of learning and affect [2,6].

In recent years, a lot of focus had been given to possible connections between affective states or emotions and learning-related parameters. Unlike learning situations in which the instructor infers affective aspects of students' responses (e.g., from facial expressions, satisfaction/frustration intonation), computer-based learning does not offer the instructor such direct means for the assessment of affect-related parameters. Therefore, a lot of efforts had been put in various directions in order to compensate for this apparent lack. We can roughly divide these methods into two large groups: methods that get information directly from the student, and methods that use indirect information about the student.

The first group of methods involves feedback from the learner obtained, for example, via (1) questionnaires or interviews, usually presented to the learner either at the beginning or at the end of the learning process [7,8]; (2) self-report, in the form of direct communication by the system with the student about his or her affective situation. Questions that are short and quick to answer might, in this case, be presented to the learner repeatedly during the learning process, thus enabling dynamic tapping of the motivational state [7,9]. Besides being subjective, these methods rely on the learner's cooperation, and this might, in turn, interrupt and interfere with the learning process.

The second group of methods does not directly involve the learner in the evaluation process. Its main methods are (1) observation of the students, either by an observer who is in the same space as the student or by a distant observer who uses a camera (in real-time) or a videotape (not in real-time) [9,10]. Speech analysis may be included in this category [11,12]; (2) expert systems, based on knowledge rules (determined a priori) regarding the learner's behavior [13]; (3) sensor system for tapping the learner's interaction with the virtual environment (e.g., mouse pressure strength, eye gaze) and physical reactions (e.g., facial expressions, skin conductivity) [14–16]; (4) analysis of the learner's interaction with the system, including dialogue analysis [17,18] and usage analysis [19–21].

Students' motivation, which is part of their emotional and affective behavior, has been suggested as one of the factors explaining individual differences in intensity and direction of behavior [22]. While it is not easy to assess motivation in face-to-face learning situations, it becomes even more challenging in computer-based learning, where there is no direct, eye-to-eye contact between the instructor and the students. Therefore, developing ways to detect motivation is especially challenging in such environments [23].

It is generally accepted that motivation is "an internal state or condition that serves to activate or energize behavior and give it direction" [24]; sources of motivation can be either internal (e.g., interestingness, enjoyment) or external (e.g., wishing for high grades, fear of parental sanctions) to the person [25]. Motivational patterns, in addition to ability, may influence the way people learn: whether they seek or avoid challenges, whether they persist or withdraw when they encounter difficulties, or whether they use and develop their skills effectively [26]. It has been shown that different motivational patterns relate to different aspects of the learning process, e.g., achievement goals (performance or mastery), time spent on tasks, performance [27–32]. Previous research on motivation, based on learner–computer interaction data, examined some variables measuring, e.g., number of pages read or tasks performed [21,33,34], response time [20,33,34], time spent on different parts of the learning environment [21,33,34], speed of performance [9], and correctness (or quality) of answers [9,20,34]. It is the intention of this study to develop a tool for measuring motivation, based on log files solely.

20.3 The Study

We designed a study for developing a log-based motivation measuring tool in a given online learning environment, and it is presented with details in this section.

20.3.1 The Learning Environments

A simple yet very intensive online learning unit was chosen as the research field. This fully online environment, which focuses solely on Hebrew vocabulary, is accessible to students who take a (face-to-face) course preparing them for the Psychometric University Entrance Exam. Log files of this environment document a large part of the activities available in the system, including client-side logging, therefore offering a broad view of learners' activity. Each year, about 10,000 students (aged 18–25) from all over Israel enroll in this online course. The material being taught in the online unit is not taught in class and students who choose not to take the online unit acquire it from a book. The system holds a database of around 5000 words/phrases in Hebrew that the student is expected to learn. The modes of learning are varied: (1) *memorizing*—the student browses a table, which includes the words/phrases and their meanings, and tries to memorize it; (2) *practicing*—the student browses the words/phrases in the table and checks whether he or she knows their meaning (the student may also use a hint); (3) *searching*—the student can search for specific words/phrases from the database; (4) *gaming*—the student plays games aimed to teach the words/phrases in an experiential way; or (5) *self-examining*—the student practices by doing self-exams that are structured like the exam he or she will finally take. As they use the different modes of learning, students may mark each word/phrase as "well known," "not well known," or "unknown." In the memorizing and practicing modes, the system presents the student only with those words that he or she didn't mark as "known."

20.3.2 Population

Log files of 2162 adults who used the online learning system during 1 month (April 2007) were analyzed. After filtering nonactive students and 0-value cases, the research population was reduced to $N = 674$.

20.3.3 Log File Description

The researched system logs a student's activity. Thus, each student is identified by a serial number (to ensure privacy, the names of the students were removed before starting the analysis). Each row in the log file documents a session, which begins by entering the system and ends with closing the application window. For each session, the following attributes are kept: starting date, starting/ending time, list of actions, and their timestamps. Actions documented are every html/asp page in the system, not including actions within Java/Flash applets (i.e., within-game pages are not documented, only the entry to a game and the next action outside it), and this is due to the limitations of the system logging mechanism. Cleaning and preprocessing, the main purpose of which is to prepare the data for initial manipulation and for visualization, were carried out (e.g., removing empty logged records, unifying date format, computing basic variables).

20.3.4 Learnograms

The *Learnogram* can be illuminated if we compare it with the medical clinic, where the electrocardiogram (ECG), for instance, allows the cardiologist to examine a graphical display of the patient's heart-related parameters over time, thus allowing him or her to learn about the patient's cardiac functions without actually seeing the heart. Since we cannot always observe the student while he or she is interacting with a computer-based (and particularly a Web-based) learning environment, we may use a mechanism (i.e., log collection) that continuously documents and graphically displays their learning-related activity, i.e., the *Learnogram*. However, the behavioral variables that can be extracted from log files of learning systems have been only little researched in terms of their association with affective aspects of learning. The process described in this chapter is another step toward bridging this gap. *Learnogram*-like representations appear in, e.g., Hwang and Wang [35], and a case study in which *Learnograms* are used as a qualitative research tool is described in Nachmias and Hershkovitz [36].

20.3.5 Process

The motivation measuring tool that this chapter presents was developed as part of a more general study of affective states while learning in a Web-based or computer-based environment. The framework consists of four consecutive phases. The first phase includes an explicit and operational definition of the affective features in question; eventually, this definition will be assessed in view of the empirical results. Next, empirical data will be collected, reflecting students' activity in the learning environment examined. These data are to be analyzed qualitatively (during the second phase), in order to find relevant variables to measure the affective state, and then quantitatively (in the third phase), for clustering according to similarity over large population. Finally, Phase IV associates the empirical clusters with the theory-based definition. The result of this is a set of variables, whose computation is based solely on the log files; at this stage, we also relate these variables to the theoretical conceptualization. Below is a description of these phases:

- **Phase I—Constructing a Theory-Based Definition**. This phase is based on litera-ture, and it aims to explicitly conceptualize the terms under study. An operational definition regarding motivation is evolved. This definition should later be related to empirical findings.

- **Phase II—Identifying Learning Variables**. The main purpose of this phase is to find as many learning variables as possible that best reflect motivation. After cleaning and preprocessing the log files, learnograms for a few students were observed by education experts in order to find variables indicating individual dif-ferences, which might be related to the research framework constructed in the previous phase. A learnogram of a basic variable (e.g., visiting different parts of a learning environment) might lead to the need to generate the learnogram of a more complex variable (e.g., cumulative activity in a certain part of the system); all of these variables are computed from the log files at a later point in time. A list of variables to be calculated based on the log files is the outcome of this phase.

- **Phase III—Empirically Clustering the Variables**. During this phase, data min-ing algorithms are applied on a newly formed dataset consisting of the calculated values of the Phase II variables, now for all the students. Then we use a cluster-ing algorithm that groups together different variables by similarity as empirically yielded by the research population (this, though, is not the only possible method and others might be considered).

- **Phase IV—Linking the Empirical Clusters to the Theory-Based Definition**. In order to link the empirical clusters with the theory-based definition, data reflect-ing the students' motivation should be collected (e.g., by questionnaires, inter-views, observations, pop-up surveys) and triangulated with the existing log-based data. This can offer a validation of the connection between the empirical data and the definition. In this sub-study, we only present a theory-based validation of the results.

File analysis, learnograms, and learning variable computations were all done using MATLAB®. Clustering analysis was done using SPSS.

20.3.6 Results

The four-phase framework described in Section 20.3.5 was implemented in the online learning environment investigated, in order to develop a log-based motivation measuring tool. Following is the description of each of the phases.

20.3.6.1 Phase I—Constructing a Theory-Based Definition

Based on the reviewed literature, we suggest conceptualizing the motivation measuring tool by reference to three dimensions: (1) *engagement*—which relates to the intensity of motivation. Although we use the same term as Beck [20] and Cocea and Weibelzahl [21], what we have in mind is a more general notion; (2) *direction*—which refers to the way motivation is preserved and oriented; (3) *source* of motivation (internal or external). Here it is important to point out that although the variables by which motivation is measured might be (almost) continuously evaluated, motivation—as the sum of many parameters— should be measured over a period of time. Hence, *engagement* is considered an average intensity, *direction* should describe the overall trend of the engagement level (e.g., increasing, decreasing, stable, frequently changing), and *source* indicates the motivation's tendency to be either internal or external.

20.3.6.2 Phase II—Identifying Learning Variables

In order to identify and define motivation-related variables, *Learnograms* of 5 students were produced from the log files, reflecting 65 days of activity for four basic variables: (1) *presence*—indicating when the student was online; (2) *pace*—a calculation of number of pages viewed per minute; (3) *learning modes*—a mapping of the viewed pages into five different learning modes; and (4) *perceived knowledge*—the number of words marked as "known" by the student. Figure 20.1 presents some sample *Learnograms*. We examined the *Learnograms* in order to identify the motivation-related computable variables. As a result, seven variables were defined, and they are detailed in Table 20.1. These variables are the basis for the analysis in Phase III.

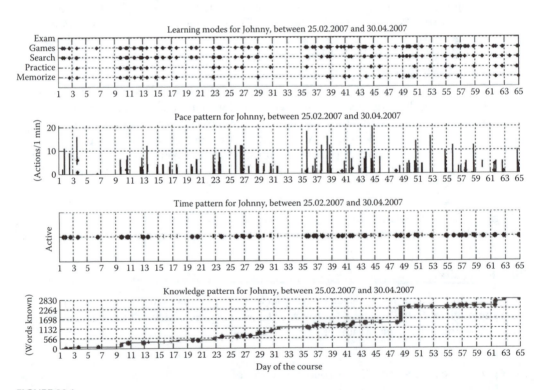

FIGURE 20.1

Four *Learnograms* for one student representing behavior over 65 days of activity in the researched learning environments. The variables presented (from bottom to top): perceived knowledge, presence, pace, learning modes.

TABLE 20.1

The Variables Defined in Phase II

Variable	Description	Unit
timeOnTaskPC	Total time of active sessions [min] divided by total time of logged data	%
avgSession	Average session duration	min
avgActPace	Average pace of activity within sessions; pace of activity per session is the number of actions divided by the session duration	actions/min
avgBtwnSessions	Average time between sessions	min
wordMarkPace	Pace of word marking: Changed number of known words from beginning to end (can be negative) divided by total time of logged data	words/min
examPC	Percentage of exam-related activity: Number of exam actions divided by total number of actions	%
gamePC	Percentage of game-related activity: Number of game actions divided by total number of actions	%

20.3.6.3 Phase III—Clustering the Variables Empirically

An empirical study for the evaluation of the identified variables from previous phase was conducted (with the same learning environment). Log files of a large population ($N = 2162$) for 1 month (April 2007) were collected and preprocessed. Students using the researched system were enrolled in different courses (varying in terms of their length, intensity, starting date, and proximity to the Psychometric exam); however, this logged segment was analyzed regardless of the student's learning stage. A filter was applied for including students with at least three active sessions ($N = 1444$). Algorithms for calculating the variables were formally written and implemented using MATLAB®.

First, the variable distributions were examined. We observed two major problems regarding this distribution which might lead to difficulties in their clustering: The first of these was a significant 0-value noise. This was especially the case for the following three variables: wordMarkPace, examPC, gamePC. Hence, cases with 0-value in either of these variables were cleaned for focusing on the positive-value cases. As a result, the dataset was reduced to $N = 674$. Second, we found skewness; hence, we used the transformations of log (timeOnTaskPC, avgSession, wordMarkPace, examPC, gamePC) and square-root (avgActPace, avgBtwnSessions).

Finally, for classifying the variables into groups by similarity, hierarchical clustering of the variables was applied using SPSS, with Pearson Correlation Distance as the measure and Between Groups Linkage as the clustering method. The clustering process is described by a dendrogram (from the Greek dendron "tree," gramma "drawing") presented in Figure 20.2. The vertical lines describe which variables/clusters were grouped together and at which stage of the algorithm (from left to right). For example, the first coupled variables were timeOnTaskPC and avgSession, and next examPC and gamePC were grouped. We decided to define three clusters: (1) timeOnTaskPC, avgSession; (2) examPC, gamePC, avgBtwnSessions, avgActPace; and (3) wordMarkPace.

20.3.6.4 Phase IV—Associating the Empirical Clusters with the Theory-Based Definition

In our research, this phase is currently based only on literature review, and has not yet been validated empirically. The variables, timeOnTask and avgSession, which form the

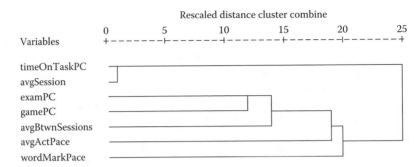

FIGURE 20.2
Dendrogram of the hierarchical clustering process.

first cluster, might be related to the extent of *engagement*, as it was previously suggested that working time might be a measure for attention or engagement [21,26].

The variables, examPC and gamePC, grouped together in the second cluster, reflect the student's *source* of motivation; it may be reasonable to hypothesize—inspired by, e.g., [37,38]—that students who tend to take self-exams frequently (related to performance goal orientation) have extrinsic motivation to learn, while those who tend to take game applications (related to learning goal orientation) are intrinsically motivated. The variables, avgActPace and avgBtwnSessions, are also clustered together with the previous two, but their closeness to *Source* of motivation is yet to be established.

The variable, wordMarkPace, indicating students' word-marking speed, forms the third cluster. According to a diagnostic rule found in de Vicente and Pain [9], high speed of activity together with high quality of performance (when staying in similarly-difficulty exercises) suggests increasing motivation. Since an increase in the number of words marked is an indication of the student's perceived knowledge (i.e., a reflection of performance), wordMarkPace might be related to the direction of motivation, i.e., *direction*.

20.4 Discussion

Many modes of delivery of online and computer-based learning exist (e.g., Intelligent Tutoring System, educational software, virtual courses, Web-supported courses, and electronic books), all are mainly based on the interaction between student and system. While using such an environment, learners leave continuous hidden traces of their activity in the form of log file records, which document every action taken. These log files hold data that can be analyzed in order to offer a better understanding of the learning process. Using these traces for investigating the learners' behavior has a great potential for serving different aspects of educational research [39,40]. Our goal in this chapter was to suggest an empirically constructed tool for log-based measuring of motivation.

In many years of educational research, it has been shown that cognitive skills crucially influence learning outcomes and achievements; however, the affective aspects of learning, which seriously determine this influence, must be understood and assessed. Such assessment becomes a great challenge in learning situations which do not include face-to-face interactions between instructor and learner. Being able to measure affect-related variables in such environments is of great importance for various parties involved: (a) the instructors, who might identify and consequently address irregularities in his or her students' affective state; (b) learning system developers, who might integrate assessment and intervention mechanisms in order to better fit the individual student's learning needs; and (c) researchers, who might extend the existing models of affective aspects of learning on the basis of empirical evidence. Over all, the main beneficiary is the learner, whose effective learning constitutes the very heart of this process.

Examining motivational aspects of learning in e-learning systems, which hold a large number of students, has a great potential, since this may tap otherwise unrecognized phenomena (e.g., a constant decrease in students' motivation in certain situations, high levels of anxiety associated with certain topics or with certain courses). Validating the presented results and scaling the variables suggested are crucial before the completion of the development of our motivation measuring tool. The proper way of doing this is by an external validation, i.e., finding the association between the variables found and independent variables measured by an external measuring tool for motivation. It is also possible to examine the validation step by referring to a different learning environment; however, in this case, a few preliminary steps are required, particularly, a replication of the clustering process, in order to validate that the new system preserves the found clusters.

Furthermore, two major limitations are to be considered. First, variables were identified in a specific learning environment; the measuring tool, hence, might be useful for similar systems, but when using it in different environments (in terms of, e.g., learning domain, instruction modes available), these variables should be converted, and their clustering should be re-examined. Second, the tool might not be complete: we only focused on seven variables but others might be considered. Identifying these variables from a segment of the learning makes it possible to employ this tool during the learning process; in this way, intervention when needed might be possible, and changes in motivation may be analyzed.

The data-mining-driven research of affective aspects of learning is only in its first stages and we feel that a long way is still ahead. Among the many difficulties, one of the major challenges is that of validating the measuring tools, and the different ways of doing so. Developing automatic log-based measuring algorithms for the different aspects of the learning process, is a core aim of our EduMining research group (http://edumining.info) and we always seek new partners in brainstorming and further research.

References

1. Craig, S., Graesser, A., Sullins, J., and Gholson, B. (2004). Affect and learning: An exploratory look into the role of affect in learning with AutoTutor. *Learning, Media and Technology, 29*(3), 241–250.
2. Kort, B., Reilly, R., and Picard, R. (2001). An affective model of the interplay between emotions and learning. In *Proceedings of IEEE International Conference on Advanced Learning Technologies*. Madison, WI, August 6–8, 2001.
3. Keller, J.M. (1983). Motivational design of instruction. In *Instructional-Design Theories and Models: An Overview of Their Current Status*, C.M. Reigeluth (Ed.), pp. 383–434. Lawrence Erlbaum Associates, Inc., Hillsdale, NJ.
4. Malone, T.W. and Lepper, M.R. (1987). Making learning fun: A taxonomy of intrinsic motivations for learning. In *Conative and Affective Process Analyses*, Vol. 3. *Aptitude, Learning, and Instruction*, R.E. Snow and M.J. Farr (Eds.), pp. 223–253. Lawrence Erlbaum Associates, Inc., Hillsdale, NJ.

5. Csikszentmihalyi, M. (1990). *Flow: The Psychology of Optimal Experience*. Harper and Row, New York.
6. Stein, N.L. and Levine, L.J. (1991). Making sense out of emotion. In *Memories, Thoughts, and Emotions: Essays in Honor of George Mandler*, W. Kessen, A. Ortony, and F. Kraik (Eds.), pp. 295–322. Lawrence Erlbaum Associates, Hillsdale, NJ.
7. del Soldato, T. and du Boulay, B. (1995). Implementation of motivational tactics in tutoring systems. *Journal of Artificial Intelligence in Education, 6*(4), 337–376.
8. O'Regan, K. (2003). Emotion and e-learning. *Journal of Educational Computing Research, 7*(3), 78–91.
9. de Vicente, A. and Pain, H. (2002). Informing the detection of the students' motivational state: An empirical study. *Proceedings of the Sixth International Conference on Intelligent Tutoring Systems (ITS 2002)*. Biarritz, France, June 5–8, 2002.
10. Baker, R.S.J.d., Corbett, A.T., Koedinger, K.R., and Wagner, A.Z. (2004). Off-task behavior in the cognitive tutor classroom: When students "game the system." *Proceedings of SIGCHI Conference on Human Factors in Computing Systems*. Vienna, Austria, April 24–29, 2004.
11. Batliner, A., Steidl, S., Hacker, C., and Nöth, E. (2008). Private emotions versus social interaction: A data-driven approach towards analysing emotion in speech. *User Modeling and User-Adapted Interaction, 18*(1–2), 175–206.
12. Campbell, N. (2006). A language-resources approach to emotion: Corpora for the analysis of expressive speech. In *Proceedings of a Satellite Workshop of the International Conference on Language Resources and Evaluation (LREC 2006) on Corpora for Research on Emotion and Affect*. Genoa, Italy, May 25, 2006.
13. Nkambou, R. (2006). Towards affective intelligent tutoring system. In *Proceedings of Workshop on Motivational and Affective Issues in ITS, in the Eighth International Conference on Intelligent Tutoring Systems*. Jhongli, Taiwan, June 27, 2006.
14. Burleson, W. (2006). Affective learning companions: Strategies for empathetic agents with real-time multimodal affective sensing to foster meta-cognitive and meta-affective approaches to learning, motivation, and perseverance. PhD dissertation. MIT Media Lab, Boston, MA.
15. D'Mello, S.K., Craig, S.D., Gholson, B., Franklin, S., Picard, R., and Graesser, A.C. (2005). Integrating affect sensors in an intelligent tutoring system. *Proceedings of Affective Interactions: The Computer in the Affective Loop, Workshop in International Conference on Intelligent User Interfaces*. San Diego, CA.
16. McQuiggan, S.W., Mott, B.W., and Lester, J.C. (2008). Modeling self-efficacy in intelligent tutoring systems: An inductive approach. *User Modeling and User-Adapted Interaction, 18*(1–2), 81–123.
17. D'Mello, S.K., Craig, S.D., Witherspoon, A., McDaniel, B., and Graesser, A. (2008). Automatic detection of learner's affect from conversational cues. *User Modeling and User-Adapted Interaction, 18*(1–2), 45–80.
18. Porayska-Pomsta, K., Mavrikis, M., and Pain, H. (2008). Diagnosing and acting on student affect: the tutor's perspective. *User Modeling and User-Adapted Interaction, 18*(1–2), 125–173.
19. Baker, R.S.J.d. (2007). Modeling and understanding students' off-task behavior in intelligent tutoring systems. In *Proceedings of Proceedings of the SIGCHI Conference on Human Factors in Computing Systems*. San Jose, CA, April 14–18, 2007.
20. Beck, J.E. (2004). Using response times to model student disengagement. In *Proceedings of ITS2004 Workshop on Social and Emotional Intelligence in Learning Environments*. Maceio, Brazil, August 31, 2004.
21. Cocea, M. and Weibelzahl, S. (2007). Cross-system validation of engagement prediction from log files. In *Proceedings of Second European Conference on Technology Enhanced Learning (EC-TEL 2007)*. Crete, Greece, September 17–20, 2007.
22. Humphreys, M.S. and Revelle, W. (1984). Personality, motivation, and performance: A theory of the relationship between individual differences and information processing. *Psychological Review, 91*(2), 153–184.

23. de Vicente, A. and Pain, H. (1998). Motivation diagnosis in intelligent tutoring systems. In *Proceedings of Fourth International Conference on Intelligent Tutoring Systems*. San Antonio, TX, August 16–19, 1998.

24. Kleinginna, P.R. and Kleinginna, A.M. (1981). A categorized list of emotion definitions, with suggestions for a consensual definition. *Motivation and Emotion, 5*(4), 345–378.

25. Deci, E.L. and Ryan, R.M. (1985). *Intrinsic Motivation and Self-Determination in Human Behavior*. Plenum, New York.

26. Dweck, C.S. (1986). Motivational processes affecting learning. *American Psychologist, 41*(10), 1040–1048.

27. Ames, C. and Archer, J. (1988). Achievement goals in the classroom: Students' learning strategies and motivation. *Journal of Educational Psychology, 80*(3), 260–267.

28. Elliott, E.S. and Dweck, C.S. (1988). Goals: An approach to motivation and achievement. *Journal of Personality and Social Psychology, 54*(1), 5–12.

29. Greene, B.A., Miller, R.B., Crowson, H.M., Duke, B.L., and Akey, K.L. (2004). Predicting high school students' cognitive engagement and achievement: Contributions of classroom perceptions and motivation. *Contemporary Educational Psychology, 29*(4), 462–482.

30. Masgoret, A.M. and Gardner, R.C. (2003). Attitudes, motivation, and second language learning: A meta-analysis of studies conducted by Gardner and associates. *Language Learning, 23*(1), 123–163.

31. Singh, K., Granville, M., and Dika, S. (2002). Mathematics and science achievement: Effects of motivation, interest, and academic engagement. *Journal of Educational Research, 95*(6), 323–332.

32. Wong, M.M.-h. and Csikszentmihalyi, M. (1991). Motivation and academic achievement: The effects of personality traits and the quality of experience. *Journal of Personality, 59*(3), 539–574.

33. Qu, L. and Johnson, W.L. (2005). Detecting the learner's motivational states in an interactive learning environment. In *Proceedings of the 12th International Conference on Artificial Intelligence in Education (AIED'2005)*. Amsterdam, the Netherlands, July 18–22, 2005.

34. Zhang, G., Cheng, Z., He, A., and Huang, T. (2003). A WWW-based learner's learning motivation detecting system. In *Proceedings of the International Workshop on Research Directions and Challenge Problems in Advanced Information Systems Engineering, at the First International Conference on Knowledge Economy and Development of Science and Technology*. Honjo City, Japan, September 17, 2003.

35. Hwang, W.-Y. and Wang, C.-Y. (2004). A study of learning time patterns in asynchronous learning environments. *Journal of Computer Assisted Learning, 20*(4), 292–304.

36. Nachmias, R. and Hershkovitz, A. (2007). A case study of using visualization for understanding the behavior of the online learner. In *Proceedings of the International Workshop on Applying Data Mining in e-Learning, at the Second European Conference on Technology Enhanced Learning (EC-TEL'07)*. Crete, Greece, September 17–20, 2007.

37. Heyman, G.D. and Dweck, C.S. (1992). Achievement goals and intrinsic motivation: Their relation and their role in adaptive motivation. *Motivation and Emotion, 16*(3), 231–247.

38. Ryan, R.M. and Deci, E.L. (2000). Intrinsic and extrinsic motivations: Classic definitions and new directions. *Contemporary Educational Psychology, 25*(1), 54–67.

39. Castro, F., Vellido, A., Nebot, A., and Mugica, F. (2007). Applying data mining techniques to e-learning problems. In L.C. Jain, T. Raymond and D. Tedman (Eds.), *Evolution of Teaching and Learning Paradigms in Intelligent Environment*, Vol. 62, pp. 183–221. Springer-Verlag, Berlin, Germany.

40. Romero, C. and Ventura, S. (2007). Educational data mining: A survey from 1995 to 2005. *Expert Systems with Applications, 33*(1), 135–146.

21

Mining Student Discussions for Profiling Participation and Scaffolding Learning

Jihie Kim, Erin Shaw, and Sujith Ravi

CONTENTS

21.1 Introduction

Online discussion boards play an important role in distance education and Web-enhanced courses. Recent studies have pointed to online discussion boards as a promising strategy for promoting collaborative problem-solving courses and discovery-oriented activities [1,2]. However, other research indicates that existing systems for online discussion may not always be fully effective in promoting learning in undergraduate courses. For example, some analyses of collaborative online learning indicate that student participation is low or weak, even when students are encouraged to participate [3,4]. As course enrollments increase, with some introductory courses enrolling several hundred students, the heavier online interaction can place a considerable burden on instructors and teaching assistants. We are developing instructional tools that can automatically assess student participation and promote interactions.

In this chapter, we present two novel tools that apply data mining and information retrieval techniques. First, we describe an approach that scaffolds undergraduate student discussions by retrieving useful information from past student discussions. We first semiautomatically extract domain terms from textbooks specified for the courses, and use them in modeling individual messages with term vectors. We then apply term frequency and inverse document frequency (TF-IDF) [5] in retrieving useful information from past student discussions. The tool exploits both the discussions from the same undergraduate course and the ones from a graduate-level course that share similar topics. Our hypothesis is that since graduate discussions are full of rich, elucidating dialogues, those conversations can be recommended as interesting references for undergraduates. We also hypothesize that we can scaffold discussions by sending messages from past students who had similar assignments or problems regarding course topics. We analyze the usefulness of the retrieved information with respect to relevance and technical quality.

The second section of the chapter presents an instructional tool that profiles student contributions with respect to student genders and the roles that they play in discussions. The discussion threads are viewed as a special case of human conversation, and roles of a message with respect to its previous message are described with respect to speech acts (SAs) such as *question, answer, elaboration,* and/or *correction* [6]. We apply two SA classifiers: question classifier and answer classifier [6]. The question classifier identifies messages that play a role of asking questions, and the answer classifier detects messages with answers in response to a previous message. We use the classification results in profiling male and female student contributions.

We performed an initial evaluation of these tools in the context of an undergraduate operating systems course offered by the computer science department at the University of Southern California (USC). The current results for the scaffolding tool indicate that past discussions from the same course contain many similar concepts that we can use in guiding the discussions. Although graduate-level discussions did not contain many similar topics, their technical quality was higher. The initial results from the profiling tool show that female participation in undergraduate-level discussions is lower than that in graduate-level discussions, and graduate female students post more questions and answers compared to undergraduate female students.

21.2 Developing Scaffolding Capability: Mining Useful Information from Past Discussions

This section describes our approach to developing an instructional tool that scaffolds student discussions by retrieving useful information from past student discussions. The new scaffolding capability is built on top of an existing question answering (QA) module that sends responses to student queries [7]. First of all, in order to handle noisy student messages and retrieve more useful information for scaffolding, we extended the answer extraction procedure to focus on technical terms. We also expanded our corpus to include graduate-level courses so that graduate student conversations as well as undergraduate ones can be used. The retrieved information can be sent out as responses when discussion threads are short or stagnant. Figure 21.1 shows the system components and steps involved in retrieving responses. The following subsections explain the steps shown in the figure.

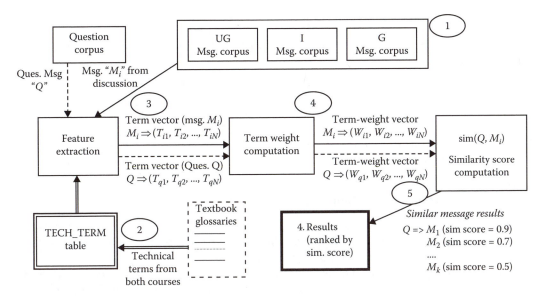

FIGURE 21.1
Mining relevant or similar messages from past discussions.

21.2.1 Step 1: Discussion Corpus Processing

We use discussion corpora from two operating systems: an undergraduate-level course and a graduate-level course. The undergraduate course is held every semester, and students and instructors have access to discussion boards to exchange information regarding various topics covered in the course. We first removed messages from administrative forums that contain nontechnical discussions. The undergraduate discussion corpus was created with data from four semesters, and consisted of 3788 messages from students and 531 messages from the instructor. The graduate discussion corpus available to us was comparatively smaller; it was obtained from two semesters and contained 957 messages. The past discussions from the two courses were divided into three corpora: (1) "UG"—undergraduate student messages, (2) "I"—messages posted by the instructor for the undergraduate course, and (3) "G"—messages from graduate student discussions. Step 1 in Figure 21.1 represents this process.

We found that discussion data from students, especially undergraduate students, are highly incoherent and noisy. The raw data include humorous messages and personal announcement as well as technical questions and answers. Student messages are very informal and there are high variances in the way they present similar information. A lot of messages on programming assignments also include programming code. Due to the noise and the highly informal nature of messages posted by students in the discussion forums, in modeling the messages for scaffolding, we use only technical terms present in the messages.

21.2.2 Step 2: Technical Term Processing

The technical terms that we use were extracted from the glossaries of the undergraduate and graduate textbooks. The glossaries were automatically scanned and processed. We created a "TECH_TERM" table that contains all the technical terms from both the courses. This corresponds to Step 2 in Figure 21.1.

21.2.3 Step 3: Term Vector Generation

Individual messages are then modeled with a term vector of the following form (Step 3 in Figure 21.1):

$$M_i = \langle T_{i1}, T_{i2}, ..., T_{iN} \rangle$$

where
  N is the total number of technical terms in the domain
  $T_{ij} = 0$ if a term is missing in that message

21.2.4 Step 4: Term Weight Computation

After term vectors are created for all messages in the corpus, the weights for the terms are computed. The weights are used in calculating similarity scores between messages, such as similarity of a new message and a message in a corpus.

In computing term weights, we use TF-IDF [5]. Messages with the same technical terms are more likely semantically related. This information is captured in term frequency (TF). TF tends to weight the commonly occurring terms more and give low weights to rare technical terms. Inverse document frequency (IDF) fixes it by introducing a general importance of the term. Equation 21.1 in Table 21.1 describes the method to compute individual TF-IDF weight values for each term. The term vector for each message is converted into a corresponding term-weight vector, where each term weight represents the TF-IDF measure for a particular technical term existing in the message (Step 4 in Figure 21.1).

Given a new message posted on the discussion board, a new term vector is created with term weights in the same way. We use cosine similarity to determine relevance between the new message and a message in the corpus (Equation 21.2 in Table 21.2). This measures the cosine of the angle between the two term-weight vectors representing the two messages. We rank messages by their scores in order to find the most relevant messages.

21.2.5 Step 5: Similarity Computation and Result Generation

We compare the given message with the messages from the three discussion corpora (UG, I, G) and compute their corresponding similarity scores. Once all the similarity scores are computed, we select the messages with the similarity score higher than 0.5. To ensure that

TABLE 21.1

TF-IDF Feature Weight Computation

$$W_{ik} = TF_{ik} \cdot \log\left(\frac{N}{n_k}\right) \tag{21.1}$$

where
  W_{ik} = TF-IDF weight for term k in document (message) M_i
  TF_{ik} = frequency of term k in document (message) M_i
  IDF_k = inverse document frequency of term k in the discussion corpus

  $$= \log\left(\frac{N}{n_k}\right)$$

  N = total number of documents (messages) in the discussion corpus
  n_k = number of messages in the discussion corpus that contain the term k

TABLE 21.2

Cosine Similarity Computation (between Document/Message Mi and Question Message Q)

$$\text{sim}(Q, M_i) = \frac{\sum_{k=1}^{n} w_{qk} \cdot w_{ik}}{\sqrt{\sum_{k=1}^{n} (w_{qk})^2 \cdot \sum_{k=1}^{n} (w_{ik})^2}} \tag{21.2}$$

where

$Q = (W_{q1}, W_{q2}, W_{q3}, ..., W_{qk}, ..., W_{qn})$
= feature-weight vector representing question message Q

$M_i = (W_{i1}, W_{i2}, W_{i3}, ..., W_{ik}, ..., W_{in})$
= feature-weight vector representing message M_i from the discussion corpus

$\text{sim}(Q, M_i)$ = similarity score between messages Q and M_i

w_{qk} = TF-IDF weight for feature term k in question message Q

w_{ik} = TF-IDF weight for feature term k in message M_i

there is some amount of technical content in the message, we retrieve the messages with at least three technical terms. The results can be sent as a response (Step 5 in Figure 21.1).

21.2.6 Step 6: Evaluation of System Responses

For evaluating usefulness of retrieved information, we created a new message corpus with a separate discussion data from a recent semester, Fall 2006. We removed administrative forums that contain nontechnical discussions as we did for existing corpora. We extracted the first messages in all the threads in the new corpus, which resulted in 207 messages. The messages were used in triggering the above procedure and retrieving relevant messages from the three corpora (UG, I, G). With UG and I, the system found responses for 132 and 71 messages, respectively. G provided answers for only 8 messages. Since there are many responses for some of the messages, the actual number of messages retrieved was large. We randomly selected 13 messages that have responses from UG and I. For the 13 messages there were 123 and 27 responses from UG and I, respectively. For G, we use all 8 messages and the system provided 13 responses for them. We designed the evaluation so that the human evaluators can perform the analysis in half a day. The evaluators had to examine about 150 message responses for the 13 questions, which took several hours.

Four human evaluators rated the system responses with respect to (1) technical quality and (2) degree of relevance to the given message. Figure 21.2 (left) shows the average ratings of technical quality. Messages with high quality would contain information pertaining to the operating systems course and related areas, and would convey some technical knowledge on the subject. Such messages may also present a deeper understanding of the subjects rather than providing shallow answers. Some student messages included humor, and other extra information besides technical discussions. This is especially true for undergraduate student discussions. The technical quality of undergraduate student messages does not seem as good as others. The messages from the instructor for the undergraduate course on the other hand are more specific and directed toward answering some questions/problems posed by students on the discussion board. The messages, in this case, contain more technical information and sometimes give detailed explanations for specific concepts or solutions to problems. However, in addition to these, the instructor corpus also contains many short messages with Yes/No answers, suggestions, or alternative approaches in response to specific questions posted by students. So, some of the

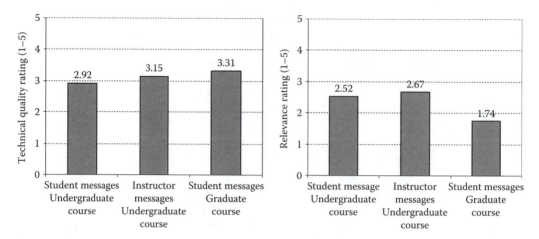

FIGURE 21.2
Evaluation results by human judges for technical quality and usefulness/relevance.

messages were rated lower than others. The number of messages retrieved from G is less. However, their technical quality seems a little better than that of the other two (3.31).

Figure 21.2 (right) shows the average ratings of relevance. In this case, the evaluators assessed the relevance of system responses to the given message. The evaluators checked "how useful the message is as a response" or "how related the message was to the given message." The UG results returned by the system tend to be less relevant (average rating ~2.52) to the given message than the ones from I (average rating ~2.67). The average rating for responses from G is the lowest (~1.74). Even though the graduate student messages tend to be more technical than the undergraduate student messages, they might not be fully relevant to the given undergraduate student message. Although there are some common topics between the undergraduate and the graduate courses, the kinds of problems that they are discussing seem different. In addition, we had a smaller set of data for G, which made it harder for the system to extract relevant results.

21.3 Profiling Student Participation with Gender Data and Speech Act Classifiers

In this section, we describe new SA classifiers that identify messages containing questions and answers [6], and use the results of the classification to report the message distribution for male and female students in two different courses.

21.3.1 Speech Act Classifiers

Within a thread, each text message plays a different role. A message may represent a question, an intermediate response, such as a clarification or correction, or a solution, such as a suggestion or answer. Inspired by the model of spoken dialogue SAs [8,9], we defined a set of SA categories that relate pairs of *text* messages in the discussion corpus. For example, a pair of messages in which the first message is an elaboration of the second is given the label "elaboration." Other SA categories include question, answer, correction, acknowledgment, etc.

We grouped the SAs to create two binary classifiers, one which identifies questions and the other which identifies answers in questions and answer-type discussion threads [6]. Using the question classifier, we identified the question messages posted by students from among all the messages in the corpus. The answer classifier was used similarly to identify the messages from the same corpus that contained answers or suggestions. Questions and answers occasionally appear in the same posts so that a particular message may be classified as both a question and an answer, that is, the identifications are not mutually exclusive.

The training set consisted of 1010 messages. The test set had 824 messages. Besides typical data preprocessing and cleaning steps taken by many natural language processing (NLP) systems, such as stemming and filtering, our system performs additional steps for removing noise and reducing variances.

We first remove the text from previous messages that is automatically inserted by the discussion board system when the user clicks on a reply-to button. We also apply a simple stemming algorithm that removes "s" and "es" for plurals. Since the corpus contains mostly technical discussions, it comprises many computer science concepts and terms including programming code fragments. Each section of programming code or code fragment is replaced with a single term called code. We then use a transformation algorithm that replaces common words or word sequences with special category names. For example, many pronouns like "I," "we," and "you" are replaced by the symbol categ_person and sequences of numbers by categ_number_seq. For "which," "where," "when," "who," and "how," we used the term categ_w_h. Similar substitution patterns were used for a number of categories like filetype extensions (".html," ".c," ".c++," ".doc"), URL links, and others. Students also tend to use informal words (e.g., "ya," "yeah," "yup") and typographical symbols such as smiley faces as acknowledgment, support, or compliment. We transform such words into consistent words or symbols. We also substitute words like 're, 'm, 've, don't, etc., with "are," "am," "have," "do not," etc. Finally, since SA tends to rely more on surface word patterns rather than technical terms used, technical terms occurring in the messages were replaced by a single word called tech_term.

For our classifiers, we use N-gram features that represent all possible sequences of N terms. That is, unigrams (single-word features), bigrams (sequence of two words), trigrams (sequence of three words), and quadrograms (sequence of four words) are used for training and building the classifier models. There were around 5000 unigrams or unique words occurring in the training corpus. Since the data was very noisy and incoherent, the feature space is larger and contains a lot of extraneous features.

We use information gain theory for pruning the feature space and selecting features from the whole set [10]. Information gain value for a particular feature gives a measure of the information gained in classification prediction, that is, how much the absence or the presence of the feature may affect the classification. First, we compute the information gain values for different N-gram features extracted from the training data (Equation 21.3 in Table 21.3). For each feature, we compute two values, one for the question classifier (called QC) and the other for the answer classifier (called AC). Subsequently, all the features (unigrams, bigrams, trigrams, and quadrograms) are sorted based on the information gain values. We use the top 200 features for each classifier. Some of the top N-gram features for QC and AC are shown in Table 21.4.

We use a linear support vector machine (SVM) implementation [11] to learn SA classifiers from the training data. Linear SVM is an efficient machine learning technique used

TABLE 21.3

Information Gain Computation for Features in Speech Act Classification

$$G(k) = -\left[P(C)\log P(C) + P(\bar{C})\log P(\bar{C})\right]$$

$$+ P(k)\cdot\left[P(C\,|\,k)\log P(C\,|\,k) + P(\bar{C}\,|\,k)\log P(\bar{C}\,|\,k)\right]$$

$$+ P(\bar{k})\cdot\left[P(C\,|\,\bar{k})\log P(C\,|\,\bar{k}) + P(\bar{C}\,|\,\bar{k})\log P(\bar{C}\,|\,\bar{k})\right] \qquad (21.3)$$

where

    k = feature term k present in message
    $\bar{k}$ = feature term k not present in message
    C = message belongs to class C (e.g., *question*)
    $\bar{C}$ = message does not belong to class C (e.g., *not a question*)
    $G(k)$ = information gain corresponding to feature k

TABLE 21.4

Top N grams Based on Information Gain

Category	1-Gram	2-Gram	3-Gram	4-Gram
QUES	?	do [categ_person]	[categ_w_h] should	do [categ_person] have to
	[categ_w_h]	[tech_term] ?	[categ_person]	do [categ_person] need to
	will	can	[categ_person] was	[tech_term] [tech_term]
	do	[categ_person]	wondering	[tech_term] ?
	confused	is there	[or/and] do [categ_person]	is there a better
		? thanks	is there a	does this mean that
			the [tech_term] ?	
ANS	Yes	look at	look at the	[categ_person] am a
	am	[or/and] do	for example,	[tech_term]
	helps	seems like	. [categ_person] should	do [categ_person] have to
	but	in [tech_term]	let [me/him/her/us] know	look at the [tech_term]
	depends	stated in	not seem to	in the same [tech_term]
				[tech_term] is not
				[tech_term]

often in text classification and categorization problems. We constructed feature vectors for all the messages in the corpus. A feature vector of a message consisted of a list of values for individual features that represent whether the features existed in the message or not. We perform fivefold cross-validation experiments on the training data to set kernel parameter values for the linear SVM. After we ran SVM, the resulting classifiers (QC and AC) were then used to predict the SAs for the feature vectors in the test set. QC tells whether a particular message contains question content or not, and AC predicts whether a message contains answer content, that is, answers or suggestions. The classification was then compared with the human annotations. The resulting QC and AC had accuracies of 88% and 73%, respectively [6].

21.3.2 Gender Classifier/Distribution

Using the new classifiers, we then analyzed student participation by gender for two discussion board datasets. The undergraduate corpus contained messages from threaded discussions in an undergraduate-level operating systems course at USC; the graduate corpus contained messages from discussions in a graduate-level operating systems course. We used the question and answer classifiers on each discussion set to identify the messages containing questions and answers, respectively, within the set. We used the results to compare types of posts (question or answer), classes (undergraduate or graduate), and students (by gender).

The undergraduate corpus contained 699 student-posted messages, out of which we identified 370 question messages and 157 answer messages. The graduate corpus contained 154 student-posted messages, out of which we identified 85 question messages and 26 answer messages.

In our analysis, we consider only those messages that are classified as either a "Question" or "Answer" or "Both" by the SA classifiers. Table 21.5 shows the gender distribution of both the total number of students registered in a course and the number of students who contribute to discussions in a course. In the undergraduate course, 89% of students are male and 11% are female; in the graduate course, 86.4% are male and 13.6% are female. Not all of the registered students participate in discussions: In the undergraduate course, 91.3% of the students who participate in discussions are male and 8.7% are female. In the graduate course, the percentage of participating female students increases to 12.5% of participating students.

Table 21.6 gives the gender distribution of the types of messages posted in both the courses. In the undergraduate course, most of the questions and answers are posted by male students. In comparison, female students in the graduate course post a higher percentage of messages, especially questions.

21.3.3 An Application of Gender Classifier/Distribution

This type of classification can help us better analyze how students are using a discussion board. For example, it could help determine if female students prefer text-based discussion

TABLE 21.5

Male/Female Student Distribution (Registered/Participating) in the Two Courses

Course	Students	Males (%)	Females (%)
Undergraduate	Among total students registered	89	11
	Among students posting messages (participating in discussions)	91.3	8.7
Graduate	Among total students registered	86.4	13.6
	Among students posting messages (participating in discussions)	87.5	12.5

TABLE 21.6

Male/Female Student Participation by Message Type

Course	Message Type	Males (%)	Females (%)
Undergraduate	Question messages	97	3
	Answer messages	96	4
Graduate	Question messages	78	22
	Answer messages	88	12

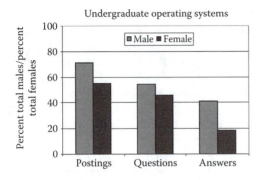
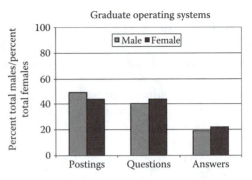

FIGURE 21.3
Comparison of participation by gender in undergraduate and graduate courses.

as a means of communication/collaboration in highly technical courses. The question is of interest to the science, technology, engineering, and math (STEM) research community, especially those interested in gender issues. We used the classifier to generate the results shown in Figure 21.3. Results are mixed: in the undergraduate course (left) female students as a group posted fewer questions and answers than male students as a group. However, the reverse was true for female graduate students (right): Though they posted fewer messages overall, a greater percentage of females posted more questions and more answers than that of males.

Graduate-level female students appear to engage more actively in discussions than undergraduate female students and utilize the discussion board as a collaborative tool to help in their learning. These results may be used for further pedagogical analysis, to develop techniques to help instructors better assess student participation from the discussions, which has the potential to increase and improve participation so as to promote a better understanding of the subject topics.

21.4 Related Work

Developing automatic natural language–based QA systems has been a field of research for many years [12,13], but QA in an open domain is still an unsolved problem. Much research in the NLP community has focused on developing techniques to understand and answer user queries. QA systems provide a general framework for parsing questions, searching documents, and retrieving relevant answers. Some QA systems employ semantic- and ontology-based approaches. Most systems assume that queries are concise, coherent, and of a particular form (e.g., a factoid question), and can be answered with short phrases. But queries posted to a discussion board often span multiple sentences, are incoherent (in the computational sense), and include extra (informal) content and lengthy descriptions, especially in technical discussions. Providing QA support for student discussions still remains a challenge.

The goals of our system include (1) referring students to relevant past discussions from related courses, (2) promoting interactions among students, and (3) aiding instructional assessment through automatic tools that assess quality and participation, all of which contribute to a better learning environment for students. Related work on dialogue modeling investigates different ways to manage continuous dialogue for personal assistants [14] or scaffold conversations in a virtual meeting space [15]. In contrast, we focus on optimizing a one-step question response by mining knowledge from archived materials asynchronously. More similarly, some systems can generate helpdesk responses using clustering techniques [16], but their corpus is composed of two-party, two-turn conversation pairs, which makes it easier to bypass the complex analysis of discussions among multiple parties.

In the area of online learning, much attention has been paid to the analysis of student learning behaviors in online communications. Various frameworks have been proposed for characterizing and analyzing computer-mediated communications in the context of collaborative discussions [17], e-mail and chat exchanges [18], knowledge sharing [19], and general argumentation [20,21], but none have been sufficiently relevant or fine grained to facilitate data mining and answer extraction in threaded discussions.

21.5 Summary and Discussion

This chapter presents some approaches for mining information automatically and building tools to help students participating in online discussions using various natural language processing and machine learning techniques. Our work focuses on technical discussions among students enrolled in operating systems courses at both the undergraduate and graduate levels. We first presented an automated way of helping students asking questions in discussion boards by retrieving useful messages and related discussions from the past both from the same course and from a graduate-level course. Next, we used automatic SA classifiers to classify student messages as questions or answers and used this to analyze the distribution of student participation by gender. We performed the analysis for both undergraduate- and graduate-level discussions and presented our results.

In order to improve the quality of the results and extract better and more relevant/related answers from past graduate discussions for questions posted by undergraduates, we plan to include more discussion data and additional features, such as topics discussed, and analyze the significance of the results. We are also looking at statistical models to infer and extract semantic information and relations from the messages posted on the discussion board. Another interesting study that we wish to perform in the future is to distinguish the answer messages based on the complexity—short answers vs. complex answers—and perform a separate analysis on each type. We also plan to extend participation profiling with topic analysis and contribution changes over time.

References

1. Scardamalia, M. and Bereiter, C., Computer support for knowledge building communities. In: T. Koschmann (Ed.), *CSCL: Theory and Practice of an Emerging Paradigm*. Mahwah, NJ: Erlbaum, 1996.
2. Koschmann, T. (Ed.), *CSCL: Theory and Practice of an Emerging Paradigm*. Hillsdale, NJ: Lawrence Erlbaum, 1996.

3. Pallof, R.M. and Pratt, K., *Building Learning Communities in Cyberspace: Effective Strategies for the Online Classroom*. San Francisco, CA: Jossey-Bass, 1999.
4. Kim, J. and Beal, C., Turning quantity into quality: Supporting automatic assessment of on-line discussion contributions. *American Educational Research Association (AERA) Annual Meeting*, San Francisco, CA, 2006.
5. Salton, G., *Automatic Text Processing: The Transformation, Analysis, and Retrieval of Information by Computer*. Reading, MA: Addison-Wesley, 1989.
6. Ravi, S. and Kim, J., Profiling student interactions in threaded discussions with speech act classifiers. *Proceedings of AI in Education Conference*, Los Angeles, CA, 2007.
7. Feng, D., Shaw, E., Kim, J., and Hovy, E.H., An intelligent discussion-bot for answering student queries in threaded discussions. *Proceedings of International Conference on Intelligent User Interfaces*, Sydney, Australia, pp. 171–177, 2006.
8. Austin, J., *How to Do Things with Words*. Cambridge, MA: Harvard University Press, 1962.
9. Searle, J., *Speech Acts*. Cambridge, U.K.: Cambridge University Press, 1969.
10. Yang, Y. and Pedersen, J.O., A comparative study on feature selection in text categorization. *Proceedings of the 14th International Conference on Machine Learning*, Nashville, TN, pp. 412–420, 1997.
11. Chang, C.-C. and C.-J. Lin, LIBSVM: A library for support vector machines. *Journal of Machine Learning Research*, 1, 161–177, 2001.
12. Hermjakob, U., Hovy, E.H., and Lin, C., Knowledge-based question answering. *Proceedings of Text Retrieval Conference*, Gaithersburg, Maryland, 2000.
13. Pasca, M. and Harabagiu, S., High performance question/answering. *Proceedings of SIGIR*, New Orleans, LA, pp. 366–374, 2001.
14. Nguyen, A. and Wobcke, W., An agent-based approach to dialogue management in personal assistants. *Proceedings of International Conference on Intelligent User Interfaces*, San Diego, CA, pp. 137–144, 2005.
15. Isbister, K., Nakanishi, H., Ishida, T., and Nass, C., Helper agent: Designing an assistant for human-human interaction in a virtual meeting space. *Proceeding of the Computer Human Interaction Conference*, Hayama-machi, Japan, pp. 57–64, 2000.
16. Marom, Y. and Zukerman, I., Corpus-based generation of easy help-desk responses. Technical Report. School of Computer Science and Software Engineering, Monash University, 2005.
17. Shaw, E., Assessing and scaffolding collaborative learning in online discussion. *Proceedings of Artificial Intelligence in Education Conference*, Amsterdam, the Netherlands, pp. 587–594, 2005.
18. Cakir, M., Xhafa, F., Zhou, N., and Stahl, G., Thread-based analysis of patterns of collaborative interaction in chat. *Proceedings of Artificial Intelligence in Education Conference*, Amsterdam, the Netherlands, pp. 716–722, 2005.
19. Soller, A. and Lesgold, A., Computational approach to analyzing online knowledge sharing interaction. *Proceedings of Artificial Intelligence in Education Conference*, Sydney Australia, 2003.
20. Feng, D., Kim, J., Shaw, E., and Hovy E., Towards modeling threaded discussions through ontology-based analysis. *Proceedings of National Conference on Artificial Intelligence*, Boston, MA, 2006.
21. Painter, C., Coffin, C., and Hewings, A., Impacts of directed tutorial activities in computer conferencing: A case study. *Distance Education*, 24(2), 159–173, 2003.

22

Analysis of Log Data from a Web-Based Learning Environment: A Case Study

Judy Sheard

CONTENTS

22.1 Introduction

Web-based learning environments in the form of a course Web site or a learning management system are used extensively in tertiary education. When providing such an environment, an educator will generally have an expectation for how it will be used by students; however, often this does not match actual usage. Students may access the learning environment at different rates or for different times, or for purposes other than those intended by their educator. A Web-based learning environment is typically complex and there are various determinants for usage, which may relate to the technology, the teaching program, or the student. Information about how students use such an environment is important for effective design of an education program, but difficult to gain using traditional evaluation methods. The aim of this study was to investigate the usage of a Web-based learning environment from analysis of student interactions with the environment. The Web-based learning environment explored was a Web site developed to support and monitor students working on a capstone project.

The questions that guided this investigation were

- How frequently and when did students access the Web site?
- What resources did students use?
- What time did students spend at the Web site?
- What were the patterns of use over the year?
- Were there any differences in usage based on gender or on course performance?

This case study will serve to illustrate data collection and preparation techniques, and the type of information that can be gained from statistical analysis of the data gathered using the techniques described in Chapter 3.

22.2 Context of the Study

Students in their final year of an IT degree at an Australian university undertake a capstone project in which they design, develop, and deliver a computer system for an external client. The project runs for two consecutive semesters and comprises one quarter of the normal workload for the final year of this degree program. Students are typically organised into groups of five for their project work, providing them with real life experience in project coordination and management. A fuller description of this course can be found elsewhere [1].

The Web Industrial Experience Resources (WIER) Web site was developed by staff in the university as a Web-based learning environment for capstone project work [2]. More information about the development of WIER is provided elsewhere. WIER offered a comprehensive range of resources to assist students with their project work. These were accessed via a page or group of linked pages on the Web site. Taking a logical perspective, these could be viewed as resources within the WIER domain. At the time of this study, there were 25 different resources identified on WIER that were accessible by students. These included a task and time recorder (Time Tracker—old and new versions), a graph to show project progress (Time Graph), a file management facility (File Manager), an event scheduling calendar (Event Scheduler) and a risk management facility (Risk Manager) and various forms of communication facilities. Also included were pages providing access to repositories of standards documents, document templates, and examples of past projects. All students were required to use WIER to at least record their project tasks and times.

To aid meaningful analysis of student usage of WIER, all pages within the Web site that were accessible by students were classified as belonging to a particular resource. For example, pages used to record or view a project time were classified under Time Tracker and the page that held the timetable of events was classified under Event Scheduler. Over 144 pages were classified in this way.

22.3 Study Method

22.3.1 Participants

WIER Web site interactions data were collected for students enrolled in an IT capstone project. In this cohort, there were 258 students organized into 53 project groups. There were 182 (71%) male and 76 (29%) female students. For the purpose of comparison, the top 25% of the students according to their final project result were classified as the *high-achieving* group and the bottom 25% were classified as the *low-achieving* group.

22.3.2 Data Collection and Integration

All online interactions with WIER were automatically collected, and centrally recorded in a database. The data collection period of 41 weeks covered the entire period of time that most of the students used WIER for their project work. The Web site was instrumented to capture details of each interaction. This involved adding code to each page on the Web site to write information to a central database. The information recorded for each interaction comprised the interaction identification, page URL, interaction time, session identification, and user identification. In addition, student demographic information and project results were recorded in the database to enable comparisons to be made on the bases of gender and course performance. Also recorded in the database was a classification for each web page as belonging to a resource to enable analysis of student usage of particular resources.

22.4 Data Preparation

The main purpose of the data preparation process was to prepare files in a suitable format for statistical analysis in a standard statistical package. The tasks involved the definition of data abstractions, the construction of data files of different abstractions, and the removal of outlier records for time-based data.

The design of the Web site and modifications made to record the interactions data enabled more information to be recorded for each interaction than is typically found in log file data. In particular, a login mechanism enabled the identification of the students and the recording of session identities. The identification of the students allowed the integration of the demographic data of the project group identity, gender, and final project results. The cleaning of the log file data only involved the removal of outliers. It was not necessary to remove irrelevant entries as each interaction that was recorded represented a single-page access. In addition, it was not necessary to determine missing data as caching was disabled and students were not able to use the back button as the post method was used on form requests.

22.4.1 Abstraction Definitions

Four different abstractions of the log file data were defined as follows:

1. *Page view*—a single interaction recorded on the log file.
2. *Session*—a sequence of interactions of a user from a login to the last interaction with the Web site before logging out or moving to another Web site and not returning.

3. *Task*—a sequence of interactions of a user within one resource, for example, the Time Tracker or File Manager. The elapsed time for a task was calculated by measuring the time interval from the first interaction within a resource until the last interaction with that resource or the first interaction with another resource within the same session.

4. *Activity*—a series of one or more interactions with the Web site to achieve a particular outcome. In the context of the WIER Web site, examples of learning activities were as follows: recording a task time in the Time Tracker, posting a newsgroup item, uploading a file to the File Manager or navigating to another resource. Not all activities were taken to completion and in many sessions there were a mixture of completed and partial activities.

The specification of the activities was a complex process involving the Web site developer and the capstone project coordinator. A software tool was written specifically for this process [3]. There were over 144 ways in which students could interact with WIER, equivalent to the number of pages on the Web site. Each possible student interaction with the Web site was examined to determine its purpose and then it was defined as an activity or a component of an activity. Using this method, every interaction was identified as part of one or more activities and a series of templates of activity abstractions was prepared. As a verification of these templates, all possible student activities on WIER were performed and each activity definition matched to the log file scripts generated. The templates may be seen as forming the educator model of the Web site [4].

22.4.2 Data File Construction

In order to perform the analysis in the statistical software SPSS (Statistical Package for the Social Sciences), it was necessary to prepare a file at each abstraction level. First, a log file containing records of individual interactions was extracted from the database. Each record contained details of the interaction and demographic data. This was, in effect, a page view abstraction file. Second, session, task, and activity abstraction files were prepared from the page-view file, using software developed for this purpose [3]. Each record on these files contained summary information of the abstraction including the time period of the session, task, or activity, and demographic data. The extraction of the learning activities from the log file of student interactions involved the identification of the sequences of interactions according to the activity templates. A total of 111 different types of activities were extracted from the log file from a possible 112 defined activities. An extra data item was included in the activity file records to indicate whether or not the activity had been completed.

22.4.3 Data Cleaning: Removal of Outliers

A filtering process was used to remove any task, session, and activity abstractions that had excessively long intervals between interactions as these had probably recorded periods of inactivity. In the preparation of the session, task, and activity abstraction files, the maximum interaction interval for each abstraction was recorded in the abstraction record. In this study, the abstraction records were filtered using a maximum interaction interval limit of 10 min, as determined from a previous study [5]. It was decided to use the same interaction interval limit for all times calculated for access to all resources or performing all activities. A refinement of this technique could vary the interaction interval limits depending on the type of resource or activity, as discussed in Redpath and Sheard [6].

22.5 Data Analysis Methods

Statistical analysis of the four abstraction files (page view, task, session, and activity) was performed using SPSS. Both parametric and nonparametric analysis techniques were used and were chosen for their appropriateness and robustness. The decisions as to the appropriateness of the techniques were based on the levels of measurement of the data items and their distributional characteristics [7]. The basic measures and descriptive and statistical analysis techniques used for the different data collected were as follows:

- *Counts and frequencies at each level of abstraction*: The frequencies of page views, sessions, tasks, and activities were used to give measures of Web site usage and were described using totals, percentages, and medians. The distributions of these frequencies over line periods and student groups showed high skewness and kurtosis, and outlying data. These indicated that medians rather than means were more appropriate measures of central tendency for these distributions.

- *Comparisons of counts and frequencies across time periods and student groups*: The frequencies of page views, sessions, tasks, and activities were compared using Mann–Whitney U and Kruskal Wallis tests. The nonconformance with normality of these distributions meant that nonparametric statistical tests were more appropriate than parametric tests.

- *Length of time of sessions, tasks, and activity abstractions*: The total time for all sessions was calculated for each student. This was used to give a measure of the mean times students spent using the Web site each week. The session, task, and activity times were used to give measures of Web site usage and were described using totals, percentages, and medians. The distribution of these times showed high positive skewness and kurtosis, indicating that medians were more appropriate descriptive statistics than means.

- *Comparisons of session, task, and activity times*: The session, task, and activity times between groups of students were compared using Mann–Whitney U and Kruskal Wallis tests. The nonconformance with normality meant that nonparametric statistical tests were more appropriate than parametric tests.

- *Counts of interactions within activity sequences*: The lengths of activity sequences were used to give a measure of activity performance efficiency. The lengths were compared using Mann–Whitney U and Kruskal Wallis tests. Spearman's rank-order correlation coefficients were used to search for relationships.

- *Percentages of completed activities*: Chi-square tests were used to test for comparisons of complete and partially complete activities.

- *Comparisons of variances of frequency distributions*: The variances of the frequency of the performance of activities between different semesters of the project were compared using Levene's homogeneity of variance test. This test does not assume conformance to normality.

22.6 Analysis Results

The aim of the study was to explore the learning behavior of the students over the course of their capstone project. The following are samples of the findings from the analysis of the data set presented at each level of abstraction. This serves to demonstrate the analysis and the type of information possible at each level of abstraction.

22.6.1 Page View Abstraction

Analysis at the page view abstraction gives basic information about student usage of the Web site. For this abstraction, counts and frequencies of interactions can be analyzed to show when and how much the students interacted with the site.

22.6.1.1 Sample Findings

There were 683,767 student interactions recorded on the WIER Web site during the 41 week data collection period of the project.

The students recorded 34,319 sessions giving a mean of three sessions per week over the 41 weeks of data collection. There was a huge variation in the number of sessions recorded per student. Over the period of the data collection, the number of sessions ranged from 32 to 604 per student. The median number of sessions for the high-achieving students was 128 compared with 76 for the low-achieving students, and a Mann–Whitney U test indicated this difference was significant ($U = 1341$, $p < 0.01$). There was no difference in the frequency of access based on gender.

22.6.2 Session Abstraction

Analysis at the session level of abstraction gives information about student engagement with the Web site. For this abstraction, the duration of sessions can be analyzed to show how long the students spent at the site and when this occurred.

22.6.2.1 Sample Findings

The mean time that each student spent on the WIER Web site per week was 15 min 17 s.

The high-achieving students spent more time than the low-achieving students using WIER. The mean time high-achieving students spent on the WIER Web site per week was 19 min and 31 s compared with 12 min and 36 s for low-achieving students. A comparison of total access times using a Mann–Whitney U test indicated a significant difference ($U = 1448$, $p < 0.01$). There was no difference in mean access times per week based on gender.

The session-level abstractions file was a convenient format for graphing the frequency of sessions. For example, the frequency of sessions over the course of the project is shown in Figure 22.1, the frequency of session over a day is shown in Figure 22.2, and the frequency of sessions over a week is shown in Figure 22.3. These graphs indicate that students used WIER more during the daytime and more on weekdays than at other times. The pattern of use over the course of the project varied greatly, but was explainable when considering the project schedule and other commitments. For example, there was high usage in weeks 2–5 when the Web site was introduced and there were a number of initial administrative tasks, and low usage occurred in weeks 15–17, which was during the exam period. Similar patterns of use were found in an earlier study of WIER [8].

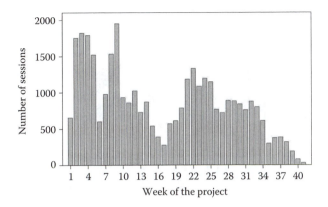

FIGURE 22.1
Frequency of sessions on WIER per week of the project.

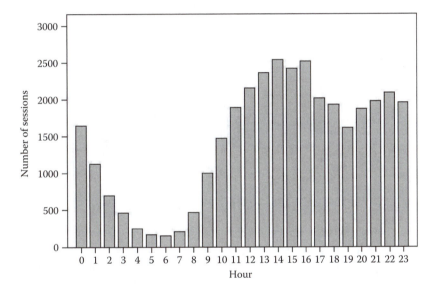

FIGURE 22.2
Frequency of sessions on WIER per hour of the day.

22.6.3 Task Abstraction

Analysis at the task level of abstraction gives information about the areas of the Web site that the students used. Using similar analysis to that used for the session analysis, analysis at this level focuses attention on the resources on the Web site and how long the students spent using these resources and when they were used.

22.6.3.1 Sample Findings

There were huge variations in the frequency of access to the different resources on the WIER Web site, as shown in Figure 22.4. The most frequently accessed resources were the Time Trackers, File Manager, and Time Graph. In addition, comparison of total access times showed that the students spent most of their time on these four resources and very

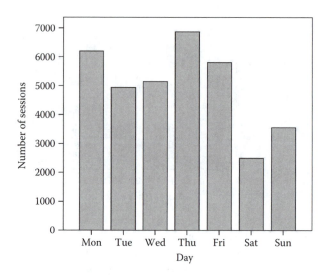

FIGURE 22.3
Frequency of sessions on WIER per day of the week.

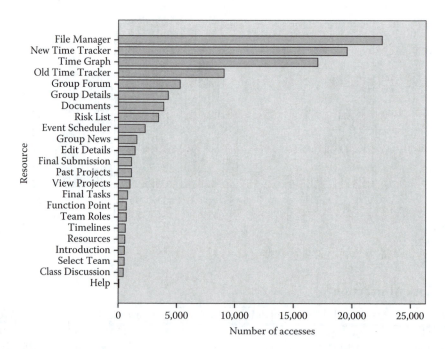

FIGURE 22.4
Frequency of access to resources.

low proportions of time on each of the other resources. There were far fewer accesses to and time spent on the communication resources (Group Forum, Group News, and Class Discussion). Further analysis showed that the File Manager was the last resource accessed in more than half the sessions, providing an indication that File Manager tasks were the main purpose of these visits [9].

The median number of accesses to the File Manager for the high-achieving students was 80 compared with 53 for the low-achieving students, and a Mann–Whitney U test indicated this difference was significant ($U=1389$, $p<0.05$). Furthermore, the high-achieving students spent more time than the low-achieving students using the File Manager. The median total time spent on the File Manager for the high-achieving students was 254 min and 18 s compared with 131 min and 19 s for the low-achieving students, and a Mann–Whitney U test indicated that this difference was significant ($U=1430$, $p<0.05$).

There was no difference in frequency of access to the File Manager based on gender, however, the female students spent more time in using the File Manager than the male students. The median total time spent on the File Manager for the female students was 195 min and 51 s compared with 156 min and 21 s for the male students, and a Mann–Whitney U test indicated this difference was significant ($U=5753$, $p<0.01$). A similar result was found with the use of the New Time Tracker. For this resource, the median total time spent for the female students was 316 min and 46 s compared with 245 min and 23 s for the male students, and a Mann–Whitney U test indicated this difference was significant ($U=5722$, $p<0.05$).

22.6.4 Activity Abstraction

Analysis at the activity level of abstraction gives information about what the students were doing during their visits. This data can also be analyzed to give information about task performance and learning behavior.

22.6.4.1 Sample Findings

Most activities were performed more by the high-achieving students. In contrast, only one activity, *download file* in the Document Templates, was performed more by low-achieving students. There were very few differences based on gender.

The activity with the highest number of occurrences was the *log time* activity in the Old and New Time Trackers. This was a mandatory activity for the purpose of recording times spent working on various project tasks. The students were expected to record their times regularly and at least once a week; however, there were indications that a number were not doing this. There was a mean of approximately three completed *log time* activities per week per student over the course of the project, with 35 students recording a mean of less than two activities per week. This indicates that these students engaged less than expected with the project work and/or the task recording facility. The differences in performance of *log time* activities according to performance and gender were tested using Mann–Whitney U tests. These indicated that the high-achieving students performed this activity more frequently than the low-achieving students in both the New Time Tracker ($U=1048$, $p<0.01$) and the Old Time Tracker ($U=458$, $p<0.05$). There were no significant differences according to gender.

To determine any trend in activity efficiency, the data collection period was divided into three 13 week periods (excluding the first and last weeks) and the sequence lengths of successful activities for these periods were compared using a Kruskal Wallis test. This indicated that the length of the sequences decreased over the course of the project, χ^2 (2, $N=752$) $=9.41$, $p<0.01$, thus indicating that the students became more efficient over time in their performance of activities. There were no differences found based on gender or performance.

Long activity sequences could indicate that students were using a resource in an inefficient way and perhaps having difficulty performing the activity. For a *log time* activity, the minimum sequence length was three interactions. Cross tabulations with a chi-square test indicated that low-achieving students recorded more sequences of length greater than three than high-achieving students, χ^2 (1, $N = 1531$) = 8.18, $p < 0.01$. This suggested that the high-achieving students used the resource more efficiently and appeared to have less difficulty in performing tasks. There was no difference based on gender.

The analyses of the frequency of activities showed that students became more regular in their work habits over the course of the IE Project. For example, the comparison of the frequency of download file and upload file activities on a weekly basis indicated that more consistent access to files occurred in the second semester than the first semester (refer Figures 22.5 and 22.6). The variations in frequencies of access were compared using Levene's test of the homogeneity of variance. This indicated a difference in the variances between the two semesters and this was significant at $p < 0.01$.

22.7 Discussion

The usage of the WIER Web site and resources in terms of frequency of access and time spent at the site provided insights into student learning behavior. The daily, weekly, and whole project patterns of access to WIER indicate that it supported a variety of work styles. Students became more regular and efficient in the performance of activities over the course of the project.

The level of the use of resources and performance of activities show that students were very functional in their use of this learning environment. Huge differences were found in the level of engagement within each resource. The students engaged most with facilities that were mandated and assessed. A notable exception was the File Manager,

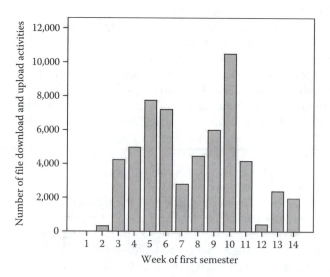

FIGURE 22.5
Frequency of file uploads and downloads per week of the first semester.

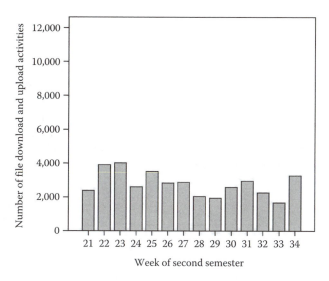

FIGURE 22.6
Frequency of file uploads and downloads per week of the second semester.

which students were not required to use, but apparently found useful. The least-used resources were those provided for communication and collaboration. Students have a number of ways to communicate and work together on project tasks and most did not choose to do this through WIER. This highlighted a mismatch between how the educators intended WIER to be used and how the students wanted to work and suggests that educator participation and guidance may be necessary to encourage students to engage in this way.

Comparisons of usage based on student performance showed a greater use of WIER by the high-achieving students, giving indications of the value of WIER for their work. As an example, the greater engagement with the Time Tracker activities by the high-achieving students appears to indicate a more thorough and explicit analysis and recording of the details of their project work. In contrast, the higher use of the download file activity in the Document Templates by the weaker students indicates that they may have been seeking extra guidance in the form of examples to follow. This type of information is potentially useful to educators. Monitoring student use of particular Web site resources can be used to determine students who are having difficulty with their work or are at risk of not achieving a successful outcome.

The analysis of activities based on gender gave further insights into diversity in behavior. The female students spent more time using the Time Tracker and File Manager, indicating they may take on more administrative roles in the project groups. This was supported by the analysis of the activities in these resources. From an educational perspective, such allocations of project roles have been found to be inappropriate by the capstone project coordinators and this particular finding encouraged the coordinators to review the role-allocation processes within the groups.

Overall, the results indicated that the capstone project coordinators' expectations were not necessarily in line with the ways students wanted to learn. Students will use and adapt technology to suit their own needs. This highlights the value in understanding student work styles and preferences in order to provide an environment that is useful and valuable to them.

22.8 Conclusions

The analysis of interactions data at page view, session, task, and activity abstractions, as demonstrated by this study of a courseware Web site, extends the type of usage analysis typically conducted on student interactions data. This type of analysis can lead to deeper insights into student learning behaviors, providing valuable information that may be used by educators and Web site designers when making decisions about their teaching programs, learning environment, and resources. The ultimate goal is to create useful and usable learning environments for students.

References

1. Hagan, D., Tucker, S., and Ceddia, J. 1999. Industrial experience projects: A balance of process and product. *Computer Science Education*, **9**(3): 106–113.
2. Ceddia, J., Tucker, S., Clemence, C., and Cambrell, A. 2001. WIER—Implementing artifact reuse in an educational environment with real projects. In *Proceedings of 31st Annual Frontiers in Education Conference*, Reno, NV, pp. 1–6.
3. Ceddia, J., Sheard, J., and Tibbey, G. 2007. WAT: A tool for classifying learning activities from a log file. In *Proceedings of Ninth Australasian Computing Education conference (ACE2007)*, Ballarat, Australia, Australian Computer Society, pp. 11–17.
4. Ceddia, J. and Sheard, J. 2005. Log files for educational applications. In *Proceedings of World Conference on Educational Multimedia, Hypermedia and Telecommunications (ED-MEDIA 2005)*, Montreal, Canada, Association for the Advancement of Computing in Education (AACE): Norfolk, VA, pp. 4566–4573.
5. Sheard, J., Ceddia, J., Hurst, J., and Tuovinen, J. 2003. Determining Website usage time from interactions: Data preparation and analysis. *Journal of Educational Technology Systems*, **32**(1): 101–121.
6. Redpath, R. and Sheard, J. 2005. Domain knowledge to support understanding and treatment of outliers. In *Proceedings of International Conference on Information and Automation (ICIA 2005)*, Colombo, Sri Lanka, pp. 398–403.
7. Burns, R. 2000. *Introduction to Research Methods*, 4th ed. 2000, London, U.K.: Sage Publications Ltd.
8. Sheard, J., Ceddia, J., Hurst, J., and Tuovinen, J. 2003. Inferring student learning behaviour from Website interactions: A usage analysis. *Journal of Education and Information Technologies*, **8**(3): 245–266.
9. Buttenfield, B.P. and Reitsma, R.F. 2002. Loglinear and multidimensional scaling models of digital library navigation. *International Journal of Human-Computer Studies*, **57**: 101–119.

23

Bayesian Networks and Linear Regression Models of Students' Goals, Moods, and Emotions

Ivon Arroyo, David G. Cooper, Winslow Burleson, and Beverly P. Woolf

CONTENTS

23.1 Introduction

If computers are to interact naturally with humans, they should recognize students' affect and express social competencies. Research has shown that learning is enhanced when empathy or support is provided and that improved personal relationships between teachers and students leads to increased student motivation.[1-4] Therefore, if tutoring systems can embed affective support for students, they should be more effective. However, previous research has tended to privilege the cognitive over the affective and to view learning as information processing, marginalizing, or ignoring affect.[5] This chapter describes two data-driven approaches toward the automatic prediction of affective variables by creating models from students' past behavior (log-data). The first case study shows the methodology and accuracy of an empirical model that helps predict students' general attitudes, goals, and perceptions of the software, and the second develops empirical models for predicting students' fluctuating emotions while using the system. The vision is to use these models to predict students' learning and positive attitudes in real time. Special emphasis is placed in this chapter on understanding and inspecting these models, to understand how students express their emotions, attitudes, goals, and perceptions while using a tutoring system.

23.2 Predicting Goals and Attitudes

The first case study demonstrates a methodology for predicting students' attitudes and goals from their behavior within the tutor. In earlier research,[6] a taxonomy of help seeking bugs and possible hints was created to encourage positive behavior. In other research,[7] a Bayesian model was used to infer students' emotions and personality in a mathematics game. Later work from these same authors[27] has used student goals collected from a pretest survey to help predict student emotions within the tutor. Instead, this work tries to understand student goals and attitudes to take remedial action upon the appearance of goals that are unproductive (e.g., performance orientation goals, or clear goals that indicate a desire to not use the system). Corrective action does not necessarily have to come from the system itself, but could consist of informing the teacher, so that he or she takes corrective action.

Crude generic descriptors of students' behavior in a tutoring system were used to predict students' goals, attitudes, and learning for a large database of student actions. Some of the behaviors may reflect unproductive students' behavior that has been studied in the past, and classified as "gaming" behavior, e.g., clicking through hints to get the right answer.[8] In this section, we present statistics that show that such dependencies do exist, describe how the Bayesian network created from data, and evaluate its accuracy.

23.2.1 Data Description

The data used in the first case study comes from a population of 230 high school students from two schools in rural and urban areas of Massachusetts. Students used Wayang Outpost, a multimedia web-based tutoring system for high school mathematics.[9–10] Wayang Outpost provides step-by-step instruction to students in the form of animations supplemented with sound, which help students solve mathematics problems. All actions taken by students or system are logged in a database in a central server, allowing researchers to extract variables such as time spent, the number of problems seen, and the speed of response for each student. Students took a mathematics pretest and then used Wayang Outpost for about 2–3 h during a week's time. After using the tutor, students took a mathematics posttest and took a survey that asked them about their goals when using the system, how they felt about mathematics and the tutoring system. Table 23.1 shows the specific questions asked to the student, with code names for each question (in bold). In addition, we identified features that describe student behaviors, specific ways in which they interacted with the system. These summaries of student behavior fall into four categories: (1) *Problem-solving behavior*, e.g., average incorrect responses, specifically for those problems where help was requested; average seconds spent in any problem and where help was requested; and average time spent between pairs of attempts. (2) *Help activity*, average hints requested per problem; average hints in helped problems (when a student asks for help, how much help is requested?); average seconds spent in helped problems (time/effort the student invested when she asked for help); the percentage of helped problems in the tutoring session (how often the student asked for help). (3) *Help timing*, when help was sought as a percentage of all helped problems: help before making an attempt, help after making an attempt, help after entering the correct answer. (4) *Other descriptors*, math pretest score, gender, time between pairs of attempts.

We may attempt to interpret these dependencies among variables to understand students' use of the system. For instance, learning gains from pre- to posttest (% improvement)

TABLE 23.1

Post-Tutor Student Goals, Attitudes, and Perceptions

Goals/Attitudes While Learning
Seriously try learn. How seriously did you try to learn from the tutoring system?
Get it over with (fast). I just wanted to get the session over with, so I went as fast as possible without paying much attention.
Challenge. I wanted to challenge myself: I wanted to see how many I could get right, asking as little help as possible.
No care help. I wanted to get the correct answer, but didn't care about the help or about learning with the software.
Help fading attitude. I wanted to ask for help when necessary, but tried to become independent of help as time went by.
Other approaches. I wanted to see other approaches to solving the problem, and thus asked for help even if I got it right.
Fear of wrong. I didn't want to enter a wrong answer, so I asked for help before attempting an answer, even if I had a clear idea of what the answer could be.
Student perceptions of the tutor.
Learned? Do you think you learned how to tackle SAT-Math problems by using the system?
Liked? How much did you like the system?
Helpful? What did you think about the help in the system?
Return? Would you use the system again if there were more problems and help for you to see? How many more times would you use it again?
Interaction with the tutor.
Audio? How much did you use the audio for the explanations?

is not correlated to "average hints seen per problem," but it is correlated to "average hints seen in *helped* problems." The trend suggests that students who search deeply for help are more likely to learn. In addition, learning gain is not significantly correlated with "time spent in a problem," but instead to "time spent in problems in which help was seen." This suggests that spending much time struggling in a problem and not seeing help will not lead to learning; instead, a student should spend significant time seeing help. Learning is negatively correlated to average incorrect attempts per problem, suggesting that students who tend to make many incorrect responses per problem will not improve much from pre- to posttest. Many of these correlations are not very strong (in general, neither of them by themselves accounts for more than 15% of the variance). However, a model that accounts for all these variables together should allow for a better prediction of the dependent variables (i.e., goals, attitudes, perceptions of the software and learning).

23.2.2 Identifying Dependencies among Variables

Bi-variate Pearson correlations were computed to search for dependencies among latent and observable variables from student behavior in the tutor. A high number of significant correlations found among help-seeking attitudes, help-seeking behaviors, perceptions of the system, gender, and other behaviors such as problems seen and reports such as how often a student heard the audio for explanations. These dependencies are among latent variables—such as significant correlations among student goals and attitudes. In addition, students' general perceptions and attitudes are significantly correlated to student behaviors in the tutor. For instance, asking for help in problems where mistakes were made seems to be a positive action and is correlated to "seriousness" and "liking of the system," though not directly associated to higher learning gains. It is also correlated to the "challenge" attitude, showing that students might want to make an attempt even if they risk a wrong answer. One interesting dependency is that a high number of mistakes per problem is correlated to a higher chance of a student saying he or she wants to "get over with" (probably just "gaming" and clicking through to get the answer). However, making a high number of mistakes in problems, where they also request help, is associated to a lower likelihood of wanting to "get over with" the session, again suggesting that failing and asking for help is associated to a positive attitude toward learning. The positive perceptions of the software, such as willingness to return to use the system, are correlated to productive behaviors that lead to higher learning gains (e.g., "average hints per problem"). Students who decide to seek for hints seem to be genuinely trying to learn.

23.2.3 An Integrated Model of Behavior, Attitude, and Perceptions

The next step is to build a model to predict a student's goals and attitudes from summaries of student interactions with the tutor. If an accurate inference of attitudes, goals, and even learning can be made while the student is using the system, then the tutor can anticipate these attitudes and take corrective action.

Bayesian belief networks (BBNs) are used to model knowledge that is uncertain, e.g., student knowledge, emotion, and teaching strategies. For example, teachers don't know which teaching actions will encourage students in the short term or inspire them in the long run.[11] Evidence that a student knows a topic might result from authentic skills, a lucky guess, or a random choice. These uncertainties necessitate that intelligent tutors reason under uncertainty. BBNs are a representation of knowledge or emotion in which every path through the space describes a collection of believed or observed facts.[12] Yet, every representation must remain incomplete due to uncertainty about learning and incomplete understanding of human emotion. Bayesian theory can roughly be boiled down to one principle: to see the future, one must look at the past. Bayesian methods reason about the probability of future events, given their past and current probabilities and enable computers to combine new data to predict values with prior beliefs about data.

Our team built a BBN to predict student emotion by starting with observed student actions and inferring the probability of unobserved (hidden) emotion (e.g., topics that students know), Figure 23.1. The correlation network first represents the observed variable (AvgIncorrect, % helped problems) as well as the unobserved variable (don't care about help, seriousness). Arcs list the probability that one variable can be inferred from another (e.g., unobserved variable from an observed variable). If an arc joins two nodes, it means the probability of all possible values for the pointed-at-node depends on the value of the previous node. If no arc joins two nodes, it means that the values for these nodes do not correlate to each other. Bayesian networks that are learned from data such as this correlation network can capture complex dependencies among variables, as they can predict the probability of some unknown (latent) variables, given a few others that have been observed. We constructed the Bayesian network shown in Figure 23.2 from the correlation graph in Figure 23.1, by (1) eliminating the correlation links among student interaction variables; (2) giving a single direction to the links from goals/attitudes to observable behavior variables; (3) providing a single direction for links between goals/attitudes variables (from the nodes that are more likely "causes" to the nodes that are more likely effects); (4) eliminating links that create cycles, basing the elimination choice on correlation strength. This resulted in the directed acyclic graph shown Figure 23.2.

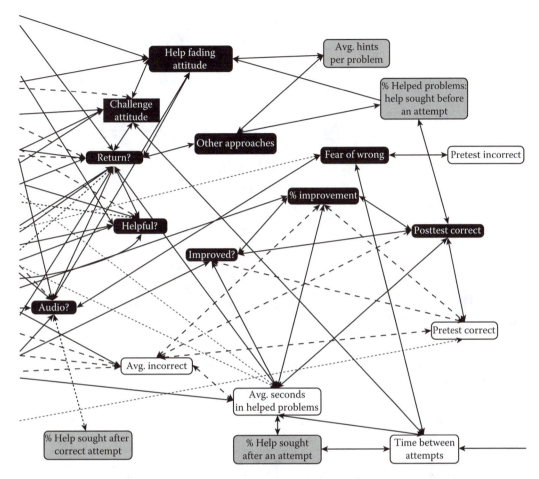

FIGURE 23.1
Part of the full network of correlations between latent and observed variables. Variables that describe a student's observed interaction style (light-colored nodes) are correlated with the students' latent attitudes, feelings, and learning (dark nodes) derived from the survey. Line weight indicates correlation: dashed line (- -) indicates a negative correlation; lines (—) indicate a positive correlation; thick lines indicate $p < 0.01$—light lines indicate correlations of $p < 0.05$.

Next, the parameters of the network were generated by (1) discretizing all variables in two levels (high/low) with a median-split; (2) simplifying the model further by discarding existing links whose connecting nodes do not pass a Chi-square test (the dependency is not maintained after making the variables discrete); (3) creating conditional probability tables (CPTs) from the cross-tabulations of the students' data ("maximum likelihood" method for parameter learning in discrete models).[12]

The probability that a student has a goal/attitude given that we know his observable actions is stated as a *conditional probability*; dependencies in the network are defined by conditional probability with one entry for each different combination of values that variables can jointly take.[11] This is represented as a table that lists the probability that the child node takes on, based on different values for each combination of values of its parents, see Table 23.2.

Assume that a BBN represents whether students have a fear of getting the problem wrong (Figure 23.2, middle row). Consider that the tutor begins with no clear knowledge

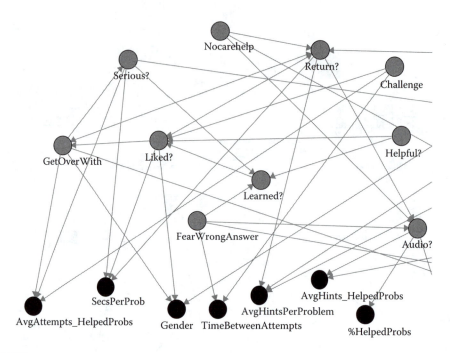

FIGURE 23.2
Part of the structure of a Bayesian network to infer attitudes, perceptions, and learning (light gray nodes). The bottom (leaf) nodes are set as evidence.

TABLE 23.2

Learning Parameters to the BBN

"Fear of Wrong"	"Challenge"	Time between Attempts	Cases	Probability	
False	False	Low	43	0.64	(1)
		High	24	0.36	(2)
	True	Low	35	0.42	(3)
		High	48	0.58	(4)
True	False	Low	8	0.50	(5)
		High	8	0.50	(6)
	True	Low	7	0.32	(7)
		High	15	0.68	(8)

Note: Maximum likelihood to learn conditional probability tables for "fear of wrong" attitude from students' data.

about whether students will express this fear in the survey: There is 50% probability that the student will state this fear or not. All nodes in this case study are binary—that is, nodes have two possible values denoted by T (true) and F (false). Either students will express this attitude in the surveys or they will not. The strength of the relationship for two nodes is shown in Table 23.2. When a hidden node, such as "Fear of wrong" is queried, its probability distribution is updated to incorporate all the leaf nodes in Figure 23.2. Two propositions P(fear of wrong) and P(time between attempts) are dependent if a change in belief about one affects belief in the other. In general, if we are interested in the probability of a proposition, *S*, and we have accumulated evidence, *E*, then the quantity to calculate is $P(S|E)$. If this conditional probability is not directly available in the knowledge base, then probabilistic inference can be used to determine it.

As an example, Table 23.2 shows the conditional probability table corresponding to the node "Time Between Attempts," which has two parents: "Fear of wrong" and "challenge," see Figure 23.2. Many interesting relationships between variables are captured, e.g., when a student reports a "challenge" attitude, the chance of spending a long time between subsequent attempts is higher than when a student does not report wanting to "challenge" herself (compare (4) to (2) and (8) to (6) in Table 23.2). When a student reports "fear of the wrong answer," there is also a higher likelihood of spending a long time between attempts (compare (8) to (4) and (6) to (2) in Table 23.2).

23.2.4 Model Accuracy

A 10-fold cross-validation was carried out to test the accuracy of the model. The following process was repeated 10 times: the conditional probability tables were learned from 90% of a random student data-fold; the remaining 10% data was used to test the model, in the following way: leaf nodes (observable student behavior within the tutor) were evidenced with the behavior that the student displayed and other student descriptors. Then, the latent nodes (goals, attitudes, learning improvement, posttest score, perceptions of the system) were inferred with the Bayesian network. Table 23.3 shows that all of the latent nodes were predicted with accuracy above random level, half of them with an accuracy of 75% or above.

23.2.5 Case Study Summary

A data-driven Bayesian model was created from a dataset of 230 high school students' logs. This model predicts latent affective and motivational variables related to the learning

TABLE 23.3

Accuracy of Predictions, 10-Fold Cross-Validation

Attribute	Accuracy	Highly Certain Predictions %Times $P(T) > 0.7$ or $P(T) < 0.3$
Get over with? (Attitude)	0.89	96%
Liked? (Perception)	0.82	80%
Learned? (Perception)	0.81	97%
Fear of wrong (Attitude)	0.81	83%
No care help? (Attitude)	0.76	92%
Help fading attitude (Attitude)	0.76	41%
Other approaches (Attitude)	0.75	59%
Gain pre-post test (Cognitive Outcome)	0.72	37%
Challenge attitude	0.70	28%
Improved? (Cognitive outcome)	0.69	57%
Return? (Perception)	0.65	34%
Audio? (Cognitive outcome)	0.58	57%
Seriousness? (Attitude)	0.54	11%

experience: their goals, attitudes, and whether they learn. We showed how a methodology that combines machine learning methods and classical statistical analysis were combined to create a fairly accurate model of students' latent variables. This model can be used in real-time so that the tutoring software can make inferences about student emotion—by keeping "running averages" of behavioral variables (e.g., average hints per problem). This provides the tutor with an estimation of students' attitudes and likely outcomes while students interact with the program. It is interesting that many of the students' negative attitudes and unlearning were expressed with different forms of "speeding" within the software (consistent with past research[11,6]). Corrective pedagogical decisions can be made by the tutoring software to change the standard course of action whenever attitudes are inferred to be negative, and the teacher can be informed via web-based report tools that are permanently updated.

23.3 Predicting Emotions

While tracing students' attitudes is valuable (e.g., the teacher could be hinted that certain students are not having a positive and potentially successful experience with the software), it seems valuable to trace more detailed and fine-grained fluctuating student emotions during a tutoring system use. Tracing emotions is a powerful approach because the tutoring system could potentially make different pedagogical moves when a student is in a certain emotional state (e.g., frustrated or bored). This section describes how students' emotions were inferred from physiological sensors (camera facial detection software, mouse pressure sensors, chair posture sensors, and skin-conductance wrist-band), see Figure 23.3, in concert with "standard" tutor context variables similar to the previous section.

23.3.1 Background and Related Work

No comprehensive, validated, theory of emotion exists that addresses learning, explains which emotions are most important in learning, or identifies how emotion influences learning.[5] Additionally, most educational technologies do not take into consideration natural affective student characteristics, e.g., interest, boredom, or surprise. Since the recognition of student emotion is a key aspect of tailored affective support, researchers have focused on the automated detection of affective states in a variety of learning contexts.[13–15] This prior research has shown promising results having detected affective states such as frustration or boredom.[15–16]

The research described in this section is based on recognizing a set of emotions, first identified by Ekman[17] from the analysis of facial expressions. These emotions (joy, anger, surprise, fear, and interest) were grounded in an educational setting and certain names changed to express emotions observed during learning. Our team produced four orthogonal bipolar axes of cognitive affect (e.g., "I feel anxious... very confident."), see Table 23.4.

Hardware sensors have the potential to provide information on students' physiological responses linked to various affective states.[18] Dialog and posture features were used to discriminate among the affective states of boredom, confusion, flow, and frustration.[18] Most prior efforts, however, have been conducted in laboratory experiment settings, and have not been brought to real educational settings such as mathematics classes in public schools.

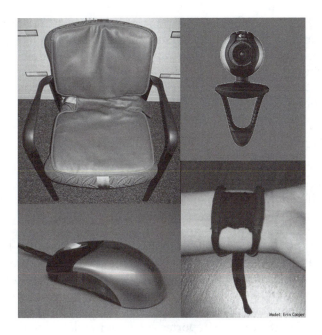

FIGURE 23.3
Sensors used in the classroom (clockwise): facial expression sensor; conductance bracelet, pressure mouse, and posture analysis seat.

TABLE 23.4

Cognitive-Affective Terms Based on Human Face Studies

Cognitive-Affective Term	Emotion Scale	Ekman's Categorization
High enjoyment	"I am enjoying this."	Joy
Little enjoyment	…	
	"This is not fun."	
High frustration	"I am very frustrated."	Anger
Little frustration	..	
	"I am not frustrated at all."	
Interest/novelty	"I am very interested."	Interest and surprise
Boredom/dullness	…	
	"I am bored."	
Anxiety	"I feel anxious"	Fear
Confidence	….	
	"I feel very confident"	

Sources: Ekman, P., Universals and cultural differences in facial expressions of emotion, in J. Cole (Ed.), *Nebraska Symposium on Motivation 1971*, Vol. 19, pp. 207–283, University of Nebraska Press, Lincoln, NE, 1972; Ekman, P., *Facial Expressions*, John Wiley & Sons Ltd., New York, 1999.

23.3.2 Data Description

We conducted two studies during Fall 2008 involving the use of sensors with the mathematics tutor Wayang Outpost. Thirty eight high school students and 29 female undergraduate students were part of this study.[19,20] Students took mathematics pretests and surveys to assess their motivation,[4] self-confidence in mathematics, and subjective mathematics value.[21] Posttest surveys also included questions that measured student perceptions of the software. Every 5 min, as long as students had finished a mathematic problem, a screen queried their emotion: "How [interested/excited/confident/frustrated] do you feel right now?" Students choose one of five possible emotion levels, where the ends were labeled (e.g., I feel anxious… very confident). The emotion queried was randomly selected (obtaining at least one report per student per emotion for most subjects).

23.3.3 Overall Results

We analyzed the relationship between the sample mean interest, excitement, confidence, and frustration reported by each student and their corresponding incoming mathematics knowledge, self-concept, mathematics value, and mastery goal orientation. Baseline feelings for mathematics reported in the pretest survey (e.g., "How frustrating is it to solve math problems?") were highly correlated with attitudes such as self-confidence in mathematics ($R = 0.7$, $p = .000$). However, emotions reported within the tutor showed only a marginally statistical significant correlation with pretest attitudes, pretest emotions, and mathematics knowledge. Instead, students' self-report of emotions depended highly on what had just occurred in the previous problem (e.g., if a student had reported "I feel frustrated," it is likely that he had several incomplete attempts in the previous problem).

Our team analyzed each student's reported emotion in relation to the following contextual variables regarding the last problem seen before the emotion self-report: number of incorrect attempts (#IncompleteAttempts), whether the problem was solved correctly in the first attempt (Solved?), time elapsed since log-on (TimeInSession), time so far using the tutor (TimeInTutor), number of hints seen in the last problem (#HintsSeen), seconds until the first attempt to answer (Secsto1stAttempt), seconds until the problem was solved correctly (SecsToSolve), presence/absence of a character that gave feedback (LearningCompanion?), and the gender of the learning companion (GenderPedAgent). Stepwise linear regression was used to identify good predictors of each emotion. Stepwise regression finds those variables that are good predictors of the dependent variable (in this case, the emotion reported) and eliminates those that don't contribute significantly to the prediction.[22]

Figure 23.4 suggests that student emotions (middle row) *can* be predicted from contextual variables (top row), as they depend significantly on what has just happened in the previous problem. *Confidence* can be predicted from #HintsSeen and whether the previous problem was solved correctly. *Frustration* can be predicted from #HintsSeen, #IncorrectAttempts, and TimeInTutor. *Excitement* can be predicted from Solved? *Interest* can be predicted from #IncorrectAttempts and the gender of the learning companion. All these statistically significant dependencies indicate that students' emotion self-reports depend on what has just happened and only marginally depend on students' incoming beliefs.

Tables 23.5 and 23.6 describe different models and variables entered with the stepwise regression method. For instance, in the first cell of Table 23.5, there are 62 reports of students' confidence. The regression model generated has a fit of $R = 0.49$. The variables found to predict confidence in this case were "solved?," "seconds to first attempt," and "seconds to solve."

23.3.4 Students Express Their Emotions Physically

As mentioned before, a set of noninvasive hardware sensors recorded students' physiological behavior.[23,24] The hardware (with the exception of the camera developed at MIT) was manufactured at Arizona State University from validated instruments first developed by the Affective Computing group at MIT. Twenty-five sets of each sensor were manufactured

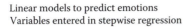

Linear models to predict emotions
Variables entered in stepwise regression

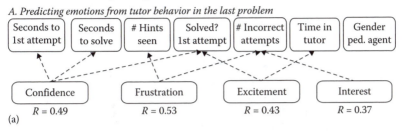

A. Predicting emotions from tutor behavior in the last problem

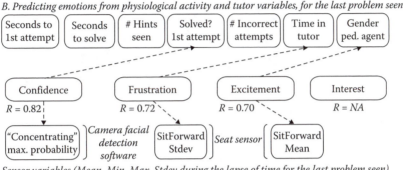

B. Predicting emotions from physiological activity and tutor variables, for the last problem seen

Sensor variables (Mean, Min, Max, Stdev during the lapse of time for the last problem seen)
(b)

FIGURE 23.4
Variables that help predict self-report of emotions. The result suggests that emotion depends on the context in which the emotion occurs (math problem just solved), and also can be predicted from physiological activity captured by the sensors (bottom row).

TABLE 23.5

Each Cell Corresponds to a Linear Model to Predict Emotion Self-Reports

	Tutor Context Only	Camera + Tutor	Seat + Tutor	Wrist + Tutor	Mouse + Tutor	All Sensors + Tutor
Confident	$R=0.49, N=62$	$R=0.72, N=20$	$R=0.35, N=32$		$R=0.55, N=28$	$R=0.82, N=17$
Frustrated	$R=0.53, N=69$	$R=0.63, N=25$	$R=0.68, N=25$	$R=0.56, N=45$	$R=0.54, N=44$	$R=0.72, N=37$
Excited	$R=0.43, N=66$	$R=0.83, N=21$	$R=0.65, N=39$	$R=0.42, N=37$	$R=0.57, N=37$	$R=0.70, N=15$
Interested	$R=0.37, N=94$	$R=0.54, N=36$	$R=0.28, N=51$		$R=0.33, N=51$	

Note: Models were generated using stepwise regression, and variables entered into the model are shown in Table 23.6. The top row lists the feature sets that are available. The left column lists the emotional self-reports being predicted. R values correspond to the fit of the model (best fit models for each emotion are in bold). N values vary because students may be missing data for a sensor. R values for Linear Regression Models (best fit models for each emotion in bold). Empty cells mean that no fit model was found for that data set. N values vary because each case corresponds to one emotion report crossed with the data for each sensor—mean, minimum value, and maximum value corresponding to each sensor for the last problem before the report. Full data for all sensors is limited to a subset of students.

for simultaneous use in classrooms in Massachusetts and Arizona. The four sensors, shown in Figure 23.3, include a facial expression recognition system that incorporates a computational framework to infer a user's state of mind,[25] a wireless conductance bracelet based on an earlier glove that sensed skin conductance developed at the MIT Media Lab, a pressure mouse to detect the increasing amounts of pressure that students place on mice related to

TABLE 23.6

Variables Entered into Each Model (These are Significant Predictors of the Emotion Reported)

	Tutor Context Only	Camera + Tutor	Seat + Tutor	Wrist + Tutor	Mouse + Tutor	All Sensors + Tutor
Confident	SolvedOnFirst HintsSeen	IncorrectAttempts thinkingMin ConcentratingMax	IncorrectAttempts SolvedOnFirst sitForwardStDev	IncorrectAttempts	IncorrectAttempts SolvedOnFirst TimeInSession	IncorrectAttempts ConcentratingMax thinkingMax
Frustrated	LearnCompanion? IncAttempts HintsSeen TimeInSession	LearnCompanion? HintsSeen TimeInSession InterestedMax thinkingMin	LearnCompanion? TimeInSession IncAttempts HintsSeen	LearnCompanion? HintsSeen TimeInSession IncAttempts	LearnCompanion? IncAttempts TimeInSession HintsSeen SecondsToSolve	unsureStdev LearnComparison? TimeInSession thinkingMin HintsSeen
Excited	Gender_LC IncorrectAttempts	IncorrectAttempts InterestedMean	IncorrectAttempts Gender_LC	Gender_LC IncorrectAttemps	Gender_LC HintsSeen IncorrectAttempts	netSeatChange interestedMin sitForwardMean
Interested	Gender_LC	Gender_LC InterestedMin HintsSeen	Gender_LC	Gender_LC	Gender_LC HintsSeen MouseStdev MouseMax	Gender_LC HintsSeen InterestedMin mouseMax

increased levels of frustration,[18] and low-cost/low-resolution, pressure-sensitive seat cushions and back pads with an incorporated accelerometer to measure the elements of a student's posture.

Our team examined the extent of the benefits of using sensor data to detect students' emotions, above and beyond, making inferences from contextual variables (time, hints, attempts, etc.) as shown above. This was addressed by analyzing the improved emotion predictions when sensor data was available compared to when inferences were limited to information about student behavior in the tutor context. One caveat is that regression works with a full set of data; not all sensors were available at all times for all students, because of several real-life classroom problems, and this resulted in approximately full data for each emotion for half of the students. Figure 23.4 shows the generated models with reduced (but complete) data set that includes all sensors. However, in order to be more precise about the potential contribution of each sensor, we created another set of models showing the contribution of each individual sensor separately, shown in Table 23.5. The second cell toward the left shows that when we add in the camera information, we can create a linear model of $R = 0.72$, accounting for 52% of the variance (more than double than without sensors). The variables that were found to predict confidence after the camera data is added were Solved? and ConcentratingMax (the maximum probability of "concentrating" for the last problem before the student confidence report, given by the facial recognition software). The third cell toward the left shows that when we consider only those emotion reports for students who also have seat posture data, the seat features (SitForwardMax, Min, Mean, and Stdev) generate a worse model.

Figure 23.5 provides an example of data analyzed from the camera for student self-reports on confidence and frustration. The left two graphs show that the facial recognition software predicts that students reporting low confidence (bottom left) are concentrating minutes before the self-report, whereas students who report high confidence (top left) do not seem to be concentrating. That is, students who are working hard trying to figure out a problem feel unsure/anxious about their ability to solve it. The right two graphs show that a student who self-reports little frustration (bottom) is predicted to be thinking before stating the self-report. The small letters (O, X, ?, F) indicate actions taken by students in the tutor (correct, incorrect, Hint, or sit forward.)

23.4 Summary and Future Work

This chapter makes several important contributions to the data mining of affective models of students using tutoring systems. In the first case described, BBNs were mined from student logs to predict student goals while using the system, with the objective of detecting unproductive goals and attitudes that don't contribute to learning. In the second case, linear models were data-mined to predict state-based fluctuating emotions that are related to longer term affective variables (e.g., self-concept and value in mathematics) known to predict long-term success in mathematics.[26] A great opportunity exists for tutoring systems to optimize not only learning, but also attitudes and goals that are related to students' emotions. Instead of asking students to say how they feel or what their goals are when using the software, we can infer what the student will say on a minute-to-minute basis. We have shown that these predictions can be enhanced with physiological data that is streamed to the tutoring software, in real time. The summaries of this physiological activity, in particular, data

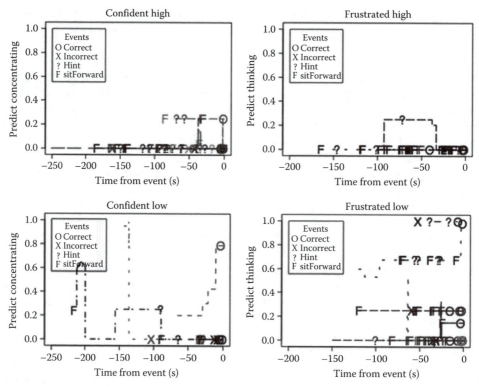

FIGURE 23.5
MindReader[25] Camera Software output stream (probabilities of concentrating or thinking) for students report-ing different confidence levels and frustration levels. The graphs show minutes of student activity *before* the self-report of high or low confidence/frustration. Note students who have low confidence are "concentrating" more than highly confident ones. Students who are not frustrated are thinking frequently. Each contiguous line represents a single student episode, and the zero point on the X-axis represents the moment of the report of confidence or frustration. The small letters (O, X, ?, F) indicate actions taken by the student (correct, incorrect, hint, or sit forward.)

streams from facial detection software, can help tutors predict more than 60% of the vari-ance of some student emotions, which is better than when these sensors are absent.

Future work consists of validating these models with new populations of students and verifying that the loss of accuracy is relatively small. The final goal is to dynamically pre-dict emotional states, goals, and attitudes of new students from these models created from previous students. We are working on pedagogical strategies to help students cope with states of negative emotion and support their return to on-task behavior[19], as well as teacher reports. Further down the line, we intend to create tutor modules that recompute these affec-tive models as new student data arrives, thus producing self-improving tutoring software.

Acknowledgments

We acknowledge contributions to the sensor software development from Rana el Kaliouby, Ashish Kapoor, Selene Mota, and Carson Reynolds. We also thank Joshua

Richman, Roopesh Konda, and Assegid Kidane at ASU for their work on sensor manufacturing.

This research was funded by two awards: one from the National Science Foundation, #0705554, IIS/HCC *Affective Learning Companions: Modeling and Supporting Emotion during Teaching*, Woolf and Burleson (PIs) with Arroyo, Barto, and Fisher; and a second award from the U.S. Department of Education to Woolf, B. P. (PI) with Arroyo, Maloy and the Center for Applied Special Technology (CAST), *Teaching Every Student: Using Intelligent Tutoring and Universal Design to Customize the Mathematics Curriculum*. Any opinions, findings, conclusions, or recommendations expressed in this material are those of the authors and do not necessarily reflect the views of the funding agencies.

References

1. Graham, S. and Weiner, B. (1996). Theories and principles of motivation. In Berliner, D. and Calfee, R. (Eds.), *Handbook of Educational Psychology*. New York: Macmillan, pp. 63–84.
2. Zimmerman, B.J. (2000). Self-efficacy: An essential motive to learn. *Contemporary Educational Psychology*, 25, 82–91.
3. Wentzel, K. and Asher, S.R. (1995). Academic lives of neglected, rejected, popular, and controversial children. *Child Development*, 66, 754–763.
4. Mueller, C.M. and Dweck, C.S. (1998). Praise for intelligence can undermine children's and performance. *Journal of Personality and Social Psychology*, 75(1), 33–52.
5. Picard, R.W., Papert, S., Bender, W., Blumberg, B., Breazeal, C., Cavallo, D., Machover, T., Resnick, M., Roy, D., and Strohecker, C. (2004). Affective Learning—A Manifesto. *BT Technical Journal*, 2(4), 253–269.
6. Aleven, V., McLaren, B., Roll, I., and Koedinger, K. (2004). Toward tutoring help seeking: Applying cognitive modeling to meta-cognitive skills. In *Proceedings of the 7th International Conference on Intelligent Tutoring Systems (ITS-2004)*. Berlin, Germany: Springer.
7. Zhou, X. and Conati, C. (2003). Inferring user goals from personality and behavior in a causal model of user affect. In *Proceedings of the International Conference on Intelligent User Interfaces*, Miami, FL, pp. 211–218.
8. Baker, R., Corbett, A.T. and Koedinger, K.R. (2001). Toward a model of learning data representations. In *Proceedings of the 23rd Annual Conference of the Cognitive Science Society*, Edinburgh, U.K., August 1–4, 2001, pp. 45–50.
9. Arroyo, I., Beal, C.R., Murray, T., Walles, R., and Woolf, B.P. (2004). Web-based intelligent multimedia tutoring for high stakes achievement tests. In J.C. Lester, R.M. Vicari, and F. Paraguaçu (Eds.), *Intelligent Tutoring Systems, 7th International Conference, ITS 2004*. Maceió, Brazil, pp. 468–477, *Proceedings. Lecture Notes in Computer Science 3220*. Berlin, Germany: Springer.
10. Arroyo, I., Ferguson, K., Johns, J., Dragon, T., Mehranian, H., Fisher, D., Barto, A., Mahadevan, S., and Woolf, B. (2007). Repairing disengagement with non invasive interventions. In *International Conference on Artificial Intelligence in Education*, Marina del Rey, CA, July 09, 2007.
11. Woolf, B. (2009). *Building Intelligent Tutors: Bridging Theory and Practice*. San Francisco, CA: Elsevier Inc./Morgan Kauffman.
12. Russell, S. and Norvig, P. (2002). Probabilistic reasoning systems, Chapter 14. In *Artificial Intelligence: A Modern Approach*, 2nd Edn. Upper Saddle River, NJ: Prentice Hall.
13. Conati, C. and Mclaren, H. (2004). Evaluating a probabilistic model of student affect. In *Proceedings of ITS 2004, 7th International Conference on Intelligent Tutoring Systems*, Lecture Notes in Computer Science, Volume 3220/2004, Berlin/Heidelberg, Germany: Springer, pp. 55–66.

14. D'Mello, S. and Graesser, A. (2007). Mind and body: Dialogue and posture for affect detection in learning environments. In *Frontiers in Artificial Intelligence and Applications*, Volume 158. Amsterdam, the Netherlands: IOS Press.

15. Graesser, A.C., Chipman, P., King, B., McDaniel, B., and D'Mello, S. (2007). Emotions and Learning with AutoTutor. In *13th International Conference on Artificial Intelligence in Education (AIED 2007)*. R. Luckin, K. Koedinger, and J. Greer (Eds.). Amsterdam, the Netherlands: IOS Press, pp. 569–571.

16. D'Mello, S.K., Picard, R.W., and Graesser, A.C. (2007). Towards an affect-sensitive AutoTutor. *Special issue on Intelligent Educational Systems IEEE Intelligent Systems, 22*(4), 53–61.

17. Ekman, P. (1999). *Facial Expressions*. New York: John Wiley & Sons Ltd.

18. Burleson, W. (2006). Affective learning companions: Strategies for empathetic agents with real-time multimodal affective sensing to foster meta-cognitive approaches to learning, motivation, and perseverance. PhD thesis, Massachusetts Institute of Technology, Cambridge, MA.

19. Arroyo, I., Cooper, D., Burleson, W., Woolf, B.P., Muldner, K., and Christopherson, R. (2009). Emotion sensors go to school. In *Proceedings of the 14th International Conference on Artificial Intelligence in Education: Building Learning Systems that Care: From Knowledge Representation to Affective Modelling*. Amsterdam, the Netherlands: IOS Press, pp. 17–24.

20. Arroyo, I., Muldner, K., Burleson, W., Woolf, B.P., and Cooper, D. (2009). Designing affective support to foster learning, motivation and attribution. Workshop on Closing the Affective Loop in Intelligent Learning Environments. In *14th International Conference on Artificial Intelligence in Education*, Brighton, U.K., July 6–10, 2009.

21. Wigfield, A. and Karpathian, M. (1991). Who am I and what can I do? Children's self-concepts and motivation in achievement solutions. *Educational Psychologist, 26*, 233–261.

22. Draper, N. and Smith, H. (1981). *Applied Regression Analysis*, 2nd Edn. New York: John Wiley & Sons, Inc.

23. Cooper, D., Arroyo, I., Woolf, B.P., Muldner, K., Burleson, W., and Christopherson, R. (2009). Sensors model student self concept in the classroom. In *International Conference on User Modeling, Adaptation, and Personalization (UMAP 2009)*, Trento, Italy, June 22–26, 2009.

24. Dragon, T., Arroyo, I., Woolf, B.P., Burleson, W., El Kaliouby, R., and Eydgahi, H. (2008). Viewing student affect and learning through classroom observation and physical sensors. In *Proceedings of the 9th International Conference on Intelligent Tutoring Systems*, Montreal, Canada, June 23–27, 2008, pp. 29–39.

25. El Kaliouby, R. (2005). Mind-reading machines: Automated inference of complex mental states. Unpublished Ph.D. thesis, University of Cambridge, Cambridge, U.K.

26. Royer, J.M. and Walles, R. (2007). Influences of gender, motivation and socioeconomic status on mathematics performance. In D.B. Berch and M.M.M. Mazzocco (Eds.), *Why is Math So Hard for Some Children*. Baltimore, MD: Paul H. Brookes Publishing Co., pp. 349–368.

27. Conati, C. and Maclaren, H. (2009). Empirically building and evaluating a probabilistic model of user affect. *User Modeling and User-Adapted Interaction, 19*(3): 267–303.

28. Ekman, P. (1972). Universals and cultural differences in facial expressions of emotion. In J. Cole (Ed.), *Nebraska Symposium on Motivation 1971*, vol. 19, pp. 207–283. Lincoln, NE: University of Nebraska Press.

24

Capturing and Analyzing Student Behavior in a Virtual Learning Environment: A Case Study on Usage of Library Resources

David Masip, Julià Minguillón, and Enric Mor

CONTENTS

24.1 Introduction

The Internet has completely changed what we understand as distance education. Information and communication technologies had a great impact on distance education and, rapidly, e-learning has become a common way to access education. Everyday, more and more people use e-learning systems, environments, and contents for both training and learning. Education institutions worldwide are taking advantage of the available technology in order to facilitate education to a growing audience. Nowadays, most educational institutions use learning management systems for providing learners with additional support in their learning process. According to Taylor [24], this is the fourth generation of e-learning systems, spaces where there is an asynchronous process that allows students and teachers to interact in an educational process expressly designed in accordance with these principles. Indeed, these e-learning systems have evolved to what we know as virtual learning environments, virtual spaces where users, services, and content converge, creating learning scenarios where multiple interactions are generated.

One of the main elements in the learning process is the digital library, a wide service that provides access to all the learning resources, ranging from books to specific documents in digital format, and serves also as a gateway for accessing other resources outside the institution. Following the recommendations from the new European Higher Education

Area (also known as the Bologna process), the learning process must become more learner-centered, rather than content-centered. Therefore, the classical model of teachers pushing content toward learners is obsolete. Instead, learners must acquire and develop competences according to a learning process based on activities specially designed to do so [1]. These activities involve the use of different content or, even better, force learners to search and decide by themselves which content is the most suitable for them. This fact promotes the use of services such as digital libraries or learning object repositories, which are also becoming a common service in most virtual learning environments and are considered to be strategic for development purposes [9]. Nevertheless, the use of the digital library is not really integrated into the learning process, as it is seen as an additional service or resource. In fact, only a small percentage of learners can be considered users of the digital library as expected. Most of the students never access the digital library or they only do it at the beginning of the academic semester. The digital library can be accessed from several places in the virtual learning environment, and this can explain the differences among learners with respect to their learning goals: do they need a specific resource in a particular moment and, therefore, they access the digital library? Or do they browse the digital library as a basic competence related to the fact of being online learners? These and other similar questions could be answered by analyzing the real usage of the digital library. One of the most interesting possibilities in any e-learning environment is tracking user navigational behavior for analysis purposes, as it may help to discover unusual facts about the system itself, improve understanding of users' behavior, and also can provide useful information for adaptation and personalization purposes. In fact, the main goal of educational data mining is reintroducing such discovered knowledge in the learning management system again, following an iterative cycle of continuous improvement [21]. As stated in [19], it is possible to improve the instructional design of learning activities if the behavior of learners in a particular context is analyzed. According to this premise, we intend to use a session classification technique for identifying learning goals within a single session, trying to find the relationship between the digital library usage and the learning scenario where it is accessed from.

This chapter is organized as follows: Section 24.2 describes the institutional environment that served as a case study for analyzing user behavior with respect to the digital library access. In Section 24.3, we describe the proposed strategy for capturing user interactions within the virtual learning environment and the further analysis on such usage data related to the digital library. Finally, the most important conclusions of this work and current and future research lines are summarized in Section 24.4.

24.2 Case Study: The UOC Digital Library

The Universitat Oberta de Catalunya (in English the Open University of Catalonia) is an institution that has emerged from the knowledge society. The mission is to provide people with training throughout their lives. The university's principal aim is to ensure that each student satisfies his or her learning needs in a virtual environment, gaining the maximum benefit from their own efforts. To this end, it offers the intensive use of information and communications technologies (ICT), thereby enabling us to overcome the barriers imposed by time and space for offering an educational model based on personalized attention for each individual student. Students, professors, and administrators interact and cooperate on the virtual campus, constituting a true university community that uses the Internet to create, structure, share, and disseminate knowledge. Within the UOC virtual campus, each subject has a virtual classroom for the teaching and learning process. Virtual classrooms are the virtual meeting points for learning activities, following a student-centered model [22]. The learning model determines the interaction produced in the virtual learning environment. The study of learners' interaction can allow us to obtain new knowledge to validate and improve the virtual learning environment design, and even the learning model itself. To characterize the users' navigation, sessions may also contribute to improve the virtual campus design.

The virtual classroom (see Figure 24.1) is the place where the students have access to all the information related to their learning process. In the classroom, they find the tools to interact and share resources with the instructor and the other students. The system notifies students about the changes that have been produced from their last visit. The virtual classroom is structured in four main areas: planning, communication, resources, and evaluation. The planning area contains the description of all the elements of the course, the learning, and the calendar of activities and assignments. The communication area provides the tools for students to communicate among themselves and with their instructor. This is where the shared mailboxes or boards can be found. In this area, they also find the list of the classroom participants and the information whether they are connected to the virtual campus at that moment. The resource area contains the links to all the necessary digital resources, as well as the listing of nondigital resources that are also a requirement of the subject. Most of those links are, in fact, links to the university digital library. Finally, the evaluation area contains the tools for assignment delivery as well as the direct accesses to the applications related to the evaluation process, like for example, the qualifications view.

The digital library integrates all resources and digital contents of the virtual campus. It allows to look up and access digital resources and to request the resources in nondigital format. The digital library can be accessed from the main menu of the virtual campus and also from the virtual classroom even though links can also be added from other learning resources as, for example, the discussion boards. To guide the study of the digital library usage, three scenarios have been established. These scenarios characterize the way students can access and interact with the library, according to the different navigation paths available in the virtual campus, which are related to different possible user behaviors. The first scenario is defined by users that log in the virtual campus and they navigate directly to the digital library using the main menu button. It includes all those students who are studying offline and need to access a resource or to look for a book, so they connect to

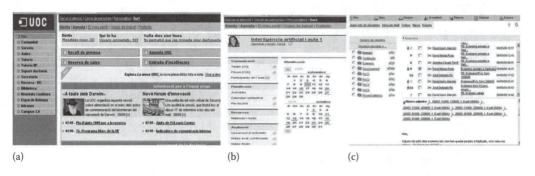

(a)   (b)   (c)

FIGURE 24.1
Screenshots of the virtual campus: (a) shows an example of the campus home page, (b) shows a virtual classroom overview, and (c) shows the interaction space of the classroom.

the virtual campus and access the digital library. The second scenario takes into account accessing the digital library from the virtual classroom. In this scenario, students access directly the resources specific to the subject via the links in the resource area of the virtual classroom. This access is very frequently used since it simplifies the navigation and search for specific resource in the digital library. The third scenario of the use of the digital library includes accessing the digital library from the discussion boards of the virtual classrooms. The messages posted in the boards can contain a link related to the discussion topic. This link could be a resource or a book in the digital library. In this work, we are interested in understanding and explaining the behavior of the students not in the digital library but their navigation before accessing it. This information will be used to improve the learning process as explained later. Basically, we will use clustering techniques in order to determine the relationship between the proposed usage scenarios and the observed navigational behavior.

Several authors [2,10,18] have proposed to analyze usage in order to provide a better support for searching and browsing, personalized services, or improving user interface design, among several possibilities. Digital libraries combine a web-based interface as a front-end with a server acting as a back-end where all the searches and queries are executed. Both the front-end and the back-end generate their own log files that are usually analyzed separately, the former for studying how users interact with the user interface and the latter for analyzing browsing and searching informational behaviors. In our case, we are not interested in predicting which learners will access the digital library and when, but in improving the understanding of the learners' needs with respect to the digital library as a basic service of the virtual classroom. The real usage of the digital library has been always a critical issue for teachers and instructional designers. Preliminary experiments [6] show that most learners do not use the digital library and other sources following a continuous basis, but they concentrate their accesses during the first days of the academic semester. Surprisingly, the results from an internal institutional survey show that the digital library is one of the most well-rated resources in the virtual campus, which is somehow contradictory with the real usage data. Therefore, it becomes necessary to analyze with more detail the real digital library usage patterns and try to establish their relationship with the other areas and elements of the virtual campus.

24.3 Educational Data Analysis

Educational data mining has attracted a lot of attention in the last few years [21]. The proliferation of learning management systems and their adoption by educational institutions has provided teachers with new perspectives for understanding how learners behave (and allegedly learn) in such learning scenarios. As most of these systems are web based, user behavior can be tracked using simple web analysis techniques and tools, although it is usually necessary to develop specific tools for analyzing a particular context, in order to capture all the richness of the interactions that occur there. Clustering is a common technique for analyzing web usage patterns [8], both combining usage and content mining [15]. For example, Chen and Chen [3] propose a personalized recommendation service for a digital library based on clustering, although such service is not linked to the learning process. In this section, we describe how usage data is acquired from the UOC web log servers and the variables extracted for analyzing user behavior. Such variables try to capture not only navigational behavior but also the structure of the different services (we call them regions) used during the learning process. Descriptive statistics are used to extract useful information from such variables and Principal Component Analysis is used to establish the most important relationships among the different regions visited by learners. Then, learners are clustered according to their navigational behavior.

24.3.1 Data Acquisition

The UOC virtual campus is a web-based learning management system with a variable number of front-ends receiving requests from the users accessing it. Each front-end acts as a web server, thus logging all user interactions in a single log file for each server. Server log files are generated on-the-fly by the 24 web servers, and these files are copied onto other server that joins them and applies the filters aforementioned above, in a 24 h basis routine, starting at 01:00 a.m. Nevertheless, a simple analysis of connection patterns reveals that the lowest server load is between 04:00 a.m. and 05:00 a.m., so consecutive log files are joined and split again at such time, in order to minimize the number of invalid sessions when analyzing a short period of time off-line, which is a common situation. These daily chunks of preprocessed log files are then the starting point for analysis purposes.

For each action, a user performs in the virtual campus, one or more lines representing such an action are logged in several servers. Furthermore, depending on the type of action, several servers might log the same action but using different information. In this work, we have used mainly the log files from the Apache servers that act as front-ends, once they have been joined in a single file that is generated each day. This file is firstly preprocessed in order to remove all those log lines that are surely not hits produced by the user, such as the load of icons, style sheets, banners, and so on. This preprocessing reduces the amount of lines by 90%. Nevertheless, during a typical week, the total number of lines that needs to be processed is still about 36 million lines, approximately 12 GB, which is indeed a very large figure. Therefore, a second preprocessing, more oriented toward narrowing the experiment, is required, following the recommendations described in Cooley et al. [5]. Furthermore, as stated in Kitsuregawa et al. [12], it is impossible to apply classical data mining techniques if the amount of valid entries to be analyzed is not drastically reduced and a distributed system is used. Therefore, there is a real need for introducing a transparent set of marks for user behavior analysis that will simplify server logs processing, as described in Mor et al. [17]. The main goal of this embedded mark system is to capture the real behavior of each user navigating through the e-learning environment, but focusing on those activities related to the learning process, that is, accessing the mailbox and the virtual classrooms, using the digital library, the learning resources, and so on. In order to achieve this goal, starting from the virtual campus initial page, a set of marks is introduced in the most likely paths followed by the learners, in order to validate such paths and trying to discover any interesting fact that might be relevant for analysis purposes. It is important to remark that the introduced marks should not interfere with the original system, and that they should be completely transparent for other possible analysis and for the final user.

These sessions show the basic information about the student navigation in the virtual learning environment. Each session contains the user id, the timestamp of beginning and the timestamp of end of the session, and all the marks that show the user navigation between the main spaces and the services of the virtual learning environment. The most important aspect of these sessions is that their format has been thought to be able to be processed by data mining algorithms and, therefore, to obtain new knowledge to characterize users regarding their navigation.

24.3.2 UOC Users Session Data Set

In this work, the data generated in a full academic semester of the UOC have been used. The academic semester consists of 136 days from the first class day to the last day, when the final marks are published. The total number of students enrolled in the UOC was 29,531. Almost all the students' activity has been received directly from the campus servers (apache logs), and preprocessed and stored in our computational resources. Nevertheless, there were some specific troubles in specific dates, where data were not received or were incomplete. More concretely, we missed 5 days of data, so our final data set is 131 days long. For each day, all the students' navigation sessions have been filtered and stored. These sessions have been finally merged in a unique data file, so a total number of 4,301,469 sessions is obtained. The large amount of activity information gathered makes the application of the most commonly used data mining algorithms intractable. Moreover, the most part of the sessions do not contribute to the students' activity analysis with respect to the digital library.

In addition, we are interested in modeling the students' activity to analyze the navigability on the different regions of the campus. More concretely, we are interested on the sessions where students use the different learning resources found in the campus, specially the library resources that are usually richer than short sessions. In this context, we define a priori six regions from the virtual campus, which aggregate the different clicks produced on a single session. The regions R_i defined are

1. The initial home page (INIT), where the student reaches the university institutional information, and has a summary of the activity of all the courses he or she is enrolled into. This page can be accessed again from any point in the virtual campus, so students use it as a "synchronization" point, when they change from an activity (i.e., reading the mailbox) to another (i.e., going to the digital library).

2. The mail box (MAIL), where private messages are stored. The student can access this service by four shortcuts situated on different parts of the virtual campus. Although most students have now other mail addresses outside the virtual campus, it is still very common that they use this one for all the official communication with other students, teachers, and so on.

3. The classroom (CLASS). In this space, the students have all the information about each subject. In addition, the Teaching Plan, a document that describes the whole learning process, can also be accessed from this region.

4. Virtual learning spaces (SPACES). These spaces are situated on each classroom, and typically can be classified as forums, debate spaces, and news boards. In fact, these spaces are special mailboxes where students can read (and sometimes write) messages that are shared among all students in the same virtual classroom.

5. The digital library (LIBRARY), where the students can find the information they need for complementing their learning process.

6. Other spaces (OTHERS). Under this term, we aggregate different administrative resources, such as secretary services, community, research, news, agenda, files, help, personalization aspects, and profile management, which are not mandatory for learning purposes.

From the whole session data set, we filter out those where there is no interaction with the digital library. The final analyzed data set has a total of 65,226 sessions, which is large enough to perform a clustering analysis. These sessions are generated by 12,446 learners (out of 29,531). From this data set, we compute the following information: the timestamp of the session; the relative session number in the current day; the total number of relevant clicks performed during the session; the initial click, that is, which one of the six regions aforementioned is visited from the initial page; the session length in seconds; the day of the week, in order to know whether students connect on weekends or holidays or not; the hour segment when they started the session, in order to know if they connect in the morning, afternoon, evenings, or at night; six values containing the probability of being in each one of the six regions, namely $P(R_i)$; and 36 values with the number of times that the student goes from each region to each other region of the virtual campus, also normalized, namely $P(R_i \rightarrow R_j)$. Notice that some of these values will be zero as the virtual learning environment does not allow learners to navigate among all the regions.

24.3.3 Descriptive Statistics

A simple statistical analysis reveals interesting facts about this data set. For example, both $P(\text{MAIL} \rightarrow \text{SPACES}) = 0$ and $P(\text{SPACES} \rightarrow \text{MAIL}) = 0$, which shows that learners do not "change" from one mailbox to another without going first to the initial page. $P(\text{LIBRARY} \rightarrow \text{SPACES})$ and $P(\text{OTHERS} \rightarrow \text{SPACES})$ are also zero, although this is caused by the virtual learning environment that does not allow some direct jumps between all regions. Nevertheless, we take also into account the order in which such regions are visited, which can be inferred from the session navigational profile, so indirect jumps are also captured.

When compared to the whole data set, the sessions visiting the digital library show several similarities. First, the number of sessions decreases along the academic semester, which is a typical navigational behavior within the virtual campus. With regards to date and time, there are more sessions on Monday and Tuesday than the rest of the week, with a minimum on Saturday and Sunday, as expected. Most sessions occur in the afternoon and the evening, which is a typical connection pattern. This might indicate that digital library sessions are not preplanned, but they occur within the typical stream of sessions each learner generates during his or her learning process.

As a preliminary data inspection technique, we have also performed a Principal Component Analysis (PCA) on the whole data set with all the original variables but the initial click, which is categorical. The session timestamp has been also shifted to reduce its magnitude, so the first day is considered to be zero. Obviously, those variables with zero variance aforementioned are not used in the PCA. We have used a Varimax rotation with the aim to explain each component with a minimum subset of the original variables, and only variables with a correlation within each component higher (in absolute value) than 0.5 are taken into account, following the recommendations of Cohen et al. [4]. The original 45 variables are reduced to 16 components whose eigenvalues are larger than one. These 16 components only explain the 69.7% of the total data variance, showing a poor internal data structuring. Furthermore, none of these components shows a significant clustering on the data, although they reveal some interesting facts about the digital library usage:

First component: $P(\text{SPACES}) + P(\text{INIT} \rightarrow \text{SPACES}) + P(\text{SPACES} \rightarrow \text{SPACES}) + P(\text{SPACES} \rightarrow \text{LIBRARY})$. This component shows a typical navigational behavior that consists in going first to read the pending messages in the specific spaces of the virtual classroom. Notice that this component also takes into account visiting the digital library once all the pending messages have been read.

Second component: $P(\text{INIT}) + P(\text{INIT} \rightarrow \text{INIT}) + P(\text{LIBRARY} \rightarrow \text{INIT})$. This component shows two interesting navigational behaviors: first, it describes those sessions characterized by the use of the INIT button as a "synchronization" point between activities. Second, it shows that learners finish their session in the digital library by reloading the initial page.

Third component: $P(\text{CLASS}) + P(\text{CLASS} \rightarrow \text{CLASS}) + P(\text{LIBRARY} \rightarrow \text{CLASS})$. This component captures those sessions that mainly occur within the virtual classroom, with the particularity that the digital library is also visited in such process.

Fourth component: $P(\text{MAIL}) + P(\text{INIT} \rightarrow \text{MAIL}) + P(\text{MAIL} \rightarrow \text{LIBRARY})$. This component captures the navigation of those learners that access their mailbox from the initial page and once they have finished with their pending mails, they visit the digital library.

Fifth component: $P(\text{CLASS}) + P(\text{CLASS} \rightarrow \text{LIBRARY})$. Finally, this component describes the navigational behavior of those learners accessing the digital library from the virtual classroom. This component is complementary with respect to the third one.

Notice that all these components use only variables related to navigation, that is, the relative day of the academic semester, session length, and the other variables described previously are not considered relevant by the PCA (for these components). Therefore, the further clustering analysis will be performed only on the 36 variables describing the probability of accessing one of the six regions of the virtual campus from another. We will not include the probability of being in a particular region as these are directly related to the other 36 navigational variables.

24.3.4 Categorization of Learners' Sessions

The proposed methodology basically consists of two parts: (1) a feature extraction step on the large-scale log data, and (2) the application of unsupervised learning algorithms to automatically categorize the users' navigational behavior. In applications dealing with large log data sets extracted from a real environment, the feature extraction step becomes crucial, and the main goal is twofold: to reduce the amount of information available to make the problem computationally tractable, and to obtain a registered knowledge representation that can be further analyzed on an algebraic subspace. Notice, that the order of the actions of a single session and even the entire length of the action vector are extremely variable. This fact complicates the application of a distance metric, that is, the application of classical unsupervised machine learning techniques.

In this work, we propose the construction of an adjacency matrix from each session. Given the different N regions of the site subject to analysis, we propose to build the $N \times N$ matrix A, where A_{ij} encodes the number of times that the user has gone from region i to region j. This simple approach allows us to encode the navigation activity of a session on an $N \times N$ feature vector $\mathbf{V}$ (the matrix A column-wise represented). Notice that the vector $\mathbf{V}$ is aligned for all the sessions obtained on the same environment, and encodes a nonparametric estimation of the likelihood of visiting the part j of the site provided that we are on i. Any distance metric can be applied to $\mathbf{V}$, given that the features are perfectly aligned.

Given the described representation of the information present on each session, the characterization of users' navigation is obtained by performing unsupervised learning on the M sessions. More concretely, a K-means clustering algorithm is applied to the M training samples [13]. In spite of its simplicity, the K-means algorithm obtains interesting clustering performance, especially with large training sets. Briefly, the K-means algorithm receives as input the training samples V, and the number of clusters to find, K. Initially, the samples are randomly assigned to any one of the K clusters. Then a set of iterative steps are performed, and at each step, the K-centroids are computed as the mean points of each cluster. Each sample is then reassigned to its closer centroid, and the centroid adjustment is iteratively performed until no samples change their cluster (convergence is guaranteed).

The K-means algorithm has two important drawbacks: first, the number of clusters K must be determined in advance and, second, the centroids are points of the space that do not directly correspond to a sample of the training set. To solve these drawbacks, we first determine a reasonable range for K, and then we will run the K-means algorithm varying K in such range. For solving the second problem, the closest point to each one of the centroids computed by the K-means algorithm will be used as the representing sample of each cluster. This approach is known as the medoid search algorithm, that is, the most centrally located object in a cluster [11]. In order to determine the minimum number of clusters needed to explain the different session profiles, we perform an iterative process creating two clusters, then three clusters, then four, and so. Then we analyze the number of sessions that change their clustered index assignment. Notice that clustered index may change from an iteration to the next, as we compute only the minimum number of sessions that have been assigned to a different cluster when the number of clusters is increased. We do not expect to find too many navigational behaviors, so we test only a few possible values for K. The minimum number of index changes occurs when five clusters are used to explain the possible navigational behaviors. Furthermore, there is a large cluster that contains all those sessions that go directly to the digital library, and this cluster is always generated when the number of clusters is increased (although it might change its index). Therefore, more than two clusters are needed to explain the different navigational behaviors, while increasing the number of clusters above four creates small clusters (only containing a 4.3% of the input sample) that do not seem to be representative. In the light of these results, and for simplicity reasons, we have selected $K = 3$ for exploratory purposes. Notice that other criteria for selecting K (see [14,20]) might yield to a different number of clusters, but this satisfies our exploratory requirements for explaining the scenarios described in Section 24.2.

Once the number of clusters has been determined, we can proceed to analyze the navigational behaviors with respect to the digital library usage. The results of the unsupervised clustering on the proposed representation yields us K adjacency matrices that are the most representative from the training set. In this work, we represent each adjacency matrix as a directed graph, where each node represents a concrete part of the virtual campus being analyzed, and each edge has associated a likelihood value to go from one part of the campus to another one. This algorithm allows us to know the most typical navigation patterns from our students, obtaining important information that could be used in other systems of the virtual campus: such as the improvement of the learning process, the campus design, or the personalization system. In addition, the graphic visualization of the proposed interface becomes straightforward. We plot each medoid session as a directed graph, with the naively approximated transition probabilities in the edges. For the sake of clarity, we purged the edges with likelihood lower than 0.001, for improving presentation. As can be seen in the Figure 24.2, the characterization of the users' navigation can be determined by three distinct graph models:

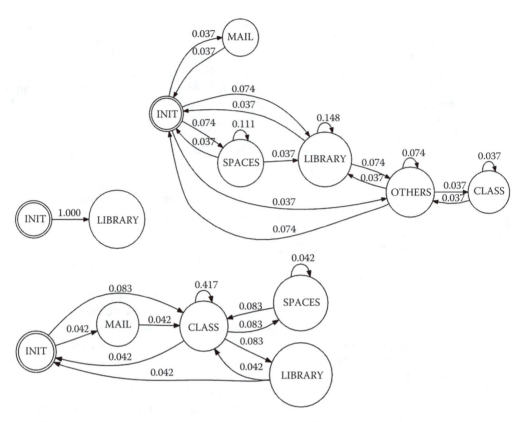

FIGURE 24.2
Directed graphs representing learners' navigation described using $K=3$ medoids.

1. The first clearly defined cluster illustrates a frequent kind of navigation on virtual learning environments, the connections of students that are only interested on checking a specific resource, usually responding to a premeditated behavior. This behavior matches with one of the defined scenarios. Notice that the graph shows that students check the virtual library, and choose to end the session just after obtaining the desired answer. This fact cannot be considered an isolated case. Notice that more than 19,000 navigational sessions behave in a similar way to the graph corresponding to cluster 3.

2. The second graph shows a navigation that might be considered a classroom-driven activity model. Students focus on the spaces found in the classroom, mainly consulting the main novelties of the different spaces of the subjects where they are enrolled. This cluster matches with the second scenario definition, where there are students that access the digital library from the classroom, using the available links to the specific course resources.

3. In the third cluster, we aggregate the samples from sessions that are focused on rich campus navigation. Students use the different resources available and eventually can check the virtual library to satisfy a punctual need. In fact, this cluster is a mixture of the two main scenarios, students that directly access the digital library and also students accessing it after visiting the discussion boards. If $K=4$ clusters were used, this group would split in the two cases mentioned.

24.4 Discussion

In this chapter, we propose a simple algorithm to model the navigation on the virtual campus, taking into account the information from the logged sessions. The proposal is centered on an exploratory study of the campus activity related to the library resources. More concretely, we propose an algorithm to extract an aligned feature set from the different students' sessions, which can be used as a previous step for any standard learning algorithm. On the other hand, the representation provided allows a straightforward graphical representation of the users' behavior using navigational graphs. We applied the *K*-means algorithm to clusterize the session data, extracting a set of prototypes that might help the visualization of the users' navigation on our exploratory study.

As every session is uniquely identified, it is possible to group sessions in recurrent visits for each user. Understanding sessions is the first step toward the creation of a personalization system [23] that takes into account not only what a user is doing in a single session but also all his or her previous activity in the virtual learning environment. In fact, learners in a virtual learning environment establish an ongoing relationship, that is, they maintain a continuous activity during a long period of time (ranging from weeks to years), changing their goals according to the context [16].

24.4.1 Future Works

The study of sessions corresponding to the students' navigation could use other feature extraction algorithms, especially those taking into account higher-order dependencies. In the current approach, we restrict ourselves to first-order navigation, considering a finite state machine where only the precedent node is used. An analysis of the second- and third-order movements among the campus regions could improve the future prediction capabilities of the model [7]. In addition, other unsupervised learning algorithms could be used to cluster the data samples.

On the other hand, we focused the exploratory study on the sessions involving the library resource. Similar studies could be performed on other specific sections of the virtual campus. In this context, the methodology proposed could be hierarchically extended to the internal sections of each region defined. For instance, the navigation inside the library could be analyzed as a hidden layer inside the LIBRARY state.

Acknowledgment

This work has been partially supported by the Spanish government project PERSONAL(ONTO) under grant ref. TIN2006-15107-C02.

References

1. Ade, J. et al. (1999). The Bologna Declaration. Available at http://www.bologna-bergen2005.no/Docs/00-Main doc/990719BOLOGNA DECLARATION.PDF
2. Bollen, J. and Luce, R. (2002). Evaluation of digital library impact and user communities by analysis of usage patterns. *D-Lib Magazine*, 8(6).

3. Chen, C.C. and Chen, A.P. (2007). Using data mining technology to provide a recommendation service in the digital library. *The Electronic Library*, 25(6), 711–724.

4. Cohen, J., Cohen, P., West, S.G., and Aiken, L.S. (2003). *Applied Multiple Regression/Correlation Analysis for the Behavioral Sciences*, 3rd edn. Hillsdale, NJ: Lawrence Erlbaum Associates.

5. Cooley, R., Mobasher, B., and Srivastava, J. (1999). Data preparation for mining World Wide Web browsing patterns. *Knowledge and Information Systems*, 1(1), 5–32.

6. Ferran, N., Casadesús, J., Krakowska, M., and Minguillón, J. (2007). Enriching e-learning meta-data through digital library usage analysis. *The Electronic Library*, 25(2), 148–165.

7. Fok, A.W.P., Wong, H.S., and Chen, Y.S. (2005). Hidden Markov model based characterization of content access patterns in an e-learning environment. In *Proceedings of the IEEE International Conference on Multimedia and Expo*, Amsterdam, the Netherlands, July 6–9, 2005, pp. 201–204.

8. Fu, Y., Sandhu, K., and Shih, M.-Y. (2000). A generalization-based approach to clustering of Web usage sessions. In *Proceedings of the International Workshop on Web Usage Analysis and User Profiling*, San Diego, CA, *Lecture Notes in Computer Science*, Vol. 1836. Berlin, Germany: Springer, pp. 21–38.

9. Joint, N. (2005). Strategic approaches to digital libraries and virtual learning environments (VLEs). *Library Review*, 54(1), 5–9.

10. Jones, S., Cunningham, S.J., and McNab, R. (1998). Usage analysis of a digital library. In *Proceedings of the Third ACM Conference on Digital Libraries*, Pittsburgh, PA, June 23–26, 1998, pp. 293–294.

11. Kaufman, J. and Rousseeuw, P.J. (1987). Clustering by means of medoids. In *Statistical Data Analysis Based on the L1 Norm*, Y. Dodge (Ed.). Amsterdam, the Netherlands: North Holland/Elsevier, pp. 405–416.

12. Kitsuregawa, M., Pramudiono, I., Ohura, Y., and Toyoda, M. (2002). Some experiences on large scale Web mining. In *Proceedings of the Second International Workshop on Databases in Networked Information Systems*, Aizu, Japan, December 16–18, 2002, *Lecture Notes in Computer Science*, Vol. 2544. Berlin, Germany: Springer, pp. 173–178.

13. Linde, Y., Buzo, A., and Gray, R. (1980). An algorithm for vector quantizer design. *IEEE Transactions on Communications*, 28, 84–94.

14. Ming-Tso, M. and Mirkin, B. (2007). Experiments for the number of clusters in K-means. In *Proceedings of the Third Portuguese Conference on Artificial Intelligence*, Guimarães, Portugal, *Lecture Notes in Computer Science*, Vol. 4874. Berlin, Germany: Springer, pp. 395–405.

15. Mobasher, B., Dai, H.H., Luo, T., Sun, Y.Q., and Zhu, J. (2000). Integrating web usage and content mining for more effective personalization. In *Proceedings of the First International Conference on Electronic Commerce and Web Technologies*, London, U.K., *Lecture Notes in Computer Science*, Vol. 1875. Berlin, Germany: Springer, pp. 165–176.

16. Mor, E., Garreta-Domingo, M., Minguillón, J., and Lewis, S. (2007). A three-level approach for analyzing user behavior in ongoing relationships. In *Proceedings of the 12th International Conference on Human-Computer Interaction*, Beijing, China, July 22–27, 2007, pp. 971–980.

17. Mor, E., Minguillón, J., and Santanach, F. (2007). Capturing user behavior in e-learning environments. In *Proceedings of the Third International Conference on Web Information Systems and Technologies*, Barcelona, Spain, March 3–6, 2007, pp. 464–469.

18. Nicholson, S. (2005). Digital library archaeology: A conceptual framework for understanding library use through artifact-based evaluation. *The Library Quarterly*, 75(4), 496–520.

19. Pahl, C. (2006). Data mining for the analysis of content interaction in web-based learning and training systems. In *Data Mining in E-Learning*, Romero, C. and Ventura, S. (Eds.). Southampton, U.K.: WIT Press, pp. 41–56, ISBN 1-84564-152-3.

20. Ray, S. and Turi, R. (1999). Determination of number of clusters in k-means clustering and application in colour image segmentation. In *Proceedings of the Fourth International Conference on Advances in Pattern Recognition and Digital Techniques*, Calcutta, India, December 27–29, 1999, pp. 137–143.

21. Romero, C. and Ventura, S. (2007). Educational data mining: A survey from 1995 to 2005. *Expert Systems with Applications*, 33(1), 135–146.

22. Sangrà, A. (2002). A new learning model for the information and knowledge society: The case of the UOC [online]. *International Review of Research in Open and Distance Learning*, 2(2). [Date accessed: 18/08/2008].

23. Smeaton, A.F. and Callan, J. (2005). Personalisation and recommender systems in digital libraries. *International Journal on Digital Libraries*, 5(4), 299–308.

24. Taylor, J.C. (1999). Distance education: The fifth generation. In *Proceedings of the 19th ICDE World Conference on Open Learning and Distance Education*, Vienna, Austria, June 20–24, 1999.

25

Anticipating Students' Failure As Soon As Possible

Cláudia Antunes

CONTENTS

25.1 Introduction

With the spread of information systems and the increased interest in education, the quantity of existing data about students' behaviors has exploded in the last decade. Those datasets are usually composed of records about students' interactions with several curricular units. On one hand, these interactions can be related to traditional courses (taught at traditional schools) that reveal the success or failure of each student on each assessment element of each unit that a student has attended. On the other hand, there are the interactions with intelligent tutoring systems (ITS), where each record stores all students' interactions with the system. In both cases, records for each student have been stored at different instants of time, since both attendance of curricular units and corresponding assessment elements, and ITS interactions, occur sequentially, in a specific order. Although this order can be different for each student, the temporal nature of the educational process is revealed in the same way: each student's record corresponds to an ordered sequence of actions and results.

Once there are large amounts of those records, one of their possible usages is the automatic prediction of students' success. Work on this area has been developed, with the research being focused mainly on determining students' models (see, e.g., [4,5]), and more recently on mining frequent behaviors [2,12]. Exceptions to this general scenario are the works [3,14,17] that try to identify failure causes. For predicting students' success, existing data per se is not enough, but combined with the right data mining tools, can lead to very interesting models about students behavior. Classification is the natural choice, since it can produce such models, based only on historical data (training datasets as the ones described above). Once these models are created, they can be used as predictive tools for new students' success.

Despite the excellent results of classification tools on prediction in several domains, the educational process presents some particular issues, such as temporality, that bring additional challenges to this task.

In this chapter, we will describe how traditional classifiers can be adapted to deal with these situations after they have been trained in full and rich datasets. We cease the opportunity to succinctly explain the classification problem and describe the methodology adopted to create ASAP classifiers (*as soon as possible classifiers*). The chapter will also include a detailed study about the accuracy of these new classifiers when compared with the traditional ones, both applied on full and reduced datasets.

In order to demonstrate that ASAP classifiers can anticipate students' failure in an interesting time window, the chapter will present a case study about students' performance recorded in the last 5 years in a subject in an undergraduate program.

The rest of the chapter is organized as follows: next, the classification problem is described, giving particular attention to the most common measures for their efficacy; in this section, the problem of ASAP classification is also introduced. In Section 25.3, a methodology for the ASAP classification is proposed. Section 25.4 presents the case study for evaluating the new methodology, concluding with a deep study on the impact of different factors. The chapter closes with a critical analysis of the achieved results and points out for future directions to solve the problem.

25.2 The Classification Problem

25.2.1 Problem Statement and Evaluation Criteria

Automatic classification of records has its roots in the area of artificial intelligence and machine learning, and aims to classify one entity in accordance to its attributes and similar historical entities.

In this manner, a *classifier* is just a function f from the set of instances I to the set of *classes* or *concepts* C, where each instance is characterized by a set of *attributes* or *variables*. Whenever the number of elements in C is finite (usually small, say k), a classifier is just a partition mechanism that splits the set of instances I into k subsets, I_k, each one corresponding to one class. Therefore, a classifier can be seen as a *model*, composed by the definition of each concept (class). In order to find such models, classification methods use a set of historical instances, with their own classification (usually known as *training set*). Once the model is discovered, and assuming that all new instances follow the same probability distribution as the training set, it may be applied to predict the class for any unseen instance.

Several have been the methods applied for discovering (or training) classifiers, all of them needing a specific *generalization language* to represent learnable models [8]. Among the most well known approaches are decision trees [11], neural networks [9], Bayesian classifiers, and more recently support vector machines [15]. All of them create a model based on the training set that can be used in classification time, without reanalyzing known instances.

In a general and simplified way, the different learning approaches can be compared following some criteria when applied to a particular problem: (1) the time spent on training the classifier, (2) the time spent on classifying an instance, (3) the tolerance to the existence of incoherencies in the training set, and (4) their accuracy. Since, some problems are best

$$Accuracy = \frac{\#\{h(x_i) = c(x_i) : x_i \in D\}}{\#\{x_i \in D\}}$$

FIGURE 25.1
Formula for accuracy.

solved with some of these approaches, and none of them are better than the others in all situations, the important issue is to know what classifier to apply in a particular domain, and how to assess its quality.

The first issue does not have a consensual answer, but the second one is perfectly defined. Indeed, the quality of a specific classifier is measured by its *accuracy* in an independent dataset (usually known as *testing set*, and represented by D in the following expressions).

Classification

	Positive	Negative
Positive	TP	FN
Negative	FP	TN

Real

FIGURE 25.2
Confusion matrix for binary classification.

The *accuracy* of a classifier h is the percentage of instances in the testing set D that are correctly classified (Figure 25.1), where $h(x_i)$ is the estimation for x_i's class and $c(x_i)$ its own classification.

In order to distinguish the ability to classify instances from different classes, it is usual to use the *confusion matrix*. This is a $k \times k$ matrix (with k the number of classes), where each entry x_{ij} corresponds to the percentage of instances of class i that are classified as in class j. Therefore, a diagonal matrix reveals an optimal classifier.

When there are only two classes, it is usual to talk about positive and negative instances: instances that implement the defined concept and the ones that do not implement it, respectively. In this case, it is usual to designate the confusion matrix diagonal entries as *true positives* (TP), and *true negatives* (TN), and the others as *false positives* (FP) and *false negatives* (FN), as depicted in Figure 25.2.

In the binary case, it is useful to use some additional measures, namely sensitivity and specificity. While the first one reflects the ability to correctly identify positive cases, the second one reveals the ability to exclude negative ones. Hence, *sensibility* is given by the ratio between the number of instances correctly classified as positives (TP) and the number of real positive instances (TP + FN), Figure 25.3.

On the other side, *specificity* is given by the ratio between the number of instances correctly classified as negative (TN) and the number of real negative instances (TN + FP), as shown in Figure 25.4. In this manner, specificity is just sensibility for the negative class.

25.2.2 Anticipating Failure As Soon As Possible

By nature of, the educational process begins with students who do not have any knowledge of the topic to be taught, and aims to end with the same student filled with that

$$Sensibility = \frac{\#\{h(x_i) = c(x_i) : x_i \in D \cap Positive\}}{\#\{x_i \in D \cap Positive\}} = \frac{TP}{TP + FN}$$

FIGURE 25.3
Formula for sensibility.

$$Specificity = \frac{\#\{h(x_i) = c(x_i) : x_i \in D \cap Negative\}}{\#\{x_i \in D \cap Negative\}} = \frac{TN}{TN + FP}$$

FIGURE 25.4
Formula for specificity.

knowledge. At the same time, students are asked to interact with the system, either almost continuously or at specific instants of time; the process occurs during some time interval. The results of these interactions are usually used to assess students' success and progress. Another important characteristic of the educational process is the fact that the success or failure of the student is determined at a particular instant of time, usually at the end of the process.

Consider, for example, the enrolment of a student to an undergraduate subject: he or she begins to interact with the curricular unit, usually with some small assignments that have a small weight on the final grade; as the time goes on, the student is confronted with harder tasks and at the end of the semester he or she has to be evaluated on a final exam and has to deliver a final project. His final mark is determined according to a mathematical formula that weights the different interactions. In this case, the best classifier is the one that corresponds to that mathematical formula, which can be represented accurately by all the referred approaches. However, despite the perfect accuracy of this method, the goal is not achieved: it is not able to predict in advance if some student will fail.

To our knowledge, in order to accomplish the goal of predicting students result in advance, the training of classifiers have to suffer some adaptations, namely on weighting the different attributes based on their instance of occurrence. In this manner, oldest attributes have higher weights in the classification than the youngest ones. However, this is against the educational process, since the classifier would be almost the reverse of the optimal one.

In the next section, a new approach is proposed, avoiding this contra-nature approach.

25.3 ASAP Classification

The amounts of data needed for training a classifier for achieving a specific accuracy has been studied thoroughly, with very interesting results (see, e.g., [16], or more recently [7] in other contexts). However, the problem of classifying instances that are partially observable, when classifiers may be trained with fully observable instances, is to our knowledge unstudied. Note that Bayesian networks are trained when such unobservable attributes exist, but this is not the problem defined here. For this reason, the problem statement is presented below.

25.3.1 Problem Statement

Let I be a set of instances, A a set of attributes, and C a set of possible classes; an instance x_i from I is described by an ordered list of m attributes from A, and is represented as $x_i = x_{i1}x_{i2}\ldots x_{im}c_i$, where $c_i \in C$ corresponds to the class of x_i.

Given a set of instances from I, described by m attributes from A, and a number of attributes n, such that $n < m$, the problem of *classifying* an instance x_i *as soon as possible* consists on determining the value of c_i—the class for x_i, considering only its first n attributes, known as the *observable attributes*.

The distinction between this formulation and the traditional formulation of classification lies in the notion of order among the attributes that characterize an instance, and the fact that the classifier for instances with m attributes have to be able to classify instances described by a fewer number of attributes.

Note, however, that nothing is said about the training process of classifiers. Indeed, the use of a training set, composed of historical records, is compatible with the notion that these historical instances are fully observable, which means, that classifiers can be trained using the traditional methods without needing any adaptation.

From this point forward, classifiers that work in the context of this formulation are denominated, *as soon as possible classifiers—ASAP classifiers*, in short.

These new classifiers can be trained using two different strategies: a first one, based on the usage of the entire set of attributes, named the *optimistic strategy*, and a second one, the *pessimistic strategy*, that train the classifier only using the observable attributes.

The pessimistic strategy converts the problem into the traditional problem of classification, by reducing each training instance from its original m-dimensional space, to an n-dimensional space, with $n < m$. Clearly, this strategy does not use all the information available at classification time. Indeed, it wastes the historical values of the unobservable attributes, existing in the training set. For this reason, it is expected that the pessimistic strategy will lead to the creation of less accurate classifiers.

On the other hand, the optimistic strategy needs to train classifiers from m-dimensional instances that can be applied to n-dimensional ones. Again, it is possible to consider two approaches, either to convert the learnt classifier, a function from A^m to C, into a function from A^n to C, or to convert the n-dimensional instances into m-dimensional ones.

Note that both approaches require some nontrivial transformation. In the case of the second approach, it tries to enrich instances that are not fully observable, which can be achieved with any method capable of estimating unobservable attributes from observable ones. Next, an approach based on Class Associations Rules (CAR) is described.

25.3.2 CAR-Based ASAP Classifiers

Association analysis is an unsupervised task, which tries to capture existing dependencies among attributes and its values, described as *association rules*. The problem was first introduced in 1993 [1], and is defined as the discovery of "all association rules that have support and confidence greater than the user-specified minimum support and minimum confidence, respectively." An *association rule* corresponds to an implication of the form $A \rightarrow B$, where A and B are propositions (sets of pairs attribute/value), which expresses that when A occurs, B also occurs with a certain probability (the rule's *confidence*). The *support* of the rule is given by the relative frequency of instances that include A and B, simultaneously. In this case, A and B are named the *antecedent* and the *consequent* of the rule, respectively. In this manner, while confidence measures the effectiveness of a rule, its support accounts for its coverage.

A CAR is an association rule, the consequent of which is a single proposition related to the value of the class attribute. In this manner, a set of CAR can be seen as a classifier. In this manner, each rule has an *accuracy* value, with the same meaning as introduced before, but that can be estimated as described in [13].

Considering the problem of ASAP classification, as described above, and adopting an optimistic strategy, the *CAR-based ASAP classifier*, proposed in this chapter, makes use of class association rules for estimating the values of unobservable attributes.

Given a set of training instances D, described by an ordered list of m fully observable attributes and a class label $y \in C$ (the set of class labels), say $a_1 a_2 \ldots a_m y$. The classification of a new unseen instance z described by the same list of attributes, but where only the first n attributes are observable (with $n < m$), by the CAR-based ASAP classifier is done as follows:

- First, a classifier is trained based on the entire training set D, for example, using decision trees learners.
- Second, for each unobservable attribute a_j,
  - It creates a subset of D, D_j, with instances characterized by attributes a_1 to a_n, followed by attribute a_j; this last attribute is set to assume the role of class.
  - And subsequently it finds the set of all classification association rules in set D_j, that satisfy chosen levels of confidence, support and accuracy, CAR_j.
- Third, for each unobservable attribute in instance z, z_i
  - It identifies the rules from CAR_i that match instance z, CAR_{zi}.
  - Among the consequents of rules on CAR_{zi}, it chooses the best value for filling in the value of z_i, say z_i'.
- Finally, in order to predict the class label of instance z, it creates a new instance with m attributes z', such that $z' = z_1 z_2 \ldots z_n z_{n+1}' \ldots z_m'$ and submits it to the learnt classifier.

Note that a similar methodology can be adopted even when other estimators are used for predicting the value of unobservable attributes. It is only necessary to define what "the best value" means. In the case of the CAR-based ASAP classifier, the best value results from combining the different matching rules and choosing the one that better matches the instance. The combination of matching rules is necessary to identify the different possible values and their corresponding interest, since possibly there are several rules that match with a unique instance.

An instance x is said *to match* a class association rule, r, designated $x|=r$, if and only if

$$x = x_1 x_2 \ldots x_n \text{ matches } r = \langle a_1 = v_1 \wedge a_2 = v_2 \wedge \ldots \wedge a_n = v_n \Rightarrow Y = y \rangle$$

$$\leftrightarrow \forall i \in \{1, \ldots, n\} : x_i \text{ is missing } \vee x_i = v_i$$

A rule better matches an instance than another one if the first is more specific than the second, which means that it has more matching attributes with the instance, and fewer missing values. In this manner, more restrictive rules are preferred. Note that despite variables x_i with $i \leq n$ are observable, some instances may present missing values for those variables, since their values may not be recorded. For example, the rule $a_1 = v_1 \wedge a_2 = v_2 \wedge a_n = v_n \rightarrow Y = y$ is a better match than $a_1 = v_1 \wedge a_2 = v_2 \rightarrow Y = y$, since it is more specific than the second one (it has an additional constraint on the value of a_n).

The major disadvantage of the methodology proposed is that the existence of rules that match with some instance is determinant for the success of the final classification. Indeed, if it is not possible to estimate the value for each nonobservable attribute, then most of the times the classifier cannot improve its accuracy.

One important advantage of CAR-based ASAP classifier is the direct influence of minimum confidence and minimum support thresholds on the number of matching rules. Definitely, with lower levels of support, the number of matching rules increase exponentially (a phenomenon well studied in the area of association analysis), and lower levels of confidence decrease the certainty of the estimation, increasing the number of errors made. In order to increase the accuracy of the estimation of unobservable attributes, a rule is selected to estimate a value, only if it has an accuracy higher than a user-specified threshold.

25.4 Case Study

In this chapter, we claim that traditional classifiers can be beaten by ASAP classifiers on predicting students' failure. In order to support this claim, some results of applying both kinds of classifiers to a specific dataset of an educational process, are described.

The dataset in study stores the results of students enrolled in the last five years, in the subject of *Foundations of Programming* of an undergraduate program at *Instituto Superior Técnico*. The dataset has 2050 instances, each one with 16 attributes. From these, 12 correspond to considered observable attributes: 11 weekly exercises and 1 test. Unobservable attributes are the project (ATT13), the exam (ATT14), and another optional exam (ATT15). All have a classification from A to F (and NA – meaning not evaluated). The last attribute corresponds to the classification obtained at the end of the semester (*Approved*—A, B, C, D or E, and *Failed*—F).

The initial dataset was split into two sets: the training set with 75% of instances and the test set with 25% of instances. Training and testing sets, named *train* and *full test set*, respectively, from this point forward, were preprocessed creating two different sets: the *small training set* and the *small testing set*. These sets have the same number of instances as the preceding sets, but fewer attributes (in this case the first 12 attributes of the original set). The small training set will be used to train the pessimistic classifier and to identify CAR rules for each unobservable attribute (by being enriched with its corresponding column); the small testing set will be used to assess the accuracy of pessimist and CAR-based ASAP classifiers.

In order to compare the results, three classifiers were trained using the C4.5 algorithm [10], implemented by J48 on the WEKA software [18]): optimal, pessimistic, and CAR-based ASAP.

The optimal classifier was trained in the full training dataset and tested in the corresponding testing set (with all attributes: observable and unobservable ones). It serves as a reference line and gives the best possible classifier for this data using C4.5 (represented in Figure 25.5—left).

The pessimistic classifier, on the other hand, was trained using a small training set and tested in the corresponding small testing set. Again, it serves as a reference line for the best model created when there is loss of information; the decision tree discovered is in Figure 25.5—right.

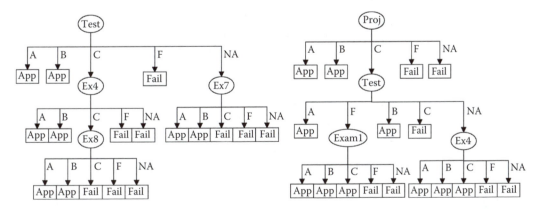

FIGURE 25.5
Discovered decision trees for optimal (left) and pessimistic (right) classifiers.

Finally, CAR-based ASAP classifier corresponds to the optimal one discovered and is tested on the estimated testing set. This set is created by extending the small testing set with estimations for unobservable attributes, creating a new full testing set.

Results confirm the expectations. CAR-based ASAP classifier presents relative success, when compared with pessimistic approaches. Indeed, for lower levels of support (0.5%), the accuracy achieved is always above the accuracy of the pessimistic classifier (Figure 25.6—left).

It is important to note that for higher levels of support, the discovered rules do not cover the majority of situations of recorded students' results. This is explained by the sparse data, resulting from the large number of evaluation moments (variables): there are only a few students with similar behaviors. In order to find them, it is necessary to consider very low levels of support.

Additionally, note that decreasing the level of confidence would decrease the quality of the discovered rules. See that for the fixed levels of support the accuracy of the classifier decreases when confidence also decreases. This is because rules with lower confidence are more generic and less predictive than the ones with larger confidence.

Another interesting result is on predicting failure: ASAP classifier (Figure 25.6—right) has always better specificity levels than the pessimistic one. This reflects the ability of our classifier to cover both positive and negative cases with the same efficacy, since it both looks for failure and success rules.

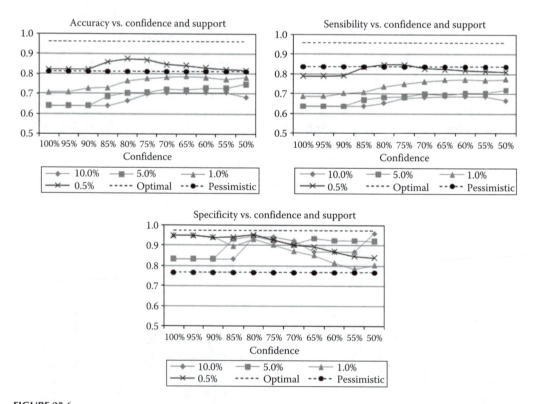

FIGURE 25.6
Accuracy, sensibility, and specificity for different levels of support and confidence (for a minimum CAR accuracy of 50%).

A look at the percentage of correct estimation of attribute values with CAR again shows that the accuracy increases with the decrease of support. However, the increase of correct values is not directly correlated with the decrease of missing values. Indeed, when confidence decreases, missing values also decrease but the correct percentage does not (Figure 25.7).

Again, this is due to the different confidence levels of discovered rules: if lower levels of confidence are preferred, then there will be more discovered rules that would cover more instances, and then they will be used to estimate more unobservable values. However, since confidence is not high, the accuracy of the rule is not enough, and missing values are replaced by wrong ones. With higher levels of confidence, the accuracy of rules will be higher, and the number of wrong values will be reduced, that is, missing values will prevail.

Note that the most important factor on the accuracy of the CAR-based ASAP classifier is the accuracy of the discovered rules. Indeed, interesting results appear when the minimum cutoff for CAR accuracy does not impair the estimation of values (Figure 25.8).

High levels of CAR accuracy exclude most of the discovered rules, which results in attributing missing values for the unobservable attribute. It is important to note that C4.5 in particular presents better results on dealing with missing values than for wrong estimations.

Another interesting fact is that the tree discovered with the pessimistic approach has the same number of leaves as the optimistic one (Figure 25.5). However, while the optimal classifier tests the primary attributes (the ones that have a minimum threshold for a

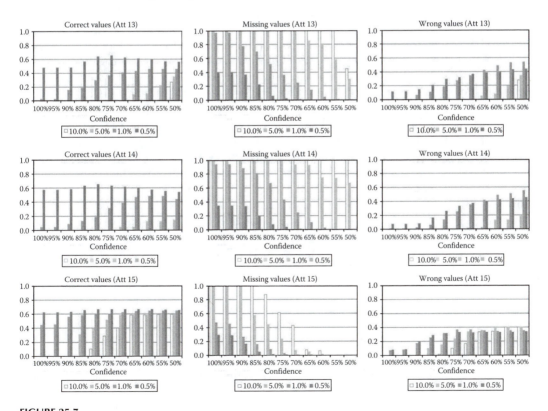

FIGURE 25.7
Impact of support and confidence on the estimation of unobservable attributes (for a minimum CAR accuracy of 50%).

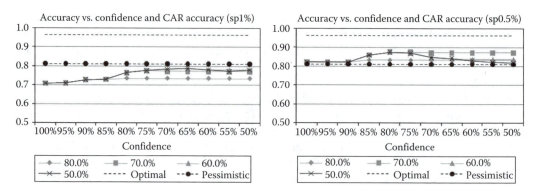

FIGURE 25.8
Impact of accuracy and confidence on the estimation of unobservable attributes.

student to have success—Project and Exams), the pessimistic one tests the attribute Test and some of the weekly exercises. Little changes on the teaching strategy (changing the order of presenting concepts) will invalidate the pessimistic classifier.

25.5 Conclusions

In this chapter, we introduce a new formulation for predicting students' failure, and propose a new methodology to implement it. Our proposal makes use of classifiers, trained as usual, using all available data, and the estimation of unobservable data (attributes) in order to predict failures as soon as possible. In our case, this estimation is based on the discovery of class association rules.

Experimental results show that our methodology can overcome the difficulties of approaches that do not deal with the entire set of historical data, and by choosing the best parameters (confidence, support, and rule accuracy), the results are closer to the optimal classifier found in the same data. However, the choice of the best parameters is a difficult task, followed by the traditional problems related with the explosion on the number of discovered rules. Other methodologies able to estimate the values of unobservable variables (the EM algorithm [6] is just one of such possibilities) can also be applied to determine *ASAP classifiers*. A study of their application, advantages, and disadvantages is mandatory in order to understand the total potential of *ASAP classifiers*.

References

1. Agrawal, R., T. Imielinsky, and A. Swami. 1993. Mining association rules between sets of items in large databases. In *Proceedings of the ACM SIGMOD Conference on Management of Data*. ACM Press, Washington, DC, pp. 207–216.
2. Antunes, C. 2008. Acquiring background knowledge for intelligent tutoring systems. In *Proceedings of the International Conference on Educational Data Mining*. Montreal, Canada, June 20–21, 2008, pp. 18–27.

3. Antunes, C. 2009. Mining models for failing behaviors. In *Proceedings of the Ninth International Conference on Intelligent Systems Design and Applications*. Pisa, Italy, November 30–December 02, 2009, IEEE Press.
4. Baker, R. and A. Carvalho. 2008. Labeling student behavior faster and more precisely with text replays. In *Proceedings of the First International Conference on Educational Data Mining*. Montreal, Canada, June 20–21, 2008, pp. 38–47.
5. Beck, J.E. 2007. Difficulties in inferring student knowledge from observations (and why should we care). In *Workshop Educational Data Mining—International Conference Artificial Intelligence in Education*. Marina del Rey, CA, 2007, pp. 21–30.
6. Dempster, A.P., N.M. Laird, and D.B. Rubin. 1997. Maximum likelihood from incomplete data via the EM algorithm. *Journal of the Royal Statistical Society Series*, 39: 1–38. Blackwell Publishing.
7. Domingos, P. and G. Hulten. 2000. Mining high-speed data streams. In *Proceedings of the Sixth ACM SIGKDD International Conference on Knowledge Discovery and Data Mining*. Boston, MA, ACM Press, New York, pp. 71–80.
8. Mitchell, T. 1982. Generalization as search. *Artificial Intelligence*, 18 (2): 223–236.
9. Nilsson, N. 1965. *Learning Machines: Foundations of Trainable Pattern-Classifying Systems*. McGraw-Hill, New York.
10. Quinlan, J.R. 1993. *C4.5 Programs for Machine Learning*. Morgan Kaufmann, San Mateo, CA.
11. Quinlan, J.R. 1986. Induction of decision trees. *Machine Learning*, 1(1): 81–106. Kluwer Academic Publishers.
12. Romero, C., S. Ventura, P.G. Espejo, and C. Hervas. 2008. Data mining algorithms to classify students. In *Proceedings of the First International Conference on Educational Data Mining*. Montreal, Canada, June 20–21, 2008, pp. 8–17.
13. Scheffer, T. 2001. Finding association rules that trade support optimally against confidence. In *Proceedings of the European Conference on Principles and Practice of Knowledge Discovery in Databases (PKDD'01)*. Springer-Verlag, Freiburg, Germany, pp. 424–435.
14. Superby, J.F., J.-P. Vandamme, and N. Meskens. 2006. Determining of factors influencing the achievement of first-year university students using data mining methods. In *Proceedings of the Eighth Intelligent Tutoring System: Educational Data Mining Workshop (ITS'06)*. Jhongali, Taiwan, pp. 37–44.
15. Vapnik, V. 1995. *The Nature of Statistical Learning Theory*. Springer-Verlag, New York.
16. Vapnik, V. and A. Chervonenkis. 1971. On the uniform convergence of relative frequencies of events to their probabilities. *Theory of Probability and its Applications*, 16(2): 264–280. SIAM.
17. Vee, M.H., B. Meyer, and K.L. Mannock. 2006. Understanding novice errors and error paths in object-oriented programming through log analysis. In *Intelligent Tutoring System: Educational Data Mining Workshop*. Jhongli, Taiwan, June, 2006, pp. 13–20.
18. Witten, I. and E. Frank. 2000. *Data Mining: Practical Machine Learning Tools and Techniques with Java Implementations*. Morgan Kaufmann, San Mateo, CA.

26

Using Decision Trees for Improving AEH Courses

Javier Bravo, César Vialardi, and Alvaro Ortigosa

CONTENTS

26.1 Introduction

Adaptive educational hypermedia systems (AEHS) seek to make easier the learning process for each student by providing each one (potentially) different educative contents, customized according to the student's needs and preferences. One of the main concerns with AEHS is to test and decide whether adaptation strategies are beneficial for all the students or, on the contrary, some of them would benefit from different decisions of the adaptation engine. Data-mining (DM) techniques can provide support to deal with this issue; specifically, this chapter proposes the use of DM techniques for detecting potential problems of adaptation in AEHS.

26.2 Motivation

Whenever possible, learning systems should consider individual differences among students. Students can have different interests, goals, previous knowledge, cultural background or learning styles, among other personal features. If these features are taken into account, it is possible to make the learning process easier or more efficient for each individual student. In this sense, AEHS [1] provide a platform for delivering educative material and activities through the web. They automatically guide students through the learning, by recommending the most suitable learning activities at every moment, according to their personal features and needs. AEHS have been successfully used in different contexts, and many online educational systems have been developed (e.g., AHA! [2], TANGOW [3], WHURLE [4], and more recently NavEx [5], QuizGuide [6] and CoMoLE [7], among others).

Most of the AEHS proposed had been tested and evaluated against nonadaptive counterparts, and many of them have shown important benefits for the students. Moreover, systems supporting e-learning are commonplace nowadays. However, AEHS have not been used in real educational environments as much as its potential and effectiveness may suggest. The main obstacle to a wider adoption of AEH technology is the difficulty in creating and testing adaptive courses. One of the main problems is that teachers need to analyze how adaptation is working for different student profiles. In most AEHS, teachers define rather small knowledge modules and rules to relate these modules, and the system selects and organizes the material to be presented to every student depending on the student profile. As a result of this dynamic organization of educational resources, the teacher cannot look at the "big picture" of the course structure easily, since it can potentially be different for each student and many times it also depends on the actions taken by the student at runtime. In this sense, teachers would benefit from methods and tools specially designed to support development and evaluation of adaptive systems.

Due to their own nature, AEHS collect records with the actions done by every student while interacting with the adaptive course. Log files provide good opportunities for applying web usage mining techniques with the goal of providing a better understanding on the student behavior and needs, and also how the adaptive course is fulfilling these needs.

With this intention, our effort is centered on helping authors to improve courses and we propose a spiral model for the life cycle of an adaptive course:

- The first step in this cycle is for the instructor (or educative content designer) to develop a course with an authoring tool and to load it in a course delivering system.

- The course is delivered to the students, collecting their interaction with the system (log files).

- Afterward, the instructor can examine the log files with the aid of DM tools. These tools help the instructor to detect possible failures or weak points of the course and even propose suggestions for improving the course.

- The instructor can follow these suggestions and make the corresponding modifications to the course through the authoring tool and load the course in the delivering system again, so that new students can benefit from the changes.

Therefore, the instructor can improve the course on each cycle. However, using DM tools to analyze the interaction data and interpreting the results, even if the tools are available, can be a daunting task for nonexpert users. For this reason, methods that help the instructors and course designers to analyze the data need to be developed.

The proposed method (key-node method) consists of using decision trees to assist in the development of AEH courses, particularly on the evaluation and improvement phase. When analyzing the behavior of a number of students using an AEH system, the author not only needs to find "weak points" of the course, but also needs to consider how these potential problems are related with the student profiles. For example, finding that 20% of the students failed a given exercise is not the same as knowing that more that 80% of the students with profile "English," "novice" failed it. In this case, the goal of our approach is not only to extract information about the percentage of students that failed the exercise but also to describe the features the students who failed have in common.

In order to show a practical use of the method, synthetic user data are analyzed. These data are generated by Simulog [8], a tool able to simulate student behavior by generating log files according to specified profiles. It is even possible to define certain problems of the adaptation process that logs would reflect. In that way, it is possible to test this approach, showing how the method will support teachers when dealing with student data.

26.3 State of the Art

In recent years, many works related to e-learning and DM areas can be found. For example, Becker and Marquardt's study [9] showcases the use of sequence analysis where student logs are analyzed in order to find patterns that reveal the different paths taken by the students. They used this information to improve the student experience. This work focuses mainly on two problems that exist in e-learning environments. The first problem is related to analyzing the student behavior determined by frequent paths followed by students. For this task, they study the log files of students by using association rules and sequential patterns. On the other hand, the second problem consists of optimizing the use of resources offered in the learning activities, for example, number of available printers. This chapter is centered on the first problem, but not by analyzing the students' paths, but by analyzing the students' interaction. Furthermore, the approach in this chapter differs from the authors mentioned above since our attention is focused on student profile. While Becker looks for navigation patterns without considering students' profiles, we try to find behavioral patterns in the outcomes (success or failure) of student practical activities in AEH courses. Merceron and Yacef published another study where association rules are extracted from data of Logic-ITA [10]. Logic-ITA is a web-based tutoring tool used to offer courses, specifically to help students in their formal logic exercises. This system can also report the progress of students to the teacher. Similar to our study, but using a different technique, Merceron and Yacef focused the work on detecting patterns of mistakes made by the students by using association rules. In a different study, they found a relation between a given number of mistakes of students applying relevance methods such as Chi-Square, cosine, and contrasting rules [11]. In this study, the association rules are used to relate the categories of the student profile to the success or failure in practical exercises. Cheong et al. proposed a methodology to analyze students' interaction logs and guess their programming intentions [12]. They use this analysis to understand why these errors occur and why students made them. They provided direct feedback to the teachers in the process of designing and teaching courses. In this analysis they got valuable insights into the ways students learn to program, that is to say, their typical mistakes and ways to overcome them. These typical mistakes are detected by exploring patterns in the attempts made by students, which are utilized to design a feedback mechanism guiding the students in the course. Romero et al. proposed to use sequential patterns to help authors or teachers to discover interesting information from students' usage information of an AEH course [13]. This information is used to improve and personalize AEH courses (recommending the next links). Further information can be found in a very complete survey developed by Romero and Ventura [14]; it provides a good review of the main works (from 1995 to 2005) using DM techniques grouped by task, in e-learning environments, both for adaptive and nonadaptive systems.

26.4 The Key-Node Method

AEHs use a model of the student to adapt the material presented and the navigation support to the student features. In this way, a student is characterized by the dimensions of his/her student model. Attributes or dimensions included in the student model are different for different AEH systems and even for different courses of the same system, and they can include, for example, previous knowledge, language, age, and learning styles, among others. If for a given adaptive course relevant attributes are, for instance, previous knowledge, language, and age, the model or profile for a concrete student can contain {"English," "advanced," "young"}.

Typically adaptive systems comprise some codification about how contents and navigation must be adapted to different student profiles. In a general way this information is coded through adaptation rules. According to these rules, each student can follow a different path of activities in an adaptive course, where a path is the sequence of activities visited by the student. From the teacher point of view, one of the main problems is to know if certain paths followed by the students reached successful results with more probability than others paths. In other words, it is possible that certain paths largely increase the possibilities of failure. Another problem is to know if these paths are related to a specific profile or, on the contrary, they represent a problem not related to the adaptation but with the course in general.

A possible way of searching for problems in the adaptation rules is finding potential symptoms of bad adaptation in the user interactions with the AEHS. In this work, we start from the assumption that problems related to the adaptation will be detected through these symptoms. As user interactions are records on logs and they are a vast quantity of data, a natural approach is to apply DM techniques, and more specifically web mining, in order to find these symptoms. The **key-node** method uses a DM technique (decision tree) in order to find potential symptoms, which indicate bad adaptation in the system. In particular, this method utilizes the C4.5 algorithm [15,16], since it provides a readable output for human beings. The **key-node** method is described as follows:

- **Step 1: Cleaning phase**. Select the records in which the type of activity is either practical activity or test. It is important that all entries must contain an indicator of success or failure of each activity.
- **Step 2: Apply the C4.5 algorithm** with the following parameters:
  - Attributes: Dimensions of *student model* and *name of activity* variable.
  - Variable of classification: *Indicator of success* variable. This indicator shows if a student passes a given practical activity or test. Two values are possible for this variable: *yes* or no. A value *yes* indicates that the student score is higher than the minimum required (specified by the teacher). Otherwise its value is *no*.

- **Step 3: Evaluate the results**. The resulting decision tree contains nodes for each attribute. In other words, the tree could be composed of nodes related to *dimensions* of student profile, and one node related to *name of activity* variable. The leaves of the tree contain the values of the variable of classification, *indicator of success*. The next steps are necessary to find the symptoms:
  - Select the leaves in which *indicator of success* variable has value no. Only these leaves are important because they indicate that many students failed a given activity.
  - Analyze each path from the previous selected leaves to the root of the tree. For each path, two steps are necessary:
    - Find in the path the node with the name of activity and store it. The problems in the adaptation should be closely related to this activity.
    - Find in the path the values of the student profile.

26.5 Tools

This section provides a short description of the tools utilized to apply the **key-node** method. In addition, a description of **ASquare** (Author Assistant Tool) is provided.

26.5.1 Simulog

Simulog is a tool that simulates log files of several student profiles, which contain symptoms of bad adaptation [8]. A symptom of bad adaptation is, for example, most of the students with profile "novice = experience" fails a given practical activity. The first step in Simulog is to load the course description. Simulog is able to extract the parameters of the adaptation from the course description. These parameters generally include the types of student profiles. Afterward, the types of student profiles and the percentage of these profiles, the number of students to be generated, the average time that a student spent in an activity, and the symptom of bad adaptation can be specified. Simulog reads the course description and, based on a randomly generated student profile, reproduces the steps that a student with this profile would take in the adaptive course.

26.5.2 Waikato Environment for Knowledge Analysis

Waikato Environment for Knowledge Analysis (Weka) is a free software project composed of a collection of machine learning algorithms for solving real world DM problems [17]. It was developed by the University of Waikato (New Zealand). The system is written in JAVA and distributed under the terms of the GNU General Public License.

Weka provides implementations of learning algorithms, such as classification techniques, association rules, and clustering. In addition, Weka includes a variety of tools for preprocessing data (transforming datasets and cleaning) and facilities of data visualization (more information can be found in Weka home page: http://www.cs.waikato.ac.nz/ml/weka/index.html).

26.5.3 Author Assistant Tool

The Author Assistant (**ASquare)** tool is based on the Weka collection of DM algorithms. This tool is able to assist the evaluation of adaptive courses. **ASquare** is used to analyze the log files generated from the student interactions with the system, and it can provide initial hints about potential problems on the course, and even suggest actions oriented to solve the problems. In this sense, **ASquare** is particularly valuable when the adaptive course is offered periodically or continuously to the students [18].

26.6 Applying the Key-Node Method

In this section, two examples show the application of **key-node** method. For these examples, two tools were used: **Simulog** and **Weka**. The first tool was used to generate the log files, and the second tool to analyze these data. In the following examples, log files are generated for a well-documented course on *traffic rules* [3].

26.6.1 Data Description

The data of the first example are the interactions of 240 simulated students, and the data of second example are of 480 students.

Table 26.1 shows the parameters of the simulation for the first example. This table indicates that 35% of the simulated students follow the Spanish version of the course and the rest 65% follow the English or German version. The percentage of both novice and advanced students is 50%. The percentage of students who are young is 50% and who are old is 50%. For example, a generated profile can be {"Spanish"; "novice"; "young"}. In other words, students with this profile are young, follow the Spanish version of the course, and have novice experience.

An entry of a log file in TANGOW is composed of several attributes: *<user-id, profile, activity, complete, grade, numVisit, action, activityType, syntheticTime, success>*. Each entry belongs to an action of the student at a given point in time. The profile field is actually an aggregated field. It is composed of age, language, and previous experience. Table 26.2 shows the description of the attributes.

Examples of entries for the student with user-id = s100 are

- <s100, young, Spanish, novice, S_Ag_Exer, 0.0, 0.0, 1, FIRSTVISIT, P, no>
- <s100, young, Spanish, novice, S_Ag_Exer, 0.0, 0.0, 1, LEAVE-ATOMIC, P, no>

TABLE 26.1

Dimensions for the Student Profile

Dimension	Values
Language	Spanish (35%), English (32.5%), German (32.5%)
Experience	Novice (50%), Advanced (50%)
Age	Young (50%), Old (50%)

TABLE 26.2

Description of the Attributes of an Entry of Log File in TANGOW

Attributes	Description
Activity	Activity id
Complete	It represents the level of completeness of the activity. If the activity is composed, it takes into consideration the completeness of all subactivities. It is a numeric parameter that ranges from 0 to 1. Value 0 indicates the activity was not completed and value 1 indicates the activity was fully completed.
Grade	The grade given to each activity. In practical (P) activities it is usually calculated from a formula provided by the teacher. In composed activities it is the arithmetic mean of subactivity grades. Value 1 indicates the activity was finished with success and value 0 indicates the activity was finished with failures.
NumVisit	Number of times the student has visited the activity.
Action	The action executed by the student; these are defined by the TANGOW system:
	"START-SESSION": beginning of the learning session.
	"FIRSTVISIT": first time an activity is visited.
	"REVISIT": any visit to the activity following the first one.
	"LEAVE-COMPOSITE": the student leaves the (composed) activity.
	"LEAVE-ATOMIC": the student leaves the (atomic) activity.
ActivityType	The type of activity: *theoretical* (T), *exercises* (P), and *examples* (E).
SyntheticTime	Time stamp generated by Simulog when the student starts interacting with the activity.
Success	Indicates whether the activity is considered successful (*yes*) or not (*no*).

These two entries show that the student s100 with profile {"Spanish"; "novice";"young"} visited the "exercises of signs of traffic policeman" activity (*S_Ag_Exer*). It has 0.0 for complete, 0.0 for grade and this is the first visit to this activity. The type "P" means that this is a practical activity. The second entry shows that the student left this activity without completing it (complete = 0.0) and having an insufficient score to pass the exercise; for this reason, success is set to *no*.

26.6.2 First Example

In this example, we studied data on 240 students generated by Simulog according to the dimensions and proportions shown in Table 26.1. In addition, the generated interaction data contain the following symptom of bad adaptation:

- Profile: Language = Spanish, Experience = novice, Age = young
- Activity: *S_Ag_Exer*
- Type of symptom: Fail
- Proportion: 70%

This symptom of bad adaptation represents that 70% of students with "language = Spanish," "experience = novice," and "age = young" fail the *S_Ag_Exer* activity. That is to say, students with profile {"Spanish"; "novice"; "young"} fail the activity "exercises of signs of traffic policeman" with 70% probability.

According to the previous method, the first step (**Cleaning phase**) was to clean the data. It consists of removing from log file the records that are not necessary for the mining

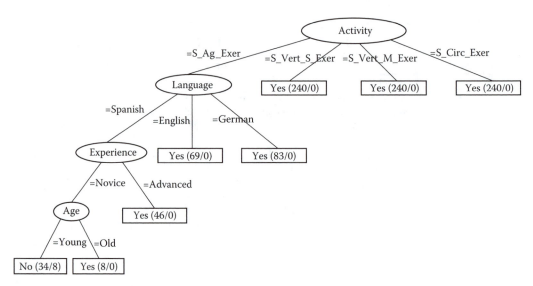

FIGURE 26.1
Decision tree for the first example.

phase. Cleaning in this case is both important and necessary for the size of data as a whole and, consequently, for the speed and accuracy with which results are obtained. Only practical activities are considered in the analysis, since these activities provide a reliable grade. The practical activities are denoted in the log file with action equals to "LEAVE-ATOMIC" and type equals to "P". As our intention is to analyze the practical activities, the records with action different from "LEAVE-ATOMIC" and type of activity different from "P" (test or practical activities) were eliminated. As a result, the final set of records contained 960 records. The second step (**Apply the C4.5 algorithm**) is to generate the decision tree. Figure 26.1 shows the obtained decision tree. This tree is composed of three nodes related to dimensions of student profile: nodes language, experience, and age; and one node related to the name of activity: node activity. The last step of the method (**Evaluate the results**) is to find the node activity and the profile, and it is described as follows:

- In the tree, only one leaf is found with the value no. This leaf has 77% of well-classified instances. The value of node activity for this leaf is *S_Ag_Exer*. Then, the student profile is formed by "age=young," "experience=novice," and "language=Spanish".

Therefore, this tree indicates that a great number of the students who follow the Spanish version of the course, who have novice experience, and who are young had many failures in the *S_Ag_Exer* activity. It is important to highlight that in this example the tree has a high percentage of well-classified instances. This fact is due to the absence of randomness effect in variable grade when a student is not related to the symptom of bad adaptation. In this case, these students always pass the activity.

26.6.3 Second Example

In this last example, data from 480 students were studied, generated by Simulog with two symptoms of bad adaptation and adding randomness effect in the variable grade.

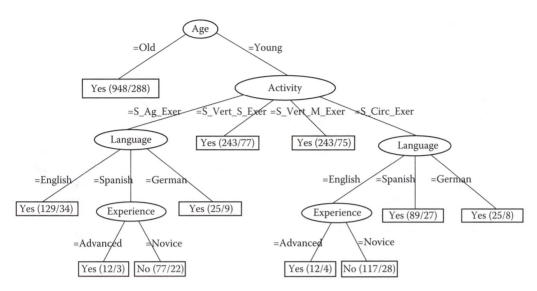

FIGURE 26.2
Decision tree for the second example.

Therefore, in this example, there are two sources of noise, which are the number of symptoms and the randomness effect. These symptoms were defined as 60% of students with profile {"Spanish"; "novice"; "young"} fail the *S_Ag_Exer* (*exercises of signs of traffic policeman*), and 60% of students with profile {"English"; "novice"; "young"} fail the *S_Circ_Exer* (*exercises of circular signs*) activity. The first phase of the **key-node** method is to proceed to clean the data (**cleaning phase**) as it is realized in the first example. The results of the cleaning phase showed 1920 records to which the algorithm of decision tree is applied in the second step (Figure 26.2 shows the decision tree). The last step of the method obtained the following outcomes:

- Two leaves with the value *no* are found in the tree. Two activities are related to these leaves: *S_Ag_Exer* and *S_Circ_Exer*. Therefore, two possible symptoms of bad adaptation can be found.
- For the first leaf *no* (related to the node "activity = *S_Ag_Exer*"), the student profile is defined by the variables "experience = novice," "language = Spanish," and "age = young."
- For the second leaf with *no* value (related to the node "activity = *S_Circ_Exer*"), the student profile is defined by the variables "experience = novice," "language = English," and "age = young".

Thus, two symptoms of bad adaptation are detected, since the proportion of well-classified instances is reasonably high in both leaves with *no* value (more than 70%). Hence, the young students with novice experience who follow the Spanish version of the course had many difficulties with *S_Ag_Exer* activity. In addition, there was another group of young students with novice experience with many difficulties in *S_Circ_Exer* activity, but the language in this group was English.

26.7 Conclusions

This work proposes a practical way, based on decision trees, to search for possible wrong adaptation decisions on AEHS. The decision tree technique is a useful method for detecting patterns related to symptoms of potential problems on the adaptation procedure.

This chapter presents two experiments intended to show the advantages of this method. They were carried out with different numbers of simulated students and also with different percentages of students failing the same exercise, all of them corresponding to a certain profile. The first experiment proves the effectiveness of decision trees for detecting existing symptoms of bad adaptation without noise in the data. The second experiment was carried out with a larger number of students. Moreover, noise was included in the data through a randomness factor in the grade variable. It was added with the objective of generating data to be closer to reality. This experiment shows the algorithm scalability and reliability. Furthermore, the method for detecting symptoms provides instructors with two types of information. On one hand, the instructor can know whether a symptom is closely related to a given activity. Then, the instructor can decide to check the activity and the adaptation around it. On the other hand, the instructor can detect whether a group of students belonging to a certain user profile (or sharing certain features) had trouble with an activity. Then, the instructor can decide either to modify the activity itself, to include additional activities to reinforce the corresponding learning, to establish previous requirements to tackle the activity or to change the course structure, that is, for students matching this learning profile, by incorporating rules to represent the corresponding adaptation for this type of students.

The usefulness of this method for detecting potential problems in AEH courses has been shown in the two examples. However, to be useful for instructors, this method ought to be supported by tools, which hide the technique details to nonexpert users in DM. In that sense, we are improving our evaluation tool, **ASquare (Author Assistant)**, by adding the key-node method [18].

It is important to highlight that the utility of decision trees showed in this chapter is not centered on the accuracy in predicting the success of students when tackling learning activities. Therefore, the percentage of well-classified events is less important than the capability of this tree to show the symptoms of bad adaptation. Finally, the two examples showed that, although decision trees are a powerful technique, they also have weak points. An important weakness is that the information extracted may not always be complete, since the algorithm C4.5 works with probabilities of events. Therefore, for complementing the information extracted it may be necessary to use this method together with other DM techniques such as association rules, clustering, or other multivariable statistical techniques. In that sense, our future work is centered on testing the combination of decision trees with other techniques for completing the information extracted from those. In this sense, we analyzed in other work if association rules provide additional information to decision trees [19]. Another important challenge is to know the threshold index of failures that indicates a symptom of bad adaptation. This last challenge is also part of our future work.

Acknowledgment

The work presented in this chapter has been partially funded by the Spanish Ministry of Science and Education through project HADA (TIN2007-64716).

References

1. Brusilovsky, P. 2003. Developing adaptive educational hypermedia systems: From design models to authoring tools. In *Authoring Tools for Advanced Technology Learning Environment*, ed. T. Murray, S. Blessing, and S. Ainsworth, pp. 377–409. Dordrecht, the Netherlands: Kluwer Academic Publishers.

2. De Bra, P., Aerts, A., Berden, B. et al. 2003. AHA! The Adaptive Hypermedia Architecture. In *Proceedings of 14th ACM Conference on Hypertext and Hypermedia*, pp. 81–84. Nottingham, U.K.: ACM Press.

3. Carro, R.M., Pulido, E., and Rodríguez, P. 1999. Dynamic generation of adaptive internet-based courses. *Journal of Network and Computer Applications* 22:249–257.

4. Moore, A., Brailsford, T.J., and Stewart, C.D. 2001. Personally tailored teaching in WHURLE using conditional transclusion. In *Proceedings of the 12th ACM Conference on Hypertext and Hypermedia*, pp. 163–164. Odense, Denmark: ACM Press.

5. Yudelson, M. and Brusilovsky, P. 2005. NavEx: Providing navigation support for adaptive browsing of annotated code examples. In *Proceedings of 12th International Conference on Artificial Intelligence in Education (AIED)*, ed. C.K. Looi, G. McCalla, B. Bredeweg, and J. Breuker, pp. 710–717. Amsterdam, the Netherlands: IOS Press.

6. Sosnovsky, S. and Brusilovsky, P. 2005. Layered evaluation of topic-based adaptation to student knowledge. In *Proceedings of 4th Workshop on the Evaluation of Adaptive Systems at 10th International User Modeling Conference*, ed. S. Weibelzahl, A. Paramythis, and J. Masthoff, pp. 47–56, Edinburgh, U.K.

7. Martín, E., Carro, R.M., and Rodríguez, P. 2006. A mechanism to support context-based adaptation in m-learning. *Innovative Approaches for Learning and Knowledge Sharing, Lecture Notes in Computer Science* 4227:302–315.

8. Bravo, J. and Ortigosa, A. 2006. Validating the evaluation of adaptive systems by user profile simulation. In *Proceedings of Fifth Workshop on User-Centred Design and Evaluation of Adaptive Systems held at the Fourth International Conference on Adaptive Hypermedia and Adaptive Web-Based Systems (AH2006)*, ed. S. Weibelzahl and A. Cristea, pp. 479–483, Dublin, Ireland.

9. Becker, K., Marquardt, C.G., and Ruiz, D.D. 2004. A pre-processing tool for web usage mining in the distance education domain. In *Proceedings of the International Database Engineering and Application Symposium (IDEAS'04)*, ed. J. Bernardino and B.C. Desai, pp. 78–87. Coimbra, Portugal: IEEE.

10. Merceron, A. and Yacef, K. 2005. Educational data mining: A case study. In *Proceedings of the 12th International Conference on Artificial Intelligence in Education (AIED)*, ed. C. Looi, G. McCalla, B. Bredeweg, and J. Breuker, pp. 467–474. Amsterdam, the Netherlands: IOS Press.

11. Merceron, A. and Yacef, K. 2007. Revisiting interestingness of strong symmetric association rules in educational data. In *Proceedings of International Workshop on Applying Data Mining in E-Learning (ADML07) held at the 2nd European Conference on Technology Enhanced Learning (EC-TEL 2007)*, pp. 3–12, Crete, Greece.

12. Cheong, M-H., Meyer, B., and Mannock, K.L. 2006. Understanding novice errors and error paths in object-oriented programming through log analysis. In *Proceedings of Workshop on Educational Data Mining at the 8th International Conference on Intelligent Tutoring Systems (ITS 2006)*, ed. C. Heiner, R. Baker, and K. Yacef, pp. 13–20, Jhongli, Taiwan.

13. Romero, C., Porras, A.R., Ventura, S., Hervás, C., and Zafra, A. 2006. Using sequential pattern mining for links recommendation in adaptive hypermedia educational systems. *Current Developments in Technology Assisted Education* 2:1016–1020.

14. Romero, C. and Ventura, S. 2007. Educational data mining: A survey from 1995 to 2005. *Expert Systems with Applications* 33(1):135–146.

15. Quinlan, J.R. 1993. *C4.5: Programs for Machine Learning*. San Mateo, CA: Morgan Kaufmann Publishers.

16. Mitchell, T. 1997. *Decision Tree Learning*. New York: McGraw Hill.

17. Witten, I.H. and Frank, E. 2005. *Data Mining Practical Machine Learning Tools and Techniques*. San Francisco, CA: Morgan Kaufmann Publishers.
18. Bravo, J., Vialardi, C., and Ortigosa, A. 2008. ASquare: A powerful evaluation tool for adaptive hypermedia course system. In *Proceedings of Hypertext Conference*, ed. P. Brusilovsky, pp. 219–220. Pittsburgh, PA: Sheridan Printing.
19. Vialardi, C., Bravo, J., and Ortigosa, A. 2009. Improving AEH courses through log analysis. *Journal of Universal Computer Science (J.UCS)* 14(17):2777–2798.

27

Validation Issues in Educational Data Mining: The Case of HTML-Tutor and iHelp

Mihaela Cocea and Stephan Weibelzahl

CONTENTS

27.1 Introduction

Validation is one of the key aspects in data mining and even more so in *educational* data mining (EDM) owing to the nature of the data. In this chapter, a brief overview of validation in the context of EDM is given and a case study is presented. The field of the case study is related to motivational issues, in general, and disengagement detection, in particular. There are several approaches to eliciting motivational knowledge from a learner's activity trace; in this chapter the validation of such an approach is presented and discussed.

The chapter is structured as follows. Section 27.2 provides an overview of validation in the context of EDM. Section 27.3 presents the case study, including previous work on motivation in e-Learning, details of data and methods, and results. Section 27.4 presents some challenges encountered and lessons learned and, finally, Section 27.5 concludes the chapter.

27.2 Validation in the Context of EDM

The term validation in EDM is used in two different meanings: (1) the validation of a model for the current context and similar users or (2) validation of a model in a new context and/ or for other users. The former is the typical evaluation of models in data mining, while the latter is more specific to social/educational research, when a model/theory is considered to be valid when it goes beyond the data on which the model has been built upon.

For the first type of validation, which is the most frequent one, different criteria are used, often depending on the methods applied. For example, when modeling student proficiency, criteria such as relative closeness to real scores and mean absolute error [5], mean absolute deviation [1], and R square and Bayesian information criterion [12] are used. For association rules, many criteria are considered as representative; for example, 12 such measures were used in [22] among which are chi-squared, correlation coefficient, and predictive association. Prediction models often use accuracy, kappa, true positives, and false positives measures [16,26].

Validation against an external measurement, such as a standardized test, was proposed in [11]. Another possibility is to use different methods and compare their results. For example, [25] compared results of three methods: (1) randomized controlled trials, (2) learning decomposition, and (3) knowledge tracing; they argue that the qualitative consistency of results provides evidence for the validity of the results and of the methods.

In contrast, the validation of a model for a new context or for a new population is less frequently used due to the difficulty of building models that could work in different contexts and/or for different users. However, there is research that investigates these aspects; for example, validation of a model for "gaming the system" was successful for new lessons (i.e., different content) and new students (i.e., different users) [4]. Validation in a different context helps to understand to what degree findings can be generalized. It can thus contribute to educational theory building by identifying relationships between concepts or patterns of behavior.

The case study presented in this chapter also investigates validation of a predictive approach in a different context, and more specifically, in a different e-Learning system. The development of the predictive approach and the validation are presented in the following.

27.3 Disengagement Detection Validation: A Case Study

27.3.1 Detection of Motivational Aspects in e-Learning

Several approaches for motivation detection from learner's interactions with e-Learning systems have been proposed ranging from rule-based approaches to latent response models. Some of these approaches are briefly presented below.

First, a rule-based approach based on ARCS Model [14] has been developed to infer motivational states from learners' behavior using a 10-question quiz [9]. A set of 85 inference rules was produced by the participants who had access to replays of learners' interactions with the system and to learners' motivational traits.

Second, another approach [18], also based on ARCS Model, is used to infer three aspects of motivation: (1) confidence, (2) confusion, and (3) effort from the learner's focus of attention and inputs related to learners' actions.

Third, engagement tracing [6] is an approach based on Item Response Theory that pro-poses the estimation of the probability of a correct response given a specific response time for modeling disengagement; two methods of generating responses are assumed: (1) "blind guess" when the student is disengaged, and (2) an answer with a certain probability of being correct when the student is engaged. The model also takes into account individual differences in reading speed and level of knowledge.

Fourth, a dynamic mixture model combining a hidden Markov model with Item Response Theory was proposed in [13]. The dynamic mixture model takes into account student proficiency, motivation, evidence of motivation, and the student's response to a problem. The motivation variable can have three values: (1) motivated; (2) unmotivated and exhausting all the hints in order to reach the final one that gives the correct answer, categorized as unmotivated-hint; and (3) unmotivated and quickly guessing answers to find the correct answer, categorized as unmotivated-guess.

Fifth, a Bayesian network has been developed [2] from log-data in order to infer variables related to learning and attitudes toward the tutor and the system. The log-data registered variables such as problem-solving time, mistakes, and help requests.

Last, a latent response model [4] was proposed for identifying the students that game the system. Using a pretest–posttest approach, the gaming behavior was classified in two cate-gories: (1) with no impact on learning and (2) with decrease in learning gain. The variables used in the model were student's actions and probabilistic information about the student's prior skills. The same problem of gaming behavior was addressed in [23], an approach that combines classroom observations with logged actions in order to detect gaming behavior manifested by guessing and checking or hint/help abuse.

27.3.2 Proposed Approach to Disengagement Detection

In previous research [8], an approach to disengagement prediction for web-based systems that covered both reading and problem-solving activities was proposed. Log files from HTML-Tutor, a web-based interactive learning environment, were analyzed. Initially, com-plete learning sessions, that is, all activities between login and logout, were analyzed [7]. However, it was found that in this setup the level of engagement could be predicted only after 45 min of activity. After such a long duration, most disengaged students would have logged out, leaving no possibility of disengagement prediction and intervention. To over-come this problem, in the subsequent studies, the sessions were divided in sequences of 10 min.

Several data mining techniques were used, showing that the user's level of engagement can be predicted from logged data, mainly related to reading pages and problem-solving activities. The fact that similar results were obtained when using different techniques and different numbers of attributes demonstrated the consistency of prediction and of the attributes used. The best accuracy, that is, 88%, was obtained using Classification via Regression on a dataset that included attributes related to reading, problem-solving, hyperlinks, and glossary. The best prediction for disengagement (with a true positive rate of 0.93) was obtained using Bayesian networks.

27.3.3 Disengagement Detection Validation

27.3.3.1 Data Considerations

To validate the approach briefly presented above, data from iHelp, the University of Saskatchewan web-based system, was analyzed. The iHelp system includes two web-based

TABLE 27.1

The Attributes Used for Analysis

Codes	Attributes
NoPages	Number of pages read
AvgTimeP	Average time spent reading
NoQuestions	Number of questions from quizzes/surveys
AvgTimeQ	Average time spent on quizzes/surveys
Total time	Total time of a sequence
NoPpP	Number of pages above the threshold established for maximum time required to read a page
NoPM	Number of pages below the threshold established for minimum time to read a page

applications, the iHelp Discussion System and iHelp Learning Content Management System, designed to support both learners and instructors throughout the learning process. The latter is designed to deliver online courses to students working at a distance, providing course content (text and multimedia) as well as quizzes and surveys. The students' interactions with the system are preserved in a machine readable format.

The same type of data about the interactions was selected from the logged information to perform the same type of analysis as the one performed on HTML-Tutor data. An HTML course was also chosen to prevent differences in results caused by differences in subject matter. Data from 11 students was used, meaning a total of 108 sessions and 450 sequences (341 of exactly 10 min and 109 less than 10 min). While at first glance a sample size of 11 students may seem rather small, it should be noted that the total time observed (i.e., more than 60 h of learning) as well as the number of instances analyzed (i.e., 450 sequences) is far more important for the validity of the results.

Several attributes (displayed in Table 27.1) related to reading pages and quizzes were used in the analysis. The terms tests and quizzes will be used interchangeably; they refer to the same type of problem-solving activity, except that in HTML-Tutor they are called tests and in iHelp they are named quizzes. Total time (of a sequence) was included as an attribute for the trials that took into account sequences of less than 10 min as well as sequences of exactly 10 min. Compared to the analysis of HTML-Tutor logs, for iHelp, there are fewer attributes related to quizzes: information about the number of questions attempted and about the time spent on them is included, but information about the correctness or incorrectness of answers given by users was not available at the time of the analysis. Two new meta-attributes that were not considered for HTML-Tutor were introduced for this analysis: the number of pages above and below a certain time threshold, described in the subsequent section; they are meta-attributes because they are not among the raw data, but they are derived from it.

27.3.3.2 Annotation of the Level of Engagement

Annotations of the level of engagement for each sequence (of 10 min or less) were made by an expert with tutoring experience, in a manner similar to the HTML-Tutor data; each sequence was annotated with the label *engaged* or *disengaged*. The expert annotated sequences based on *all logged attributes*, not just the ones used in the analyses. Besides these annotations, two additional rules related to the two new attributes (regarding the number of pages that are above or below a threshold, depending on time spent reading) were used.

These rules were applied after having obtained the expert annotations and as a result of a common pattern observed for both HTML-Tutor and iHelp. Consequently, the two new meta-attributes were added to investigate their contribution to prediction and their potential usage for a less time-consuming process for annotation.

Initially, we intended to use the average time spent on each page across all users, as suggested by [19], but analyzing the data, we have seen that some pages are accessed by a very small number of users, sometimes only one; this problem was also encountered in other research (e.g., [10]). Consequently, we decided to use the average reading speed known to be in between 200 and 250 words per min [20,21]. Out of the 652 pages accessed by the students, five pages needed between 300 and 400s to be read at average speed, 41 pages needed between 200 and 300s, 145 needed between 100 and 300s, and 291 needed less than 100s. Some pages included images and videos; however, only two students attempted to watch videos, one giving up after 3.47s and the other one watching a video (or being on the page with the link to a video) for 162s (almost 3min). Taking into account this information, less than 5s or more than 420s (7min) spent on a page were agreed to indicate disengagement.

For the HTML-Tutor logs, the level of engagement was established by human experts that looked at the log files and established the level of engagement for each sequence (of 10min or less), in a manner similar to the analysis described by [9]. The same procedure was applied for iHelp, plus the two aforementioned rules.

Accordingly, the level of engagement was determined for each sequence of 10min or less. If in a sequence the learner spent more than 7min on a page or test, the learner was considered disengaged during that sequence. In relation to pages accessed less than 5s, a user was considered disengaged if two-thirds of the total number of pages were below that time.

With HTML-Tutor, the rating consistency was verified by measuring inter-coding reliability. A sample of 100 sequences (from a total of 1015) was given to a second rater and results indicated high inter-coder reliability: percentage agreement of 92%, Cohen's kappa measurement of agreement of 0.826 ($p < 0.01$), and Krippendorff's alpha of 0.845 [15]. With iHelp only one rater classified the level of engagement for all sequences.

27.3.3.3 Analysis and Results

Using the attributes described in Section 27.3.3.1, an analysis was conducted to investigate disengagement prediction with iHelp data and to compare the results with the ones from HTML-Tutor. Waikato Environment for Knowledge Analysis (WEKA) [24] was used to perform the analysis. The same methods (presented below) as the ones used in our previous research were applied and four datasets were used: (1) Dataset 1 including all attributes and all sequences; (2) Dataset 2 was obtained from Dataset 1 by eliminating the two additional attributes (NoPgP, NoPgM); (3) Dataset 3 included all attributes, but only sequences of exactly 10min; and (4) Dataset 4 was obtained from Dataset 3 by eliminating the two additional attributes (NoPgP, NoPgM). Dataset 2 and 4 were used to compare the results with the ones from HTML-Tutor. Table 27.2 presents the datasets with the corresponding attributes and sequences.

The eight methods [17,24] used for the analysis are (1) Bayesian networks with K2 algorithm and maximum three parent nodes (BN); (2) Logistic regression (LR); (3) Simple logistic classification (SL); (4) Instance-based classification with IBk algorithm (IBk); (5) Attribute Selected Classification using J48 classifier and Best First search (ASC); (6) Bagging using REP (reduced-error pruning) tree classifier (B); (7) Classification via Regression (CvR) and

TABLE 27.2

Datasets Used in the Experiment

Dataset	Sequences	Attributes
Dataset 1	All sequences	NoPages, AvgTimeP, NoQuestions, AvgTimeQ, Total time, NoPpP, NoPM
Dataset 2	All sequences	NoPages, AvgTimeP, NoQuestions, AvgTimeQ, Total time
Dataset 3	Only 10 min sequences	NoPages, AvgTimeP, NoQuestions, AvgTimeQ, Total time, NoPpP, NoPM
Dataset 4	Only 10 min sequences	NoPages, AvgTimeP, NoQuestions, AvgTimeQ, Total time

(8) Decision Trees (DT) with J48 classifier based on Quilan's C4.5 algorithm. The experiments were done using 10-fold stratified cross-validation iterated 10 times.

Results are displayed in Table 27.3, including accuracy and its standard deviation across all trials, true positive (TP) rate for disengaged class, precision (TP/(TP + false positive)) for disengaged class, mean absolute error, and kappa statistic. In our case, TP rate is more important than precision because TP rate indicates the correct percentage from *actual* instances of a class, and precision indicates the correct percentage from *predicted* instances

TABLE 27.3

Experiment Results Summary

Dataset	Measure	BN	LR	SL	IBk	ASC	B	CvR	DT
Dataset 1	Accuracy	89.31	95.22	95.13	95.29	95.44	95.22	95.44	95.31
	Std. Dev	4.93	2.78	2.82	2.98	2.97	3.12	3.00	3.03
	TP rate	0.90	0.95	0.95	0.94	0.94	0.94	0.95	0.95
	Precision	0.90	0.95	0.95	0.96	0.97	0.97	0.96	0.96
	Error	0.13	0.07	0.10	0.05	0.08	0.08	0.08	0.07
	Kappa	0.79	0.90	0.90	0.91	0.91	0.90	0.91	0.91
Dataset 2	Accuracy	81.73	83.82	83.58	84.00	84.38	85.11	85.33	84.38
	Std. Dev	5.66	5.03	5.12	4.85	5.08	5.17	5.13	5.07
	TP rate	0.78	0.82	0.81	0.79	0.77	0.79	0.80	0.78
	Precision	0.86	0.86	0.86	0.89	0.91	0.91	0.91	0.91
	Error	0.22	0.24	0.26	0.20	0.25	0.23	0.23	0.25
	Kappa	0.64	0.68	0.67	0.68	0.69	0.70	0.71	0.69
Dataset 3	Accuracy	94.65	98.06	97.91	98.59	97.65	97.65	97.76	97.47
	Std. Dev	4.47	2.18	2.69	2.11	2.64	2.64	2.65	2.58
	TP rate	0.95	0.97	0.96	0.98	0.96	0.96	0.96	0.96
	Precision	0.94	0.99	0.99	0.99	0.99	0.99	0.99	0.99
	Error	0.07	0.02	0.04	0.02	0.05	0.04	0.03	0.03
	Kappa	0.89	0.96	0.96	0.97	0.95	0.95	095	0.95
Dataset 4	Accuracy	84.29	85.82	85.47	84.91	84.97	85.38	85.26	85.24
	Std. Dev.	5.77	5.90	5.88	5.95	5.61	5.80	5.96	5.91
	TP rate	0.78	0.77	0.76	0.77	0.75	0.76	0.75	0.75
	Precision	0.88	0.92	0.92	0.89	0.92	0.92	0.92	0.92
	Error	0.18	0.22	0.23	0.20	0.25	0.23	0.24	0.24
	Kappa	0.68	0.71	0.70	0.69	0.69	0.70	0.70	0.70

TABLE 27.4

The Confusion Matrix for Instance Based
Classification with IBk Algorithm

		Predicted	
		Engaged	**Disengaged**
Actual	**Engaged**	180	1
	Disengaged	4	155

in that class. In other words, the aim is to identify as many disengaged students as possible. If an engaged student is misdiagnosed as being disengaged and receives special treatment for remotivation, this will cause less harm than the opposite situation.

The results presented in Table 27.3 show very good levels of prediction for all methods, with accuracy varying between approximately 81% and 98%. There are similar results for the disengaged class, the TP rate and the precision indicator for disengaged class varying between 75% and 98%. The mean absolute error varies between 0.02 and 0.25; the kappa statistic varies between 0.64 and 0.97, indicating that the results are much better than chance. In line with the results for HTML-Tutor, the fact that very similar results were obtained from different methods and trials demonstrates the consistency of the prediction and of the attributes used for prediction. The results for Dataset 1 and 3 are better than the ones from Dataset 2 and 4, suggesting that the two new meta-attributes bring significant information gain.

The highest accuracy was obtained using Instance-based classification with IBk algorithm on Dataset 3: 98.59%; the confusion matrix for this method is presented in Table 27.4. For the disengaged TP rate, the same method performs best on the same dataset: 0.98.

Investigating further the information gain brought by the two meta-attributes, attribute ranking using information gain ranking filter as attribute evaluator was performed and the following ranking was found: NoPgP, AvgTimeP, NoPages, NoPgM, NoQuestions, and AvgTimeQ. Hence, the meta-attributes seem to be more important than the attributes related to quizzes. The information gain contributed by NoPgP is also reflected in the decision tree graph displayed in Figure 27.1, where NoPgP has the highest information gain, being the root of the tree.

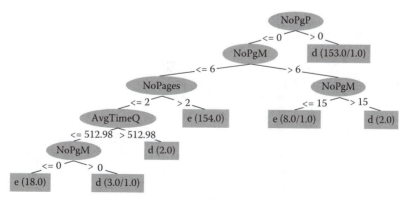

FIGURE 27.1
Decision tree graph for Dataset 3.

27.3.3.4 Cross-System Results Comparison

Comparing the results of iHelp to the ones of HTML-Tutor, an improvement for Datasets 1 and 3 and a small decrease for Datasets 2 and 4 are noticed. For ease of comprehension, some of the results from HTML-Tutor log-file analysis were included. These are only for the dataset with the attributes related to reading and tests, and they are presented in Table 27.5.

The decrease for Dataset 2 and 4 may be due to the two missing attributes related to quizzes: number of correct and number of incorrect answers that were available for HTML-Tutor. The increase for Datasets 1 and 3 could be accounted by the contribution of the two new attributes.

The two missing attributes related to correctness or incorrectness of quiz responses may improve even more the prediction level. Looking at their role in prediction for HTML-Tutor, using three attribute evaluation methods with ranking as search method for attribute selection, these two attributes were found to be the last ones. Thus, according to chi-square and information gain ranking, the most valuable attribute is average time spent on pages, followed by the number of pages, number of tests, average time spent on tests, number of correctly answered tests, and number of incorrectly answered tests. OneR ranking differs only in the position of the last two attributes: number of incorrectly answered tests comes before number of correctly answered tests. The attribute ranking using information gain filter for iHelp attributes shows similar positions for attributes related to reading and tests, meaning that attributes related to reading come before the ones related to tests. This suggests that the two missing attributes in iHelp are not essential, but if available they could improve the prediction level. Table 27.6 summarizes the similarities and differences between the findings from iHelp and HTML-Tutor.

TABLE 27.5

Experiment Results Summary for HTML-Tutor

	BN	LR	SL	IBk	ASC	B	CvR	DT
Accuracy	87.07	86.52	87.33	85.62	87.24	87.41	87.64	86.58
TP rate	0.93	0.93	0.93	0.92	0.93	0.93	0.92	0.93
Precision	0.91	0.90	0.90	0.91	0.92	0.92	0.92	0.91
Error	0.10	0.12	0.12	0.10	0.10	0.12	0.12	0.11

TABLE 27.6

Similarities and Dissimilarities between iHelp and HTML-Tutor

Characteristic	iHelp	HTML-Tutor
Prediction based on reading and tests attributes	81%–85% with no information on correctness/incorrectness of quizzes and no additional attributes 85%–98% with the two additional attributes	86%–87%
Attribute ranking	Number of pages above a threshold	Average time spent on pages
	Average time spent reading	Number of pages
	Number of pages read/accessed	Number of tests
	Number of pages below a threshold	Average time spent on tests
	Number of questions from quizzes	Number of correctly answered tests
	Average time spent on quizzes	Number of incorrectly answered tests

Even with the mentioned differences, the fact that a good level of prediction was obtained from similar attributes on datasets from different systems using the same methods indicates that engagement prediction is possible using information related to reading pages and problem-solving activities, information logged by most e-Learning system. Therefore, our proposed approach for engagement prediction is potentially system independent and could be generalized for any web-based system that includes both types of activities.

27.4 Challenges and Lessons Learned

In defining our approach to disengagement detection, one of the major challenges encountered was the definition of disengagement in terms of the actions of learners when interacting with web-based learning environments. The type of web-based systems investigated, that is, systems that provide both reading and problem-solving activities, presents an even bigger challenge. Most frequently, research on motivation focused exclusively on problem-solving activities, often characterized by a clearly defined structure that, to a certain degree, facilitates the assessment and modeling of motivational characteristics. To overcome this problem, we used human experts that assessed the level of engagement of learners based on their actions and annotated the data; these annotations were subsequently used in building the prediction models. As observed in other research [3], without labeled data it is difficult to validate models.

Another challenge was the subject domain; most previous research was conducted in fields such as mathematics or programming, which are more systematic and, therefore, more "controllable" than nontechnical domains. In our approach, the domain was HTML, which is at the junction between technical and nontechnical domains. Still, what seemed a disadvantage may prove to be beneficial, in the sense that the characteristics of this domain may allow an easier generalization across other domains, including nontechnical ones; however, this requires further investigation. One important lesson learned from the case study presented is that a lack of domain structure does not necessarily mean that user activity is impossible to model; nevertheless, the modeling process involves more exploration and is, perhaps, closer to typical data mining, which aims to discover information hidden in the data.

Another challenge was the validation process and its aim was to validate the approach and the attributes involved in the detection of disengagement rather than the models initially built. The disadvantages involved in this course of action are twofold: (1) the model(s) needs to be built for every new system and (2) annotations are needed to do that. However, the big advantage is that knowledge about the relevant attributes is available and this offers the possibility of building disengagement detectors for web-based systems that include both reading and problem-solving activities. The other way to generalize would be to use models built for other systems and change them or provide them with adaptive mechanisms for the new environment; however, current research indicates that this is still a difficult task, while our proposed approach, although involving some effort, is feasible.

In relation to the above-mentioned challenge, the lesson learned is that two stages are needed when aiming to develop an approach that could be extended beyond the data it was initially built on. The first step is an exploratory one, involving research about the relevant attributes and methods, while the second one involves the practical, implementation issues. For example, when developing an approach, the use of several methods serves the purpose of inspecting the consistency of results, while in practice it is best to work with one method.

27.5 Conclusions

In this chapter, issues related to validation in EDM were presented and discussed in the context of a case study on disengagement detection. The proposed approach for disengagement detection is simple and needs information about actions related to reading and problem-solving activities, which are logged by most e-Learning systems. Because of these characteristics, we believe that this approach can be generalized to other systems, as illustrated in the validation study presented in this chapter. The similarity of results across different data mining methods is also an indicator of the consistency of our approach and of the attributes used.

References

1. Anozie N. and Junker, B.W., Predicting end-of-year accountability assessment scores from monthly student records in an online tutoring system. In Beck, J., Aimeur, E., and T. Barnes (eds.), *EDM: Papers from the AAAI Workshop*. Menlo Park, CA: AAAI Press, pp. 1–6. Technical Report WS-06-05, 2006.
2. Arroyo, I. and Woolf, B.P., Inferring learning and attitudes from a Bayesian network of log file data. In *Proceedings of the 12th International Conference on Artificial Intelligence in Education*, Amsterdam, the Netherlands, pp. 33–34, 2005.
3. Baker, R.S.J.D. and Carvalho, A.M.J.A.D., Labeling student behavior faster and more precisely with text replays. In *Proceedings of 1st International Conference on Educational Data Mining*, Montreal, Canada, pp. 38–47, 2008.
4. Baker, R.S.J.D., Corbett, A.T., Roll, I., and Koedinger, K.R., Developing a generalizable detector of when students game the system. *User Modeling and User-Adapted Interaction* 18(3), 287–314, 2008.
5. Beck, J. E. and Sison, J., Using knowledge tracing in a noisy environment to measure student reading proficiencies. *International Journal of Artificial Intelligence in Education* 16, 129–143, 2006.
6. Beck, J., Engagement tracing: Using response times to model student disengagement. In *Proceedings of the 12th International Conference on Artificial Intelligence in Education*, Amsterdam, the Netherlands, pp. 88–95, 2005.
7. Cocea, M. and Weibelzahl, S., Can log files analysis estimate learners' level of motivation? In *Proceedings of ABIS Workshop, ABIS 2006—14th Workshop on Adaptivity and User Modeling in Interactive Systems*, Hildesheim, Germany, pp. 32–35, 2006.
8. Cocea, M. and Weibelzahl, S., Eliciting motivation knowledge from log files towards motivation diagnosis for adaptive systems. In *Proceedings of 11th International Conference on User Modeling*, Corfu, Greece, pp. 197–206, 2007.
9. De Vicente, A. and Pain, H., Informing the detection of the students' motivational state: An empirical study. In *Proceedings of the 6th International Conference on Intelligent Tutoring Systems*, Biarritz, France and San Sebastian, Spain, pp. 933–943, 2002.

10. Farzan, R. and Brusilovsky, P., Social navigation support in e-Learning: What are real footprints. In *Proceedings of IJCAI'05 Workshop on Intelligent Techniques for Web Personalization*, Edinburg, Scotland, pp. 49–56, 2005.

11. Feng, M., Beck J., Hefferman, N., and Koedinger, K., Can an intelligent system predict math proficiency as well as a standardized test? In *Proceedings of 1st International Conference on Educational Data Mining*, Montreal, Canada, pp. 107–116, 2008.

12. Feng, M., Heffernan, N.T., and Koedinger, K., Addressing the testing challenge with a web-based e-assessment system that tutors as it assesses. In *Proceedings of the 15th International World Wide Web Conference*, Edinburgh, Scotland, pp. 307–316, 2006.

13. Johns, J. and Woolf, B., A dynamic mixture model to detect student motivation and proficiency. In *Proceedings of the 21st National Conference on Artificial Intelligence (AAAI-06)*, Boston, MA, pp. 163–168, 2006.

14. Keller, J.M., Development and use of the ARCS model of instructional design. *Journal of Instructional Development* 10(3), 2–10, 2007.

15. Lombard, M., Snyder-Duch, J., and Campanella Bracken, C., *Practical Resources for Assessing and Reporting Intercoder Reliability in Content Analysis Research*, 2003. http://www.temple.edu/mmc/reliability (accessed November 6, 2006).

16. Mavrikis, M., Data-driven modelling of students' interactions in an ILE. In *Proceedings of 1st International Conference on Educational Data Mining*, Montreal, Canada, pp. 87–96, 2008.

17. Mitchell, T.M., *Machine Learning*. McGraw-Hill, New York, 1997.

18. Qu, L., Wang, N., and Johnson, W.L., Detecting the learner's motivational states in an interactive learning environment. In *Proceedings of the 12th International Conference on Artificial Intelligence in Education*, Amsterdam, the Netherlands, pp. 547–554, 2005.

19. Rafter, R. and Smyth, B., Passive profiling from server logs in an online recruitment environment. In *Proceedings of the IJCAI Workshop on Intelligent Techniques for Web Personalization*, Seattle, Washington, pp. 35–41, 2001.

20. ReadingSoft.com found at HYPERLINK, http://www.readingsoft.com

21. TurboRead Speed Reading found at HYPERLINK, http://www.turboread.com

22. Ventura, S., Romero, C., and Hervas, C., Analysing rule evaluation measures with educational datasets: A framework to help the teacher. In *Proceedings of 1st International Conference on Educational Data Mining*, Montreal, Canada, pp. 177–186, 2008.

23. Walonoski, J. and Heffernan, N.T., Detection and analysis of off-task gaming behavior in intelligent tutoring systems. In *Proceedings of the 8th International Conference in Intelligent Tutoring Systems*, Jhongli, Taiwan, pp. 382–391, 2006.

24. Witten, I.H. and Frank, E., *Data Mining. Practical Machine Learning Tools and Techniques*, 2nd edn., Morgan Kauffman Publishers, Elsevier, Amsterdam, the Netherlands, 2005.

25. Zhang, X., Mostow, J., and Beck, J.E., A case study empirical comparison of three methods to evaluate tutorial behaviors. In *Proceedings of the 9th International Conference on Intelligent Tutoring System*, LNCS, Vol. 5091, Montreal, Canada, pp. 122–131, 2008.

26. Zhang, X., Mostow, J., Duke, N., Trotochaud, C., Valeri, J., and Corbett, A., Mining free-form spoken responses to tutor prompts. In *Proceedings of 1st International Conference on Educational Data Mining*, Montreal, Canada, pp. 234–241, 2008.

28

Lessons from Project LISTEN's Session Browser

Jack Mostow, Joseph E. Beck, Andrew Cuneo, Evandro Gouvea,
Cecily Heiner, and Octavio Juarez

CONTENTS

28.1 Introduction

Intelligent tutoring systems' ability to log their interactions with students poses both an opportunity and a challenge. Compared to human observation of live or videotaped tutoring, such logs can be more extensive in the number of students, more comprehensive in the number of sessions, and more exquisite in the level of detail. They avoid observer effects, cost less, and are easier to analyze. The resulting data is a potential gold mine [4]—but mining it requires the right tools to locate promising areas, obtain samples, and analyze them.

For example, consider the data logged by Project LISTEN's Reading Tutor [5,6], which listens to children read aloud, and helps them learn to read [7–10]. As Figures 28.1 and 28.2 illustrate, each session involves taking turns with the Reading Tutor to pick a story to read with its assistance. The Reading Tutor displays the story one sentence at a time, and records the child's utterances for each sentence. The Reading Tutor logs each event (session, story, sentence, utterance, ...) into a database table for that event type. Data from tutors at different schools flow overnight into an aggregated database on our server. For example, our 2003–2004 database includes 54,138 sessions, 162,031 story readings, 1,634,660 sentences, 3,555,487 utterances, and 10,575,571 words. This data is potentially very informative, but orders of magnitude larger than is feasible to peruse in its entirety.

We view educational data mining as an iterative cycle of hypothesis formation, testing, and refinement. This cycle includes two complementary types of activities. One type

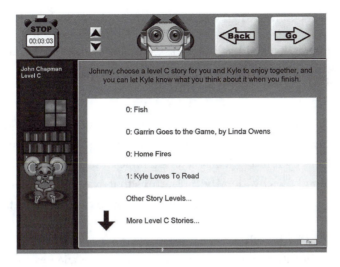

FIGURE 28.1
Picking a story in Project LISTEN's Reading Tutor.

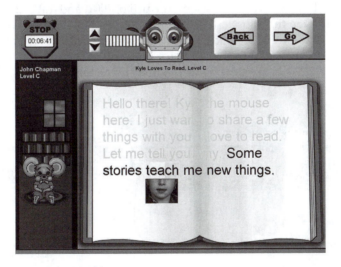

FIGURE 28.2
Assisted reading in Project LISTEN's Reading Tutor.

of activity involves aggregate quantitative data analysis, whether confirmatory or exploratory. For example, embedded experiments [5,11–13] compare alternative tutorial actions by selecting randomly among them and aggregating outcomes of many trials. Knowledge tracing [14] and learning decomposition [15] analyze growth curves by aggregating over successive opportunities to apply a skill. The Pittsburgh Science of Learning Center's (PSLC) DataShop [16] summarizes performance and learning curves aggregated by student, problem, problem step, and/or skill.

In contrast, the other type of activity involves in-depth qualitative analysis of individual examples. For conventional educational data in the form of test scores, this type of exploratory data analysis might try to identify individual students' patterns of correct and incorrect answers to individual test items, or (if available) what they wrote on the test paper in the course of working them out. For data logged by an intelligent tutoring system detailing its interactions with students, such analysis might try to identify significant sequences of tutorial events. In both cases, the research question addressed is descriptive [17, p. 204]: "What happened when ...?" Such case analyses serve several purposes; a few examples are listed below:

- Spot-check tutoring sessions to discover undesirable tutor–student interactions.
- Identify and characterize typical cases in which a specified phenomenon occurs.
- Develop a query by refining it based on examples it retrieves.
- Formulate hypotheses by identifying features that examples suggest are relevant.
- Sanity-check a hypothesis by checking that it covers the intended sorts of examples.

28.1.1 Relation to Prior Research

An earlier program [18] attempted to support case analysis by viewing interactions logged by Project LISTEN's Reading Tutor. As Tables 28.1 and 28.2 illustrate, the viewer displayed a table of tutorial interactions at a user-selected level of detail—computers, launches, students, sessions, stories, sentences, utterances, words, or clicks. For example, Table 28.1 lists stories encountered in a particular session on April 5, 2001, and Table 28.2 lists sentences encountered during the first story. Some columns of this table contained hyperlinks that let the user drill down to a table at the next deeper level of detail. For example, clicking on the hyperlink labeled 6 in the Sentence Encounters column of the first row of the table shown in Table 28.1 caused the viewer to display the table of six sentence encounters

TABLE 28.1

Activities in a Session

Start Time	Num Sent Encount	Num Sentences	Title	Exit Through
04-05-2001 12:24:25	6	40	How to Make Cookies by Emily Mostow.	end_of_activity
04-05-2001 12:28:14	14	56	One, two	end_of_activity
04-05-2001 12:31:34	5	112	Pretty Mouse by Maud Keary	select_response

Source: Mostow, J. et al., Viewing and analyzing multimodal human-computer tutorial dialogue: A database approach, in *Proceedings of the Fourth IEEE International Conference on Multimodal Interfaces (ICMI 2002) IEEE*, Pittsburgh, PA, 2002, pp. 129–134. First presented June 4, 2002, at the *ITS 2002 Workshop on Empirical Methods for Tutorial Dialogue Systems*, San Sebastian, Spain. © 2002 IEEE. With permission.

Note: The table contains a row for each activity in the session, and a column for each field displayed: the start time of the activity; the number of sentences read; the number of sentences in the story (including word previews and reviews before and after the story proper); the story title; and how the story encounter ended. Information about time spent on the story, reader level, story level, and who picked the story has been omitted here to save space.

TABLE 28.2

Sentence Encounters in a Story [18]

Start Time	Duration	Num Actions	Num Utterances	SentenceStr
04-05-2001 12:24:25	00:00:01	3	0	OVEN
04-05-2001 12:24:27	00:00:01	3	0	BATTER
04-05-2001 12:24:28	00:00:44	47	4	First get the batter
04-05-2001 12:25:12	00:00:24	20	4	Next put all the ingredients in
04-05-2001 12:25:37	00:00:33	3	2	Then put it in the oven
04-05-2001 12:26:11	00:00:40	3	3	Last eat them

Source: Mostow, J. et al., Viewing and analyzing multimodal human-computer tutorial dialogue: A database approach, in *Proceedings of the Fourth IEEE International Conference on Multimodal Interfaces (ICMI 2002) IEEE,* Pittsburgh, PA, 2002, pp. 129–134. First presented June 4, 2002, at the *ITS 2002 Workshop on Empirical Methods for Tutorial Dialogue Systems,* San Sebastian, Spain. © 2002 IEEE. With permission.

Note: This table has a row for each sentence encounter in the activity, including individual word previews and reviews, and a column for each field shown, namely, the sentence encounter's start time and duration, the number of tutor and student actions during it, the number of student utterances recorded, and the text of the word or sentence.

shown in Table 28.2. This ability to generate a table on demand with a single click spared the user the effort of writing the multiple database queries, including joins, required to generate the table.

However, the viewer suffered from several limitations. It displayed a list of records as a standard HTML table, which was not necessarily human-understandable. Although tables can be useful for comparing events of the same type, they are ill-suited to conveying the heterogeneous set of events that transpired during a given interaction, or the context in which they occurred. Navigation was restricted to drilling down from the top-level list of students or tutors, with no convenient way to specify a particular type of interaction to explore, and no visible indication of context. Finally, the viewer was inflexible. It was specific not just to the Reading Tutor but to one particular version of it. The user could not specify which events to select, how to summarize them, or (other than by deciding how far to drill down) which details to include.

28.1.2 Guidelines for Logging Tutorial Interactions

Our experience led us to develop the following guidelines for logging tutorial interactions [19]. They support multiple purposes, such as using logged information in the Reading Tutor itself, generating reports for teachers [20], mining the data by constructing queries to answer research questions [15,21], and browsing data as reported previously [1,3] and developed further in this chapter.

28.1.2.1 Log Tutor Data Directly to a Database

Intelligent tutoring systems commonly record their interactions in the form of log files, and so did the Reading Tutor prior to 2002. Log files are easy to record, flexible in what information they can capture, (sometimes) human-understandable to read, and useful in debugging. However, they are unwieldy to aggregate across multiple sessions and computers, difficult to parse and analyze in ways not anticipated when they were designed, and generally cumbersome and error-prone to process [5]. Consequently, more and more researchers have discovered the hard way that easy, accurate, efficient mining of educational data requires converting it from log files into a database representation. Indeed, the viewer described in Section 28.1.1 operated on a database extracted rather painfully from Reading Tutor log files.

Logging tutorial interactions directly to a suitably designed and indexed database instead of to log files eliminates the need to parse them—previously a major time sink and error source for Project LISTEN. Starting with the 2003–2004 school year, the Reading Tutor has logged its interactions to a database, making the process of analyzing them easier, faster, more flexible, less bug prone, and more powerful than analyzing conventional log files. This practice has enabled or facilitated nearly all the dozens of subsequent papers listed on the Publications page of Project LISTEN's website at www.cs.cmu.edu/~listen.

Moreover, logging straight to a database supports immediate efficient access. This capability is essential for real-time use of logged information—in particular, by the tutor itself. In fact, the original impetus for re-architecting the Reading Tutor from a stand-alone application into a client of a shared database server was to free students from being constrained to use the Reading Tutor only on the particular machine that they had enrolled on and that had their records. The Reading Tutor now relies at runtime on student model information logged directly to a shared MySQL database server located on-site at the school or on campus at Carnegie Mellon. In contrast, although the PSLC DataShop uses a database, it generates the database by parsing tutor logs encoded in XML, whether as files processed after the fact, or as messages processed in real time.

Logging directly to a database is not entirely risk free. To mitigate the risk of database corruption, each server uses a standard MySQL feature to log each day's transactions to a file. In the event of database corruption more serious than MySQL's repair command can fix, we can use these files to regenerate the database from scratch.

28.1.2.2 Design Databases to Support Aggregation across Sites

To merge separate databases from multiple schools into a single database, a nightly script on the MySQL server at each site sends the day's file of transactions to our lab server, which simply re-executes them on the aggregated database. To make this solution possible, each table must be able to combine records from different sites. Therefore the Reading Tutor uses student IDs unlikely to recur across different classes or schools, so as to distinguish data from different students. In practice, IDs that encode student gender, birthdate, and length of first and last names tend to suffice. Similarly, the Reading Tutor uses computer, ID, and start time to identify events, instead of numbering them from 1 independently at each site.

28.1.2.3 Log Each School Year's Data to a Different Database

The database for each school year holds data logged by that year's version of the Reading Tutor from multiple computers at different schools. Each year's version of the Reading Tutor adds, omits, or revises tables or fields in the previous year's database schema, and therefore requires its own archival database. This practice accommodates differences between successive versions of the Reading Tutor, as new versions add or change fields or tables. It also facilitates running a query on one school year's data at a time, for example to develop and refine a hypothesis using data from 1 year, and then test it on data from other years.

Also, each team member has his or her own database to modify freely without fear of altering archival data. Making it easy for researchers to create new tables and views that are readily accessible to each other is key. This step enables best practices to propagate quickly, whereas version skew can become a problem if researchers keep private copies of data on their own computers.

28.1.2.4 Include Computer, Student ID, and Start Time as Standard Fields

The key insight here is that student, computer, and time typically suffice to identify a unique tutorial interaction of a given type. Together they distinguish the interaction from those of another type, computer, or student. (We include computer name in case the student ID is not unique, and also because some events, such as launching the Reading Tutor, do not involve a student ID.) There are two reasons this idea is powerful. First, these fields serve as a primary key for every table in the database, simplifying access and shortening the learning curve for working with the data. Second, nearly every tutor makes use of the concepts of students, computers, and time, so this recommendation is broadly applicable.

28.1.2.5 Log End Time as well as Start Time

This additional information makes it possible to compute the duration of a non-instantaneous event, measure the hiatus between the end of one event and the start of another, and determine if one event starts before, during, or after another event—capabilities essential for the Session Browser, in particular, to infer hierarchies of events based on temporal relations among them (as Section 28.3 will discuss). Many tutors log start times but not end times. For instance, logging the end time of an event can be problematic for a web-based tutor that does not know when the student leaves a page or window. Without information about event end times, one cannot use them to infer the hierarchical structure of events, and must instead rely on detailed knowledge of control flow in the specific tutor.

Logging the end time of an event in the same record as its start time is a bit burdensome to implement, because it requires the tutor to remember until the end of the event what information to log about it, in particular when it began. In fact to ensure that each event is logged even if the tutor crashes during it, the Reading Tutor logs the event at start time and updates it later to fill in the end time. Although logging start and end times to different records might seem simpler because it reduces the amount of state the tutor must remember at runtime, it merely replaces this requirement with the messier task of matching up start and (possibly missing) end times after the fact.

28.1.2.6 Name Standard Fields Consistently Within and Across Databases

Naming fields consistently in successive versions of the tutor makes them easier for the Session Browser to extract. Thus most of the tables in a Reading Tutor database have fields named machine_name, user_id, start_time, and (for non-instantaneous events) end_time. Timestamps in MySQL (at least in the version we use) are limited to 1 s resolution, so tables that require higher resolution encode the milliseconds portion of start and end times in separate integer-valued fields named sms and ems, respectively. It's fine to add new tables and fields as the tutor and its database schema evolve, but keeping the names of the old ones facilitates reuse of code to display and analyze tutor data.

28.1.2.7 Use a Separate Table for Each Type of Tutorial Event

Using a separate table for each event type (e.g., story, sentence, utterance, click) lets us include fields for features specific to that event type. Thus, the story table includes a field for the story title; the sentence_encounter table has a field for the text of the sentence; the utterance table has a field for the filepath of the audio recording of the utterance; and the student_click table has a field for the word the student clicked on.

28.1.2.8 Index Event Tables by Computer, Student ID, and Start Time

Database indices enable fast retrieval even from tables of millions of events. For example, given computer name, student ID, and start time, retrieval from the 2003–2004 table of 10,765,345 word hypotheses output by the speech recognizer takes only 15 ms—3000 times faster than the 45.860 s it would take to scan the table without using indices.

28.1.2.9 Include a Field for the Parent Event Start Time

A field for an event's parent in the record for the event makes joins easier to write and faster to execute. For example, the sentence_encounter_start_time field of the record for a read word makes it easier and faster to find the sentence encounter containing the word than by querying for the sentence encounter that started before the word and ended after it.

28.1.2.10 Logging the Nonoccurrence of an Event Is Tricky

"Subjunctive logging" means recording what could have happened but did not. A discussion at the ITS2006 Educational Data Mining Workshop defined this term as "what the system's other options were" (http://www.educationaldatamining.org/datalogged.html). However, it can also encompass actions the student could have done but did not [19]. Either way, tutor designers and data miners should be aware that recording some nonevents can greatly simplify later analyses.

For example, when the Reading Tutor gives help on a word, it chooses randomly among the types of help available. This set of choices depends on the word—for instance, the Reading Tutor cannot give a rhyming hint for the word *orange* because none exists, nor can it decompose a monosyllabic word into syllables. We compared the efficacy of different types of help based on how often the student interrupted to request a different type of help [22], or read the word fluently at the next opportunity [23]. However, a "level playing field" comparison requires comparing different types of help *on the same set of words*. Otherwise, the comparison can be skewed unfairly. For example, rhyming words tend to be monosyllabic and hence easier on average than multisyllabic words. Unless carefully taken into account, this difference in scope of applicability may masquerade as a difference in efficacy that spuriously favors rhyming hints over syllabification. Unfortunately, the Reading Tutor logged only the type of help it actually gave on a word, not the alternatives it could have chosen. Consequently, we had to reconstruct them based on the lexical properties of the word. Our level playing field comparisons would have been both easier and more trustworthy if each time the Reading Tutor gave help on a word by choosing randomly among the types of help available, it had logged all of them, not just the type it chose.

Just as it can be useful to log actions the tutor didn't do, it can be useful to log actions the student didn't do. For example, the Reading Tutor logs each word it heard the student read. But it is also important to know which words of text the student skipped. However, the precise time at which the student did *not* read a skipped word is undefined, so the Reading Tutor logs its start and end time as null. Fortunately, the Reading Tutor also logs the skipped word's sentence_encounter_start_time, and the position in the text sentence where it should have been read. These two pieces of information about the skipped word are non-null, enabling analysis queries and the Session Browser to retrieve words as ordered in the sentence, whether or not the student read them.

28.1.3 Requirements for Browsing Tutorial Interactions

To address the limitations of the event viewer described in Section 28.1.1, we developed the Session Browser described in this chapter. The Session Browser is a Java™ program that queries databases on a MySQL server [24], both running on ordinary personal computers. To avoid the ambiguity of the word "user," we will instead use "researcher" to refer to a Session Browser user, and "student" to refer to a Reading Tutor user.

How should researchers explore logged interactions with an intelligent tutor? Our previous experience suggested the following requirements for the content to display (1–2), the interface to display it (2–3), and the architecture to implement the Session Browser (4):

1. Specify a phenomenon to explore.
2. Display selected events with the context in which they occurred, in dynamically adjustable detail.
3. Summarize interactions in human-understandable form.
4. Adapt easily to new tutor versions, tasks, and researchers.

The rest of this chapter is organized as follows. Sections 28.2 through 28.5, respectively, explain how the Session Browser satisfies each requirement listed above. To illustrate its various features, we use the event depicted in Figure 28.2, as well as real examples based on children's tutorial interactions with Project LISTEN's Reading Tutor and our own research interactions with the Session Browser. Section 28.6 summarizes contributions and limitations, and evaluates the Session Browser against several criteria.

28.2 Specify a Phenomenon to Explore

First, how can an educational data miner specify what to explore? Sections 28.2.1 through 28.2.3 describe three different ways a researcher can indicate which tutor events to examine in the Session Browser.

28.2.1 Specify Events by When They Occurred

To explore what the Reading Tutor and student were doing on a given computer at a given point in time, the researcher can fill in the form shown in Figure 28.3 with the name of the computer, the ID of the student, and the date and time at that point, and click the *Process the form* button. The Session Browser then retrieves all events logged by the Reading Tutor that occurred on that computer, involved that student, and included that point in time. It performs this retrieval by querying the table for each event type for events that started at or before that point and ended at or after it.

Student ID
Machine Name
Date (format m/d/y h:m:s am/pm)
sms
Process the form

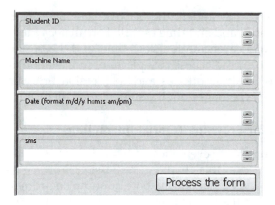

FIGURE 28.3
Event form.

Using this feature requires knowing the precise time when the event of interest occurred. We knew the computer and user_id that generated the screenshot in Figure 28.2, but did not know exactly when. What to do?

28.2.2 Specify Events by a Database Query

We need a well-defined, expressively powerful language to specify phenomena of interest and a computationally efficient search mechanism to find instances of them. Rather than invent a new language for this purpose, we exploit the expressiveness of an existing database query language [24] and the efficiency of database retrieval. Typing in a query and clicking the *Run* button causes the Session Browser to execute the query on the database server and display the table of results it returns. The Session Browser maintains a history of these queries to make them easy to review and reuse.

To specify the event shown in the screenshot, we used the fact that it showed the Reading Tutor sounding out the word *teach*. Based on this fact, we formulated the query shown in Figure 28.4.

As Figure 28.5 shows, the Session Browser displays the query results in a table with a numbered row for each record and a column for each field of "help_given" in the database, including the name of the computer that recorded it, the time at which the tutor decided to help, the times at which the help started and ended, the word helped, the type of help, what the tutor said or showed, the identity of the student, and so on.

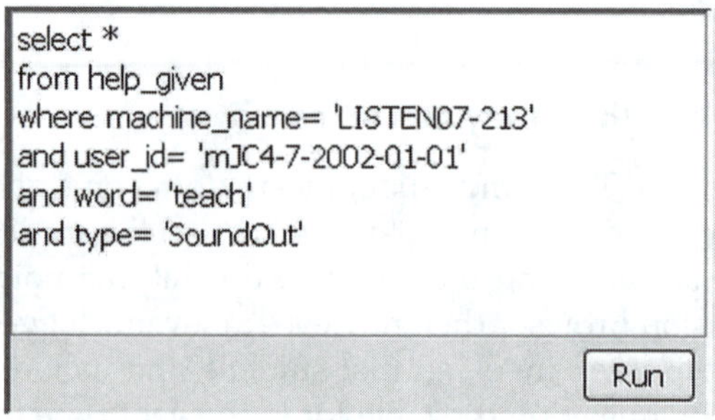

select *
from help_given
where machine_name= 'LISTEN07-213'
and user_id= 'mJC4-7-2002-01-01'
and word= 'teach'
and type= 'SoundOut'
Run

FIGURE 28.4
Event query.

Num...	Machine...	Decided_Time	dms	Start_Time	sms	End_Time	ems	Word	Type	Help_Text	User_ID
1	LISTEN07-...	2009-03-12 1...	654	2009-03-1...	670	2009-03-...	874	teach	SoundOut	T+EA+CH/T+IY+CH	mJC4-7-2
2	LISTEN07-...	2009-03-12 1...	874	2009-03-1...	905	2009-03-...	62	teach	SoundOut	T+EA+CH/T+IY+CH	mJC4-7-2
3	LISTEN07-...	2009-03-12 1...	626	2009-03-1...	641	2009-03-...	642	teach	SoundOut	T+EA+CH/T+IY+CH	mJC4-7-2
4	LISTEN07-...	2009-03-13 1...	9	2009-03-1...	40	2009-03-...	457	teach	SoundOut	T+EA+CH/T+IY+CH	mJC4-7-2
5	LISTEN07-...	2009-03-13 1...	507	2009-03-1...	538	2009-03-...	690	teach	SoundOut	T+EA+CH/T+IY+CH	mJC4-7-2
6	LISTEN07-...	2009-03-13 1...	859	2009-03-1...	890	2009-03-...	198	teach	SoundOut	T+EA+CH/T+IY+CH	mJC4-7-2
7	LISTEN07-...	2009-03-13 1...	531	2009-03-1...	562	2009-03-...	152	teach	SoundOut	T+EA+CH/T+IY+CH	mJC4-7-2

FIGURE 28.5
Table of events returned by query.

To translate the result of a query into a set of tutorial events, the Session Browser scans the labels returned as part of the query, and finds the columns for student, computer, start time, and end time. As recommended in Guideline 1.2.6 above, the Session Browser assumes standard names for these columns, e.g., "user_id" for student, "machine_name" for computer, and "start_time" for start time. If necessary, the researcher can apply this naming convention after the fact, e.g., by inserting "as start_time" in the query in order to relabel a column named differently.

An extensively used tutor collects too much data to inspect all of it by hand, so the first step in mining it is to select a sample. For instance, this query selects a random sample of 10 from the table of student utterances:

```
select * from utterance
order by rand()
limit 10;
```

Whether the task is to spot-check for bugs, identify common cases, formulate hypotheses, or check their sanity, our mantra is "check (at least) ten random examples." Random selection assures variety and avoids the sample bias of, e.g., picking the first 10 examples in the database. For example, random examples quickly revealed Session Browser bugs not manifest when using the standard test examples used previously.

Our queries typically focus on a particular phenomenon of interest, such as the set of questions that students took longest to answer, or steps where they got stuck long enough for the Reading Tutor to prompt them. Exploring examples of such phenomena can help the researcher spot common features and formulate causal hypotheses to test with statistical methods on aggregated data.

For example, one such phenomenon was a particular student behavior—namely, clicking *Back* out of stories. The Reading Tutor has *Go* and *Back* buttons to navigate forward or backward in a story. In the 2004–2005 version, the *Go* button advanced to the next sentence, and the *Back* button returned to the preceding sentence. We had previously observed that students sometimes backed out of a story by clicking *Back* repeatedly even after they had invested considerable time in the story. We were interested in understanding what might precipitate this presumably undesirable behavior. This query finds a random sample of 10 stories that students backed out of after more than 60 s:

```
select * from story _ encounter
where Exit _ through = 'user _ goes _ back'
and unix _ timestamp(end _ time) - unix _ timestamp(start _ time) > 60
order by rand()
limit 10;
```

28.2.3 Specify Events by Their Similarity to Another Event

A third way to specify events is by their similarity to an event already displayed in the event tree. Right-clicking on the event and selecting *Show command for similar* or *Show and run similar* generates a query to retrieve them, and spawns a new Session Browser window to run the query and display its results, as Figure 28.6 illustrates. Displaying the query lets the researcher edit it if desired.

Right-clicking on the highlighted help_given event in the top window and selecting *Show command for similar* brings up a new instance of the Session Browser with a query that looks for other help events with the same values as the user-selected fields of the original event, in this case machine_name, user_id, and the word *teach*:

```
select * from help _ given
where machine _ name= 'LISTEN07-213'
and user _ id= 'mJC4-7-2002-01-01'
and word= 'teach';
```

Running this query returns the list of matching events, one of which is highlighted in the bottom window and consisted of giving the hint *Rhymes with peach*.

Here "similar events" means events that have the same type as the original event, and share the same values for the subset of fields checked off in the displayed record. For example, consider a help_requested event where the Reading Tutor sounded out a word the student clicked on. If similarity is defined as having the same user_id and word, the Session Browser can retrieve the student's history of help on that word. By selecting different subsets of fields, the researcher can direct the Session Browser to find events when the same student clicked on any word, or the Reading Tutor sounded out a word, or anyone clicked on the same word. In Figure 28.6, the researcher has specified "similar" as the same student on the same computer getting any type of help on the word *teach*. For example, in the highlighted event, the Reading Tutor gave the hint *rhymes with peach*.

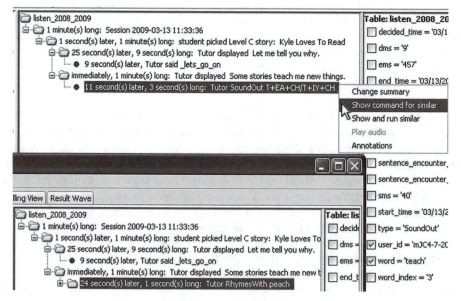

FIGURE 28.6
Specifying events by similarity to another event.

28.3 Display Selected Events with the Context in Which They Occurred, in Adjustable Detail

As Figure 28.5 illustrated, the Session Browser lists field names and values for each event as a numbered row in the results table. To select one or more events from this table to focus on, the researcher uses standard click and drag mouse gestures to highlight them.

As Figure 28.7 shows, the Session Browser also displays all fields of the current focal event in a more spacious vertical format. However, both displays (the results table and the attribute-value list of field values) support only limited understanding of the event, because they lack context. What is the context of a set of events? Our answer is: "its chain of ancestors"—i.e., the higher-level events during which they started. For example, the ancestors of a help_request event include the utterance, sentence, story, and session in which it occurred.

How can we discern this hierarchical structure of student–tutor interaction? The initial implementation of the Session Browser computed this hierarchy using its hardwired schema of the Reading Tutor database to determine which events were part of which others. This knowledge was specific to the particular tutor, increasing the work to develop the original Session Browser and reducing its generality. Moreover, such knowledge may even depend on the particular version of the tutor, making it harder to maintain the Session Browser across multiple tutor versions. At first, we pondered how to declare this knowledge in a form we could input to the Session Browser. But then our programmer (Andrew Cuneo) had an elegant insight: we could eliminate the need for such declarations simply

FIGURE 28.7
Attribute-value list for an event record.

by exploiting the natural hierarchical structure of nested time intervals, which Section 28.3.1 now defines.

28.3.1 Temporal Relations among Events

As Figure 28.8 shows, we define various relations between a student or computer's events based on their time intervals.

28.3.1.1 The Ancestors of a Descendant Constitute Its Context

- A *descendant* starts during its *ancestor* but does not include it. That is, the descendant must start after its ancestor starts, and/or end before it ends. The ancestor is part of the context in which the descendant started, even if the descendant continued after the ancestor ended.
- The *context* of one or more events is the set of all their ancestors.

28.3.1.2 Parents, Children, and Equals

- A *child* is a minimal descendant of a *parent*, and a parent is a minimal ancestor of its children, i.e., the children's ancestors do not overlap with their parent's descendants.
- If an instantaneous event occurs at the point where one ancestor ends and another begins, we define the parent as the earlier ancestor.
- *Equals* span the same time interval. They therefore share the same parents and children. As Section 28.4.4 will discuss, we represent annotations as pseudo-events that are equals of the events they describe.

28.3.1.3 Siblings

- A *younger sibling* has the same parent(s) as its *older sibling(s)* but starts later.
- An *eldest child* has no older siblings.

28.3.1.4 Duration and Hiatus

- The *duration* of a non-instantaneous event is the difference between its start and end times.

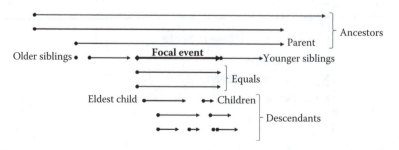

FIGURE 28.8
Time intervals with various temporal relations to a focal event.

- The *hiatus* between a parent and an eldest child is the difference between their start times.
- The hiatus between successive siblings is the difference between the older sibling's end time and the younger sibling's start time.

28.3.1.5 Overlapping Events

What if two events overlap in time, but neither one contains the other? Section 28.3.1.1 above defines whichever event starts earlier as the ancestor of the other event. This relation is not transitive: just because event 2 starts during event 1 and event 3 starts during event 2 does not guarantee that event 3 starts during event 1. In order to make context trees intuitive, we first explored alternative ways to treat overlapping events.

One alternative is to treat overlapping events as siblings, i.e., require that an ancestor contain the entire descendant, not just its beginning. This approach makes the ancestor relation transitive. But then events that occur during the overlap are descendants of both siblings, and therefore appear in both their event trees when expanded, which is visually confusing. (Similar replication occurs with equal events, which have identical sets of descendants; to avoid the confusion, we are simply careful when browsing an event context to expand only one of the equals.)

To avoid such awkward replication, we decided to sacrifice the transitivity of the ancestor relation and define one overlapping event as the ancestor of the other. How to choose? Based on the intuition that the ancestor should be a larger-grain event, we at first chose whichever event was longer in duration. However, if the longer event starts later, the hiatus from the start of the ancestor to the start of the descendant is negative, which we found made it harder to understand the order of events. We therefore adopted the ancestor criterion defined in Section 28.3.1.1 above. Fortunately, the overlapping-event case is relatively rare in our data, thanks to the predominantly hierarchical structure of the Reading Tutor's interactions with students.

28.3.2 Displaying the Event Tree

How can we generate a dynamic, adjustable-detail view of hierarchical structure in a human-understandable, easily controllable form? Given a focal event or set of events, the Session Browser at first displays only its context, i.e., its ancestors. Thus, as Figure 28.9 illustrates, the context of the help event depicted in the screenshot in Figure 28.2 includes only the session, story, and sentence during which it occurred, not any of their other descendants—except as we now explain.

When the Session Browser analyzes the table of query results, it looks not only for columns named "start_time" or "end_time," but also for columns whose names end with

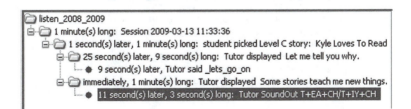

FIGURE 28.9
Event tree shows context of the highlighted event.

"start_time" or "end_time." We assume that these times identify related events, so we add them to the set of selected events whose context the Session Browser will display. In this particular case, the columns come from a help_given event, which specifies a sentence_encounter_start_time but not a sentence_encounter_end_time. Therefore, the Session Browser includes in the set of selected events any instantaneous event(s) with sentence_encounter_start_time as start (and end) time—namely, the audio_output event "Tutor said_lets_go_on," which is represented without an end_time and is therefore instantaneous so far as the Session Browser is concerned. Its start time coincides with the end_time of the previous sentence encounter "Let me tell you why," which is therefore its parent (by the second rule in Section 28.3.1.2 above) and shown as such in the event tree.

28.3.2.1 Computing the Event Tree

To compute the context of a focal event, the Session Browser retrieves its ancestors from the tables for the various event types. That is, it queries each such table for events that contain the start time of the focal event. We adapted a standard expandable tree widget to display event trees. Bullets mark terminal nodes. Given a set of events to display, the Session Browser sorts it by the ancestor relation, then by start time, so that siblings are ordered from eldest to youngest. It maps each event to a node in the tree widget and links it to the nodes for its parent(s), equal(s), and child(ren).

28.3.2.2 Expanding the Event Tree

The context tree initially appears with the ancestors of the focal event(s) ancestors only partially expanded, with their other descendants omitted for brevity. The folder icon marks an event as not yet fully expanded. Clicking on the + or – next to a nonterminal node expands or collapses it, respectively.

Collapsing and re-expanding a partially expanded event reveals the rest of its children. For instance, expanding the node for the "Let me tell you why" sentence encounter reveals the utterances that occurred during it, as Figure 28.10 illustrates. The ability to selectively expand or collapse nodes in the event tree lets the researcher drill down to events and details of interest without drowning in irrelevant details.

When the researcher first expands the current focal event by clicking on the + next to it, the Session Browser computes its children on the fly. This process is similar to computing the context of a focal event, and in fact uses the same expansion procedure, but in the opposite

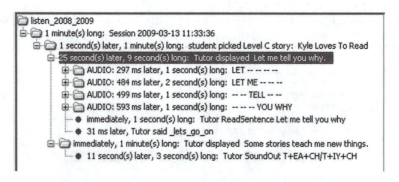

FIGURE 28.10
Hierarchical context and partially expanded details of (another) highlighted event.

direction—from parent to children instead of vice versa. To retrieve the descendants of an event, the Session Browser queries the table for each event type for events that start during it.

28.4 Summarize Events in Human-Understandable Form

We have already described the event trees we use to display the hierarchical structure of tutorial interaction. But how do we summarize individual events?

28.4.1 Temporal Information

Temporal properties are common to all events, so we display them in the same way for all event types. An event's absolute start and end times seldom matter except for time-of-day or time-of-year effects. Therefore we generally display them only in the event's attribute-value list.

In contrast, the duration of an event is a simple but informative universal measure. For example, a long story encounter suggests persistence. A long sentence encounter suggests difficulty in reading it. The hiatus between two events is sometimes as informative as the events themselves because it reflects effort, hesitation, confusion, inactivity, or off-task behavior.

Precise times seldom matter for a duration or hiatus. Therefore for readability and brevity, we round them to the largest nonzero units (days, hours, minutes, seconds, or milliseconds).

Figure 28.11 summarizes a real story encounter that ended with the student backing out of the story by repeatedly clicking *Back*. The fact that most of the sentence encounters just

FIGURE 28.11
What occurred before backing out of a story?

beforehand lasted 14–39 s reflects very slow reading, averaging a few seconds per word. The fact that the subsequent hiatuses from when the Reading Tutor displayed a sentence to when the student clicked *Back* were less than 100 ms long indicates that the student was clicking repeatedly as fast as possible.

28.4.2 Event Summaries

The complete attribute-value list for an event occupies considerable screen space, as Figure 28.7 illustrated. Therefore the Session Browser displays this information only for the event currently selected as the focus.

In contrast, it displays all the one-line summaries for an event tree at once. What information should such summaries include? How should it be displayed? How should it be computed?

The answers depend on the type of event. We observed that although the Reading Tutor's database schema has evolved over time, the meaning of table names is nevertheless consistent across successive versions and between databases created by different members of Project LISTEN. Therefore, we wrote one function for each table to translate a record from that table into a one-line string that includes whatever we think is most informative. Ideally, these functions are simple enough for researchers to modify to suit their own preferences. The default string for a table without such a function is just the name of the table, e.g., "Session" or "Story_encounter." Most functions just display one or more fields of the record for the event. For example, the function for a session just shows its start time. However, some summary functions incorporate information from other tables. For example, the function for a story encounter retrieves its title from a separate table containing information about each story. The summary for an utterance retrieves aligned_word events during the utterance to show which words of the sentence were heard, as in "Then it pulls the – – – –."

28.4.3 Audio Recordings and Transcription

Special-purpose code identifies events that have audio recordings logged directly to the database or to a separate .wav file, or displays "Audio not available" if the audio file has not yet been archived to our data repository. An event with audio available is marked AUDIO, as shown in Figure 28.10. Clicking on the node plays the audio.

Clicking the "Result Wave" tab displays the recorded audio's waveform and, if available, its transcript, as shown in Figure 28.12. The researcher can zoom in and out of the wave form, click and drag to select a portion of it, play it back, and add or edit its transcript, which is stored in a separate database table. Once transcribed, an event can include its transcript in its summary, as the focal event in Figure 28.13 illustrates.

28.4.4 Annotations

Right-clicking on an event and selecting Annotations brings up a table listing its current annotations, as in Figure 28.13. Clicking on an annotation lets the user edit or hide its value. Clicking on the blank bottom row of the *Annotate a Record* table lets the user add a new attribute.

The annotation feature is relatively recent (August 2008). So far we have used it primarily for two published analyses. One analysis examined students' free-form answers to comprehension questions [25]. The annotations specified how an expert teacher would respond, what features of the answer called for this response, and what purpose it was intended to achieve. The purpose of the analysis was to identify useful features of students'

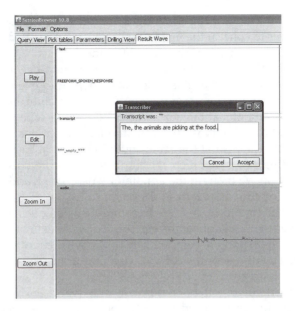

FIGURE 28.12
Audio transcription window.

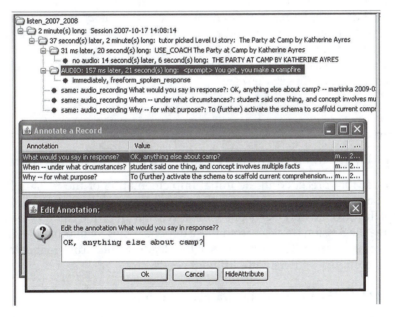

FIGURE 28.13
Annotations of an event.

free-form answers to try to detect automatically. In the other analysis [26], two human judges hand-rated children's recorded oral reading utterances on a four-dimensional fluency rubric, with one attribute for each dimension. The purpose of this analysis was to provide a human "gold standard" against which to evaluate automated measurements of oral reading fluency. The reason for having a second judge was to compute inter-rater reliability, so it was important for the two judges' ratings to be independent. We used the ability to hide attributes to conceal the first judge's ratings, and added a parallel set of four attributes for the second judge to rate the same utterances.

We implement annotations by representing them as pseudo-events in order to use the same code that retrieves regular events, integrates them into event trees, and displays them. Therefore, the Session Browser stores the attribute, value, author, and date of an annotation as a record in a global table of annotations, along with the annotated event's computer, student, and time interval. An event and its annotations are equals as defined in Section 28.3.1.2, so they appear at the same depth in the event tree.

Prior to implementing the annotation mechanism, we wrote special-purpose queries to collect the information we thought the annotator would need, and exported the resulting table into an Excel spreadsheet for the annotator to fill out. For example, the Reading Tutor recorded students' free-form answers to comprehension questions [25]. We sent our expert reading teacher the transcribed answers in a spreadsheet with columns to fill in to describe how she would respond to each answer, under what circumstances, and for what purpose. We included columns for the context we thought she would need, such as which prompt the student was answering.

The annotation mechanism offers a number of advantages over the spreadsheet approach. First, it eliminates the need to write special-purpose queries (typically complex joins) to assemble the context needed by the annotator, because the Session Browser already displays event context. Second, it avoids the need to anticipate which context the annotator will require, because the annotator can use the Session Browser to explore additional context if need be. Third, storing annotations in the database instead of in a spreadsheet supports the ongoing arrival and transcription of new data. Sending spreadsheets back and forth is a cumbersome batch solution. In contrast, storing annotations directly in the database makes it easier to keep up with new data. A simple query enables the annotator to enumerate events not yet annotated.

28.5 Adapt Easily to New Tutor Versions, Tasks, and Researchers

Like the viewer that preceded it, the initial implementation of the Session Browser was specific to a particular version of the Reading Tutor, a particular database structure, and particular paths through and views of the data. We now describe changes we have implemented to free the Session Browser from these dependencies by making it more flexible so that it can accommodate different versions of the Reading Tutor, different data exploration tasks, and different researchers with different needs.

28.5.1 Input Meta-Data to Describe Database Structure

How can the Session Browser obtain the information it needs about a database of tutor interactions? Its generic architecture enables it to make do with readily available meta-data, a few assumed conventions, and a little code.

The Session Browser was originally implemented with references to specific event tables, but has evolved to be more generic. When the researcher selects a database, the Session Browser queries the MySQL server for its meta-data, namely, the list of tables in the database, the fields in each table, and their names and data types. Similarly, when the Session Browser queries the MySQL server for a list of events, it returns the same sort of meta-data along with the results of the query. By following the data-logging guidelines in Section 28.1.2, we exploit the assumption that the names and meanings of fields are mostly consistent across database tables and over time. Thus the code assumes particular field names for student, machine, and start and end times, but overrides this convention for exceptions. For example, the normal method to extract the start time of an event looks for a field named Start_time, but is overridden for particular tables that happen to call it something else, such as Time for instantaneous types of events, or Launch_time for the table that logs each launch of the Reading Tutor.

As explained in Section 28.3.2, the method to compute the context of a selected target event is as follows: First, extract its student, computer, and start time. Then query *every* table of the database for events that involve the same student and computer and contain the start of the target event. Finally, sort the retrieved records according to the ancestor relation, and display them accordingly by inserting them in the appropriate positions in the expandable tree widget. The method to find the children of a given event fires only when needed to expand the event node. It finds descendants in much the same way as the method to find ancestors, but then winnows them down to the children (those that are not descendants of others).

Rather than query every table to find ancestors and descendants of a given event, a more knowledge-based method would know which types of Reading Tutor events can be parents of which others. However, this knowledge would be tutor- and, possibly, version-specific. In contrast, our brute force solution of querying all tables requires no such knowledge. Moreover, its extra computation is not a problem in practice. Our databases consist of a few dozen tables, the largest of which have tens of millions of records. Despite this table size, the Session Browser typically computes the context of an event with little or no delay.

28.5.2 Which Events to Include

Besides drilling down in the event tree, as described in Section 28.3.2.2, the user can specify more globally which types of events to display. As shown in Figure 28.14, clicking on the *Pick tables* tab displays three menus in successive columns—one for databases, one for tables, and one for fields.

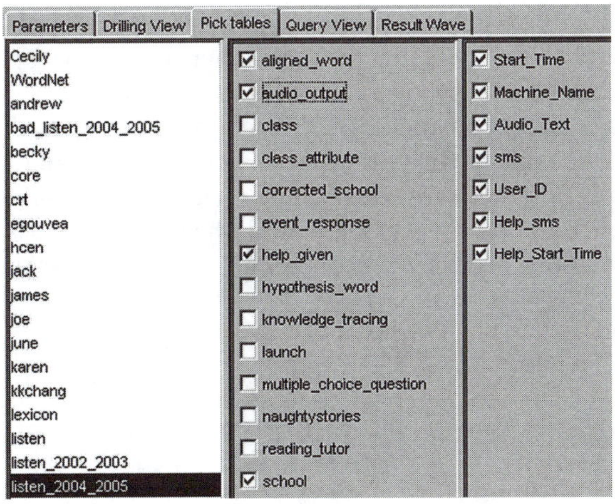

FIGURE 28.14
Select database and tables.

The databases menu shows the currently selected database(s). We have a separate database for archival data from each school year. In addition, each member of our research team has a personal database so as to protect archival data when using it to build and modify new tables, which may augment archival tables with additional derived information. Selecting a personal database in addition to an archival database causes the Session Browser to include it as well when searching for an event's ancestors or descendants.

The tables menu lists the tables in the most recently selected database. We assume a database has a different table for each type of event. The checkbox for each table in the selected database specifies whether to include that type of event in the event tree. For example, turning on the *audio_output* table tells the Session Browser to include the Reading Tutor's own logged speech output in the event tree, which is an easy way to view the tutor's side of the tutorial dialogue. The ability to select which tables to include in the event tree helps focus on the types of events relevant to the particular task at hand by excluding irrelevant details.

The checkboxes do not distinguish among events of the same type. For instance, a user might want the event tree to include the tutor's spoken tutorial assistance (e.g., *"rhymes with peach"*) but not its backchanneling (e.g., *"mmm"*). User-programmable filters would allow such finer-grained distinctions, but not be as simple as using check boxes to specify which event types to include. So far, the check boxes have afforded us sufficient control.

Mousing over a table in the tables menu displays its list of fields in the fields menu. We use this feature primarily as a handy reminder of what fields are in a given table. However, we can also uncheck the box next to a field to omit that field when displaying the attribute-value list representation for an event record. For example, the audio_recording table includes a field for the audio input logged by the tutor. The value of this field can occupy enough memory to cause a noticeable lag in retrieving it from the database server. Unchecking the field to omit it from the display avoids this lag. In fact, unlike other fields, the default setting for this particular field is to leave it unchecked.

28.5.3 Make Event Summaries Customizable by Making Them Queries

We initially implemented the summary for each type of event in Java. However, this approach made it difficult to modify event summaries on the fly. We therefore reimplemented event summaries as queries that the researcher can edit or replace by right-clicking the event and selecting *Change summary*. This operation immediately updates the summaries for all events of that type, including those already displayed. Although the event summary queries are specific to the particular structure of the database, the mechanisms for editing and interpreting them are generic, and enable researchers to change event summaries on the fly to include the aspects relevant to the particular task at hand.

Some summary functions are very simple. For example, the Session summary query is

```
select "Session", start_time from session
where machine_name=@this.machine_name@
and user_id=@this.user_id@
and start_time=@this.start_time@
and sms=@this.sms@;
```

We added the construct @this.*field*@ to refer to a field of the event being summarized. The Session Browser replaces this construct with regular MySQL before executing the query. Combined with the generic mechanism for event duration and hiatus, this query produces summary lines such as "34 second(s) long: Session 2008-10-01 14:31:46."

Other queries are more complex. For example, the summary line for an utterance shows text words the speech recognizer accepted in UPPER CASE, substitutions in lower case, and omitted words as –. (The omission of a word constitutes the nonoccurrence of an event as discussed in Section 28.1.2.10.) The query to summarize an utterance is

```
select if (center _ context=1, upper(target _ word),
        if (aligned _ word <> '<UND>', lower(aligned _ word), '—'))
from aligned _ word
where Machine _ name = @this.machine _ name@
and utterance _ start _ time = @this.start _ time@
and utterance _ sms = @this.sms@
and user _ id = @this.user _ id@
order by target _ word _ number;
```

For example, a summary of one utterance for the sentence "Don't ya' forget to wear green on St Patrick's Day!" is

no audio: 4 second(s) earlier, 4 second(s) long: DON'T YA start_forget(2f_axr) TO WEAR
– – – – – –

Here "start_forget(2f_axr)" is a phonetic truncation recognized instead of "forget."

28.5.4 Loadable Configurations

The selections of which events to explore, which tables to include, and how to summarize them constitute a substantial amount of program state. The Session Browser lets the researcher name, store, and load such configurations, including which database and tables are currently selected, the summary function for each event type, the current query, and the number of the most recently selected row in the results table. When it loads the configuration, it regenerates the context of this event. The configuration does not specify which nodes to expand, but provides enough state to regenerate the event tree quickly.

At first we stored each configuration as a file on the client machine where it was generated. However, we modified the Session Browser to store configurations in the same database where it stores annotations, after finding multiple reasons to share them, as we now discuss.

28.5.4.1 Resume Exploration

A configuration provides enough information to resume exploration at the point where it was suspended. This capability is useful for explorations too extensive to complete in a single session. Storing the configuration on the database server instead of on the Session Browser client lets researchers access it from different client machines, which makes it easier for them to share.

28.5.4.2 Replicate Bugs

The ability to share configurations quickly proved useful in reporting and replicating bugs. Upon encountering buggy Session Browser behavior, the researcher can simply save the current configuration, send its name to the developer, and continue working. Loading the named configuration recreates a state useful (and often sufficient) for replicating the bug.

28.5.4.3 Support Annotation by Non-Power-Users

The ability to encapsulate and name a complex configuration makes it possible to use the Session Browser without knowing how to write queries or set up configurations. This capability enables less technically skilled personnel to use the Session Browser for task assignments such as transcription and annotation. The researcher creates and names a configuration that specifies the appropriate database(s) to query, the query to retrieve the events to transcribe or annotate, and the subset of tables to include in event trees. The transcriber or annotator simply loads the named configuration and performs the assigned transcription or annotation as described, respectively, in Sections 28.4.3 and 28.4.4, using the Session Browser's graphical user interface to select and browse events returned by the query. The researcher can design the query to keep track of completed vs. remaining work by restricting it to return only events still to be processed.

28.6 Conclusion

We conclude by summarizing research contributions, acknowledging some limitations, and evaluating the Session Browser.

28.6.1 Contributions and Limitations

This chapter describes an implemented, efficient, fairly general solution to a major emerging problem in educational data mining: how to explore vast student–tutor interaction logs. We identify several useful requirements for a Session Browser to support such exploration.

28.6.1.1 Specify a Phenomenon to Explore

We frame this problem as specifying a set of events, and describe three ways to specify events: by when they occurred, by database query, or by similarity to another event. Other ways may also be useful, such as an easy way to point out a constellation of related events and search for similar constellations.

28.6.1.2 Display Selected Events with the Context in Which They Occurred, in Dynamically Adjustable Detail

Our key conceptual contribution uses temporal relations to expose natural hierarchical structure.

The success of this approach is evidence for specific guidelines for logging tutorial interactions, enumerated in Section 28.1.2. The key recommendations are **log directly to databases** (28.1.2.1) rather than to files, and **log events as time intervals** (28.1.2.5), not as instantaneous.

An event's chain of ancestors can provide informative context. However, we often want to know what happened just before a focal event in order to explore what might have precipitated it. At present, revealing this type of context involves expanding the event's ancestors more than is convenient, necessary, or desirable. Instead, it may be useful to display just the older sibling of each ancestor, and to expand it selectively. The Session Browser could locate all events that occurred within a specified time (e.g., 1 min) before the focal event, but there might be too many of them to display intelligibly. It might be safer to display the last N events prior to the focal event, for some manageable value of N.

28.6.1.3 Summarize Interactions in Human-Understandable Form

Screen area and human attention are scarce resources in displaying complex tutorial interactions, so it is important to summarize events clearly, concisely, and flexibly. We use duration and hiatus to expose temporal relations among events, user-editable summary queries to convey key event features, and manual annotations to add human observations.

28.6.1.4 Adapt Easily to New Tutor Versions, Tasks, and Researchers

We described several useful types of customization motivated by experience with the Session Browser: selecting which databases and tables to include, editing event summary functions, and defining reusable configurations. The greater the extent to which knowledge of tutor database structure is input as meta-data from the server rather than baked into the code by the developers, the more easily the Session Browser can adapt to new versions of the Reading Tutor, and perhaps eventually to other tutors.

28.6.1.5 Relate Events to the Distributions They Come From

The Session Browser displays features of particular events rather than aggregate properties of sets of events. It may be useful to extend it to relate events in the event tree to the overall distribution of events in the database. How typical is the particular value of a field for the type of event in question? For instance, it may be useful not only to display the fact that a story encounter ended by backing out of the story, but to put it in perspective by including the percentage of story encounters that end in that way, whether overall or for that student, that story, that level, or some other subset of events. This notion could be applied throughout the Session Browser to retrieve, select, expand, and describe events based on typicality or atypicality.

28.6.2 Evaluation

Relevant criteria for evaluating the Session Browser include implementation cost, efficiency, generality, usability, and utility.

28.6.2.1 Implementation Cost

Implementation took only several person-weeks for the tutor-specific prototype and about the same for its generalized interval-based successor presented in 2005. Judging by the number of subsequent versions, it took roughly twice as much work since then to add improvements such as configurations, transcription, annotation, equal events, specification by similarity, user-editable event summarizers, and multi-selection of databases to query and events to display.

28.6.2.2 Efficiency

Running both the database server and the Session Browser on ordinary PCs, we routinely explore databases with data from hundreds of students, thousands of hours of tutorial interaction, and millions of words. The operations reported here often update the display with no perceptible lag, though a complex query to find a specified set of events may take several seconds or more.

28.6.2.3 Generality

Structural evidence of the Session Browser's generality includes its largely tutor-independent design, reflected in brevity of code (103 .java files totaling 799 kB, with median size

4 kB) and relative scarcity of references to specific tables or fields of the database. Both these measures would improve by deleting unused code left over from the initial tutor-specific implementation. Empirical evidence of generality includes successful use of the Session Browser with archival databases from different years' versions of the Reading Tutor as well as with derivative databases constructed by members of Project LISTEN. Other researchers have not as yet adapted the Session Browser to databases from tutors besides the Reading Tutor, in part because most tutors still log to files, not databases.

However, it may be feasible to use the Session Browser with data in PSLC's DataShop [16] logged by various cognitive tutors. These tutors typically log in XML, which a PSLC translation routine parses and imports into a database. Datashop users don't even need to know the structure of the database; they just need to output or convert log data into PSLC's XML format, and to be sure that the log details are sufficient.

The PSLC Datashop database has a logically and temporally hierarchical event structure (imputed by its XML translator), which generally obeys the semantic properties required by the Session Browser. Tutorial interaction could lack such structure if it consisted of temporally interleaved but logically unrelated events, or were based primarily on other sorts of relations, such as the anaphoric relation between antecedent and referent in natural language dialog. However, tutorial data from the PSLC Datashop appears to have hierarchical temporal structure.

We are currently investigating the feasibility of applying the Session Browser to that data by modifying it and/or the PSLC database to use compatible representations, e.g., one table per event type, with fields for student, machine, and event and start–end times, and conventions for naming them. If so, the Session Browser could apply to many more tutors—at least if their interactions have the largely hierarchical temporal structure that it exploits, displays, and manipulates.

28.6.2.4 Usability

The Session Browser is now used regularly by several members of Project LISTEN after at most a few minutes of instruction. Usability is hard to quantify. However, we can claim a 10- or 100-fold reduction in keystrokes compared to obtaining the same information by querying the database directly. For example, clicking on events in the list of query results displays their context as a chain of ancestor events. Identifying these ancestors by querying the database directly would require querying a separate table for each ancestor. Moreover, the Session Browser's graphical user interface enables users to explore event context without knowing how to write queries, and stored configurations make it easy for them to retrieve events to transcribe or annotate.

28.6.2.5 Utility

The ultimate test of the Session Browser is whether it leads to useful discoveries, or at least sufficiently facilitates the process of educational data mining that researchers find it helpful and keep using it. We cannot as yet attribute a publishable scientific discovery to a eureka moment in the Session Browser, nor do we necessarily expect one, because scientific discovery tends to be a gradual, multi-step process rather than a single flash of insight. However, the Session Browser has served as a useful tool in some of our published research. Time will clarify its value for us and, if it is extended to work with Datashop-compatible tutors, for other researchers as well.

Acknowledgments

This work was supported in part by the National Science Foundation under ITR/IERI Grant No. REC-0326153 and in part by the Institute of Education Sciences, U.S. Department of Education, through Grants R305B070458, R305A080157, and R305A080628 to Carnegie Mellon University. Any opinions, findings, conclusions, or recommendations expressed in this publication are those of the authors and do not necessarily reflect the views of the Institute, the U.S. Department of Education, or the National Science Foundation, or the official policies, either expressed or implied, of the sponsors or of the United States Government. We thank the educators and students who generated our data, the members of Project LISTEN who use the Session Browser, the contributors to the 2005 papers on which much of this chapter is based [1–3], Thomas Harris for exploring the feasibility of using the Session Browser with data from PSLC's DataShop, and Ryan Baker and the reviewers for helpful comments on earlier drafts.

References

(Project LISTEN publications are available at www.cs.cmu.edu/~listen)

1. Mostow, J., Beck, J., Cen, H., Cuneo, A., Gouvea, E., and Heiner, C., An educational data mining tool to browse tutor-student interactions: Time will tell!, in *Proceedings of the Workshop on Educational Data Mining, National Conference on Artificial Intelligence*, Beck, J. E. (Ed.), AAAI Press, Pittsburgh, PA, 2005, pp. 15–22.
2. Mostow, J., Beck, J., Cen, H., Gouvea, E., and Heiner, C., Interactive demonstration of a generic tool to browse tutor-student interactions, in *Interactive Events Proceedings of the 12th International Conference on Artificial Intelligence in Education (AIED 2005)*, Amsterdam, the Netherlands, 2005, pp. 29–32.
3. Mostow, J., Beck, J., Cuneo, A., Gouvea, E., and Heiner, C., A generic tool to browse tutor-student interactions: Time will tell!, in *Proceedings of the 12th International Conference on Artificial Intelligence in Education (AIED 2005)*, Amsterdam, the Netherlands, 2005, pp. 884–886.
4. Beck, J. E., *Proceedings of the ITS2004 Workshop on Analyzing Student-Tutor Interaction Logs to Improve Educational Outcomes*, Maceio, Brazil, August 30–September 3, 2004.
5. Mostow, J. and Aist, G., Evaluating tutors that listen: An overview of Project LISTEN, in *Smart Machines in Education*, Forbus, K. and Feltovich, P. (Eds.), MIT/AAAI Press, Menlo Park, CA, 2001, pp. 169–234.
6. Mostow, J. and Beck, J., When the rubber meets the road: Lessons from the in-school adventures of an automated Reading Tutor that listens, in *Scale-Up in Education*, Schneider, B. and McDonald, S.-K. (Eds.), Rowman & Littlefield Publishers, Lanham, MD, 2007, pp. 183–200.
7. Mostow, J., Aist, G., Burkhead, P., Corbett, A., Cuneo, A., Eitelman, S., Huang, C., Junker, B., Platz, C., Sklar, M. B., and Tobin, B., A controlled evaluation of computer- versus human-assisted oral reading, in *Artificial Intelligence in Education: AI-ED in the Wired and Wireless Future*, Moore, J. D., Redfield, C. L., and Johnson, W. L. (Eds.), IOS Press, San Antonio, TX, Amsterdam, the Netherlands, 2001, pp. 586–588.
8. Mostow, J., Aist, G., Huang, C., Junker, B., Kennedy, R., Lan, H., Latimer, D., O'Connor, R., Tassone, R., Tobin, B., and Wierman, A., 4-Month evaluation of a learner-controlled Reading Tutor that listens, in *The Path of Speech Technologies in Computer Assisted Language Learning: From Research Toward Practice*, Holland, V. M. and Fisher, F. P. Routledge (Eds.), New York, 2008, pp. 201–219.
9. Poulsen, R., Wiemer-Hastings, P., and Allbritton, D., Tutoring bilingual students with an automated Reading Tutor that listens, *Journal of Educational Computing Research* 36(2), 191–221, 2007.

10. Mostow, J., Aist, G., Bey, J., Burkhead, P., Cuneo, A., Junker, B., Rossbach, S., Tobin, B., Valeri, J., and Wilson, S., Independent practice versus computer-guided oral reading: Equal-time comparison of sustained silent reading to an automated reading tutor that listens, in *Ninth Annual Meeting of the Society for the Scientific Study of Reading*, Williams, J. (Ed.), Chicago, IL, June 27–30, 2002.

11. Aist, G., Towards automatic glossarization: Automatically constructing and administering vocabulary assistance factoids and multiple-choice assessment, *International Journal of Artificial Intelligence in Education* 12, 212–231, 2001.

12. Mostow, J., Beck, J., Bey, J., Cuneo, A., Sison, J., Tobin, B., and Valeri, J., Using automated questions to assess reading comprehension, vocabulary, and effects of tutorial interventions, *Technology, Instruction, Cognition and Learning* 2, 97–134, 2004.

13. Mostow, J., Beck, J. E., and Heiner, C., Which help helps? Effects of various types of help on word learning in an automated Reading Tutor that listens, in *Eleventh Annual Meeting of the Society for the Scientific Study of Reading*, Reitsma, P. (Ed.), Amsterdam, the Netherlands, 2004.

14. Corbett, A. and Anderson, J., Knowledge tracing: Modeling the acquisition of procedural knowledge, *User Modeling and User-Adapted Interaction*, 4, 253–278, 1995.

15. Beck, J. E. and Mostow, J., How who should practice: Using learning decomposition to evaluate the efficacy of different types of practice for different types of students, in *Ninth International Conference on Intelligent Tutoring Systems*, Montreal, Canada, 2008, pp. 353–362. Nominated for Best Paper.

16. Koedinger, K. R., Baker, R. S. J. d., Cunningham, K., Skogsholm, A., Leber, B., and Stamper, J., A data repository for the EDM community: The PSLC DataShop, in *Handbook of Educational Data Mining*, Romero, C., Ventura, S., Pechenizkiy, M., and Baker, R. S. J. d. (Eds.), CRC Press, Boca Raton, FL, 2010, pp. 43–56.

17. Shavelson, R. J. and Towne, L., *Scientific Research in Education*, National Academy Press, National Research Council, Washington, DC, 2002.

18. Mostow, J., Beck, J., Chalasani, R., Cuneo, A., and Jia, P., Viewing and analyzing multimodal human-computer tutorial dialogue: A database approach, in *Proceedings of the Fourth IEEE International Conference on Multimodal Interfaces (ICMI 2002) IEEE*, Pittsburgh, PA, 2002, pp. 129–134. First presented June 4, 2002, at the ITS 2002 *Workshop on Empirical Methods for Tutorial Dialogue Systems*, San Sebastian, Spain.

19. Mostow, J. and Beck, J. E., Why, what, and how to log? Lessons from LISTEN, in *Proceedings of the Second International Conference on Educational Data Mining*, Córdoba, Spain, 2009, pp. 269–278.

20. Alpern, M., Minardo, K., O'Toole, M., Quinn, A., and Ritzie, S., Unpublished Group Project for Masters' Lab in Human-Computer Interaction, 2001.

21. Beck, J. E., Chang, K.-m., Mostow, J., and Corbett, A., Does Help help? Introducing the Bayesian evaluation and assessment methodology, in *Ninth International Conference on Intelligent Tutoring Systems*, Montreal, Canada, 2008, pp. 383–394. ITS2008 Best Paper Award.

22. Heiner, C., Beck, J. E., and Mostow, J., When do students interrupt help? Effects of time, help type, and individual differences, in *Proceedings of the 12th International Conference on Artificial Intelligence in Education (AIED 2005)*, Looi, C.-K., McCalla, G., Bredeweg, B., and Breuker, J. (Eds.), IOS Press, Amsterdam, the Netherlands, 2005, pp. 819–826.

23. Heiner, C., Beck, J. E., and Mostow, J., Improving the help selection policy in a Reading Tutor that listens, in *Proceedings of the InSTIL/ICALL Symposium on NLP and Speech Technologies in Advanced Language Learning Systems*, Venice, Italy, 2004, pp. 195–198.

24. MySQL, Online MySQL Documentation at http://dev.mysql.com/doc/mysql, 2004.

25. Zhang, X., Mostow, J., Duke, N. K., Trotochaud, C., Valeri, J., and Corbett, A., Mining freeform spoken responses to Tutor prompts, in *Proceedings of the First International Conference on Educational Data Mining*, Baker, R. S. J. d., Barnes, T., and Beck, J. E. (Eds.), Montreal, Canada, 2008, pp. 234–241.

26. Mostow, J. and Duong, M., Automated assessment of oral reading prosody, in *Proceedings of the 14th International Conference on Artificial Intelligence in Education (AIED2009)*, Dimitrova, V., Mizoguchi, R., Boulay, B. d., and Graesser, A. (Eds.), IOS Press, Brighton, U.K., 2009, pp. 189–196.

29

Using Fine-Grained Skill Models to Fit Student Performance with Bayesian Networks

Zachary A. Pardos, Neil T. Heffernan, Brigham S. Anderson,
and Cristina L. Heffernan

CONTENTS

29.1 Introduction

The largest standardized tests (such as the SAT or GRE) are what psychometricians call "unidimensional" in that they are analyzed as if all the questions are tapping a single latent trait. However, cognitive scientists such as Anderson and Lebiere [1] believe that students are learning individual skills and might learn one skill but not another. Among the reasons, psychometricians analyze large-scale tests in a unidimensional manner, such as our colleagues have done with item-response models [2,4], is that student performance on different skills is usually highly correlated, even if there is no necessary perquisite relationship between these skills. We are engaged in an effort to investigate if we can do a better job of predicting student performance by modeling skills at a fine-grained level. Four different *skill models** are considered: one that is unidimensional, WPI-1; one that has five skills, WPI-5; one that has 39 skills, WPI-39; and our most fine-grained model that has 106 skills, WPI-106. We will refer to a tagging of skills to questions as a skill model. We will compare skill models that differ in the number of skills and use Bayesian networks to see how well the different models fit a dataset of student responses collected via the ASSISTment system.

---

* A *skill model* is referred to as a "Q-matrix" by some AI researchers [5] and psychometricians [19].

There are many researchers in user modeling and educational data mining communities working with Intelligent Tutoring Systems who have adopted Bayesian network methods for modeling knowledge [3,7,12,21]. Even methods not originally thought of as Bayesian network methods turned out to be so; Reye [18] showed that the classic Corbett and Anderson "Knowledge tracing" approach [8] was a special case of a dynamic belief network. While we make use of knowledge tracing in our analysis, other notable work takes a different approach. Wilson's learning progressions [20], for example, tracks different levels of knowledge within a concept map based on misconceptions detected according to the student's multiple-choice answer selection. A student's progress is tracked longitudinally across concept maps. This approach would perhaps be the strongest when there are clear misconceptions to track. We instead follow in the tradition of Anderson and VanLehn–style cognitive tutors where knowledge is treated as a binary random variable and where the subject of skill granularity is most relevant.

We are not the first to do model selection based on how well the model fits real student data [10,12]. Nor are we the only ones concerned with the question of granularity. Greer and colleagues [11] have proposed methods of assessment using different levels of granularity to conceptualize student knowledge. However, we are not aware of other work prior to this* work where researchers attempted to empirically answer the question of "what is the right level of granularity to best fit a dataset of student responses."

29.1.1 Background on the MCAS Test

The Massachusetts Comprehensive Assessment System (MCAS) is a state-administered standardized test that covers English, math, science and social studies for grades 3–10. We focused on the 29 multiple-choice questions of the 8th grade mathematics test only. Our work related to the MCAS in two ways: First, we built our tutor content based upon 300 publicly released items from previous MCAS math tests. Second, we evaluated our models by predicting students' scores on the 8th grade 2005 MCAS test taken at the end of the school year. The MCAS test is of particular importance to students and teachers in Massachusetts because students must pass the test in order to graduate high school.

29.1.2 Background on the ASSISTment System

The ASSISTment system is an e-learning and e-assessing system. In the 2004–2005 school year, over 600 students used the system about once every two weeks. Eight math teachers from two schools would bring their students to the computer lab, at which time students were presented with randomly selected MCAS test items. Each tutoring item, which we call an ASSISTment, is based upon a publicly released MCAS item to which we have added "tutoring." Students get this tutoring, referred to as scaffolding, when they answer an original question incorrectly.

We believe that the ASSISTment system has a better chance of showing the utility of fine-grained skill modeling due to the fact that we can ask scaffolding questions that break the problem down in into parts, allowing us to tell if the student answered incorrectly because he or she did not know one skill versus another. Figure 29.1 shows a student being presented with a geometry question from the 2003 MCAS. After the student answers incorrectly he is

---

* This chapter is an expansion of work presented at the workshop on Educational Data Mining held at the 18th International Conference on Intelligent Tutoring Systems (2006) in Taiwan [13] and the 11th International Conference on User Modeling (2007) in Corfu, Greece [14].

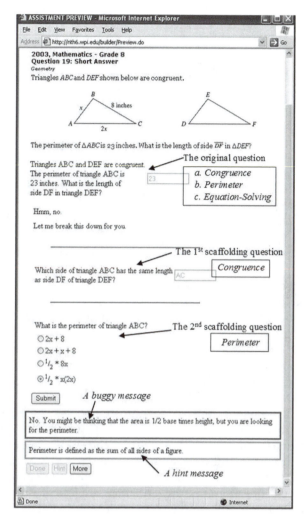

FIGURE 29.1
An ASSISTment showing the original question and the first two scaffolds.

presented with scaffold questions that break the original problem into separate skills. On average, students in our 2004–2005 dataset answered 100 original questions and 160 scaffold questions. A student's response was only marked as correct if he or she answered the question correctly on the first attempt without assistance from the system. The MCAS items from the 2005 test, publically released in June of 2005, were tagged with skills shortly after release but before we received any of the students' official scores for the test from the state.

29.2 Models: Creation of the Fine-Grained Skill Model

In April of 2005, our subject-matter expert, Cristina Heffernan, with the assistance of the second author, set out to code skills and tag all of the 300 existing 8th grade MCAS items with these skills [17]. Because we wanted to be able to track learning between items, we

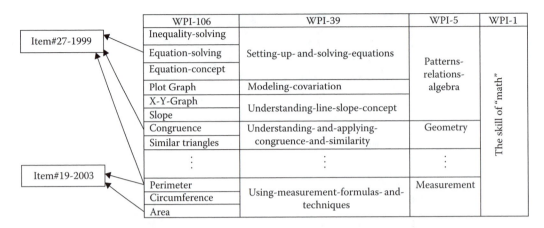

WPI-106	WPI-39	WPI-5	WPI-1
Inequality-solving			
Equation-solving	Setting-up- and-solving-equations	Patterns-relations-algebra	
Equation-concept			
Plot Graph	Modeling-covariation		The skill of "math"
X-Y-Graph	Understanding-line-slope-concept		
Slope			
Congruence	Understanding- and-applying-congruence-and-similarity	Geometry	
Similar triangles			
⋮	⋮	⋮	
Perimeter	Using-measurement-formulas- and-techniques	Measurement	
Circumference			
Area			

FIGURE 29.2
Questions are tagged with the WPI-106 that is mapped to the other skill models.

came up with a number of skills that were somewhat fine-grained but not so fine-grained that each item had a different skill. Therefore, we imposed upon our subject-matter expert the restriction that no one item would be tagged with more than three skills. This model is referred to as the April Model or WPI-106, due to the fact that when she was done, there were 106 knowledge components that that model attempted to track. We also wanted to use coarser skill models so we borrowed skill names from The National Council of Teachers of Mathematics and the Massachusetts Department of Education who use broad classifications of 5- and 39-skill sets. The 5- and 39-skill classifications were not tagged to the questions. Instead, the skills in the coarse-grained models were mapped to skills in the finest-grained model in a "is a part of" type of hierarchy, as opposed to a prerequisite hierarchy [6]. The appropriate question-skill tagging for the WPI-5 and WPI-39 models could therefore be derived from the WPI-106, as illustrated in Figure 29.2. Items could be tagged with up to three skills. The state's own choice of skill tags for an item was not used because their model only allows a question to be tagged with a single skill. Comparing a single skill per question model to a multi skill per question model would not be a fair comparison.

29.2.1 How the Skill Mapping Was Used to Create a Bayesian Network

Our Bayesian networks consisted of three layers of binomial random variable nodes, as illustrated in Figure 29.3. A separate network was created for each skill model. The top layer nodes represent knowledge of a skill that was set to a prior probability of 0.50. This model is simple and assumes all skills are as equally likely to be known prior to being given any evidence of student responses. Once we present the network with evidence, it can quickly infer probabilities about what the student knows. The bottom layer nodes are the question nodes with conditional probabilities set *ad hoc* to 0.10 for the probability of answering correctly without knowing the skill, guess, and 0.05 for the probability of answering incorrectly if the skill is known, slip. The intermediary secondary layer consists of AND* gates that, in part, allowed us to only specify a guess and slip parameter for the

---

* An "ALL" gate is equivalent to a logical AND. Kevin Murphy's Bayes Net Toolbox (BNT) evaluates MATLAB®'s ALL function to represent the heolean node. This function takes a vector of values as opposed to only two values if using the AND function. Since a question node may have three skills tagged to it, the ALL function is used.

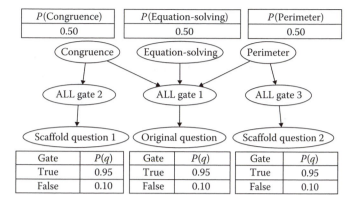

FIGURE 29.3

Example of the Bayesian network topology for an ASSISTment question with two scaffolds. $P(q$=True|Gate=False) is the guess. $P(q$=False|Gate=True) is the slip.

question nodes regardless of how many skills were tagged to them. Our colleagues [2] investigated using a compensatory model with the same dataset but we found [15] that a conjunctive, AND, is very well suited to model the composition of multiple skills. When predicting MCAS test questions, a guess value of 0.25 was used to reflect the fact that the MCAS items being predicted were all multiple-choice (one correct answer out of four), while most of the online ASSISTment system items have text-input fields as the answer type. Future research will explore learning the parameters from data.

29.2.2 Model Prediction Procedure

A prediction evaluation was run for each model, one student at a time. The students' responses on the tutor were presented to the Bayesian network as evidence and inference (using exact join-tree) was made on the skills to attain knowledge probabilities. To predict each of the 29 questions, we used the inferred skill probabilities to ask the Bayesian network what the probability was that the student would get the test question correct. We calculated a *predicted score* by taking the sum of the probabilities for all test questions. Finally, we found the percent error by taking the absolute value of the difference between predicted and actual score and dividing by 29. The *Average Error* of a skill model is the average error across the 600 students. Table 29.1 demonstrates how the error was calculated. Notice that the predicted probability of answering correctly, $P(q)$, is the same for test questions of the same skill (e.g., questions 1 and 2). Also notice test question 3 involves two skills, patterns and measurement, and the $P(q)$ of that question is lower than the $P(q)$ of questions with only one of either skill because of the conjunctive (AND) model of skill composition being used.

29.3 Results

An early version of the results in this section (using approximate inference instead of exact inference and without Section 29.3.1) appears in a workshop paper [13]. The mean absolute difference (MAD) score is the score between the predicted and the actual score. The under/over prediction is our predicted average score minus the actual average score on the test.

TABLE 29.1

Tabular Illustration of Error Calculation

Test Question	Skill Tagging (WPI-5)	User 1 P(q)	User 2 P(q)	...	User 600 P(q)	Average Error
1	Patterns	0.2	0.9	...	0.4	
2	Patterns	0.2	0.9	...	0.4	
3	Patterns and measurement	0.1	0.5	...	0.2	
4	Measurement	0.8	0.8	...	0.3	
5	Patterns	0.2	0.9	...	0.4	
:	:	:	:	:	:	
29	Geometry	0.7	0.7	...	0.2	
	Predicted score	14.2	27.8	...	5.45	
	Actual score	18	23	...	9	
	Error	10.34%	19.42%	...	12.24%	**17.28%**

TABLE 29.2

Model Prediction Performance Results for the MCAS Test

Model	Error	MAD	Under/Over
WPI-39	12.86%	3.73	↓ 1.4
WPI-106	14.45%	4.19	↓ 1.2
WPI-5	17.28%	5.01	↓ 3.6
WPI-1	22.31%	6.47	↓ 4.3

Results were statistically significantly separable from each other at the $p < 0.05$ level.

The results in Table 29.2, show that the WPI-39 had the best accuracy with an error of 12.86% that translates to a raw score error of 3.73. The finest-grain model, the WPI-106, came in second followed by the WPI-5 and finally the WPI-1. We can conclude that the fine-grain models are best for predicting the external test but that the finest-grain model did not provide the best fit to the data. An analysis [16] of error residuals revealed that test questions that were poorly predicted had a dramatically higher percentage of correctness on the test than questions on the ASSISTment system relating to the same skill. These ASSISTment system questions all had text-input fields (fill in the blank) question types. The conclusion drawn was that the multiple-choice question type of the test made some questions much easier than their ASSISTment system counterparts to an extent not captured by the guess and slip of the model. This disparity in difficulty likely attributed to the consistent under prediction of performance on the test. Learning the guess and slip parameters of the tutor and test questions can help correct for this variation in performance. All results in Table 29.2 were statistically significantly separable from each other at the $p < 0.05$ level.*

---

* We compared [16] this Bayesian method to a mixed-effects [9] test prediction that was run with the same data and found that the best mixed-effects model came up 0.05% short of the Bayesian method's best model. Both approaches agreed that the two finest-grained models were most accurate. Internal fit was not run with the mixed-effects approach.

TABLE 29.3

Model Prediction Performance
Results for Internal Fit

Model	Error	MAD	Under/Over
WPI-106	5.50%	15.25	↓ 12.31
WPI-39	9.56%	26.70	↓ 20.14
WPI-5	17.04%	45.15	↓ 31.60
WPI-1	26.86%	69.92	↓ 42.17

Note: Results were statistically significantly
separable from each other at the
$p < 0.05$ level.

29.3.1 Internal/Online Data Prediction Results

To answer the research question of which level of granularity is best for predicting student performance *within the system,* we measured the internal fit. The internal fit is how accurately we can predict student answers to our online question items. If we are able to accurately predict a student's response to a given question, this brings us closer to a computer-adaptive tutoring application of being able to intelligently select the appropriate next questions for learning and/or assessing purposes.

The internal fit prediction was run, again, for one student at a time. The processes was similar to an N-fold cross validation where N is the number of question responses for that student. The network was presented with evidence minus the question being predicted. One point was added to the internal total score if the probability of correct was greater than 0.50 for the question. This was repeated for each question answered by the student. The mean absolute difference between predicted total and actual total score was tabulated in the same fashion, as shown in Table 29.1; however, it is worthwhile to note that not all users answered the same number of questions, so the MAD did not have greater variance. All the differences between the models in Table 29.3 were statistically significantly different at the $p < 0.05$ level.

We can see from the results in Table 29.3 that the WPI-106 model predicted responses on the tutor with high accuracy and that prediction error decreased as the granularity of the model increased. The internal fit errors for the WPI-1 and WPI-5 are similar to their MCAS score prediction errors, while the WPI-39 and, especially, the WPI-106 were able to excel at internal fit prediction. We explore an explanation for this in the discussion section. We can also observe the under prediction of all models that again suggests there is room for improvement by learning better parameter values for the network.

29.4 Discussion and Conclusions

It appears that we have found strong evidence that fine-grained models can provide better tracking of student knowledge than coarse-grained models as measured by their ability to predict student performance. For predicting student performance on the tutor system, the finer-grained the model is, the better. However, when predicting the statewide standardized test scores, the second finest-grained model achieved the best prediction. The

Top 5 hard knowledge components

WPI 8th grade math fine-grained model click to sort by	Skill meter	Rate click to sort by	#Record click to sort by
Surface-area	▪	8%	35
Congruence	▬	18%	16
Inverse relations	▬▬	31%	32
Pythagorean-theorem	▬▬	33%	54
Division-fraction	▬▬▬	42%	21

FIGURE 29.4
Class skill report generated by the WPI-106 fine-grained skill model.

error of the coarse-grained WPI-1 and WPI-5 models remained relatively steady between predicting the test and responses within the tutor. We believe that the finer-grained models' reduced performance on test prediction might be due to questions on the tutor with a much higher difficulty than questions of the same skill on the test. The skill of 'Venn-Diagram' from the WPI-106, for example, has two questions on the ASSISTment system, both of fill in the blank–type answers with an average correctness of 18.2% on the system. A similar 'Venn-Diagram' question appeared on the state standardized test in multiple-choice form and recorded a correctness of 87.3% on the test. Coarser-grained models may be less susceptible to this variance in difficulty because knowledge estimates are averaged over a wider variety of questions. Thirty-five questions and eight WPI-106 skills, including 'Venn-Diagram,' are represented by the WPI-39 skill of 'understanding-data-presentation-techniques.' Eighty-three questions and sixteen of the WPI-106 skills, including 'Venn-Diagram,' are represented by the WPI-5 skill of 'data-analysis-statistics-probability.'

Some of our colleagues have perused item-response models for this very dataset [2,4] with considerable success. We think that item-response models do not help teachers identify what skills a students should work on, so even though they might be very good predictors of student responses, they suffers in other ways. Part of the utility of fine-grained modeling is being able to identify skills that students have mastered and those they still need to master. An example of a class skill report presented to a teacher is shown in Figure 29.4.

We think that this work is important in that while adapting fine-grained models is hard, we have shown that fine-grained modeling can produce a highly accurate prediction of student performance. Future work on this topic should include learning guess and slip parameters that provide a better fit to the data. Also worth investigating would be using a temporal Bayesian network. Using a temporal framework would allow for learning to be modeled and would take into account that a student's most recent responses should be weighted more heavily in assessing their current state of knowledge.

Acknowledgments

This research was made possible by the U.S. Department of Education, Institute of Education Science "Effective Mathematics Education Research" program grant #R305K03140, the Office of Naval Research grant #N00014-03-1-0221, NSF CAREER award to Neil Heffernan, and the Spencer Foundation. All of the opinions in this article are those of the authors and not those of any of the funders. This work would not have been possible without the assistance of the 2004–2005 WPI/CMU ASSISTment team that helped make possible this dataset. The first author is an NSF GK-12 fellow.

References

1. Anderson, J. R. and Lebiere, C. (1998). *The Atomic Component of Thought*. Erlbaum, Mahwah, NJ.
2. Anozie, N. O. and Junker, B. W. (2006). Predicting end-of-year accountability assessment scores from monthly student records in an online tutoring system. *Proceedings of the AAAI-06 Workshop on Educational Data Mining*, Boston, MA. AAAI Technical Report WS-06-05, pp. 1–6.
3. Arroyo, I. and Woolf, B. (2005). Inferring learning and attitudes from a Bayesian Network of log file data. *Proceedings of the 12th International Conference on Artificial Intelligence in Education*, Amsterdam, the Netherlands, pp. 33–40.
4. Ayers, E. and Junker, B. W. (2006). Do skills combine additively to predict task difficulty in eighth grade mathematics? In Beck, J., Aimeur, E., and Barnes, T. (eds.), *Educational Data Mining: Papers from the AAAI Workshop*. Menlo Park, CA: AAAI Press. Technical Report WS-06-05, pp. 14–20.
5. Barnes, T. (2005). Q-matrix method: Mining student response data for knowledge. *Proceedings of the AAAI-05 Workshop on Educational Data Mining*, Pittsburgh, PA, 2005. AAAI Technical Report #WS-05-02.
6. Carmona, C., Millán, E., de-la Cruz, J.-L.P., Trella, M., and Conejo, R. (2005). Introducing prerequisite relations in a multi-layered Bayesian student model. In Ardissono, L., Brna, P., and Mitrovic, A. (eds.), *User Modeling*. Lecture Notes in Computer Science, Vol. 3538. Springer, Berlin, Germany, pp. 347–356.
7. Conati, C., Gertner, A., and VanLehn, K. (2002). Using Bayesian networks to manage uncertainty in student modeling. *User Modeling and User-Adapted Interaction*, 12(4), 371–417.
8. Corbett, A. T., Anderson, J. R. & O'Brien, A. T. (1995). Student modeling in the ACT programming tutor. In Nichols, P., Chipman, S., and Brennan, R. (eds.), *Cognitively diagnostic assessment*. Erlbaum, Hillsdale, NJ, pp. 19–41.
9. Feng, M., Heffernan, N. T., Mani, M., and Heffernan, C. (2006). Using mixed-effects modeling to compare different grain-sized skill models. In Beck, J., Aimeur, E., and Barnes, T. (eds.), *Educational Data Mining: Papers from the AAAI Workshop*. AAAI Press. Technical Report WS-06-05. ISBN 978-1-57735-287-7, pp. 57–66.
10. Mathan, S. and Koedinger, K. R. (2003). Recasting the feedback debate: Benefits of tutoring error detection and correction skills. In Hoppe, U., Verdejo, F., and Kay, J. (eds.), *Artificial Intelligence in Education: Shaping the Future of Learning through Intelligent Technologies, Proceedings of AI-ED 2003*. IOS Press, Amsterdam, the Netherlands, pp. 39–46.
11. McCalla, G. I. and Greer, J. E. (1994). Granularity-based reasoning and belief revision in student models. In Greer, J. E. and McCalla, G. I. (eds.), *Student Modelling: The Key to Individualized Knowledge-Based Instruction*. Springer-Verlag, Berlin, Germany, pp 39–62.
12. Mislevy, R.J. and Gitomer, D. H. (1996). The role of probability-based inference in an intelligent tutoring system. *User-Modeling and User Adapted Interaction*, 5, 253–282.
13. Pardos, Z. A., Heffernan, N. T., Anderson, B., and Heffernan, C. L. (2006). Using fine-grained skill models to fit student performance with Bayesian networks. *Workshop in Educational Data Mining held at the Eight International Conference on Intelligent Tutoring Systems*, Taiwan. http://www.educationaldatamining.org/ITS2006EDM/EDMITS2006.html
14. Pardos, Z. A., Heffernan, N. T., Anderson, B., and Heffernan, C. (2007). The effect of model granularity on student performance prediction using Bayesian networks. *Proceedings of the 11th International Conference on User Modeling*. Springer, Corfu, Greece, pp. 435–439. http://www.educationaldatamining.org/UM2007.html

15. Pardos, Z. A., Heffernan, N. T., Ruiz, C., and Beck, J. (2008). The composition effect: Conjunctive or compensatory? An analysis of multi-skill math questions in ITS. *Proceedings of the First Conference on Educational Data Mining*, Montreal, Canada, pp. 147–156. http://ihelp.usask.ca/iaied/ijaied/AIED2007/AIED-EDM_proceeding_full2.pdf

16. Pardos, Z. A., Feng, M., Heffernan, N. T., and Heffernan-Lindquist, C. (2007). Analyzing fine-grained skill models using Bayesian and mixed effect methods. In Luckin, R. and Koedinger, K. (eds.), *Proceedings of the 13th Conference on Artificial Intelligence in Education*. IOS Press, Amsterdam, the Netherlands, pp. 626–628.

17. Razzaq, L., Heffernan, N., Feng, M., and Pardos, Z. (2007). Developing fine-grained transfer models in the ASSISTment system. *Journal of Technology, Instruction, Cognition, and Learning*, 5(3), 289–304.

18. Reye, J. (2004). Student modelling based on belief networks. *International Journal of Artificial Intelligence in Education*, 14, 63–96.

19. Tatsuoka, K. K. (1990). Toward an integration of item response theory and cognitive error diagnosis. In Frederiksen, N., Glaser, R., Lesgold, A., and Shafto, M. G. (eds.), *Diagnostic Monitoring of Skill and Knowledge Acquisition*. Lawrence Erlbaum Associates, Hillsdale, NJ, pp. 453–488.

20. Wilson, M. (2009). Measuring progressions: Assessment structures underlying a learning progression. *Journal of Research in Science Teaching*, 46(6), 716–730.

21. Zapata-Rivera, J.-D. and Greer, J. E. (2004). Interacting with inspectable Bayesian models. *International Journal of Artificial Intelligence in Education*, 14, 127–163.

30

Mining for Patterns of Incorrect Response in Diagnostic Assessment Data

Tara M. Madhyastha and Earl Hunt

CONTENTS

30.1 Introduction

It is a popular belief in education that students come into a classroom with ideas about the material they are taught that can alter or interfere with their understanding of a topic. A dramatic example is the video *A Private Universe*, where Harvard students in cap and gown are asked to describe the cause of the seasons. Invariably, they fall back on the misconception that seasons are caused by the distance of the earth from the sun [1]. It is recommended that teachers should check the extent to which students hold erroneous concepts throughout instruction, ideally to deliver personalized feedback to students. One such approach, developed by Minstrell, is called "diagnostic instruction" [2,3]. It is based on the idea of delivering multiple-choice questions to students where each question (and corresponding responses) attempts to "diagnose" a particular type of thinking. If the thinking is incorrect, the teacher then uses the diagnosis to select an appropriate intervention. In Minstrell's framework, these types of fine-grained incorrect thinking are called "facets" and are catalogued by topic. Student facets should theoretically result in predictable behaviors; facets are defined as only "slight generalizations from what students actually say or do in the classroom" [2]. A similar model-based feedback approach is often implemented in intelligent tutoring systems, which recognizes incorrect responses and provides targeted feedback (e.g., Andes [4], ASSISTment [5]).

However, feedback based on incorrect multiple-choice responses can potentially assume an untested assumption—that students hold consistent incorrect beliefs, resulting in predictable responses, which must be individually addressed (as opposed to correcting the mistake with a very limited model of student knowledge and reteaching the material).

Students may frequently choose the same incorrect answer to a single question, but it does not necessarily mean that they are doing so because of a firm misunderstanding and will therefore answer other questions with the same consistent error. For readability, we will call these consistent errors "misconceptions" throughout this chapter, noting that a pattern of consistent errors does not actually need to correspond to a logical misconception in the educational sense—it can be evidence of a consistent pattern of fragmented understanding or a basic heuristic. We ask the following question: do students hold consistent misconceptions in the timeframe of a single assessment? We examine data collected over a period of 2.5 years from the DIAGNOSER [6], a web-based software system that delivers diagnostic questions to students, to determine the answer to this question.

30.2 The DIAGNOSER

The data we describe comes from the DIAGNOSER instructional tools [7]. This web-based assessment system is the second generation of a tool originally designed and prototyped by Hunt and Minstrell [8] that a teacher could use to diagnose student difficulties in science. The system consists of short sets of questions designed to elicit middle school and high school student thinking around specific concepts in physics (grades 6–12). The DIAGNOSER system matches incorrect responses to questions to "facets," or descriptions of common ideas within a topic. The teacher then uses the facet patterns for individuals or for a class to select "prescriptive activities" to challenge students' misconceptions and help move them to the target level of understanding. All DIAGNOSER questions and materials referred to in this chapter are available at www.diagnoser.com by clicking on "Teacher login" to register.

Figure 30.1 shows an example diagnostic question on position and distance from a paper assessment. Questions in the online system are presented in a *question set*, designed to diagnose ideas within one central topic, called a "facet cluster" (e.g., "average speed"). Multiple-choice responses may correspond to different facets within a facet cluster, or they may represent uncoded reasoning. DIAGNOSER also supports numerical response questions, for which certain common responses are mapped to facets. Each question set has between 6 and 13 questions, some of which are conditionally delivered based on facets diagnosed in other questions.

Table 30.1 shows how the responses to the question in Figure 30.1 should be interpreted by a teacher. For example, a student who responds "5 meters" might be confusing the ideas of position and distance, responding to the question with the final position. Each facet is then mapped to a corresponding pedagogical intervention that a teacher may use to address it.

30.3 Method

We wish to determine whether students are consistent when reasoning using misconceptions. We examine this issue in two parts. First, we consider the consistency of reasoning across pairs of questions. Operationally, we ask: if we know a student's incorrect

During lunch your science teacher has 30 min to run errands down the corridor in preparation for the afternoon classes. Your teacher's motion is shown in the position versus time graph below.

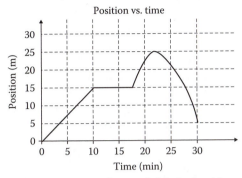

What is the total distance your teacher traveled during lunch?

a. 5 m

b. 20 m

c. 25 m

d. 45 m

e. 60 m

FIGURE 30.1
Example diagnostic question targeting concepts of position and distance.

TABLE 30.1

Facet Descriptions Corresponding to Example Question in Figure 30.1

Response	Description
(a)	Student determines the distance traveled by giving the final position.
(b)	Student reports the farthest position traveled minus the end position as the distance traveled.
(c)	Student reports the farthest position as the distance traveled.
(d)	Student correctly determines the distance traveled for motion in one direction from a graphical representation.
(e)	The student determines distance by adding several positions along the trajectory.

multiple-choice response* to one question, does this help us to predict his or her response to another question? For example, if a student says that a truck exerts more force upon a fly that collides with its windshield than the fly does on the truck, we intuit that the student might be thinking that greater force inflicts greater damage. We might predict that when we ask the student to compare the force of a hammer upon a nail, the student will respond that the hammer exerts more force than the nail. We use the concept of conditional entropy to quantify the additional "information" gained from knowing a response to a question. We mine the data from an atheoretical perspective.

---

* We use the term "response" throughout this chapter to refer to a specific multiple choice selection, not merely whether the question was answered correctly or not.

This is pedagogically very important because teachers who use facet theory to guide instruction implicitly assume that such predictions would hold, and gauge their interventions accordingly. Similarly, an intelligent tutoring system could successfully base automatic feedback on the underlying conceptual model. Students who can reason consistently can learn from an experiment set up to demonstrate the flaws in their thinking. If, in the opposite extreme, students answer diagnostic questions randomly, there is no information to suggest an appropriate intervention beyond reteaching the material.

Second, patterns that span more than two questions may exist. To identify the prevalence of patterns, we extend the concept of entropy to the problem of defining the consistency of responding across several questions. Because some responses are conceptually "closer" to each other than others, simple mining for patterns will yield far more patterns than is pedagogically important. Our intuition is that if students are responding with some, but not perfect, consistency, their response patterns should fall into clusters, where the patterns within clusters are more similar to each other than they are to the response patterns in other clusters. Note that these clusters are mathematically defined clusters of responses, in contrast to "facet clusters" that are used in the DIAGNOSER system. If this were the case, teachers could use the misconceptions that characterize each cluster, rather than misconceptions that characterize individual items, to identify what interventions are appropriate.

A traditional approach to this analysis would use item-response theory to fit a model to the different incorrect responses (e.g., [9]). However, as written, DIAGNOSER question sets intended for use in a classroom setting, do not provide a sufficient number and difficulty of questions to obtain reliable estimates of facet difficulty. Furthermore, this approach assumes that the relative difficulty of responses is the same for all students, which is an assumption that DIAGNOSER explicitly rejects. We have extended a single question set as a proof of concept that in fact such an approach can be used to model diagnostic responses, and that at lower levels of mastery, students are inconsistent in their facet responses [10].

The entropy-based analysis described in this chapter is novel but, we believe, appropriate to mining data from similar model-based assessment or tutoring systems.

In the context of an assessment, consider the questions X and Y, which have response alternatives $X_1, X_2 \ldots X_{k(X)}$ and $Y_1, Y_2 \ldots Y_{k(Y)}$ where $k(X)$ and $k(Y)$ are the number of allowable responses to X and Y. Define $N(X_i)$ as the number of students choosing alternative X_i and $P(X_i)$ as the probability of choosing alternative X_i.

The entropy associated within each question X is

$$H(X) = -\sum_{i=1}^{k(X)} P(X_i) * \log_2(P(X_i)) \tag{30.1}$$

Next, let $N(X_iY_j)$ be the number of cases of responses X_i to question X and Y_j to question Y $(i = 1 \ldots k(X), j = 1 \ldots k(Y))$. Then

$$P(Y_j \mid X_i) = \frac{N(X_iY_j)}{\sum_{v=1}^{k(Y)} N(X_iY_v)} \tag{30.2}$$

It follows that the entropy of Y, given that the response to X was X_i is

$$H(Y \mid X_i) = -\sum_{Y_i}^{k(Y)} P(Y_j \mid X_i) * \log_2(P(Y_j \mid X_i)) \tag{30.3}$$

The conditional entropy of question Y given knowledge of the response to question X is

$$H(Y \mid X) = -\sum_{i=1}^{k(X)} P(X_i) * H(Y_j \mid X_i) \qquad (30.4)$$

We can use the entropy function to quantify the uncertainty within a question, and then consider the information (or lack of uncertainty) that we can gain from knowing responses to another question. This is the difference between the entropy of a question and the conditional entropy, given that the response to a second question is known:

$$T(XY) = H(Y) - H(Y|X) \qquad (30.5)$$

This is a measure of the extent to which responses to question X can be used to predict responses to question Y. It is an effect size measure, i.e., it does not depend on the number of cases.

Let us consider what this means given two questions X and Y on a test. If the response to Y can be completely predicted by knowledge of the specific responses to X ($X_1...X_k$), the entropy of Y conditional upon X is zero. In information-theoretic terms, the mutual information will be maximized. If the response to Y is independent of the response to X, there will be no difference between the terms, and the response to X tells us nothing about how students will respond to Y.

We can use the concept of entropy to place students into clusters according to their responses to a set of multiple-choice questions to minimize the entropy of the entire system. For example, suppose there is just one question and half of the students respond A, and half respond B. By our definitions above, we see that the entropy of this random variable is 1.0. If we can cluster the students into two groups, those who selected A and those who selected B, we can reduce the conditional entropy of the system, given that group membership is known, to zero.

More formally, we seek to minimize the expected entropy. We calculate the expected entropy by multiplying the entropy of each cluster (the sum of the entropies of each attribute) by the probability that an item falls into that cluster. Finding the optimal clustering is an NP-complete problem. Efficient implementations of entropy-based clustering have been described and implemented, such as COOLCAT [11] and LIMBO [12], and as we scale to large datasets, we will need to evaluate such algorithms.

We evaluate the effectiveness of the clustering by calculating the categorical utility (CU) [13] function, which gives an idea of how predictive the clustering is, penalized by the number of clusters. The CU function is itself built up from a lower-order statistic, the Δ index introduced by Goodman and Kruskal [13,14]. The Δ index is simply the decrease in the number of erroneous predictions of a variable's value that is obtained by knowing which cluster the case being predicted is in, using the strategy of probability matching. This is best seen by an example. Suppose that on a particular two-choice question half the respondents say "Yes" and half say "No." Given this information, one expects to make an error in prediction half the time. Suppose further, though, that on the basis of other variables, respondents are clustered into two groups, A and B. In cluster A, 80% of the respondents respond "Yes" and 20% respond "No." If you guess according to the distribution of responses, given the knowledge of cluster A, you will guess "Yes" 80% of the time and be right 80% of those guesses, and you will guess "No" 20% of the time and be right 20% of those guesses. Your correct guess rate will be $0.8*0.8+0.2*0.2=0.68$. The Δ index for the cluster is $0.68-0.50=0.18$.

The formula for the Δ index is given as follows, where C is one of k clusters, A_i is the question i, and each A_i can assume j values, V_{ij}:

$$\Delta(C, A_i) = \sum_{k=1}^{n} P(C_k) \sum_{j} P(A_i = V_{ij} \mid C_k)^2 - \sum_{j} P(A_i = V_{ij})^2 \tag{30.6}$$

The CU function is the average of the Δ values for each of the n clusters. This introduces a penalty factor that increases with the number of clusters:

$$CU(C) = \frac{1}{n} \sum_{i} \Delta(C, A_i) \tag{30.7}$$

Therefore, the larger the CU function, the better the clustering, in the sense that knowledge of the cluster helps to predict the responses to the questions.

30.4 Results

We examined responses to questions students took in DIAGNOSER over a period of approximately two years. These sets included questions in the subjects of motion of objects, nature of forces, forces to explain motion, and human body systems. We considered only those question sets that have been taken at least 200 times, and removed question set responses from experimenters or teachers. Students occasionally retake question sets after study; we included these responses in our analysis. Explaining 2D motion was taken the least ($N=200$) and position and distance 1 was taken by the most students ($N=5540$). In all, there were over forty-thousand completed question sets ($N=40237$).

In the DIAGNOSER, some questions are offered conditionally; only students who obtain a certain response on one question are presented with the next. For pair-wise analysis, we considered only the subset of students who complete each pair of questions. In addition, some questions allow a diagnosis of "unknown," meaning that the facet represented by that response is unknown (e.g., when students type in a numerical response that does not correspond to a postulated reasoning strategy). Because unknown facets have no corresponding instructional interventions, we limited our pair-wise analysis to question pairs where both responses have been diagnosed with known facets through multiple-choice responses. For cluster analysis, missing questions and unknown responses are part of the response pattern.

The final subset of data represents student responses in well-developed and tested modules where consistent relationships between pairs of diagnosed responses are most likely to be found. We examine relationships among questions completed by each student within each question set, which is intended to take about 20 min to complete during a class. Therefore, there is little chance that instruction will affect the consistency of incorrect response at this timescale.

30.4.1 Pair-Wise Analysis

We calculated the information gained from knowing an incorrect response to question X to predict a response to Y for every possible pair of questions X and Y that met the criteria described above in every question set. In pedagogic terms, we check to see whether knowledge of a specific incorrect response (linked to a specific facet) predicts a student's subsequent responses to related questions (linked to specific related facets). If a student's reasoning in answering a question does not predict his or her subsequent responses, it is unlikely that an intervention targeted to addressing the diagnosed facet will be effective. In simple terms, the students might be more confused than we think they are. We examined all pairs within a question set rather than limiting our analysis to pairs, which pedagogical content experts have judged, to diagnose the same facets because students do not reason like experts, and they may find similarities where experts do not. Furthermore, a consistent pattern of fragmented understanding is also of pedagogical utility and would not correspond to identically selected facets. Finally, no information is lost with this decision to expand the scope, because we include the sub-analysis of more tightly coupled questions, particularly those where a student is asked to select the reasoning for a response to a previous question.

First, we consider the magnitude of the additional information one might gain about Y by knowledge of X (information gain) as a fraction of what we know from Y alone. Figure 30.2 shows, for each question set, the conditional entropy ($H (Y|X)$) and corresponding

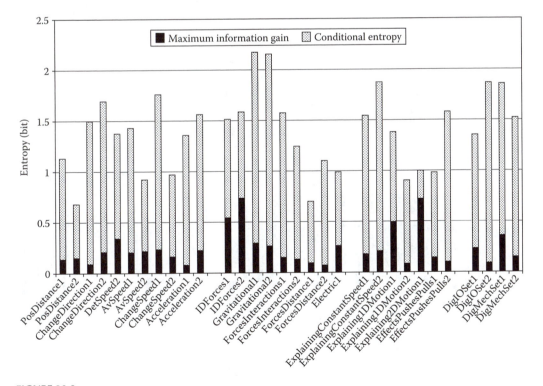

FIGURE 30.2
The conditional entropy (in bits) and corresponding information gain for the question pair within each question set that had the maximum information gain.

information gain (T (XY)) for the question pair within the set that had the maximum information gain. By Equation 30.8, the sum of the conditional entropy and information gain (the height of each bar) is the entropy for question Y. The information gain is quite small, in bits, meaning that for the most highly predictable pair of questions in each set, knowing the student's response to the first question did not significantly help predict the response to the second question. In the extreme, if the response to the first question of the pair completely predicts the response to the second question, the conditional entropy would be zero.

Ultimately, however, we are less interested in the maximal information gain than in the conditional entropy. Low conditional entropy indicates that the responses to a question are highly determined by the responses to another question.

Figure 30.3 shows the conditional entropy (in bits) and the corresponding information gain for the question pair (X,Y) in each question set with the smallest conditional entropy. The conditional entropy H ($Y|X$) added to the information gain T (XY) is the entropy for Y. With a few exceptions, the smallest conditional entropy is not very low. Where it is low, the entropy of the question is low in the first place (e.g., where students largely choose a single response because the question is very easy or the distracters are not attractive).

One question pair, in the set Explaining2DMotion1, stands out in both Figures 30.2 and 30.3 with a low conditional entropy and high information gain. This indicates that the first question in the pair is an excellent predictor of responses to the second question of the pair. This occurred because the second question of the pair asks students to explain their reasoning for their response, providing good cues for consistent responses. This is

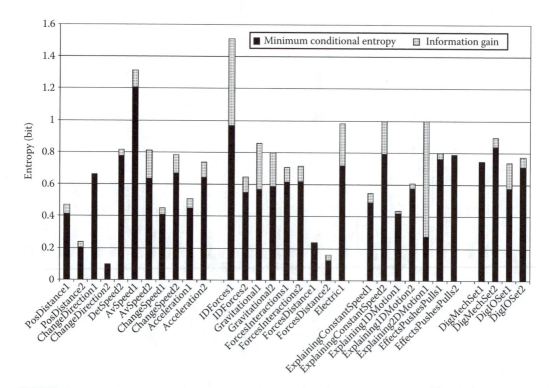

FIGURE 30.3
The conditional entropy (in bits) and the corresponding information gain for the question pair in each question set with the smallest conditional entropy.

an example of a question pair where the content of the questions is closely related. There is also an alternative: "I do not see my reasoning in this list" that was chosen very frequently, but eliminated from analysis because it did not correspond to a known diagnosis. We see high information gain in this case only because we consider only a small subset of responses.

In summary, we saw little evidence from entropy-based pair-wise analysis that incorrect responses successfully predict other responses beyond that which would be expected by random chance. There are several possible explanations for this finding. First, although the questions are judged by content experts to be related in a facet cluster, it may be that students do not reason consistently until they gain a certain level of understanding. Evidence for this has been provided by research on a similar dataset [10]. Second, as we will explore in the next section, consistent reasoning strategies may span multiple questions.

30.4.2 Entropy-Based Clustering

Overall, the information gained across pairs of questions was low. However, distinct patterns of thought may not be visible from the inspection of pairs of ideas. In this section, we extend the concept of entropy to the problem of defining consistency of responding across several questions. Evidence of multiple clusters with unique, albeit noisy, response patterns supports the concept of individual student diagnosis (and corresponding "treatment" of the ideas represented by responses that characterize the cluster).

Figure 30.4 shows the CU functions for each clustering for the question sets in each of the four areas. Of 27 sets, in 11 cases, a two-cluster solution was best. In another 11 cases, a three-cluster solution was best. There were five sets in which a four- or five-cluster solution was slightly better than a three-cluster solution; e.g., the question sets within forces to explain motion: effects of pushes and pulls 1 and 2.

A multiple cluster solution is only evidence of unique patterns of thought if the response patterns that represent each cluster are interpretable as pedagogically consistent ideas. In the two-cluster solutions, one cluster represents students who respond mostly correctly (assuming that correct responses occur frequently) and the remaining cluster represents students who tend toward incorrect responses. In the three-cluster solutions, there are high- and low-ability clusters and a cluster that represents the most common pattern of response. In other words, most cluster results support the interpretation of facets as a linear construct, where certain facets represent primitive understanding and others represent correct/mostly correct understanding, rather than a constellation of equal, but different ideas. Figure 30.5 shows the percentage of reduction in entropy obtained for each question set by optimal clustering. Low reductions in entropy indicate that the clusters do not hold together particularly well, and are not very informative about the patterns of response within the cluster. This is consistent with our observation that clusters of two or three are aligned with ability.

We turn our attention to the sets with higher-order cluster solutions and higher reductions in entropy. There are only two question sets where the reduction of entropy was greater than 35%: Change in Direction 2, and Effects of Pushes and Pulls 2. These two question sets had the lowest entropy of all sets before clustering. This happens when there are few multiple-choice questions (we do not consider open-ended or numerical fill-in questions), when the questions have few possible responses, when most students answer questions correctly, or any combination of these conditions. In Change in Direction 2, there are two fill-in questions, two questions with only three responses, and one question that diagnoses only one facet (so in effect, there are only two possible responses to it). With the

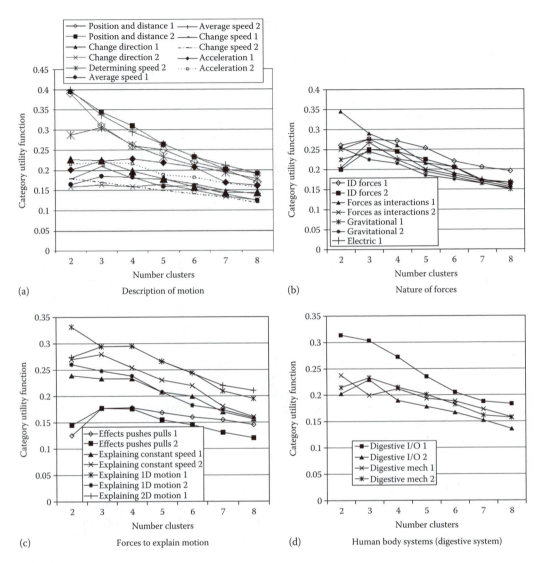

FIGURE 30.4
Category utility function curves for DIAGNOSER question sets: (a) Description of motion, (b) nature of forces, (c) forces to explain motion, (d) human body systems (digestive system).

response space so constrained, the five-cluster solution that was optimal had one cluster where responses are mostly correct, three clusters each representing the most common error to each of the questions with three or fewer responses, and one "entropy" cluster with a high variation of responses.

Effects of Pushes and Pulls 2 has only six multiple-choice questions, four of which have only three multiple-choice responses. Of the four clusters in the optimal solution, one cluster was mostly correct, two clusters included the most common error to two of the questions with three multiple-choice responses, and one was an "entropy" cluster with a high variation of responses.

The results of our cluster analysis do not support the existence of unique patterns of thought. Rather, clusters form by ability levels.

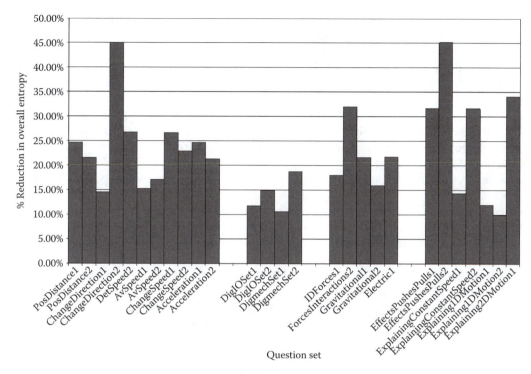

FIGURE 30.5
Percentage reduction in overall entropy for best clustering.

30.5 Discussion

We have found little evidence from either pair-wise analysis of questions or clustering analysis that students, on the whole, have systematic misconceptions that can be diagnosed by the patterns of facets within the time frame of a single assessment. We are not the first to notice this. This result is consistent with work by Tatsuoka [15] describing the inconsistency with which students use procedural rules to solve arithmetic problems until they reach mastery (i.e., use the correct rules). Hallhoun and Hestenes [16] noted that the common sense conceptual systems of students have much less internal coherence than naïve theories, which, although incorrect, are internally consistent (e.g., Aristotelian reasoning). Facets are in fact designed to capture fine-grained and inconsistent fragments of knowledge and reasoning [2], similar to ideas proposed by diSessa [17], although the proposed interventions assume facets are actually evidence of consistent reasoning. Thus, this analysis suggests that student reasoning is fragmented and inconsistent, within a broad representative sample of 6–12 graders taking physics in middle or high school.

These results have serious implications for pedagogical intervention. Predictable responses to diagnostic questions allow teachers to use instructional strategies that ask students to commit to ideas and then engage in experiments to test their hypotheses. Tutoring systems can provide feedback based on an underlying model of incorrect student understanding. In the extreme, if a student answers every question completely randomly, there is no pattern to the responses, and no information to be exploited. Absence of predictability, evidenced by low information transmission, is evidence against the pedagogical utility of targeted interventions based on facets of reasoning. Sleeman [18] compared human tutoring using diagnosed "bugs" in algebraic solutions with reteaching and did not find a significant difference. From a cognitive point of view, for some students, classroom time might be better spent on reteaching than on diagnosis and intervention.

Although we did not look for them specifically in this chapter, there are probably certain ideas that are particularly difficult to understand (e.g., the cause of the seasons), that do warrant specific attention. However, there is no evidence from our analysis that students structure most knowledge in this way. We have not examined the relationship of ability to consistency. In general, it may be sufficient merely to know what content poses significant problems at different levels of ability and to address these in the classroom, spending less time on individual diagnosis. This analysis considered facets in the context of assessments from a purely cognitive point of view. We have not considered the effect of facet-based instruction on engagement and motivation, which is an important component of classroom instruction. It may be that the action of listening to student's incorrect ideas, and then testing them with activities and interventions, may increase student interest in the subject and motivation to learn. This may transfer to automated feedback within a tutoring system. Anecdotal reports suggest that many students who are required to take physics in middle and high school may not be particularly excited about it.

We have also not considered individual differences among students. It is possible that some students may reason more systematically than others, but are not motivated enough to monitor and correct their own incorrect understandings. For these students, diagnostic instruction might work exceptionally well—motivating students to learn from testing their misconceptions.

References

1. M.H. Schneps, P.M. Sadler, S. Woll, and L. Crouse, *A Private Universe*, South Burlington, VT: Annenberg Media, 1989.
2. J. Minstrell, Facets of students' thinking: Designing to cross the gap from research to standards-based practice, in *Designing for Science: Implications for Professional, Instructional, and Everyday Science*, K. Crowley, C.D. Schunn, and T. Okada (eds.), Mawah, NJ: Erlbaum, 2001.
3. E. Hunt and J. Minstrell, Effective instruction in science and mathematics: Psychological principles and social constraints, *Issues in Education*, 2, 1996, 123–162.
4. K. VanLehn, C. Lynch, K. Schulze, J.A. Shapiro, R. Shelby, L. Taylor, D. Treacy, A. Weinstein, and M. Wintersgill, The Andes physics tutoring system: Lessons learned, *International Journal of Artificial Intelligence in Education*, 15, 2005, 147–204.
5. L. Razzaq, M. Feng, G. Heffernan, K.R. Koedinger, B. Junker, S. Ritter, A. Knight, C. Aniszczyk, S. Choksey, T. Livak, E. Mercado, T. Turner, R. Upalekar, J.A. Walonoski, M.A. Macasek, and K.P. Rasumssen, The assistment project: Blending assessment and assisting, in *Proceedings of the 12th International Conference on Artificial Intelligence in Education*, C.K. Looi, G. McCalla, B. Bredeweg, and J. Breuker (eds.), Amsterdam, the Netherlands: ISO Press, 2005, pp. 555–562.
6. FACET Innovations, *Welcome to Diagnoser: Instructional Tools for Science and Mathematics*. www.diagnose.com.
7. J. Minstrell, R. Anderson, P. Kraus, and J.E. Minstrell, Bridging from practice to research and back: Tools to support formative assessment, in *Science Assessment: Research and Practical Approaches*, J. Coffey, R. Douglas, and C. Sterns (eds.), NSTA Press, Arlington, VA, 2008.

8. E. Hunt and J. Minstrell, The DIAGNOSER project: Formative assessment in the service of learning. Paper presented at the International Association for Educational Assessment, Philadelphia, PA, 2004.
9. C. Huang, Psychometric analysis based on evidence-centered design and cognitive science of learning to explore student's problem-solving in physics, unpublished dissertation, December 2003.
10. K. Scalise, T. Madhyastha, J. Minstrell, and M. Wilson, Improving assessment evidence in e-learning products: Some solutions for reliability, *International Journal of Learning Technology*, in press.
11. D. Barbará, Y. Li, and J. Couto, COOLCAT: An entropy-based algorithm for categorical clustering, in *Proceedings of the 11th International Conference on Information and Knowledge Management*, McLean, VA: ACM, 2002, pp. 582–589.
12. P. Andritsos, P. Tsaparas, R.J. Miller, and K.C. Sevcik, LIMBO: Scalable clustering of categorical data, in *Advances in Database Technology* (*EDBT 2004*), Crete, Greece, 2004, pp. 531–532.
13. B. Mirkin, Reinterpreting the category utility function, *Machine Learning*, 45(2), November 2001, 219–228.
14. L.A. Goodman and W. Kruskal, Measures of association for cross classifications, *Journal of the American Statistical Association*, 49, 1954, 732–764.
15. K.K. Tatsuoka, M. Birenbaum, and J. Arnold, On the stability of students' rules of operation for solving arithmetic problems, *Journal of Educational Measurement*, 26, 1989, 351–361.
16. J.A. Halloun and D. Hestenes, Common sense concepts about motion, *American Journal of Physics*, 53, 1985, 1056–1065.
17. A.A. diSessa, *Knowledge in Pieces*, University of California, Berkeley, CA, 1985.
18. D. Sleeman, A.E. Kelly, R. Martinak, R.D. Ward, and J.L. Moore, Studies of diagnosis and remediation with high school algebra students, *Cognitive Science*, 13, July 2005, 551–568.

31

Machine-Learning Assessment of Students' Behavior within Interactive Learning Environments

Manolis Mavrikis

CONTENTS

31.1 Introduction

Enhancing an interactive learning environment (ILE) with personalized feedback within and between activities necessitates several intelligent capabilities on behalf of its adaptive components. Such capabilities require means of assessing students' behavior within the ILE.

This chapter presents a case study of the use of educational data-mining (EDM) techniques to assess the quality of students' interaction in terms of learning, and subsequently to predict whether they can answer a given question without asking for help. Such an approach, based on data, provides an objective and operational, rather than intuitive or *ad hoc*, measure and can empower intelligent components of an ILE to adapt and personalize the provided feedback based on students' interactions. The next section, after describing briefly the ILE (WaLLiS) used as a test bed for the research presented here, further motivates the necessity for such capabilities on behalf of the system. The section also presents the datasets and provides background and justification for the machine-learning method, Bayesian network (BN), which was primarily employed.

Section 31.3 presents details of the development of two interrelated BN, their accuracy and comparisons with other techniques and, in particular, with decision trees. The last section discusses the use of the developed models in WaLLiS and raises issues around the application of such models relevant to EDM researchers in general. In addition, it presents future work that provides insights to improve and automate the development of similar models in related work.

31.2 Background

31.2.1 The Interactive Learning Environment WaLLiS

WaLLiS is a web-based environment that hosts content that includes theory or example pages, as well as interactive and exploratory activities [1]. Apart from the typical components of the system that deliver the material and the tree-based navigation of the content, WaLLiS provides adaptive feedback that takes into account students' errors and common misconceptions. The feedback is designed to help them progress and complete the activities. This way, a problem that students cannot solve is turned into a teaching aid from which they learn by practicing. In that sense, WaLLiS is similar to other Intelligent Tutoring Systems (ITS) (e.g., [2]), which have the potential to improve student learning.

However, research on students' interactions within ILE shows that their behavior is neither always optimal nor beneficial to their learning [3,4]. In particular, the analysis of students' working within WaLLiS indicated that students' help seeking behavior played a particular role in learning [4]. The importance of help seeking is further supported by the studies of human–human and classroom interactions (e.g., [5]), as well as other research in ITS [6,7]. Moreover, a combination of qualitative research and statistical analysis indicates that part of the evidence that human tutors employ to adapt their pedagogical strategies comes particularly from help requests for questions on which the tutors estimate that a student's request for help is superfluous [4,8]. This estimation is mostly based on the quality of previous interactions. Therefore, in principle, an operational way to assess the quality of students' interaction in terms of learning as well as a way to predict whether students can answer a given question without asking for help, seems an important requirement for an intelligent component of an ILE. The main aim of the case study presented here was to develop such a component and to investigate its use.

31.2.2 Datasets

WaLLiS is integrated in the teaching of various courses of the School of Mathematics of the University of Edinburgh. The datasets that facilitated the research discussed here are from the second year module "Geometry Iteration and Convergence" (GIC) and, in particular, its last part that introduces "Conic Sections." Although students are familiar with the system from other courses, the materials taught in this part are unknown to them and constitute a rather individual unit, which is taught solely through WaLLiS. This way, for the data analysis reported here, it was possible to establish not only the indicators of prerequisite knowledge but also that any performance results are reasonably (if not solely) attributed to the interaction with the system and not other external factors. In particular, with the collaboration of the lecturer, certain questions on the students' final exam were designed to test long-term retention.

Accordingly, it was possible to conduct machine-learning analysis based on datasets collected through the application of WaLLiS over 3 years (2003–2005). These are referred to as GIC03, GIC04, and GIC05. The students who interacted with the system were 126, 133, and 115, respectively. The GIC04 and GIC05 data collection aimed at collecting, apart from students' interactions, their performance. This was assessed by averaging (a) the students' marks on an impromptu assessment they had to complete right after their interaction with the system and (b) their mark on a final exam purposefully designed to probe learning that can be attributed to the system.

It is evident that data collection under realistic conditions entails several challenges that result in discarding some data. Due to the way the datasets were collected (i.e., remotely over the internet and not during a controlled laboratory study), they can be quite noisy. The methods used for data collection are subject to bandwidth availability, appropriate security settings and other client and server-side concerns (see [9]). In addition, some students did not consent to their data being recorded. For other students, it could not be established whether they were familiar with the system, so their data were discarded since their behavior was quite different. After this data cleaning process, the GIC03, GIC04, and GIC05 datasets comprised 106, 126, and 99 students, respectively.

31.2.3 Employing Bayesian Networks for Student Modeling

The long-term interest of the research presented here is to develop a model that can be employed, in real-time, within the ILE to enhance its feedback capabilities. In order to decide on the exact modeling approach, initial investigations employing cross-validation in the GIC03 and later with GIC04 as a test set were performed. These supported the claim that a machine-learning algorithm could be used to automatically predict with reasonable accuracy whether students' help requests are necessary and whether their interaction is beneficial. From all the approaches attempted (decision trees, BN, classification via regression), the BN and the decision tree were the most accurate ones with no significant difference. While, in principle, implementing a model based on decision trees has the potential to increase the flexibility when providing feedback (i.e., specific rules would fire under specific circumstances), it is not clear whether communicating to the students the reasons behind the ineffective interaction would have any effect. In particular, if one takes into account that the results suggest that in at least 30% of the cases the system could be wrong, explaining the exact reasons could have negative effects.

Based on the above, BN was preferred not only because of the slightly higher accuracy but also because the highly probabilistic nature of what we would like to predict. BN is the perfect candidate for employing its outcomes in an evidence-based probabilistic framework such as the one described in [10] and combine it with other similar models, which previous research suggests were successful. For example, BNs have been used successfully to predict students' skills based on observable behavior on relevant problems [11,12], for selecting which problems to present to students [13] or, more generally, to predict the students' problem-solving behavior [14,15].

However, handcrafting a BN, deciding on prior probabilities and for the structure of the network is quite a complex and time-consuming process. While previous research has shown that it is possible to learn models from simulated data of students' responses on problems (e.g., [16]), doing so requires a thorough understanding of possible student actions, which is not always possible in a complex learning environment. Other attempts include learning a model through actual responses from, say a pencil-and-paper pretest [17]. The research presented here employs similar techniques but capitalizes on the datasets with the actual usage of the system and therefore allows the development of a model of students' interactions with the particular system that goes beyond the prediction of skills and allows the prediction of latent variables from a quite complex interaction.

31.3 Assessing Students' Behavior

31.3.1 Predicting the Necessity of Help Requests

Predicting whether a student needs help or not in a given educational situation is a far-from-trivial task. In the context of educational technology, this information is particularly crucial for ITS [6] and definitely not a unique issue to the research discussed here. Because of its complexity, different researchers address it in different ways depending on the special characteristics of the system under consideration and the overall context. For example, as mentioned in the Background, in the CMU tutors (see for example, [18]) the problem is approached as an attempt to estimate the probability that a skill has been mastered (also known as knowledge tracing [12]). Similarly, [14,19] describe systems where BNs are used to predict students' knowledge during their interaction. The approach presented here is different. The model predicts students' necessity to ask for help on an item given their previous interaction. Furthermore, it is learned based on data of all students' interactions with previous interaction with the system.

As discussed in the previous section, the GIC datasets were collected from studies where students have no previous knowledge of the material. Therefore, it does not seem too bold to assume that students who do not ask for help and answer a question correctly with the first attempt have learnt either from carefully reading the material in the system or from the interaction with the related items. In other words, all other characteristics of a student being equal, similar interactions should have enabled students to answer without any help. The opposite is not necessarily true. Students who ask for help without an attempt to answer are not included in the data since there are many explanations behind their help request. Individual differences between students and affective characteristics, rather than just knowledge of an answer, influence whether a student requests help or not. Using these data for machine learning would not necessarily provide additional instances that demonstrate whether a student really needed help or not. In addition, it was decided to limit the prediction only on help requests prior to the first attempt to answer a question. Further attempts are quite complex and depend again on the students' understanding of the feedback, whether they read it or not, and several other factors, which add noise to the prediction.

Given the above assumptions and in order to learn a more accurate model from the data, both GIC03 and GIC04 datasets were used as training sets. In an attempt to have a simple model and a method that could be generalized to other courses of WaLLiS or other ILEs, only a few aspects of the interaction were considered as features for the learning task. These should be available across courses in WaLLiS and are quite common in other ILEs as well. Accordingly, vectors containing the following variables were constructed: (a) time spent on related pages (*trp*), (b) time spent on attempt (tsa), (c) student previous knowledge (*prev*), (d) a rule-based measurement of the degree of "completeness" of the goals of interactions on related pages (rel), (e) difficulty of the item (*diff*), and (f) the type of the answer required (mcq, blank, matrix) (*answertype*).

The Boolean class learned represents whether the student seems to be able to answer correctly without any help. Its value therefore, is FALSE when students provided completely wrong answers (not from the usual misconceptions), or answered wrongly very quickly demonstrating, in a sense, that they only answer in order to "game" the system into providing feedback (c.f. [3]). The value of the class is TRUE when a student's answer was correct or partially correct. The final set of data comprises 1230 instances (the class of 429 of which was FALSE).

The Waikato Environment for Knowledge Analysis (WEKA*) was employed for learning the model. In WEKA, learning a BN is considered as a learning task of finding an appropriate classifier for a given dataset with a class variable and a vector of attributes [20]. While there are several approaches for learning the structure of the network, *conditional independence test-based structure (ICS) learning* was preferred. In particular, the ICS algorithm [21] follows a two-stage process of first finding an appropriate network structure and then learning the probability tables. It starts from a complete undirected graph for each pair of nodes and then considers subsets of nodes that are neighbors to the pair. If independence is identified, the edge between the pair is removed from the network structure and the arrows are directed accordingly (i.e., from each node of the pair to the node that justified the removal of the link). The remaining arrows are directed based on common sense graphical rules (see [21] for more details).

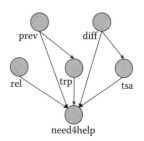

FIGURE 31.1
BN for predicting unnecessary help requests.

The conditional independence tests of ICS left out the variable *answertype* from the model as irrelevant. Feature selection also confirmed the relevance of all variables apart from *answertype*. The final model learned appears in Figure 31.1. To evaluate the result, the GIC05 dataset (with 590 instances) was employed as a test set (see accuracy report in Table 31.1).

Further investigation with the data showed that deriving a different model per activity that WaLLiS provides improves the results substantially (see Table 31.2). The main reason behind this, is the fact that some of the variables do not play the same role in every item (e.g., the influence of the related items page is not always the same on subsequent items) and, therefore, one model cannot accommodate all the items. To construct the different models, the data were split by item and the variables *difficulty* and *answertype* were removed. This process simplified the models considerably and, therefore, separate models were preferred for the actual implementation.

Although further investigation and research could improve the model's accuracy, it was considered adequate for implementation and further testing. Its application and how the results could be improved and automated are further discussed in the last section. The model is employed as a feature in relevant machine-learned predictors of affect (see [22]) and plays a particular role as a feature in the model described in the next section.

TABLE 31.1

Classification Accuracy, Kappa Statistic and Recall Values for BN and Decision Trees for Predicting Superfluous Help Request in Any Activity

		BayesNet		J4.8	
		Cross	Test Set	Cross	Test Set
	Accuracy	67.64	66.52	65.84	64.05
	Kappa	0.317	0.318	0.30	0.23
Recall	True	0.60	0.56	0.59	0.5
	False	0.74	0.76	0.71	0.72

---

* The Waikato Environment for Knowledge Analysis—http://www.cs.waikato.ac.nz/~ml

TABLE 31.2

Average Classification Accuracy, Kappa Statistic and Recall
Values for BNs and Decision Trees to Superfluous Help
Requests Per Activity

		BayesNet		J4.8	
		Cross	Test Set	Cross	Test Set
	Accuracy	69.12	67.61	67.84	63.05
	Kappa	0.36	0.35	0.34	0.27
Recall	True	0.74	0.71	0.72	0.66
	False	0.62	0.62	0.60	0.58

31.3.2 Predicting the Benefit of Students' Interactions

Similar to the development of the previous model, the problem of measuring the benefit of students' interactions in terms of learning is also quite complex and not unique to the research presented here. For example, [23] employ BN to assess the effectiveness of a learner's exploratory behavior in an exploratory environment based on hand-crafted conditional probability tables. The approach presented here develops a machine-learned model that predicts whether a given student's interaction with the system is beneficial *to their learning*, based on data from interactions of all students in relation to their answers in posttest questions linked to specific items in the system.

The features for machine learning are chosen based on a combination of qualitative analysis, and were decided based on the predictive power that similar features had in other related research (e.g., [3,6]). Some features (e.g., time spent per page) relate to aspects for which an absolute measurement does not provide any useful information. One approach that is often adequate is to estimate the standard deviation of the distance of the value under question from a mean or centroid value. However, when there is a need of taking into account several measurements (e.g., the speed between hint requests throughout an activity), comparison across students and across events is needed in order to obtain a relative distance of a whole vector of values. In such cases, one approach is to employ the Euclidean distance under the assumption that the points are normally distributed. However, this is not the case for some of the variables in our data. Therefore, in order to have more realistic comparisons, the Mahalanobis distance [24] is employed, which provides a measurement for the distance between elements of whole vectors. Compared to the traditional Euclidean distance, the Mahalanobis distance utilizes group means and variances for each variable as well as the correlations and covariance of the dataset [25]. Formally, the distance of a vector $x = (x_1, x_2, ..., x_n)^T$ from another vector, $y = (y_1, y_2, ..., y_n)^T$ with covariance matrix S is defined as $D(x) = \sqrt{(x-y)^T S^{-1}(x-y)}$.

Table 31.3 shows the list of features that were considered for learning the model. The Boolean class learned represents whether a student answered correctly the related posttest question. To achieve a mapping between the actions in the system and the answers in the posttest question, the answers are assessed across four basic skills and three to five sub-steps that have a direct correspondence with the steps of the questions in WaLLiS. In the cases where students did not answer parts of the questions, the missing answers are considered as wrong (i.e., the Boolean variable is FALSE). In addition, some students did not interact with certain steps or whole items in WaLLiS and, therefore, their data were excluded (most of these students did not answer the posttest question either, and the few

TABLE 31.3

Features Considered for Learning the Model of Beneficial Interaction

1. Help frequency
2. Error frequency
3. Tendency to ask for help rather than risk an error, i.e., help/errors+help as in [26]
4. No need for help but help requested (according to the previous section) (true/false)
5. Answertype—the type of the answer required (mcq, blank, matrix, checkbox)
6. Previous attempts in items related to the current skill
    - If this was the student's first opportunity to practice this skill, −1.
    - If no previous attempt was successful, 0.
    - Otherwise, a measure of the degree of completeness of the goals of related items (if there were no related items then the standardized score of their exam in prerequisite of this skill)
7. Time in standard deviations off the mean time taken by all students on the same item.
8. Speed between hints—The Mahalanobis distance of the vector of times between hints from the vector of mean times taken by all students on the same hints and item3
9. Accessing the related example while answering (true/false)
10. Self-correction (true/false)
11. Requested solution without attempt to answer (true/false)
12. Reflection on hints (defined as the time until next action from hint delivery) (calculated as in point 8, using the Mahalanobis distance)
13. The number of theoretical material lookups that the student followed when such a lookup was suggested by the system (−1 if no lookups were suggested)

who did, provided wrong answers). The final set of data contains 472 instances from GIC04 and 352 from GIC05.

For similar reasons as the ones presented in the previous section, BNs were preferred. To facilitate the algorithm's search, feature selection is employed in advance to remove irrelevant and redundant features. Although (as expected) similar structures and accuracies are learned, whether the full set of data are employed or not, simpler models are always preferred. In fact, the simplified model achieved slightly better accuracy on a 10-fold cross-validation check and slightly better accuracy on the test set. By removing redundant features, the remaining ones were easier to comprehend. This allowed a more informed ordering of the variables, which can affect the search for the structure of the ICS algorithm.

The list of reduced variables is shown in Table 31.4 and the final model in Figure 31.2. Its accuracy report, as well as comparisons with decision trees are presented in Table 31.5.

TABLE 31.4

Variables After Feature Selection from Table 31.1

1. Tendency for help
2. Need for help
3. Self-correction
4. Example access
5. Average reflection time
6. Speed for hints
7. Error frequency

31.4 Application and Future Work

As discussed in the Introduction, the model was developed to empower WaLLiS with an objective and operational way of predicting unnecessary help requests and a measurement of students' interaction with the material. The immediate benefit of the two models was their use for further adaption of the feedback, interventions, and suggestions for studying further material. Second, as presented in [22], the models were used to improve the detection of students' affective characteristics.

One has to bear in mind that, in the approach presented here, both learning and evaluation are performed off-line and the models were implemented prior to their integration

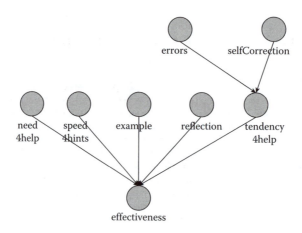

FIGURE 31.2
BN for predicting beneficial interaction.

TABLE 31.5

Classification Accuracy and Kappa Statistic for BN and Tree
Induction to Predict Beneficial Interaction

		BayesNet		J4.8	
		Cross	**Test Set**	**Cross**	**Test Set**
	Accuracy	70.11	68.23	66.52	65.843
	Kappa	0.40	0.36	0.318	0.313
Recall	True	0.72	0.73	0.714	0.686
	False	0.67	0.62	0.605	0.626

with the system. Therefore, speed of learning was not relevant. However, speed becomes important when automating the learning of the model to occur at run-time while students are interacting with the ILE. Feature selection, therefore, becomes relevant since, by reducing the available features, it speeds up the learning process significantly.

The Bayesian models were integrated in the system.* Their output is utilized by a diagnostic agent, the outcomes of which are taken into account by the feedback mechanism in order to adapt its actions (for more details the reader is referred to [4]). As already mentioned, the accuracy of the models was considered adequate for implementation. However, as it should be the case in all EDM approaches, such decisions should not be taken solely on the grounds of accuracy but should be based on a careful balance of the likely educational consequences of any incorrect predictions.

In the case of WaLLiS and the model of unnecessary help requests, particular importance was given to the recall of instances classified as FALSE (i.e., where the model would predict that a student does not need help). The high values indicate less false negatives (i.e., less cases where a student needs help but the model predicts that they do not). For the model of beneficial interaction, we were interested in high recall of instances classified as TRUE to have as less true negatives as possible (i.e., less cases where the model would predict that the student's interaction is beneficial when it is not). Nevertheless, it was decided to take

---

* JavaBayes http://www.cs.cmu.edu/javabayes/is used in WaLLiS to query the models that result from the offline processing from WEKA.

an approach as unobtrusive and as less preventive as possible. If one takes into account that in some cases a model is wrong, it is obvious, but paramount, to use these predictions in a way that has the fewest negative educational consequences. Accordingly, when students solicit suggestions on what to study next, the prediction of beneficial interaction is employed assisting the system to prioritize the available items. In other cases, the prediction is employed for providing suggestions about which items to study next or for interacting again with the same item. As for the prediction of unnecessary help requests, this is not employed directly (e.g., to stop students from asking for help) but rather through the model of beneficial interaction and in other models of affect prediction [22].

The aforementioned decisions may seem specific to the case study presented here but they are relevant to designers of systems that take into account outcomes of EDM research. Similar issues are raised in [3,6,13]. The challenge is to strike a balance between an approach that utilizes the predictions from the models in an informative way and a more preventative approach that may be required in some cases. When highly uncertain machine-learned decisions are taken, it may be better, in some circumstances, not to communicate this information with the student directly. Models such as the ones developed here could have other applications. For example, the prediction of the benefit of the interaction could be used in open-learner modeling or in classroom environments to provide useful information for teachers on the basis of which they can adapt their own teaching.

Future work will focus on improving the accuracy of models and automating the process. In addition, by providing access to designers and other stakeholders of the ILE (e.g., lecturers), they can also query the model and draw some conclusions about the nature of the students' interaction with the system. It is clear that approaches such as the ones presented here have the potential to contribute to a deeper understanding of complex behaviors. Apart from improving the adaptivity of the intelligent components of the system, machine-learned models of students' behavior could also help in the system's redesign by targeting, for example, the types of actions that fail to lead to a beneficial interaction.

References

1. Mavrikis, M. and Maciocia, A., WALLIS: A web-based ILE for science and engineering students studying mathematics, in *Workshop of Advanced Technologies for Mathematics Education in 11th International Conference on Artificial Intelligence in Education*, Sydney Australia, 2003.
2. Koedinger, K., Anderson, J., Hadley, W., and Mark, M., Intelligent tutoring goes to school in the big city, *International Journal of Artificial Intelligence in Education* 8, 30–43, 1997.
3. Baker, R. S., Corbett, A. T., Koedinger, K. R., and Wagner, A. Z., Off-task behavior in the cognitive tutor classroom: When students "Game The system," in *Proceedings of ACM CHI 2004: Computer-Human Interaction*, Vienna, Austria, pp. 383–390, 2004.
4. Mavrikis, M., Modelling students' behaviour and affective states in ILEs through educational data mining, PhD thesis, The University of Edinburgh, Edinburgh, U.K., 2008.
5. Karabenick, S. A., *Strategic Help Seeking Implications for Learning and Teaching*, Lawrence Erlbaum Associates, Mahwah, NJ, 1988.
6. Aleven, V. and Koedinger, K. R., Limitations of student control: Do students know when they need help? in *Proceedings of Fifth International Conference on Intelligent Tutoring Systems*, Montreal, Canada, pp. 292–303, 2000.
7. Aleven, V., McLaren, B., Roll, I., and Koedinger, K. R., Toward tutoring help seeking: Applying cognitive modeling to meta-cognitive skills, in *Intelligent Tutoring Systems*, Maceió, Brazil, pp. 227–239, 2004.

8. Porayska-Pomsta, K., Mavrikis, M., and Pain, H., Diagnosing and acting on student affect: The tutor's perspective, *User Modeling and User-Adapted Interaction* 18 (1), 125–173, 2008.

9. Mavrikis, M., Logging, replaying and analysing students' interactions in a web-based ILE to improve student modelling, in *Artificial Intelligence in Education: Supporting Learning through Intelligent and Socially Informed Technology* (*Proceedings of the 12th International Conference on Artificial Intelligence in Education, AIED2005*), Looi, C., McCalla, G., Bredeweg, B., and Breuker, J. (eds.), IOS Press, Amsterdam, the Netherlands, Vol. 125, p. 967, 2005.

10. Morales, R., Van Labeke, N., and Brna, P., Approximate modelling of the multi-dimensional learner, in *Proceedings of the Eighth International Conference on Intelligent Tutoring Systems*, Jhongli, Taiwan, pp. 555–564, 2006.

11. Arroyo, I., Murray, T., Woolf, B., and Beal, C., Inferring unobservable learning variables from students' help seeking behavior, in *Proceedings of the Seventh International Conference on Intelligent Tutoring Systems*, Maceio, Brazil, pp. 782–784, 2004.

12. Corbett, A. and Anderson, J., Student modeling and mastery learning in a computer-based programming tutor, in *Proceedings of the Second International Conference on Intelligent Tutoring Systems*, Montreal, Canada, pp. 413–420, 1992.

13. Mayo, M. and Mitrovic, A., Using a probabilistic student model to control problem difficulty, in *Proceedings of Fifth International Conference on Intelligent Tutoring Systems*, Montreal, Canada, pp. 524–533, 2000.

14. Conati, C., Gertner, A., Vanlehn, K., and Druzdzel, M., On-line student modeling for coached problem solving using Bayesian networks, in *User Modeling: Proceedings of the Sixth International Conference*, Jameson, A., Paris, C., and Tasso, C. (eds.), Sardinia, Italy, 1997.

15. Collins, J., Greer, J., and Huang, S., Adaptive assessment using granularity hierarchies and bayesian nets, in *Proceedings of the Third International Conference on Intelligent Tutoring Systems*, Montreal, Canada, pp. 569–577, 1996.

16. Jonsson, A., John, J., Mehranian, H., Arroyo, I., Woolf, B., Barto, A., Fisher, D., and Mahadevan, S., Evaluating the feasibility of learning student models from data, in *AAAI Workshop on Educational Data Mining*, Pittsburgh, PA, 2005.

17. Ferguson, K., Arroyo, I., Mahadevan, S., Woolf, B., and Barto, A., Improving intelligent tutoring systems: Using expectation maximization to learn student skill levels, in *Proceedings of the Eighth International Conference on Intelligent Tutoring Systems*, Jhongli, Taiwan, pp. 453–462, 2006.

18. Anderson, J. R., Corbett, A. T., Koedinger, K. R., and Pelletier, R., Cognitive tutors: Lessons learned, *The Journal of the Learning Sciences* 4 (2), 167–207, 1995.

19. Vanlehn, K. and Martin, J., Evaluation of an assessment system based on Bayesian student modeling, *International Journal of Artificial Intelligence in Education* 8 (2), 179–221, 1998.

20. Bouckaert, R. R., Bayesian networks in Weka, Technical Report 14/2004, Computer Science Department, University of Waikato, Hamilton, New Zealand, 2004.

21. Verma, T. and Pearl, J., An algorithm for deciding if a set of observed independencies has a causal explanation, in *Proceedings of the Eighth Conference on Uncertainty in Artificial Intelligence*, Stanford, CA, pp. 323–330, 1992.

22. Mavrikis, M., Maciocia, A., and Lee, J., Towards predictive modelling of student affect from web-based interactions, in *Artificial Intelligence in Education: Building Technology Rich Learning Contexts that Work* (*Proceedings of the 13th International Conference on Artificial Intelligence in Education, AIED2007*), Luckin, R., Koedinger, K., and Greer, J. (eds.), Los Angeles, CA, IOS Press, Amsterdam, the Netherlands, Vol. 158, pp. 169–176, 2007.

23. Bunt, A. and Conati, C., Probabilistic student modelling to improve exploratory behaviour, *User Modeling and User-Adapted Interaction* 13, 269–309, 2003.

24. Mahalanobis, P. C., On the generalized distance in statistics, *Proceedings of Natural Institute of Sciences* 2, 49–55, 1936.

25. De Maesschalck, R., Rimbaud, J., and Massart, D. L., The Mahalanobis distance, *Chemometrics and Intelligent Laboratory Systems* 50, 1–18, 2000.

26. Wood, H., Help seeking, learning and contingent tutoring, *Computers & Education* 33, 2–3, 1999.

32

Learning Procedural Knowledge from User Solutions to Ill-Defined Tasks in a Simulated Robotic Manipulator

Philippe Fournier-Viger, Roger Nkambou, and Engelbert Mephu Nguifo

CONTENTS

32.1 Introduction

Domain experts should provide relevant domain knowledge to an intelligent tutoring system (ITS) so that it can assist a learner during problem-solving activities. There are three main approaches for providing such knowledge. The first one is cognitive task analysis that aims at producing effective problem spaces or task models by observing expert and novice users [1] to capture different ways of solving problems. However, cognitive task analysis is a very time-consuming process [1] and it is not always possible to define a complete or partial task model, in particular when a problem is ill-structured. According to Simon [2], an ill-structured problem is one that is complex, with indefinite starting points, multiple and arguable solutions, or unclear strategies for finding solutions. Domains that include such problems and in which tutoring targets the development of problem-solving skills are said to be ill-defined (within the meaning of Ashley and coworkers [3]). Constraint-based modeling (CBM) was proposed as an alternative [4]. It consists of specifying sets of constraints on what is a correct behavior, instead of providing a complete task description. Though this approach was shown to be effective for some ill-defined domains, a domain expert has to design and select the constraints carefully. The third approach consists of steps to integrate an expert system into an ITS [8]. However, developing an expert system can be difficult and costly, especially for ill-defined domains.

Contrarily to these approaches where domain experts have to provide the domain knowledge, a promising approach is to use knowledge-discovery techniques to automatically learn a problem space from logged user interactions in an ITS, and to use this knowledge base to offer tutoring services. A few efforts have been made in this direction in the field of ITS [5,6,17,21–23]. But they have all been applied in well-defined domains. As an alternative, in this chapter, we propose an approach that is specially designed for ill-defined domains. The approach has the advantage of taking into account learner profiles and does not require any form of background knowledge. The reader should note that a detailed comparison with related work is provided in Section 32.5.

This chapter is organized as follows. First, we describe the CanadarmTutor tutoring system and previous attempts for incorporating domain expertise into it. Next, we present our approach for extracting partial problem spaces from logged user interactions and describe how it enables CanadarmTutor to provide more realistic tutoring services. Finally, we compare our approach with related work, discuss avenues of research, and present conclusions.

32.2 The CanadarmTutor Tutoring System

CanadarmTutor [8] (depicted in Figure 32.1) is a simulation-based tutoring system to teach astronauts how to operate Canadarm2, a 7-degrees-of-freedom robotic arm deployed on the International Space Station (ISS). The main learning activity in CanadarmTutor is to move the arm from a given configuration to a goal configuration. During the robot manipulation, operators do not have a direct view of the scene of operation on the ISS and must rely on cameras mounted on the manipulator and at strategic places in the environment where it operates. To move the arm, an operator must select at every moment the best cameras for viewing the scene of operation among several cameras mounted on the manipulator and on the space station.

To provide domain expertise to CanadarmTutor, we initially applied the expert system approach by integrating a special path-planner into CanadarmTutor [8]. The path-planner can generate a path avoiding obstacles between any two arm configurations. The path-planner makes it possible to track a learner solution step by step, and generate demonstrations when necessary. However, the generated paths are not always realistic or easy to follow, as they are not based on human experience, and they do not cover other aspects of the manipulation task such as selecting cameras and adjusting their parameters. Also, it cannot support important tutoring services such as estimating knowledge gaps of learners as there is no knowledge or skills representation.

In subsequent work, we attempted to describe how to manipulate Canadarm2 as a set of rules with a rule-based knowledge-representation model by applying the cognitive

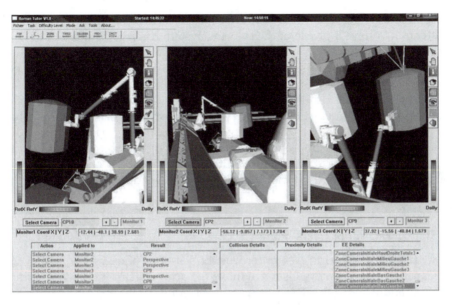

FIGURE 32.1
The CanadarmTutor User Interface.

task-analysis approach [9]. Although we described high-level rules such as how to select cameras and set their parameters in the correct order, it was not possible to go into finer detail to model how to rotate the arm joint(s) to attain a goal configuration. The reason is that for a given robot manipulation problem, there is a huge number of possibilities for moving the robot to a goal configuration and because one must also consider the safety of the maneuvers and their easiness, it is very difficult to define a "legal move generator" for generating the moves that a human would execute. In fact, some joint manipulations are preferable to others, depending on several criteria that are hard to formalize such as the view of the arm given by the chosen cameras, the relative position of obstacles to the arm, the arm configuration (e.g., avoiding singularities), and the familiarity of the user with certain joint manipulations over others. It is, thus, not possible to define a complete and explicit task model for this task. Hence, CanadarmTutor operates in an ill-defined domain as defined by Simon.

The CBM approach [4] may represent a good alternative to the cognitive task analysis approach. However, in the CanadarmTutor context, it would be very difficult for domain experts to describe a set of relevance and satisfaction conditions that apply to all situations. In fact, there would be too many conditions and still a large number of solutions would fit the conditions for each problem. Moreover, the CBM approach is useful for validating solutions. But it cannot support tutoring services such as suggesting next problem-solving steps to learners, which is a required feature in CanadarmTutor.

32.3 A Domain Knowledge Discovery Approach for the Acquisition of Domain Expertise

Our hypothesis is that a data-mining approach for learning a partial problem space from recorded user interactions can overcome some problems related to the ill-defined nature of a procedural learning domain. Our approach consists of the following steps. Each time a user attempts to solve a problem, the tutoring system records the attempt as a *plan* in a database of user solutions. Then humans can display, edit, or annotate plans with contextual information (e.g., required human skills to execute the plan and expertise level of those skills). Thereafter, a data-mining algorithm is applied to extract a partial task model from the user plans. The resulting task model can be displayed, edited, and annotated before being taken as input by the tutoring system to provide tutoring services. This whole process of recording plans to extract a problem space can be performed periodically to make the system constantly improve its domain knowledge. Moreover, staff members can intervene in the process or it can be fully automated. The next sections present in detail each step of this process and how they were applied in CanadarmTutor to support relevant tutoring services.

32.3.1 Step 1: Recording Users' Plans

In the first phase, the tutoring system records the solutions of users who attempt an exercise. In CanadarmTutor, an exercise is to move the arm from an initial configuration to a goal configuration. For each attempt, a *sequence of events* (or *plan*) is created in a sequence database. We define an event $X = (i_1, i_2, \ldots, i_n)$ as a set of one or more actions $i_1, i_2, \ldots, i_n$ done by a learner that are considered simultaneous, and where each action can specify an integer parameter value (this could be extended to several parameters or other types of values: see [15] for more details). In CanadarmTutor, we defined 112 such actions that can be recorded including (1) selecting a camera, (2) performing an increase or decrease of the pan/tilt/zoom of a camera, and (3) applying a rotation value to an arm joint. Formally, we define a sequence of events (based on the definition of Hirate and Yamana [10]) as $s = \langle (t_1, X_1), (t_2, X_2), \ldots, (t_v, X_v) \rangle$ where each event X_k is associated with a timestamp t_k indicating the time of the event. In CanadarmTutor, timestamps of successive events are successive integers (0, 1, 2...). An example of a partial sequence recorded for a user in CanadarmTutor is $\langle (0, rotateSP\{2\}), (1, selectCP3), (2, panCP2\{4\}), (3, zoomCP2\{2\}) \rangle$, which represents decreasing the rotation value of joint SP by two units, selecting camera CP3, increasing the pan of camera CP2 by four units, and then its zoom by two units.

To annotate sequences with contextual information, we have extended the notion of sequence database with dimensional information as suggested by [11]. A sequence database having a set of dimensions $D = D_1, D_2, \ldots, D_p$ is called a multidimensional database (MD-Database). Each sequence of an MD-Database is called an MD-Sequence and consists of a plan and annotations. Annotations are a list of values for each dimension. Values can be symbols or the value "*," which subsumes all other values. Such a list of dimension values is called an MD-Pattern and is denoted by $d_1, d_2, \ldots, d_p$. Table 32.1 shows an example of a toy MD-Database containing six learner plans annotated with five dimensions. In this table, the single letters a, b, c, and d denote actions. The first dimension "Solution state" indicates if the learner plan is a successful or buggy solution. In the case of CanadarmTutor, values for this dimension are produced by the tutoring system (see Section 32.5). The four other dimensions of Table 32.2 are examples of dimensions that can be added manually. Whereas the dimension "Expertise" denotes the expertise level of the learner who performed a sequence, "Skill_1," "Skill_2," and "Skill_3" indicate whether any of these three specific skills were demonstrated by the learner when solving the problem. This example illustrates a five-dimensional MD-Database of three main types (skills, expertise level, and solution state). However, our framework can accept any kind of learner information or contextual information encoded as dimensions. For example, learner information could

TABLE 32.1

An MD-Database Containing Six User Solutions

		Dimensions				
ID	Solution State	Expertise	Skill_1	Skill_2	Skill_3	Sequence
S1	Successful	Novice	Yes	Yes	Yes	$\langle(0,a), (1,b\ c)\rangle$
S2	Successful	Expert	No	Yes	No	$\langle(0,d)\rangle$
S3	Buggy	Novice	Yes	Yes	Yes	$\langle(0,a), (1,b\ c)\rangle$
S4	Buggy	Intermediate	No	Yes	Yes	$\langle(0,a), (1,c), (2,d)\rangle$
S5	Successful	Novice	No	No	Yes	$\langle(0,d), (1,c)\rangle$
S6	Successful	Expert	No	No	Yes	$\langle(0,c), (1,d)\rangle$

TABLE 32.2

Some Frequent Patterns Extracted from the Dataset of Table 32.1 with *minsup* = 33%

		Dimensions					
ID	Solution State	Expertise	Skill_1	Skill_2	Skill_3	Sequence	Supp.
P1	*	Novice	Yes	Yes	Yes	$\langle(0,a)\rangle$	33%
P2	*	*	*	Yes	Yes	$\langle(0,a)\rangle$	50%
P3	*	Novice	Yes	Yes	Yes	$\langle(0,a), (1,b)\rangle$	33%
P4	Successful	*	No	*	*	$\langle(0,d)\rangle$	50%
P5	Successful	Novice	*	*	Yes	$\langle(0,c)\rangle$	33%
P6	Successful	Expert	No	*	No	$\langle(0,d)\rangle$	33%

include age, educational background, learning styles, cognitive traits, and emotional state, assuming that the data is available. In CanadarmTutor, we had 10 skills, and used the "solution state" and "expertise level" dimensions to annotate sequences (see Section 32.4 for more details).

32.3.2 Step 2: Mining a Partial Task Model from Users' Plans

In the second phase, the tutoring system applies the data-mining framework to extract a partial problem space from users' plans. To perform this extraction, an appropriate method is needed that considers many factors associated with the specific conditions in which a tutoring system such as CanadarmTutor operates. These factors include the temporal dimension of events, actions with parameters, the user's profile, etc. All these factors suggest that we need a temporal pattern-mining technique. According to [12], there are four kinds of patterns that can be mined from time-series data. These are trends, similar sequences, sequential patterns, and periodic patterns. In this work, we chose to mine sequential patterns [13], as we are interested in finding relationships between occurrences of events in users' solutions. To mine sequential patterns, several efficient algorithms have been proposed. These have been previously applied, for example, to analyze earthquake data [10] and source code in software engineering [24]. While traditional sequential pattern-mining (SPM) algorithms have as their only goal to discover sequential patterns that occur frequently in several transactions of a database [13], other algorithms have proposed numerous extensions to the problem of SPM such as mining patterns respecting time constraints [10], mining compact representations of patterns [14,16,24], and incremental mining of patterns [24]. For this work, we developed a custom SPM algorithm [15] that combines several features from other algorithms such as accepting time constraints [10], processing databases with dimensional information [11], and mining a compact representation of all patterns [14,16], and that also adds some original features such as accepting symbols with parameter values. We have built this algorithm to address the type of data to be recorded in a tutoring system offering procedural exercises such as CanadarmTutor. The main idea of that algorithm will be presented next. For a technical description of the algorithm, the reader can refer to [15].

The algorithm takes as input an MD-Database and some parameters and find all MD-Sequences occurring frequently in the MD-Database. Here, sequences are action sequences (not necessarily contiguous in time) with timestamps as defined in Section 32.3.1. A sequence $sa = \langle (ta_1, A_1), (ta_2, A_2), ..., (ta_n, A_n) \rangle$ is said to be contained in another sequence $sb = \langle (tb_1, B_1), (tb_2, B_2), ..., (tb_n, B_m) \rangle$, if there exists integers $1 \leq k1 < k2 < \cdots < kn \leq m$ such that $A_1 \subseteq B_{k1}, A_2 \subseteq B_{k2}, ..., A_n \subseteq B_{kn}$ and that $tb_{kj} - tb_{k1}$ is equal to $ta_{kj} - ta_{k1}$ for each $j \in 1 ... n$ (recall that in this work timestamps of successive events are successive integers. e.g., 0, 1, 2...). Similarly for MD-Patterns, an MD-Pattern $Px = dx_1, dx_2, ..., dx_p$ is said to be contained in another MD-Pattern $Py = dy_1, dy_2, ..., dy_p$ if for each $i \in 1 ... p$, $dy_i =$ "*" or $dy_i = dx_i$ [11]. The relative support of a sequence (or MD-Pattern) in a sequence database is defined as the percentage of sequences (or MD-Patterns) from D, which contain it. The problem of mining frequent MD-Sequences is to find all the MD-sequences such that their support is frequent, defined as greater or equal than *minsup* for an MD-Database D, given a support threshold minsup. As an example, Table 32.2 shows some patterns that can be extracted from the MD-Database of Table 32.1, with a *minsup* of two sequences (33%). Consider pattern P3. This pattern represents doing action *b* one time unit (immediately) after action *a*. The pattern P3 appears in MD-Sequences S1 and S3. It has thus a support of 33% or two MD-Sequences. Because this support is higher or equal to *minsup*, P3 is frequent. Moreover, the annotations for P3 tell us that this pattern was performed by novice users who possess skills "Skill_1," "Skill_2," and "Skill_3," and that P3 was found in plan(s) that failed, as well as plan(s) that succeeded.

In addition, as in [10], we have incorporated in our algorithm the possibility of specifying time constraints on mined sequences such as minimum and maximum time intervals required between the head and tail of a sequence and minimum and maximum time intervals required between two successive events of a sequence. In CanadarmTutor, we mine only sequences of length two or greater, as shorter sequences would not be useful in a tutoring context. Furthermore, we chose to mine sequences with a maximum time interval between two successive events of two time units. The benefits of accepting a gap of two is that it eliminates some "noisy" (non-frequent) learners' actions, but at the same time, it does not allow a larger gap size that could make patterns less useful for tracking a learner's actions.

Another important consideration is that when applying SPM, there can be many redundant frequent sequences found. For example, in Table 32.2, the pattern "*, *novice, yes, yes, yes* $\langle (0,a) \rangle$" is redundant as it is included in the pattern "*, *novice, yes, yes, yes* $\langle (0,a), (1,b) \rangle$" and it has exactly the same support. To eliminate this type of redundancy, we have adapted our algorithm to mine only *frequent closed sequences*. "Closed sequences" [14,16,24] are sequences that are not contained in another sequence having the same support. Mining frequent closed sequences has the advantage of greatly reducing the number of patterns found, without information loss (the set of closed frequent sequences allows reconstituting the set of all frequent sequences and their support) [14]. To mine only frequent closed sequences, our SPM algorithm was extended based on [14] and [16] to mine closed MD-Sequences (see [15]).

Once patterns have been mined by our SPM algorithm, they form a partial problem space that can be used by a tutoring agent to provide assistance to learners, as described in the next section. However, we also provide a simple software program for displaying patterns, editing them, or adding annotations.

32.3.3 Step 3: Exploiting the Partial Task Model to Provide Relevant Tutoring Services

In the third phase, the tutoring system provides assistance to the learner by using the knowledge learned in the second phase. The basic operation that is used for providing assistance is to recognize a learner's plan. In CanadarmTutor, this is achieved by the plan-recognition algorithm, presented next.

```
RecognizePlan(Student_trace, Patterns)
    Result:= Ø.
    FOR each pattern P of Patterns
        IF Student_trace is included in P
            Result = Result ∪ {P}.
    IF Result:= Ø AND length(Student_trace) ≥ 2
        Remove last action of Student_trace.
        Result:= RecognizePlan(Student_trace, Patterns).
    Return Result.
```

The plan-recognition algorithm *RecognizePlan* is executed after each student action. It takes as input the sequence of actions performed by the student (*Student_trace*) for the current problem and a set of frequent action sequences (*Patterns*). When the plan-recognition algorithm is called for the first time, the variable *Patterns* is initialized with the whole set of patterns found during the learning phase. The algorithm first iterates on the set of *Patterns* to note all the patterns that include *Student_trace*. If no pattern is found, the algorithm removes the last action performed by the learner from *Student_trace* and searches again for matching patterns. This is repeated until the set of matching patterns is not empty or the length of *Student_trace* is smaller than 2. In our tests, removing user actions has improved the capability of the plan-recognition algorithm to track learner's patterns significantly, as it makes the algorithm more flexible. The next time *RecognizePlan* is called, it will be called with the new *Student_trace* sequence and just the set of matching patterns found by the last execution of *RecognizePlan*, or the whole sets of patterns if no pattern matches.

After performing preliminary tests with the plan-recognition algorithm, we noticed that in general, after more than six actions are performed by a learner, it becomes hard for *RecognizePlan* to tell which pattern the learner is following. For that reason, we made improvements to how the CanadarmTutor applies the SPM algorithm to extract a knowledge base. Originally, it mined frequent patterns from sequences of user actions for a whole problem-solving exercise. We modified our approach to add the notion of "problem states." In the context of CanadarmTutor, where an exercise consists of moving a robotic arm to attain a specific arm configuration, the 3D space was divided into 3D cubes, and the problem state at a given moment is defined as the set of 3D cubes containing the arm joints. An exercise is then viewed as going from a problem state P_1 to a problem state P_f. For each attempt at solving the exercise, CanadarmTutor logs (1) the sequence of problem states visited by the learner $A = P_1, P_2, ..., P_n$ and (2) the list of actions performed by the learner to go from one problem state to the next visited problem state (P_1 to P_2, P_2 to P_3, ..., P_{n-1} to P_n).

After many users perform the same exercise, CanadarmTutor extracts sequential patterns from (1) sequences of problem states visited and (2) sequences of actions performed for going from a problem state to another. To take advantage of the added notion of problem states, we modified *RecognizePlan* so that at every moment, only the patterns performed in the current problem state are considered. To do so, every time the problem state changes, *RecognizePlan* will be called with the set of patterns associated with the new problem state. Moreover, at a coarser-grain-level tracking, the problem states visited by the learners is also achieved by calling *RecognizePlan*. This allows connecting patterns for different problem states. We describe next the main tutoring services that a tutoring agent can provide based on the plan-recognition algorithm.

32.3.3.1 Assessing the Profile of a Learner

First, a tutoring agent can assess the profile of the learner (expertise level, skills, etc.) by looking at the patterns applied. If, for example, 80% of the time a learner applies patterns with value "intermediate" for dimension "expertise," then CanadarmTutor can assert with confidence that the learner expertise level is "intermediate." In the same way, CanadarmTutor can diagnose mastered and missing/buggy skills for users who demonstrated a pattern by looking at the "skill" dimensions of patterns applied (e.g., "Skill_1" in Table 32.2). In CanadarmTutor, assessing the profile of a learner is done with a simple student model that is updated each time *RecognizePlan* finds that a student followed a pattern. The estimations contained in such a student model could be used in various ways by a tutoring system. The tutoring service described in the next section presents an example of how to use this information.

32.3.3.2 Guiding the Learner

Second, a tutoring agent can guide the learner. This tutoring service consists in determining the possible actions from the current problem state and proposing one or more actions to the learner. In CanadarmTutor, this functionality is triggered when the student selects "What should I do next?" in the interface menu. CanadarmTutor then identifies the set of possible next actions according to the matching patterns found by *RecognizePlan*. The tutoring service then selects the action among this set that is associated with the pattern that has the highest relative support and that best matches the expertise level and skills of the learner. If the selected patterns contain skills that are not considered mastered by the learner, CanadarmTutor can use textual hints that are defined for each skill to explain the missing skills to the learner. In the case where no actions can be identified, CanadarmTutor can use the aforementioned path-planner to generate solutions. In this current version, CanadarmTutor only interacts with the learner upon request. But it would be possible in future versions to program CanadarmTutor so that it can intervene if the learner is following a pattern that leads to failure or a pattern that is not appropriate for his or her expertise level. Different criteria for choosing a pattern could also be used for suggesting patterns to learners. Testing different tutorial strategies is part of our current work.

32.3.3.3 Letting Learners Explore Different Ways of Solving Problems

Finally, a tutoring service that has been implemented in CanadarmTutor is to let learners explore patterns to learn about possible ways to solve problems. Currently, the learners can explore a pattern with an interface that list the patterns and their annotations, and provides sorting and filtering functions (e.g., to display only patterns leading to success). However, the learner could be assisted in this exploration by using an interactive dialog with the system, which could prompt them on their goals and help them go through the patterns to achieve these goals. This tutoring service could be used when the tutoring system wants to prepare students before involving them in real problem-solving situations.

32.4 Evaluating the New Version of CanadarmTutor

We conducted a preliminary experiment in CanadarmTutor with two exercises to qualitatively evaluate its capability to provide assistance. The two exercises consist of moving a load with the Canadarm2 robotic arm to one of the two cubes (Figure 32.2a). We asked 12 users to record plans for these exercises. The average length of plans was 20 actions. Each plan was annotated with "Solution state" and "Expertise level" information semi-automatically by CanadarmTutor: annotated solutions with skills information by hand. In our experiment, we included 10 skills that consist of familiarity with some important cameras and joints, and some more abstract skills of being good at evaluating distances, and at performing plans of manipulations requiring precise movements. From the set of annotated plans, CanadarmTutor extracted sequential patterns with the algorithm. In a subsequent work session, we asked the users to evaluate the tutoring services provided by the virtual agent. All the users agreed that the assistance provided was helpful. We also observed that CanadarmTutor often correctly inferred the estimated expertise level of learners, a capability not available in the previous version of CanadarmTutor, which relied solely on the path-planner.

As an example of interaction with a learner, Figure 32.2b illustrates a hint message given to a learner upon request during scenario 1. The guiding tutoring service selects the pattern that has the highest support value, matches the student actions for the current problem state, is marked "successful," and corresponds to the estimated expertise level and skills of the learner. The given hint is to decrease the rotation value of the joint "EP," increase the rotation value of joint "WY," and finally to select camera "CP2" on "Monitor1." The values on the right column indicate the parameter values for the action. In this context, the values "2" and "3" mean to rotate the joints 20° and 30°, respectively (1 unit equals 10°). By default, three steps are shown to the learner in the hint window depicted in Figure 32.2b. However, the learner can click on the "More" button to ask for more steps or click on the "another possibility" button to ask for an alternative.

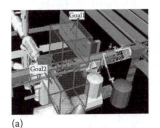
(a)

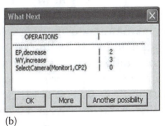
(b)

FIGURE 32.2
(a) The two scenarios. (b) A hint offered by CanadarmTutor.

It should be noted that although the sequential pattern algorithm was applied, only one time in this experiment after recording each learner's plan, it would be possible to make CanadarmTutor apply it more often, in order to continuously update its knowledge base, while interacting with learners.

32.5 Related Work

This section compares our approach with related work.

32.5.1 Other Automatic or Semiautomatic Approaches for Learning Domain Knowledge in ITS

A few approaches have been described for learning domain knowledge from demonstrations in ITS [5,6,17,21–23].

Demonstr8 by Blessing [23] can infer simple production rules from pairs of inputs and outputs. However, rules can only have two arguments, and each rule action is defined as a single function from a predefined set of LISP functions such as adding two numbers. Moreover, demonstrators have to constantly indicate to Demonstr8 their goal and subgoals during demonstrations so that it can link rules together. Blessing [23] applied Demonstr8 for the task of multicolumn subtraction, and admitted that the approach would be hard to apply for more complex domains, or domains where not all reasoning is done within the user interface of the tutoring system (e.g., CanadarmTutor).

A second example is the Behavior Recorder [5], which allows an author to create a problem space by demonstrating the different correct or erroneous ways of solving a problem. The problem spaces produced by the Behavior Recorder are graphs where nodes are problem states and links are learner actions for passing from one state to another. The major limitation of the Behavior Recorder is that it does not perform any generalization. For a given problem, it simply integrates raw solutions in a graph, and the graph is problem specific.

Jarvis et al. [6] designed a system that can extract general production rules from a set of demonstrations, given that authors provide a minimal set of background knowledge. This background knowledge comprises functions and conditions to create, respectively, the "IF" and the "THEN" parts of the learned rules. During demonstrations, demonstrators have to label the values that they manipulate in the user interface (e.g., define an integer as a carry in a multicolumn subtraction). Some limitations of the approach are that (1) the search for rules is an exhaustive search with a complexity that increases quickly with the number of functions and conditions to consider, (2) rules produced are sometimes over general, and (3) the approach was applied only in well-defined domains such as fraction addition [6].

Another example is the virtual agent SimStudent [21], which can learn production rules from demonstrations. Similar to the work of Jarvis and Nuzzo-Jones and Demonstr8, SimStudent requires authors to define operators and predicates to be used to create rules. During demonstrations, demonstrators have to indicate the name of each rule to be learned and the elements in the user interface to which the rule is applied. Rules that are learned are general and can be applied to several problems. SimStudent is designed for well-defined domains where a task can be described as production rules, and providing background knowledge or information during demonstrations can be a demanding task.

For building constraint-based tutors, a few systems have been described to learn constraints from demonstrations. One, named CAS [22], takes as input a domain ontology, and problems and solutions, both annotated with concept instances from the ontology. CAS then extracts constraints directly from the restrictions that are defined in the ontology. CAS was successfully applied for the domains of fraction addition and entity-relation diagram modeling. But the success of CAS for a domain depends directly on whether it is possible to build an ontology that is appropriate and detailed enough, and this is not necessarily the case for all domains. In fact, ontology modeling can be difficult. Moreover, as previously mentioned, constraint-based tutors can validate solutions. But they cannot suggest next problem-solving steps to learners.

A last method that we mention is the work of Barnes and Stamper [17], which was applied for the well-defined domain of logic proofs. The approach of Barnes and Stamper consists of building a Markov decision process containing learner solutions for a problem. This is a graph acquired from a corpus of student problem-solving traces where each state represents a correct or erroneous state and each link is an action to go from one state to another. Then, given a state, an optimal path can be calculated to reach a goal state according to desiderata such as popularity, lowest probability of errors, or shortest number of actions. An optimal path found in this way is then used to suggest to a learner the next actions to perform. This approach does not require providing any kind of domain knowledge or extra information during demonstrations. However, since all traces are stored completely in a graph, the approach seems limited to domains where the number of possibilities is not large. Moreover, their approach does not support more elaborated tutoring services such as estimating the profile of a learner by looking at the actions that the learner applies (e.g., expertise level), and hints are not suggested based on the estimated profile of a learner. We believe this to be a major limitation of their approach, as in many cases, an ITS should not consider the "optimal solution" (as previously defined) as being the best solution for a learner. Instead an ITS should select successful solutions that are adapted to a learner profile, to make the learner progress along the continuum from novice to expert.

In summary, in addition to some specific limitations, all systems mentioned in this section have one or more of the following limitations: they (1) require defining a body of background knowledge [6,21–23], (2) have been demonstrated for well-defined domains [5,6,17,21–23], (3) rely on the strong assumption that tasks can be modeled as production rules [6,21,23], (4) do not take into account learner profiles [5,6,17,21–23], (5) learn knowledge that is problem specific [5,17], and (6) require demonstrators to provide extra information during demonstrations such as their intentions or labels for elements of their solutions [6,22].

Our approach is clearly different from these approaches as it does not possess any of these limitations except for generating task models that are problem specific. We believe that this limitation is an acceptable trade-off, as in many domains a particular collection of exercises can be set up to be administered to many students. Also, it is important to note that our approach allows manual annotation of sequences if needed.

The approach of Barnes et al. shares some similarities with our approach as it needs to be applied for each problem, and authors are not required to provide any kind of domain knowledge. But the approach of Barnes et al. also differs from ours in several ways. The first important difference is that our approach extracts partial problem spaces from user solutions. Therefore our framework ignores parts of learner solutions that are not frequent. This strategy of extracting similarities in learners' solutions allows coping with domains such as the manipulation of Canadarm2 where the number of possibilities is very large, and user solutions do not share many actions. In fact, our framework builds abstractions of learners' solutions, where the frequency threshold *minsup* controls what will be excluded from these abstractions. A second important difference is that the abstractions created by our framework are generalizations as they consist of subsequences appearing in several learner solutions. This property of problem spaces produced by our framework is very useful as it allows finding patterns that are common to several profiles of learners or contexts (e.g., patterns common to expert users who succeed in solving a problem, or common to users possessing or lacking one or more skills). Conversely, the previously mentioned approaches do not take into account the profile of learners who recorded solutions.

32.5.2 Other Applications of Sequential Pattern Mining in E-Learning

Finally, we mention related work about the application of SPM in the field of artificial intelligence in education (AIED). This work can be divided into two categories.

The first category is work on discovering patterns that will be interpreted by humans. For example, Kay and coworkers [20] mined sequential patterns from group work logs to discover patterns that would indicate good or bad group behavior in collaborative learning, so that human tutors could recognize problematic behavior in early stages of learning sessions. Similarly, Antunes [25] extracted sequential patterns to identify the deviations of individual student behaviors from a curriculum comprising several courses in a university setting. In this case, a sequence is the list of courses followed by a student. From these sequences, several sequential patterns were found. For instance, one pattern is that whenever some students failed a course in the fourth semester, they chose a particular economy course next [25]. Romero et al. [26] proposed an information visualization tool that has a similar purpose. It allows visualizing routes that learners follow within a curriculum. Different parameters such as frequency define the routes that are displayed. The approach was applied in a web-based ITS to visualize navigation patterns.

A second category of work uses SPM to help build systems for recommending learning activities to learners. For instance, Su et al. [27] described a system based on the idea of suggesting learning activities to learners based on what "similar" learners did. Their approach consisted of (1) extracting sequential patterns from the learning patterns of each student, (2) clustering students who exhibited similar learning patterns into groups, and (3) building a decision tree for each group from the patterns found for learning activity recommendation. A system with a similar aim was developed by Kristofic and Bielikova [7]. This system uses patterns found in learner navigation sequences to recommend concepts that a student should study next.

All work mentioned in this section is different from ours, as it does not attempt to learn domain knowledge.

32.6 Conclusion

In this paper, we have presented an approach for domain knowledge acquisition in ITS, and shown that it can be a plausible alternative to classic domain knowledge acquisition approaches, particularly for a procedural and ill-defined domain where classical approaches fail. For discovering domain knowledge, we proposed to use an SPM algorithm that we designed for addressing the type of data recorded in tutoring systems such as CanadarmTutor. Since the proposed data mining framework and its inputs and outputs are fairly domain independent, it can be potentially applied to other ill-defined procedural domains where solutions to problems can be expressed as sequences of actions as defined previously. With the case study of CanadarmTutor, we described how the approach can support relevant tutoring services. We have evaluated the capability of the new version of CanadarmTutor to exploit the learned knowledge to provide tutoring services. Results showed an improvement over the previous version of CanadarmTutor in terms of tracking learners' behavior and providing hints. In future work, we will perform further experiments to measure empirically how the tutoring services influence the learning of students.

Because the problem spaces extracted with our approach are incomplete, we suggest using our approach jointly with other domain knowledge acquisition approaches when possible. In CanadarmTutor, we do so by making CanadarmTutor use the path-planner for providing hints when no patterns are available. Also, we are currently working on combining our data-mining approach with the rule-based model that we implemented in another version of CanadarmTutor using the cognitive task analysis approach [9]. In particular, we are exploring the possibility of using skills from the rule-based model to automatically annotate recorded sequences used by the data-mining approach presented in this paper.

We also plan to use association rule mining as in a previous version of our approach, to find associations between sequential patterns over a whole problem-solving exercise [18]. Mining association rules could improve the effectiveness of the tutoring services, as it is complementary to dividing the problem into problem states. For example, if a learner followed a pattern p, an association rule could indicate that the learner has a higher probability of applying another pattern q later during the exercise than some other pattern r that is available for the same problem state.

Finally, we are interested in mining other types of temporal patterns in ITSs. We have recently published work [19] that instead of mining sequential patterns from the behavior of learners, mines frequent sequences from the behavior of a tutoring agent. The tutoring agent then reuses sequences of tutorial interventions that were successful with learners. This second research project is also based on the same algorithm described here.

Acknowledgments

Our thanks go to FQRNT and NSERC for their logistic and financial support. Moreover, the authors would like to thank Severin Vigot, Mikael Watrelot, and Lionel Tchamfong for integrating the framework in CanadarmTutor, the other members of the GDAC/ PLANIART teams who participated in the development of CanadarmTutor, and the anonymous reviewers who provided many comments for improving this paper.

References

1. Aleven, V., McLaren, B. M., Sewall, J., and Koedinger, K. 2006. The Cognitive Tutor Authoring Tools (CTAT): Preliminary evaluation of efficiency gains. In *Proceedings of the Eighth International Conference on Intelligent Tutoring Systems*, Jhongli, Taiwan, June 26–30, 2006, pp. 61–70.
2. Simon, H. A. 1978. Information-processing theory of human problem solving. In *Handbook of Learning and Cognitive Processes*, Vol. 5. *Human Information*, W.K. Estes (Ed.), pp. 271–295. Hillsdale, NJ: John Wiley & Sons, Inc.

3. Lynch, C., Ashley, K., Aleven, V., and Pinkwart, N. 2006. Defining ill-defined domains; A literature survey. In *Proceedings of the Intelligent Tutoring Systems for Ill-Defined Domains Workshop*, Jhongli, Taiwan, June 27, 2006, pp. 1–10.
4. Mitrovic, A., Mayo, M., Suraweera, P., and Martin, B. 2001. Constraint-based tutors: A success story. In *Proceedings of the 14th Industrial & Engineering Application of Artificial Intelligence & Expert Systems*, Budapest, Hungary, June 4–7, 2001, pp. 931–940.
5. McLaren, B., Koedinger, K.R., Schneider, M., Harrer, A., and Bollen, L. 2004. Bootstrapping novice data: Semi-automated tutor authoring using student log files. In *Proceedings of the Workshop on Analyzing Student-Tutor Logs to Improve Educational Outcomes*, Maceió, Alagoas, Brazil, August 30, 2004, pp. 1–13.
6. Jarvis, M., Nuzzo-Jones, G., and Heffernan, N.T. 2004. Applying machine learning techniques to rule generation in intelligent tutoring systems. In *Proceedings of Seventh International Conference on Intelligent Tutoring Systems*, Maceió, Brazil, August 30–September 3, 2004, pp. 541–553.
7. Kriatofic, A and Bielikova, M. 2005. Improving adaptation in web-based educational hypermedia by means of knowledge discovery. In *Proceedings of the 16th ACM Conference on Hypertext and Hypermedia*, Bratislava, Slovakia, September 6–10, 2005, pp. 184–192.
8. Kabanza, F., Nkambou, R., and Belghith, K. 2005. Path-planning for autonomous training on robot manipulators in space. In *Proceedings of International Joint Conference on Artificial Intelligence 2005*, Edinburgh, U.K., July 30–August 5, 2005, pp. 35–38.
9. Fournier-Viger, P., Nkambou, R., and Mayers, A. 2008. Evaluating spatial representations and skills in a simulator-based tutoring system. *IEEE Transactions on Learning Technologies*, 1(1): 63–74.
10. Hirate, Y. and Yamana, H. 2006. Generalized sequential pattern mining with item intervals, *Journal of Computers*, 1(3): 51–60.
11. Pinto, H. et al. 2001. Multi-dimensional sequential pattern mining. In *Proceedings of the 10th International Conference on Information and Knowledge Management*, Atlanta, GA, November 5–10, 2001, pp. 81–88.
12. Han, J. and Kamber, M. 2000. *Data Mining: Concepts and Techniques*. San Francisco, CA: Morgan Kaufmann Publisher.
13. Agrawal, R. and Srikant, R. 1995. Mining sequential patterns. In *Proceedings of the International Conference on Data Engineering*, Taipei, Taiwan, March 6–10, 1995, pp. 3–14.
14. Wang, J., Han, J., and Li, C. 2007. Frequent closed sequence mining without candidate maintenance, *IEEE Transactions on Knowledge and Data Engineering*, 19(8):1042–1056.
15. Fournier-Viger, P., Nkambou, R., and Mephu Nguifo, E. 2008. A knowledge discovery framework for learning task models from user interactions in intelligent tutoring systems. In *Proceedings of the Sixth Mexican International Conference on Artificial Intelligence*, Atizapán de Zaragoza, Mexico, October 27–31, 2008, pp. 765–778.
16. Songram, P., Boonjing, V., and Intakosum, S. 2006. Closed multidimensional sequential pattern mining. In *Proceedings of the Third International Conference Information Technology: New Generations*, Las Vegas, NV, April 10–12, 2006, pp. 512–517.
17. Barnes, T. and Stamper, J. 2008. Toward automatic hint generation for logic proof tutoring using historical student data. In *Proceedings of the Ninth International Conference on Intelligent Tutoring Systems*, Montreal, Canada, June 23–27, 2008, pp. 373–382.
18. Nkambou, R., Mephu Nguifo, E., and Fournier-Viger, P. 2008. Using knowledge discovery techniques to support tutoring in an ill-defined domain. In *Proceedings of the Ninth International Conference on Intelligent Tutoring Systems*, Montreal, Canada, June 23–27, 2008, pp. 395–405.
19. Faghihi, U., Fournier-Viger, P., and Nkambou, R. 2009. How emotional mechanism helps episodic learning in a cognitive agent. In *Proceedings of IEEE Symposium on Intelligent Agents*, Nashville, TN, March 30–April 2, 2009, pp. 23–30.
20. Perera, D., Kay, J., Koprinska, I., Yacef, K., and Zaiane, O. 2008. Clustering and sequential pattern mining of online collaborative learning data. *IEEE Transactions on Knowledge and Data Engineering*, 21(6): 759–772.

21. Matsuda, N., Cohen, W., Sewall, J., Lacerda, G., and Koedinger, K. 2007. Performance with SimStudent: Learning cognitive skills from observation. In *Proceedings of Artificial Intelligence in Education 2007*, Los Angeles, CA, July 9–13, 2007, pp. 467–478.

22. Suraweera, P., Mitrovic, A., and Martin, B. 2007. Constraint authoring system: An empirical evaluation. In *Proceedings of Artificial Intelligence in Education 2007*, Los Angeles, CA, July 9–13, 2007, pp. 467–478.

23. Blessing, S. B. 1997. A programming by demonstration authoring tool for model-tracing tutors. *International Journal of Artificial Intelligence in Education*, 8: 233–261.

24. Yuan, D., Lee, K., Cheng, H., Krishna, G., Li, Z., Ma, X., Zhou, Y., and Han, J. 2008. CISpan: Comprehensive incremental mining algorithms of closed sequential patterns for multi-versional software mining. In *Proceedings of the Eighth SIAM International Conference on Data Mining*, Atlanta, GA, April 24–26, pp. 84–95.

25. Antunes, C. 2008. Acquiring background knowledge for intelligent tutoring systems. In *Proceedings of the Second International Conference on Educational Data Mining*, Montreal, Canada, June 20–21, pp. 18–27.

26. Romero, C., Gutiarrez, S., Freire, M., and Ventura, S. 2008. Mining and visualizing visited trails in web-based educational systems. In *Proceedings of the Second International Conference on Educational Data Mining*, Montreal, Canada, June 20–21, pp. 182–186.

27. Su, J.-M., Tseng, S.-S., Wang, W., Weng, J.-F., Yang, J. T. D., and Tsai, W.-N. 2006. Learning portfolio analysis and mining for SCORM compliant environment. *Educational Technology & Society*, 9(1): 262–275.

33

Using Markov Decision Processes for Automatic Hint Generation

Tiffany Barnes, John Stamper, and Marvin Croy

CONTENTS

33.1 Introduction

In this chapter, we present our novel application of Markov decision processes (MDPs) for building student knowledge models from collected student data. These models can be integrated into existing computer-aided instructional tools to automatically generate context-specific hints. The MDP method is straightforward to implement in many educational domains where computer-aided instruction exists and student log data is being generated, but no intelligent tutors have been created. In this chapter, we demonstrate the creation of an MDP-Tutor for the logic domain, but the methods can be readily translated to other procedural problem-solving domains. We first demonstrate how to create an MDP to represent finding optimal solutions. We then show how to use this MDP to create a hint generator, and illustrate a feasibility study to determine how often the generator can provide hints. This feasibility technique is a valuable contribution that can be used to make decisions about the appropriateness of MDPs for hint generation in a particular problem-solving domain. The chapter concludes with a discussion of the future of using MDPs and other data-derived models for learning about and supporting student learning and problem solving.

33.2 Background

Our goal is to create data-driven, domain-independent techniques for creating cognitive models that can be used to generate student feedback, guidance, and hints, and help educators understand students' learning. Through adaptation to individual learners, intelligent tutoring systems (ITSs), such as those built on ACT-R, can have significant effects on learning [1]. ACT-R Theory is a cognitive architecture that has been successfully applied in the creation of cognitive tutors, and contains a procedural component that uses production rules to model how students move between problem states [1]. Through a process called **model tracing**, cognitive tutors find a sequence of rules that produce the actions a student has taken. This allows for individualized help, tracks student mastery (using the correctness of the productions being applied), and can provide feedback on recognized errors.

In general, most of these ITSs include models that are domain or application specific, and require significant investment of time and effort to build [22]. A variety of approaches have been used to reduce the development time for ITSs, including ITS authoring tools (such as ASSERT and CTAT), or building constraint-based student models instead of production rule systems. ASSERT is an ITS authoring system that uses theory refinement to learn student models from an existing knowledge base and student data [3]. Constraint-based tutors, which look for violations of problem constraints, require less time to construct and have been favorably compared to cognitive tutors, particularly for problems that may not be heavily procedural [21]. However, constraint-based tutors can only provide condition violation feedback, not goal-oriented feedback that has been shown to be more effective [28].

Some systems, including RIDES, DIAG, and CTAT use teacher-authored or demonstrated examples to develop ITS production rules. In these example-based authoring tools, domain experts work problems in what they predict to be frequent correct and incorrect approaches, and then annotate the learned rules with appropriate hints and feedback. RIDES is a "Tutor in a Box" system used to build training systems for military equipment usage, while DIAG was built as an expert diagnostic system that generates context-specific feedback for students [22]. CTAT has been used to develop example-based tutors for subjects including genetics, Java, and truth tables [16]. CTAT researchers built SimStudent, a machine learning agent that learns production rules by demonstration and is used to simulate students [17]. CTAT has also been used with student data to build initial models for an ITS, in an approach called Bootstrapping Novice Data (BND) [19]. However, expert example-based approaches cannot be easily generalized to learn from student data, and considerable time must still be spent in identifying student approaches and creating appropriate hints.

Machine learning has been used in a number of ways to improve tutoring systems, most extensively in modeling students and in tutorial dialog. In the ADVISOR tutor, machine learning was used to build student models that could predict the time students took to solve arithmetic problems, and to adapt instruction to minimize this time while meeting teacher-set instructional goals [8]. Jameson et al. similarly predict a user's execution time and errors based, in part, on the system's delivery of instructions [15]. Mayo and Mitrovic use a Bayesian network model and predict student performance, and use a decision-theoretic model to select appropriate tutorial actions in CAPIT [18]. The DT-Tutor models focus of attention, affect, and student knowledge of tasks and domain rules to predict the topic and correctness of a student's next action, and uses this with decision theory to make decisions about tutor actions [23]. All of these systems use probabilistic networks to model student learning and behavior, and combine these models with decision-theoretic approaches to make choices for the next tutorial actions.

Other applications use educational data mining techniques to discover patterns of student behavior. Baker has used educational data mining on labeled tutor log data to discover detrimental gaming behaviors to avoid learning in ITSs [4]. Soller uses hand-labeled interactions to train a Hidden Markov Model classifier to distinguish effective interactions in collaborative learning tasks from ineffective ones [26]. Amershi and Conati have applied both unsupervised and supervised learning to student interaction and eye-tracking data in exploratory learning environments to scaffold building models of effective student learning behavior [2], and applied their educational data mining model to two different learning environments. Other educational data mining approaches discover patterns by clustering student test scores or solution data labeled by correctness, and present these patterns to educators [14,24].

MDPs have been used specifically to model tutorial interactions, primarily for dialogue, but also to model how to offer intelligent help in more general software applications. Chi, VanLehn, and colleagues have built MDPs to model the dialogue acts of human tutors, and compared them with their Greedy-RL tutor to investigate what tactics (such as elicit or tell actions) are most effective for supporting learning [9]. Hui and colleagues use MDPs to model decisions for a simulated help assistant, balancing the costs of interaction including factors such as bloat, visual occlusion, information processing, and savings [13]. In contrast, our MDPs are used as models of target student behavior and use them to generate hints for students.

Deep Thought [10] and the Logic-ITA [20] are two CAI tools to support teaching and learning of logic proofs. These tutors verify proof statements as a student enters them, and provide feedback on clear errors. Logic-ITA provides students with performance feedback upon proof completion, and considerable logging and teacher feedback [20]. Logic-ITA student data was also mined to create hints that warned students when they were likely to make mistakes using their current approach [20]. Another logic tutor called the Carnegie Proof Lab uses an automated proof generator to provide contextual hints [25]. We have augmented Deep Thought with a cognitive architecture derived using educational data mining, that can provide students feedback to avoid error-prone solutions, find optimal solutions, and inform students of other student approaches.

Similar to the goal of BND, we seek to use student data to directly create **model tracers** for an ITS. However, instead of feeding student behavior data into CTAT to build a production rule system, we directly build data-derived **model tracers** (DMTs) for use in tutors. To do this, we have generated MDPs that represent all student approaches to a particular problem, and use these MDPs directly to generate hints. This method of automatic hint generation using previous student data reduces the expert knowledge needed to generate intelligent, context-dependent hints. The system is capable of continued refinement as new data is provided. In this chapter, we demonstrate the feasibility of our hint-generation approach through simulation experiments on existing student data and pilot studies that show that the automatically generated hints help more students solve harder proof problems.

Barnes and Stamper used visualization tools to explore how to generate hints based on MDPs extracted from student data [5]. Croy, Barnes, and Stamper applied the technique to visualize student proof approaches to allow teachers to identify problem areas for students [10,11]. Our feasibility study for hint generation on simulated students indicated valuable trade-offs between hint specificity and the amount of source data for the MDP [6].

Our method of automatic hint generation using previous student data reduces the expert knowledge needed to generate intelligent, context-dependent hints and feedback, and provides the basis for a more general DMT that learns as it is used. Although our approach is currently only appropriate for model tracing and generating hints for specific problems with existing prior data, we believe that machine learning applied to MDPs may be used to create automated rules and hints for new problems in the same domain. We illustrate our approach by applying MDPs to support student work in solving formal logic proofs.

MDP-Tutors work best in situations where CAI already exists, problems consist of a series of related steps and are most often solved using similar strategies, and log data is readily available. Many CAI tools exist for math and science problems, which often have multiple related steps but involve a limited number of problem-solving strategies. For the best hint generation, it is best if errors and correct solutions are labeled or detected. However, the MDP method can be used to analyze problems and build probabilistic MDP-Tutors without this information [7].

We have created and describe here our MDP-Tutor for the logic proofs domain, but other researchers have applied our techniques to generate student feedback as well. Fossati and colleagues have used MDPs to model student behavior in the iList linked list tutor, and use these models to choose tutorial feedback such as that given by human tutors [12]. The tutor represents linked lists in a graphical form that students can manipulate in order to gain a better understanding of the concepts without the need for large amounts of programming. The iList tutor uses the MDP method to provide proactive feedback, indicating whether the student's current approach is likely to be successful.

33.3 Creating an MDP-Tutor

The purpose of creating an MDP from data is to build a model of knowledge in a problem-solving domain. The data-derived MDP is then used as a model tracer by matching student work to that in the MDP. A unique feature of an MDP as a domain model is that, at any state in the MDP, we know an "optimal" solution to the problem being solved if it has been discovered in the past. Therefore, while we are tracing student work, the MDP can be used to determine the "best" approach that will take the student from their current state to the goal. We work with content area experts to build an automatic hint generator that presents aspects of this best-from-here approach to provide context-specific hints. Together, the MDP, model tracer, and hint generator are added to a CAI to create an MDP-Tutor.

In this section, we illustrate the creation of an MDP-Tutor from a CAI tool. Deep Thought is a custom graphical CAI tool for solving logic proofs, and has been used in logic courses since before 2000 [10]. In Deep Thought's graphical interface, shown in Figure 33.1, students solve logic proofs by clicking on proof statements (rectangles in the left pane) and logic rules (buttons on the right) to generate new proof statements. The goal is to connect the premises (not (T and L), if not T then not N, not (E or T), given at the top of the screen) to the conclusion (not N, given at the bottom of the screen). Each step in the proof is saved with a time stamp, the generated statement, the source statement(s) and rule used to derive it, and whether the step was correct or not. We leverage this log to create states for our MDP.

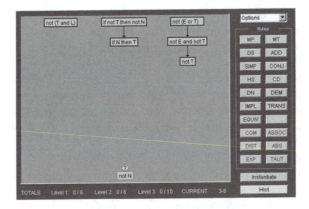

FIGURE 33.1
Deep Thought Logic Tutor with problem 3.6 partially completed.

33.3.1 Constructing the MDP from Data

An MDP is defined by its state set S, action set A, transition probabilities T: S×A×S → [0,1], and a reward function R: S×A×S → $\Re$ [27]. The goal of using an MDP here is to determine the best policy, or set of actions the model should take at each state *s* to maximize its expected cumulative utility (V-value), which can be calculated recursively using equation (1). In our case, we wish the policy to find the best sequence of actions that students have taken to solve the given problem. For a particular point in a student's logic proof, a state consists of the list of statements generated so far, and actions are the rules used at each step. Actions are directed arcs that connect consecutive states. Therefore, each proof attempt can be seen as a graph with a sequence of states connected by actions. For example, the sequence of states for the attempt shown in Figure 33.1 is given below. The actions taken join state 1 to 2 (TRANS), 2 to 3 (DEM), and 3 to 4 (SIMP).

1. not(T and L), if not T then not N, not (E or T)
2. not(T and L), if not T then not N, not (E or T), if N then T
3. not(T and L), if not T then not N, not (E or T), if N then T, not E and not T
4. not(T and L), if not T then not N, not (E or T), if N then T, not E and not T, not T

In other problem-solving domains, a mapping of cumulative logs of derived statements and the actions taken to derive them can be used to create MDP states and actions. Care must be taken to ensure that the granularity of MDP states is appropriate; in our case we did not map every click in the interface to a state. The granularity of existing logs, if they can be read and understood relatively easily by a content expert, provides a general guide to the content of MDP states. If states are too fine-grained, the MDP can become quite large and the hints generated may not map into meaningful problem-solving steps. If states are too coarsely grained, then the hints generated may be too general. States can be considered to be ordered or unordered, depending on the relevance of step order in the problem domain.

While creating MDP states, consideration must also be given to how to record errors. Deep Thought detects incorrect steps, and once a message is displayed, the step is removed from the screen. We therefore save this as a state in the MDP, but as a "leaf" where it is understood that the error state is entered and then the interface is restored to the prior state. In other CAI tools where errors may persist in the problem-solving environment, either because they are not detected or not removed, error states could be incorporated into the MDP just as other states are. However, the retention of erroneous information in a state must be carefully considered when generating hints about what a student should do next. When the reward and expected reward values are assigned, as described below, it is important to penalize only the states in which an error originally occurs, and not those that follow it.

Once state representations are determined and student attempt graphs are constructed, we combine these attempts into a single graph that represents all of the paths students have taken in working a proof, by taking the union of all states and actions, and mapping identical states to one another. We also create an artificial "goal" state and connect the last state in each successful problem solution to this goal state. Next, value iteration is used to find an optimal solution to the MDP. For the experiments in this work, we assign a large reward to the goal state (100) and negative rewards (penalties) to incorrect states (–10) and actions (–1), resulting in a bias toward short, correct solutions such as those an expert might work. We have also proposed two other reward functions to deliver different types of hints [4], including functions that

1. Find frequent, typical paths. To derive this policy, we assign high rewards to successful paths that many students have taken. Vygotsky's theory of the zone of proximal development [29] states that students are able to learn new things that are closest to what they already know. Presumably, frequent actions could be those that more students feel fluent using, and may be more understandable than expert solutions.

2. Find least error-prone paths. To derive this policy, we assign large penalties to error states, which lower the overall rewards for paths near many errors.

After setting the chosen rewards, we apply the value iteration using a Bellman backup to iteratively assign values $V(s)$ to all states in the MDP until the values on the left- and right-hand sides of Equation 33.1 converge [27]. $V(s)$ corresponds to the expected reward for following an optimal policy from state s. The equation for calculating values $V(s)$ is given in equation (1), where $R(s,a)$ is the reward for taking action a from state s, and $P_a(s, s')$ is the probability that action a will take state s to state s'. In our case, $P_a(s, s')$ is calculated by dividing the number of times action a is taken from state s to s' by the total number of actions leaving state s.

$$V(s) := \max_a \left(R(s,a) + \sum_{s'} P_a(s,s') V(s') \right) \tag{33.1}$$

Once value iteration is complete, the values for each state indicate how close to the goal a state is, while probabilities of each transition reveal the frequency of taking a certain action in a certain state. The optimal solution in the MDP from any given state can then be reached by choosing an action to the next state with the highest value.

33.3.2 The MDP Hint Generator

An MDP built using data from several semesters will reflect a diversity of student approaches to solving a given problem. We can use this MDP to perform model tracing as a student is working a proof. When a new student solves a problem, we match each step to the states in the MDP using a matching function. When a match occurs, we then use the matched state to generate a potential hint sequence. If the student asks for help, we can direct that student to optimal, frequent, or simply away from error-prone paths, based on that particular student and/or path. Similar to constraint-based tutors [21], if a student is solving a proof in a way that is not already present in the MDP, we simply add their steps to the model. If such a student does commit an error, only default feedback will be given. We have proposed a number of matching functions, including exact matches with order preserved, unordered matches, and those with less than 100% overlap [6]. The degree of overlap between actual student work and its matched state in the MDP determines the specificity of hints that we can generate based on the match.

Once a matching function is constructed, we generate a hint sequence that takes advantage of the state values in the MDP to determine the next state(s) needed to best arrive at the problem solution. With domain experts, we write a sequence of hint templates. Based on the next best state, hint templates can suggest the action to take, aspects of the next state, or how the current state can be used to get to the next state. For a given state in Deep Thought, we use the next best state to generate a sequence of four hints. Table 33.1 shows the four hints that would be generated based on the state in Figure 33.1. Each time the hint button is pressed, the next hint is given. Once a student performs a correct step, the hint sequence is reset. For each hint request, we record the time, hint sequence number, and the total number of hint requests.

If no match to the current state exists in the MDP, we can disable the hint function, or we can iteratively remove the last step of the problem until a match is found. Although we have not implemented this capability into the Deep Thought MDP-Tutor, we have observed that some students take this approach when they reach an impasse but a hint is not available; they simply delete steps until the hint button becomes active.

Together, the MDP, matching function, and hint templates comprise a hint generator that can create individualized hints for a particular problem. When the hint generator is added to a CAI, we create an MDP-Tutor.

TABLE 33.1

Deep Thought Hint Sequence Template and Example Data

Hint	Hint Text (Source Data BOLD)	Hint Type
1	Try to derive **not N** working forward	Indicate goal expression
2	Highlight **if not T then not N** and **not T** to derive it	Indicate the premises to select
3	Click on the rule **Modus Ponens (MP)**	Indicate the rule to use
4	Highlight **if not T then not N** and **not T** and click on **Modus Ponens (MP)** to get **not N**	Bottom-out hint

Source: Barnes, T. J. et al., A pilot study on logic proof tutoring using hints generated from historical student data, in Baker, R. S. J. d., Barnes, T., and Beck, J. E. (Eds.) *Educational Data Mining 2008: 1st International Conference on Educational Data Mining, Proceedings.* Montreal, Quebec, Canada. June 20–21, 2008, pp. 197–201. Available online at: http://www.educationaldatamining.org/EDM2008/index.php?page=proceedings

33.4 Feasibility Studies

To explore the capability of our method to generate automated hints, we divided a set of 523 attempts on a logic proof problem from four semesters of a logic course into training and test sets, where the training set was used to generate the MDP as described above, and the test set was used to explore hint availability. For each state in a test set, there are two requirements for a hint to be available: (1) there must be a "matching" state in the MDP and (2) the "matching" state must not be a leaf in the MDP. The closer the match between a test state and the corresponding MDP state, the more context-specific the hint based on that match will be.

We considered four matching functions: (1) ordered (exact), (2) unordered, (3) ordered minus the latest premise, and (4) unordered minus the latest premise. An ordered, or exact, state match means that another student has taken the same sequence of steps in solving the proof. An unordered state match means that there is a state with exactly the same premises, but they were not necessarily reached in the same order. An "ordered-1" match looks for an exact match between the student's previous state and an MDP state. An "unordered-1" match looks for an unordered match between the student's previous state and an MDP state. Once a match is made, we generate a hint based on knowing the next optimal (highest reward value) step from the matching state. The more specific the match, the more contextualized the hint.

To determine hint availability, we calculated the "move matches": the number of test set states, or "moves," including duplicates, that have matches in the MDP, divided by the total number of test set states. Move matches give us a measure of the percentage of the time a particular student will be able to attain a hint while working a proof.

We conducted two experiments to test the feasibility of automated hint generation. The first is something like a cross-validation study, comparing the hints we can generate using various semesters of data for MDP creation. As shown in Table 33.2, on average, for 72% of moves, we can provide highly contextualized (ordered) hints using just one semester of data. With two semesters of data, we can provide these hints almost 80% of the time, but this only increases to 82% for three semesters of data. If we wished to provide hints after collecting just one semester of data, we could provide less contextualized hints for those who do not have ordered matches in the MDP. There is a nearly identical benefit to providing hints using unordered versus ordered-1 matches, increasing the match rate to almost 80% [6].

TABLE 33.2

Comparison of % Move Matches Across # Source Semesters and Matching Techniques

Matching	1-sem. MDPs	2-sem. MDPs	3-sem. MDPs
Ordered	72.79%	79.57%	82.32%
Unordered	79.62%	85.22%	87.26%
Ordered-1	79.88%	87.84%	91.57%
Unordered-1	85.00%	91.50%	93.96%

Source: Barnes, T. and Stamper, J., *J. Educ. Technol. Soc.,* Special Issue on *Intelligent Tutoring Systems,* 13(1), 3, February 2010. With permission.

TABLE 33.3

Algorithm for One Trial of the Cold Start Experiment to Test
How Quickly Hints Become Available

1. Let Test = {all 523 student attempts}.
2. Randomly choose and remove the next attempt a from the Test set.
3. Add a's states and recalculate the MDP.
4. Randomly choose and remove the next attempt b from the Test set.
5. Compute the number of matches between b and MDP.
6. If test is nonempty, then let a:=b and go to step 3. Otherwise, stop.

The second study was a simulation of creating MDPs incrementally as students work
proofs, and calculating the probability of being able to generate hints as new attempts are
added to the MDP. This experiment explores how quickly such an MDP is able to provide
hints to new students, or in other words, how long it takes to solve the cold start problem.
For one trial, the method is given in Table 33.3.

For this experiment, we used the ordered and unordered matching functions, and
plotted the resulting average matches over 100,000 trials. As shown in Figure 33.2, unordered matches have a higher number of matches, but for both ordered and unordered
matching functions, the number of move matches rises quickly, and can be fit using power
functions.

Table 33.4 lists the number of attempts needed in the MDP versus target hint percentages. For the unordered matching function, the 50% threshold is reached at just eight

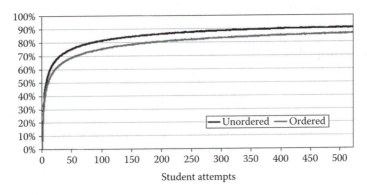

FIGURE 33.2
Percentage of moves with hints available as attempts are added to the MDP. (From Barnes, T. and Stamper, J.,
J. Educ. Technol. Soc., Special Issue on *Intelligent Tutoring Systems*, 13(1), 3, February 2010. With permission.)

TABLE 33.4

Number of Attempts Needed to Achieve Threshold % Hints Levels

	50%	55%	60%	65%	70%	75%	80%	85%	90%
Unordered	8	11	14	20	30	46	80	154	360
Ordered	11	15	22	33	55	85	162	362	?

Source: Barnes, T. and Stamper, J., *J. Educ. Technol. Soc.*, Special Issue on *Intelligent Tutoring
Systems*, 13(1), 3, February 2010. With permission.

student attempts and the 75% threshold at 49 attempts. For ordered matching, 50% occurs on attempt 11 and 75% on attempt 88. These data are encouraging, suggesting that instructors using our MDP hint generator could seed the data to provide hint generation for new problems. By allowing the instructor to enter as few as 8–11 example solutions to a problem, the method could automatically generate hints for 50% of student moves.

Together, the two feasibility studies presented here provided us with evidence that using an MDP to automatically generate hints could be used with just one semester of data for a particular problem. The quality of the hints is assured by our collaborative construction of hints with domain experts, but as described in the next section, we evaluated the effects of our automatically generated hints with students using the Deep Thought MDP-Tutor.

33.5 Case Study: The Deep Thought Logic MDP-Tutor

In order to evaluate the method with students, a hint generator was added to the Deep Thought CAI to create an MDP-Tutor for several Deep Thought problems. MDPs were generated using Deep Thought data for four Level 3 problems from Deep Thought, 3.2, 3.5, 3.6, and 3.8, from two Deductive Logic philosophy courses: spring 2007 (30 students) and summer 2007 (20 students). The characteristics of these training datasets are given in Table 33.5. Forty students in the spring 2008 course were assigned to work these four problems. We hypothesized that, with hints, a higher percentage of students would complete the proofs. Figure 33.3 shows the percentage of solution attempts that are complete for the source (2007) and hints (2008) groups. For 2008, the attempt and completion rates were 88% and 83%, respectively, out of 40 students. For 2007, these rates were at most 48%, out of 50 students. This may be due to a novelty effect. For all problems but 3.5, there was a slightly higher percentage complete with hints. Problem 3.5 showed much higher completion rates for the hints group, as shown in Figure 33.3.

In the feasibility study, we predicted that proof MDPs built using 16–26 attempts on problem 3.5 have a probability of providing hints 56%–62% of the time [6]. In this experiment, if a student had pressed the hint button after every move taken, a hint would have been available about 48% of the time. This is lower than our prediction. However, the existence of the hint button may have changed student behavior. We were encouraged by the comparison of this rate with the hint availability when students requested hints. In this

TABLE 33.5

Problem Descriptions for Deep Thought Problems

Problem	3.2	3.5	3.6	3.8
Attempts	16	22	26	25
Average length	11.3	18.8	8.0	11.9
Std deviation length	4.0	12.4	5.9	3.1
Min length	7	10	4	7
Max length	18	58	30	19
Expert length	6	8	3	6
Errors	0.9	3.1	1.1	1.1
Time to solve	4:25	9:58	3:23	6:14

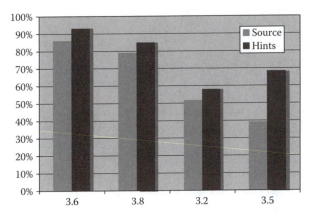

FIGURE 33.3
Percent attempt completion between the source and hints groups. (From Barnes, T. J. et al., A pilot study on logic proof tutoring using hints generated from historical student data, in Baker, R. S. J. d., Barnes, T., and Beck, J. E. (Eds.) *Educational Data Mining 2008: 1st International Conference on Educational Data Mining, Proceedings*. Montreal, Quebec, Canada. June 20–21, 2008, pp. 197–201. Available online at: http://www.educationaldatamining.org/ EDM2008/index.php?page=proceedings)

study, hints were delivered for 91% of hint requests. This suggests that hints are needed precisely where we have data in our MDPs from previous semesters. We plan to investigate the reasons for this surprising result with further data analysis and experiments. It is possible that there are a few key places where many students need help. Another explanation is that, when students are performing actions that have not been taken in the past, they may have high confidence in these steps.

Based on these results (see Table 33.6), we conclude that the hint generator is particularly helpful for harder problems such as 3.5, where students might give up if hints were not available. The hint generator may also encourage lower performing students to persevere in problem-solving.

TABLE 33.6

Hint Usage and Availability by Problem, Including All
Solution Attempts in Spring 2008

Problem	3.2	3.5	3.6	3.8
Attempts	69	57	44	46
% Moves w/ avail. hints	44.2%	45.8%	51.2%	48.7%
% Hints delivered	90.3%	91.4%	94.3%	92.2%
Average # hints	6.82	8.03	3.57	6.63
Min # hints	0	0	0	0
Max # hints	22	44	17	37
Std deviation # hints	2.44	3.68	2.03	1.88

Source: Barnes, T. J. et al., A pilot study on logic proof tutoring using hints generated from historical student data, in Baker, R. S. J. d., Barnes, T., and Beck, J. E. (Eds.) *Educational Data Mining 2008: 1st International Conference on Educational Data Mining, Proceedings*. Montreal, Quebec, Canada. June 20–21, 2008, pp. 197–201. Available online at: http://www.educational datamining.org/EDM2008/index.php?page=proceedings

33.6 Conclusions

In this chapter, we have demonstrated how to augment a CAI with a data-driven automatic hint generator to create an MDP-Tutor for logic proofs. We have also discussed our feasibility studies to verify sufficient hint availability, and a pilot study showing that augmenting the DT-tutor with hints helps more students complete difficult logic proof problems. Using these methods, MDP-Tutors can be created from CAIs in procedural problem-solving domains. Our approach has been used by other researchers in a linked lists tutor called iList, where the MDPs generated based on student work were used to select hints like those given by human tutors, including warning students when their current action is unlikely to lead to a successful problem solution [12].

There are a number of new directions we are exploring with the method. As discussed above, we plan to explore using different reward functions for different types of students when generating hints, including (1) expert, (2) typical, and (3) least error prone. The reward function we have used herein reflects an expert reward function, where the value for a state reflects the shortest path to the goal state. Alternatively, when the "Hint" button is pressed, we could select a personalized reward function for the current student based on their student profile. If we have identified the student as an at-risk student, we may select the "least error-prone" reward function for generating hints. On the other hand, high-performing students would likely benefit from expert hints, while students between these two extremes may benefit from hints reflecting typical student behavior. If there is sufficient data, we can create separate MDPs for students in particular groups, such as high, low, and medium performers on a previous exercise, learning styles, GPA, or other factors, and use these to generate personalized hints. These hints would be contextualized both within the problem and by student characteristics. We also envision using MDPs to create higher level user models that could be applied to a variety of different problems, and to generate statistics to be used in knowledge tracing.

References

1. Anderson, J. and Gluck, K. 2001. What role do cognitive architectures play in intelligent tutoring systems? In D. Klahr and S. Carver (eds.), *Cognition & Instruction: 25 Years of Progress*, pp. 227–262, Erlbaum, Mahwah, NJ.
2. Amershi, S. and Conati, C. 2009. Combining unsupervised and supervised machine learning to build user models for exploratory learning environments. *Journal of Educational Data Mining*, 1(1): 18–71.
3. Baffes, P. and Mooney, R.J. 1996. A novel application of theory refinement to student modeling. *Proceedings of the AAAI-96*, pp. 403–408, Portland, OR, August 1996.
4. Baker, R., Corbett, A.T., Roll, I., and Koedinger, K.R. 2008. Developing a generalizable detector of when students game the system. *User Modeling and User-Adapted Interaction*, 18 (3): 287–314.
5. Barnes, T. and Stamper, J. 2007. Toward the extraction of production rules for solving logic proofs. In C. Heiner, T. Barnes, and N. Heffernan (eds.), *Proceedings of the 13th International Conference on Artificial Intelligence in Education, Educational Data Mining Workshop (AIED2007)*, pp. 11–20, Los Angeles, CA.
6. Barnes, T. and Stamper, J. 2009. Automatic hint generation for logic proof tutoring using historical data. *Journal of Educational Technology & Society, Special Issue on Intelligent Tutoring Systems*, 13(1), 3–12, February 2010.

7. Barnes, T. and Stamper, J. 2009. Utility in hint generation: Selection of hints from a corpus of student work. In V. Dimitrova, R. Mizoguchi, B. du Boulay, and A.C. Graesser (eds.), *Proceedings of 14th International Conference on Artificial Intelligence in Education, AIED 2009*, pp. 197–204, IOS Press, Brighton, U.K., July 6–10, 2009.

8. Beck, J., Woolf, B.P., and Beal, C.R. 2000. ADVISOR: A machine learning architecture for intelligent tutor construction. *Seventh National Conference on Artificial intelligence*, pp. 552–557, AAAI Press/The MIT Press, Menlo Park, CA.

9. Chi, M., Jordan, P.W., VanLehn, K., and Litman, D.J. 2009. To elicit or to tell: Does it matter? In V. Dimitrova, R. Mizoguchi, B. du Boulay, and A.C. Graesser (eds.), *Proceedings of 14th International Conference on Artificial Intelligence in Education, AIED 2009*, pp. 197–204, IOS Press, Brighton, U.K., July 6–10, 2009.

10. Croy, M. 2000. Problem solving, working backwards, and graphic proof representation. *Teaching Philosophy*, 23(2): 169–187.

11. Croy, M., Barnes, T., and Stamper, J. 2007. Towards an intelligent tutoring system for propositional proof construction. In P. Brey, A. Briggle, and K. Waelbers (eds.), *Proceedings of 2007 European Computing and Philosophy Conference*, Enschede, the Netherlands, IOS Publishers, Amsterdam, the Netherlands.

12. Fossati, D., Di Eugenio, B., Ohlsson, S., Brown, C., Chen, L., and Cosejo, D. 2009. I learn from you, you learn from me: How to make iList learn from students. In V. Dimitrova, R. Mizoguchi, B. Du Boulay, and A. Graesser (eds.), *Proceedings of 14th International Conference on Artificial Intelligence in Education, AIED 2009*, IOS Press, Brighton, U.K., July 6–10, 2009.

13. Hui, B., Gustafson, S., Irani, P., and Boutilier, C. 2008. The need for an interaction cost model in adaptive interfaces. In *Proceedings of the Working Conference on Advanced Visual Interfaces*, AVI '08, pp. 458–461, Napoli, Italy, May 28–30, 2008, ACM, New York.

14. Hunt, E. and Madhyastha, T. 2005. Data mining patterns of thought. In *Proceedings of the AAAI 22nd National Conference on Artificial Intelligence Educational Data Mining Workshop (AAAI2005)*, Pittsburgh, PA.

15. Jameson, A., Grossman-Hutter, B., March, L., Rummer, R., Bohnenberger, T., and Wittig, F. 2001. When actions have consequences: Empirically based decision making for intelligent user interfaces. *Knowledge-Based Systems*, 14: 75–92.

16. Koedinger, K.R., Aleven, V., Heffernan. T., McLaren, B., and Hockenberry, M. 2004. Opening the door to non-programmers: Authoring intelligent tutor behavior by demonstration. In *Proceedings of the 7th Intelligent Tutoring Systems Conference*, pp. 162–173, Maceio, Brazil.

17. Matsuda, N., Cohen, W.W., Sewall, J., Lacerda, G., and Koedinger, K.R. 2007. Predicting students performance with SimStudent that learns cognitive skills from observation. In R. Luckin, K. R. Koedinger, and J. Greer (eds.), *Proceedings of the International Conference on Artificial Intelligence in Education*, pp. 467–476, Los Angeles, CA, IOS Press, Amsterdam, the Netherlands.

18. Mayo, M. and Mitrovic, A. 2001. Optimising ITS behaviour with Bayesian networks and decision theory. *International Journal of Artificial Intelligence in Education*, 12: 124–153.

19. McLaren, B., Koedinger, K., Schneider, M., Harrer, A., and Bollen, L. 2004. Bootstrapping Novice data: Semi-automated tutor authoring using student log files. In *Proceedings of the Workshop on Analyzing Student-Tutor Interaction Logs to Improve Educational Outcomes, Proceedings of the 7th International Conference on Intelligent Tutoring Systems (ITS-2004)*, pp. 199–207, Maceió, Brazil.

20. Merceron, A. and Yacef, K. 2005. Educational data mining: A case study. In *12th International Conference on Artificial Intelligence in Education*, IOS Press, Amsterdam, the Netherlands.

21. Mitrovic, A., Koedinger, K., and Martin, B. 2003. A comparative analysis of cognitive tutoring and constraint-based modeling. *User Modeling, Lecture Notes in Computer Science*, Vol. 2702, pp. 313–322. Springer, Berlin, Germany.

22. Murray, T. 1999. Authoring intelligent tutoring systems: An analysis of the state of the art. *International Journal of Artificial Intelligence in Education*, 10: 98–129.

23. Murray, R. C., VanLehn, K., and Mostow, J. 2004. Looking ahead to select tutorial actions: A decision-theoretic approach. *International Journal of Artificial Intelligence in Education*, 14, 3,4 (December 2004), 235–278.

24. Romero, C., Ventura, S., Espejo, P.G., and Hervas, C. 2008. Data mining algorithms to classify students. In *Proceedings of the First International Conference on Educational Data Mining*, pp. 8–17, Montreal, Canada, June 20–21, 2008.
25. Sieg, W. 2007. The AProS project: Strategic thinking & computational logic. *Logic Journal of IGPL*, 15(4): 359–368.
26. Soller, A. 2004. Computational modeling and analysis of knowledge sharing in collaborative distance learning. *User Modeling and User-Adapted Interaction*, 14(4): 351–381.
27. Sutton, S. and Barto, A. 1998. *Reinforcement Learning: An Introduction*, MIT Press, Cambridge, MA.
28. VanLehn, K. 2006. The behavior of tutoring systems. *International Journal of Artificial Intelligence in Education*, 16(3): 227–265.
29. Vygotsky, L. 1986. *Thought and language*, MIT Press, Cambridge, MA.

34

Data Mining Learning Objects

Manuel E. Prieto, Alfredo Zapata, and Victor H. Menendez

CONTENTS

34.1 Introduction

Data mining techniques are applied in education with several perspectives. Many of them are oriented to facilitate students' work or adapt existing systems to their needs. We are interested to improve teachers' and instructional designers' activities. Learning objects (LOs) are of great importance at present, since they are the building blocks of different types of computer-based learning systems. In this chapter, a new approach of data mining used in e-learning is presented. A method and tool to extract and process relevant data from LOs is introduced. A major question is intended to be solved: which data must be considered to be processed to discover important rules about usability of LOs in different environments?

34.2 Introduction: Formulation, Learning Objects

An increasing interest exists about the use LOs to facilitate the reutilization, distribution, and personalization of educational contents in the Internet. LOs promote the portability and the interoperability of learning resources between the e-learning systems. They are widely used in learning management systems and in distance education, but they are also used as aids in business training and even in various forms of informal education.

Even after several years of research and development there is no consensus on the exact LO definition [1,2]; hence, it can be described as follows:

- Any entity, digital or non-digital, which can be used, reused, or referenced during technology-supported learning [3].
- A structured and independent media resource that encapsulates high-quality information to facilitate learning and pedagogy [4].
- Any digital resource that can be used as support for learning [5].

The definitions are diverse but, in general, all of them consider LOs as recyclable media content items that have an educational purpose. We consider an LO as any digital entity developed with instructional design intentions, which can be used, reused, or referenced for learning.

Many LOs are produced, but their availability cannot be guaranteed sometimes due to a lack of metadata, or because they are not properly organized or categorized. Its reusability is limited because the information about their content is not standardized and very often is either absent or incomplete.

Metadata generation, evaluation, or search are frequent activities that can provide relevant data about LOs in order to determine their use in different environments. It is important, therefore, to provide methods and tools adapted to analyze LOs from their educational dimensions points of view.

The use of data mining techniques has produced good results specially with models that can assess student's knowledge and skills from observation [6] or in automatic generation of hints for students using their historical data [7]. On the other hand, in studies [8,9] geared to provide mechanisms for adjusting the systems, to the learner's individual needs, were presented.

This chapter presents the advances in knowledge discovery activity, applying the knowledge discovery in databases (KDD) and, particularly, the data mining (DM) techniques to the information that can be drawn from LOs. The following results are presented:

- A classification scheme of data categories of LOs
- The LOs management system "AGORA"
- A method for LO data mining
- The results of a pilot implementation of the method to data gathered from AGORA

34.3 Data Sources in Learning Objects

Information about LOs is diverse and often poorly structured. To conduct studies about characteristics, design, and use of LOs, it is necessary to have an appropriate framework.

Efforts in this direction generally considered the objects only partially, especially for not covering its multiple computational or pedagogical aspects as well as their design and use. In recent years we have focused, among other things, to determine a set of attributes that can represent main LOs characteristics as fully as possible. We propose a characterization of LOs, based on three data categories to be processed:

- Metadata
- External assessments
- Information obtained when managing LOs

34.3.1 Metadata

Metadata contains primary and objective information about LOs. They represent a way of characterizing introspective object's analysis. Metadata standards facilitate reusability, search, and adaptation to different environments. However, in many cases, metadata are missing, incomplete, or poorly constructed. Main standards and specifications cover various aspects such as follows:

- Packaging (e.g., IMS CP [10] and SCORM Content Package 2004 [11])
- Labeling (e.g., IMS MD [12], IEEE-LOM [3])
- Sequencing (e.g., IMS Simple Sequencing [13])

SCORM 2004 is one of the most widely used packaging specifications. It is based on IMS metadata, a profile application of IEEE Learning Object Metadata (LOM) specification. LOM is a specification, encoded in XML, which describes a set of metatags used to represent metadata. These metadata are teaching and learning oriented, but they are insufficient to suit the needs of various educational systems.

In LOM, tags can be filled with two types of values: those for "controlled vocabulary" and the "free text" values. Labels are formalized in an XML multi-scheme that implements the specification and, in this way, LOM provides a mechanism for adjusting the specification called "application profile," which must meet the following restrictions:

- It must preserve data types and the element's value areas of the basic scheme.
- It cannot define new data types or value areas for the added elements.

LOM-ES [14] is a Spanish application profile that contains several extensions, especially new labels and vocabularies. It is used in LOs classification according to a set of rules including taxonomies and thesaurus that permits to specify, among others, discipline, idea, prerequisite, educational objective, accessibility restrictions, instructional level, or skills level. LOM-ES supports the development of several important services such as the LOs search and retrieval in federated repositories, or content previewing. We used LOM-ES for data analysis including 15 attributes as aggregation, interactivity levels, semantic density, structure, and language. Nevertheless, the general method proposed is also applicable when using other schemes or specifications.

34.3.2 External Assessments

Evaluation schemes respond to the practices used in behavioral sciences to assess the quality of resources and practices in education. LOs are also subject to the application of such techniques, mostly based on expert assessments. Data obtained from LOs by this route are mostly subjective and based on the use of questionnaires to measure impacts in learning results.

There are no internationally recognized standards or schemes to assess the quality or usability of LOs. Some systems are oriented to assess particular technological or pedagogical attributes.

Our proposal seeks to contribute in this regard. A methodology was developed and also an instrument that involves the assessment of the most important aspects of learning objectives from the pedagogical point of view, as well as the technical features not included in metadata.

The MECOA [15] (in Spanish means quality evaluation model for learning objects) contains 22 attributes that include those relating to the interface, the current level of content, the matching resources with the learning goal, the type of educational activity, or the degree of difficulty in dealing with the content. This method is also applicable when using other schemes for quality assessment.

34.3.3 Information Obtained When Managing Learning Objects

In this category, we include all data obtained from systems that support the management LOs. An important example of this is the repository management system. But, there are other applications able to collect relevant LOs data. Nowadays we consider the following:

- Search engines and meta-searchers
- Automatic metadata generators
- LOs composition systems
- Repository management systems

The AGORA system [16], which is briefly presented in the following section, is an attempt to provide an unified platform for the LOs management whose intention is to facilitate the design and use of such resources by teachers and instructional designers.

34.4 The Learning Object Management System AGORA

The framework AGORA (from a Spanish acronym that means help for the management of reusable learning objects) aims to provide an infrastructure that supports the development of instructional design activity. Particularly, it provides solutions for LOs management. As result of the project, an operational version of the system has been designed, implemented, and tested. The main components of AGORA are

- A knowledge base consisting of instructional ontologies. The initial version includes models of instructional design and methodology for the population, editing, and refinement of instructional engineering ontologies.
- A system for automatic discovery of knowledge about instructional design based on KDD techniques. This chapter presents details of this subsystem.

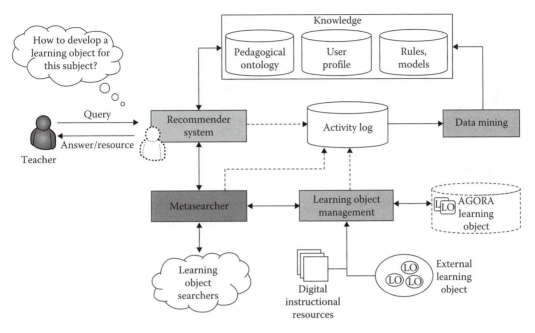

FIGURE 34.1
AGORA architecture.

- A module for LOs management. It aims at cataloguing, development, and processing LOs based on accepted international standards. It includes mechanisms for automatic metadata generation and a repository management system.
- A semantic meta-search engine specialized in e-learning resources available in multiple repositories through a semantic approach that improves the chances of getting relevant results according to the user's instructional needs.
- A method and a tool for assessing the quality of digital learning resources.
- A recommender system capable of supporting LOs design, search, recovery, and reuse activities based on the resource development requirements and the teachers' profiles.

AGORA Architecture is shown in Figure 34.1.

34.5 Methodology

We take as reference a methodology that contains the same stages contained in the general process for data mining [17]; particularly, for e-learning applications we propose a data mining methodology for course management systems (CMS) that focuses on the study of learner's interactions [8].

We propose a data mining process for LOs and its characteristics. This method contains four stages with data: collect, preprocess, apply data mining and interpret, evaluate, and deploy the results. We considered the AGORA platform as case of study (Figure 34.2).

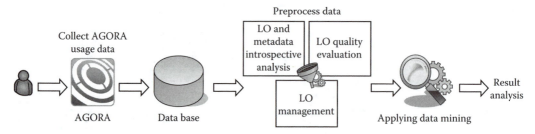

FIGURE 34.2
Scheme learning objects KDD.

34.5.1 Collect Data

The information used for the study is obtained from the AGORA platform log files. In AGORA, teachers generate, search, evaluate, and interact with LOs. Examples of the values recorded into the system are the user name, activity name, action time, activity duration, given parameters, etc. All these data are a rich source of knowledge about patterns, characteristics, and profiles of the users, resources, and tasks.

34.5.2 Preprocess the Data

It is important to adapt data during preprocessing stage, considering the nature of the available information about LOs. This contains major differences of this method with regard to preceding ones.

The details of all four preprocessing activities and our tests are presented below.

34.5.2.1 Select Data

For the study, we used data obtained from a set sample of 60 LOs from a total of 580 stored objects. These objects were published in the AGORA platform by 155 teachers of public and private universities of Mexico, Argentina, Chile, and Spain. LOs were selected taking into consideration their biggest amount of attribute data available.

34.5.2.2 Create Summarization Tables

Four tables were defined. Three of them obtained from data categorizing LOs (metadata, evaluations, and management). The fourth table was based on the merging of the previous three.

In the metadata analysis, attributes were based on the standard LOM-ES. (However, some categories were not included, due to limits in the current version of AGORA).

For the quality evaluation table, the attributes were based on the MECOA quality assessment method, including indicators for LOs evaluation from a pedagogic perspective and some computational attributes not included in metadata.

For the management table, the attributes were based on the available information about the teachers' behavior patterns regarding their manipulation of LOs. Some teachers' profile data are also included.

For the merged table, attributes from the three previous categories were included.

34.5.2.3 Data Discretization

The data discretization was done only in the log activity user. Labels were generated for the different attribute tables. In the metadata and MECOA tables, their values are labeled by default. These labels facilitate the field edition. They also help in the later interpretation of results. To decide if this activity is necessary an expert is consulted to get an adequate discretization; for example, the labels for MECOA tables were generated with the help of education experts.

34.5.2.4 Data Transformation

Data tables were transformed into datasets, which were exported to ARFF format (attribute-relation file format), allowing a best portability for the application of data mining algorithms. These data are now described in detail.

The first dataset was formed from the LOs metadata information. For this set, 15 attributes were used from the LOM-ES standard with 60 LO instances. Examples of this group of attributes are structure, format, and interactivity level.

For the second set, the information generated from LO evaluations was used. For this set, 22 attributes were established, all of them based in the MECOA model and 60 LO instances. Examples of this group of attributes are information quality, cognitive process, and references.

The third set was created by means of the activity carried on by teachers with LOs. The set uses 22 attributes based on the activity of the teachers, their profiles, and the classes they give. Examples of this group of attributes are educational experience, discipline, and resources downloaded.

The fourth dataset is the result of merging all the previous sets, and it is shaped by 59 attributes and all the 60 instances. The data was cleaned and transformed into an adequate format for the data mining process.

34.5.3 Apply Data Mining and Interpret Results

For this stage, we used WEKA (Waikato Environment for Knowledge Analysis) [18] that provide data mining algorithms for clustering, classification, and association. In this section, for each algorithm used in the study, the test characteristic and results obtained are shown. These results can be presented in the form of tables or graphs.

34.5.3.1 Clustering Algorithms

For clustering testing, the following algorithms were used: SimpleKmeans [19] and EM (expectation maximization) [20]. Eight tests were realized with EM and SimpleKmeans algorithms. In each test, the number of clusters was calibrated to generate the greater amount of clusters having mutually exclusive attributes. In Figure 34.3, some clusters obtained are presented.

34.5.3.2 Classification Algorithms

We considered some of the attributes that define the clusters as a class. This is achieved using ID3 (induction decision trees) [21] and J48 [22] algorithms. These tests are intended to verify the effectiveness in the classification rules generation from both systems and thus provide corroboration if rules are similar.

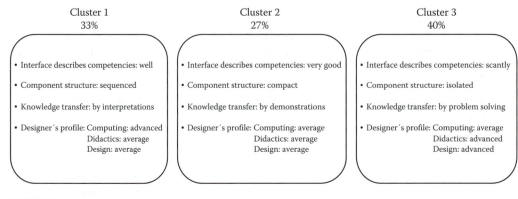

FIGURE 34.3
Clustering results.

Various tests were verified with ID3 and J48 algorithms with the already mentioned datasets. In accordance with the attribute's main pedagogical impact from the expert's points of view, respective classification attributes were defined for LOs:

- Semantic density, whose labels are very low, low, medium, high, very high
- Knowledge transfer, whose labels are examples, demos, applications, interpretations, none

We obtained a set of IF-THEN-ELSE rules from the algorithms. After an analysis, we eliminated those rules that were with irrelevant information. Tables 34.1 and 34.2 show some of the best rules obtained.

TABLE 34.1

Some of the Best Rules Obtained with the ID3 Algorithm

Rules—Generated	Rules—Interpretation
Considering the *semantic density* as classification attribute	
format = PPT; knowledge transfer = demonstrations; media balance = regular => *high*	The LO has a *high semantic density* if it does fulfill the next requirements: has a PPT format, contains demonstrations, and the media balance is regular.
format = SWF; media balance = basic; structure = atomic => *high*	The LO has a *high semantic density* if it does fulfill the next requirements: has an SWF format, the media balance is basic, and the structure is atomic.
format = PDF; educational resource type = reading => *very low*	The LO has a *very low semantic density* if it does fulfill the next requirements: has a PDF format and is used as a reading in class.
Considering *knowledge transfer* as classification attributes	
conceptual structure = index; motivation = introduction to problem; format = DOC => *interpretations*	The LO provides *interpretations for the knowledge transfer* if it does fulfill the next requirements: contains an index, introduction to a problem, and has a DOC format.
conceptual structure = symbology; initiative = programmed answers => *applications*	The LO provides *applications for the knowledge transfer* if it does fulfill the next requirements: contains symbols and programmed answers.
semantic density = medium; information quality = deep => *applications*	The LO provides *applications for the knowledge transfer* if it does fulfill the next requirements: medium semantic density and excellent information quality.

TABLE 34.2

Some of the Best Rules Obtained with the J48 Algorithm

Rules—Generated	Rules—Interpretation
Considering the *semantic density* as classification attribute	
format = PDF; user contribution = publisher; type contribution = publisher editor; => *low* (7.0/4.0)	The LO has a *very low semantic density* if it does fulfill the next requirements: has a PDF format, the user publishes and corrects the resource.
contribution = creator; modality = blended learning => *high* (4.0)	The LO has a *high semantic density* if it does fulfill the next requirements: the user designs the resource and is used in blended learning.
user contribution = publisher; type contribution = publisher editor; format = HTML; result = knowledge; conceptual structure = graphics => *very high* (3.0)	The LO has a *very high semantic density* if it does fulfill the next requirements: the user publishes and corrects the resource, has a HTML format, knowledge transfer, and contains graphs.
Considering *knowledge transfer* as classification attributes	
components = integrated; semantic density = medium => *applications* (11.0/5.0)	The LO provides *application for the knowledge transfer* if it does fulfill the next requirements: integrated components and medium semantic density.
components = integrated; semantic density = low; problems solution = yes => *applications* (2.0)	The LO provides *applications for the knowledge transfer* if it does fulfill the next requirements: integrated components, low semantic density, and contains problem solutions.
components = integrated; semantic density = high => *examples* (10.0/3.0)	The LO provides *examples for the knowledge transfer* if it does fulfill the next requirements: the components are integrated, and high semantic density.

34.5.3.3 Association Algorithms

For the association rules generation we executed the Apriori algorithm [23]. For this algorithm, we determined the generation of 100 rules, which have a minimum support of 0.3 and minimum confidence of 0.9 as parameters.

We obtained a set of IF-THEN rules from the algorithms. After an analysis, we eliminated those rules that were with irrelevant information. Table 34.3 shows some of the best rules obtained.

TABLE 34.3

Some of Best Rules Obtained with the APriori Algorithm

Reliability	Rules—Generated	Rules—Interpretation
0.98	version = final; environment = classroom => *aggregation level* = 1	*If* the LO consists of the final version and is used in presencial learning, *then* aggregation level is basic.
0.99	structure = atomic; version = final; environment = classroom => *aggregation level* = 1	*If* the LO consists of atomic structure, final version, and is used in presencial learning, *then* aggregation level is basic.
0.97	aggregation level = 1; version = final; easy navigation = security => *environment* = *classroom*	*If* the LO is basic and security navigation *then* it is used in presencial learning.
0.98	version = final; level = vocational training => *aggregation level* = 1	*If* the LO consists of final version and is oriented to professional training *then* aggregation level is basic.

34.6 Conclusions

In this chapter, we presented an adapted methodology for the application of data mining techniques to LOs, trying to discover relevant characteristics in its design and usage characteristics.

For this method, the learning object management system AGORA was used for evaluating LO data from three main perspectives: metadata, quality assessments, and several management activities. Some tests were carried out using clustering and classification algorithms. Particular details about processing LOs data were presented.

The method and results allow improving the work of teachers in designing and searching, and also in the management of LOs required for their activities. This proposal seeks to obtain knowledge about the possibilities of using data mining technologies in education, improving the work of teachers, and instructional designers.

It shows that the use of methods and data mining techniques are useful for the discovery of knowledge from information available in LOs. For example, it is possible to generate rules from information related to user profiles. The rule set can be used to improve certain processes, such as searching, sequencing, and editing of LOs.

Clustering tests provided us with relevant information about the attributes that define each group. The classification and association tests supplied information significant of the key attributes that provide information to the LOs rules.

The obtained rules allow the development of classifiers to improve the search mechanisms in AGORA. For example, information relating to user profiles and their needs may be considered as filters for the recommendation of resources or users with similar needs.

This is a first approach to redefine attributes and consider other information sources to supplement LOM and allows us to establish what elements are crucial to classify, suggest, or recommend action values in a learning management system.

Acknowledgments

This work is partially supported by AECID A/016625/08 Project (Spain), YUC 2006-C05-65811 project FOMIX CONACYT (México), Consejo Nacional de Ciencia y Tecnología CONACYT (México), Consejo de Ciencia y Tecnología del Estado de Yucatán CONCyTEY (México) Programa de Mejoramiento del Profesorado PROMEP (México).

References

1. Knolmayer, G.F., Decision support models for composing and navigating through e-learning objects. In *The 36th Annual Hawaii International Conference on System Sciences (HICSS'03)*, Big Island, Track 1, HI, 2003.
2. Mohan, P., Reusable online learning resources: Problems, solutions and opportunities. In *The Fourth IEEE International Conference on Advanced Learning Technologies (ICALT'04)*, Joensuu, Finland, pp. 904–905, 2004.

3. Institute of Electrical and Electronics Engineers, L.T.S.C. Draft standard for learning object metadata, IEEE, 1484.12.1, 2002. http://ltsc.ieee.org/wg12/files/LOM_1484_12_1_v1_Final_Draft.pdf (accessed December 15, 2008).

4. Nugent, G., Soh, L.-K., Samal, A., Person, S., and Lang, J., Design, development, and validation of a learning object for CS1. In *The 10th Annual SIGCSE Conference on Innovation and Technology in Computer Science Education,* Lisbon, Portugal, ACM, Caparica, Portugal, 2005.

5. Wiley, D., Connecting learning objects to instructional design theory: A definition, a metaphor, and a taxonomy. *The Instructional Use of Learning Objects,* Wiley, D.A. (ed.), Association for Educational Communications and Technology, Bloomington, IN, 2002.

6. Desmarais, M., Villareal, A., and Gagnon, M., Adaptive test design with a naïve bayes framework. In *First International Conference on EDM,* Montreal, Canada, 2008. http://www.educationaldatamining.org/EDM2008/uploads/proc/5_Desmarais_17.pdf (accessed December 18, 2008).

7. Barnes, T., Stamper, J., Lehman, L., and Croy, M., A pilot study on logic proof tutoring using hints generated from historical student data. In *First International Conference on EDM,* Montreal, Canada, 2008. http://www.educationaldatamining.org/EDM2008/uploads/proc/22_Barnes_41a.pdf (accessed December 18, 2008).

8. Romero, C., Ventura, S., and García, E., Data mining in course management systems: Moodle case study and tutorial. Department of Computer Sciences and Numerical Analysis, University of Córdoba, 2007. http://sci2s.ugr.es/keel/pdf/specific/articulo/CAE-VersionFinal.pdf (accessed October 10, 2008).

9. Ventura, S., Romero, C., and Hervás, C., Analyzing rule evaluation measures with educational datasets: A framework to help the teacher. In *First International Conference on EDM,* Montreal, Canada, 2008. http://www.educationaldatamining.org/EDM2008/uploads/proc/18_Ventura_4.pdf (accessed December 2, 2008).

10. IMS Global Learning Consortium, IMS content packaging, 2004. http://www.imsglobal.org/content/packaging/cpv1p1p4/imscp_bestv1p1p4.html (accessed December 20, 2008).

11. Advanced Distributed Learning. Sharable Content Object Reference Model (SCORM), Overview, 2004. http://www.adlnet.org/index.cfm?fuseaction=scormabt (accessed october 15, 2008).

12. IMS Global Learning Consortium. Learning design specification, 2003. http://www.imsglobal.org/learningdesign/ldv1p0/imsld_infov1p0.html (accessed December 20, 2008).

13. IMS Global Learning Consortium. IMS Simple sequencing, 2003. http://www.imsglobal.org/simplesequencing/index.html (accessed December 20, 2008).

14. Blanco, J.J., Galisteo del Valle, A., and García, A., Perfil de aplicación LOM-ES V.1.0. *Asociación Española de Normalización y Certificación (AENOR),* 2006. http://www.educaplus.org/documentos/lom-es_v1.pdf (accessed December 16, 2008).

15. Prieto, M.E. et al., Metodología y herramientas para la evaluación de la calidad de los recursos para tele-aprendizaje en la formación de profesores, *Internal Report.* Agencia Española de Cooperación Internacional para el Desarrollo, Proyecto AECI A/8172/07, 2008.

16. Prieto, M., Menéndez, V., Segura, A., and Vidal, C. 2008. Recommender system architecture for instructional engineering. In *First World Summit on the Knowledge Society,* Athens, Greece, pp. 314–321, September 24–28, 2008.

17. Fayyad, U., Piatetsky-Shapiro, G., and Smyth, P., *The KDD Process for Extracting Useful Knowledge from Volumes of Data,* ACM, New York, 1996. http://www.citeulike.org/user/imrchen/article/1886790 (accessed November 18, 2008).

18. Witten, I. H. and Frank, E., *Data Mining: Practical Machine Learning Tools and Techniques,* Morgan Kaufman, San Francisco, CA, 2005.

19. MacQueen, J., Some methods for classification and analysis of multivariate observations. In *Proceedings of the Fifth Berkeley Symposium on Mathematical Statistics and Probability,* Berkeley, CA, pp. 281–297, 1967.

20. Dempster, A., Laird, N., and Rubin, D., Maximum likelihood from incomplete data via the EM algorithm. *Journal of the Royal Statistical Society,* 39(1), 1–38, 1977.

21. Quinlan, J. R., Induction to decision trees. *Machine Learning*, 1(1), 81–106, 1986.
22. Ye, P. and Baldwin, T., Semantic role labeling of prepositional phrases. In *The Second International Joint Conference on Natural Language Processing*, Jeju Island, Korea, pp. 779–791, 2005.
23. Agarwal, R., Imielinski, T., and Swami, A., Mining association rules between sets of items in large databases. In *Proceedings of the 1993 ACM SIGMOD International Conference on Management of Data*, Washington, DC, pp. 207–216, 1993.

35

An Adaptive Bayesian Student Model for Discovering the Student's Learning Style and Preferences

Cristina Carmona, Gladys Castillo, and Eva Millán

CONTENTS

35.1 Introduction

In the last years, a considerable number of online educational data designed as *learning objects repositories** has been implemented (e.g., MERLOT [1] and ARIADNE [2]). Using learning object repositories is a way to increase the flexibility and manageability of rich libraries of learning resources available online from academic institutions, publishers, and organizations. In such repositories, learning objects are shared across different learning environments and can be accessed on demand either by learners or instructors.

One of the key issues concerning the use of learning object repositories is the retrieval and searching facilities of learning objects. One approach is to *"filter"* and *"sort"* the learning objects according to the student's learning style and preferences, so he or she can make a better use of them. To this end, students' learning styles can be acquired using one of the existing psychometric instruments. Then, some decision rules are established. Such rules represent the matches between learning styles and educational objects. Following this idea, some educational hypermedia systems have implemented different learning style models for a better adaptation of their educational resources to their users (e.g., MANIC [4], AES-CS [5], INSPIRE [6], iWeaver [7], TANGOW/WOTAN [8], WHURLE [9], and CS383 [10]). However, as argued in [11], "There are no proven recipes for the application of learning styles in adaptation." First, in the majority of these approaches,

---

* The learning object metadata [3] is a standard to specify the syntax and semantics of learning objects using a set of attributes that adequately describe them.

assumptions about the student's learning style are static, that is, once acquired, they are no longer updated with evidence gathered from the student's interactions with the system. The rules included in the decision models do not change either. Thus, the model is used for adaptation, but it is unable to adapt itself with new evidences. Second, during the interaction with the system, the student could change his or her preferences for another kind of learning object that no longer matches with his or her inferred learning style, a problem known as *concept drift* [12]. In these scenarios, *adaptive decision models*, capable of better fitting the current student's preferences, are desirable.

The main contribution of our approach is that the model presented is adaptive, i.e., the initial acquired information about the student's learning style and preferences is updated according to the results of the student's interactions with the system. We use all the background knowledge available to build an initial *learning style model* and a *decision model* for each particular student. The *learning style model*, represented as a Bayesian network (BN) [13] and based on the Felder–Silverman learning style model [14], classifies students in four dimensions: *processing, perception, input,* and *understanding*.

To initialize the learning style model, we use the Felder and Solomon Index of Learning Style Questionnaire [15]. Completing the questionnaire is not mandatory for the student, so if he or she chooses not to answer it, we use the uniform distribution. Then, the student's selections are set as evidences in the model, triggering the evidence propagation mechanism and getting up-to-date beliefs for the learning styles. This learning style model was first introduced in [16]. For the decision model, we use a BN classifier [17] that represents the matches between learning styles and learning objects in order to decide if a resource is interesting to a student or not. We use a subset of metadata attributes to represent a learning object [3], in particular, those related with the learning style dimensions: *Format, Learning Resource Type, Interactivity Level, Interactivity Type,* and *Semantic Density*.

We learn an initial classifier from data randomly generated by some predefined rules. Then, when the student selects a resource (and eventually gives feedback), we will incorporate this information to the model in order to reflect more accurately the current preferences. Moreover, our decision model is capable of adapting quickly to any change of the student's preferences. This proposal is an improvement of the approach proposed in [18] and was first presented in [19], where the learning style once acquired was not updated and the decision model was modeled using an adaptive naive Bayes classifier.

In Section 35.2, we explain the design of the learning style model. Section 35.3 is devoted to the description of the decision model. Next, in Section 35.4, we briefly describe the whole process aimed at selecting the proper learning objects for a student each time he or she makes a topic selection. Finally, we conclude with a summary and a description of ongoing and future work.

35.2 The Learning Style Model

Learning styles can be defined as the different ways a person collects, processes, and organizes information. We choose the Felder–Silverman Learning Style Model [14] to model learning styles since it is one of the more popular models and has been implemented in many e-learning systems, for example [8–10]. The Felder–Silverman model classifies students in four dimensions: *active/reflective* (processing), *sensing/intuitive* (perception), *visual/verbal* (input), and *sequential/global* (understanding). To determine a student learning style, Felder and Soloman proposed the index of learning style questionnaire [15]. The questionnaire classifies student's preferences for each category as *mild*, *moderate*, or *strong*. The results of this test, if the student has chosen to take it, are used to initialize the learning style model. In general, the use of tests to initialize student models has some drawbacks. First, students tend to choose answers arbitrarily. Second, it is really difficult to design tests capable of exactly measuring "how people learn." Therefore, the information gathered through these instruments encloses some grade of uncertainty. Moreover, this information, as a rule, is no longer updated with evidences gathered from the student's interactions with the system.

Our approach uses a BN to model the student's learning style [21,22], instead of acquiring it by a psychometric test. A BN [23] is composed of two components: the *qualitative part* (its structure) and the *quantitative part* (the set of parameters that quantifies the network). The structure is a directed acyclic graph whose nodes represent random variables, and the arcs represent dependencies (causal influence relationship) between the variables. The parameters are conditional probabilities that represent the strength of the relationships. The Bayesian learning style model allows observations about the user's behavior to discover learning styles automatically using the inference mechanisms. In these works, the BN structure is designed by the experts and the parameters are specified from data obtained from both the expert and the log files.

We propose to design the learning style model using a hybrid approach. The four dimensions of the learning styles model are initialized according to the initial test results. We then observe the student's selections of different learning objects to set them as evidences in the BN. Therefore, whenever new evidences about the preferences of the student arrive (student's selections and feedback) the propagation mechanism is automatically triggered and gets up-to-date beliefs for the learning style. Thus, we can refine the initial values for the student's learning style acquired by the initial test as the student interacts with the system, thus becoming more and more confident over time. In our BN model, we consider three types of variables:

1. *Variables to represent the student's learning style*—one variable for each dimension of the model: *Input* = {visual, verbal}; *Processing* = {active, reflective}; *Perception* = {sensing, intuitive}; *Understanding* = {sequential, global}.

2. *Variables to represent the selected learning object*—one variable for each metadata attribute that we consider significant for modeling learning style (see Table 35.1):

TABLE 35.1

Learning Style vs. Learning Object Type Attribute

	Visual	Verbal	Sensing	Intuitive	Sequential	Global	Active	Reflective
Exercise	□	■	■	□	■	□	■	□
Simulation	■	□	■	□	■	□	■	□
Questionnaire	□	■	□	■	■	□	■	□
Figure	■	□	■	□	□	■	□	■
Index	□	■	■	□	□	■	□	■
Table	■	□	■	□	□	■	□	■
Narrative-Text	□	■	□	■	■	□	□	■
Exam	□	■	■	□	■	□	■	□
Lecture	□	■	□	■	■	□	□	■

SelectedFormat = {text, image, audio, video, application}; *SelectedLearningObjectType* = {exercise, simulation, questionnaire, figure, index, table, narrative text, exam, lecture}; *SelectedInteractivityLevel* = {very-low, low, medium, high, very-high}; *Selected InteractivityType* = {active, expositive, mixed}; *SelectedSemanticDensity* = {very-low, low, medium, high, very-high}.

3. *A variable representing the student rating for that learning object*—the student can rate the selected object from 1star to 5stars: *SelectedRating* = {star1, star2, star3, star4, star5}.

Regarding the relationships between the variables, we consider that the student's learning style determines the student's learning objects selections and that the selected learning object and the student's learning style determine the rating value for that learning object. Before the selection of the learning object, the student only knows its format and the activity it implements. We consider that the student's selection shows his or her preferences for a particular kind of learning object, and the preferences are influenced by the student's learning style. Only after selecting and viewing the learning object the student can rate it. After having explored several possibilities for modeling the learning style dimensions, we choose to model each dimension separately, thus obtaining four BN models as depicted in Figure 35.1.

To define the a priori distribution for nodes representing the learning style dimensions, we use the score obtained by the student in the initial test if the student took the test, or a uniform distribution, otherwise. To estimate the conditional probabilities between learning style dimensions and each learning object attribute, we use some "matching tables" previously defined by an expert. These tables allow us to match learning styles with learning object's attributes. An example of such a matching table for the *SelectedLearningObjectType* variable is shown in Table 35.1.

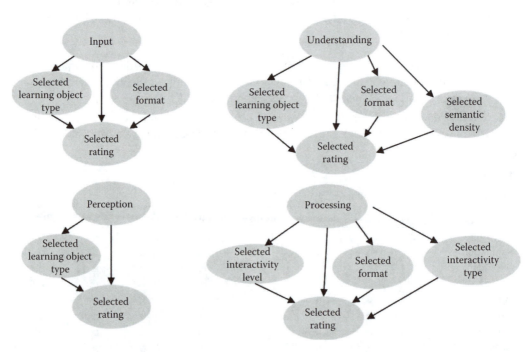

FIGURE 35.1
Modeling the four dimensions of the learning style.

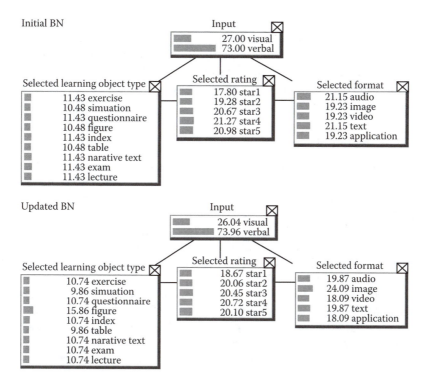

FIGURE 35.2
Updated beliefs for the input dimension after the student's selection.

For instance, suppose a student takes the initial test and obtains for the *Input* dimension: *visual* = 3 and *verbal* = 8. This student is classified as *verbal-moderate*. Next, every time the student makes a selection, the *sequential update algorithm* [13] is triggered in order to incorporate the new information into the BN model. That makes it possible to refine the initial beliefs for the student's learning style accordingly. If the student changes his or her preferences, that is, he or she begins to select objects that do not match with our current estimation of his or her learning style, this network is able to interpret and account for this information and update the model. Figure 35.2 shows how the beliefs of the BN are updated after several students' selections.

35.3 The Decision Model

The decision model helps to determine whether a given resource is appropriate for a specific learning style or not. This model uses a BN classifier, and its behavior is quite similar to a content-based recommender system.* The information about the resource (the item to

---

* A recommender system tries to present to the user the information items he or she is interested in. To do this, the user's profile is compared to some reference characteristics. These characteristics may be from the information item (the content-based approach) or the user's social environment (the collaborative-filtering approach).

recommend) and the user's learning style (the user's features) are presented to the classifier as input, having as output a probability that represents the appropriateness of the resource for this student (or how interesting the item is for this user). There are two issues that are crucial in the definition of the decision model. First, the *cold-start problem*, that is, the problem of obtaining the data to build the initial model. Second, the adaptation procedure for updating the model with new data.

35.3.1 Building the Initial Model

The acquired information about the student's learning style helps us to initialize the DM. To this end the system's author must establish the rules to match learning styles with the proper resource's characteristics. In this implementation, such rules are extracted from the tables previously explained (see Table 35.1 for an example). After that, the predefined matching rules are used to generate some training examples. These examples are described through ten attributes: the first four represent the *student's learning style*, the next five represent the *learning object*, and the last one is the class. The possible values for each attribute are presented in Table 35.2.

For instance, the example *1,4,3,1,6,2,1,2,5,1* means that a student, with a *strong preference* for VISUAL, a *moderate preference* for INTUITIVE, a *mild preference* for SEQUENTIAL, and a *strong preference* for ACTIVE, likes a resource implementing the learning activity TABLE in the format IMAGE with an *Interactivity Level* VERY-LOW and *Interactivity Type* EXPOSITIVE; and with *Semantic Density* VERY-HIGH. Finally, the generated examples can be used to learn a model (classifier) that gives the minimum error rate.

We choose the class of *k*-Dependence Bayesian Classifiers (*k*-DBCs) [20] to represent our decision model. A *k*-DBC is a BN, with a naive Bayes* structure that allows each attribute to have a maximum of *k* attribute nodes as parents. To define the initial model, we carried out some experiments in order to select the best classifier among the BN classifiers belonging to the *k*-DBCs that best fits the training examples generated from the predefined

TABLE 35.2

Establishing the Attributes and Their Possible Values

Attributes	Values
Input	visualStrong (1); visualModerate (2); balanced (3); verbalModerate (4); verbalStrong (5)
Perception	sensingStrong (1); sensingModerate (2); balanced (3); intuitiveModerate (4); intuitiveStrong (5)
Understanding	sequentialStrong (1); sequentialModerate (2); balanced (3); globalModerate (4); globalStrong (5)
Processing	activeStrong (1); activeModerate (2); balanced (3); reflectiveModerate (4); reflectiveStrong (5)
Learning Object Type	Exercise (1); simulation (2); questionnaire (3); figure (4); index (5); table (6); narrative text (7); exam (8); lecture (9)
Format	Text (1); image (2); audio (3); video (4); application (5)
Interactivity Level	Very-low (1); low (2); medium (3); high (4); very-high (5)
Interactivity Type	Active (1); expositive (2); mixed (3)
Semantic Density	Very-low (1); low (2); medium (3); high (4); very-high (5)

---

* A naive Bayes is a BN with a simple structure that has the class node as the parent node of all other feature nodes.

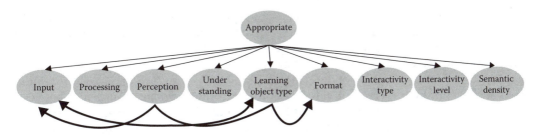

FIGURE 35.3
Initial decision model.

rules extracted from matching tables. We generated several datasets using an increasing number of instances (3125, 6250, 9375, 12500, 15625, 18750, and 21875) and generated 10 samples for each setting. For each dataset, all the possible learning styles are represented. Since there are 4 attributes for the learning style and each one has 5 values, we obtain 625 different learning styles. We generated datasets with 5, 10, 15, 20, 25, 30, and 35 examples for each learning style. The learning object characteristics were generated randomly and the obtained examples were classified according to the matching rules. We then learn different models from the generated data: the naive Bayes and several k-DBCs varying k from 1 to 5. To learn the k-DBCs, we apply, in conjunction with a score, a hill-climbing procedure as explained in [25]. In the experiments, we use different scores (BAYES, MDL, and AIC) with a 10-fold cross validation. From the error rates obtained with each model and each score, we found that the best model was a 2-DBC. From $k > 2$, the accuracy does not improve significantly, which may indicate that we found a 2-degree of dependence in these domains. Regarding the score function, the AIC score produces the low error rate, but the model generated is very complex, almost every node has two parents (besides the class), so we chose the model generated using the BAYES score because of its simplicity and good performance. The error rate for the 2-DBC model with the BAYES score is 6.3%. The structure of the chosen model is shown in Figure 35.3. In addition to the relationships between the class and the attributes, we found other dependences between the attributes.

35.3.2 Adapting the Model

During further interactions of the user with the system, the initial model is adapted using the data generated from the user behavior. In order to compose the required examples with the correct class, we need to obtain some feedback about how much the student likes or dislikes a particular resource. To this end we observe the ratings of the visited resources. Whenever we obtain new labeled examples, they can be used to update the model. We are very interested in adapting the model in such a way that the most recent observations gathered through relevant feedback represents the current user's preferences better than the older ones. To this end, we propose an adaptation of the iterative Bayes algorithm [24] included in the adaptive prequential learning framework (AdPreqFr4SL) for BN classifiers [25] to this particular task. As shown in many experiments, the most important characteristic of the AdPreqFr4SL is its ability to improve the predictive performance with new data and deal with concept drift scenarios. Particularly, iterative Bayes performs an optimization process based on an iterative updating of the BN's parameters. In each iteration, and for each example, the corresponding conditional probabilities are updated so as to increase the probability on the correct class. Given an example, an increment is computed and added to all the corresponding counters of the predicted class and proportionally sub-tracted to the counters of all the other classes. If an example is correctly classified then the increment is positive and equal to 1–P(predicted|X), otherwise it is negative. Experimental evaluation showed consistent reductions of the error rate. The main idea we propose is to use the student's ranks instead of the categorical class values for the adaptation procedure. We consider different increment values according to the *quantitative differences* between the observed class and the predicted class. For instance, if a learning object is classified as *appropriate* with a high probability (*5star*) and the student rates this learning object as *4star*, then we use an increment with a value greater than the value used when the student ranks this resource as *1star*.

35.4 Selecting the Suitable Learning Objects

The whole process (see Figure 35.4) to select the proper learning objects for a given topic according to the *student's characteristics* (knowledge level, learning style, and preferences) and the *characteristics of the learning objects* (as defined in the learning object metadata) is performed according to the following steps:

1. *Filtering:* When a student logs in, we use some deterministic rules to filter those learning objects that match the student's preferred language defined in his or her profile.

2. *Prediction*: When the student selects a topic, we filter the learning objects and apply a third filter to obtain the learning objects for that topic that matches the student's knowledge level. After that, the current decision model is used to classify each selected object as *"appropriate"* or *"not appropriate"* for the student. To do it, examples including the learning style attributes (inferred from the learning style model) and the learning object's characteristics are automatically generated and classified by the decision model. Since we use a probabilistic classifier, the learning objects can be easily ranked to be shown to the student.

3. *Adaptation*: All the learning objects explain the same topic, so when the student selects a particular learning object we assume that it should be interesting to the student, especially by its characteristics. To obtain more feedback, we also suggest to the user to explicitly rate each learning object. Whenever we will obtain new evidences about the real student preferences for a particular learning object, we will use this information to adapt both the learning style model and the decision model.

35.5 Conclusions and Future Work

We have presented an adaptive user model aimed at discovering the student's preferences about the educational materials based on learning styles. This model is very suitable in e-learning systems that need to "filter" the great volume of information available,

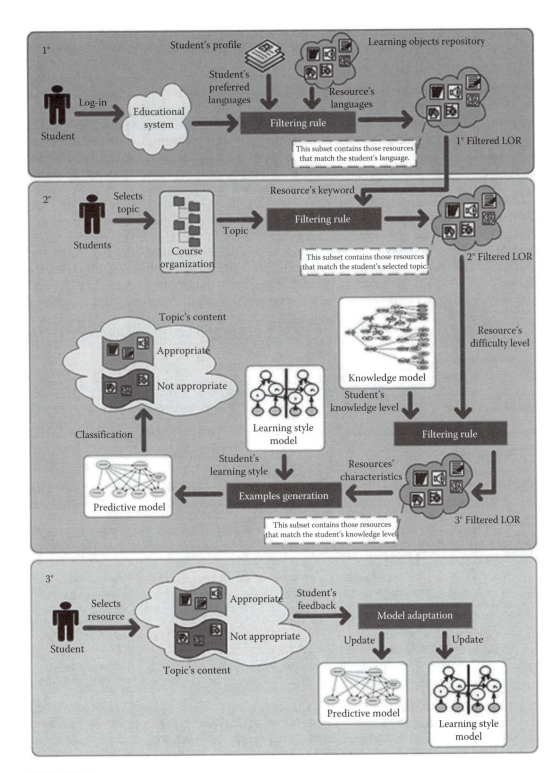

FIGURE 35.4
The selection of learning objects task.

so that their users can make a better use of it. To discover the user's preferences, we use the information about learning styles represented in the student's Bayesian learning style model. The advantage of using a Bayesian model is that this allows refining the initial beliefs acquired by the initial test by observing the student's selections over time, thus computing up-to-date learning style for each student. On the other hand, we use an adaptive BN classifier as the decision model to determine whether a given resource is appropriate for a specific learning style or not. We described the experiments carried out to obtain an initial model, thus solving the cold-start problem. For each student, we initialize the decision model from data generated from the matching tables (set of rules defined by an expert that represents the matches between learning styles and learning objects). Each individual decision model is then adapted from the observations of the student's selections and ranks over time. Moreover, the model is also able to adapt itself to changes in the student's preferences. Although the proposed model has not yet been evaluated using data generated from experiments with real students, we believe that both BN and adaptive BN classifiers are suitable choices to model learning styles and students' preferences in e-learning. Using the proposed models allows dealing with the uncertainty inherited in the acquisition of this information about a particular user and also with the unexpected changes of the students' behavior over time. In future work, we plan to carry out experiments with simulated students and also in the context of a real e-learning system with real students in order to evaluate the performance of our proposal.

References

1. Merlot, http://www.merlot.org. URL last accessed on January 2008.
2. Ariadne, http://www.ariadne-eu.org/. URL last accessed on January 2008.
3. IEEE Learning Technology Standards Committee. IEEE standard for learning object metadata. IEEE. http://ltsc.ieee.org/wg12/files/LOM_1484_12_1_v1_Final_Draft.pdf. URL last accessed on January 2008.
4. Stern, M.K. and Woolf, B.P. Adaptive content in an online lecture system. *Proceedings of the International Conference on Adaptive Hypermedia and Adaptive Web Based Systems* (*AH2000*), Trento, Italy, pp. 227–238, 2000.
5. Triantafillou, E., Pomportsis, A., and Demetriadis, S. The design and the formative evaluation of an adaptive educational system based on cognitive styles. *Computers & Education* 41 (2003) 87–103.
6. Papanikolaou, K.A., Grigoriadou, M., Kornilakis, H., and Magoulas, G. D. Personalizing the inter-action in a Web-based educational hypermedia system: The case of INSPIRE. *User-Modeling and User-Adapted Interaction* 13(3) (2003) 213–267.
7. Wolf, C. iWeaver: Towards learning style-based e-learning in computer science education. *Proceedings of the Fifth Australasian Computing Education Conference* (*ACE2003*), Adelaide, Australia, pp. 273–279, 2003.
8. Paredes, P. and Rodriguez, P. The application of learning styles in both individual and collaborative learning. *Proceedings of the Sixth IEEE International Conference on Advanced Learning Technologies* (*ICALT'06*), Kerkrade, the Netherlands, pp. 1141–1142, 2006.
9. Brown, E., Stewart, C., and Brailsford, T. Adapting for visual and verbal learning styles in AEH. *Proceedings of the Sixth IEEE International Conference on Advanced Learning Technologies* (*ICALT'06*), Kerkrade, the Netherlands, pp. 1145–1146, 2006.

10. Carver, C.A., Howard, R.A., and Lane, W.D. Enhancing student learning through hypermedia courseware and incorporation of student learning styles. *IEEE Transactions on Education* 42(1) (1999) 33–38.
11. Brusilovsky P. and Millán, E. User models for adaptive hypermedia and adaptive educational systems. *The Adaptive Web: Methods and Strategies of Web Personalization, LNCS* 4321 (2007) 3–53.
12. Webb, G., Pazzani, M., and Billsus, D. Machine learning for user modeling. *User Modeling and User-Adapted Interaction* 11 (2001) 19–29.
13. Jensen, F.V. and Nielsen T. *Bayesian Networks and Decision Graphs*. Springer Verlag Inc., New York, 2007.
14. Felder, R.M. and Soloman, B.A. Learning styles and strategies, 2003. URL last accessed on January 2008. http://www.ncsu.edu/felder-public/ILSdir/styles.htm
15. Felder, R.M. and Soloman, B.A. Index of learning style questionnaire (ILSQ). URL last accessed on January 2008. http://www.engr.ncsu.edu/learningstyles/ilsweb.html
16. Carmona, C., Castillo, G., and Millán, E. Designing a dynamic Bayesian network for modeling student's learning styles. *The Eighth IEEE International Conference on Advanced Learning Technologies (ICALT 2008)*, Santander, Spain, pp. 346–350, 2008.
17. Friedman, N., Geiger, D., and Goldszmidt, M. Bayesian network classifiers. *Machine Learning* 29(2–3) (1997) 131–163.
18. Castillo, G., Gama, J., and Breda, A.M. An adaptive predictive model for student modeling. *Advances in Web-Based Education: Personalized Learning Environments*, Chap. IV, London, UK: Information Science Publishing, 2005.
19. Carmona, C., Castillo, G., and Millán, E. Discovering student preferences in e-learning. *International Workshop on Applying Data Mining in e-Learning (ADML'07)*, Crete, Greece, pp. 33–42, 2007.
20. Sahami, M. Learning limited dependence Bayesian classifiers. *Proceedings of the Second International Conference on Knowledge Discovery and Data Mining (KDD-96)*, Portland, OR, AAAI Press, Menlo Park, CA, pp. 335–338, 1996.
21. García, P., Amandi, A., Schiaffino, S., and Campo, M. Evaluating Bayesian networks' precision for detecting students' learning styles. *Computers & Education* 49 (2007) 794–808.
22. Dan, Y. and XinMeng, C. Using Bayesian networks to implement adaptivity in mobile learning. *Proceedings of the Second International Conference on Semantics, Knowledge, and Grid (SKG'06)*, Guilin, China, p. 97, 2006.
23. Pearl, J. *Probabilistic Reasoning in Expert Systems: Networks of Plausible Inference*. San Francisco, CA: Morgan Kaufmann Publishers, Inc., 1988.
24. Gama, J. Iterative Bayes. *Discovery Science—Second International Conference*, LNAI, Vol. 1721, Tokyo, Japan, pp. 80–91, 1999.
25. Castillo, G. and Gama, J. Adaptive Bayesian network classifiers. *International Journal of Intelligent Data Analysis* 13(1) (2009) 39–59.

Index